LIBERATING VOICES

LIBERATING VOICES

A Pattern Language for Communication Revolution

Douglas Schuler

The MIT Press
Cambridge, Massachusetts
London, England

For information about special quantity discounts, please e-mail special_sales@mitpress.mit.edu

This book was set in Stone Serif and Stone Sans on 3B2 by Asco Typesetters, Hong Kong.
Printed and bound in the United States of America.

Library of Congress Cataloging-in-Publication Data

Schuler, Douglas.
Liberating voices : a pattern language for communication revolution / Douglas Schuler.
    p.   cm.
Includes bibliographical references and index.
ISBN 978-0-262-19579-9 (hardcover : alk. paper) — ISBN 978-0-262-69366-0 (pbk. : alk. paper)
1. Communication—Social aspects. I. Title.
HM1206.S38   2008
303.48′33—dc22   2007039867

10 9 8 7 6 5 4 3 2 1

Contents

Preface

Growing up in a middle-class neighborhood in Los Angeles, I frequently heard comments like, "When I was young, we never locked our doors," which I ascribed to clueless adults. (I had an attitude before I knew that a person could have one.) Another one was the hackneyed observation that "the weather has been weird lately." Even at that age, I was enough of a scientist to sense that any single weather anomaly didn't constitute "weird weather."

I had other prejudices in addition to my overflowing bounty of skepticism for the sensibilities of adults. One notable prejudice was my distaste for the volumes of inflexible rules that I had not written or otherwise ratified whose sole purpose (apparently) was to make life uninteresting and mechanical. For whatever reason, the forbidden activities generally had infinitely more allure than the ones that were ordained.

Now, forty years later, my own children are returning the favor of questioning the rules that I present as received wisdom. Beyond this, both kids (now moving inexorably into grown-upness) are seemingly always on the ready to point out the staleness of my jokes or the feebleness with which I attempt to understand their slang.

Besides indulging my nostalgic reflections on the process of moving from youth to maturity (who me?!) I believe that there are some relevant observations that can be made based on this brief look backward.

One observation, of course, is the strength and durability of one's own prejudices—and the difficulty of understanding them, let alone circumventing them. My parents, for example, may have had some good advice for me from time to time. It is also possible that I would have something reasonable to share with the next generation. But for all of that, the mental and emotional wall that I had erected (or was erected for me by, say, genes or brain chemistry) provided a profound filter on what I heard and what meaning, if any, I assigned to what I heard that I will never be able to fully understand. Individually and collectively, we are all locked into systems of interpretation that make it difficult to change our mental and other habits, even when our very existence is threatened.

Another observation is that I, like other people, believed implicitly that the current state (youth, for example) was eternal; the world was out there and was a given; the rules could be resisted but not actually changed. In general things actually do not change—especially at the behest of people. In other words, the weather never really gets "weird."

Of course, if anybody asked me if I thought that things change, I would have answered affirmatively. Deep inside, however, I believed that the 1950s (my earliest years) were eternal, and although the 1960s were quite unlike the decade that preceded them, I never totally got beyond the idea that the world was on automatic. (And "history"—at least the way it was taught and my abiding conviction that it was unalterably tedious—did nothing to alleviate my feeling that humankind was inexorably plodding through the millennia.)

Of course I am asserting that I am not the only person to have these feelings. I am also suggesting that groups of people, organizations, and institutions are also likely to share these feelings, including the immaturity of thinking that what they do is right and that any and all other approaches are wrong. Unfortunately dogged inertia and other shortcomings of human beings are not particularly newsworthy. Throughout humankind's epochs-long trudge, there has been a sort of dreary meta-stability: the more things changed, the more they stayed the same. Although there were indications that this could change, certainly the specter of humankind actually destroying the world—or at least profound chunks of it—was not something that we could plausibly contemplate until quite recently. That was God's job!

I have reluctantly come to acknowledge that many of the myths of childhood may not be true, even if the majority of the people in the world still cleave to them. People can change rules, and they can change their habits. And more rules and habits can be changed and more people can be engaged in the process—if they choose to. Human existence does not have to mean an eternal treadmill of futility. Nor does exploitation of nature and other people have to be the defining characteristic of our species.

I have been fortunate to have witnessed—and even, quixotically, to have tried to influence—an exciting and unparalleled period of technological creativity. We have witnessed the unveiling and widespread adoption of an amazing and unprecedented communication system that can theoretically connect not only all inhabitants on earth, but also the world's culture and knowledge, including an immense amount of scientific data on our planet and beyond that presumably could be put to good use. If, however, we set aside these rose-colored glasses, a host of challenges awakes us from our reverie. These challenges are so immense that if we are honest with ourselves, we must readily admit that they may yet undo all that has been built. For the first time in our long history, we have the means by which to bring about global destruction. The two sides of our nature—intellect, creativity, and understanding versus greed, suspicion, and violence—are now starkly pitted against each other. Our social creativity must now at least equal our technological creativity. We are going to need all the help we can get.

We can count on the Internet for some of this help—not the Internet exactly as it is now, or the Internet in the absence of other communication and information systems (public libraries, for example), or the Internet as a magical force that does the right thing by itself, without human intention or interaction, but the Internet as one aspect of an information and communication fabric animated by human intelligence and the need to address shared concerns. It will not be easy. The agenda now seems to be largely driven by parochial desires and short-term needs. I am dismayed (but not surprised) by the corporate dedication to colonizing the Internet and making it "theirs" and not "ours," just another aspect, of course, of their hugely successful campaign to concentrate media ownership in a few hands. I am similarly disappointed (but not necessarily surprised) by the hordes of incredibly brilliant people toiling in the vineyards of the computer industry who are unwilling or unable to contemplate what a truly responsive Internet might look like, to think beyond their company's bottom line and whatever slogan or mantra is making its rounds among the cyber-cognoscenti at the moment.

The Internet is and is likely to continue to be a reflection of humanity, with its myriad needs, prejudices, and interests. This will encompass the sacred and the profane, the authentic, thoughtful and healing, as well as the close-minded, venal, and violent. Without conscious intervention, the Internet will likely reflect and succumb to the power structures that currently exist outside it, a complex of resources and institutional inertia that supports the desires of the few over the needs of the many.

Of course, everything moved too fast to monitor (let alone understand) it all. Moreover, my personal prejudices colored everything I have witnessed, just as other people's prejudices colored what they witnessed. In some cases, I was not surprised: the nearly immediate commercialization of the Internet, for example. I was disappointed when the National Science Foundation decided to commercialize the Internet with no public discussion. I was saddened by the silence of civil society that was unaware of the momentous decisions that were being made before it was possible for ordinary people to have any idea of what they might be losing. In other cases, I was surprised and thoroughly impressed with the resilience, brilliance, and dedication of civil society that was appropriating the Internet for their work striving against (at least the way I see it) militarism, greed, bumbling leadership, insensitivity, racism, and the other isms. The rapid growth of community networks was exciting, as was the explosive growth of Indymedia. The Internet will undoubtedly continue to reflect the wide dimensions of humankind in some unequal sense. But we can demand more. What is stopping us from developing something that is more like an *agora* that supports education, deliberation, mutual problem solving, and the free expression of ideas for everybody, and less like a shopping channel raised to some infinite power?

Engaging in this type of work is a little like straddling an immense chasm with technology development on one side and social activism on the other. I have always thought that the two sides belonged together, but there seemed to be immense pressure to choose one over the other. And choosing one is tempting; for one thing, the rules of the game are clearer for either of the two sides than they are for the murky place where the two sides overlap. Working in the computer industry or having a voice in the technological direction it goes seems to require unquestioning faith in the product it is producing. But a little voice keeps barging in that reminds me of my reservations. On the other side of the chasm is the skeptical voice that says that technology cannot solve problems by itself, that technology is often a distraction, and that much of the rhetoric is self-serving hype.

Occasionally this voice has gotten me in trouble. It has spiked job opportunities on a few occasions, but mostly it has just annoyed people. I was not playing along and "didn't get it." I was just trying to be difficult. And so on. It was this little voice, however, that reminded me that the Internet does not replace face-to-face relationships. It was this little voice that said that new does not equate to good, no more than old means good. But following this voice to its logical extremes was not appropriate either. The little voice must be tempered with other voices. If, for example, the trajectory of the Internet is shaped only by the technocrats because the more socially motivated wanted to retain their technological virginity, the Internet would be even less likely to meet society's real needs.

The technocratic, corporate, and neoliberal rhetoric has been intense, and some has been quite articulate and persuasive. I have watched as the rhetoric took hold and had immense power over the first generation of the Internet released from the labs. Acknowledging the absolutely critical importance of information and communication, *and acting on this knowledge,* is key to selecting from humankind's possible futures.

About the Patterns

I was amazed to see how quickly this pattern language book project started to come together when it actually started to really come together. And it was exciting to see how the authors became suddenly aware—and pleasantly surprised—that their patterns connected with other patterns in the book much more deeply and coherently than they had anticipated.

Since the way we use the terms *pattern* and *pattern language* in this book may be misleading, I'll describe both briefly here and revisit them in more depth later. It should be noted that we owe a tremendous debt to Christopher Alexander who developed both concepts, which were used to great effect in his magisterial book about architecture and urban planning, *A Pattern Language* (Alexander, Ishikawa, and Silverstein 1977). A *pattern* is a concise discussion of a solution to a problem in some area of focus, which in our case is information and communication for social change. A pattern contains suggestions about how to think about solving the problem and about how to take action to alleviate the problem. Each pattern is presented in a consistent format: each has a title, a description of the problem it is designed to address, the context within which it is used, and a discussion that explores the motivation for the pattern and how the pattern can be put to use. A *pattern language* is an organized collection of patterns that together express a broad coherent response to a large number of related problems. In many, if not all, cases, people will use several patterns in conjunction with each other when trying to solve a particular problem.

While it can honestly be said that the pattern language described in this book is the work of hundreds of people, who built on the musings, experiments, and struggles of thousands more, the final responsibility for this enterprise must fall on me. Pattern authors are responsible for their individual patterns, but many of the patterns and the chapters before and after chapter 8, which contains the patterns, are mine. Some of the authors are more "radical" than I am, while others are less so. I say this because I feel obligated to provide the coauthors with whatever distance from me or the other authors they may want or need. Some will feel that I was too critical, and some will feel that I was too timid. Nonetheless, I believe that most, if not all of them, support on some level the audacious objective of this book: to play some meaningful role in the repair of an increasingly dysfunctional world.

Although the structure of the patterns promotes a degree of consistency, there is a difference in styles among them, a pleasant reminder of the diversity of viewpoints. Also, the examples are unequally drawn from U.S. experience or, for that matter, built on examples in Seattle, where I live. Ideally there would be an even distribution of coverage around the world. To this end, I have tried to use examples from outside the United States whenever possible. But even in the age of the Internet, the local exists—and I hope it always will.

I wanted to apologize for not mentioning all of the great projects around the world that demonstrate aspects of the patterns It is a testament to humankind's engaged compassion and intelligence that a book even one hundred times this size could not contain them all. I also want to apologize for the limited space that was allotted for individual patterns. The page limit was restrictive, but everybody did their part to keep the size of the book manageable. The *Liberating Voices* Web site, http://www.publicsphereproject.org/patterns/, should help to rectify these unavoidable transgressions. On the Web site, pattern authors can expand their patterns almost indefinitely. Other people can contribute new patterns that they believe are supportive of the broader effort. Generally we are envisioning the site as a shared resource that will help various communities use the pattern language effectively and to help them interact with others around the world on the evolving communications revolution project.

The Future of the Patterns

What is needed in the years ahead? Of course, the other contributors to this effort and I would like to secure support for this work as a whole. Ideally the patterns will be used more as patterns, and we will have an opportunity to evaluate their effectiveness. This should help improve the patterns and the pattern language accordingly. Ultimately we hope that civil society will be strengthened through the use of the patterns this book. This project places faith in the people, and nothing of any magnitude can be accomplished without them.

We are also hoping to convene face-to-face meetings on the pattern language and related projects. The conscious development of collective intelligence is an intriguing possibility, and I hope that this book can play a role. It will be interesting to see how the pattern authors and others in the community can devise new ways of working together to make progress on their goals.

Ideally this book would have been, like its predecessor, *A Pattern Language* (1977) by Christopher Alexander, Sara Ishikawa, and Murray Silverstein, a work of art and a work of genius. Although this book has likely fallen short of that goal, the work it describes, however imperfectly, does not fall short of those high honors. The active, engaged, intelligent, and possibly naive work that information and communication activists are taking on throughout the world is becoming increasingly widespread. The application of nonviolent and just principles to help build a world that works for all is noble and beautiful. Who knows? The vast, principled, ad hoc, and largely uncoordinated project that millions of people are working on might succeed. It is one project, and we are allies. A better world is possible.

Acknowledgments

The National Science Foundation (NSF) helped support this work with two grants. The Ethics and Values Studies office of the NSF helped support the Directions and Implications of Advanced Computing conference in 2001 and several of the other ten DIAC symposia that helped develop the groundwork and the community for this work. The NSF supported my trip to Malmo, Sweden, where I first presented this project. The Evergreen State College where I teach ("The last great experimental college in the American Empire," according to Cornel West) provided two grants: one to assist with the development of the book and one to explore how pattern languages could be used in education, particularly as a way to encourage the development and integration of knowledge within a collective and constructivist framework. I also thank Computer Professionals for Social Responsibility (CPSR). Although we did not always see eye-to-eye, the relationship has been enduring and fruitful. CPSR sponsored the Directions and Implications of Advanced Computing symposia, hosted the Public Sphere Project Web space (thank you, Carl and Ed!), and helped in innumerable other ways. I've been working with CPSR for over twenty years and I've been ready for a reinvigorated and assertive "CPSR 2.0" for a good fifteen of them! Are you?

I thank people who have helped advance several of my admittedly iffy propositions over the years. Many have been supportive, while others were scratching their heads. Val Brown did an amazing job of editing the first draft of this manuscript and keeping engaged in the project for several years. John Adams put in an enormous number of hours on so many thankless tasks. Ken Gillgren was extremely steady and helped me through the periods when too much material was due in too brief a time. Andrew Dearden helped throughout the process, but was immeasurably productive at a critical period with the organization of the patterns. Stewart Dutfield was a reliable and enthusiastic contributor for years, as were John Thomas, Burl Humana, Justin Smith, and others. Fiorella de Cindio helped organize a meeting in Milan and in general is a tireless worker for an inclusive and intelligent civil society. And Scott Rose has volunteered his time developing several Web sites and applications for DIAC conferences and this project for over twenty years. Scott developed the online pattern management system, while several others, like Allen Williams, Abram Bender, Jeff Shieber, and even me, developed specialized applications that built on the core. I also relied on a number of people for advice and other assistance, including Peggy Holman, Nancy White, Mike Powell, Åke Walldius, Peter Blomquist, Todd Davies, Peter Dorman, Ron Eglash, Greg Paine, Jonathan Lawson, Andrew Clement, Ed Johnson, Roxi Bruner, Allen Acevedo, Shea Kaufman, and Bradie Derrenger. Beverly Miller, Jessica Pugsley, Melissa Crouse, and Thomas Van Roosendaal also helped greatly with the manuscript.

Thanks of course to all of the authors (approximately eighty-five of them) who contributed patterns to this book. Thanks also to everybody who contributed a pattern or pattern idea to the Web site. There are over four hundred of them, and I am hoping that this community will continue the pattern language work that we have started. A much longer list of contributors is on the Web. If you do not see your name there, please tell me. My intention is to acknowledge everybody who has helped, and my bad memory should not get in the way of that.

I thank Bob Prior for being flexible with me and generous with the patterns in a way that is in keeping with the spirit of the project. Bob, unlike other editors, felt that it was important to maintain the open accessibility of the patterns on the Web, for which I am very grateful. I also thank Valerie Geary, Nathan Hohenstein, Colleen Lanick, Alyssa Larose, Beverly Miller, Sandra Minkkinen, Sharon Deacon Warne, and others, particularly for their willingness to be flexible as they worked on a somewhat unorthodox book.

I feel quite fortunate to be able to count as colleagues a remarkable group of people from around the world (thank you, Internet!) who are able to promote and pursue the development of computer systems without forsaking their ideals. They are too numerous to list here, and the group is growing daily. Without this group of people around to assure me that I was not crazy—or at least not the only one with crazy ideas—I am not quite sure what I would have done. Certainly solidarity and community provide enduring incentives throughout efforts like these.

Finally I thank my family—including my mother, Donna, and mother-in-law, Flo—and my wife of twenty-seven years. Although Terry was not happy (nor was I) with the thousands of hours that I plowed into this project, she (mostly) supported all of this. Our two kids, now mostly grown-up, looked at this effort with some amusement. I hope that they and others in their generation will step up to the challenges that my generation has at least sporadically picked up and successfully face them. There is a lot of work to be done.

Rainy/Sunny Seattle
January 2008

LIBERATING VOICES

1 Communication Revolution

Humankind's centuries-long journey is punctuated with revolutions large and small, where the general order is perturbed, and the lives of the people who are born later are profoundly different from those who live through those revolutionary times. It now appears that we are living in such an era. As we are constantly reminded, we are in the midst of a revolution in the ways that our species communicates and how it creates and shares information. Although we acknowledge the truth of that statement, we do not say "the communication revolution," because that implies that a single revolution is underway when, in fact, a million revolutions, some well publicized and some virtually unknown, are simultaneously coexisting and coevolving. Generally, in fact, thinking of "communication revolution" as a single revolution is tantamount to accepting the official version of communication revolution that, through obeisance to state and corporate leadership (and perhaps some well-deserved blind luck), the people of the world will naturally become more prosperous, democratic, and happy. We can trust the business and government elites to solve any problems that may emerge. They will sort it all out—don't worry! And in the meantime, buy and enjoy their vast array of dazzling products and services!

This book is devoted to the demolition of the official version of information and communication systems at the dawn of the twenty-first century and to the construction of alternative visions. Without denying the positive impacts that elite people can and do make, this book is dedicated to a radical orientation in which ordinary people assert their rights, and their responsibilities, as citizens of the world. It is my contention that the collective intelligence of the world's citizens, built on values, creativity, and courage, is also desperately needed now. In part this is necessary to curb the excesses of the world's elites, many of whom have drunk too deeply and too eagerly of their own self-congratulatory rhetoric and ideology and, as a result, sacrificed the common good, knowingly as well as unknowingly, to enhance their own privilege and power.

This book concentrates on communication as a crucial arena in the battle for equality and justice. Communication is key to any collective enterprise, and it is for that reason that we invite you to the communication revolution that is already yours to win. Our only request is that you acknowledge and take seriously your role as an active participant. This is a diffuse and distributed movement. It needs leaders and followers, and people in this work frequently shift in and out of both roles. Everybody is needed in this struggle as we work to liberate the voices, and the thoughts and actions, of people around the world as humankind lurches warily and ill prepared into the uncertainties of the century that has just begun.

Do Not Believe Everything You Think

Countless written and spoken words assert that humankind is now living in a new age within a new society that has been characterized as the "information society" (by Daniel Bell and others) and as "the network society" (by Manuel Castells and others) and by many other labels as well. What many of these new conceptualizations have in common is the centrality of information and communication. This book takes a radical perspective that humankind can create roles for itself in relation to information and communication rather than simply laboring under existing ones. Rather than adopt these new labels for our time as master narratives and thereby relegate humans to the role of spectators in their own lives, in performances scripted masterfully and unerringly by the wielders of power, technology, and capital, this book presents a collection of new ideas crafted by people who believe that people can be creative and ethical and caring animators, not merely robots that buy, sell, obey, toil, and die according to their programs.

This book presents the first draft of a language for a communications revolution. It is intended to be an everyday guide for people who are working to shape a better future. Like this book, many of them are focusing on the information and communication systems that reflect and shape—for better or for worse—what humankind thinks and does. These communications revolutionaries are peaceful but insistent. They are working in a million places on a million projects. Their contributions are large and small, their ideas old and new, and their perspectives theoretical and extremely practical at the same time. The diversity is precisely the point: the objective of this book and the broader pattern language project is to characterize this unruly and uncoordinated revolution by integrating the totality of their efforts.

This language differs from a general theory primarily by its insistence on a formulation that stops well short of precision and certainty. The favored intellectual objective in the hard sciences is the ever better, but never complete, explanation of an objective and unchanging reality. Einstein's $E = mc^2$ may be the most elegant (and abstract) example of an equation that sums it all up, but its elegance is of little use to most of the world's inhabitants. Instead the practical world that humankind inhabits is almost indescribably complex and dynamic: it is unknowable in fundamental ways, messy and full of contradictions. Rather than summing it up, we spend our lives making it up as we go along.

The structure of our language acknowledges the enormity of this world: a world that can be seen as comprising three deeply interconnected and enmeshed worlds of distinctive as well as shared characteristics. The first world is physical and measurable and ultimately provides our sustenance. It includes natural elements like air, sunlight, water, and soil, as well as physical products of humankind like roads, buildings, books, pesticides, and bombs. The second world is the world of individual and social communication and interpretation, a world also complex—and messy. Paradoxically it guides our perception, but it itself can change over time. Within this world some people learn and grow wise; others may become banal, stupid, uncaring, and brutal. The third world is the world of the knowledge that we collectively create and recreate over time, a world of theories, disciplines, data, language, policies, institutions, laws, and taboos.

Our language, formulated as a pattern language (described below), is intended to address all three worlds. It is messy like the three worlds—and that stands to reason: it is inextricably linked to them. And it makes no guarantees. It defines no specific destination (which would be futile) or specifications for utopia. Nor does it assert a mystical purpose. Rather, it advocates a universe of ordinary and plausible actions that are likely to further complicate a complicated world, to push it in directions that may ultimately be important within the complex and poorly understood ecosystems of the three worlds and their interactions. It offers us tools not to define the world that we live in but to create it.

We named our pattern language *Liberating Voices* to signify its descriptive and prescriptive functions. Pattern languages comprise patterns, and each pattern is an encapsulated, peaceful revolt. Each pattern contains within it a built-in confrontation with a problem, and the application of the pattern is intended to help us overcome the problem and bring us closer to a more humane existence. The problem described in each pattern contains features of the world that we think need changing, features that perpetrate the status quo, with its system of few winners and many losers, a category that seemingly includes most people and the natural environment. The last part of the pattern is the solution, which summarizes the ideas that people are using to confront the problem, wrestle with it, and make some progress at subduing it, while the problem resurrects itself in another form. A pattern, then, is a form of seed. It contains a reflection of current work and thinking, as well as the vision of a future in which the seeds have sprouted and borne fruit.

Obsolete Assumptions

Until very recently most people assumed that the ways in which information was created and destroyed, modified, stored, and shared, were givens. Like the weather, they did not change—at least not through conscious intervention by ordinary people. But just as people are gradually acknowledging that human activities can affect the weather, people are also learning that human activities can affect the information and communication environment—and vice versa. Moreover, like our impact on the weather, some of the changes that we are inducing may be hazardous to our mental, emotional, and physical health.

The assumptions that we make are often made by default; they are supplied ready-made by the culture. Many people remain unfortunately oblivious to the fact that humankind's communicative activities are in large measure conventionalized and institutionalized. These activities do not remain constant, however. They differ tremendously depending to some degree on the circumstances surrounding their origins. Spoken language, for example, is hundreds of thousands of years old. The World Wide Web, in contrast, is a few decades old at most. And although the information and communication environment is certainly the result of a collective effort (human language was not invented by scientists in a research laboratory), some contributors to this effort have had more influence than others, especially in our own time. Consider, for example, the clout of three men—Rupert Murdoch, Silvio Berlusconi, and Bill Gates—that seemingly overshadows the effects of millions, if not billions, of other less powerful people around the world.

The common—although false—assumption that some type of objective, or neutral, and reliable information environment exists now or existed at some point in history is slowly dissipating. Until recently only a handful of propagandists, social critics, pragmatics, paranoids, and advertising pitchmen would see through this convenient fiction. Now society is rapidly learning new lessons about communication. For one thing, as Claude Shannon (1949) made clear, communication and information take material forms. So although a single bit of information can be teeny-tiny, it nevertheless requires matter and energy to store and distribute it. Hence the vast "server farms" of Google or Facebook and other popular Web sites become necessary. From an economic point of view, information in a book, disk drive, or DVD becomes "content," generic stuff that can be sold—hopefully at the highest price. Seen at the societal level, information and communication, at least in the developed world, are becoming ubiquitous and inescapable at the same time that they are becoming increasingly commercial and corporatized.

But quantity does not always translate into quality. When, as pioneering critics like George Gerbner (1998) pointed out, people get a large amount of their information (hence their ideas, beliefs, attitudes, interests, cultural biases, and so forth) from electronic sources with anonymous origins, then human culture has gone through a fundamental and historic shift. When the primary objective of those anonymous sources is accumulating money, votes, or influence, the always-on electronic environment represents an enormous amount of actual and potential influence. As these systems become more ubiquitous worldwide, the fact that they are corruptible, corrupting, and often corrupt should, at the very least, raise grave concerns about potential misuse. In fact given this immense power, it would seem derelict not to consider how those vast systems could be reconceptualized as collective assets of culture and wisdom, which, in theory, could put humanity and the natural environment ahead of the never-ending pursuit of cash.

Media Intervention

Recently, however, and with little warning, the cloud of ignorance appears to be breaking up—at least slightly. Signs that communication is the new battleground for freedom of ideas are coming in from all sides. At the same time it would be hard to assign a precise date to the first salvo of the struggle. One reasonable marker might be the unexpectedly large public outcry in the United States in 2003 when the Federal Communications Commission (FCC) issued new plans to allow large media companies to control an even larger share of the media market in U.S. cities and towns. After being besieged with vast volumes of blisteringly critical comments from people across the political spectrum, the extraordinarily business-friendly Congress in a surprise move pounced on the FCC and demanded a change in the policy with a lopsided 400 to 21 vote. A more recent example is the struggle for Net neutrality in which diverse organizations, including mutually antagonistic groups such as MoveOn and the Christian Coalition, joined forces to keep the major telecommunications corporations in the United States from reconstituting the Internet in ways that would be more subservient to their bottom line.

Why those sudden outbursts of revolt? It is not difficult to generate plausible hypotheses. Perhaps people had finally reached their boiling point. Perhaps the lessons of media critics like Ben Bagdikian, Robert McChesney, Noam Chomsky, Edward Herman, and Herbert Schiller had finally penetrated the consciousness of enough people. Perhaps the reality was getting too obvious to ignore, and the media refuseniks were finally attaining a critical mass. Ben Bagdikian brought the concept of the ever increasing "media monopoly" (1992) to our attention, while Chomsky and Herman presented their findings on "manufacturing consent" (1988), including the vast sums that the U.S. military spends directly to influence the U.S. public.

The Internet, moreover, was at the same time providing an increasing bonanza of new perspectives, which flourished in the fertile and undomesticated brine of cyberspace. Inquisitive readers could more easily find alternative and independent points of view within the U.S. and the foreign press that had previously been beyond the reach of the vast majority of Americans. In the run-up to the invasion of Iraq, for example, outlets such as the U.K. *Guardian* provided a welcome tonic amid the din of drum beating in the U.S. corporate media. Another explanation could be that people complained to Congress and the FCC because they could: people who had become increasingly aware of serious malfunctions in the official information sphere had both the motivation and the technical means ("click to send your comments") to mount an attack when they encountered an overt and tangible policy affront.

The realization that consumers of news and other content are part of a complicated informational ecosystem has vastly complicated our intellectual landscape. It is hard enough to think about the information within a message without contemplating the biases, constraints, and other underlying features of the messenger who brought it to you. In the past, if CBS television told its viewers in the United States that something was true, *it was true*. If a story was not mentioned on the nightly news, an event in question was presumed to have never happened, and it certainly was not news. Now in an era when venerable institutions like the *New York Times* proffer subdued and belated apologies for slipshod and erroneous coverage of events with national and international implications—like Florida's highly dubious vote tallies in the 2000 U.S. presidential election or planted reports of weapons of mass destruction in Iraq, which helped provide palatable rationale cover for the Bush administration's invasion—readers and media consumers of all types must now acknowledge, happily or not, the additional responsibility of questioning each piece of reportage that they receive. Moreover, as people in developed and developing countries are increasingly recognizing the importance of the media as the powerful arbiter and shaper of public consciousness it is, battlegrounds suddenly are made visible where virtually none existed before and, just as suddenly, everybody becomes a potential warrior within that arena.

One skirmish in the war for information integrity can serve as an example. In 2005 a document from the U.K., the now-famous Downing Street Memo containing the claim that the United States was "fixing intelligence" to justify its invasion of Iraq was leaked to the public. The document was ignored by the mainstream U.S. press for over a month. Finally, after an extensive campaign by U.S. progressives, the media, in lockstep, belatedly determined that "fixing intelligence" to justify an invasion might in fact be news after all. Even then, professional journalists Michael Kinsley in the *Los Angeles Times* and Dan Millbank in the *Washington Post* impugned those amateurs who had the audacity to express an opinion on what was or was not "news" and to prod the professional media into reporting on what they believed was important.

Becoming the Media

The public's new-found engagement with mass media, however innovative and paradigm challenging it may be, would still be playing a submissive position, tacitly acknowledging that traditional mass media systems with their deep reserves of power, privilege, and resources are firmly in control, if the public's actions were limited to occasional reactions to dubious journalistic actions and practices. In other words, while it might be possible to influence the activities of the media conglomerates now and again, their basic trajectory may ultimately remain unchanged. It does appear, however, that the public's work in shaping the evolving information and communication environment is extending far beyond playing cat and mouse with traditional media systems. The signs are beginning to become clearer that people are taking the suggestion of punk musician Jello Biafra seriously: "Don't fight the media. Become the media."

Breaking out from under the deep shadow of the large media systems will not be easy, and we cannot know now if any efforts to do so will be successful in the future. We do know with reasonable certainty that sporadically challenging their hegemony, however important that remains, will not suffice; creating viable competition is absolutely necessary. Fortunately, this is apparently what is now happening. Distaste and distrust of mainstream and popular media are high and increasing, and so is interest in both consuming and producing independent media. But success breeds jealousy, and any substantial growth in historically negligible independent media, especially if it cuts into the market share of large commercial systems, may threaten the independent nature, if not the very existence, of this fledgling enterprise. User-supplied content is seen as an important area for economic growth, and even the largest, most predatory corporations have begun sniffing around in that area.

We have already seen corporate offerings that cultivate edgy, independent-looking products like fruit juice with funky labels; preripped, prestained, and prepatched pants; and out-of-focus, jarring videos and television shows with the gritty handheld look. Even less savory approaches to protecting media monopolies exist as well; several countries have explored or actually established laws that bar people who are not officially certified in one way or another from practicing journalism, thus containing dissent in the name of professional standards. Independent efforts can be killed in other ways with the stroke of a pen by friends in the legislature (of course, friendly but uncertified journalists can be smuggled into important press briefings, as was demonstrated when Republican operative Jeff Gannon attended Bush press conferences); when the threats are deemed significant enough by the powers that be, journalists can themselves be killed outright, a phenomenon that is not as rare as it ought to be (see any issue of *Index on Censorship* for a depressing eye-opener).

Several new civic approaches are emerging that run counter to the commercial-corporate-broadcast model, and many blur traditional boundaries like those between consumer and producer and between inaction- and action-based media. The profusion of new models signals an exciting and defining period of time; some of these models will survive and thrive, even as many will disappear or remain impotent at the margins; some will be subsumed by powerful institutions, while others, I hope, will promote a vibrant civil society with positive social change on behalf of people and the environment.

One important development is the establishment of alternative news sources. The community networks movement (Grundner 1993, Schuler 1996) of the 1990s provided the first widespread expression of civil society in cyberspace. The explosion of the World Wide Web, its commercialization, and the unpackaging and repackaging of community network services, coupled with the dearth of resources, all contributed to the decline in the movement (Schuler forthcoming). The birth of the Indymedia movement in the aftermath of the Seattle demonstrations against the World Trade Organization in 1999 signaled a second-generation civic phenomenon. By employing a similar platform at individual locations around the world and, at the same time, being loosely linked to each other, independent media activists have created a worldwide network, technologically and socially, of approximately 180 locations around the world that simultaneously promotes independence (and the power of local autonomy and on-the-ground knowledge and context) and solidarity (and the power of cooperation and global framing). The proliferation of blogs has added to the vibrancy of new media forms in cyberspace. Although blogs started (and many remain) as idiosyncratic and personal online diaries, the blogging community quickly devised ways to create an interlinked collective information environment now commonly called the blogosphere, which, for better or worse, has become a factor in public deliberation and consciousness.

The blogosphere, for example, "reacted instantaneously, and often furiously" (Skolnik 2006) in reaction to the Bush administration's alleged deal with three of the four largest local and long-distance telecommunications corporations to secretly collect records of telephone calls made by millions of U.S. citizens.

Another recent development is the use of communication in organizing actions. The opposition to the World Trade Organization in Seattle in the waning days of the twentieth century is generally considered to be the first successful use of the Internet and electronic communication by civil society in organizing on a large scale. It is vitally important to acknowledge that the online component was accompanied by extensive training and other focused face-to-face meetings (Starhawk 2002). And in early 2003, days before the United States invaded Iraq, two different kinds of events opposed to the war—angry mass street demonstrations and subdued and pensive candlelight vigils—took place nearly simultaneously in hundreds of locations worldwide.

Robert Muller, former assistant secretary general of the United Nations, remarked on this enormous incipient potential of the citizenry by saying, "Never before in the history of the world has there been a global visible, public, viable, open dialogue and conversation about the very legitimacy of war" (Wolner 2003). He was describing the unprecedented movement that arose spontaneously around the world. What this represents, perhaps more than anything else, is the advent of an immensely powerful force that Muller called a "merging, surging, voice of the people of the world" and James Moore of Harvard's Berkman Center for Internet & Society called "an emerging second superpower, which is 'a new form of international player,' constituted by the 'will of the people' in a global social movement." Although the Bush administration was apparently not impressed by this worldwide renunciation of violence, this event may signal the possibility of a larger, more effective, and more coherent force for peace and human values that could yet emerge.

Not Just a Media Referendum

Since the media serve as the public face of government and other powerful elites worldwide, I focused on it considerably earlier in this chapter. The media, however, are, like everything else, embedded in other systems. What we have is a rough equilibrium between what the owners are willing to produce and what the mass audience is willing to consume. The elites control the media to a large extent. They write the policies that guide it, determine what is acceptable, and manage almost the entire edifice, including the Internet to a large degree. And millions of nonelites spend a good deal of their time consuming the available product (apparently whenever they have a chance). The point of this is acknowledging that the industry elites would likely be responsive to the demands of the nonelites if enough of them would demand it. The other point is that to a large degree, the media that we are stuck with (at this point in time) exist within cultural and social environments, and changing these environments can ultimately help change the media as well, an important task but far from the only one before us. Ultimately we must not only think about how to make the media more accountable, we must consider what kinds of media, and other information and communication systems, we need. The better we understand that, the more likely are our chances of success in reshaping the world.

The Liberating Voices pattern language project is best seen as another experiment in the struggle to help build a better world. In chapter 2, we describe the project at a fairly general level starting with its motivation.

2 Invitation to a Revolution

A good case can be made for the view that humankind is participating in a staggering and inexorable million-year march to mass extinction and ecocide. For nearly all of our history, this march has been slow. The pace, however, has quickened considerably. For that reason many people are especially concerned by the wars, genocides, famines, and other crises that are all too common. Others anticipate that the crises of the future are likely to be far worse than those of today. When people pause to consider the world's ills, their emotional responses vary greatly. Some may experience dread or anger or hopelessness. Some may feel fortunate to have escaped a good portion of the misery; some people in fact may feel superior to those who are in the clutches of despair and violence, as if their inherent goodness or that of their religion, culture, or country somehow explains it all, somehow makes the situation seem natural or inevitable. Other people are outraged by the everyday brutality, insensitivity, and ignorance that tolerates—or even encourages—these catastrophes, and others may even be tempted to help if that were at all viable, if the time or resources could be made available, or approaches could be identified that had some reasonable likelihood of success existed. Unfortunately, most, if not all, of the options that people see before them in this area seem futile. It is understandable that their attention is readily drawn elsewhere.

Project Motivation and Rationale

Our hope for this project was that we could develop at least a partial antidote for the futility, cynicism, escapism, fear, and indifference that afflict people in the developed and developing world alike. The need seemed great for an alternative vision of interacting with other people on the planet. We wanted to encourage people to engage with the critical issues of our era, issues with deep roots in the past and looming impacts in the future. These are the issues in general that have been shielded from most of us, reserved for people with more resources, connections, education, whose hands seemingly belonged on the levers of power. If the people and institutions that are steering the good ship Earth, possibly onto the shoals of global catastrophe, were doing a reasonably credible job, the rest of us could tolerate some degree of corruption, the occasional feast on the fruits of war, for example. We could live like the hobbits in Bag End, ignorant and smug, while Frodo and his band were off slaying dragons, vanquishing evil on our behalf. Unfortunately the hobbit lifestyle isn't working. Frodo, Gandalf, and the others have gone missing, and the hobbits must cast aside their cloak of ignorance.

But this need is not new. Despite Superman and John Wayne and countless white-hatted cowboys riding off into the sunset without accepting even a dollar for their service, actions of the people against tyranny, stupidity, and brutality are required again and again. For although citizens can be selfish, fractious, and as inert as pebbles, it is ultimately through their actions that most genuine positive social change is accomplished. Although the poor and the powerless can and do work for social change, the rich and the powerful are in excellent positions to do good for the world as well. Fortunately there is enough work for everybody. At least that is my contention.

The fundamental impetus for this entire endeavor may be an ongoing attempt to answer the question, "What is the best way to live one's life?" This seems less esoteric and more answerable than other classic fundamental questions like, "What is life?" or "What is the meaning of life?" This project and, in particular, all of the work on the patterns was born of a desire to explore, interpret, and act on the nature of today's world and put forth an active, engaged, thoughtful, and multifaceted challenge to the inertia of business as usual.

Making some progress on the question, whether thinking as an individual or as part of a community or organization, involves some understanding of personal and collective attributes such as environment, interests, talents, resources, opportunities, and aspirations as well as the environment in which one lives and works. As it has been presented so far, this approach is broad enough to be universal; it could be applied to anybody in any time period, culture, or situation. To make the approach more useful, however, the contextual information needs to be introduced, and this is where interpretation comes into play. No two people will interpret the same situation in the same way. But since interpretation is important according to the formula given above, we are faced with the inherent and eternal dilemma of acting in what we have called the messy second world of individual and social communication and interpretation. At some point we must follow the advice of noted rural architect Samuel Mockbee (quoted in Design Stance, pattern 44): *Be bold and proceed.*

There are worldviews that prefer the pursuit of understanding to action. These worldviews are embraced by scholars whose life is consumed with the pursuit of knowledge, with each piece of newly revealed information providing additional motivation for the hunt for more information. Mystics' personal desire to embrace or become one with the universe or the infinite leads them to meditation, rituals, or other processes whose intent is disregarding the reality (or materiality) of life as generally perceived. There are problems on the other end of the "understanding" scale as well. An inflexible understanding based on rigid ideology or religious dogma is also problematic. This type of programmed worldview can often be characterized by racism, hatred of "the other," an inability to compromise or acknowledge another point of view, and blind obedience to authority. Some people have amazing strategies for the prevention of learning. But one does not have to be a red-necked racist to have a rigid, nonlearning worldview. Scientists (even!) can believe that their knowledge is superior to that of other people and that their interpretations of events, judgments, opinions, and so forth in areas not so delimited by scientific knowledge are also better.

This project is intended to be socially ameliorative. We intend to promote it by focusing attention on the world and its problems and how people might engage fruitfully in addressing these problems. The context for the project and its goals call for equal measures of reflection and engagement on issues relating to the global environmental crisis, war and militarism, and the widening disparity between rich and poor. These acute maladies have come to a head at a time when more or less unimpeded capitalistic ideology holds sway over much of the world's economic activity and, indeed, ways of looking at the world itself, often including, I would add, the practices of the teacher, physician, and even the scientist. Unfortunately at a time when the need for starkly and honestly facing the awesome problems that face us, even in places where discussion and dissent are nominally tolerated, the political dialogue has been turned into polarizing slogans, wedge issues, and focus group–hardened sound bites.

Within this de facto moratorium on civic and public thinking, an already massive communications empire is propagating rapidly to all reaches of the world (unevenly and not without scattered resistance) to an unprecedented degree of global concentration. This global web of information and communication represents threats as well as opportunities. As the product and by-product of vast corporate and economic forces, this expanding infrastructure is unlikely to consciously or unconsciously promote the type of information that supports social amelioration and transformation. If the media corporations and other powerful elites are totally free to take information and communication systems in the directions of their (or the market's) choosing, they are unlikely to place needs of people and the planet over their own needs. On the contrary, these commercial systems are intended primarily to sell products and make money for their owners and stockholders: entertainment is preferred over news, racial and sexual stereotyping is common. Starlets and scandals are less boring (God forbid!) than discussion or analysis.

So although the Internet and other digital communication will continue to change over time, its role as the fundamental glue linking communication systems worldwide is unlikely to change in the near future. For that reason, citizens must struggle to ensure that the current war over the media, unlike virtually all those (see, for example, McChesney 2000) that have preceded this one, is not lost. Control of the information and communication sphere must never be ceded to powerful entities beyond the reach of the people. People must be able to access that sphere and participate fully in the conversations that take place within it. This sphere must furthermore be infused with values and intelligence that humankind needs today. Ideally the sphere should be a tool and a foundation for invigorated and engaged civic intelligence.

Social Knowledge and Patterns

While the exact degree of humankind's effects on the world cannot be fully known, everybody would agree that the past actions of humans have helped to bring about today's state of affairs. While individuals throughout time act in a variety of ways–they write, fight, procreate, invent, study, pray, and the like–it is only through collective action (coordinated or otherwise, conscious or otherwise) that things–especially the big things with big, long-lasting effects–actually get done. It is the immense importance of collective action that led us to focus on information and communication, for it is only through communicating and sharing information that collective action is even possible.

For that reason, the design and development of an area of intense focus was information and communication systems that are responsive, useful, and ultimately life affirming. The first thing we realized was that there are millions of relevant efforts already underway worldwide that are creating and discovering important information, ideas, and paradigms. We also realized that other efforts are sometimes recreating and rediscovering much of this knowledge. In general, it was clear that efforts often did not build effectively on each other. For that reason, we felt the need to help promote the consolidation and integration of that knowledge, creation of shared agendas, and the building of community among the world's advocates for living communication. It was the feeling that millions of people are working on one big project that encouraged us to initiate this one.

It soon became clear what basic criteria would drive the project. It would have to be a collaborative enterprise in which values and advocacy would be key elements, not indirect side effects. It would focus on information and communication systems, and the project would not establish artificial lines between research and action; policy, service, and technology design; between disciplines and communities within the academy; and between the academy and the rest of the world. Based on discussions with several people, notably Erik Stolterman, then with the University of Umea in Sweden, it was established that we would use the Directions and Implications of Advanced Computing (DIAC) Symposium as the initial forum for these ideas. This made a lot of sense since the discussions during that forum had helped spawn the initial insights for an integrative project on information and communication. We also realized that the pattern language approach developed by Christopher Alexander and his colleagues for their popular book, *A Pattern Language* (1977), would provide a nearly perfect intellectual as well as structural framework for a project with the objectives that we had. So in November 2001, Computer Professionals for Social Responsibility's DIAC-2002 symposium program committee embarked on an ambitious participatory project. We issued a call for patterns and announced that the long-range goal is the construction of a large, structured collection of knowledge that represents the wisdom of a widely distributed, very loosely knit community of activists, researchers, policymakers, and technologists from around the world. The original domain of the pattern language project was civic and community information and communication, and this label, however unwieldy, would probably suffice today. We look more closely at the route that we took based on these ideas in more detail in a later chapter. In the next few paragraphs, we briefly examine the idea of patterns as social knowledge.

Based on the observation that knowledge is inherently social, the sum total of the knowledge systems that operate in the world is a social and collective rather than individual enterprise. After determining that the focus of the project would be on the social (the arena where the more formal-sounding concepts of information and communication actually perform), we also determined that the context that structures how information and communication systems are actually designed, developed, deployed, regulated, and used throughout society is essential. If, for example, healing people who have diseases is one function of a doctor, then teaching people how to be doctors is also part of the continuum we could call "Freedom from Disease," which is concerned with fighting the root causes of disease, whether biological, educational, legal, or economic. After all, how useful would it be to find the cure for a disease when the people who contract the disease cannot afford the cure or even, if the real "cure" for the disease is clean water, a luxury item in much of the developing world.

We looked at the activities that people are engaging in to promote positive change, especially those that are applicable in a wide variety of situations. These are patterns in the same way that Alexander envisioned in *A Pattern Language*, his holistic work on architecture and urban design. At the same time, we wanted to avoid totalizing concepts or meaningless abstractions. For that reason, we emphasized linking theory and practice and a focus on local problems and outcomes that could be evaluated and reevaluated frequently and could, thus, be key to an ongoing learning process. And since patterns are inherently responses to given, typical situations, they contain ways in which to help understand the environment as well as ways to act on it.

Patterns are an attempt to choose life over death. Employed intelligently, they can inject life into ailing environments. In living systems, diversity is the key to life. Each pattern in the pattern language is intended to inject life into systems that are often barren, often life destroying, and often, apparently, beyond our control. Nobody knows where the system is going in the long run, but many fear that if we do not change our course, we will arrive where we're heading. This project consciously adopts a principled approach that intelligently, sensitively, and seriously attempts to shape the future in ways that are sustainable and life affirming. We believe this is a better strategy than competing ones that go in the opposite direction by following the trajectories that are responsible for the worrisome problems that we now face. One assumption of the project is that most people would really like to "do the right thing" and that most people would agree what these "right things" are. Peace, adequate food, health, security for everybody, environmental sustainability, justice, and so forth are among the values that most people share. Patterns are descriptions of what exists and prescriptions for what should be done. Patterns, then, are a logical response to the needs I have described. The quantity of them ensures that they meet the requirement for knowledge diversity. They are also the result of the conscious social construction of diversity.

3 Anticipating the Critics

Like death and taxes, criticism is inevitable. In this chapter, we briefly respond to some of the questions and issues that have been raised in relation to this enterprise so far. Some of these have come up regularly since the project began, and some are relatively new. Colleagues who support the general thrust and intent of the project have posed many of these. Many also have been raised by myself and the members of the editorial board based on their experiences helping to formulate the language. In the future, especially if this project garners any type of exposure, people who are opposed to this project–and the broader project we are attempting to portray and support–will offer additional criticisms, undoubtedly harsher ones. At any rate, thinking about these questions and the issues they raise has been extremely useful to us and will continue to be useful as the project unfolds.

We have divided the issues and questions roughly into four categories, personal, philosophical, political, and pragmatic, that we discuss in this chapter. We encourage readers to entertain a good mix of skepticism and optimism, much the same as we did as we developed this pattern language, as they traverse these pages.

Personal Issues

The first set of issues is related to perspective from the personal or individual point of view. These are issues that arise when people think about themselves or other individual people in relation to this project:

I do not really get it.
Isn't this idea hopelessly naive?
Why should ordinary people get involved with this project?
What can one person do?
I disagree with your perspective, your progress, and your goals.

I Do Not Really Get It
One of the most commonly voiced concerns about this project that I have heard from people is that they that do not get it. They are interested in the topics, but the project sounds

amorphous and abstract. A good part of the problem, I suspect, was that people made assumptions about the project that were based more on a mental model that they had constructed of the project and less on what was actually said. I am not blaming them for that. After all, that phenomenon is common: everybody sees what he or she wants—or expects—to see and hears what they expect to hear. I also readily (although not always happily) admit that my explanations have not always been as good as they should be. It is well known that a short sound bite or 10-second pitch is often required; without it, you are still sputtering after the people you are trying to convince have left the elevator. Another reason for the confusion is that the words *pattern* and *language* (and the use of them together) have somewhat specialized connotations within this project. Most people have a concept of a pattern, usually a graphic image that one can see and a language that is written or spoken using words. Neither of these common connotations is very useful here. In fact if people ask for an explanation of the project, I generally ask first if they are familiar with Alexander's original pattern language. If they are, my task is far simpler.

The explanation generally has two parts: a pattern is something that regularly occurs; a language is a way to describe how elements of some type—usually words, but, in our case, patterns, are used together to create a meaningful whole. But why do we persist in calling it a pattern language when less confusing terminology could be used? The best response is that we use the expression *pattern language* to describe our work because the product is a pattern language, not something else. The other reason, which is more ethically binding than the first, is that we want to acknowledge our debt to Alexander and his colleagues who have built an entire intellectual world of urban design on this concept, whether they would be satisfied with our efforts or not. It seems to us that using another expression would be dishonest.

The most important thing to know about this project (regardless of what a pattern language is exactly and why we adopted its form and structure for our purposes) is that we are trying to bring together a wide range of ideas (the patterns) that we believe can be used by themselves, but particularly in conjunction with each together, in innumerable ways that will be shaped by the people who use them and the situation that they are used in, to help bring forth a world that is more just, equitable, and sustainable than the one we live in today.

The broad nature of this quest means that we need to bring together a variety of disciplines or modes of thinking, including economics, education, media, public health, and sociology, which are often sequestered from each other. And while the project may seem amorphous and abstract, we have tried to present patterns that, while not formulaic or presented in a cookbook style, have practical (as well as thought-provoking) uses and can be applied with good effects. Although the broad concept may seem diffuse, we believe that once anyone "gets it," they really get it.

Isn't This Idea Hopelessly Naive?

While we hope the answer to this question is *no*, the answer to the question, *Isn't the project naive?* is undoubtedly *yes* because the project is based on the idea that progress in collective thinking can in fact be made. Yet if the belief associated with the project was that of unbridled hope and expectations that everything would work out, it is all good, or that utopia is just around the corner, that indeed would be hopelessly naive, especially considering humankind's destructive and exploitive past and the current dangerous trajectories that seem to be growing worse. If, however, this work, as part of a larger project, merely represents a partial approximation of what it would take to get our species back on track, the project cannot honestly be seen as hopelessly naive.

Nevertheless, while admitting to the unrealistic possibilities of humankind actively choosing life over death, health over disease, and cooperation over exploitation, we also base our work on the complement of the Yiddish truism that states that things can always get worse: things can always get better. How much better things actually do get (if they go in that direction at all) will depend on individuals and on individuals working with others. We hope it will not be a question of what one person can do but rather what one people can do.

Why Should Ordinary People Get Involved with This Project?

The short answer to the questions of *Why should ordinary people get involved with this project? Why all of us? Why not just leave it to them?* is that we need the ordinary people. They can be creative, dedicated, and active, or they can be inert deadweight. Just as readily, they can be obstacles to positive social change, even that which benefits them. But it would be impossible to build a culture in which it was harder to exploit people or the environment without the strong voice of ordinary people. And without some degree of engagement from people, no positive social change, regardless of where it originated, would be possible. Most—if not all—of society's progressive movements and social accomplishments, from banning slavery to securing rights for people with disabilities to environmentalism, have originated with civil society. The powerful institutions of the world often do not seem to have the imagination, social conscience, or the interest in making these changes on their own.

Powerful organizations and people are not going away, but they do need to be legitimate, accountable, and monitored. At both the personal level and institutional and national levels, the adage that power corrupts seems as close to a fact of life as anything else I can contemplate. People and organizations have a tendency to extract "rents" whenever they can. If I have control over something (even if it is not really mine) why shouldn't I extract from you whatever price I demand for it?

What Can One Person Do?

To my mind, answering the question, *What can one person do?* would go something like this. First, it is possible for one person to accomplish a lot. History is filled with biographies of people with humanity, perseverance, vision, courage, leadership, and, not incidentally, luck who have made enduring, positive impressions on the world. But although there are many well-known role models, who, for example, helped usher in a great social movement, there are millions of lesser-known people who were also instrumental. Positive social change is not created by one or two great leaders, but by thousands and millions of people making positive contributions, large and small. Unfortunately it is also true that one might not be able to see or understand how their seemingly small actions contributed to larger social changes. This is why we need to identify and make more widely known actions that people can take that contribute to the greater good and are satisfying to the person who is making the effort, including providing rewards or other positive feedback for the effort. This, I believe, makes answering the question in a positive way much easier while presenting the three necessary preconditions for being able to answer it that way: (1) there must be positive actions that can be taken, (2) society (at least some aspects of it) must value and encourage these actions, and (3) opportunities must exist for people who are not necessarily saints or martyrs. The good acts would be satisfying to the doer and thus carry their own reward in addition to any external rewards.

I Disagree with Your Perspective, Your Proposals, and Your Goals

In order to reply, I would need to know more about your criticisms. I dismiss several out-of-hand. One is that we are heading in the right (i.e., correct) direction. Another is that people in control will save us. I do want to point out that many of the arguments in this book are neither left nor right. The physical environment, for example, is shared by people of all political and religious persuasions. If the solutions you posit hinge to a large degree on unregulated capitalism, divine intervention, use of military force, the total absence of government, or benign dictators, we are in serious disagreement. Finally, if you are opposed to the objectives of this book, you will likely find hundreds of assertions and suggestions throughout the book that you strenuously detest. Ideally from my point of view, readers who keep an open mind and persevere will be completely or partially won over by our compelling arguments. Barring this, perhaps they will find ideas in the book that could be used to co-opt or countermand our objectives. Dedicated (and pragmatic) opponents could absorb the ideas in the book to "understand the enemy" and use our insights as a helpful guide for the next generation of strategies and tactics to defeat our "radical" goals of justice, peace, and sustainability. If they diligently support exploitation, militarism, and environmental degradation, it should be possible to ensure the emergence of the next dark ages.

Philosophical Issues

Philosophical issues are related to the big questions of existence, knowledge, and purpose. The specific issues range from questions about our choice of focus for the project, its breadth and the way we have framed it, to the nature of people and society, to the nature of knowledge itself and its adequacy for describing the world and social action. Here is a list of philosophical issues that are addressed briefly below.

The topic is too big.
The topic is framed poorly.
You cannot change human nature.

The Topic Is Too Big

Is this folly? Are we biting off too much? Saving the world is understandably considered to be a naive proposition. For one thing, it implies that there is a simple binary choice, with nothing between saving the world and not saving the world. It also implies that there is a single act of saving that could be done, and presumably the world would thereby be saved. Finally, of course, the world is not really just one thing, so visualizing the two states, the saved and the nonsaved, is no trivial matter. Claiming to have the answer to a question like that is undoubtedly folly. I hope you are not looking for it! Biting off too much is always possible. But whether we have taken on too much, we believe that a good case can be made for a holistic treatment of information and communication in society today. There are a number of places where we could have drawn arbitrary boundaries (for example, by considering cyberspace only), but we elected not to do so. In fact, as one reviewer of our book proposal noted, "The very reason for using the rubric *pattern* is to be able to work across many material and informational domains."

It is obvious that the vast world that this book and this enterprise are attempting to grapple with in a meaningful way is too immense to be adequately covered. This criticism could probably be leveled against any serious work of nonfiction; the "real world" though "real," is far too complex for adequate treatment. We necessarily traded some specificity for holism.

The claim that making progress in the social or environmental realms is simply impossible is powerful and somewhat plausible. And if the world situation degenerates into pandemics, nuclear war, or total environmental collapse, it would be tempting to claim that it was impossible to stem the inevitable and sheer vanity to think we should try. On the other hand, one could just as easily advance the counterclaim that we did not try hard enough. As with some of the other issues, a lot depends on how the concepts are defined. In this case, we need to consider progress. While we do not accept it as an inevitable trajectory of humankind (far from it!) or even a concept with any clear-cut or measurable meaning, we do believe that progress is something that occurs, often within a region bounded temporally and geographically, if and when, for example, wars become less frequent and less destructive, or when people are exploited less or starvation becomes less common. The main trouble with the "impossibility" argument is that it is impossible to prove or disprove or, indeed, derive any utility at all from its invocation.

The Topic Is Framed Poorly

Some arguments can fall into this category. One argument is directed at the idea that we explicitly incorporated values into this work or that our objective is positive social change. Although information and communication are central to our era and especially to the project under discussion here, by themselves they are only plumbing. If values are banished from the discussion, then the rules of the game, whatever they are at that moment, become paramount. The rules then trump the values that all the world cultures advance (but do not necessarily always respect) and people become cogs in a machine within a machine. But values seem to vary from person to person and from culture to culture. This argument is an important one, and one not dismissed easily. At the same time, not being to answer this (at least partially unanswerable) question with precision is not sufficient to halt all human intervention. Having said that, we can assume a certain near universality of values against exploitation and violence against people and nature. Values, whatever they actually are, must resolve themselves in practice.

Another criticism takes the opposite point of view: that the project seems academic, unusable, sterile, mechanistic, and overly logical. Are we ignoring emotions? What role do emotions play anyway? This question is important and not easily answered. Emotions such as anger, compassion, shame, and envy play a large part in social movements—and in resistance to them. This has been a focus in works like *Rethinking Social Movements* (Goodwin and Jasper 2004), which have been critical of efforts to understand social change solely through rational and mechanistic models. Although we have stressed the cognitive aspects of the pattern language work and have worked hard to make this presentation coherent and logical, it would be a mistake to think that we are advocating a mechanistic, wholly rational approach to social change. Nor are we seeking or advocating a purely rational theory as an ultimate objective of this work. We do not believe that objective is advisable or even possible. We are acutely aware of severe limitations to this approach, in addition to the structural constraints on our individual and collective knowledge, that cannot be circumvented, for example, with faster computers or better simulations. Whether or not it has been adequately addressed here, emotion will continue to play a large role in social movements. Although emotion can be exploited and should not be seen as the sole determinant of action any more than pure reason, it will be present when people are working together on projects such as those suggested by the pattern language. This mutual work will uncover truths that will likely never be uncovered through a purely rational description or program.

You Cannot Change Human Nature

One of the most difficult classes of problems to address, and to my mind, impossible to answer, has to do with the nature of humankind: whether, for example, humankind is intrinsically evil or whether men will always wage war. (Women are included in the humankind label and so are possible harborers of evil. But it is men who typically wage war.) The problem with this criticism, as with others, is that it is masquerading as an either-or choice, a point that I assume is not lost on the people making the argument. Of course, conflicts, even lethal ones, over resources, for example, will never vanish completely. I am willing to acknowledge that some types of conflicts and competition are actually inherent in our species. How could it be otherwise? I would also agree that an inherent aggressive nature will have some tendency to promote aggression, a regrettable inertia toward self-destruction of our species. Yet the ultimate outcome of this inescapable aspect of all of us need not inexorably lead to nuclear annihilation or destruction of the earth. Ironically the under-appreciated but awesome force of habit that seems to play a huge role in the behavior of people and organizations gives me reason for hope and for despair—hope because it means that if we can change our habits, then we can change our culture. If, for example, war could be deinstitutionalized and delegitimized, perhaps by changing the rewards that sometimes accrue to war wagers, we could perhaps abandon it to the dustbins of history. Acknowledging that force of habit can lead to despair, the archetype for human beings becomes neither the angel nor the devil but the addict.

When pressed, people may offer other truisms to support the impossibility of positive social change. These include such thoughts as people are too stupid (or lazy or evil or something else) at their core, the world's organizations are too powerful, and any actions we take invariably create antiactions from them, as well as the idea that humankind has simply passed too many tipping points beyond which we cannot put the genie back in the bottle (that ominous and genuinely threatening cliché) of, for example, nuclear weapons and global warming.

Whether human nature contains the germs of progress is a question with elements of sociology (particularly social movements) and history (when and how do new historical paradigms or world models come into being?). This book endorses two basic notions. First, the sum total of lots (and lots) of individual actions that promote positive social change can ultimately result in a social and environmental world that has more of the characteristics that we would like to see. Second, the pattern language in the book, like the pattern language approach in general, accepts the primary importance of human willingness to improve the human condition.

It is possible that, as Immanuel Wallerstein believes, the emergence of a new world model within a relatively short period of time (historically) is more or less assured due to several factors (described in more detail in chapter 4). Could the efforts advocated with the patterns in this book help provide a catalyst for a paradigm or world model shift? Could they be useful in choosing human directions during a massive shift? Could they cause such a shift?

In this project, we focus on the intersection of three main themes: the use of information and communication systems by ordinary people, a strengthened civil society, and a better society (or even a society that is not getting worse as quickly). The first question might be, "Why focus on communication and information?" The main reason is that the topic is fundamental. It underlies most, if not all, of our activities, and it is universal: all people in all societies engage in this activity. While it is certainly possible to indulge in too much talk and not enough action, it is hard to imagine human action that was not informed by information and communication. It is even harder to imagine human action that helps advance human needs and aspirations that was not influenced to a strong degree by information and communication.

Talk, as the aphorism informs us, is cheap, but we disregard its powerful potential at our own peril. Even cheap talk can have catastrophic consequences. From the talk-radio-fueled right-wing militias in the United States, to terrorist recruitment, to vast, overt, orchestrated propaganda public relations blitzes on behalf of powerful elites whether it be Milosevic's Serbia or Bush's America can help spur the world into violent, apparently endless, and self-perpetuating bloodshed. And talk, loose and unquestioned and endlessly repeated, forms the basis of deep-seated prejudices and habitual cognitive reflexes that substitute for thinking and serve essentially as sleeper cells that can be awakened by nationalist or fundamentalist rhetoric by politicians and propagandists who know the code and can use the media to awaken their minions.

Therefore we are seeking patterns that address talk in all of its guises and milieus. People must improve their ability to resist being swept along by coded speech designed to bypass the brain's reasoning centers. We also need to change the circumstances that surround and influence the production of these messages. Presumably the patterns to address situations between wars would differ from those that would be useful in times immediately preceding an invasion or a slaughter of innocent people by paramilitaries, for example. People also must actively work to shape information and communication systems that better support human needs. Information and communication systems are intended to promote action, not substitute for it.

Although there are undoubtedly others floating around the world today, there are several common reasons that are provided as to why ordinary people should not worry about the environment, social justice, peace, and other big issues facing citizens of the earth today. One of them, that the market will take care of any problems that may arise, has remarkable staying power in the United States, although it is unclear where the blind faith ends and where the pecuniary self-interest begins. The other magic bullet that will cure our ills is technology, which today goes hand in hand with money. The unfortunate reality, hidden from the public by the media, is that free markets and technology have succeeded in widening the gap between rich and poor to obscene levels.

The questions that ultimately will have the greatest consequences relate to what we do with the information we receive and how, in the broadest sense, we communicate with each other. In short, the type of world we attempt to create will be helped or hindered by the information and communication capabilities that are available to us.

We have encountered several comments that focus on problems related to our reliance on the pattern language concept. Although these comments would not necessarily undermine any of the arguments raised within individual patterns or these chapters, any claims that we make that are based on a close correspondence to the pattern language concepts could be at risk. In later chapters we discuss the similarities and differences between our work and Alexander's. In a nutshell, we believe that the pattern and the pattern language (as defined by Alexander and his colleagues) provides especially appropriate frameworks for representing the information associated with this project. Furthermore *A Pattern Language*, the book containing the most developed version of Alexander's pattern language, expresses—as does our book—the important need for citizen intervention in shaping the future. We part company, or at least appear to, with some of their bolder philosophical claims, notably that there exists a pattern language for doing things right, a process that all people can use to shape information and communication systems correctly, a "timeless way of building" information and communication systems and that systems created or shaped in this way will necessarily exhibit the "quality without a name."

Political Issues

The issues in this section are political in two senses: the politics inherent in a participatory project like this and the politics of the patterns as they relate to the rest of the world. As with the issues in the other sections, these issues overlap with others and are not so neatly contained within one category.

How were the patterns selected?
Whose knowledge is being represented?
Is this just recycled Western or neoliberal ideology?

How Were the Patterns Selected?

This simple question hides a great number of important issues. As we discuss in more detail in later chapters, the evolution from an idea in someone's mind to a pattern in this published set of patterns (and the online sets as well) has taken several routes. The process has been very open: literally anybody with access to a Web browser can submit a pattern concept to the online system (and anybody without this access could conceivably ask somebody who did have access to post it for them). People can, and have, joined various discussion lists as well or volunteered for the editorial advisory board. Nevertheless, the selection of the patterns, although informed by guidance and insight from the advisory committee, was ultimately made by me. Project governance admittedly has been administered by a (hopefully) "benevolent dictator" who has final say over what patterns ended up in this book (although subsequent editions could be done differently). Although the idea of complete equality of all participants seems impossible as well as not necessarily ideal, the idea of more participation, more egalitarianism, and more diversity seems immensely desirable, if not totally practical, and worth pursuing and exploring intellectually. Obviously this point of view is in keeping with the overall philosophy of this project and, indeed, some of the patterns in the pattern language, a topic that we reopen in later chapters of this book. It is also worth mentioning that if this book had been developed by a large committee, possibly by consensus, it may have been more watered down and contained more platitudes in the end.

Whose Knowledge Is Being Represented?

The question of whose knowledge is being represented is one of the most important issues to raise. (We discuss this explicitly in Voices of the Unheard, pattern 83.) It is also one of the most difficult to answer in a satisfactory way. The main problem is that, as in a meeting, the decisions are made by those who show up. There are many reasons that people are not able to "show up," including, predominantly, language barriers (the project was conducted in English) and access to the Internet (often an economic barrier). Unfortunately this naturally resulted in less participation by people in developing countries. These are criticisms that must be taken seriously, especially in a work that explicitly sets out to address problems with inequitable access to information and communication. We have done the best we could. We have solicited patterns and reviews of patterns from people with experience and knowledge about the situations in developing countries. Nevertheless, the proof of our success (or lack thereof) will ultimately be ascertained from the quality of the patterns themselves. Also, we plan for the project to evolve. Extending the representation outward to accommodate other voices (and other voices in other languages) is key as we move forward.

Finally we mention a last (but important) barrier to pattern authorship: the barrier of professionalism and education. For the most part, the pattern authors have been faculty members of colleges and universities or students or graduates of those institutions. Submitting a pattern (an unfamiliar entity in its own right) can be daunting, especially considering who else may be posting on the system. So although the system will allow anybody to post patterns, the professional standards called for implicitly for the online submissions and explicitly for the patterns in this book are a palpable barrier to participation. This problem is not exclusively one of the pattern language, however, nor is it likely to soon stop being a significant barrier (which is part of the motivation behind Translation, pattern 15). We have asked authors to avoid jargon in their pattern verbiage and make their writing as clear as possible without dumbing down their thoughts. It is an assumption throughout this book that many ideas or findings in the sciences, social sciences, and humanities are not actually as difficult to understand as they are made out to be. If jargon were pitched out and obtuse language replaced by clear writing (which is not necessarily easy for anybody to produce), much of that problem would be solved. To increase the participation among nonacademics, the idea of mentors in pattern writing is a good one. We also feel that increasing the number of venues is also an important idea.

Isn't All of This Just Recycled Western or Neoliberal Ideology?

This last issue is a perennial concern, and we have tried to address it throughout. I feel that the criticism in these chapters of the "Western" models (especially of global capitalism and the ruling classes) would clear us of the neoliberal accusation. But there is also criticism from another corner, that authoritarian regimes can be fine and their inhabitants are dwelling happily within their realms. While we acknowledge this viewpoint, we respectfully disagree for two reasons. The first is that unanswerable rulers are inexorably drawn into corruption. The second is that authoritarian rule is too inflexible and hidebound to deal with exigencies of today's emergencies; the skills, values, and civic imagination of people are required. And, finally, to those who think that there is no environmental crisis or that poor people deserve their poverty, I can only say that no answer could penetrate your mind anyway, so I will not bother trying.

Pragmatic Issues

We end this chapter with a wide range of pragmatic issues that have to do with how the patterns are developed and used and how they are evaluated and, possibly, modified. Pragmatic issues have to do with how things work out in the real world as opposed to any imagined ideal one. Pragmatic issues are not likely to be show-stoppers and are more likely to be resolved by adjusting our actions based on how we could have done better in certain areas.

How useful are the patterns?
How will the patterns and the pattern language change over time?
Why a book?

How Useful Are the Patterns?

Many of these issues are discussed in more detail in the chapter 9, following the patterns themselves. Usefulness is, of course, a complex issue. In our case, it raises issues related to, first and foremost, accessibility of the patterns. This boils down to how the people who should find the patterns useful actually locate the information (and how easily, either in the book or at the Web site) and once they found the pattern whether they were able to readily understand the pattern and use it as an insight for productive thinking or as an impetus for productive action. We also need to find out the conditions of pattern use. Were they discussed in a group? Were the patterns used individually, sequentially, or many at the same time?

In our case, evaluation cannot truly be separated from other actions on behalf of the project. For example, thinking about who the potential users should be is a component of evaluation and activism. In other words, at the same time we would evaluate whether we reached these users, we would be devising a strategy to reach them. At the same time we evaluated how useful the language is, we would try to make it more useful to readers.

Also it must be said that in the long run, one can never know the effects of something because it is impossible to know what impact was made on, say, a pattern reader and what the reader did with the information and so on. Although this was not the original intent, the main users of patterns might actually never have looked at any of the patterns directly; they may be using a service or information resource developed by somebody who employed the patterns.

It must also be acknowledged that the pattern language is not generally the original source of the information within the patterns. The pattern language is a particular ensemble of ideas that we have woven together in a particular way that we hope will be useful. And following on from that, we really need, at least ultimately, to ask whether bringing all these ideas together and the concept itself of bringing all these ideas together was useful and if the particular organizing approach of the pattern language was useful.

Evaluation therefore is part of evolution, the subject of the next question.

How Will the Patterns and the Pattern Language Change over Time?

Evaluation is part of evolution, but that does not tell the whole story. We are saying, as Christopher Alexander and the developers of the original pattern language said, that the pattern language consists of hypotheses, and they change over time. At the same time, Alexander uses terms like *timeless*, and the pattern language book in the latest edition is no different than it was in its original 1977 edition.

Part of the story behind this is the fact that the domain of communication and information itself is changing and will continue to change. To some degree, that in itself will force changes in the way we use—and react to, sometimes in opposition—communication and information systems. Some of our patterns will become obsolete over time and will need changing or removing. This is not to say that everything will change, however. We expect that many of our patterns express the timelessness of the human condition with respect especially to information and communication systems, as well as the inextricable connection that humans have to them.

At the same time, however, we have tried to acknowledge the tentativeness of our pursuit from the start. The fact that we offer this as our best guess and best attempt, and not as received truth, may put some people off. Seeking truth, like other important enterprises, is a journey, and it is hard won, if won at all. For these reasons, we have tried to embody evolution and incremental development in this project from the onset.

Why a Book?

Finally, the question of why a book is needed at all has been raised. Would it be easier—and better—to just publish the patterns online? The book is a frozen entity in time; unlike the Web, it is not dynamic—a feature that has its own virtues. A book, as a static artifact (revising and editing notwithstanding), is also not readily susceptible to the Orwellian prospect of being modified by the powers that be to something more of their liking. And although books (especially new, hardcover, non-best-sellers) are often expensive and beyond the reach of many people (especially in developing countries), they may be in a library where they can be borrowed, or they may be given or lent to other people in an actual transfer of a physical, durable object (see Durable Assets, pattern 58).

This book and the work described in it, like the new media forms described in the first chapter, blur many of the same boundaries. The pattern language orientation provides a solid framework for an online environment that we could use to develop the project collaboratively. Much of the verbiage in this book, particularly the patterns that constitute the main part of this book, were developed online and will continue to be freely available online to anybody with a Web browser. We also hope to develop additional online technology to facilitate the ongoing collaborative evolution of the pattern language. The other boundary that we intend to ignore is the one that separates action and inaction, engagement and reflection. We are not merging the two poles into one; rather, we are acknowledging and promoting the inseparability and potential synergy of the two.

Our pattern language project is a type of secular guide to living an engaged life; it is pragmatic and value based, and it provides directions, not an explicit destination, or a side effect, or a distraction. We are developing a holistic and far-reaching answer to the question, "How can people and civil society use information and communication to improve social and environmental health and well-being around the world?" We believe that our approach has several attributes that distinguish it from others. The first is that we are building the case that this is a recognition of, as well as a part of, one big project (perhaps subconsciously inspired by the universality of "One Big Union" vision promoted by the International Workers of the World in the early 1900s) that has yet to be conceptualized as such. Within this perspective, we are attempting to explicitly identify people, actions, issues, ideas, and locations that have not been connected historically—but should be—using the pattern language framework. And although we welcome the assistance of the elite, the focus and orientation of this project is on the common man and woman—the grassroots, that is, a bottom-up, participatory approach that involves everybody, everywhere at once. Perhaps it goes without saying that this is a never-ending project.

The next chapter goes into more depth as to what we are dealing with and why. Specifically it expands on the three worlds that we introduced in chapter 1.

4 The End of the World as We Know It

The two interpretations of the title of Immanuel Wallerstein's 1999 book, *The End of the World as We Know It,* aptly capture two important realities and challenges of our era. Certainly the world that we know is changing. For one thing, the social part of the world is becoming more closely linked through culture, commerce, media, and war as the human population becomes larger, more urbanized, more unequal, and seemingly more polarized. The physical part of the world is changing as well. There is a growing list of endangered species and diminishing resources (like forests, fish stocks, and fresh water), looming pandemics, more toxic waste, and alarming changes in the earth's climate presumably precipitated by its human multitudes.

At the same time that the world is changing (the "end of the world as we know it"), the systems of knowledge, communications, discourse, inquiry, and perception that humankind uses to make sense of the world are also changing. Hence the ways in which we know the world are changing at the same time as the world itself is changing. And when our world and the ways in which we know it are both rapidly changing into unfamiliar forms, humankind is faced with the seemingly impossible task of understanding the nature of the changes. The task is made more difficult when the patterns of thought and action (embodied in our minds, culture, and transcriptions of knowledge) that we necessarily employ to prosecute that impossible task are incoherent, incomplete and self contradictory. When the world is changing in ways that belie the assumptions about the world that have evolved over the centuries and guide our everyday behavior, the need to appropriately and expeditiously revise our views of the world (which in turn will influence our thinking and activities) is as difficult as it is urgent. One can briefly note the lack of success that humankind has had in understanding and adapting to major threats (including, of course, the ones that it has directly caused such as war and resource depletion and despoliation) proactively, thoughtfully, or equitably. Indeed, it has established ongoing material and intellectual support to perpetuate destructive aspects of current society through the development and maintenance of powerful social institutions. The term *institutionalize*, in fact, now signifies the notion of habitual and unimaginative ways of thinking that are particularly inflexible in their response to new circumstances.

Three Worlds from One

In keeping with Wallerstein's insights, it is useful to think of three somewhat distinct though interacting worlds as we advance the case for the pattern language project: (1) the world "out there" that humans can observe or otherwise perceive, (2) how humans think and communicate, and (3) what humans know about the other two worlds. These worlds also have similarities and major differences to the three worlds—of physical objects, subjective experiences, and products of the human mind—proposed by Popper (1972). Each of the worlds I am proposing is intimately related to the other two, yet because each world seems to follow its own logic, each can be thought of as somewhat independent of the other two. John Dewey (1938) suggests as much in his discussion on what types of inquiry are most suitable for biological and cultural explorations. Dewey's logic of inquiry is an exploration of how this third world should be constituted in order to reflect in meaningful ways the other world(s). It is our contention that an improved understanding of these worlds (including an appreciation of what we do not know) and their relationships is required for humankind is to make genuine progress. This discussion helps to provide context and direction to the pattern language as it evolves.

The first world is the world that we live in—what we generally refer to as the environment. It includes the physical world of life on earth consisting of animals, plants, and so forth and the weather, earth forms, and physical phenomena ranging from atoms and subatomic particles to galaxies. This world also includes the physical structures that humankind has constructed over the years. This is a world that humans must live with—and contend with. It is a world that sustains the other two but often suffers silently as a result of repetitive and unwise interaction. Nevertheless, this world has ways of passing its insults back to those who insult it–or at least to their descendants.

Human physicality—how we digest food and grow muscles, for example—is best thought of as belonging to the first world. The psychology of individuals and the sociology of groups, by contrast, belong in the second world of human interpretation—in particular, the emotional, cognitive, and sentient world of people. Importantly for the perspective of this book, the second world is animated through individual and collective action. It changes not only through the generation or acquisition of knowledge but through praxis: "reflection and action upon the world in order to transform it" (Freire 1974). Human emotion and cognition are active causal components in propelling interpretations, actions, interactions, and outcomes toward our desired ends of social progress. Although difficult in practice, we are considering this world in the absence of knowledge (which we include in the third world described below).

The third world is the world of (transcribed and otherwise) human knowledge, here separated from the world of human individual and social interpretation even though the two are thoroughly inseparable, because of its incredible influence and, especially, how the force it exerts sometimes makes it seem as if it is an independent force (which also can be usefully viewed as independent). This is the world that, along with the communicative and interpretive aspects of the second world, describes how we know the other two worlds. It is the second of the two meanings in Wallerstein's book title.

The pattern language project should take these worlds into account. Indeed the product is part of the third world described above. If and when any of the three worlds changes, so should the pattern language. Thus the pattern language is not being presented as timeless or immutable, but rather as a reflection and an actor within a complex and dynamic environment comprising these three worlds. The three worlds model should not be envisioned as a snapshot of reality that imposes its strictures; instead it is more like an abstract playing field in which people can work to effect change. We briefly explore these worlds as they affect the pattern language, hinting at the deep interactions between them.

Impossibility of "Knowing Reality"

Everything we have in our brain came originally from our senses, but our senses and our understanding of what we have sensed is incomplete; our eyes, for example, are useful only for visible wavelengths. Frazier (1995) points out several significant barriers to comprehending the world that start even before the information reaches the brain:

Our eyes transmit to our brains poor resolution, upside-down, mainly monochrome, moving two-dimensional images which the brain converts into a three-dimensional colored model which moves with us but is static relative to our eye movements. The brain censors out our obtrusive nose, fills in the gaps where the bundle of optic nerves leaving our eyes causes a blind spot, employs a rich repertory of tricks such as size constancy which prevents someone appearing to shrink as they move away, is easily deceived by false perspective and other illusions. Then the ultimate trick is played and the brain gives us the feeling that this virtual model in our brains is actually "out there" and incorporates other information from the senses such as vibration in the air which it conveniently converts into sounds also "out there"

Our brain evolved to meet the reality that existed millions of years ago (and we are as helpless to change this as we are to change the circumstances that have already occurred). And we share many of our emotions with our nonhuman relatives, emotions that probably have evolved to address issues of survival more than to address needs for comprehensive knowledge and flawless reasoning.

Our mind has been largely constructed before we have any knowledge of so-called free choice. We (individually and as a species) dwell in the tiniest temporal and spatial zone, which necessarily constrains what we can know. And ultimately our mind is very much shaped by the collective mind that we call culture.

We See What We Want (or Expect) to See

Human beings everywhere create systems of knowledge that are used to understand, explain, and so forth. Our knowledge systems become our reality. Seemingly intangible, they become material and authoritative; they determine what we see and how we interpret what we see, that is, what it means; they guide policy; they justify actions. They represent a type of cognitive and cultural inertia that police themselves and the rest of society, for it is these systems that dictate what is good, proper, and *possible*.

At the core of the human brain, near the base of the spinal column, is a "reptilian brain" that controls breathing and other vital functions. The limbic brain, built around the reptilian brain, is found in all mammals. It is this part of our brain that generally decides long before any conscious (or reasoned) consideration of actual virtues or flaws takes place whether we like or hate somebody at first glance. This is where our value judgments are formed and some of our earliest habits and inclinations are rooted. This part of the brain is also responsible for our emotions and, especially because it is largely inaccessible to our probing, is the area of the brain that receives the most attention from propagandists.

Finally, although our brain is intricate and wondrous, it is finite—and some are apparently more finite than others. And not only is our brain small, it is prone to errors. To a large degree we construct our own reality to the extent that our own life circumstances, constraints, aspirations, and habits seek and allow. In spite of all our limitations, part of humankind's problem is that it thinks it knows everything. Although it is difficult for us to admit, our knowledge is— and always will be— partial and uncertain. This truism should not prevent us from taking action; that is not an option. It should, however lead us to explore where the dominant ideas and forces are taking us. Paradoxically, acknowledging our cognitive limitations may be one of the most important steps toward wisdom and more effective civic intelligence.

The Physical World

It does not take long for us to be reminded that the three worlds are not separate. The realization dawns at the moment that we attempt to describe some aspect of the physical world and the impossibility of describing it without relying on the other two worlds arises. Having noted that our understanding of the physical world is constrained by our interpretation, we can at least acknowledge that the physical world is incredibly vast, complicated, and interlinked. Any reader of this book currently exists in an intimate and intensely interactive relationship with an immediate environment. At the same time we really have little knowledge about how the physical world in its entirety works, although humankind's knowledge has changed considerably in the past century. Each living thing on Earth, from a cell to a seed to an organism, is apparently waiting for signs or signals, which initiate actions and trigger other signs and signals and so on in a vital, fascinating, and infinitely complex choreography. Humankind, for example is just now beginning to understand the immensely important carbon cycle that links phytoplankton, currents, trees, moss, and weather (and just about everything else) and shapes much of life on earth.

The Human World

The human world is the world that describes how humans interact with each other and the rest of the physical world. It describes how humans go about obtaining and interpreting information. For our purposes, this world does not include the actual information that is in play. This world does not include what people are actually thinking about— just how they do it. This world describes the habits of action, patterned habits of thinking, and an advanced ability to rationalize that individuals have. It describes the ways that we have learned, consciously and otherwise, how to deal with the necessities of life and its all-too-finite resources. Interestingly, this world includes physical actions and reactions of humans when there are communicative or interpretive aspects.

Humans are social animals. From a basic family unit to civilizations, humans organize themselves in collectives to perform whatever tasks the unit deems necessary. Current European censuses, for example, "recognize 10,000 to 20,000 unique occupational roles" (Tainter 1990). These tasks generally include an approach toward the production and allocation of goods and services, that is, an economic system. Religions, education, and culture are collective inventions. So, too, is language, a remarkable collective achievement that allows humans to communicate and, perhaps more important, to engage in distributed cognition. The abilities to defend themselves from attack or to mount attacks are collective achievements. Social movements that aim to change the status quo are collective, as, of course, are the forces that maintain it.

Sociologists have identified two important concepts, socialization and the social image, that are relevant to the human world. Two somewhat extended quotations (Lindblom 1990) provide a view of the negative side of each. While each concept is unavoidable in any society, they generally oppose change or deviance of any sort from the unchallengeable soul that lies at the core of society.

Regarding, as they do, socialization as necessary for the viability of society, many people see it as benign, often, for example, characterizing it as an educational process. But societies "teach" ways of looking at the world not only by enlightening the new generation about life's many opportunities but by inducing or coercing the new generation not to consider some possibilities. They "teach" the rules of the game not solely by an illuminating instruction but by coercive enforcement that cuts off probing.

The features of the social image that everyone seems to agree to are: (1) It is expressed in symbols (mostly verbal) and their accompanying emotional affects; (2) it is often implicit and always incompletely articulated in linguistic form; (3) it is systematically instilled in each generation through various agencies of socialization and education; (4) it is an ordering device, ensuring common meanings and responses by means of stereotyped metaphors, models, myths, or other symbolic devices; (5) it is most difficult to recognize as something other than reality or experience; (6) it is impossible to test or evaluate as well as difficult to question; (7) it is anonymously authored; and its absence would mean idiocy or insanity. (From Larry D. Spence, The Politics of Social Knowledge, [University Park, Pennsylvania State University Press, 1978])

For our purposes, we want to understand how people work together in complex ways and how certain ideas and activities are institutionalized and enforced. What exists now is the product of evolving systems of thought and interactions and engagements where various actors, such as armies, churches, commercial enterprises, and, increasingly, large media systems, work harder and with more resources than most others to instill the ideas and activities that they endorse (often not explicitly). The ultimate question, of course, is whether those actors are going to work with or against the rest of us.

The Knowledge World

A collection of ideas, worldviews, knowledge systems, or other viewpoints that coexist define an environment of sorts, an ecosystem where alliances are formed and battles are waged. Within this environment some of the viewpoints will thrive and dominate while others recoil, cringe, shrivel, and die. A diversity of knowledge systems seems key to survival. However, a diversity of dysfunctional and mutually incoherent and unintelligible systems with no common goals or desire to strike compromises can also be problematic. While a monoculture is anathema, stagnant, and death inviting, a bad mix of ideas can be deadly and corrosive to new ideas and vitality.

Slogans and other social clichés do not exist in a vacuum. They generally arose for a reason and will persist for as long as people and organizations are willing to employ them. There are plenty to choose from, including the "hidden hand" and the "wisdom of the market." One interesting example is the "tragedy of the commons" (Hardin 1968). Although the idea was presented in essentially a speculative essay, it has been elevated to the status of an immutable law. Hardin's preoccupation with human "breeding" allowed him to neglect the fact that people consume and pollute at unequal rates. Jared Diamond (2008), for example, reminds us that "with 10 times the population, the United States consumes 320 times more resources than Kenya does." Presumably the idea received this hero's welcome because it argued against common property, a forbidden notion among orthodox capitalists.

The scientific community (specifically, the *hard*, that is, not *social*, science community) presents a fascinating case study in our brief look at the knowledge systems. This community is a fairly recent addition historically, and its body of knowledge is founded on a different model from, say, religious or commercial systems. Scientists have been extremely successful in unlocking many secrets that have been fundamental to transportation, communication, medicine, and the development of weapons of unfathomable power. Dishonest scientific practice, such as the falsification of data, is often publicly exposed and disgraced. Stringent requirements for making testable predictions from theory, for replicable results, have earned substantial legitimacy.

Several new developments are afoot that could change the face of science. One is the privatization of science. This means two things: that scientific work is increasingly being supported by commercial interests (pharmaceutical companies, for example) and that the results are being kept private. These violate the de facto social contract that has been understood by the scientific community and the public. We can judge science not only by its criteria of honesty, testability, replicability, and objectivity, but also by the effects of its choices of what to study in the first place. For example, research funded by the tobacco industry may be conducted in a scientific manner, but its methods and the phenomena under study may be carefully chosen to yield results that can be interpreted favorably to the sponsors. Funding is not equally available to all areas of scientific research. Wallerstein's (1999) comments underscore these points well when he asks the social science community to

recognize that science is not and cannot be disinterested, since scientists are socially rooted and can no more escape their minds than their bodies. It must recognize that empiricism is not innocent, but always presumes some a priori commitments. It must recognize that our truths are not universal truths and that if there exist universal truths they are complex, contradictory, and plural. It must recognize that science is not the search for the simple, but the search for the most plausible interpretation of the complex.

When Worlds Collide

The worlds I have described are not autonomous or totally distinct from each other, nor are they palpable like the graphic depiction of a globe that often is used to portray worlds. This section briefly discusses some of the major ways in which the three worlds influence each other. Although each to some degree abides by its own mutable and immutable set of rules, they are in deep, perpetual, and unavoidable interaction. Each world interacts with each of the others; each influences the others with some general patterns of behavior.

The Human World Influences the Physical World   At a basic level, the human world influences the physical world by extracting and transforming resources: what the human world needs—or what it thinks it needs. The extraction process can damage or poison the environment and deplete resources, thus setting up conditions for more degradation. It can even create a new global climate regime. It can transform the physical world ultimately through farming, construction, or war. The human world can upset existing natural balances and cyclical processes, thus affecting the habitats and lives of many animals, including humans. Of course humans can—or at least attempt to—make changes that promote biodiversity or other approaches to environmental health.

The Human World Influences the Knowledge World   The human world creates, discusses, argues about, institutionalizes, and prioritizes certain types of knowledge development. As we have defined it, the world of knowledge would not exist without the world of humans. Creation and destruction are the most profound forms of influence.

The Physical World Influences the Human World   The physical world provides the basic conditions of living: gravity, atoms, and all the rest. It also provides all physical sustenance. The necessities of living in it prompted the evolution of our bodies and our minds. The natural part of it inspires and teaches people like artists, storytellers, scientists, and religious figures. It can be healing, and it can be threatening.

The Physical World Influences the Knowledge World It is conjectured that many of humankind's central notions—of cycles, order, complexity, symmetry, and so on—were inspired by the physical world. The physical world today provides scientists with data to measure and monitor and presents phenomena to understand and question. The prospect of widespread climate change has shifted research priorities and may ultimately lead to shifts, planned or unplanned, into new economic regimes as well. Of course, the human world must intervene for any of these influences to occur.

The Knowledge World Influences the Physical World The knowledge world has given us technology, global capitalism, the idea of free markets, and mass media. There are obvious clear links between the knowledge system and the physical world. Historically, however, it would have been impossible for the knowledge world to influence the physical world directly. Now, with the invention of computers (and actually some feedback devices before them), it is possible to develop software that causes some action to occur when some particular measurement from the physical world is detected. As Albert-Laszlo Barabasi points out (2002), "Millions of measuring devices, including cameras, microphones, thermostats and temperature gauges, light and traffic sensors, and pollution detectors are popping up everywhere, feeding information into increasingly fast and sophisticated computers. Experts predict that by 2010, there will be around 10,000 telemetric devices for each human on the planet." If software is programmed to learn or adapt over time and does so inaccurately or inappropriately, it may come at a time when we forget (or the original programmers change jobs or die) what actions were programmed.

Knowledge World Influences the Human World How the knowledge world influences the human world is a story that may never be written satisfactorily. The changes may be happening too quickly and too unpredictably for them to be properly understood. The global reach of media is an interesting place to look because we are in the midst of the fastest and most profound shift in the way that people obtain information. While nearly all that was perceived by people worldwide a century ago was direct (nonmediated) and "real," a large and growing amount of people's time is now spent interacting with commercially produced mass media. It is unclear what the long-term (or even short-term) effects of global mediation will be on individual cognition and perception or on more difficult to measure capabilities such as collaborative problem solving, social capital, and attitudes toward other people. As scientists learn more about how the brain works and attitudes and habits are formed, social engineering may be possible through drugs or other approaches. The U.S. military, for example, has vastly improved the killing efficiency of its soldiers over the past hundred or so years (Grossman 1995). Finally, the knowledge world is where many of the decisions are made about how resources are distributed. It is well documented that mental illness is increasing worldwide at unprecedented levels (Lancet Global Mental Health Group 2007). Although the answers to this troubling development might not be easy to find, experts seem to agree that this phenomenon is not getting the attention it deserves.

The Three Worlds All Influence Each Other Improving our collective understanding of these three worlds and how they interact, including our collective understanding of what we do not understand, is key to our survival. We disavow this advice at our own peril. The human world and the knowledge world relate strongly to their own respective worlds, but rarely without the involvement of the other. Knowledge does not change without human interaction and reflection.

Knowledge System Clashes

It is the knowledge world (although the physical world is always present) that predominantly sets up the direct and modifiable conditions under which the human world exists today. In other words, although we depend on the physical world to provide us with food, much of the world is starving because the rules of the human and knowledge world ensure that the distribution of food is unequal. A society using the scientific method as an intellectual tool and a worldview that promoted dominion over nature is likely to become materially different from a group that thinks otherwise, one, for instance, that believes that spirits are responsible for everything that happens or that humans should live in harmony with nature.

Local Effects, Global Implications

Although the meanings we assign to our perceptions and experiences are at least to some degree socially conditioned, we experience our environment personally and locally. The food we put in our mouths, the weather where we live, the challenges that we face here and now are likely to loom larger than those that are remote, unseen, and unknown. The dangerous nature of this exclusively local focus is becoming increasingly obvious. For one thing, nonlocal events—smog in Asia, for example—can have strong effects locally—in the western hemisphere. Noxious chemicals or other pathogens that are imperceptible can enter our bodies, resulting in consequences that are all too perceptible. One of our best strategies might be conceptualizing what a global view might actually entail and begin, at least as a provocative thought experiment, exploring what this global view might mean.

Scientific Uncertainty: The Fox and the Rabbit Story

Many people are familiar with figure 4.1, which shows the waxing and waning of fox and rabbit—or at least some type of predator-prey—populations. The graph is produced by a simple computer simulation in which there are only two types of animals: foxes and rabbits.

Let us say that when the world begins, there are few foxes but rabbits are plentiful. This is great for a fox because his favorite meal is just about everywhere he looks. The abundance of rabbit meat allows the foxes to multiply their numbers considerably. Being a rabbit always looking over your shoulder for hungry foxes is less fun, but the graph does not address that. (Look up the Alternative Progress Indexes, pattern 46, and The Good Life, pattern 3, which do.) While the fox population is burgeoning, the rabbit population is in decline. Suddenly—or so it must seem—there are zillions of foxes and rabbits are sparse. Of course in the lonely world of a computer simulation, the hapless fox, so fat and sassy in years gone by, finds

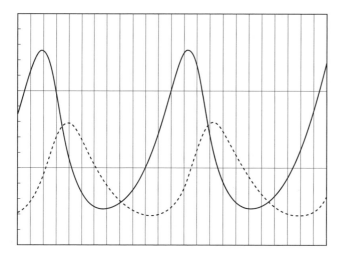

Figure 4.1
Theoretical fluctuations in fox and rabbit populations. The more volatile rabbit population is depicted by
the curves with the higher amplitude.

himself among lots (and lots) of his own inedible company. There is little or nothing for him
and his brethren to eat. Over time, the graph returns to a familiar state, and mathematical
equations are again demonstrated to be elegant and regular.

We could wonder, however, what happened to the foxes. Apparently they did not hunt
down every last rabbit, for if they had, both foxes and rabbits would go extinct. (Remember
in the model that the foxes, unlike the rabbits, need to eat, and rabbits are the only thing in
this world that foxes can eat.) What the graph does not convey is the anguished thoughts
that the virtual foxes entertained or the desperate measures they contemplated when their
very survival was threatened.

This is a tiny version of view of reality that scientists try to construct using mathematics
and computer modeling. And while it does show a dynamic and the interrelationships
between interacting entities within an environment, it also shows a regularity that could be
misleading if applied to the real world too liberally. The example also highlights the absence
of the complexity that any real interaction or local variation would entail. Neither does it
allow for any deviation; the foxes cannot decide to become vegetarians, for example.

We tell the fable of the rabbits and the foxes not because scientists (or even ordinary
people) would believe the literal truth of the model but to illustrate a simple model on which
more complicated models are built. Unfortunately, although complicated models are likely
to retain the flaws of earlier assumptions, they are unlikely to be replaced because of the large
investments of time and money and people's familiarity with them. One observation from
Wilson (2002), a marine scientist, recounts the successes of this approach: "The history of
technological advance over the past 200 years illustrates the power of this method. But

unlike civil engineering and the many other fields that have flourished using a reductionist approach, the sciences dealing with complex natural and human systems such as marine fisheries have not been able to develop a track record that generates broad social trust." He goes on to describe the challenges we face if we expect to carry on in that way, "The difficulty of the scientific problem in a complex, quickly changing, and highly adaptive environment such as the ocean should not be underestimated. It has created pervasive uncertainty that has been magnified by the strategic behavior of the various human interests who play in the game of fisheries management."

Fundamentalisms

Ideally, representatives of the various battling knowledge systems would be working together on common concerns about the future, but from different perspectives and different approaches. Instead, many seem to be dedicated to the destruction (or the denigration) of other systems of knowledge. Worse, many are interested in promoting violence against other groups or, at least, the cultivation of fear and loathing, which if not lending directly to violence help sustain an environment that precludes cooperation. Dogged insistence on simplistic slogans is not a threat in its own right (merely a type of intellectual deadweight—like rowing a boat with the anchor dragging the bottom of the lake); people's active resistance to accepting knowledge derived from common sense, minority groups, and those whose ethnicity, skin color, or deity of choice does not appeal, is more problematic.

Regardless of the accuracy of the diagnosis regarding the fundamentalization of the world, the importance of meaning to people and cultures seems impossible, and possibly suicidal, to ignore. While it is not the intent of this project to define meaning for people or establish what it ought to be, it seems clear that humankind has historically found meaning in a variety of pursuits and orientations that are not likely to be obsolete because of mass media, global capitalism, or the Internet. Humankind typically draws on a relatively small number of activities to provide meaning in their lives. Historically ordinary life provided meaning, and a conscious quest for meaning was not necessary. It is arguably some of humankind's more unfortunate inventions, tangible and abstract, such as slavery, exploitation, loss of community, and consumerism, that have robbed people of the meaning they need.

The quest for a shared pattern language is intended to help reintroduce meaning into people's lives. Some of the ways that meaning is cultivated and maintained in societies are linked to the mysteries of life, and find expression through nature, artistic expression, conviviality, study, and service to one's family, the community, and the rest of the world. Artistic and intellectual achievement, conviviality, community, service, usefulness, and love are in fact timeless and irreplaceable.

Tight Linkages and Emergent Network Properties

In network theory, there is a phenomenon that occurs when a certain threshold based on the degree of connectedness among a number of nodes is surpassed. When this happens, all of the nodes in the network abruptly and unexpectedly become close neighbors (Watts 2003). We now know more about communication networks than we used to. Their degree of interconnectedness and the speed by which this connectivity is increasing suggests that a startling new world, one filled with pleasant and unpleasant surprises, may be just ahead. The speed with which new information, including rumors or computer viruses, can be disseminated to the extremities of the particular network or networks it resides within can initiate severe disruptions, causing, for example, a run on the banks. The tight linkage of economic data (especially that generated and distributed by computer networks) can send massive shock waves through the world's economic institutions; a cascade of automated decisions or a short circuit on the electrical grid can cause crippling effects in a region far away.

A system essentially on unknown hair-trigger alert is open to gaming by malicious manipulators as well. The energy hustlers at Enron routinely toyed with the state of California, promoting rolling brownouts and other types of troublesome and unexpected perturbations while bringing in hundreds of millions of dollars for themselves. Chaotic changes à la "butterfly effect," in which the flutter of a butterfly's wings in Brazil causes severe storms thousands of miles away, are nothing new. However, the number of possible routes through which a small effect can be magnified—or ganged with other small effects—along with the speed through which the rogue information can be propagated and the distance it can traverse, has increased significantly. Globalization and information technologies have created opportunities for the butterfly effect to take wing as an apparent design objective. New hair-trigger events have become a central component in the configuration.

Networking of course can take many forms. It may be the world's biosphere, where the network's nodes are living creatures who dwell within an incredibly intricate web of signals. It could also be the world's economy, with its elaborate system of balances, debits and credits, interest accruing, and transfers of funds exceeding $1 trillion a day. Computers and digital networks are woven into complex systems that are essentially beyond human control or understanding. Putting our future "on automatic" with ever more complex systems in de facto decision-making roles does not seem wise given these deficiencies.

Collapses: The Fox and the Rabbit Writ Large

Jared Diamond, in his book *Collapse* (2005), raises the critical question indicated by the book's subtitle, *How Societies Choose to Fail or Succeed*. Diamond focuses on environmental factors in his analysis, basically the destruction or overuse of the environment due to population growth or increased per capita impact of people, but acknowledges that other contributing factors are always present. He includes both hostile neighbors and friendly trade partners to his list of presumed causes of societal collapse (the latter, because relying on trade with one or a small number of partners can be problematic if the trading suddenly stops). The last item in the five-point framework that he uses to analyze societal collapse is "the society's responses to its environmental problems," which he notes "always prove significant." Diamond then uses a road map consisting of a sequence of collective capabilities that are echoed to some degree in our Civic Intelligence pattern (1) and, indeed, throughout the pattern language.

Tainter's book, *The Collapse of Complex Societies* (1990), as well as Diamond's, concentrates on complex societies whose social roles are highly specialized and numerous, sometimes numbering more than 1 million. Certainly collapse is so much more spectacular and unexpected (since adapting was the modus operandi of these societies) in complex societies like ancient Rome than when a simple village containing small numbers of people and few social rules collapses. It goes without saying, perhaps, that current society, which could now be said to encompass the entire world, is certainly complex. But for the intriguing and illuminating insights, both books (Tainter's in particular, because he is dealing with ancient societies) focus on societies that existed more or less in isolation. Thus the inhabitants of Easter Island cut down "their" last tree. So while it still makes sense to consider habitats in our own backyards, in our current globalized era, the need or greed of one society can fell the last tree or land the last fish in the territory of another nation altogether. And while there still may exist elsewhere another tree for the cutting or another fish for the frying, the message of both books is that complex societies can unconsciously bring about their own collapse through social or environmental disregard.

World System Shift

While our approach does not assume that any particular society will dominate in the future, the threats or challenges that we will likely face in the near future suggest that new forms of thinking and of organizing will be needed. One important question that Diamond posed is what we will do to anticipate and prepare for these challenges. The approaches that we consider now—before the challenges are upon us in full force—are likely to be far different from those we devise during a major upheaval.

We would like to discuss the possibility that a major transformation, if not a collapse, is on the horizon. Immanuel Wallerstein is a cofounder of world systems theory, which looks at human history from a long-view perspective. One of his more impressive case studies is the more-or-less sudden massive and historic shift from the feudal system that had persisted in Europe for over a thousand years into the wholly new and totally unanticipated historical system that has come to be known as capitalism (1974).

Far from being a historical curiosity of little relevance today, the historically rapid transformation from one vast system that affected all facets of daily life to another quite different system is salient today. Although the capitalistic world system appears to be at the top of its form, Wallerstein offers a provocative portfolio of evidence suggesting that capitalism's days may be numbered as feudalism was before it. Interestingly, much of Wallerstein's case centers on the diminishing amount of exploitable resources, including labor, worldwide which provide the fuel for the capitalist engine.

If humankind is incapable of envisioning and implementing a new world system that works for all, then what is the point of thinking about the future or engaging in the types of activities that this book and its contributors recommend?

The Vision

Envisioning a better world has preoccupied a modest (and occasionally influential) number of scholars, prophets, artists, charlatans, lunatics, activists, and even ordinary people over the centuries. This exercise helps establish the idea that a future that is better than the present is possible. It can present new ideas that are added to the collective imagination and acted on later. And utopian thinking paradoxically can place critical focus on the real world by demonstrating (implicitly) the great distance between the real and the ideal.

Although our effort to create a pattern language, like the utopian visions, is aimed at creating a better world, our vision focuses not on a specific end result but on our activities that are designed to move us incrementally closer to a better world. On a basic level, we would like to create a language that supports cultures that encourage cooperation and collaborative problem solving and discourage war, violence, and aggression—probably by addressing the root causes, delegitimizing war as a viable option, and transforming the institutions whose goal or by-product is war and violence. The culture would strive to diminish social dominance by building bridges between people and providing opportunities for disadvantaged people. We would need to shape institutions and policies in education and media that promote these reforms while helping to develop new mental models that allow us to think more effectively about developing these new cultures.

Humankind is celebrated for its abilities to develop reasonable, even exceptional, solutions to local problems, that is, solutions that work for the most part. But these apparent solutions do not work all of the time, they would not work for every situation that looked similar, and they would not necessarily work in a global sense. Also, of course, humans have a tendency to inappropriately adopt "solutions"—like going to war—as a response to *their* problems—like unpopularity among the electorate. This may address a problem that they might have but unleash a cascade of other problems that in the broader scheme of things are much more problematic than the original problem.

What will it take to actually start making progress?

At the most general level, we would like our work here to highlight the positive ways that people are creating nonviolent and nonexploitive trajectories for humankind. We hope that our work will help strengthen the activities that we have identified, encourage more activities like them, and help set up conditions that engender new collaborative actions.

Opportunities: If We Do Not Change Direction, We'll Get Where We Are Heading

We live in an era replete with challenges—problems of seeming intractability that have grown in magnitude to encompass the entire world. Surveying the scene, what openings exist for a program like ours? How big is our opportunity, and what can be done to leverage it? How could it be expanded or contracted? There has been an enormous worldwide outburst for activities that support a more just and sustainable world. Unfortunately, at the same time, the forces opposed to that have also shown dedication.

As Margaret Keck and Kathryn Sikkink report in their enlightening book on transnational advocacy networks (1998), many people around the world are working on projects to make the world better for the simple reason that they want to do the right thing. Keck and Sikkink characterize these networks by four key attributes: "the centrality of values or principled ideas, the belief that people can make a difference, the creative use of information and the employment by non-governmental actors of sophisticated political strategies in targeting their campaigns."

Transnational advocacy networks are a natural place to focus attention given the philosophy and objectives of this project. For one thing, their involvement is likely not to be based on the prospect of power or financial reward. This is not to say that there is no place for people with money or government affiliations, or that people and organizations are somehow expected to operate without funds. We are saying that people who are motivated by the force of their conviction and concern are less likely to pack their bags when funding is down and that they are presumably less likely to succumb to diverting influences. And since these networks are generally "looser" in many ways (they are not, for example, strict hierarchies and do not have rigid membership rules) than other organizations, they can absorb new points of view more readily and accommodate people from many backgrounds. Likely participants include nongovernmental organizations; community, civic, and spiritual activists; policymakers; journalists; artists (visual, performing, and others); academics, researchers, theorists, and social critics; media producers; and religious and other concerned people. Finally, because they are networks, they are more likely to distribute new ideas to other organizations and locations than traditional organizations that operate only locally and confine their communications accordingly.

Information and Communication Focus

Why is it important to look specifically at information and communication systems? There are actually two questions embedded in that question. The first is why the whole of information and communication systems can—and should—be considered as a whole. The second is why the totality of information and communication systems can be considered—somewhat independent of other concerns—as *a*, perhaps *the*, key element in any social change project. To begin to address these questions, it is important to think first of what we mean by information and communication systems.

Information and *communication* are terms that convey two perspectives of a single phenomenon that deserves its own term. *Information* is a noun; it refers to the stuff stored (like a song on your iPod) or transferred (like an HTML page loading into your browser). *Communication* is more like a verb; it refers to a process; it is what people do with the *stuff*—the information —when they are interacting with other people. Information would be useless without communication and communication impossible without information. Each term is meaningless without the other, yet no obvious set-subset relationship exists. Some people believe that communication is a subset of information; others think the converse is true. It may also be the case that either term could subsume the other. But which one? And would readers understand?

It is tempting to use the word *media* to describe the sum of our information and communication systems. After all, what makes *media* especially suited to what it is used to describe? The use of the term would spare the writer from writing, and the reader from reading—at least as it relates to this volume—the term "information and communication systems" over and over. And, after all, *media* is generic and increasingly ubiquitous. The term, however, is generally reserved for mass media, such as commercial radio or television or newspapers, and is not related to the diverse connotations that constitute the rest: the fewer than mass, the "traditional," the nonautomated, the nonprofit, the independent, the alternative, the one-off. Thus, we resisted the temptation to use a simple term and are again stuck with the longer term.

Both terms, *information* and *communication*, are abstract and general. They are relevant in discussing how two or more entities transfer meaning from one to another, how things— people, animals, minds, the computers on the Internet or, indeed the nodes in any network—come to influence or shape the behavior of others. Obviously no positive social change project (let alone any project that people work on together) could be conceived or implemented without information or without communication. And no war could be waged, no modern weapon built, no system of enslavement or exploitation maintained, without information and communication either.

So we determined that information and communication represented a potentially fertile foundation for developing a useful, holistic social change agenda. However, information and communication at the lowest level of analysis are devoid of content and value. Hence, an agenda (or theory, language or whatever) that concentrated solely on information and communication and omitted content and values could never be a social change agenda, nor could a similar agenda that omitted *action*. Consequently, Liberating Voices, while concentrating on information and communication, addresses how information is interpreted, why certain things need attention, and what should be done with the information.

And why information and communication *systems*? *Systems*, at least as the term is used here, implies an organization of components, however transient it might be, that in regularized ways acts on inputs and produces an internal change (or is ignored) or an external product. Using systems as our focus allows us to explore how change could occur by breaking a phenomenon into (semi-) discrete components connected by lines of communication and analyzing how and why changes happen within components and how they ultimately (often working in concert with others) influence the whole. Using the idea of systems also allows us to speak of a whole, which in all cases is only part of something larger. In either case, there are limitations to the extent of what we can learn.

Theories of the Information Society

According to Frank Webster (1995), who has extensively studied how information is being conceptualized in modern sociological analysis, we may distinguish five definitions of an information society, each of which presents criteria for identifying the new: technological, economic, occupational, spatial, and cultural. There is a sixth definition of an information society. Not that there is more information today (there obviously is), but rather that the character of the information is such as to have transformed how we live. The suggestion here is that theoretical knowledge and information are at the core of how we conduct ourselves.

In this book, we are not so much claiming that a new age is here (as, say, Daniel Bell, Manuel Castells, or Bill Gates might claim) as we are that a new world is possible and that we might be able to secure it. The advice therefore is not, "Get used to it and adapt," for it is the new reality, or understand it as to better profit from it, but to accept responsibility that the future is ours to create. Our premise is that the work can be rewarding, challenging, and fun—but not that it will be easy.

We are proposing that information and communication systems, which include face-to-face communication, mass media, new forms of media including Internet-based systems like blogs, existing institutionalized forms like public libraries or urban daily newspapers, demonstrations, and other forms of dissent, give significant and coherent structure to inquiry (the knowledge world) and interpretation and action (the human world) in ways that, say, cyberspace cannot. These fields resonate profoundly with how people and organizations come to make a difference in the world

Despite the timelessness of information and communication, we must note that one of the main assumptions of this project is that many of the opportunities that exist now will not exist in the future. The Internet is an obvious example of an opportunity that may have a limited shelf life. Let us not forget that other media forms have sprung into life lusty, anarchic, and free. The Internet has become in a few short years a largely commercial medium. At this point, however, thousands of thriving social spaces reside on the Internet in addition to tens of thousands (at least) of liberatory and oppositional and socially ameliorative projects. Currently (circa 2008) the Internet's protocols are still open, and people from all (or nearly all) countries are aboard, admittedly to varying degrees.

Finally, as the Wallerstein quote below articulately asserts, the huge number of challenges represent opportunities as well as threats. Before we can be prompted through fear and paranoia into a stampede of adrenaline-triggered reactions, let's assert our intelligence and humanity and move forward.

We are faced today, as we have been faced at other points of the demise of historical systems, with historic choices in which our individual and collective inputs will make a real difference in terms of the outcome. Today's moment of choice is, however, in one way different than previous such moments. It is the first one in which the entire globe is implicated, since the historical system in which we live is the first one that encompasses the entire globe. (Wallerstein, *The End of the World as We Know it*)

To a large degree we are advocating putting our fate into the hands of the people. Of course this is not and cannot be the whole story. "The people" are not always wise. They can be misled by propaganda and charismatic leaders, and they can be ignorant about the issues through lack of opportunity or skills, personal inclination, or active propagandization. Finally, people of power, higher educational attainment, and organizational stature are not to be discounted, ignored, or scapegoated; they too can have ideas and energy, compassion and creativity, that can be put to important uses. (Nevertheless, it is their ready access to levers of power that gives them more opportunities to multiply negative effects and maximize their own wealth, power, and prestige—sometimes unethically or illegally.)

Yet "the people" who are not necessarily distinguished individually by their money or other forms of power have a reasonably good track record for social progress. Civil society has spearheaded many, if not all, of the great social innovations, from banning slavery to the forty-hour workweek, to environmentalism and beyond, and for generally manifesting a live-and-let-live attitude for their fellow earthlings. A compelling reason for the appeal to "the people" is that nothing important will happen without them.

If the people are participants in a broad peaceful social movement to face our challenges openly and thoughtfully, it may be possible to create a world that works better for all of us. If the vast multitudes of our brethren are opposed to the project or even merely indifferent, there is less hope. I am tempted to say that there would be no hope without them, for three reasons. First, I have little faith in the ability of those in power to be compassionate, creative, or vigilant for the common good. Second, I am skeptical of so-called reforms that are forced on people. Third, I consider the accidental sorting out of problems, miraculously orchestrated through the strict attention to maximizing personal gain or by the net effects of people everywhere following their "instinct" and doing what seems most fun or interesting at any given moment, to be statements of pure sophistry.

Given that civil society—the people and their organizations—must play a strong role, a leadership role, and that globalization in the social and environmental spheres is a fait accompli that must now condition our ways of thinking and perceiving, we must ask what is out there to galvanize us all and provide order to our efforts. A theory that captured it all and either explained precisely for each of us what future actions we should all take or otherwise created a vision under which it became clear to all which steps to take and when might be ideal. I do not believe that such a theory exists or is even possible. Perhaps one could comb the world's great texts, talk to all the religious and secular leaders, and craft a good approximation. But even if such a theory were developed or discovered, the world is unlikely to embrace it.

At this point in the story, we have determined that we need a broad-based intellectual effort to characterize current and proposed social change activities that seem both important and effective and are based on information and communication. But how to identify, describe, and organize it in a useful way? In the next chapter we examine the approach we ultimately adopted.

5   Pattern Languages

All of my life I've spent making living structure in the world.
—Christopher Alexander (1996)

According to Google there are hundreds of thousands of Web pages that contain the phrase "pattern language." The popularity of the idea of a pattern language is due almost entirely to Christopher Alexander, professor emeritus of the Architectural and Urban Studies Department at the University of California at Berkeley, who has been championing a more integrative and human-centered approach to architecture for over forty years. (This is why I often refer to the pattern language concept as "Alexander's," even though he worked with many colleagues on various aspects of it.) Since at least the early 1960s, when he was writing his *Notes on the Synthesis of Form* (1964), Alexander has been interested in uncovering the principles behind the development of towns and buildings that are "able to come alive" (1977). He and his colleagues were not interested only in studying these principles, however. Their strategy was identifying and animating these principles by describing them in straightforward, useful, accessible, and compelling ways, which they then shared with others. The belief was that if people put these ideas to work, the built environment would ultimately become more beautiful and life affirming.

This chapter weaves these basic ideas into a brief history of the pattern language concept. The overall philosophy is too rich to be fully described here, and I address only those aspects that are relevant to our work in Liberating Voices. This chapter provides background information on the pattern language concept in general to help explain its use in the social and physical environments.

The Birth of *A Pattern Language*

In 1968, Alexander, with colleagues Sara Ishikawa and Murray Silverstein, published *A Pattern Language That Generates Multi-Service Centers*, the first publication containing the idea of pattern languages. This book was a fascinating prelude to the enormously popular (and more polished) *A Pattern Language*, which came nine years later, in 1977. The original design for the centers presents a "prototype for multi-service center buildings" at a time when the idea of offering multiple community services, particularly to low-income communities, under one roof, was being explored in several U.S. cities. The report is billed as a prototype, which the authors assert is a "system of generated principles, which can be richly transformed according to local circumstances but which never fail to convey their essentials." They say that "the ultimate purpose of a prototype design, then, is to provide guidelines for which will generate a large number of specific buildings." The pattern language book is actually presenting and promoting three things: designs for community service centers in specific communities, a prototype for multi-service centers (in the form of patterns and a pattern language), and the concept of the pattern language as a viable approach to characterizing complex ensembles of knowledge.

This set of principles is what Alexander and his colleagues began calling a pattern language, and each principle within the set was called a pattern—each an encapsulated approach for addressing a specific need or solving a specific problem. They also make it clear that to some degree, patterns are portable. Most, if not all, of the patterns could be used in other architectural contexts. Indeed, several patterns, such as Necklace of Community Projects (16), Windows Overlooking Life (18), and Pools of Light (63), also show up in the 1977 book, *A Pattern Language*, which has 253 patterns. Patterns can be combined in various ways to generate structures that are especially appropriate for any specific conditions, giving the grammatical nature of the pattern set—hence the use of the word *language* for the collection of principles that are deemed patterns. The patterns debuted in their 1968 book, and all the patterns that followed contain, like a seed, certain elements that must be present for the pattern to be structurally correct. But just as a sentence like, *Green dreams exhume electronic cigarettes with happy purple avarice,* can be grammatically correct but meaningless, patterns in the Alexandrian sense must meet certain conditions beyond formal structural requirements in order to be bona-fide patterns.

The main thing is that the pattern must be useful, and it must describe phenomena that occur over and over in successful buildings. To this end, certain information must be present within the pattern. The information that is distributed within the pattern includes why (what problems the pattern is intended to address and why this approach is appropriate), and when, where it should be used, who should use it, and how it should be used. This information is placed within formalized pattern language elements that typically include title, problem, context, discussion, and solution or their equivalents. The patterns in the book are presented using a specific structure to portray the information. Each pattern has two parts: a pattern statement and a problem statement. The problem statement is subdivided into an "if" part and a "then" part, that is, if the conditions X occur, then we should do Z in order to solve problem Y.

Pattern languages are more than a list of patterns. For one thing, they are linked to one another. If, say, a person uses pattern A, then she may also want to use pattern C or D. Although the definition and purpose of the links (which Alexander called "connections") vary from pattern language to pattern language, it is the idea that a grammar of sorts exists that helps tie the patterns together into a language. In the pattern language for the multi-service centers, for example, each pattern has its own icon, and the relationships among the sixty-four patterns are shown in a complex network of interrelationships (figure 5.1).

Pattern languages are holistic. A pattern language that is about buildings addresses more than physical structure. The *Multi-Service Centers* authors, for example, make it clear that "our report deals with the spatial organization; but since human and spatial organization cannot properly be separated, many of the specifications given in this report, go deeply into questions of human organization as well." In other words, they acknowledge the fact that architecture is intended for some human purposes, and they use patterns to consolidate the connections between the physical structure ("patterns of space") and how people will use the structure ("patterns of events").

The tone and thrust of the first pattern language book, with its emphasis on community self-help and antiauthoritarianism, reflected the tenor of the 1960s, when it was published. Although times have changed since then, these themes and values, among others, are still critical to human existence and are unapologetically reflected in Liberating Voices. It is an interesting exercise to think of what patterns could be in their book and ours and where the patterns could overlap, through, for instance, community media production capabilities within a multi-service center.

Pattern Languages Are Discovered

After being favorably impressed with the multi-service center book, which described a new approach to planning, the University of Oregon in 1970 selected the Center for Environmental Structure to lead the school's new planning initiative. The initiative resulted in an approach, described in *The Oregon Experiment* (Alexander et al. 1975), that was specifically designed for the university and adopted as the university's master plan in the early 1970s. According to the university's Web site, "The purpose of developing a pattern language was to provide a non-technical vocabulary of design principles that would allow those who work, study, and/or live in buildings to communicate effectively with the planners and designers of those buildings" (University of Oregon 2005). This experience, incidentally, led to the last book in the series of three books discussed below.

During the early 1970s, Alexander and his team did extensive work for the Bay Area Rapid Transit (BART) project in the San Francisco area. They also developed an intriguing project in which a group of families were engaged as designers and builders of their own homes in Mexicali, Mexico, during that period.

In 1977, with the publication of Alexander's groundbreaking book *A Pattern Language,* the concept of the pattern language became known far beyond the West Coast of the United States. The majority of the book is taken up with 253 discrete but interrelated planning, architectural, and construction patterns that covered a huge conceptual area, from the division of the world's land mass to what types of things one might put in one's own room.

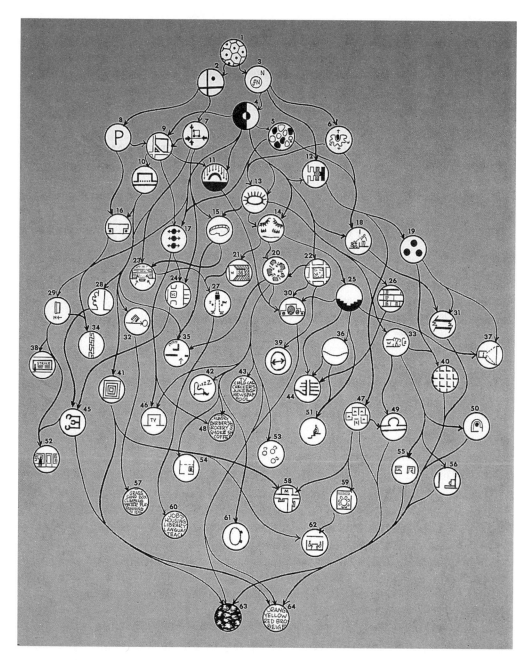

Figure 5.1
Multi-service center pattern network

159 LIGHT ON TWO SIDES OF EVERY ROOM **

. . . once the building's major rooms are in position, we have to fix its actual shape: and this we do essentially with the position of the edge. The edge has got its rough position already from the overall form of the building- WINGS OF LIGHT (107), POSITIVE OUTDOOR SPACE (106), LONG THIN HOUSE (109), CASCADE OF ROOFS (116). This pattern now completes the work of WINGS OF LIGHT (107), by placing each individual room exactly where it needs to be to get the light.

Figure 5.2

Alexander's contention was that these patterns can be used by both professionals and novices to design and build towns and dwellings that are beautiful, life affirming, and timeless.

Figure 5.2 is an inexact depiction of one of the patterns (159) in Alexander's book, Light on Two Sides of Every Room, taken from his pattern language Web site. This shows an illustration of the pattern, the title, and a paragraph showing links to other patterns. The two asterisks after the title related to a rating system (from one asterisk to three asterisks) developed by the authors to indicate the degree to which they thought the pattern was a true invariant that "describes a deep and inescapable property of a well-formed environment."

This pattern describes what the authors believe is indispensable in any successful room. While they acknowledge that their experiments in this area have been informal, they strongly believe that "people will always gravitate to those rooms which have light on two sides. The pattern also discusses why this is so ("it allows us to read in detail the minute expressions that flash across people's faces," for example) and explores what implications the patterns has on building shapes.

Whatever the reason, the pattern language concept struck a deep chord. The book has been enormously popular with the public, and its sales have actually increased over the years

(Saunders 2002). Clearly *A Pattern Language* was successful in ways that vastly exceeded the multi-service center publication. For one thing, the book included photographs of places that filled readers with longing, especially as they contemplated the spaces in the photographs, which evoke exactly what Alexander had intended them to evoke—places where one could exist, that felt comfortable (like home?) yet alive and somewhat mysterious at the same time. This feeling could be compared with the mundane, if not outright stultifying, place where the reader actually was at that moment.

A Pattern Language seemed magisterial with its red, Bible-like hard cover (no paperback edition has been printed) and its array of tempting patterns, each evocative in its own way. The book was a call to arms for people to confront the construction industry and the architectural establishment to force them to listen to people who wanted some control over the spaces they lived in. The main point was that the patterns contained both criticism and remedy. The patterns asked why something undesirable was happening rather than something else that was desirable and necessary, and then gave a solution that was worded in such a way that it could be implemented in many different ways but still have similar positive effects. Alexander made it clear in plain words what he felt was right and why. By raising these questions, Alexander was implicitly inviting people into a broader discussion and critique of all the physical spaces that humankind inhabits. But beyond asking the broadest questions he could about our man-made environment, he issued an invitation to people to discuss these issues and participate in the design and construction of their own spaces. Alexander, in answering his own questions, laid out an entire program: a theory of an architecture wanting to promote conviviality, an agenda that he believed would improve—and repair—our artificial (and, he would argue, depressing and illness producing) environment.

Projects such as Alexander's that made expansive claims and recommendations about society's overall health would incite more criticism than equally expansive counterprojects. Alexander claimed (tongue in cheek) that a competing pattern language, that included patterns such as Long and Narrow, Daylight at One End Only, Fluorescent Lights at 10 Foot Centers, Flat Concrete Wall, and Plywood Wall Surface, was used in the design of his original office at Berkeley (Alexander 1979). We examine some of these criticisms, including some of Alexander's own, later in this chapter after examining the concepts in a bit more detail and discovering what people working in other domains have done with them.

Patterns and Pattern Languages

All patterns in the Alexandrian sense share the same basic structure. Patterns can be thought of as "semistructured" chunks of information (Malone 1987) that have five main elements: name, problem, context, solution, and discussion. It is through the use of this common (though minimal) structure that the power and usefulness of the pattern language can emerge. Alexander's use of the word *language* is also simpler than it first seems. The language is simply the way that the patterns are related to each other and how patterns are used in conjunction with each other, much as words are components of spoken or written language.

Although Alexander's use of the words *pattern* and *pattern language* has its own logic, the use of the two common words in this specialized form is not immediately apparent. It is fair to say that the concepts are not made clear by looking at conventional meanings. We are using those terms in describing this book both to acknowledge their intellectual origin and because there is no obvious substitute that is preferable to the originals. Doug Lea (2000), a software engineer who specializes in pattern languages, put it another way: "You can call them anything you like, but it's too late to change what people call them." Here from Alexander's book, *The Timeless Way of Building* (1979), is a somewhat concise definition of a pattern: "Each pattern is a three-part rule, which expresses a relationship between a certain context, a problem, and a solution" (p. 247).

And here are two definitions that convey a bit more of the timeless nature that Alexander was trying to convey with the patterns and the way they connect to the real world:

Each pattern describes a problem which occurs over and over again in our environment, and then describes the core of the solution to that problem, in such a way that you can use the solution a million times over, *without ever doing it the same way twice*. (Alexander et al. 1977, my emphasis)

The pattern is, in short, at the same time a thing, which happens in the world, and the rule which tells us how to create that thing, and when we must create it. It is both a process and a thing; both a description of a thing which is alive, and a description of the process which will generate that thing." (Alexander 1979)

A pattern is designed and intended to supply direction for interpreting and acting on processes. Hence, even for institutions of normal and unchallenging activities, the patterns promote change in the sense that they suggest actions to be undertaken in a given situation. Nevertheless, many patterns cause changes in external situations, and these are more likely to help ultimately in broad social change or paradigm shifts.

The patterns in Alexander's pattern language are related in two basic ways. The first is that the 253 patterns are numbered sequentially; number 1 (Independent Regions) is the most general, and the last one, number 253 (Things from Your Life), is the most specific. The patterns are grouped within smaller categories as well. Patterns 1 through 7 are global patterns, for example, and patterns 35 through 40 deal with housing that is "based on face-to-face human groups." The patterns are also linked to each other experientially. Using the pattern for light coming into a room, there are references to other patterns that come before it in the listing of the language: Wings of Light (107), Positive Outdoor Space (106), and others. At the end of the pattern is a paragraph that describes which of the patterns this pattern is related to that follow the pattern. Thus, the patterns are all linked to each other much as paragraphs in a story or links to Web pages are, as well as actually, linked to each other. A pattern language comprises patterns, but a pattern language is not just a collection of patterns; it is an ecology of patterns: "A pattern language is a network of patterns that call upon one another. Patterns help us remember insights and knowledge about design and can be used in combination to create solutions" (Alexander et al. 1977).

Each pattern is a whole. The collection of patterns becomes a language when the patterns work together to create a larger whole just as words are used together to create meaningful sentences (Alexander 1979). Alexander emphasizes the creative power of patterns that can be used "over and over again" to generate meaningful structures. The generative capability helps to bring forth the life that Alexander believes must be immanent in the structures we inhabit. He also believes that the patterns, far from restraining creativity, promote it. They enable individuals and communities to reuse and interpret the knowledge recorded in the patterns in their particular context without ever doing it the same way twice. Patterns, like words, help give form to our thinking and, like words, can be used over and over in different ways, but each sentence is constructed in a specific context and must be sensitive to that context.

A pattern language is not an autonomous system. In *A Pattern Language*, Alexander states that *The Timeless Way of Building* and *A Pattern Language* are "two halves of a single work." The insights and ideas in *The Timeless Way of Building* and the explanatory (nonpattern) text within *A Pattern Language* provide motivation and theory as well as practical descriptions on how to use the patterns. The chapters in this book that precede the Liberating Voices pattern language, and the chapters that follow it, serve a similar function by providing rationale, context, history, suggestions for use, and possible directions for the project.

Second-Generation Pattern Languages

On the second page of *A Pattern Language*, the authors state, "In this book, we present one possible pattern language," suggesting that pattern languages could be developed in fields besides architecture. Nevertheless, several years elapsed after the first pattern language and their use within a major community of practice outside architecture and planning. Software professionals in the field of object-oriented programming sensed the value of gathering inter-related ideas together using the organizational power of patterns and the pattern languages and adopted those ideas for their own domain. This close historical linkage between computers and pattern languages is not widely known. In 1987, Kent Beck and Ward Cunningham wrote a paper for OOPSLA, the main object-oriented conference, entitled, "Using Pattern Languages for Object-Oriented Programs." Other researchers in the object-oriented programming community soon followed up on the ideas (including Gabriel 1996; Gamma, Helm, Johnson, and Vlissides 1995; Coad 1992; Anderson 1993; Coad and Mayfield 1993; and Anderson, Coad, and Mayfield 1994). Alexander was surprised that the computing community was so enamored of patterns. He relates the story that executives in the computer industry offered him $3,000 just to have lunch with him. Computing professionals of other persuasions also became interested in pattern languages, notably in the area of human-computer interaction (Tidwell 1999; Borchers 2001).

In the mid-1990s Cunningham developed The Portland Pattern Repository, an application on the Web that would enable software engineers to share their patterns with other programmers. The desire to share ideas and experience among the members of the community led Cunningham to transform the pattern repository concept and the application into a "radically something-something database application," which he christened a Wiki-Wiki, Hawaiian for "quick" or "hurry." This base software technology is the basic foundation of the Wikipedia, the online encyclopedia that was built on the unusual (and startling) idea that people could—and would—work together collectively and without pay, mostly anonymously, to construct a complex, exhaustive, and useful artifact.

Pattern languages in other domains soon followed, in line with the social and ethical orientation that Alexander favored. Working with Alexander, Stuart Cowan of the Ecotrust Foundation in Portland, Oregon, developed an impressive pattern language of seventy-two interrelated patterns that define "a comprehensive and consistent map of a sustainable region, one which may be adapted to the infinite variation of local circumstances" (http://www.conservationeconomy.net/).

Today on the Web there are dozens of domains where pattern languages have been attempted. While many of those seem to be in a perpetual undone state and many have apparently never been used, they nevertheless serve some useful purpose such as research or reflection.

In Defense of Pattern Languages

A Pattern Language was a wide-ranging manifesto that challenged the entire way that buildings are conceptualized, planned, designed, and built in the United States and in the rest of the developed world. As a repudiation of nearly everything that was being done in this area, this stance was bound to attract detractors. The book's enormous success that seemingly erupted from nowhere was also more likely to raise defensive hackles than from that of a less popular offering.

Since our work is largely based on that of *A Pattern Language*, looking at the criticism that Alexander's approach garnered should be helpful. The majority of the criticism, some of it quite scathing, regarding pattern languages has come from the architectural community. Apparently builders, urban planners, and software developers were not as viscerally disturbed by Alexander's challenge. Although, interestingly enough, Alexander himself is the source of some of the strongest criticisms of the work, we turn first to some of his fellow architects.

In a 2002 book review of *A Pattern Language*, twenty-five years after its original publication, William Saunders, the editor of the *Harvard Design Magazine*, states that although the book "could very well be the most read architectural treatise of all time, yet in the architectural schools I know, it is as if this book does not exist." The objections in print are quite varied. A common criticism is around Alexander's claims of universality with words like *timelessness* and claims that the truth of the patterns was empirically proven. There were also claims of completeness such as that *A Pattern Language* "contains all the patterns necessary for an entire community" (Alexander et al. 1975). Other architects accused Alexander of universalizing the whole of the human community or presenting a single pattern language to cover the entire world of architecture. A closer reading of Alexander's writing reveals that his intention was not to develop a universalist or monolithic program. Indeed, the title of the book, "*A* Pattern Language" (rather than *The* Pattern Language), reflects this openness. The book was a demonstration of how a pattern language could be used to make fundamental architectural issues explicit and tractable and enable a particular community to use, extend, and further develop their understandings: "So long as the people of a society are separated from the language which is being used to shape their buildings, the buildings cannot be alive.... If we want a language which is deep and powerful, we can only have it under conditions where thousands of people are using the same language, exploring it, making it deeper all the time. And this can only happen when the languages are shared" (Alexander 1977). In *The Timeless Way of Building* (1979), Alexander discusses how different cultural and environmental settings give rise to different patterns.

I argue that if there is a correspondence between a community and a pattern language, then today, when communities are more diverse that they used to be, the pattern language for new hybrid communities requires new hybrid pattern languages. For example, consider contemporary Los Angeles, where only a tiny percentage of people could claim to have any family roots older than, say, 100 years in that area.

Another claim is that the pattern language is inherently conservative, traditionalist, or romantic. It reflected a longing to go back to some other time or place. The trouble, of course, is that you "can never go home again." A related accusation leveled against Alexander is that he favors genteel, bourgeois living. He advocates home ownership, single-family homes, and gardens, which are impractical housing situations for poor people given today's winner-take-all economic realities. Saunders (2002), for example, has ample disdain for Alexander's "New Age flower-child wistfulness" when Alexander speaks of the health benefits that are associated with a deeper connection with nature. There is currently, however, substantial support for Alexander's position (e.g., Barlett 2005).

There are many reasons that an architect might find Alexander's manifesto objectionable. For one thing, the focus on both pattern ideas and strong user involvement is an implicit threat to the autonomy and authority of the professional architect, a threat that Alexander makes explicit in *The Production of Houses* (Alexander et al. 1985). The truth is that rather than being artists expressing their inner thoughts, architects are likely to be embedded in vast economic systems beyond their control. These systems often discourage architects from, say, working with poor people or for the public interest. Alexander more or less rejected this system, declared it to be bankrupt, and appealed directly to the public. In conversation with Grabow (1983) he stated, "The crux of the matter is that in all these fields or realms of activity that impinge directly on the shape of the environment—in design, in money, in politics, in construction and in geometry—the processes that exist today are wrong; and unless one changes those processes, one is not actually changing anything at all" (Grabow 1983). Although Ingrid King (1993), a colleague of Alexander, remarked:

"People have innate sensibilities with respect to space" their role in the process is limited to that of consumer.

Alexander's disappointment with the results of the pattern language were discussed extensively in Steven Grabow's book (1983). Grabow reported that Alexander himself noted that the houses that people created with the pattern language were not beautiful and did not seem to be "alive." Whether or not Alexander holds this view, it seems unrealistic to me to expect that people would abruptly create beautiful structures where ugly (or, at least, nonbeautiful) ones had been produced previously. My belief is that positive changes can happen incrementally, and the ultimate benefit would be in the way that people think about architecture as much or more than the quality of the architecture itself. In a thoughtful and engaging exegesis of the enemies of use of pattern languages, Kimberly Dovey (1990) discusses several "isms," including "pessimism":

Anyone with a reasonable understanding of the range of forces aligned against the implementation of the pattern language may well conclude that the task is futile and defect to the enemy in the form of pessimism. Many would not argue with the desirability of the pattern language approach but with its possibility, with its utopianism in the negative sense of "not of this world." Pessimists are perhaps the most numerous of all enemies and they contribute the added danger of becoming a self-fulfilling prophecy. One could argue that I have done little more in this paper than to add to the ranks of pessimists. However, I am not pessimistic and my aims are otherwise.

One reason for optimism is that the aspects of Alexander's work that make it seem irrelevant to mainstream discourse and difficult to implement are precisely those that make it applicable to global environmental design problems. For instance one of the arguments used against Alexander is that he proposes an owner-built environment that is impractical in the current context. Alexander does not propose the necessity of such a process, only its possibility, in a global context of over a billion poorly housed people and massive unemployment. The pattern language is one of the few current architectural theories that offers a potential theoretical ground for a world faced with severe problems of physical and social ecology.

The Liberating Voices project adopted the basic model from *A Pattern Language* as the best way to move forward our aim of an open civic and community communication. The pattern language work that Alexander pioneered has proved to be remarkably inspirational to people interested in the structures we inhabit to software developers, researchers, among others. At the same time we have seen fit to take a different tack in order to preclude some problems. We discuss these departures from Alexander's work in chapter 6 along with the process that we undertook to develop the Liberating Voices pattern language.

6 Liberating Voices as a Work in Progress

This chapter tells the story of the Liberating Voices project, how and why it started, and how it developed over time. It outlines our hopes and expectations and the tasks and activities that we undertook for attaining those goals. Evaluation and recommendations are discussed later. We describe what we did over the past six years, including online work, face-to-face meetings, and our ongoing (volunteer) software development of the pattern language infrastructure for this work. We also discuss how and where and why the Liberating Voices project differs from Alexander's. Readers who are not about to launch a similar project might feel tempted to forgo certain sections of this chapter. They should feel free to yield to this temptation and skip ahead to the next chapter, which previews the pattern language, or even to the patterns themselves in chapter 8.

Pattern Language Development

Rationale for Pattern Language
We decided to develop a pattern language for our own purposes. Ultimately it was an approach for uncovering, characterizing, refining, revising, organizing, linking, and publicizing the collective wisdom of a widely distributed, very loosely knit community of activists, researchers, policymakers, and technologists from around the world. There was a shared belief that information and communication systems offer massive challenges, as well as opportunities, for human society. And although civil society was intensely active in this area, we believed that it could be done more effectively and there could be better integration of the myriad efforts.

We hoped to capitalize on the intense interest as well as the influence of civil society worldwide and the increasing penetration of the Internet with its immense potential for global collaboration. This called for a network-based representation of the wide variety of thoughts and approaches related to community and civic uses of information and computer technology (ICT) worldwide. To this end, we determined that patterns as developed by Alexander would meet our needs by encouraging diverse and interdisciplinary approaches to problem solving while allowing differences of opinion, as well as parallel development.

Ideally this effort could be used in a way to help orient the work of lots of people without the need for outside or top-down coordination. Ideally it would help build a community of people who were interested in research as well as social and political action. If the participatory process unfolded as planned, the community that collaborated in the process would be stronger and smarter and therefore better equipped to deal with the issues before them. Ideally the effort would attract and inspire people from various academic disciplines, social movements, nongovernmental organizations, and geographical areas so as to constitute a thriving open action and research network (see also pattern 45 with that name in this book).

Domain and Scope

The focus (or domain) of our pattern language project is civic and community information and communication. This description is too long. Worse, it sounds dry and academic. "Democratic communication" might be a better characterization (although civic and community information and communication are needed everywhere, not just in democratic countries), and "living communication," adopting Alexander's characterization, is more compelling still. The core of the concept was that certain forms of information and communication systems and ways of thinking about them are likely to be more effective at promoting conviviality in the widest sense. These systems would be more authentic and more equitable, in marked contrast to commercial television and other media that are constructed by professionals with commercial, not civic or community, allegiances. Unfortunately their function is predominantly selling things, whether it is cars, dog food, or propaganda. Thus the patterns we set out to discover and characterize would support the six community core values that I advanced in my *New Community Networks* book (Schuler 1996): conviviality and culture; lifelong education; strong democracy; health and well-being; economic equity, opportunity, and sustainability; and open information and communication.

There are vast, powerful systems of information and communication whose goals are in contrast to those in this book. Although neither the systems nor the people and institutions that perpetuate them are necessarily evil, the systems are often oppressive. They can crowd out other forms of information and communication, particularly those that are not commercial and are not backed by vast resources and power. For that reason, critique of those systems, as well as approaches for challenging them, are also included in this pattern language. Ideally such a pattern language would assist people and organizations to shape and reshape information and communication systems to better meet human needs. Many of the activities that could play a role in this are listed below (this list also provides good clues for how and what should be included in the language):

- How to think about information and communication systems intelligently and creatively
- How to identify information that people need, even if it is not available yet
- How to locate information and communication systems that meet human needs
- How to think about information and communication strategically
- How to engage effectively with small groups and organizations, among others, as allies

- How to engage effectively with opposing groups
- How to engage effectively with media producers and other institutions
- How to shape integrated information and communication systems policy
- How to design and develop information and communication systems and manage them effectively
- How to design information and communication systems that help society address its problems

We believe that the Liberating Voices pattern language is a step forward in representing an integrated critique of current information and communication systems, as well as a vision of how things could be.

Research Perspectives

From the start of this project, we have pursued a holistic product. In this section, we offer a much abbreviated look at some of the research communities that have informed this project. If this section accomplishes nothing more than conveying the richness and complexity of the world that we are trying to understand and help share and the importance of working together, it will be successful.

We have been—and still are—interested in contributions from people in any academic (or nonacademic) discipline and the community in general. However, we have taken many cues from the political economy community, which often provides useful critique that is unlikely to be covered in other places. Civil society sets out to prove that another world is possible. Computer science specialties such as computer-supported cooperative work (CSCW) study how computers can be used to help support collaborative (generally professional) tasks that people do together. Or they develop participatory designs (see the patterns in this book) that advocate a more equitable partnership between developers and the ultimate users of software and other artifacts in its design (Schuler and Namioka 1993).

The principles behind participatory design have been key to the original conception as well as the realization of the Liberating Voices project. Insights from the science, technology, and society (STS) community help us understand how artifacts are designed, developed, and used, as well as the social context that surrounds those processes. Media studies perform similar chores for media and media systems, and media activism takes critical insights and transforms them into action. Community studies help us understand the importance of the bonds of communities and community informatics. Gurstein (2000) takes these truths and works with them to help develop systems for people and communities. This in turn creates a new more information-centric era, itself a key approach to understanding our era and an important area of research within sociology. Political scientists and others study social activism, who gets involved, for what reasons, and how they operate—and sometimes even succeed. Add the studies of the commons—how do, or do not, people come together to share resources equitably. And add studies of institutional transformations, and we begin to understand how we can begin to change institutions to make them more intelligent and responsible (Ostrom 1990, Bollier 2002). Finally we add biologists, ecologists, climatologists (among many other scientists), public health professionals, educators, artists, and others who are pushing the borders and boundaries and devising new ways to look at thinking itself and new ways to collaborate, characterize, probe, and, we hope, understand the world better.

All of these groups, besides seeking to address a shared set of issues, eternal questions, vocabulary, and cultural touchstones, have established attitudes, values, and philosophies. These preexisting attitudes exert an immense, abiding influence on the practice of that discipline within a community. No single organization or way of thinking can provide all the answers to the questions that the pattern language seeks to address. Over the past half-dozen years, we have gathered ideas from many sources all over the world and worked with authors to turn them into useful patterns. We also made the system open so as to encourage contributions from the fields described above and encouraged people from these fields to contribute ideas that we suggested and ideas that they believed in. It has been our hope all along that when the language was finished (a state that we imagine will never be reached, but the journey reaches an important milestone with the publication of this book), the patterns will all work together harmoniously. The result will be a system of knowledge that simplifies the entire enterprise without masking the complexity that will encourage future innovation. At least that is our hope.

Assumptions

Ideally the patterns in this pattern language will be used by many people at the same time. Most of them are already being used, and by people who have never heard of our effort. Obviously there is no central authority telling everybody what they should be doing. To a large degree, we have no choice but to rely on people to do the right thing. On the other hand, total individualism would be a disaster; the problems that we hope to address are immense, and coordination is critical. For that reason, we are advancing a number of approaches within the pattern language that are designed to promote collaboration and coordination. Also, the patterns in this language are to some degree neutral. They can be used with greater or lesser success by people who are polluting a lake as well as those who are trying to clean it.

We are relying on the idea that people with good information and good intentions, and with participatory communication systems, will choose to do the right thing. Unfortunately this is not a sure thing. We are not assuming a benign universe in which all our good intentions are allowed to go forward without interruption. We are assuming, however, that the big players such as national governments and corporations are not the only players in the realm of information and communication. The new force of civil society has grown enormously over the past few decades, and its resources are vast. Its force, however, is not as concentrated or as focused as that of government or business, and it cannot draw on armed entities such as militias or police to do its bidding.

Rhetoric promoting a stronger, bolder, and more unified civil society aside, this project does not assume that any particular institution is inherently opposed to this work. Thus churches, governments, businesses, labor unions, the media, and schools, for example, are all capable of assisting in a struggle for a better world—should they choose to do so. None of these should go away, yet all of them may need to change. Institutions, organizations, or individuals who insist that their viewpoints, goals, and methods are without flaw, because they are sanctified by God, validated through pure deduction, bolstered by frozen ancient texts, or enforced at gunpoint, and who typically regard any effort to exert influence over them as an attack, are inherently part of the problem—at least according to the assumptions that this project is based on: assumptions that knowledge is incomplete and that nobody has a monopoly on the truth.

This project makes the assumption that unchecked power represents a serious problem (if not now, then soon) that requires serious attention. And when powerful institutions exhort we the people to extreme actions, such as going to war or abolishing the institutions that are designed to monitor and check the exercise of power, we must exercise timely precaution and skepticism. The biggest claim that we can make is that we think a better world is possible, to borrow the mantra of the World Social Forum (Sen et al., 2004). This is both a small and a large claim: small because it makes no guarantees and does not say precisely how we will reach this improved state; large because it makes a claim that cannot be proven and relies on people of all persuasions from all over the world. The assumption that people will think wisely has important implications, including the idea that people are capable of questioning the will or wisdom of authority as well as the reliability of conventional wisdom. Thus there is an inherent wariness toward authority. There is also an inherent wariness toward those who suggest that "everything must change" and to those who blindly venerate everything that is old. Some things must change, but not everything must change.

Our enterprise is a project, not a study. It recommends actions, proposes points of view, and encourages active and engaged participation. It is partisan, not objective. And since complete objectivity is impossible, we believe that honesty, rigor, and humanity in our thought and actions should guide this project.

Project Approach

Liberating Voices takes much of its philosophical as well as its structural underpinnings from the basic model that Christopher Alexander and his colleagues developed. One of the most notable benefits is that the pattern language model is a logical and compelling way to organize complex, intellectually related material. Whereas Alexander and his colleagues were dealing primarily (or at least ostensibly) with the world of physical structure, our project explores and constructs patterns in a different domain. The patterns we have constituted do not focus on beautiful and timeless physical structures but on inclusive and useful information and communication systems. And just as Alexander's work did not represent the built environment as a province solely for professional activity but as something that belonged to everybody, our project adopts a similar grandiose vision: to reclaim information and communication as a shared right, a shared cultural legacy, and a shared tool to be used for improving humankind's civic intelligence. Beyond that, one of our goals has been to help strengthen the research and activist communities by involving them in a participatory project that uses a combination of electronic and face-to-face venues. We also hope this effort will help build the community by uncovering deep connections between people and projects that have been unknown to each other. By consciously trying to build the activist community and the capacity for social change and social amelioration, we are moving down paths with our approach that were not explicitly pursued by Alexander and his colleagues. I do not remember whether all of this came up when I described our basic concept to Alexander in the summer of 2001. My only abiding memory is that he was very enthusiastic; he brought up numerous opportunities and challenges that such a project might face. At any rate I remember being quite pleased as I walked down from his house in the Berkeley Hills that the man who is primarily associated with the pattern language concept had been so encouraging.

Over time the project was transformed into the large-scale participatory project that it ultimately became. Certainly I have been interested in the idea of collective intelligence for a long time: in the classroom, in society at large, and in the possible potential of online collaborative technologies that bring together compelling and informing user interfaces, relative efficiency, and rich outcomes (unlike voting, for example, a winner-take-all situation that yields a single answer, like selecting one card from a deck of cards). At any rate, Erik Stolterman, a friend and colleague, made the original suggestion at a Seattle coffeehouse that all people who wished to present at the symposium I was organizing should be required to submit a pattern rather than an abstract or research paper.

The symposium series, DIAC (Directions and Implications of Advanced Computing), sponsored for Computer Professionals for Social Responsibility (CPSR), began exploring these ideas in 1987. Based on our successes with the DIAC symposia over the years, we had some confidence that developing a useful and compelling pattern language would be possible. We devised strategies (listed below) for developing and disseminating the pattern language in conjunction with the conference. Here, from the DIAC-2002 Web site, is a list of activities that we believed would help reach our goals:

- Use patterns as an orienting theme for a conference and information structure.
- Use a common format to facilitate pattern integration.
- Develop and refine social processes that support the development of patterns and the pattern language.
- Develop an easy-to-use Web application that supports every aspect of the process.
- Publicize the Web site, and encourage people to post their patterns.
- Employ Web-based and print-based dissemination.

A central idea behind the common structure was that although individual patterns could be compelling and useful, a common structure would make it easier to integrate them into a collective body of knowledge that was readily accessible. And since the patterns are stored in an online database, many interesting possibilities for computer mediation and collaboration emerge. We hoped that this overall project would help inspire scholars to think about their research in terms of social implications and actual social engagement. We also hoped that the common enterprise would help build social networks that include research, practice, and advocacy.

Pattern Language Development Process

In *A Pattern Language* (1977), Alexander, Ishikawa, and Silverstein make the strong claim that "buildings will not be able to come alive, unless they are made by all the people in society, and unless these people share a common pattern language, within which to make this common pattern language alive itself." Replacing "buildings" with "information and communication systems" provides a good glimpse at our basic thesis and our inspiration. Our approach could be summed up as a gradual building up of the patterns themselves, followed by assembling a pattern language informed by our collective knowledge. The pattern language development process consists of several generic tasks: pattern solicitation and collection; pattern discussion and deliberation, and pattern language development.

Pattern Solicitation and Collection In late 2001, the DIAC-2002 program committee released a call for patterns that was sent to various electronic lists. The committee contained thirty-four people from Argentina, Bangladesh, Canada, England, Germany, Ghana, Italy, Japan, Mexico, Netherlands, Russia, Sweden and the United States. Nearly all committee members were academics involved in research and activism related to information and communication technology. The call was designed to appeal to a wide variety of people and to broadly describe the issues that we were interested in addressing.

Unfortunately the open-ended nature of the appeal and the introduction of patterns proved to be confusing to many, if not most, of the contributors. Although the confusing nature of the call, specifically the content and style of what people were expected to submit, was an impediment, the biggest problem was undoubtedly that the main audience, academics, were being asked to contribute in a form that was alien to them in structure, tone, and content. For one thing, conference papers are supposed to contain new, specific findings that are "objective," while patterns can contain generalizations based on traditional or folk knowledge and offer recommendations based on values.

To support the collection, display, and general management of the pattern ideas while keeping the administrative burden as low as possible, we set up an online pattern management system. Designed by Douglas Schuler and Scott Rose (and implemented by Rose), the system allowed anybody with access to the Web to open a password-protected author account for managing any number of patterns. Authors could edit their patterns at any time. They could indicate whether their pattern should be reviewed, whether it should be made public, and whether identifying information or contact information should be displayed with the pattern.

Ultimately we were very satisfied with the response to the call for patterns. As of February 1, 2002, approximately 150 patterns had been submitted to the online system. People from Ghana, India, United Kingdom, United States, Mexico, Australia, Germany, Sweden, South Africa, Malaysia, France, Brazil, Japan, and other countries submitted patterns in the first batch. A survey of patterns at that point showed we were at least partially vindicated in the first phase of our own quest for a coherent and holistic pattern language. The patterns submitted at that point were beginning to form a cohesive set of patterns that seemed to belong together. There was also a sense that many implicit conceptual links tied the pattern submissions together in useful ways. There were, for example, several submissions that addressed the idea of deliberation, from the town to the global level, and this idea is presented in this book. On the other hand, the community network theme was overrepresented.

In-Person Pattern Discussion and Deliberation   Because people were generally unfamiliar with the pattern language concept, we decided to make it clear that knowledge about patterns would not be a requirement. At the conference, we convened a variety of pattern-related activities including panel discussions by people with pattern language experience. Stuart Cowan, for example, who developed the Conservation Economy pattern language for Ecotrust in Portland, Oregon, gave a keynote presentation.

Opportunities for participatory development of the pattern language were available alongside more traditional conference activities like presenting papers. An example was a two-day session that relied on Owen's "open space technology," where meeting agendas are created by the meeting attendees themselves (Owen 1997). We provided three notebooks, each containing the entire collection of (abridged) patterns, and used the walls of the room for the display and rearrangement of patterns. New patterns, submitted via the Web site from off-site or on-site via wireless laptop computers, were printed and added to the collection in "near" real time.

Participants at the open space session moved the patterns around, placed similar ones together, and proposed names using sticky notes to the emerging clusters. Moving the patterns around and discussing them is likely to help the development of the pattern language. It can provide clues as to how people would use the patterns since those in the same cluster are more likely to be integrated together into new patterns based on their content. The second use of pattern clusters is to identify who might be interested in the resulting pattern language.

Pattern Refinement   Ideally each pattern submission would receive the necessary attention to ultimately turn it into a full-fledged pattern. We discovered that exposing the patterns in progress to the world on a working Web site can help address that problem but is not sufficient by itself. The review system also had problems. In my attempt to make it easy to use, I introduced a lot of checkboxes where a reviewer could indicate flaws in the pattern easily—perhaps too easily. Ultimately we used a combination of the open system and reviews that we solicited. Unfortunately a review system that is open to everybody can reinforce a "thou shalt not" attitude that stifles creativity. The pattern's title itself offered useful suggestions for refinement. For example, experience taught us that the pattern title should be a noun or noun phrase about something that the writer advocates. For example, Digital Divide would not be a pattern in our language, whereas Digital Bridge could be. Patterns are supposed to represent one thing, not one thing *and* another thing. In many cases a pattern with an *and* in its title should be turned into two patterns. A preposition can cause another red flag to be raised because it implies some qualification or watering down of the pattern's essence. Community Networks sounds like a reasonable title, whereas Community Networks In Mukilteo is too specific to be a pattern. Community networks in developing countries, however, are likely to be different from community networks in developed countries and thus could be a legitimate pattern. Likewise, community networks in a democratic or tolerant country are likely to be different from those in fascist, theocratic, or lawless states.

Pattern Ordering and Validation   When Alexander collected his patterns into a pattern language, he was faced with the question of how the set should be organized. Digital information (on the Web, for example) has more inherent flexibility: it can be ordered in countless ways but is still generally ordered in some way. (Ordering and characterizing, two approaches to organizing collections, are strongly related to each other.) Characterizing (or categorizing) is often the prelude to organizing; it is the process of identifying features of the collection that are relevant to the people who use it. We found four plausible, possibly overlapping, ways of categorizing the patterns. First, we could use core themes (digital divide, research for action, education, globalism and localism, media critique, social movement, community action) or categories (orientation, social learning and intelligence, organization, engagement, products and projects, resources). Second, computers could be used to help generate the categories using, for example, keywords or "significantly improbable phrases." Third, people could guide the process through an ad hoc, "constructed" approach with questions such as "If you used this pattern, what pattern would you use next?" for example. Finally, the patterns could be arranged according to some generic scheme or arranged along some continuum, alphabetically, for example, or in order of submission.

One plan that seemed reasonable was to let the patterns more or less sort themselves by using the categories that authors had indicated for their patterns as the key to sorting them. First, we placed the categories into a rough order of generality (where **orientation** *is-more-general-than* **social learning** *is-more-general-than* **intelligence**, and so on). Then we assigned thirty-two to orientation, sixteen to social learning and intelligence, and so on down to two to products and projects and one to resources. Then when those values were summed, each pattern was assigned a number from 1 to 63 that represented how general each was. This approach implicitly stipulated that the more categories that were checked, the more general that particular pattern was. Of course, this approach more or less tacitly assumes that the categories (or whatever) are the de facto classification and ordering plan. Although this approach did not seem to particularly resonate with people (and was replaced by the modified sort mentioned above), it is not clear that the ordering of the 253 patterns in *A Pattern Language* would have been obvious if it was not made clear through categories and captions. Based on our experience, however, it does seem possible for authors to check various boxes where they thought their pattern belonged according to various dimensional attributes, thus allowing the patterns (albeit with some assistance from their authors) to sort themselves.

Alexander and his colleagues in *A Pattern Language* arranged their patterns from most general (Independent Regions) to most specific (Things of One's Own). Why did Alexander choose this approach? He did not, for example, divide the patterns according to education, health, or some other category, nor did he arrange the patterns by roles (architects, planners, or home owners for example). For one thing, he wanted to show that one pattern helped complete another and there is a natural order of building where one thinks at the grander level first and then moves inexorably toward more detail. Our motives are different. We want to encourage people working outside their familiar territories (i.e., their comfort zones) to explore alternatives. Alexander's patterns generally addressed physical structures, so arranging them from biggest to smallest seemed relatively straightforward. Information and communication, in contrast, are abstract. The big-to-small ordering based on physical size that makes sense in *A Pattern Language* seems to make less sense here.

If, however, we think big in nonphysical ways, then it is not difficult to come up with several viable ways to impose this dimension on nonphysical entities. (Unfortunately, as we will soon see, these various ways to characterize *big-small*, each of which defines a dimension on which to compare patterns, are not necessarily commensurable. In other words, the various dimensions we can identify do not necessarily have anything to do with each other.)

The most important dimension we can identify is probably the *general-specific* dimension: a pattern that describes more is "bigger" than one that describes less. Another important dimension has to do with leverage, that is, what influence it potentially has, This is conceptually similar to Donella Meadows' s "Places to Intervene in a System" (1997), where the nine different "places" (or "leverage points") are far more likely to yield different results than others. (The "biggest" place to intervene is "the mindset or paradigm out of which the goals, rules, feedback structures arise," by the way.) A bigger result translates into longer influence, larger numbers of people, forests, and so forth that are affected, and a pattern with a "bigger influence" would end up closer to the beginning of the pattern sequence. A third and last (although it is possible to name many more) dimension is how often it is applicable. One of our pattern proposals, Neighborhood Assembly, might be applicable nearly any time (as often, say, as a town meeting in the New England states of the United States is convened). In practice, however, the need to activate the pattern generally happens only in extraordinary circumstances or times of crisis, like during the economic meltdown in Argentina in 2001.

On July 25, 2004, Andrew Dearden from Sheffield and I spent the better part of a day refining a set of categories that could be listed in a general order from most general to most specific and placing all the patterns that existed at the time into one of the categories. A conversation with John Adams resulted in the interesting idea that the categories could be thought of as types of meta-patterns that are linked to each other and have a number of regular patterns underneath each of them.

The 253 patterns in *A Pattern Language* are subsumed under three main areas (Towns, Buildings, and Construction) that we call categories or headings. The category scheme that Andrew and I identified that day is basically the same one we are using here. We adopted nine categories and, like Alexander's, arranged them in a defensible way from biggest to smallest. We begin with Theory, the most general, and work down to Tactics, which are more specific, more context-based, and usually done only sporadically. Following are the nine categories that we adopted, which I explain in more detail in chapter 8:

Theory
Organizing Principles
Enabling Systems
Policy
Collaboration
Community and Organizational Building
Self-Representation
Projects
Tactics

In *A Pattern Language*, Alexander does one more thing with the listing. He weaves "captions" in within the patterns. For example, here is a "caption" from *A Pattern Language* that describes what is to be done during this phase of the design.

Now, with the paths fixed, we come back to the buildings: within the various wings of any one building, work out the fundamental gradients of space, and decide how the movement will connect the spaces in the gradients;

The names of patterns 127–135 (Intimacy Gradient, Indoor Sunlight, Common Areas at the Heart, Zen View, and so on) follow that caption.

In figure 6.1, the grammar of the pattern language listing is made clear. Both Alexander's pattern listing and ours conform to this. After starting, there is a heading or category. Alexander's begins with "Towns," and ours begins with "Theory." The heading is followed by one caption, then one or more pattern names, and so on. Although we got to the idea of captions late in the game, we have created a reasonable approach that helps demonstrate the holism of the system.

A Pattern Language contains 253 patterns ranging in scale from the global to the intimate, personal, and private. As a collection, the patterns cover a lot of ground. But is the set complete? Alexander acknowledged that it was not and that different pattern languages would be needed for different situations. The Liberating Voices pattern language has 136 patterns,

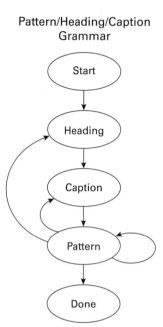

Pattern/Heading/Caption
Grammar

Figure 6.1
Pattern language grammar. This shows the myriad ways that the pattern titles and captions can tell a story that brings all of the patterns together.

and we readily acknowledge that it is not complete. Over 400 pattern proposals have been submitted, and many address themes as important as those in this book. No language, pattern or otherwise, can really be said to be complete. The concept simply does not apply.

But although our pattern language is not complete, we of course do not want gaping holes. Unfortunately there is no foolproof way to identify what is missing from a pattern language. As we proceeded, we employed a bricoleur approach to any task before us. One approach was to simply ask people for their ideas. Ultimately we assembled a list of topics that needed at least nontrivial representation within the pattern language: accessibility, attitudes and ways of thinking, civic engagement, commons, communities, community development, economics, education, emergency, environmentalism, the future, gender and ethnicity, government, health, human rights, information and community technology, computer-supported cooperative work and human-computer interaction, institutions, labor, media, policy, social services, theory, and urban and minorities. A perusal of the patterns will reveal that some of these topics received less attention than they deserved.

Pattern Context and Links   As we know, pattern languages are not just collections of patterns. For one thing the domain that is being addressed needs to be sufficiently covered and adequately described. In addition to the patterns having a strong correspondence to the domain, the patterns themselves must work and fit together sensibly. In other words, they must be perceived as being a coherent body of knowledge, and the patterns must be linked so that two or more patterns can be employed effectively and efficiently in any situation.

The Liberating Voices patterns were not developed exclusively by a team of authors with general knowledge of other patterns (as with *A Pattern Language*) nor did the authors generally check to see how (if at all) their pattern fit, did not fit, or even duplicated patterns that had already been submitted, before they submitted the patterns. For that reason, we had to develop a viable approach to integrating the patterns.

Since links between patterns are essential to a pattern language, three questions arise in relation to the participatory, somewhat open-ended approach we employed. First, what types of links exist between patterns, and how are they implemented? This pattern language has an online version where a reader can click rather than flip through to consult another pattern. Second, who determines what links exist that connect one pattern to others and, third, where in the pattern should the information go?

Links can be a general term for any relationship between, almost invariably, two (although links that point to multiple objects from one are certainly conceivable) objects—patterns in our case. Generally links are intended to show a relationship between two objects. If the relation describes the relation from A to B and not the relation from B to A, then it is directional, like the links between two Web pages. If the link is equally valid in either direction, it is bidirectional.

Pattern Development

As part of our effort to involve large numbers of people and build on opportunities afforded by the new media, we have been incrementally developing an online environment for the patterns. This environment is ideally intended to help develop a complete pattern language from assorted immature pattern ideas into a living ecosystem of mature patterns.

The pattern management system that we developed contains four major subsystems: pattern submission, pattern reviewing, pattern language presentation, and pattern language administration. It was developed subsystem by subsystem as needed rather than as a comprehensive set of specifications at the onset, since the intended uses of a system often change. For example, the system was initially designed for the 2002 DIAC conference, but has been used ever since as a general-purpose pattern management system. The four subsystems are discussed below followed by a discussion on the developments that we added after the initial system was implemented.

The pattern information is stored in a database that allows selective retrieval (for example, all patterns that have been indicated as "media critique"), text search, and the display the patterns in a consistent way. Ultimately it would be interesting to perform some algorithmic manipulation of patterns (for example, to identify similar or dissimilar patterns).

Each author can have any number of patterns under development (I currently have nearly one hundred, including many placeholders). The editing screen for an individual pattern allows the author to control whether the pattern should be reviewed by the DIAC-2002 program committee (during the period before submission for committee review was closed), whether the pattern was ready for public display, and whether author name or e-mail address was displayed.

Pattern Reviewing Subsystem

The reviewing subsystem allowed virtually all reviewing and selecting functions (for the conference) to be done over the Web. There are two basic roles: administrator and reviewer. The administrator is able to add to and remove reviewers and assign reviewers to specific patterns. Only those patterns marked by the author as ready for review were reviewed. The administrator is able to mark a pattern "closed for review," which disallows additional reviewing.

The reviewers do not see names or other identifying characteristics of pattern authors when they review the submitted patterns, and reviewers are not able to see the reviews of other reviewers. Each pattern was rated by each reviewer according to the following criteria: significance to advancement of knowledge, clarity, innovation, social implications, and suitability as a pattern. The reviewers could also provide information on the proposals they review. There is a text box to include comments to other reviewers (which are not given back to authors) and a text box for comments that are made available to authors. Reviewers are also able to edit their reviews online.

Pattern Language Administration

The administrator has a global view of the entire pattern system and can inspect and delete patterns (if, for example, a clearly inappropriate pattern had been entered). There are also several report capabilities related to the reviewing process. The system shows each pattern and whether its reviewers are done and which reviewers still need to review. It also shows all the pattern proposals ordered by the averaged scores of the five criteria. Both reviewer and author comments are shown on these reports. Each pattern has a radio button with four choices (recommended for acceptance, not recommended for acceptance, accepted, not rated), which can be set only by the administrator. The system generates different messages depending on this choice, and the administrator uses these messages to send to each submitter. The entire database is also downloadable as a spreadsheet.

Two Pattern Languages

Just because we used a pattern language does not mean that our language (or the route we took) would necessarily look like Alexander's, and it does not. Separated by thirty years and focusing on different domains, Alexander's approach and ours are similar in many ways. In this section, we examine both projects at fairly general levels, noting prominent similarities and dissimilarities between the two approaches from several perspectives: the domain; the process; the product; the goals, claims, and expectations of the projects.

The domain of *A Pattern Language* and the domain of *Liberating Voices* are vast in scope and influence, and both are inseparable from human society and civilization. It is impossible to imagine humankind without the things that we have physically built to live with and within, and it is equally impossible (more so, probably) to imagine humankind without the things that were cognitively and emotionally built to help us live with and within an environment filled with socially constructed meaning.

Building a campaign or movement is not like building a house; the environment is more fluid, and the possible responses at any instant are more numerous in the first case.

With his vision of an all-encompassing pattern language, Alexander challenged the entire architecture profession and community. He also challenged the building industry, the financial industry that was behind the building industry, and others. It was the architectural community, however, that felt most immediately and personally challenged.

We too are trying to be utopian in the sense that we are being critical of the status quo and offer visions of the alternative, utopian world that we prefer to the current one. One difference between the two utopian visions is that Alexander's is more of a portrayal or assertion of utopia as it could be, and Liberating Voices is an assertion of utopia and what we need to get there. So in Alexander's world, the houses are pleasant, and they support conviviality. There are not too many cars—or slums or homeless people—and it is even safe to sleep in public (APL pattern 194). Obviously I am not trying to discount the value of livable, convivial spaces for people, a brilliant and compelling vision. Certainly if everybody in the world were housed in such a way, the world would be better than it is. Alexander's fundamental premise, largely implicit, is that the right type of built environment will necessarily lead to the right sort of behavior.

Alexander's patterns such as Necklace of Community Services are addressing more than the purely physical environment. The 1968 multi-service center book conveys quite plainly how fundamental humanism can be imbued in physical spaces. But the books collectively do not address how, for example, people in a low-income community could ensure that such a facility was actually constructed and consequently maintained at adequate funding levels in their community. How did we try to avoid the pitfalls acknowledged by Alexander, as well as the other doubts expressed by members of the civic and community information and communication technology community? For one thing, we explicitly called for patterns that address the larger systems that current information and communication systems are embedded within. These patterns dealing with policy, education, or media critique, for example, are explicitly intended to influence the conditions under which information and communications systems must exist. Alexander shows what a better built environment looks like—and how to think about it and use patterns to build it—but not how to get to a place where one *can* use his pattern language. The Liberating Voices project, by comparison, shows, or tries to show, how to get there, less of what an end product would look like.

Like Alexander's, this project is utopian: it is attempting to move society in a direction that many current powerful social forces and ideologies are working against. This critical issue, along with the other important issue of whether progressive change can be institutionalized, should not be left aside indefinitely. A parallel question raised by Peter van den Besselaar (personal correspondence) is whether pattern languages are inherently conservative and inhibit progressive change.

We find ourselves unable to make the same strong claims about the pattern language that we are building as Alexander makes about his. For one thing, it is difficult to say that some of our patterns relating to computer use are timeless, when computers are a very recent addition to our communication sphere. Maintaining an intellectually skeptical perspective compels us to think of this as a research project with multiple hypotheses; our optimistic spirit holds on to the hope that this work will hold some of the power that Alexander's work has. In other words, pattern languages like Alexander's, but in thousands of other domains, could emerge (we hope!) from employing Liberating Voices patterns, more then we could expect positive social change to emerge necessarily from communities and societies like those hypothesized in *A Pattern Language*.

7 Looking into Liberating Voices

In chapter 6, we discussed how we developed the Liberating Voices pattern language. In this chapter, we introduce what we developed: the Liberating Voices pattern language itself and its constituents—the patterns, the links that connect the patterns, and the way everything is organized into a language. This chapter also discusses the organization of the patterns (which appear in the next chapter) from the most general at the beginning of the list to the most specific at the end. Each pattern has links to other patterns that are related to it in some way. Those patterns can be used together at the same time or one after the other. This chapter also discusses how in general the patterns could be used in real and in hypothetical situations.

Applying the Language

Social and environmental activists throughout the world are simultaneously working on a project of staggering magnitude: the aim is no less than retooling the whole informational and communicational environment to meet human needs better. If the project is successful, this new communications environment would be a key factor in helping humankind repair the environment, prevent wars, reverse the spread of poverty, and heal the wounds between and among people. In an era of intense media consolidation against a backdrop of seemingly ubiquitous and intractable problems of disease, war, environmental degradation, and injustice, people everywhere are challenging the media titans and other advocates for Liberating Voices antipatterns. Liberating voices belongs to the people working on a myriad projects to create a communication sphere capable of supporting the civic intelligence humankind will need if it is to address the challenges it faces.

These activists may be involved with newspapers for the homeless, community radio, communication policy, or any number of other projects that rely fundamentally on information and communication. There is a widespread and growing feeling that the mainstream communication systems that connect us with the information and ideas that we use every day are not what they should be. The creative impulse to build a better tomorrow is frustrated by media systems that often distort and denigrate. The water flowing from their pipes, though constant and omnipresent, seems to be actively thwarting the thoughts and actions that are most needed.

However diverse and disconnected that people and organizations seem to be, through their inventing, critiquing, exposing, imagining, probing, protesting, discussing, and adjusting, they are invisibly moving toward a larger, all-encompassing web. The web has innumerable strands, feelers, and forays. It is this central realization that a larger enterprise is taking hold that propels this project forward. We have acknowledged that the aims of this project are undeniably vast and seemingly quixotic. At the same time, we are cautiously optimistic enough to suggest that this marvelous loom of insight and engagement can be coaxed into a more energetic and productive existence. The chances for success are greater now than at any other time in history because of a communication web that is both technological and social. And it seems to be getting more powerful and more intelligent. This web will need dexterity and strength to withstand attacks from above, as well as challenges, such as apathy and cynicism, that emanate from below. We believe that the possibility for a major positive transformation exists and hope that *Liberating Voices* is a major step in that direction.

The purpose of this project is to help support and develop the wide range of activities that can influence the information and communication systems governing many aspects of our lives. Graphically this effort could be portrayed as the intersection of civil society, positive social change, and information and communications systems. A functional model would show the various components mutually interacting. Beyond that, this work is intended to help people better understand the immense role that information and communication systems play in sustaining social ills and the opportunities that now exist for overcoming them.

In *The Timeless Way of Building* (1979), the first volume of the three books on the pattern language, Alexander discusses three general characteristics of the patterns in their language: patterns of events, patterns of space, and patterns are alive.

We have also conceptualized information and communication systems in a broad way. As a reminder, here again are the basic areas that the pattern language should take into account:

• Information and communication systems that address community core values (for example, law, medicine, education)
• Information and communication systems that create and maintain conditions for open communication throughout a society
• Any activity that is fundamentally based on information (for example, economics, psychology, and science)

So, for example, when we talk about the physical environment, we talk about how we measure it, make models of it, discuss it, interpret it, and think about it, not what to do with or to it. A pattern is a story—a special type of story but a story nevertheless. Like stories, patterns come in many shapes and sizes. Most important, patterns, like stories, make sense in some situations and not in others. Just as ribald stories would be out of place at a funeral, some patterns are appropriate for some communities and some are more appropriate in others.

If we characterize the patterns in Liberating Voices at the same level of abstraction as Alexander did in *The Timeless Way of Building*, our pattern language should include patterns of interactions, patterns of relationships, patterns of community, patterns of representation, patterns of interpretation, and patterns of exchange. And as with the patterns in *A Pattern Language*, our patterns should be alive. They should depict transformations that support and actively promote life and health, and beyond that, the patterns themselves, as a system that is alive, should call on and strengthen the other patterns within the pattern language.

Liberating Communities

Communication is the bridge that brings communities together and the chasm that keeps them apart. One of the objectives of this project is helping to build a larger, more inclusive and intelligent global community that includes people from all cultures. We recognize that an injury to one is an injury to all. The project offers an antidote to the splintering, whether indigenously or exogenously inspired, of people in a profession, community, or nation. It opposes the enrichment of any one group at the expense of others or of the earth.

Patterns are intended to make their mark on the world. They characterize what is and what could be. Their domain is a galaxy of civic and community opportunities revolving around information and communication. Since patterns can be activated during times of opportunity, they, by their nature, can initiate interactions between people. Interactions in turn lead to relationships and the building of communities. Patterns, then, can be thought of amplifying nodes within a vast social network. And how these social networks function as a vibrant, energetic and resilient organism helps delineate possible futures.

One objective of this project is supporting the development of the community of activists who express their wisdom and experience through the patterns. This community is virtual in the old sense of the word. It is a community of journalists, community activists, policy-makers, educators, artists, media professionals (and amateurs), technologists, and citizens that is waiting impatiently to be realized. Our hope is that this project helps animate and enhance this nascent collective.

Although we would like everybody to actively take part in this project, we feel that the list above is a good broad characterization of the communities that conceivably would find the patterns and the pattern language compelling and useful to their work. But beyond that listing, it seems that anybody or any organization that was interested could identify with the role of ordinary citizen, especially since we characterize them as "people who are concerned" or "who want to be informed" as well as "people who are looking for ways to engage positively with important issues" or "who are interested in redirecting or reorienting some of their activities." But beyond the ordinary citizen, there are people who work in particular communities of practice that have special interests, perspectives, or commitments that significantly overlap with much of this project. We look first at educators and then proceed through several others on the list.

The line separating educators from researchers is not obvious or well recognized, nor is the line between students and educators, and neither of the boundaries is as distinct as is often assumed. Educators generally place more emphasis on presenting information and knowledge, while the role of researchers is more exploratory and the role of students less authoritative. All three are substantially involved in information and communication; it is their stock and trade, their ends and their means.

Many of the patterns, including Teaching to Transgress (20), Experimental School (89), and Citizenship Schools (96), are directly about education, and those may help educators and researchers with their craft, possibly even help them rethink aspects of what their role is or what their objectives could be. Other educators and researchers also will find useful information within other patterns. The Social Responsibility (8) pattern, for example, could be used as part of a general exploration within university business schools where the Enron and other scandals of the past few years are unfortunately regarded as historical relics that we would never expect to see again—anomalous rather than symptomatic in any way to how business is practiced today. Also, the work presented here is intended to be conducted by a community or communities. So along with using patterns, the patterns, subsets of patterns, or the pattern language itself can be objects of study as well, or what Ann Bishop and Chip Bruce call Community Inquiry (see pattern 122 with this name in chapter 8).

Journalists and others involved in media production and consumption, either working for existing institutions or independently, should find a number of patterns that apply to their work. A vast number of journalists are doing a tremendous job of bringing the truth to the rest of us in the face of daunting odds. However, the job of journalism is rarely examined in the light of the issues of civic communication raised in this book. There is a need for information and communication systems that are useful for addressing the problems of the world and support self-motivated seekers and presenters of information. The need for a different type of journalism arises. Journalists are generally embedded in a vast system with assumptions about their role: what is news, what will sell, what the owners or advertisers want them to say, and what the role of the journalism consumer is or ought to be. At the same time that journalists retune their practices to make them more responsive to urgent human needs, consumers of journalistic products need to shift their point of view from passive bystander to active participant.

As Margaret Keck has pointed out (2002), civic innovations that promote equity and fairness among people and a sustainable approach toward the environment are generally a collaborative achievement of civil society and progressive policymakers working within government. Like everything else, government is an imperfect institution, naturally enough as a reflection of humankind's imperfection. Nevertheless, government—and, perhaps most important, the people working within government—can have integrity, values, and dedication. These are indispensable in any significant positive social change. Chapter 8 contains a number of patterns that explicitly address the creation and maintenance of policy. Virtually all of the patterns in the language have policy implications.

Technology (including information and communication technology) has generally been ignored or resisted by civil society. Technology has often been seen as neutral and inevitable, too complicated, or, simply a function of progress. For whatever reason, information and communication technology was generally left to the instincts of government and business, while those of us who paid any attention watched from the sidelines, with confusion, awe, even anticipation or horror. The Internet has opened up a staggering number of opportunities for dramatically flattening the ratio of information producers to consumers, as well as increasing the size and physical reach of conversations between nonelites. While it is certainly true that the vast majority of people in the world have never used a computer, let alone own one, this is not necessarily a permanent condition. If people do ultimately acquire the access universally proclaimed as inevitable by the technopundits, it will be because people got organized and kept applying pressure. They used the Grassroots Public Policy Development (73) and other germane patterns intelligently and forcefully.

People seem to be realizing that the medium of the Internet is not like others. Its ability to host ever new forms of community demonstrates that it is clearly a meta medium. The Internet has not yet settled down into a more or less permanent configuration like broadcast television. It is breathing and alive, like an animal pacing right outside the door, a shape-shifting animal that could morph into something quite threatening if you looked away for a moment. Vastly cheaper and more powerful computers have democratized access to sophisticated media production capabilities. The price, for example, of creating a film is orders of magnitude less expensive than it was just twenty years ago.

At the very deep core of what makes the Internet alive are the protocols at its heart. Protocols, the rules for transferring information, for computers to hook up with other computers, allow nearly infinite promiscuity, where every computer can pile on and be part of a data stream population explosion. It is these protocols, or rules, that allow, even encourage, it all to happen. It is these protocols, not owned by Microsoft, Wal-Mart, the Department of Defense, or Google, that support the current orgy of sociotechnological innovation.

The protocols that live at the atomic level of the Internet can also help breath the necessary civic spirit into another community: technologists. Without feeding into stereotypes, I think it can be said that many technologists really like technology and prioritize it over other more human competitors for their time and attention. It doesn't have to be that way.

The computer technology crowd has always had the spirit of counterculture wafting around its edges. Part of this is due to the continual rising to technological challenges. Part of this is due to the values of a sharing community, a type of us-versus-them anarchism. There do seem to be a number of software engineers and others with technical interests who have decided that they are willing to forsake more remunerative avenues of employment to develop new interfaces, databases, applications, models of social interaction, and protocols for civil society and social change. The needs that they are designing for are not just the needs that individual people have. They are needs shared by billions of inhabitants on the planet. Some of these efforts provide free public domain versions of expensive commercial software that has been tailored to noncommercial users. Others develop tools and systems for independent and alternative media and journalists. Others invent whole new paradigms: the open source movement, Wikipedia, MoveOn, and the like.

And technologists are using their skills to provide free wireless networks, telecenters, and other types of community technology centers in developing countries and neglected urban and rural regions and to nonprofit and other community and activist groups. Within this pattern language, Online Community Services Engine (62), Citizen Access to Simulations (48), and Open Source Search Technology (125) have just scratched the surface. Clearly the window of opportunity is open now. There may be a new application, service, or approach for supporting online collaborative work lurking just below the surface of most of these patterns.

Finally, we should mention the community—existing and, the hope is, growing and continuing to mature and coalesce—around the idea of patterns and pattern languages. This community is interdisciplinary and is interested in pattern languages as a way to conceptualize complex systems of knowledge that help integrate the three worlds. Ideally this community will help oversee the next step in the evolution of the pattern language as a useful and influential focus for positive social change in the years ahead. This language was created by a community. Who constitutes that community, and how will it grow? What brought it together? What future plans exist?

The opportunities for civil society and the communities that constitute it have never been greater. Some of these opportunities have been seized on, but many have not. It is up to the individuals and communities that understand the importance and possibilities of information and communication systems to see that we take full advantage of these opportunities—while we still have them.

Roles and Opportunities

It is easy to see that there are roles that we all could play and actions that we all could take that would encourage the birth of a better world. Ideally society would develop alternative and rewarding opportunities for improving the world while making the opportunities to cause further damage less attractive and less rewarding. This would make it easier and less painful for a person to consider working in areas that explicitly sought and advanced societal ameliorization. (See the Opportunity Spaces (33) and the Economic Conversion (41) patterns for more discussion.) We realize, of course, that these opportunities are unequally distributed. Far from being open to all or based entirely on merit, the benefits accrue largely to those who have an adequate amount already. These benefits may be derived from the resources (money, for one) that can be drawn on, particularities of birth (economic class and society, family life, ethnicity), whom you know, allegiances (political party member, fraternity brother), and even spontaneous opportunities that come from being in the right place at the right time.

The communities discussed above are, of course, subject to the constraints and opportunities that will depend on unique circumstances. The will to transcend the givens of an era, region, culture, or regime is also unequally distributed. The same goes for the ability (or even desire) to work on the edges or gray areas that lie at the boundaries of acceptability and non-acceptability. These edges are still edges, even in places where being there is not punishable by death.

There are several additional factors to consider when people are thinking about becoming more actively engaged in public issues. The first relates to the degree of autonomy that the individual enjoys. A person whose parents have influence in the community, for example, is likely to have more room to move, hence more autonomy, than one without this advantage. Some situations have inherently more access to the levers of power. Certainly different societies mete out different punishments for people who veer out of the comfort zone and different rewards for obedience as well. What support structures exist for "deviant" activities? What support is available to help people begin to explore what they can do to encourage positive change?

Using the Language

This section discusses the critical issue of use. After all, the whole endeavor has been motivated by the idea that the patterns and the pattern language would be useful. We begin this section with a scenario that shows how multiple patterns could be used to assist in a complex, long-term project. After that, we discuss ways that patterns in general can be used and a strategy for selecting and employing individual patterns.

Scenarios

Early in the project, people in the pattern language e-mail list identified a number of scenarios that might be suitable for drivers of the pattern language project. Clearly they were not inspired solely by the patterns that existed at the time, as a number of them seem to require patterns that do not exist in our language. Some of these scenarios that do not seem to be covered by the pattern language, and some that do are listed below.

• A social scientist in Brazil needs to explain that simply putting more computers in classrooms will not improve education and is probably not the first step in any effort to do so.
• A citizen in the United States is afraid that currently flawed voting machines may make elections meaningless.
• A group of concerned citizens is trying to design a workable path away from the current campaigning system that requires huge contributions for media coverage followed by undue influence of contributors.
• A research manager is trying to help bridge the cultural gaps and differences in time horizons between researchers and the consultants they are trying to help.

• A charity wants to promote a message about improving housing provision for people with disabilities and wants to use information and communication technology to get its message to a broad audience—in particular, local government councils and housing associations.

• A mutual support group for people suffering from a rare medical condition wants to set up a virtual space for online support

• Members of an environmental lobbying group want to coordinate their media work and organize themselves more efficiently.

• A group of separate community groups or charities using shared offices wants to make effective use of information and communication technology for internal office management.

• A small group on a housing project wants to establish a sense of community and encourage skills and economic development in their locality.

• A group of community members (mixing individuals and established organizations) wants to generate and coordinate informed opposition to loss of communal facilities.

• A coalition wants to stop a war—and prevent the next one.

• A group of community members wants to generate informed opposition to a proposed industrial plant.

• A group dedicated to increasing civic capability to discuss and resolve problems wants to develop social capital and social entrepreneurialism in an environment in which people find it hard to leave their homes to participate in social dialogue unless their self-interest is at stake.

• Libraries or school districts want to collaborate to achieve what once were called economies of scale but are now the benefits of pooling resources virtually.

• An environmental group wants to develop an informed body of participants who can provide high-quality environmental monitoring in a locality.

• A citizens' advice bureau seeks to offer comprehensive civic information, interpreted for each client's circumstances.

• A practitioner initiates a global virtual collaborative effort to write a book.

   The scenario that follows illustrates the use of several patterns together in a not uncommon situation. Although all situations have their own unique set of factors (and patterns are not employed the same way every time), we believe that this scenario is plausible:

Imagine that people in a low-income neighborhood in the United States based on their own local knowledge suspect that asthma and other diseases are taking a much higher-than-normal toll on the people in their neighborhood. Using the Big Picture Health Information (27) pattern, they begin to understand in deeper way the importance of identifying and publicizing health information (such as the connection between pollution and health) that people can understand and build on. The concerned people from the community form a task force using ideas from Civic Capabilities (85), Sense of Struggle (104), and Shared Vision (101) in order to develop a common framework that encourages effective organizing. After meeting several times in a Great Good Place

(119), the community decides to develop Indicators (29), which provide them with important measurements that help them diagnose their community's health and begin to assume more control of their future. The group then discovers the Citizen Science (37) pattern, which provides them with some insight on how citizens can participate in a research process that is educational and empowering. They start performing their own air quality monitoring, which yields useful information to help catalyze social action in the neighborhood and bring about long-lasting change. They use the Open Action and Research Network (45), which describes how small groups can work together by integrating their actions to accomplish a lot more than they could accomplish working individually, and Grassroots Public Policy Development (78), which helps them develop policy that helps get the toxics out of their neighborhood and gets funding for the cleanup and medical treatment for those who are ill. Finally, they come upon the Civic Intelligence (1) pattern, which provides a general framework for thinking about how local circumstances are connected to those outside the local community and how to use this knowledge effectively. Although the discovery of the pattern and the relevance that it may have for the community came last in this case, it may come earlier or not at all in others. The importance is that they created a lexicon that they used for their own purposes. (And, of course, they could have used Homemade Media (110), Peaceful Public Demonstrations (133), Citizen Journalism (91), Community Inquiry (122), or any number of other patterns.)

Parameters

In this section we discuss how to use the patterns. The basic process is the same but several parameters (including what uses one has in mind for the patterns, whether it is for a new or existing project or process, and whether an individual or a group will be working on it) are likely to have an impact on how they are used.

Generic Pattern Uses   Any pattern can be used in a variety of ways. While the author of each pattern probably has an idea of how the pattern could, will, or, even possibly, how it should be used, readers are likely to have their own ideas about how they'd like to use the pattern. Although this was obviously not the intent of the pattern authors or of me, a reader whose aim and worldview were antithetical to the positions we are advocating could study these patterns with the aim of subverting them, possibly by devising antipatterns (as discussed in chapter 10).

Regardless of the idiosyncratic uses of the patterns that people develop, there are several generic uses to which the patterns can be put. Unlike Alexander's patterns, which were intended to be used by people who are designing or building an actual building or landscape, the Liberating Voices patterns can be applied to a much larger range of activities. These generic uses (which are likely to overlap considerably in any situation) include research, discussion, service development, policy development, institutional development, activism, resource (e.g. online information) development, technology development or personal or collective education and learning. For example, patterns that address monitoring (Earth's Vital Signs, 26), indicators (Alternative Progress Indexes, 46), deliberation (World Citizen Parliament, 40), or collaboration (International Networks of Alternative Media, 43) all suggest technology development and participatory opportunities. Also, for many patterns, a federated network of organizations all working on projects that advance that particular pattern could be developed.

Process

Since the Liberating Voices pattern language has just now been assembled as a pattern language, there are only preliminary observations of its actual use. Alexander in *The Timeless Way of Building* and in *A Pattern Language* suggests that people select a small subset of the language that they believe they should work with. Using that subset, the "builder" should then deliberately use one pattern at a time to build the structure. Our domain, while containing concrete elements (computers, books, or libraries, for example) is in general more abstract than Alexander's. Also, in our quest for a more effective characterization of our domain for policy, research, and activism, we have consciously expanded our sphere to address the broader societal forces that Alexander's original approach, by his own admission, did not include. In the ongoing Liberating Voices project we will strive to solicit comments from people using the pattern language, share these with others, and revise our recommendations as necessary.

General Approaches

This section describes general approaches to pattern language use, thus augmenting recommendations that are found in the individual patterns. It also stresses that no precise, step-by-step set of instructions exists since people will ultimately use the language in creative ways that no one anticipated. Browsing the patterns will undoubtedly be a way for readers to understand the language's essence. Different readers will focus on different patterns that speak to them differently, depending on their interests and circumstances. In this way, each reader builds an idiosyncratic lexicon that appeals to him or her.

The discussion here assumes that the pattern will be used as a basis for action. Obviously if you are not going to implement the pattern, your process will differ from one that focuses on implementation. Also in a building situation (the broad context in *A Pattern Language*), one might design this, then that, and so on toward an end, a result that incorporates several patterns (but used one at a time). In a communication setting, one might concentrate on one pattern over and over. For example, an organization might adopt the Civic Intelligence (1) pattern and use it in a variety of ways, but generally as a way to help inform it in collaborations with other groups.

A slightly more formal process is recommended when looking for patterns to address a problem. People working on projects should think about the problems that they would like to address and gather a group of patterns that might apply. Through the pattern contexts, the patterns should map onto the problem space. Although the patterns are not precise recipes, we present some general guidelines for identifying and working with one or more patterns to develop an appropriate plan.

A pattern is intended to be used to address a problem in a given context. A context is a product of various forces, including people and communities, that are involved in the situation, either by making an impact or experiencing the impacts of others. Similarly, the problem facing the potential pattern user should be similar to the problem described within the pattern. Therefore the first task is ascertaining whether the match exists. After all, if there is no problem to solve, why use the pattern at all?

An individual or group will identify patterns that appeal to them in some way. This may be because they are already using a similar approach or because it sounds intriguing. It may recommend something they would like to consider or something they were already planning to do. If they are already working on a project related to the pattern, they probably will want to read the pattern looking for insights and examples as well as challenges that they may encounter. The links to other patterns—listed at the end of each pattern—may provide ideas about possible collaborators and what types of patterns might be good to explore in the future.

Generally more than one pattern will be selected from the language for further consideration. Although the existence of a link shows that a reasonable connection exists, the absence of a link does not mean that no connection exists. It may be that we did not notice the connection when we were establishing the links. Presumably your plan will be to integrate the new patterns into your or your organization's worldview and work practices; if not, you should treat the adoption of a pattern as a new project. If the pattern seems too alien to the established ways of doing things, the difficulty of successfully employing it increases significantly. If you do decide to proceed, you may want to examine the forces that are acting against it and with it in your own specific context and what to do about them before you start. If, for example, you work for a traditional newspaper company and you would like to explore how Citizen Journalism (91) could be employed, you need to think about who with the newspaper would be able to help coordinate the new activities and how other stakeholders would react to a new journalistic approach. If the plan is to integrate the pattern, you will want to think about how it will be combined. If a group is planning to work with a new pattern, there needs to be agreement on what needs to be done and a brief plan (see Shared Vision, 101). It may turn out that launching several projects might be best.

If one big project is selected rather than smaller ones, the challenge of working several patterns at the same time arises. And the patterns themselves can be used to organize discussions among people who are working together. At any rate, the adoption of any patterns should proceed from an analysis of the group's resources, core competencies, interest level, and, in general, reasonableness of integrating the new work within the existing context and institution.

The union or universe of the context statements includes a vast number of situations but ideally addresses the most common, persistent, and urgent ones. Although through our use of prose-oriented context statements we avoid the trap of a seemingly cut-and-dried portrayal of contexts (that, for example, a form-oriented approach using radio buttons and check boxes would suggest), we have tried to promote a consistent approach to context statements within the patterns. Thus a context generally embraces three components: (1) salient features of the environment, (2) salient features of the person or a group of people (including the skills, resources, and attributes of those who are interested or affected by the context and the problem, and (3) the objectives of the person or group. There are a number of strong arguments for specifying context statements (and other portions of the patterns and the pattern language). One benefit is that the language would be more "complete" or "valid," and make the patterns and the language more accessible, compelling, convincing, or effective to users.

Based on the contexts, a variety of patterns are relevant at any given time. As Ganz (2004) has described, "Access to a diversity of approaches not only offers multiple routines from which to choose but also contributors to the 'mindfulness' that multiple solutions are possible." Ganz presents a rich collection of useful suggestions drawn from many sources in his paper, "Why David Sometimes Wins" (2004), which was the motivation for the Strategic Capacity (34) pattern.

One of the most important things to do is to read the pattern carefully, paying attention to the rationale, the examples, the problems it is trying to address, and the challenges that are likely to arise. To some degree, patterns represent idealized approaches that do not address the specifics of any given situation. They do not include precise, step-by-step instructions. For those reasons, although the patterns represent an important first step, it is important to realize that it is only a first step and many more steps must follow.

These first steps include conducting more research: read the references, check the Web sites, or even contact people who have worked in the area directly. How did other people working on similar projects organize their work? What resources did they use? What challenges did they face, and what words of wisdom—or caution—do they offer? Also along those lines, it might make sense to call or write to some people who are involved in the pattern or join (or start) an e-mail list devoted to that topic.

The person or group develops plans and actions that interact with other people and groups, which then react in supporting or dissenting actions. By working on the pattern, the person or group necessarily connects with a greater audience, which could be the media, discussions, meetings, or collaborations with other groups, among many other possibilities If the ideas within the pattern are employed successfully, the context will undergo some change. The problem will be diminished in some way and the forces that define the context, including the communities, will also change. (And if the employment of the pattern is not successful, it could also trigger an unwanted change, including a redoubling of the anti-pattern efforts, thus exacerbating the original problem.)

The next chapter contains the first version of Liberating Voices pattern language. The authors (eighty-five at last count) of these patterns are hopeful and confident that people will find them useful. At the same time, we realize that nothing is perfect and that these patterns cannot dodge that inevitability. We are asking our readers to read these patterns, think about them, and try to use them. Beyond that, we invite all of our readers to participate in the ongoing process of improving the existing patterns and playing a role in the generation of future ones.

8 The Patterns

The patterns in this chapter constitute the Liberating Voices pattern language. They have been selected from the pool of over 400 submitted patterns. Of course, there is no final pattern language; it will evolve as circumstances change and we refine our thinking. And people and organizations that use this pattern language will assemble their own language, based on patterns here and ones that make sense to them given the particularities of their situation.

The patterns are categorized from the most general (Theory) to the most specific (Tactics):

Theory   Theory is the most general level of the patterns in the language. In a broad way, these patterns express the assumptions that we are making about the world and, most important, how we intend to engage in the world.

Organizing principles   Organizing principles are less general than theory but still quite abstract. They can motivate and inform any enterprise, yet they themselves are not corporeal. They are ideas that we can employ to orient our work in a meaningful way.

Enabling systems   Enabling systems are concrete expressions of our objectives, often integrating institutions and technological systems. They are enabling because they actively encourage the multiplication of ideas and actions on which people can help create a better society.

Policy   Although largely invisible, policy nevertheless is a major force on our lives. As a set of public rules, guidelines, and programs, policy creates and demolishes barriers. It represents an arena of public affairs that, ironically enough, is often closed to the public.

Collaboration   How effective people are in their pursuits depends on how well they can work together. This realization motivates the patterns in this section and in the next. People and groups—both informal and formal—must actively engage with the world outside to achieve their goals. This, of course, can assume many forms, from the purely cooperative to the openly combative.

Community and organizational building   A group is effective insofar as it integrates the insights, knowledge, skills, interests, and resources of its members. Beyond this, a group must reflect on its own state, including its aims, methods of interpreting, decision making, and planning, and adjust its behavior accordingly. An effective group, moreover, must understand and adapt as well as shape the environment in which it finds itself.

Self-representation   The world contains a vast diversity of viewpoints and voices. By focusing on the need for people to regain control over how their culture, region, and selves are viewed by others, the patterns celebrate and strengthen that diversity while seeking ways to reduce conflict and encourage dialogue and understanding.

Projects   These patterns represent tangible projects that any community can initiate. Although these are generic in some way, the local situation will vary in every case.

Tactics   These patterns describe activities that can be particularly effective even if only applied sporadically. They are limited in space and time, yet they can focus attention, unite disparate efforts, and help create conditions for future collaborations. These patterns appear last but are not insignificant. Indeed one of our most important tasks is discovering more of these tactics.

Theory

1. Civic Intelligence
2. The Commons
3. The Good Life

Organizing Principles

As we move forward, we realize that certain perspectives can be used to help ensure that our work is purposeful.

4. Social Dominance Attenuation
5. Health as a Universal Right
6. Global Citizenship
7. Political Settings
8. Social Responsibility
9. Matrifocal Orientation
10. Collective Decision Making
11. Memory and Responsibility
12. Working-Class Consciousness
13. Back to the Roots
14. Demystification and Reenchantment
15. Translation
16. Linguistic Diversity
17. Education and Values
18. Dematerialization

Society needs to change in many ways. The following patterns set out some routes toward this end.

19. Transforming Institutions
20. Teaching to Transgress
21. Fair Trade
22. Sustainable Design

23. Antiracism
24. Spiritually Grounded Activism
25. Cyberpower

If we are to have a chance at succeeding in our objectives, information of various types will be needed, and it must be available to the widest audience.
26. Earth's Vital Signs
27. Big-Picture Health Information
28. Whole Cost
29. Indicators

Coming together to make the changes that are necessary requires venues in which this can happen.
30. Public Agenda
31. Democratic Political Settings
32. Big Tent for Social Change

People must have access to information, discussion venues, and, in general, opportunities for bettering themselves and the whole of society.
33. Opportunity Spaces

To be prepared to engage in these struggles, individuals and organizations need to improve a great number of skills and capacities.
34. Strategic Capacity
35. Media Literacy
36. Participatory Design
37. Citizen Science
38. Mobile Intelligence
39. Technocriticism

Enabling Systems
Now that the world is so tightly connected, the need to develop better support for global systems is becoming critical.
40. World Citizen Parliament
41. Economic Conversion
42. Strengthening International Law
43. International Networks of Alternative Media

We must build intelligence from the ground up.
44. Design Stance
45. Open Action and Research Network
46. Alternative Progress Indexes
47. Meaningful Maps

48. Citizen Access to Simulations
49. Culturally Situated Design Tools
50. Conversational Support across Boundaries
51. Truth and Reconciliation Commissions
52. Online Deliberation

Communities under stress need different kinds of support.
53. Alternative Media in Hostile Environments
54. Mutual Help Medical Web Sites
55. Indigenous Media
56. Peace Education

Globalization does not obviate the need to support the local community as well.
57. Intermediate Technologies
58. Durable Assets
59. Public Library
60. Digital Emancipation
61. Community Networks
62. Online Community Service Engine
63. Community Currencies

Policy
Some basic principles are needed to underpin public policy and make it open and account-able.
64. Transparency
65. Privacy
66. Media Diversity
67. Ethics of Community Informatics

Some policy is best advanced through systems.
68. Free and Fair Elections
69. Equal Access to Justice
70. E-Consultation
71. Participatory Budgeting

Global economic systems mean that vast amounts of money are being transferred every day. How can this phenomenon better serve the public good?
72. Transaction Tax
73. Powerful Remittances

Society runs on information, and access to certain types of information is essential.
74. Positive Health Information
75. Accessibility of Online Information

76. Open Access Scholarly Publishing
77. Mobile Information and Computer Technology Learning Facilities

The community itself should lead in other initiatives.
78. Grassroots Public Policy Development
79. Multiparty Negotiation for Conflict Resolution
80. Users' Information Technology Quality Network
81. Academic Technology Investments

Collaboration
Collaboration can often be better served when new ways of looking are employed.
82. Wholesome Design for Wicked Problems
83. Voices of the Unheard
84. Design for Unintended Use

Building intelligence capabilities is essential to improving the effectiveness of our collaborations.
85. Civic Capabilities
86. Strategic Frame
87. Value-Sensitive Design
88. Future Design
89. Experimental School
90. Service-Learning
91. Citizen Journalism
92. Document-Centered Discussion

We need to develop and strengthen institutions and programs that promote collaborations.
93. Citizen Diplomacy
94. Mirror Institutions
95. Patient Access to Medical Records
96. Citizenship Schools
97. Community-Building Journalism

Community and Organizational Building
Organizations must take part in collective learning.
98. Informal Learning Groups
99. Appreciative Collaboration
100. Sustainability Appraisal
101. Shared Vision

We need to think about organizations that can motivate and orient our work.
102. Community Animators
103. Online Antipoverty Community
104. Sense of Struggle

Self-Representation

Thinking about ourselves in a new light will mean redefining the ways that we are depicted.

105. Self-Help Groups

106. Self-Designed Development

107. Engaged Tourism

108. Appropriating Technology

And although much of the work that we are advocating is outwardly directed, much of it needs to be home grown as well.

109. Control of Self-Representation

110. Homemade Media

111. Arts of Resistance

112. Labor Visions

113. Universal Voice Mail

Stories belong to communities and our shared human experience. It is time to take them back and rediscover—and reinvent—stories.

114. The Power of Story

115. Public Domain Characters

116. Everyday Heroism

Projects

Building a new world requires new spaces and places to encourage innovation and collaboration. Here are three—and there are likely to be countless others.

117. Community Telecenters

118. Thinking Communities

119. Great Good Place

Communities are being confronted with new situations that they have not anticipated or adequately dealt with. The following patterns are intended to help them roll up their sleeves and get to work.

120. Soap Operas with Civic Messages

121. Emergency Communication Systems

122. Community Inquiry

123. Illegitimate Theater

124. Environmental Impact Remediation

Some of this work will require technology development.

125. Open Source Search Technology

126. Socially Responsible Computer Games

127. Open Source Everything

Some will involve engaging the powerful.

128. Power Research
129. Citizens' Tribunal

Tactics

Many of these tactics involve probing and engaging.

130. Whistle-Blowing
131. Tactical Media
132. Media Intervention
133. Peaceful Public Demonstrations

Many involve learning with a mission.

134. Activist Road Trip
135. Follow the Money

Finally, although these patterns are intended to help people engage with the world with dedication, strength, creativity, and love, it is not really possibly—or desirable—to engage all the time. Do not forget that for your actions and thoughts to be effective, you must periodically take a break and think things over.

136. Retreat and Reflection

Theory

Problem   The human race has multiplied tremendously since its origins in Africa millions of years ago. During its stay on earth, it has changed the world dramatically through social and technological innovation. In spite of great success in increasing its numbers and gaining dominion over much of the planet, the problems that humankind has created—war, famine, environmental degradation, injustice, and a host of others—may be increasingly immune to its attempts to correct them. Unfortunately there is ample evidence that the economic and political elites of the world are not able—or willing—to address these problems effectively, humanely, and ecologically responsibly. Civil society is emerging as an important force to address these problems, but in spite of best intentions, civil society efforts are often disjointed, duplicative, inflexible, ineffectual, and destructively competitive.

Context   The social and the natural environment face profound challenges at the dawn of the twenty-first century. Society often develops intelligent collective responses to collective problems, often through citizen activism. Civil society and ordinary citizens are often at the forefront of the creation and adoption of new paradigms, ideas, tactics, and technologies that are used to address shared problems and create a better future.

Discussion   In early 2003, days before the United States invaded Iraq, Robert Muller, former assistant secretary general of the United Nations, called attention to the incipient potential of the citizenry: "Never before in the history of the world has there been a global visible, public, viable, open dialogue and conversation about the very legitimacy of war" (Twist 2003). He was describing the unprecedented movement that arose simultaneously in hundreds of places around the world. What this movement represents is the advent of an immensely powerful force. Muller called it a "merging, surging, voice of the people of the world." And James Moore (2003), a multifaceted scholar, activist, and businessperson, called this same phenomenon the "second superpower" whose "beautiful but deeply agitated face ... is the worldwide peace campaign," and "the body of the movement is made up of millions of people concerned with a broad agenda that includes social development, environmentalism, health, and human rights." Both are expressions of pent-up desire and a will to work for a better world, and both are manifestations of civic intelligence.

To meet the need for civic problem solving, governments, companies, nongovernmental organizations (NGOs) citizens, and ordinary people are beginning to acknowledge the vast problems that humankind now faces and are devising new strategies, tactics, and paradigms to ameliorate them. To help with these daunting tasks, a growing array of sociotechnical information and communication systems is being developed. People and organizations need both general paradigms and specific ideas to help them devise tactics and strategies that further their objectives while working cooperatively with other people and organizations.

Civic intelligence, like Daniel Goleman's *Emotional Intelligence* (1995) or the various types of intelligences identified by Howard Gardner in *Frames of Mind: The Theory of Multiple Intelligences* (1983) (or even erotic intelligence, the cover story in a recent edition of the *Utne Reader* (September/October 2003)), is a type of intelligence, one with a specific focus; it can be used to explore and invigorate a flexible and powerful competence that goes beyond the traditional notion of intelligence (which is typically equated to what IQ tests measure) in several important ways. Civic intelligence is a type of intelligence that focuses on the betterment of society as a whole, not just on individual aggrandizement. Moreover since it is a capability of society as a whole, its manifestation is collective and distributed throughout the population. The boundary between one person's "intelligence" and another person's "intelligence" is permeable, indistinct, and constantly shifting. Ideas in your mind today might be central to my understanding of the world tomorrow. How "intelligent" would one person be without interacting with other people directly (through discussion or argument) or indirectly (through reading books, watching television, or pondering works of art) or with the nonhuman world (observing nature, for example).

Civic Intelligence builds on what we know about how people learn and maintain knowledge about the world and their place within it. Intelligent behavior in individuals is rich and multifaceted. It involves perception, monitoring, deliberating, remembering and forgetting, categorizing, coming up with new ideas and modifying old ones, negotiating and discussing, making decisions, testing hypotheses, and experimenting. Society as a whole engages in analogous activities, and these are embedded in our institutions, traditions, artifacts, and conversations. That these activities of collective intelligence exist is indisputable. Less obvious but also true is the fact that they are all subject to change. The idea that they could and should be consciously improved is the heart of this pattern. This recommendation is bolstered by the findings of Jared Diamond, the prominent historian and author at the University of California at Los Angeles, who has extensively studied how societies face challenges with potentially catastrophic consequences. Somewhat incredibly, Diamond's research reveals that the "commonest and most surprising" of the four ways in which societies fail to address their problems is their "failure even to try to solve a problem that it has perceived," even one that ultimately results in that society's collapse. To avoid that mistake, we must go beyond examining how we as a society collectively think and take a critical look at how our knowledge and ideas are—and could be—channeled into actions.

The number of organizations exhibiting civic intelligence today is vast and growing. There were ten times more transnational advocacy organizations in 2000 then there were in 1900 (Keck and Sikkink 1998). Not only are these organizations more numerous, but they are increasingly thoughtful and forward looking. While in the past, protest may have been simply opposed to something, it is not uncommon today for organizations to develop sophisticated analyses and policy recommendations. In an earlier exploration of civic intelligence (Schuler 2001), six dimensions were identified (orientation, organization, engagement, intelligence, products and projects, and resources) in which organizations and movements that demonstrate civic intelligence are likely to differ from those that do not. The set of attributes associated with those dimensions that tend to characterize civic intelligence organizations and movements is a first approximation of a descriptive model of civic intelligence. Some notable examples (among tens of thousands) include the worldwide Indymedia network, the World Social Forum, the Global Fund for Women, Jubilee 2000, Science for the People, and New Tactics in Human Rights. Civic intelligence can also be manifested locally. The graphic at the beginning of the pattern, for example, shows how neighborhood art—in this case a mural about the causes and effects of asthma—can be educational and lead to political engagement and other proactive civic activities. Many of these efforts are of necessity holistic, multidisciplinary, and entrepreneurial since the people and organizations that the efforts would ideally engage with cannot necessarily be expected to do what might be considered the right thing. In an interesting turn of events, the idea of collective intelligence, which is not necessarily aligned with civic intelligence (also a form of collective intelligence), is now receiving attention from various quarters. One group, the cyber pundits, are hoping it will be the "next big thing." Tim O'Reilly (2006), publisher of O'Reilly books and the man who coined the expression "Web 2.0," defines it as "the business revolution in the computer industry caused by the move to the Internet as platform, and an attempt to understand the rules for success on that new platform. "There is another side of this growing interest in collective intelligence as well. This approach is less concerned with making money and more about solving global problems. While these two groups have different aspirations, both of their revolutionary visions are often based on side-effects or technical aspects, such as new algorithms, semantic webs, or tipping points. Both groups seem to place less faith in the value of collaboratively working together and shy away from trying to address the problems that humankind is facing by actually addressing the problems.

A complementary model (illustrated below and described in more detail at http://www .publicsphereproject.org/civint/model-functional.html) of civic intelligence that depicts its primary functional processes has also been proposed (Schuler 2001). This model (or framework) is an amalgam of concepts from social change theory and models of education and human learning. The model is aimed at providing useful exploration in these areas as opposed to offering an algorithm or mechanism that always behaves accurately and produces precise results. Generally the two models are to be used in tandem: the descriptive model describes the what, while the functional model describes the how. The functional model contains three main components: the environment, which includes everything that is relevant to the organization yet outside the organization; the mental model (or core), which corresponds to the sum of knowledge that the organization uses; and the remaining constituents of the organization, including its resources (e.g., people) and, most important, the interactive processes under the control of the organization that link the environment and the mental model. The functional model contains eight types of interactive processes that a movement, organization, or other group exhibits when engaging in civic intelligence:

1. Monitoring   How the organization acquires new relevant information nonintrusively.

2. Discussion and deliberation   How organizations discuss issues and determine common agendas, "issue frames" (Keck and Sikkink 1998), and action plans with other organizations. The mental model of any participants or the organization itself can change as a result of the interactions.

3. Engagement   How the organization attempts to make changes through varying degrees of cooperation and combativeness.

4. Resource transfer   How noninformational resources like volunteers and money are acquired from the environment.

5. Interpretation of new information   How new information is considered and how it ultimately becomes (or does not become) part of the core. New information can also include information about the organization.

6. Maintenance of mental model (includes resource management)   How the organization maintains its organizational integrity by consciously and unconsciously resisting change over time.

7. Planning and plan execution   How a campaign is initiated, carried out, and monitored.

8. Modification of mental model   How the core itself is scrutinized by participants in the organization and modified. Another term for this is *organizational learning*.

The effectiveness of each of these processes will help determine the effectiveness of the entire organization. For that reason, it is important to develop surveys and other types of diagnostic tools that can help organizations use the civic intelligence paradigm effectively. This information could be key in evaluating actions or developing plans. Some of the other uses of this knowledge are inventorying civic intelligence initiatives of geographical regions or thematic activist areas, convening interorganizational workshops, designing curricula, planning campaigns, or even developing new organizations. One of the most important uses of this information is metacognition: examining and evaluating how the processes are used within an organization and changing them as necessary.

The physical, social, and intellectual environment is changing rapidly. Intelligence, more than anything else, describes the capacity to influence and adapt to its environment. Organizations with civic missions have the responsibility to keep their principles intact while interacting effectively with other organizations, both aligned with and opposed to their own beliefs and objectives.

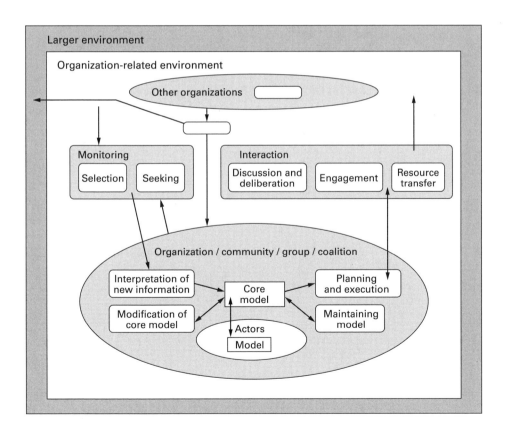

Solution   An effective and principled civic intelligence is necessary to help humankind deal collectively with its collective challenges. People need to develop and set into motion theories, models, and tools of civic intelligence that can help integrate thought and action more effectively.

Linked patterns   Social Dominance Attenuation (4), Global Citizenship (6), Social Responsibility (8), Collective Decision Making (10), Memory and Responsibility (11), Teaching to Transgress (20), Sustainable Design (22), Earth's Vital Signs (26), Strategic Capacity (34), Citizen Science (37), Open Action and Research Network (45), Transparency (64), Media Diversity (66), Open Access Scholarly Publishing (76), Grassroots Public Policy Development (78), Strategic Frame (86), Citizen Journalism (91), Mirror Institutions (94), Citizenship Schools (96), Community Animators (102), Emergency Communication Systems (121), Community Inquiry (122), Retreat and Reflection (136).

2 The Commons

Problem One of the biggest problems in contemporary life is the unchecked growth of market values as a way to govern resources and ourselves. This is resulting in the privatization and commodification, or "enclosure," of the commons. Resources that morally or legally belong to everyone are increasingly coming under the control of markets. Not only does enclosure result in higher prices and the need to ask for permission to use something previously available to all, it shifts ownership and control to private companies. The market efficiencies that businesses seek can be illusory, however, because they often depend on unacknowledged subsidies from the commons (e.g., discount access to public resources) and the displacement of costs onto the commons (pollution, social disruption, harm to future generations). Enclosure does not add value in the aggregate; it merely privatizes value at the expense of the common wealth.

Context *The commons* is a useful term for contemporary political discourse because it provides a new lexicon for resituating market activity in a social and political context. It helps us identify resources that should not be alienated for market use but should be "owned" (in a civic or democratic sense) by everyone. Our culture has no serious vocabulary for contextualizing the free market in a social framework; it assumes that it is a universal, ahistorical force of nature. The commons helps rectify this conceptual problem by offering a rich, countervailing template to the market paradigm, one that can speak about the economic and legal aspects of a commons as intelligibly as its social and personal aspects.

Discussion The commons insists that certain things should not be alienated—that is, sold and converted into money. Thus, it is inappropriate to express the value of a worker's life or an endangered species as a dollar sum in a cost-benefit analysis. It may be morally repugnant to sell off the naming rights of public institutions much as it is considered unacceptable to allow people to sell their bodies, babies, ova, or genes.

The commons gives us a language for talking about extra-market values and their importance. The commons, for example, allows us to talk about the human necessities of life—food, water, fuel, medicine—that may otherwise be seen as market commodities alone. The commons allows us to talk about the need for open spaces that haven't been turned into "property" available to all; if too much of that space—for example, scientific knowledge, musical works, or cultural symbols—is locked up through copyrights, patents, or contracts, it can greatly impede future creativity and progress. We are already seeing the effects of such enclosure in medical research as a result of overly broad patents on basic research.

By contrast, when information and creativity are not seen as "property" or as something that can be purchased, as we see most frequently on the Internet, the resulting collaborations and exchanges generate a huge surplus value that can be enjoyed by everyone, and not be privatized. This is one reason there is such an epic struggle underway on the Internet: nonmarket modes of creativity and production are frequently more efficient in a strict economic sense, compared to conventional real-world markets. There is a cornucopia of the commons, not a tragedy, as economists otherwise claim.

There is a wide variety of effective commons management models that belie the "tragedy of the commons" metaphor invoked by Garrett Hardin in his famous 1968 essay. While Hardin was talking about an open access regime in which no one owns or manages a shared resource, an actual commons has specific rules and social norms for preventing overuse, excluding outsiders, and managing the resource in long-term, sustainable ways.

Increasingly the Internet is the host for countless self-organized commons such as free and open source software, social networking communities, Wikipedia, Craigslist, and Web sites for sharing photos, videos, and other creative work. One useful tool in creating these commons are creative commons licenses, which enable ordinary people to freely share their creative works while retaining copyrights for commercial purposes.

The public library and the land trust are familiar, highly effective types of commons. More people are starting to realize that public spaces like parks, community gardens, farmers' markets, and festivals are also important to the economic and social health of a community. There is a dawning awareness that commons-based infrastructure like wireless Internet access is an important way to use a public resource, the airwaves, to help people connect with each other.

Despite the different ways in which commons and market create value, the two do not necessarily operate in separate and distinct spheres; rather, they are interdependent. The point is to strike an appropriate balance between the two so that the value-creating capacities of each can be optimized.

There are many other types of legal and institutional solutions for managing the commons, although most are not mentally grouped with other legal or institutional models as commons solutions. It is time for more people to see the kinship of these solutions and their holistic advantages over the so-called free market.

Solution Using "the commons" as a new discourse helps reframe the terms of discussion for many issues and declare our personal stake in protecting shared public resources. It helps draw new linkages among disparate market enclosures and in this sense helps fragmented public interest constituencies develop a new, shared language. At the same time, the discourse of the commons validates a number of specific governance models—civic institutions, stakeholder trusts, legal mechanisms, social customs and norms—that can help us protect and manage our common assets effectively. The emerging commons sector will not replace corporations or markets, but it will complement and temper them. In so doing, it will provide benefits that corporations cannot supply: healthy ecosystems, economic security, stronger communities, and a participatory culture. And it will curb the corporate invasion of realms that we hold dear: nature, our minds, our food, and our democracy.

Linked patterns Back to the Roots (13), Linguistic Diversity (16), Big-Picture Health Information (27), Democratic Political Settings (31), Alternative Progress Indexes (46), Open Access Scholarly Publishing (76), Citizen Journalism (91), Public Domain Characters (115), Great Good Place (119), Open Source Search Technology (125).

3 The Good Life

Problem   What is the good life? An answer to that question has so many variations today that the competition among answers can often paralyze the imaginations of people who want to work toward positive social change. How can one break through the noise and violence of such competition and begin moving global society deliberately in a positive direction?

Context   People who hope for a better world feel the need for a shared vision of the good life, a vision that is flexible enough for innumerable individual circumstances but comprehensive enough to unite people in optimistic, deliberate, progressive social change. Ideally this shared vision of the good life should promote and sustain conviviality and solidarity among people, as well as feelings of individual effectiveness, self-worth, and purpose. A shared vision of the good life is never complete, but is always adapting; it should be in harmony with the human condition, which means that it encompasses suffering, loss, and conflict, as well as pleasures, reverence, and common goals of improvement. An emergent framework for the modern good life is based on some form of humanism, particularly pragmatic or civic humanism, but with room for a spiritual dimension of the mind that does not seek domination over the minds of others. Finally, the environmental crises of the planet require a broad vision of a good life that can harmonize human aspirations with natural limits. And all of this needs to be an ongoing and open-ended conversation, best suited to small geographical groups, such as towns and neighborhoods, that can craft and then live an identity that reflects their vision of a good life.

Discussion   Ever since people began to understand the implications of the time limits of the human life, there has been speculation on what constitutes the best use of this time, a human life span—in other words, What is the "good life?"

Throughout human history and even today, the answer to this question for most people is provided by God and by ritual. That is, the fundamental guide for how to live life is religion expressed through ritual—not only the formal rituals of religious practice but the small daily rituals of an existence permeated with conventions derived from religious guidance. For billions of people today, this is so ingrained in their psyches that doubt about what constitutes the good life is absent—or else a personal secret.

But there are many other meanings attached to the phrase "the good life." Aristotle argued that the good life is the *bios theoretikos*, the contemplative life, in which the *aristos*, the "best man," spends his life contemplating the order of the cosmos and his place in it. This was transformed by Christianity into the life of the cloister, in which monks and nuns were meant to spend their lives contemplating the wonder of God's work. But it was also embedded in the practice of philosophy in the Western tradition, both metaphysical and otherwise, so that there is still today a strong Aristotelian association between the "good life" and the life of the mind.

It was in Renaissance Italy that Western thinkers first ventured a potential break between the idea of the good life and religion, by suggesting that the best example of a good life was a man of *virtu*, or the earthly qualities of courage, deliberate action, and command—someone who would be remembered in history rather than rewarded in heaven. Machiavelli derided Christianity as a belief of meekness and submission, while he advocated a robust republican humanism that celebrated worldly success and the ability to turn one's life into a kind of work of art, not unlike the famous works of art of his time.

The great break of modernity, the separation of modern thinking with that of the past, is the idea that the good life is a matter of individual choice—"the pursuit of happiness," as the U.S. Declaration of Independence puts it. English rationalists, Marxian communists, and even conservative thinkers like Edmund Burke all shared this premise: the goal of life is happiness and self-fulfillment.

Thus, it has been the explosion of interpretations of the path to happiness that has produced so many competing conceptions of the good life. For many people today, the phrase "the good life" conjures up fantasies of unlimited wealth, leisure, and luxury. This has certainly been the interpretation of marketers in a consumerist economy like that in the United States.

Yet for large numbers of people, the "good life" means simplicity and even austerity, an escape from the stress and bustle of urban life, pure air and water, the conviviality of a small, rural community, and good health. This is a model promoted by a series of books written in the 1930s by Scott and Helen Nearing, who moved to a farm in Vermont in 1932 and then published *The Good Life* (1970), a book about "simple, frugal and purposeful living," which they followed with more books and national speaking tours. The Good Life Center, a modern example of the Nearings's work, is still in operation in Harborside, Maine. Elements of this interpretation of the good life are now found in the Slow Food movement of southern Europe (and in some groups in the United States) and its spin-off in Italy, the Slow Cities (Città Slow) movement. This trend has even acquired a label: "downshifting."

The challenge of the current situation in the modern world is to develop the vision of a good life that is not antitechnological or antispiritual but is serious about the limits of the global environment and critical of the emptiness, anomie, and hectic "busy-ness" of consumerism. But cities are not going away—they are growing around the world—so we need models of the good life that embrace urban living; indeed, population density is likely to be a necessity in the future.

There is an emerging concept of what might be called "reverent humanism," borrowing terms from philosophers Paul Woodruff (2002) and Luc Ferry (2005). This proposes a blend of rational and practical humanism with an appreciation of the transcendent, whether it be beauty, the law, or the ineffable spirit of human perseverance. Such a worldview depends on the support of a social context, a community of equals engaged in open-ended dialogue that rejects absolute knowledge—a modernized version of the *res publica,* the ideal of the Italian Renaissance. The inspiring ideas of the Slow Food movement bring in the pleasures of good food, drink, conviviality and ecological balance, while globalization and communications technologies, especially the Internet, make possible a sharing of innovations and the development of an appreciation for diversity and peace.

Solution   A revitalization of the idea of the good life should reinvigorate the ancient appeal of civic humanism, or "reverent humanism," that can embrace human potential, limits to consumerism yet technological innovation, diversity, and transcendence. The development of such an ideal should be a project, explicit or implicit, among groups dedicated to progressive social change. And "living the change you want" should become an essential part of the mission of all such groups.

Linked patterns   Back to the Roots (13), Demystification and Reenchantment (14), Spiritually Grounded Activism (24), Technocriticism (39), Alternative Progress Indexes (46), Peace Education (56), Appreciative Collaboration (99), Great Good Place (119), Retreat and Reflection (136).

Organizing Principles

Problem   Social dominance is arguably at the heart of many, if not most, of humankind's most shameful enterprises. It is embodied in ideology, economics, policy, education, the media, social perception and interactions, culture, and even technological artifacts. In general, the less dominant group will have fewer opportunities for advancement, poorer health and shorter life spans, smaller incomes, and higher likelihood of being incarcerated, and they will live under more violent conditions than people do in more dominant groups. Society as a whole also suffers from high levels of inequality: the more equal the distribution of assets, the more economic growth the society will have (Dugan 2004; Ferreira 1999). Political violence is also tied to social inequality (Gurr 1971). At its most extreme, social dominance encourages oppression and wars, genocide, mob violence, and environmental destruction.

Context   This pattern pertains to any society, region, or organization where social dominance is entrenched—in other words, virtually everywhere.

Discussion   As humans evolved, our species unwittingly took on characteristics that have persisted for centuries. Over the millennia, some aspects of our genetic makeup, as well as some psychological and cultural characteristics, were encouraged, while others were halted or slowed. As we all know, these basic changes generally came about hundreds of thousands of years ago, when humans lived in small numbers and clung together in small bands for survival. That situation, once the norm, is now present only in the rarest of circumstances. We have been bred for a time and place that existed eons ago, an era that could be recreated only through pandemics, global war, massive climate change, or some combination.

One consequence is the myriad institutional structures that perpetuate dominance of one group over others. The authors of a book on social dominance (Sidaneous and Pratto 1999) make the case that our social psychology seems to propel us naturally toward oppression. Unfortunately, at least for those who believe that racism and other insidious "isms" would make excellent candidates for the dustbins of history, there are several factors that help keep social dominance in vogue. The first is that there does seem to be a measurable propensity ("generalized ethnocentrism") that shows up in some percentage of any population for strong group identification; people in this group believe that their group is superior to others and that they must stick together. When in positions of power, they generally promote laws and attitudes that favor their group over others. They will also encourage and cleave to a variety of "legitimizing myths," such as social Darwinism ("survival of the fittest"), manifest destiny, "clash of civilizations" (Huntington 1988), and a myriad racial, gender, and ethnic stereotypes, as social frames that help perpetuate social dominance.

The second is that racial (and other) stereotypes are easily and readily (and subconsciously) learned, generally at an early age, before advanced cognitive abilities come into play that could question the accuracy and the value of the stereotypes. Third, the stereotyping trigger is effortlessly and (again) subconsciously activated when "appropriate," thus making these people the hapless targets of manipulative politicians and others who can reach out to these people with tailored messages. Finally, unfortunately, there is some evidence that people in dominated groups, due to a combination of factors, will in many cases adopt characteristics that are specified by the stereotype, thus helping unconsciously to reinforce the stereotype ("behavioral asymmetry"). All of these factors help support, at least indirectly, the maintenance of institutions that operate under a variety of processes, mechanisms, and biases that serve to maintain the machinery of social dominance.

Once the holistic model that Sidaneous and Pratto (1999) propose (possibly with modifications) is well understood, it should be possible to run society's social domination machines in reverse. Along these lines, it is important to note that according to many people who study this field, approaches to attenuating social dominance will require widespread, multisectoral actions that include integrated legislative, economic, and educational efforts among and across dominant and nondominant groups. Here is a list of approaches that can be undertaken—while keeping in mind that articulation between these approaches will be critical if any progress in reducing social dominance is to be made over time:

• Role-reversal exercises. Examples include "walk a mile in their shoes," where state legislators "became" welfare recipients for a day, and an event in Wisconsin where youth in disadvantaged neighborhoods interrogated judges and police officers in a mock courtroom situation.
• Additional research. Identify, for example, markers or other classification schemes that sort people into two groups and see how the markers are used implicitly or explicitly in policy, the media, and other areas.
• Development and promulgation of social frames like "love thy neighbor," "turn the other cheek," human family, equal opportunity, and multiculturalism help characterize the theme.
• Fighting local discrimination in, for example, education or public service.
• Moving beyond tokenism. There is evidence that hiring one or two people from a less dominant group can backfire.
• Childhood education. Children need multicultural education and familiarity with different cultures and groups. Seeing a diverse society at an early age and not growing up with active stereotyping is good.
• Lawsuits as a tool to fight social dominance by business and government.
• Disciplining the media by fighting stereotypes through solidarity networks. Establishing networks of people from diverse communities to support and inform each other, advocate and collaborate.
• Religious connection. Remind people of their religion's commitment to human rights and brotherhood and would with in the church for social change.

According to Sidaneous and Pratto (1999), "arbitrary-set divisions" (divisions devised by cultures themselves according to their own decisions, like caste, religion, and race, unlike divisions shared by all cultures, basically gender and age, on which to discriminate) "largely only occur in societies in which people are able to generate and sustain an economic surplus." These societies employ divisions of labor that apparently lead to various forms of arbitrary-set-based social dominance techniques and institutions. One of the most difficult challenges of such a society is checking the power of its most powerful members.

While many people would argue that some degree of social dominance will probably always occur in society, there are also many people who believe that a meaningful attenuation in social dominance is not only possible but necessary. Fighting against social dominance will always be an uphill battle: the forces that will rally against your campaign are, by definition, powerful and well financed and cozy with the media, government, and other elites. They will also have a ready supply of slogans handy to bring their minions into the fray. Sometimes trumping our own intrinsic nature to favor our own and even going against what may seem like our own best interest (maximizing short-term gain at another's expense) is the best long-range approach. And approaches that are win-win should be accompanied with public education that preempts the inevitable claim that the approach is discriminatory.

Although social dominance may be intrinsic to humankind, there are some grounds for hope. Some countries, Sweden, for example, have more or less eliminated social dominance based on gender. Studies relating to health care in Japan, New Zealand, Denmark, and Sweden also show that proper health care can be reached for all of a nation's citizens even if some social inequality still exists within that society.

Solution   Serious, ongoing, and engaged commitment to social nondominance is the core to solving the problems of social dominance. A society that genuinely wants to reduce its own inequity is obviously more likely to adopt new policies and perspectives over the long haul than one that begrudges every dime spent on schools for poor people or health care for the elderly and the foreign born. Understanding how the machines of social dominance function provides important clues for the development of a counter machine.

Linked patterns   Civic Intelligence (1), Health as a Universal Right (5), Matrifocal Orientation (9), Linguistic Diversity (16), Fair Trade (21), Antiracism (23), Cyberpower (25), Opportunity Spaces (33), World Citizen Parliament (40), Peace Education (56), Accessibility of Online Information (75), Voices of the Unheard (83), Online Antipoverty Community (103), Control of Self-Representation (109), Labor Visions (112), Everyday Heroism (116), Illegitimate Theater (123), Power Research (128).

5 Health as a Universal Right

Problem The crisis in health care worldwide has reached catastrophic proportions. Each day 9,000 people die from AIDS and 11,000 children die from malnutrition. Over 1 billion people have no access to clean water and half the people in the world live on under $2 (U.S.) per day. The worsening conditions of the world's impoverished people provide almost ideal conditions for the cultivation of disease, including those that could reach epidemic or pandemic proportions. In addition, a somewhat invisible epidemic of depression and other mental illnesses is taking a heavy toll on people throughout the developing world.

Context The economic divisions between people have become astronomical, and they are still widening. Within this context, the majority of people are literally living from one day to the next. Understandably, the health of these people is severely compromised. People everywhere and in all walks of life have cause for alarm.

Discussion Environmental changes are adding strains to the already imperiled lives of the world's poorest people. "Droughts will worsen. We will see deforestation, forest fires, a loss of diversity, and degradation of the environment "according to Michel Jarraud, secretary general of the World Meteorological Organization (Stevenson 2006). Not surprisingly, the poorest, and hence most vulnerable, people are often the first victims of the severely declining standards of health in much of the developing world. Paul Epstein (2006) of Harvard Medical School said,

Today climate instability and the exhaustion of resources (forests, soils, water, biodiversity), together with the growing inequity and deepening poverty, are resulting in the emergence, resurgence and redistribution of infectious disease, stalking humans, plants and animals. The conditions are not sustainable, and the mounting social and economic costs are creating convergent agendas among members of civil society, international institutions and the economic sector.

Why are things different today? For one thing, the sheer number of people on the planet seems to be approaching the limits of the world's capacities. Unfortunately the trends are heading in the wrong direction. Furthermore the activities of people everywhere are more closely linked. It is no longer true that we live in isolated communities. The close links, although often geographically remote, allow the causes of ill health (although diffuse and multiple) to be quite removed from the people who ultimately become sick.

Clearly humankind has a moral obligation to establish health as a human right. That is a reasonable first step. More important, humankind has the obligation to act forcefully and diligently as if it actually believed that health was an inalienable human right. However, as Garrett and Rosenstein (2005) report, global health as an issue is "not only for do-gooders." They go on to say, "A self-interest component to the global health debate has clearly emerged—thankfully, because purely altruistic efforts often fall short of international support and sustainability. The interconnected nature of the world makes ignorance of issues such as deadly infectious diseases not only immoral, but self-destructive."

Health must not, however, be viewed solely as providing medical care after disaster or disease strikes. While it is true that a pill or injection can save a life, the person whose life has just been saved will soon return to an environment that leads inexorably to poor health, compromised ability to work gainfully, and a diminished life span. Nor is health something that can be attained solely through research. A focus on the cure for this or that disease can be a type of welfare program for Western researchers. It is a search for a magic silver bullet or technocratic approach that, while often very important, will be effective only in conjunction with other approaches.

Extreme and persistent poverty is the primary cause of ill health and premature death around the world. If people were not in desperate poverty, if they earned an adequate living, the incidence of disease would plummet. Especially today health is linked to poverty. This poverty is not confined to individuals, but covers large sections of the world's rural areas, towns, and cities and, indeed, entire countries. A person who enters the hospital in many parts of the world is likely to find infection, unsanitary conditions, and a scarcity of drugs, bandages, surgical equipment, and other vital medical supplies.

Paul Farmer is one the most articulate and hardest-hitting advocate for health care for all of the world's inhabitants, especially those who are the poorest and most vulnerable. He identifies structural inequalities that often originate in the first world as sources of the great misery that now exists in the third. The roots of the problem are likely to lead further upstream than exposure to a microbe in polluted water to a bank in London, an energy company in Houston, or a government office in Washington, D.C. As part of his work and study, Farmer traveled to prisons in the former Soviet Union and to Haiti, Chiapas, the poorest state in Mexico, and other marginalized locations around the world to work with people in need of medical care and to witness firsthand how health conditions were being met—or not met—around the world. In his book *Pathologies of Power* (2003), he proposes a new agenda for health and human rights with five facets:

- Make health and healing the symbolic core of the agenda.
- Make provision of services central to the agenda.
- Establish new research agendas.
- Achieve independence from powerful governments and bureaucracies.
- Secure more resources for health and human rights.

Farmer's agenda is comprehensive, holistic, and ambitious. At the same time, it seems that anything less would be insufficient. Nongovernmental organizations (NGOs) and philanthropists, no matter how well heeled, will not be able to do this work by themselves. The multipronged approach resembles the Open Action and Research Network (45) pattern—but writ very large. He is not unrealistic about the chances for success. He lists a number of significant challenges to this agenda, including the possibility that increasing the involvement of NGOs will help hasten "the withdrawal of states from the basic business of providing housing, education, and medical resources usually means further erosion of the social and economic rights of the poor."

The new agenda would take a mammoth effort that would integrate direct care, research, and popular mobilization. Ultimately Farmer's recommendations could provide an umbrella for many types of efforts. Health care professionals could take sabbaticals in developing countries to assist with health care. Religious people could put renewed vigor into projects to alleviate human suffering. The more than 400 billionaires in the United States (and elsewhere) could follow the lead of Bill Gates and others and donate substantial amounts of their amassed riches to the effort. At the same time, the rest could agitate for health-related initiatives including cheaper drugs from multinational pharmaceutical companies and authentic foreign aid that is not based on arms or oil.

Garrett and Rosenstein (2005) point out that "with very few exceptions, the disease amplifiers in the world today are manmade and therefore humanly controllable.... Exotic animal markets, unclean urban water supplies, lack of proper sewage systems, and unstable, conflict-ridded environments provide excellent breeding grounds for infectious diseases to spread and wreak havoc on vulnerable populations. Yet it would be short sighted to think of infectious disease as a problem for solely the poor and powerless. These diseases do not discriminate; they are undeterred by state borders, party affiliation, or socioeconomic status. With air travel and human migration on the rise, so too is the possibility that deadly microbes can and will circumnavigate the globe with speed and precision."

Solution   Humankind is faced with the massive problem of declining public health. It needs to redirect resources from activities that exacerbate the crisis to ones that overcome it. Ideologies, however dear, as well as ingrained habits and pursuit of short-term self-interest, are likely to defeat any grand initiatives such as this. Regardless of whether that suspicion reflects cynicism or just realism is irrelevant, we must persevere.

Linked patterns   Social Dominance Attenuation (4), Social Responsibility (8), Matrifocal Orientation (9), Big-Picture Health Information (27), Whole Cost (28), Public Agenda (30), Strengthening International Law (42), Indigenous Media (55), Positive Health Information (74), Online Antipoverty Community (103), Sense of Struggle (104), Labor Visions (112), Soap Operas with Civic Messages (120), Power Research (128).

Problem   Rights and responsibilities as narrowly defined by citizenship in a particular nation-state can result in an us-against-them mind-set, leading to biased interpretations of information, and even paranoia and hostility to other countries. This understanding can also be used to deny the reality or meaning of oppression and suffering in other countries and to eschew responsibility for helping to redress these problems. Citizenship also determines access to health care, education, and other rights—rights that arguably should be universal. A narrow interpretation of citizenship implicitly cedes power to national governments whose defense of national interest can sometimes be used against its own citizens who have no legal access to a "higher authority," and can restrict the participation of citizens in global affairs and problem solving.

Context   In the waning years of the twentieth century, people worldwide increasingly began to notice the world outside their own. At the same time nation-states, facing the new realities of economic globalization, seemed to be losing their ability—as well as their interest—in promoting the welfare of their own citizens and the natural world. As John Urry (1999) stated, "More generally, global money markets, world travel, the Internet, globally recognized brands, globally organized corporations, the Rio Earth summit, 'global celebrities' living as global citizens and so on, all speak of modes of social experience which transcend each nation-state and its constitution of the national citizen." Global climate change, natural resource depletion, economic inequity, and other vast problems that humankind now faces can be added to that list.

Discussion   Citizenship is generally described as the formal relationship, usually codified in law, of a person (the citizen) and a state and often is delineated in terms of rights and responsibilities. Its site has shifted from the Greek city-state, where the idea first took hold, to the modern nation-state, whose birth is linked to the 1648 Treaty of Westphalia, which established the convention that countries and its citizens do not interfere in the internal affairs of other countries.

Many nationalist political movements—the eighteenth-century American Revolution through the twentieth-century Palestinian Liberation struggle—emphasize national identity and citizenship to assert their right to self-determination and political autonomy from oppressive colonial states. But history is also rife with examples of nationalism used to oppress and remove minority, and sometimes majority, populations. At the same time, the liberal concept of citizenship based on a shared national identity offers the promise of overcoming religious and ethnic divisions. From the perspective of economically disadvantaged and oppressed subpopulations, however, the promise of inclusivity and shared interests has fallen flat.

The transnational realm of global capital in a free-market world, requires global civic response. As national laws are superseded by international treaties and trade agreements, individuals' rights and obligations become governed by global institutions—the reality that citizens of debt-ridden nations are well aware of. The question is not whether we are global citizens. The question is what form our citizenship will take. What are our rights and responsibilities toward global governing institutions and structures? Should governing bodies be directly elected by the governed? How will the rights of the weakest be protected from the strongest in the global polity? What counts as a right? What responsibilities do global citizens have to one another?

We need to ask what types of globalization are empowering to individuals and define and construct ones likely to lead to collective problem solving. Currently there are few opportunities for people to help address shared problems. Unfortunately this lack of opportunity comes at time when many problems are global in nature and require global thinking and acting. In addition to preventing people (and their ideas and other resources) from contributing to the general welfare, narrow versions of citizenship are used to establish arbitrary categories of deservedness. Our narrow version of citizenship makes it less likely that global solutions that work for everybody are developed. The opposite, in fact, is more likely: that collective dilemmas are "resolved" in ways that are relatively bad for everybody—or nearly everybody.

There are two useful avenues for people to explore to make headway toward realizing this pattern. The first is to assume the role and responsibilities without seeking permission from an authoritative source; obtaining permission would of course be impossible given that no authoritative source exists that can bestow such a designation. Assuming this role means thinking—and acting—globally, adopting the perspective that the world is densely interconnected, its general health is important, and well-intentioned and well-informed citizens can play a positive role. The second is to actively work toward some formal recognition of global citizenship by, for example, helping to define and develop the intellectual and administrative scaffolding that does not currently exist. Both of these paths could be undertaken individually or through working with existing or new organizations that work in these areas.

When Diogenes, the Greek philosopher, stated that he was a citizen of the world, he was refusing, according to Martha Nussbaum (1994), "to be defined simply by his local origins and group memberships, associations central to the self-image of a conventional Greek male; he insisted on defining himself in terms of more universal aspirations and concerns." But to some scholars, the nation-state is the rightful and permanent wellspring of citizenship, and alternative conceptualizations, however tentative and speculative, are damned as heretical. Michael Walzer (2002), for example, finds it difficult to contemplate the idea since "no one has ever offered me [world] citizenship, or described the naturalization process, or enlisted me in the world's institutional structures, or given me an account of its decision procedures (I hope they are democratic), or provided me with a list of the benefits and obligations of citizenship, or shown me the world's calendar and the common celebrations and commemorations of its citizens." As an ironic and unintended side effect of this critique,

Walzer provided a useful (if overly formal) laundry list of practical objectives that proponents of global citizenship need to consider.

Ann Florini (2005) builds a case that the Internet may help create a global consciousness analogous to the nationalist consciousness that the printed word helped inspire. The printing press led to a reconciliation of regional differences and a cheaper and faster way to reach constituencies that were too remote for effective collaboration. This then played a strong role in the development of the nation-state and, hence, nation-state-based citizenship. In similar fashion, Florini surmises that a new global consciousness could help usher in broader, more inclusive notions of citizenship. And although these are more likely to be dynamic, idiosyncratic, and short-lived, new Web sites are springing into existence every day. The Internet makes it easier to learn about foreign perspectives, and although they can be as hidebound as their domestic counterparts, they help reveal the immense diversity of viewpoints on earth as well as the universality of concerns facing people everywhere.

Are there examples of de facto global citizenship? Organizations like "No person is illegal" and the "Without Borders" groups are getting closer to that ideal. Are there practical experiments that could be done now? The growth of universal declarations, supporting human rights, for example, helps explain why the time might be fairly ripe for thinking like this.

The concept of global citizenship currently lacks the administrative and legalistic trappings of national citizenship. Nevertheless, from Diogenes to the present day, the pursuit and adoption of global citizenship, however demeaned and underinstitutionalized it is at present, continues to provide a compelling vision to millions of people around the world—people who are officially noted as belonging to individual, specific countries. The bottom line, however, for everybody interested in these issues is that people must think beyond the borders of the countries in which they hold citizenship.

As with other patterns in this category, the journey toward the goal will be incremental, perennial, lurching, and met by setbacks as well as successes. There are tasks for many people with a wide variety of roles and responsibilities; professionals like lawyers, think tank and NGO staff, government officials, and academics can engage with the public on these issues in addition to their more specialized and technical concerns. There are hosts of organizations and projects in which people can engage. Communication with people in other countries is especially important because this helps ensure that people realize that people in other countries are not abstract nonpersons. This, of course, represents a major hurdle: many people because of poverty, language barriers, or other reasons cannot easily engage with people outside their region.

Solution Martha Nussbaum, in her 1994 discussion on the Stoics in "Patriotism and Cosmopolitanism," refers to the fact that each of us dwells, in effect, in two communities: the local community of our birth and the community of human argument and aspiration that "is truly great and truly common, in which we look neither to this corner nor to that, but measure the boundaries of our nation by the sun" (Seneca, De Otio).

Linked patterns   Civic Intelligence (1), Linguistic Diversity (16), Dematerialization (18), Fair Trade (21), Sustainable Design (22), Big Tent for Social Change (32), Opportunity Spaces (33), World Citizen Parliament (40), Strengthening International Law (42), International Networks of Alternative Media (43), Digital Emancipation (60), Free and Fair Elections (68), Transaction Tax (72), Multiparty Negotiation for Conflict Resolution (79), Service-Learning (90), Citizen Diplomacy (93), Citizenship Schools (96), Engaged Tourism (107), Citizens' Tribunal (129), Activist Road Trip (134).

7 Political Settings

Problem The venues of political action are changing dramatically with the proliferation of new kinds of nongovernmental organizations, the broadening coverage of the Internet, and the actions of governments to redefine and often reduce the scope of their direct interventions. We need concepts to describe these changes and assess their implications, both negative and positive, for democratic participation.

Context Innovative political or social action fits into the existing field of popular and governmental activity. What political settings—as gatherings to inform, discuss, assert, dispute, debate, and decide important public matters—are available? What are their biases about who can participate, how matters are discussed, and what issues can be raised? Where do particular settings fit in the hierarchy of power? How do economic and cultural forces and physical threats influence the process? Will a new action create a new setting or alter an existing one? By asking questions like these, activists will better grasp the changes they are asking people to make, and researchers can analyze the changing shape and structure of political space over long or short spans of time.

Discussion Political settings are the basic physical units of collective political action. Each instance of a political setting has its own unique location in space and time. Many recur on a regular basis. Meetings and demonstrations are common types of political setting. Here are two recent examples from reports about political change in Venezuela. One is a small-scale political setting, a barrio meeting; the other describes two large-scale, competing political marches:

The Meeting
Nidia Lopez stood on one side of the brick shack. It was like one of the thousands that made up the barrio of Andres Bello. The barrios, or slums, are where the majority of the Venezuelan population lives. Thirty people looked at Nidia. Some of them stood outside in the mud. The building was too small to fit them all.

Nidia spoke, and her voice was clear and loud. She said, "There are twenty-three families living on the street in this barrio. In eight years what has this government done for them? In three years what has this committee done for them? They need help now! What are we going to do for them now?"

The "we" that Nidia was talking about was the Urban Land Committee for the Andres Bello barrio. The Urban Land Committees ... exist everywhere there are barrios in Venezuela and barrios are everywhere in Venezuela.

When barrio problems are discussed ... the most common suggestion is to get organized. At the Andres Bello meeting, barrio resident Hector Madera said, "When the people of our barrio have a problem they mustn't rely on the media, or go and whisper in the ear of a friend in a Chavista party, we need to organize ourselves."

Nidia Lopez felt the best way the Andres Bello CTU could help the twenty-three homeless families was to take the appeal to the president. Everybody else in the meeting argued it was more important that organization happen first.

The families should ... discuss with each other about what they wanted. They should also talk with the owner of the mansion. Only then should they approach the government for assistance if they still needed it.

Madera said the barrios needed to organize together: "When organized we can involve the people from nearby barrios, like Chapellin, and get their support. We will help them and them us. Together we solve our problems ourselves. We can march together." (Holland 2006)

The Marches

Venezuelans celebrated International Workers' Day yesterday with two large marches that wound through the streets of Caracas. One in support of the Chavez-led "Bolivarian Revolution," and the other with the opposition. This marks the sixth year in a row that Venezuelan workers have held separate marches on May 1st.

The opposition march was led by the Confederation of Venezuelan Workers (CTV) which, according to the Venezuelan daily *El Universal,* called for the participants to march for increased salaries, back-pay, a dignified social security system, and freedom for CTV President Carlos Ortega, who was sentenced last year to 16 years in prison for his role in the two-month 2002–3 oil industry shut down.

"Things are turbulent. With this government everything is turbulent," yelled 15 year CTV veteran, Israel Masa, from the opposition march. "That's why we are marching—to demand transparency in the next elections, because we in the opposition know that we are the majority and that we are the true democrats."

The pro-government march was led by the National Workers Union (UNT) and officially entitled, the "Bolivarian March Against Imperialism and Free Trade Agreements," highlighting the international importance of today's celebrations, and calling attention to the recent motives for Venezuela's withdrawal from the Community of Andean Nations.

"This demonstration is a struggle against imperialism and the conspiratorial plans of U.S. imperialism against Venezuela," announced Venezuelan National Assembly Representative Dario Vivas ... at the start of the march. "The people of Venezuela are ready to do whatever necessary to guarantee our liberty." (Fox 2006)

As these two examples show, the respective contexts—social structure, rules of entry and action, physical layout, and cultural expectations—heavily influence the quality of participation and the content of decisions and messages. "Political setting" is a particularly useful concept for describing political action in context, the venues of face-to-face political communication that are the building blocks of public political life. They encompass all occasions in which issues and needs of general importance to a community or a society are discussed, contested, and decided. They may be open and democratic, but very often they explicitly or implicitly bar certain groups, certain perspectives, and certain issues. It is important to investigate how they filter participants and ideas.

Although many of meetings and debates that seek to influence community-wide matters take place in government institutions, an increasing proportion occur in voluntary associations, social movement groupings, and invitation-only meetings. Internet discussions demonstrate the growing importance of virtual political settings and raise questions about how they differ from face-to-face meetings and how uneven access to computers affects political outcomes. The rules and culture of each setting influence the quality of communication, deliberation, and decision making it embodies. Are they open or secret? Which voices do they amplify or exclude? What about women, poor people, people of low status, different cultures and religions? What is their impact?

The idea of political setting draws on ecological psychology's concept of behavior settings, but it puts the focus on activity that aims to influence public policy. It opens the door to exploration of the evolving pattern language exemplified in the face-to-face political actions from below that are emerging in meetings and demonstrations around the world with all their limitations as well as their strengths.

Solution Seeing and analyzing popular politics through the lens of political settings promises to generate a useful and realistic view of the political resources available for popular action and the obstacles that such action faces.

Linked patterns Collective Decision Making (10), Transforming Institutions (19), Democratic Political Settings (31), Opportunity Spaces (33), World Citizen Parliament (40), Strengthening International Law (42), Online Deliberation (52), Self-Help Groups (105), Great Good Place (119), Community Inquiry (122), Power Research (128).

8 Social Responsibility

Problem Things do not get better by themselves. Without purposeful intervention, organizations of all kinds lose sight of their social responsibilities.

Context Any organization that sees itself without social responsibility will change only in the face of financial penalty or purposeful intervention. Where social benefits form all or part of an organization's purpose, this alone does not guarantee positive achievements. Any organization with a shared vision of social responsibility, whether a for-profit corporation or a nonprofit group working for the public good, needs to deliver what it promises. A passion for principles drives the efforts of individuals and citizen groups to make corporations, professions, and governments more responsive; the more open and accountable they are, the more responsive they will become.

Discussion The striving for social responsibility takes many forms. Grameen Bank and its founder, Muhammad Yunus, received the 2006 Nobel Prize for furthering peace and human rights by providing economic opportunities that conventional banks would not. Working Assets preassigns a portion of its revenues to activist causes. Socially responsible investing uses published criteria to recommend investment vehicles and initiate stockholder actions in support of particular principles.

Advocacy organizations pursue a wide variety of principles. The Saltwater Institute advocates five values: (1) family and community responsibility, (2) respect and appreciation for the natural world, (3) service and stewardship, (4) the necessity for work and productivity, and (5) an intentional commitment to goodness (www.saltwater.org/our_story/beliefs.htm). Scientists for Global Responsibility opt for openness, accountability, peace, social justice, and environmental sustainability, while Computer Professionals for Social Responsibility address technological problems in the light of technology-related principles.

Until the late nineteenth century, corporate charters in the United States confined a company to a specific purpose in the common good. For example, an 1823 act of the New York legislature incorporated the Delaware and Hudson Canal Company with a charter to build and maintain, with private investment, a canal between the Delaware and Hudson rivers and to charge regulated fees for the transport of coal and other goods. Any other activity by the corporation, such as setting up a bank, required an amendment to its charter (Whitford 1905). A recent form of the socially responsible corporate charter is the Community Interest Company.

In 1970, the economist Milton Friedman wrote that "the social responsibility of business is to maximize its profits." Invoking the authority of Adam Smith to claim that society most benefits if everyone pursues selfish advantage, Friedman helped pave the way for some businesses to ignore the wider impacts of their pursuit of low costs, increasing sales, and big financial returns and to consider themselves accountable only to owners and regulators. In turn, this gave rise to the tyranny of the financial bottom line; any attempt at purposeful social progress needs to overcome the myth that social progress takes place of its own accord.

Activism on behalf of principles other than self-interest or convenience is necessary to remind selfish businesses of their social responsibility and prevent other organizations from losing touch with theirs. This activism can take place outside the organization, in citizen groups and political platforms, or within the organization as the individual actions of the tempered radical (Meyerson and Scully 1995) and in the form of changes to policy and governance. In these efforts, the struggle of advocacy is at least as important as the specific principles being advocated. Social responsibility does not depend on any one principle of conduct.

To be socially responsible is to be accountable to a full range of interested parties for the achievement of clearly stated goals. It calls for (1) clear vision, values, and strategy for a better future; (2) understanding and management of expectations; (3) actions compatible with vision and values; (4) monitoring of outcomes; (5) accountability for results; and (6) a culture and governance that make this possible. A socially responsible organization acts on the basis of clear values, which may explicitly include measurable results, transparency and accountability (Grameen Foundation n.d.).

Any organization has internal and external stakeholders: customers and constituencies that both contribute to and benefit from the organization's work. For example, the Citizens Advice Bureau (2004) considers stakeholders to include potential and actual clients, volunteers, staff, partners, policymakers, and government bodies. No two of these customers or constituencies have the same expectations. A socially responsible organization makes itself accountable to stakeholders according to the unique expectations of each group and consistently with its values and strategy.

Accountability to stakeholders measures actual performance against predetermined goals. It does not simply describe what an organization has achieved in the past but requires commitment to achievements in advance. To be accountable is to measure indicators of performance that affect stakeholders and to make the results transparent—that is, to report outcomes to stakeholders as evidence that the organization is fulfilling its goals and enacting its values. One example is a set of performance indicators for microfinance institutions (Women's World Banking 2008).

Any organization devoted to serving others is measured every time someone walks in or logs on—indeed, whenever anyone even drives past the building or happens on the Web site. A commitment to achieve social benefits does not absolve a nonprofit from thinking of the people it serves as customers and to consider its relations with them as marketing (Brinckerhoff 2003). To clearly understand perspectives from outside the organization is a first step toward measuring and improving the organization's impact.

Social responsibility requires accountability, but for what and to whom? Several frameworks exist for measures of accountability. The balanced scorecard (Kaplan and Norton 1992) suggests four linked categories: financial, customer, internal business, and innovation and learning. These categories are linked to strategy because improvement in any one will benefit all the others (except that no direct relationship is claimed between the first and the last). Epstein and Birchard (1999) propose three categories: financial, operational, and social.

A stakeholder scorecard (Epstein and Birchard 1999) uses the major stakeholders as categories of performance measures. This approach directly measures how the organization serves its stakeholders and orients strategy toward those with an interest in the outcomes. Stakeholders may fall into predetermined categories, such as shareholders, customers, employees, and communities; alternatively, they may simply appear as a list of specific categories of stakeholder most important to the organization.

No organization, whether for-profit or nonprofit, is socially responsible simply by virtue of its intent to achieve social benefits. Action consistent with the organization's espoused values demands a culture—ethical assumptions, values, beliefs, and behaviors—that pervades the organization from top to bottom. Without a culture of demonstrable consistency between espoused and practiced values, claims to social responsibility are at best window dressing, and at worst a symptom of a demoralized, failing, and unethical organization. By contrast, a culture of accountability makes an organization more effective and more sustainable; social responsibility demands nothing less.

Solution   Whether from without or within, advocate for principles to help for-profit corporations realize their social responsibility in addition to the responsibility they feel toward stockholders, and to spur nonprofit organizations, government bodies, and professions to keep their social responsibility in view. The principles of openness and accountability are always applicable.

Linked patterns   Civic Intelligence (1), Health as a Universal Right (5), Memory and Responsibility (11), Transforming Institutions (19), Spiritually Grounded Activism (24), Big Tent for Social Change (32), Economic Conversion (41), Strengthening International Law (42), Alternative Progress Indexes (46), Transparency (64), Participatory Budgeting (71), Transaction Tax (72), Voices of the Unheard (83), Strategic Frame (86), Service-Learning (90), Shared Vision (101), Whistle-Blowing (130), Follow The Money (135).

Problem Because almost all contemporary societies are androcentric (male centered), women's needs, interests, ideas, and perspectives on the world are often ignored or trivialized. Androcentrism perpetuates a patriarchal system that oppresses women and severely constrains (and damages) men's lives as well. An orientation toward social change that gives voice to women's perspectives and strives to replace patriarchy with an egalitarian, matrifocal society would go a long way toward creating a just and peaceful world for all.

Context Although societies differ in the degree and form that male dominance takes, male privilege is generally maintained through systems of beliefs, laws, discriminatory practices, and cultural norms (including direct or indirect perpetuation of male violence). Patriarchy concentrates social, political, and economic power in the hands of men at the expense of women. Because gender oppression is ancient and insidious, a conscious effort is needed to recognize the gendered dimensions of social problems. Looking at the world with a matrifocal orientation can help create contexts in which women-centered analyses of social problems are fully incorporated into problem-solving processes.

Discussion A matrifocal orientation to social change draws directly on women's experience and knowledge and puts the needs of oppressed women at the center of social transformation. Matrifocal societies, real and imagined, do not challenge patriarchy by offering its mirror image, with women in positions of dominance over men. Rather, they embrace values traditionally seen as feminine: peace, nurturance, cooperation, and care for those most in need. A matrifocal society is one in which dominance over others is not supported as either an individual or collective goal. The needs and contributions of women are valued equally with those of men. Women's interests are not special interests but human interests. Social distinctions between males and females may be minimized (depending on the culture), and those biological and social differences that remain do not inhibit women's full participation in the society. A matrifocal orientation to social change recognizes that "the rising of the women means the rising of the [human] race" (Oppenheim 1911).

The need for women's voices to be heard in order for society to become more just has been recognized by progressive social reformers for centuries (and probably longer). This awareness led to the development of women-centered movements throughout the world. As a social and political orientation, this pattern is reflected in both feminist organizing in first world nations and community-centered women's organizing in third world nations. Historically, many third world women's organizations have been concerned with conditions of economic hardship, displacement, and state-sponsored violence that affect their communities as a whole, while first world feminist groups have focused more exclusively on women's social and political rights. In recent decades, the issue of violence against women has been a common theme of transnational women organizing (Keck and Sikkink 1998). Regardless of the issue, whenever women organize with the goal of creating a more just and sustainable society, they are endeavoring to insert their voices and their perspectives into the public debate. By doing so, they are subverting the androcentric norm of male power and female silence.

Las Madres de Plaza de Mayo, for example, an Argentinean women's organization that protested the disappearances and other abuses during Argentina's "dirty war," was able to subvert androcentric norms in Argentina after initially making use of them. The simultaneous cultural respect for motherhood and the perceived political irrelevance of women allowed mothers and grandmothers of disappeared children to protest relatively unhindered at a time when public demonstrations were officially illegal. By also making themselves visible beyond national borders, Las Madres fostered a successful international advocacy network to pressure the Argentinean government to become more democratic and to investigate the tens of thousands of state-sponsored murders that occurred during the 1970s and early 1980s. The powerful example of Argentinean mothers refusing to be silent has inspired other women's groups, such as Women in Black in Israel and elsewhere, to stand out publicly against state-sponsored violence.

Not surprisingly, many organizations that can be described as having a matrifocal orientation have been women's organizations. But this is not required by the pattern. Labor groups reflect a matrifocal orientation when they strive for gender equity policies, family leave policies, the right to organize in traditionally female occupations, and increased female union leadership. Antiglobalization groups demonstrate a matrifocal orientation when they recognize the significant impact of trade policies on women and give voice to women's knowledge as farmers, workers, parents, and preservers of culture. Environmental groups like the Chipko movement in India and ecofeminists in the United States reflect a matrifocal orientation when they draw on and amplify the voices of women, highlight reproductive issues as environmental issues, and speak with reference to the future of all children on the planet.

Regardless of whether a group consists of men or women or both, having a matrifocal orientation means that people ask, "How is the problem we perceive exacerbated by patriarchy, and how has our way of responding to it been limited by patriarchal thinking?" Resisting androcentric norms by putting women's perspectives in the center rather than at the periphery of social debates is a first step toward undermining patriarchy and the social ills it perpetuates.

One problem with this pattern is its potential to reinforce male-female dichotomies. Whenever people speak up for traditionally feminine goals and values—particularly when they use the role of motherhood for political leverage—they run the risk of reifying patriarchal beliefs about the essential nature of women. Many reactionary movements have argued that their goals and strategies are in the best interests of women, and female voices are often used to promote these messages. Many Western feminists, for example, have been hesitant to organize under the banner of motherhood not only because many women choose not to be mothers, but also because such representations may inadvertently bolster the idea that motherhood is women's single most important function in society. Activists who use a matrifocal orientation must be careful to distinguish between biological femaleness and matrifocal goals. There are many males who value peace, nurturance, care for those in need, collaborative problem solving, and an end to reward-oriented hierarchies. There are also many females who are not interested in creating a just society and prefer to amass what benefits they can within the current social order; some fully support patriarchy. *Matrifocal* is not synonymous with *female* or *maternal*.

A second problem with a matrifocal orientation is the misperception that everyone who adopts it will, or should, agree on particular social goals and political strategies. They will not. What is shared by people who adopt a matrifocal orientation is a consciousness that overcoming problems of violence, economic oppression, and gender oppression requires replacing patriarchy with an alternative social order and that increasing women's participation in the public sphere is one step in such a transformation.

Solution   A matrifocal orientation keeps the system of patriarchy visible so that alternatives can be imagined and created.

Linked patterns   Social Dominance Attenuation (4), Health as a Universal Right (5), Memory and Responsibility (11), Fair Trade (21), Public Agenda (30), Alternative Progress Indexes (46), Media Diversity (66), Transaction Tax (72), Strategic Frame (86), Mirror Institutions (94), Self-Help Groups (105).

Problem Divided decision making underlies the disrupted personal relationships, fragmented communities, atomized specializations, and compartmentalized organizations that have become standard in Western society. A potential antidote, a united holistic focus, is rejected as impractical. Yet to resolve any serious issue in any community for the long term, the collective voices of individuals, community, experts, and organizations working toward a shared goal are required for a harmonious response to the disrupted social and natural environments of our time.

Context At both global and local scales, major changes in the world's social and natural environments are threatening hopes of a healthy and sustainable human future. Sources as varied as the World Bank, the World Social Forum, and the combined Research Institutes of the United States are giving the highest priority to integrative thinking that links all the interests in constructive decisions (World Bank 2001, U.S. Research Council 1992). Studies of attempts at such a synthesis found each contributing group acting as if it was a separate knowledge culture, with a different language, timescale, and sources of truth (Brown 2006).

Discussion Case studies of the different knowledge cultures involved in Western decision making provide details of the ways decisions are made about the future. Individuals reflect on their own lived experience. Communities provide firsthand knowledge of the effects of change. Specialized knowledge is objective and reliable, within single frameworks. Organizational knowledge offers the political and administrative systems that can ensure the desired change. Holistic knowledge illuminates the essence or core purpose. Yet all of these are needed for mutual decisions toward a healthy, just, and sustainable future (Brown 2006).

Each knowledge culture was found to reject the contributions of the others. Individual knowledge is dismissed as anecdote, community knowledge as gossip, specialist knowledge as jargon, organizational knowledge as political intrigue, and holistic knowledge as mysticism. Yet all five knowledge cultures have to learn to accept each other's contribution if there is to be a constructive synthesis. A sustainable synthesis calls for commitment to respecting their individual contributions while strengthening their connections. This represents a fundamental change in the way we think.

Tools found to assist in this transformational change include David Bohm's rules of dialogue: maintain open communication, suspend judgment, separate inquiry and advocacy, clarify assumptions, listen to yourself, and remain open to the unexpected (Bohm 1996). Concerted change requires all the knowledge cultures to join in the stages of open learning, as described by David Kolb: developing principles, defining parameters, designing for potential and doing, and reviewing the new practice (Keen, Brown, and Dyball 2005).

These suggested strategies for collective thinking were tested in three sites: an isolated desert town wanting a green town park, a tightly packed beachside suburb needing to control oceans of tourist waste, and an indigenous community wishing to become self-supporting. Three years later, all had achieved their goals and established pathways for collective thinking.

Solution   Collective decision making toward a humane sustainable future requires commitment to synthesis: individuals, community, specialists, and organizations reach a shared understanding on (2) collective learning: the knowledge cultures learn from one another, following the stages of Kolb's open learning cycle; (3) future direction: all parties work toward a shared ideal state; and (4) dialogue: all participants use Bohm's rules of dialogue in all communication.

Linked patterns   Civic Intelligence (1), Political Settings (7), Indicators (29), Economic Conversion (41), Strengthening International Law (42), Open Action and Research Network (45), Meaningful Maps (47), Conversational Support Across Boundaries (50), Grassroots Public Policy Development (78), Multiparty Negotiation for Conflict Resolution (79), Voices of the Unheard (83), Civic Capabilities (85), Document-Centered Discussion (92), Self-Designed Development (106).

Problem   Although the evils of the past continue to haunt us in the present, society is often unable or unwilling to deal with historical injustice. Thus, although specific incidents of invasion, slavery, apartheid, and genocide may appear to be receding into the irretrievable past, they are never altogether absent from humankind's collective memories. As Robert Putnam (2000) states, "Networks of civic engagement embody past success at collaboration which can serve as a cultural template for future collaboration." Unfortunately these cultural templates include past failures as well. Evil patterns of behavior from the past are often recycled all too regularly. Can humankind escape this cycle?

Context   Societies are the sum total of their past events. The events of the past that have not been successfully reconciled haunt the present. Projects that endeavor to help address social problems may be well served by examining historical memory and reconsidering how to respond appropriately.

Discussion   Our memory of the past must guide the responsibility we accept in the present for the future. Without this linkage over time, I could steal your belongings with no guilt or responsibility. Of course, this has happened on a large scale throughout history. One group will murder, displace, or enslave another and enjoy the fruits of their sins for lifetimes. Each passing day tends to legitimize, but never really erase, history's misdeeds.

Misremembering history is institutionalized. It is important to understand the motivation and the implications of intentional (let alone unintentional) misrepresentation of history. Thus in the United States, the enslavement of Africans and the devastation of Native American communities, as well as the militaristic forays of recent years, from saturation bombing of civilian Japanese populations in World War II to the catastrophic Vietnam War to the recent illegal invasion of Iraq, are generally downplayed and sugar-coated. According to these rewriters of history, Americans always proceed with the best of intentions, perhaps marked by an occasional yet guiltless misstep. With ubiquitous misinformation, how could the next generation fully understand their country, with its successes and failures, and make wise decisions in the future?

What can or should people do to reconcile past sins and heal historical trauma? Although this question has rarely been addressed throughout history, the large number of projects now in progress shows one hopeful sign of our era. According to Richard Falk (2004), the Holocaust perpetrated by Nazi Germany, and directed against Jews primarily as well as against the Roma, gays, and other groups, marked a central historical marker in this regard. Since that time, movements for redress of war crimes of Japan against China, redress for indigenous people throughout the world, and tribunals against war crimes have been launched.

People are engaging in innovative projects that help them confront and understand and, hopefully, reconcile the present and future. Some of these examples include the courageous work of Las Madres de Plaza de Mayo who publicly confront the abuse of power with photographs of "the disappeared" from Argentina's "dirty war" (shown in the introductory graphic of this pattern) to seek justice and reconciliation with the past.

Other examples to explore include the Seder ritual celebrated by Jews around the world, the postwar efforts in Germany to come to terms with the past, the truth and reconciliation work in postapartheid South Africa and around the world, and the reparations efforts to help compensate African Americans for the enslavement of their ancestors.

Veran Matic (2004) eloquently described why the B92 radio station he works for in Serbia, in the former Yugoslavia, keeps working the way they do:

- If we do not grasp our recent past, we will build our present and our future on false assumptions, beliefs and stereotypes.
- If we do not face the errors of our past we will again seek excuses for our present in the same place Milosevic sought them—the guilt of others, global conspiracy and so on, rather than in the weaknesses of the society. These weaknesses must be faced in order to understand reality.
- If we do not fully comprehend our reality, reform programs will be based on false premises.

• The problems of the repressed past will boomerang, like the permanent problem of lack of cooperation with the Hague Tribunal, or the problem of mafia and police links, or problems with the business elite who amassed their wealth through privileges granted by Milosevic.

• Without a radical break with the past there will be no change in the cultural model under Milosevic, which has overwhelmed the entire society, from culture, through education, to the media.

• Unless we face the past, we will never know what is good for us and what is bad for us.

• By not facing the past, we neglect our duty to the future, leaving new generations to pay our debts, just as our generations have paid for the repression of the past of World War II in our country. This gave rise to new vengeance forty years later.

• And, finally, without engagement we will be unable to demonstrate authentic belief and strong will to institute changes that should benefit every single individual.

"Forgetting" the past is not desirable and in reality is impossible. Although Matic is speaking specifically about recent injustice in the former Yugoslavia, his message is universal. Through hard work by all concerned, healing historical wounds can be accomplished. Although it may seem impossible, those who have inherited the results of yesterday's actions must relive, insofar as it can be done, the past, sacrificing as necessary to set a more just course for the future.

Solution   Think about and confront memory in creative, productive, and sensitive ways. Cultivate and assume responsibility. Actively work to reconcile the trauma of the past to guide a better tomorrow.

Linked patterns   Civic Intelligence (1), Social Responsibility (8), Matrifocal Orientation (9), Back to the Roots (13), Demystification and Reenchantment (14), Linguistic Diversity (16), Spiritually Grounded Activism (24), Truth and Reconciliation Commissions (51), Ethics of Community Informatics (67), Voices of the Unheard (83), Strategic Frame (86), Homemade Media (110), The Power of Story (114), Community Inquiry (122), Citizens' Tribunal (129), Retreat and Reflection (136).

Problem   The need for a global consciousness, solidarity, and collaboration among working people in every country of the world is a critical task for confronting the economic, political, and social challenges the working class faces. The deepening contradictions of imperialism with the U.S. war in Iraq and the push to militarize Asia and the rest of the world are opportunities for bringing working people together.

Context   The man-made failure of the catastrophe for the U.S. Gulf Coast is an example of the need of working people to take control of their lives and society.

Discussion   One important tool in this process of international working-class globalization is not only joint collective action by workers throughout the world but the use of film, art, and media technology to bring working people together.

The training of workers in every industry and every country for this work is the task ahead, and the success of this project requires that this be an international campaign based on grassroots struggle in collaboration with regional, national, and international labor. The Labortech and Labor Media conferences (www.labortech2004.org) in many countries have been important in training and building these international links. They have taken place in Vancouver, B.C., Canada; Moscow, Russia; Seoul, Korea; and many cities in the United States.

In the United States and Europe and parts of Asia, these resources are readily available, but at the same time, workers in every country of the world must have the means and ability to concretely link up internationally. The developments of LaborNets, online news and resources portals, in Japan, Korea, Austria, Germany, Turkey, Denmark, and the United States have been a growing vehicle for developing labor festivals and labor technology conferences.

Laborfests have been held annually in Japan, Turkey, Argentina, Bolivia, Brazil, and in the United States. A Labor Media conference is also held in Korea. New Laborfests are also being planned in the coming years in Denmark and Costa Rica. These Laborfests and international working-class film and video festivals are a useful vehicle for bringing forward international labor solidarity and education.

These festivals, which could be held in every city of the world, provide a venue and concrete means for linking through film, music, and culture the collective experiences and consciousness of workers throughout the world. The rebellions of workers in Latin America and the fight against capitalist globalization have been a theme that exposes the commonality of all the attacks the working class faces.

The important need to use media, both TV and radio, to link workers around the world is also growing. The same economic policies that harm the working class—such as deregulation, privatization, deunionization, and the promotion of casual labor—are at work in every country of the world.

The failure of workers in the United States to begin to challenge the basic assaults that they face is the responsibility of the corporate unionists, who control the resources and apparatus of the trade unions. The failure to provide a concrete alternative program and agenda is a major impediment to any form of national and international resistance. The need for an international collaboration is also connected to develop the means for the international working class to take control of their destiny. Airline workers worldwide, longshore workers, medical workers, teachers, public workers, and telecommunication workers face the same type of attacks, but they have been hobbled by a lack of international collaboration and collective joint action.

The experience of the Liverpool dockers' strike in 1995 that led to the formation of an international labor action in solidarity as well as a Web-based international solidarity campaign was crucial in building international support (Brazil 1997). This was carried on in 1997 when the Korean Confederation of Trade Unions (KCTU) and its supporters established an international Web page in support of its general strike. The Web page in Korean and English became a critical tool in building direct support action for workers around the world, as well as an information portal on the struggle and a way for unions and workers worldwide to show their solidarity on the Web.

KCTU has been the most active national union federation in the world in the last ten years. It has sought collective cultural action and direct labor action to defend its interests. It called for and carried out a national strike of its members against casualization, the institutionalization of casual and temporary work, on November 23, 2005. International action by workers throughout the world would be an important step in building this collective action about an issue that affects and harms working people worldwide.

The KCTU also hosts and organizes a yearly festival on November 12 in commemoration of the death of labor organizer Chun Taeil with a mass mobilization and a national eight-hour cultural media art celebration. This event, which is held at the Korean Broadcasting

Company Stadium, brings together the experiences of the working class through a cultural and theatrical production that is choreographed to the minute over eight hours. Such a festival that ties together the song, poetry, music, and art of struggle and should be held in every country. The power of this collective expression is an important element in breaking down the corporatized isolation, marginalization of workers, and humanity as well as the commodification of music, art, and cultural expressions for profit of the multinationals.

The growing privatization of the Internet and the threat to censor and control of the Internet has been growing. In the Liverpool dockers' strike, the shipping corporations tried to stop information from being posted. In Korea, the government sought to shut down the Korean Labornet (www.nodong.net). The German government raided the Internet servers of the German Labornet in 2005 with charges that terrorists had used the network (Labournet Association and LabourNet Germany Net Daily 2005). There was no substance to these charges. In 2005 the Canadian Telus Corporation prevented millions of users from accessing the labor Web pages of the Canadian Telecom Union (Barrett 2005). This censorship comes not only from corporate and antiunion media but also from technology corporations that want to control the use of these communication tools. One of the most striking uses of new technology to harass workers was the use of Samsung cell phones to spy on Samsung workers who were seeking labor advice from attorneys off the company's properties, and this was exposed in a labor documentary called "Big Brother Is Watching You" (2006).

In the United Kingdom, the executive council of the FBU banned members from using the public Web site of an opposition grouping opposing labor management collaboration and "partnerships" (Brazil 1997). The international collective voices of working people have the power to overcome the different languages, cultures, and borders that now exist. In fact, this is crucial for a new renaissance of collective self-consciousness that is vital for transforming the current dynamics. The future reorganization of the world economy into one controlled by the working class requires the use of these tools now to build this collective and democratic power.

The use of the Internet as not only a communication tool but broadcasting tool is at a relatively early stage. A twenty-four-hour labor video and radio channel in all languages of the world is realizable with the expansion of the Internet, and this is now happening with a twenty-four-hour labor radio channel in Korea (www.nodong.org). International collaboration in action and on a cultural level must be linked with the use of communication technology and a labor media strategy that focuses on how these technologies can empower the working class and farmers, as well as how they can confront the global propaganda blitz by capitalist media against the interests of the people.

Solution   The international collective voices of working people have the power to overcome the different languages, cultures, and borders that now exist. In fact, this is crucial for a new renaissance of collective self-consciousness. The future reorganization of the world economy into one controlled by the working class requires the use of these tools to build this collective and democratic power. The need to defend democratic communication rights and protections is fundamental, and education and direct action are necessary to accomplish this work.

Linked patterns   Fair Trade (21), Big Tent for Social Change (32), Strategic Capacity (34), Participatory Design (36), Citizen Science (37), Economic Conversion (41), International Networks of Alternative Media (43), Open Action and Research Network (45), Strategic Frame (86), Community-Building Journalism (97), Sense of Struggle (104), Labor Visions (112), Thinking Communities (118), Power Research (128), Follow the Money (135).

13   Back to the Roots

Problem   Humankind has developed incredibly complex intellectual, cultural, physical, and technological artifacts over the years. This has put a wide chasm between our present status and our roots, where we all were closer to nature, closer to the source and sustenance of our lives.

Context   These are some of the roots that all humankind shares: Fire and the hearth. Running water, bubbling or still water. Ice and steam. The sea and the ancient life within it. The sun, moon, stars, comets and planets. Soil, mud, sand, rocks. Mountains, caves, dunes, swamps. Plant (huge trees, alpine flowers, cactus and lichen) and animal life (frogs, monkeys, lemurs, spiders, rats, ants, bats, mosquitoes, cassowaries, camels, penguins and pigs). Hunger, food, nourishment, thirst, cells, the body, the rhythms and phases of life; the family; culture, music, art, and stories. Love, knowledge, wonder, mystery, language, perception. We cannot foreswear them because they are part of us.

Discussion   In *A Pattern Language* (1977), Alexander and his colleagues described three patterns devoted specifically to water—Access to Water (25), Pools and Streams (64), and Still Water (71)—as well as Sacred Sites (24) and Tree Places (171). Yet in a review of Alexander's work in a *Harvard Design Magazine* review, Saunders (2002) faults Alexander's "New Age flower-child wistfulness" when Alexander speaks of the health benefits associated with a deeper connection with nature.

In cities and in other developed areas around the world generally, many of humankind's roots are barely visible. In the United States, for example, only 2 percent of people who live in rural areas are engaged in farming. Even more astounding is the fact that "rural" is no longer rural: a large percentage of rural dwellers live within twenty-five miles of a city. But far from being a nostalgic look back, discovering, cultivating, and building on our radical center can be a wellspring for creative preparations for the future.

We are learning the hard way that "estrangement from the animate earth has negative consequences for human functioning" (Barlett 2005), and people are making strides toward a closer touch. City dwellers are now demanding "pea patches" and other urban gardening opportunities. People are learning the value of having plants close by when, for example, convalescing from disease, operation, or abuse (Stuart 2005). In South Central Los Angeles, an economically disadvantaged part of the city close to the scene of the Rodney King riots of 1992, fourteen acres of land that were destined to become home for a giant trash-to-energy incinerator were purchased by the city through eminent domain for $4.8 million. Through a series of events, the city granted temporary use of the land for community gardens that turned into twelve years, and some 350 families have cultivated the urban farm since that day. In 2006, in spite of large public demonstrations, the farm, lungs for the city in a car-centric metropolis, was reclaimed by the city to be sold back to the original owner. The land will be used for light manufacturing or warehouses (Hoffmann and Petit 2006).

In the introduction to her excellent book (2005), Peggy Barlett recounts many of the ways through which we have lost or nearly lost our connections to our roots and the possible perils that such losses may engender. She also shows how the benefits from reconnecting spread in unexpected ways:

"As volunteers clean up a trash-filled urban stream, for example, they absorb a new concept of watershed. They learn that parking lots, driveways, and lawn chemicals affect water quality and stream insect life. People who might have never thought about mayflies or runoff water temperature develop a new relationship to the stream ecosystem and indicators of its health (Barlett 2002).

Concerns about urban air quality also draw attention to the ecological matrix of life. Trees provide "services" by removing air pollutants, retaining storm water, cooling temperatures, and providing habit and food for other species. Restoration work of prairies and forests builds attachment to the natural world in a more grounded local way than a more diffuse embrace of nature in the abstract" (Light and Higgs 1997).

According to Barlett, "Modern cities make distance from nature possible for a larger group than in the past." She also raises the idea that "urban place is a locale as well for the enactment of human hierarchy. Distance from the natural world may be connected to power over the lower classes and their labor." Certainly the arts, the priesthood, the seats of government, and the banks are often found in cities.

One intriguing, if disturbing, hypothesis is that our very patterns of thought and reasoning—our abstractions, human-centrism, and economic calculations—may exclude nature and our roots. Barlett, for examples, shows how anthropology, sociology, and the other social sciences exclude humankind's connections with other life forms, natural phenomena, and own past. Of course from a capitalist perspective, nature has value only when it has a price and potential for profit. Unfortunately many people find themselves priced out of their own land and their own cultural legacy. Access to unexploited and unspoiled nature, our common roots, is increasingly the domain of the wealthy. The most dangerous of these tendencies, however, may be that we forget our own history as a part and product of nature and hence our ability to reformulate a more harmonious connection with nature.

How are we supposed to employ this pattern? For most of humankind's progress through the centuries, nature was abundant and humankind scarce. Nature was something that could be "conquered." Some of the world's religions informed us that God intended us to have dominion over nature. We cannot really go back to the primeval time of our roots, and we do not want to. We will not and cannot abandon our cities and return to a pure state of nature. But at the same time we must boldly explore the idea of living in closer harmony with nature and the forces of life that we implicitly think we can ignore.

Yet for the timelessness and presumed innocence of our roots, immense damage has been wrought over time in the name of roots: blood, tradition, purity, the soil. We know that people from the city are not "better" than people from the country. We also know that the reverse is not true, for actually many people in the country have also lost their sense of nature. We do not invoke the idea of roots to pit one group against another but to relate the two in common bonds.

Barlett believes that "there are unanticipated benefits to collective and individual well-being with the reconnection to the natural world, an often-neglected dimension of the emerging paradigm shift toward a more sustainable society" and "part of a shifting paradigm that locates humankind within the biosphere." Thinking holistically, we can imagine and create new opportunities for reconnecting with our roots that have unxpected benefits: "a community garden in New York City may replace an abandoned lot and come to be a social focus for many who live nearby." Barlett again: "Community gardens not only provide nutritious food and conviviality with neighbors, but can build a different sense of self through a new awareness of growing cycles, weather and human agency." The South Central Farmers and their struggle to maintain the urban farmland provide a living example of the difficulty of actually realizing this pattern.

Solution Barlett presents "several layers of connections to nature," including knowledge, emerging emotional attachment, purposeful action, new personal choices, and ethical action and commitments to political action. The plants that we eat have literal roots that climb backward, down through the soil, searching for nutrients. Humankind's roots also reach back through time and space and are likewise deep and eternal.

Linked patterns The Commons (2), The Good Life (3), Memory and Responsibility (11), Demystification and Reenchantment (14), Dematerialization (18), Sustainable Design (22), Earth's Vital Signs (26), Strategic Frame (86), Community Animators (102), The Power of Story (114), Activist Road Trip (134), Retreat and Reflection (136).

Problem   For vast numbers of people, virtually every social, political, and economic system has become mystifying in its complexity. On the other hand, some of humankind's most deep-seated mysteries have become disenchanted in the sense of no longer conveying profound meaning and connection with society as a whole. This reduces political discourse to a battle of special interests, allows the marketplace to dominate in the determination of value, and limits the creativity and energy available to address fundamental challenges.

Context   This pattern addresses the ethical application of communications systems, processes, and tools to clearly distinguish that which is conditionally unknown—gaps in understanding or perception that can be addressed by gaining new knowledge, skill, or experience —and that which is essentially unknowable as the source of profound mystery and fascination. The intent is to transparently convey meaning in a way that invites, encourages, and supports free and unfettered engagement in the human enterprise.

Discussion   The floodgates of information have opened wide, and every channel and venue of communication is awash in conflicting data and analysis. In this gap between fact and meaning, some people have learned to apply an amazing sophistication in the use of communications tools to manipulate logic and shape opinions, distorting even the smallest ambiguity into a mystifying argument that freezes the status quo and preserves the current imbalance of power and influence. In the satiric film *Thank You for Smoking,* the tobacco lobbyist instructs his son, "If you argue correctly, you are never wrong."

The impact of mystifying communications can be seen in the debate over global warming. A 2006 survey on the attitude of the American public on global warming by the Pew Research Center for the People and the Press found that "roughly four-in-ten (41 percent) believe human activity such as burning fossil fuels is causing global warming, but just as many say either that warming has been caused by natural patterns in the earth's environment (21 percent), or that there is no solid evidence of global warming (20 percent)" and that "public opinion about global warming is deeply polarized along political lines." If you happen to enjoy a position of relative comfort, it is easy to become complacent and detached—despite the mounting international scientific evidence indicating the strong influence of human activity. The double-speak of Orwell's *1984* has come to life in political and ideological spin control.

This reveals a fundamental challenge of communications in our times. Statistics and scientific evidence alone do not change human behavior or engage people, at a visceral and passionate level, in the resolution of intractable challenges and at worst can be manipulated to create a mystifying fog that stifles effective intervention.

At the same time, nearly everyone has experienced at one time or another defining moments of sheer fascination and mystery that reveal a profound sense of connection—the birth of a child, the death of a loved one, an unexpected encounter with the sheer vastness of space or the intricate complexity of nature, accompanied by the inescapable feeling of being a participant in this vastness and awe-inspiring complexity. While the meaning of these experiences does not depend on formal religious belief or spiritual affiliation, the expression of this meaning falls into the realm of symbol, song, and poetry. It is a reenchantment—of the world, science, life, nature, art—that reawakens a sense of wonder that in itself makes sense, an intuitive appreciation for the sheer mystery of life and for the opportunity to be part of how that mystery continues to unfold and enliven human events, relationships, and structures. As Gablik (1991) states, reenchantment "refers to that change in the general social mood toward a more pragmatic idealism and a more integrated value system that brings head and heart together in an ethic of care, as part of the healing of the world."

The pragmatic idealism of reenchantment provides a far different and, ironically, more practical foundation for forming public consensus around serious problems such as global warming. The recent strengthening of collaborations bringing together otherwise conflicting evangelical and progressive wings of Christianity around stewardship of the earth is one sign of how foundational awe and wonder can lead to a willingness to change behaviors and social structures responsibly.

Solution   Develop and incorporate methods to elicit reenchantment—including, perhaps, personal stories, poetry, music, and art—and reframe complex issues in the context of a shared experience of wonder and mystery.

Linked patterns   The Good Life (3), Memory and Responsibility (11), Back to the Roots (13), Spiritually Grounded Activism (24), Opportunity Spaces (33), Media Literacy (35), Technocriticism (39), Transparency (64), Voices of the Unheard (83), Community-Building Journalism (97), The Power of Story (114).

15 Translation

Problem People who speak different languages cannot understand each other without benefit of translation. A related problem, which may be more insidious, arises when two or more people think they are speaking the same language when they are not. "Languages," furthermore, are of various types, in addition to what we usually think of: English, Japanese, or Hindi, for example. Some people seem to speak only "technical" or "postmodern academician," which can be incomprehensible to those outside those cultures. Finally, there is often an implied pecking order in which one language and its speakers are viewed as dominant or more important while other languages (and its speakers) are devalued and bear an unequal share of the burden of understanding.

Context This pattern applies in any situation where two or more languages are employed. Here "language" is applied broadly. For example, with global climate change looming, scientists must be able to effectively engage in two-way conversations with nonscientists; social scientists must be able to do the same if their work is to have relevance and resonance. Translation takes place when any two worlds of discourse are bridged. Thus, this pattern includes translation between systems of knowledge (e.g., theorist and practitioner) as well as translations between different languages.

Discussion Umberto Eco tells us that "A text is a machine for eliciting translations" (2001). Without a text or other snippet of communication, translation is impossible. With it, translation is indispensable.

Although cultures are maintained through a variety of institutions, the use of a common language may be the deepest and most abiding tie that binds a culture together. Language is a reflection of and a window into culture.

Of course, people speak many languages; children may invent secret words to describe the world they see and would like to see, slang is shared by youth culture, academic disciplines use certain phrases to participate in a shared intellectual pursuit, and religious communities have expressions of sacred and profane ideas of special significance.

If, however, every person in the world spoke only one language, a language that had no words in common, then each group would be a group by itself, cut off from the rest of the social world. Trade would be virtually impossible, as would diplomacy and sharing of intellectual creations, technological and artistic. War is one social activity that probably would not be hampered by this barrier to communication (although negotiating an end to the hostilities would be extremely difficult, even impossible).

Thus translation is a bridge that connects two or more cultures or two or more people. Translation allows two or more groups or people to come to a common understanding, and it allows them to take advantage of the special or expert knowledge of the other.

Translation is also a social process embedded in particular social contexts and subjected to the dictates of that context. For example, the burden of translation is often expected to fall on the lower-status or less dominant group. Thus, many people expect Spanish speakers in the United States to learn English. People who lack fluency in the dominant language (English, BBC English, or technospeak, for example) are often considered ignorant.

Umberto Eco (2001) captures a key difficulty in translation:

Equivalence in meaning cannot be take as a satisfactory criterion for a correct translation, first of all because in order to define the still undefined notion of translation one would have to employ a notion as obscure as equivalence of meaning, and some people think that meaning is that which remains unchanged in the process of translation. We cannot even accept the naive idea that equivalence in meaning is provided by synonymy, since it is commonly accepted that there are no complete synonyms in language. *Father* is not a synonym for *daddy*, *daddy* is not a synonym for *papà*, and *père* is not a synonym for *padre*.

As Eco makes clear, words in languages do not have one-to-one equivalence. For that reason, successful translation relies on a reasonable yet partial solution (actually a type of negotiation) to a number of interdependent problems. Totally accurate translation is impossible, but imperfect translation is ubiquitous—and essential. Moreover, the context of the words in the sentence or the sentence in the paragraph, or whatever else is being translated, all within the context of the inspiration and intent and audience, is relevant when translating.

Translation therefore is not a mechanical act, but a skilled and empathetic re-rewriting or reperforming of a text or utterance or intention in which an understanding of the two cultures being bridged is essential. More precisely, an understanding of the two respective audiences, intended and otherwise, the vocabulary they employ, their education, biases, fears, and so forth are all central to a good, solid, and mutually satisfactory translation.

Although the following quotation is specifically examining the differences of psychology and sociology by their focus of individuals and collective bodies, respectively, it captures a central question in translation:

To address the problem of different and incommensurable perspectives in the human sciences, two issues need to be considered. First, we must find a way to link perspectives without simply reducing one to another.... Attempts to account for complex human phenomena by invoking a perspective grounded in a single discipline are as unlikely as were the attempts of each of the three blind men to come with *the* true account of an elephant. The goal, then, is to arrive at an account—a kind of "translation at the crossroads"—that would make it possible to *link, but not reduce,* one perspective to another. (Wertsch 1998)

Solution   Think about the critical role of translation, and, if possible, become a translator—or at least when the need arises where you can help bridge a gap of understanding. From the point of view of social amelioration, translations between two particular cultures may be more immediately necessary than two others. But all cultures ultimately must have connections, and mutual understanding is necessary, if not sufficient, for a positive future.

Linked patterns   Linguistic Diversity (16), Strengthening International Law (42), Culturally Situated Design Tools (49), Conversational Support across Boundaries (50), Accessibility of Online Information (75), Open Access Scholarly Publishing (76), The Power of Story (114), Soap Operas with Civic Messages (120), Activist Road Trip (134).

Problem   Over the past century, many of the world's languages have disappeared. When a language is lost, part of the world's knowledge and culture is also irrevocably lost. Beyond the losses incurred thus far, there is evidence that the trend is increasing, as languages such as English, Spanish, and Swahili are displacing languages that are less prominent in the world's media and cultural spheres. Losing humankind's linguistic diversity diminishes our collective ability to perceive and think about the world in a holistic, multifaceted, and rich way.

Context   Everybody who communicates with other people employs language. To a large extent, the language that we use places constraints on what and how we think. Everybody has a stake in promoting linguistic diversity, although some people are better positioned to help.

Discussion   In 1992, Michael Krauss, a language professor at the University of Alaska, Fairbanks, predicted that half of the world's languages would become extinct within the next century. Although languages periodically have become extinct throughout history, the frequency of language death today is unprecedented. Krauss reported that of the twenty tongues still known to the state's indigenous people, only two of were being taught to children. A 1990 survey in Australia cited by W. Wayt Gibbs (2002) "found that 70 of the 90 surviving Aboriginal languages were no longer used regularly by all age groups. The same was true for all but 20 of the 175 Native American languages spoken or remembered in the U.S. The Ethnologue, an Internet resource that lists over 7,000 languages currently in use worldwide, contains over 400 languages thought to be in imminent danger of extinction.

It may be that our everyday familiarity with language prevents us from respecting the fact that "any language is a supreme achievement of a uniquely human collective genius, as divine and endless a mystery as a living organism," Krauss (1992) reminds us. Linguistic diversity can be thought as analogous to biological diversity. In that vein, Krauss asks his readers, "Should we mourn the loss of Eyak or Ubykh any less than the loss of the panda or California condor?"

Many of the imperiled languages are those of indigenous people. Unfortunately for the rest of us, the worldviews of indigenous people, especially in relationship to the environment, are vantage points we cannot afford to lose. David Crystal, writing in *Language Death* (2000), states that "most westerners are infants in their knowledge of the environment, and how to behave toward it, compared with the indigenous peoples, for whom the environment is part of the business of survival." It is a sobering thought to ponder how much the mass media may be determining what is in our "environment" and, hence, in our "knowledge of the environment." Is it true that Americans have sixty-three words for *shopping*?

Linguists are now employing a variety of techniques to document the world's endangered languages before they are lost forever. This usually involves fieldwork in which a dictionary and grammar guide are produced. Often recordings are made of native speakers. But looking beyond the last-ditch capture of a language before it dies forever, linguists are using a variety of techniques to try to build back a viable language community. A program devised by Leanne Hinton (2001) acquired funding to pay both fluent indigenous speakers and younger learners.

David Crystal (2000) lists six factors that he believes can help resuscitate an endangered language. An endangered language will progress if its speakers:

1. Increase their prestige within the dominant community.
2. Increase their wealth relative to the dominant community.
3. Increase their legitimate power in the eyes of the dominant community.
4. Have a strong presence in the educational system.
5. Can write their language down.
6. Can make use of electronic technology.

Hans-Jurgen Sasse (Gibbs 2002) believes that "collective doubts about the usefullness of language loyalty" among the speakers of a language can presage its demise. The speakers themselves can, of course, strive to maintain their language. The world outside that language community can play a role by respecting linguistic diversity, often by dropping prejudices and a bias for monolingualism. David Crystal believes that this bias is, at least to some degree, a product of colonialism and is now being promoted by economics. When bilingualism flourishes, speakers can participate in the world beyond their language community intellectually and commercially while maintaining their own community, identity, and heritage.

As with other thorny problems, no single answer exists. Solutions that work in some places have no effects in others. Education of one sort or another will play a large role in language maintenance because the language must be passed on from older to younger generations. Artistic and other forms of cultural expression can serve as an outlet for creative impulses that the world beyond their community can enjoy as well.

Solution   Linguists are often at the forefront of the struggle for linguistic diversity. It was linguists who first alerted us to these issues and have helped develop methods to archive linguistic resources. Nonlinguists have important roles to play as well. We need to become aware of humankind's diminishing linguistic diversity and work to preserve and enhance it.

Linked patterns   The Commons (2), Social Dominance Attenuation (4), Global Citizenship (6), Memory and Responsibility (11), Translation (15), Education and Values (17), Conversational Support across Boundaries (50), Indigenous Media (55), Grassroots Public Policy Development (78), Control of-Self Representation (109), The Power of Story (114).

17 Education and Values

Problem Education necessarily promotes and replicates values in numerous ways. Often teachers and administrators use the asymmetrical power relationships inherent in most educational settings to promulgate their own set of values. But even when they are not deliberate in this effort, they nevertheless communicate their values. Neither the conscious nor the unconscious promulgation of values is typically designed with thought to the appropriateness of these values for the future. This does not imply that newer values are always better than older values, but some values of the past must be rethought in the light of burgeoning global populations, diminishing natural resources, and the danger and ultimate futility of armed conflict.

Context To avoid simply having students parrot platitudes without deep understanding, an approach to values education has been proposed that uses moral dilemmas for discussion and encourages participation in communities where conflicts and resolutions will be a natural outgrowth (Nucci and Weber 1991). While the issue of values in education has always been important, our contemporary context raises its priority. The world is changing at a rapid pace, and many of today's implicit values are counterproductive to a viable future (e.g., judging an individual's worth by the size and power of his or her automobile; believing that a child must live constantly in an environment kept at 70 to 72 degrees Fahrenheit; that authority is always right and must be obeyed; that the way to success is to follow the crowd). Indeed, many values promulgated by society are contradictory. For instance, American society encourages overindulgence in high-fat, high-sugar foods and simultaneously insists that only people with perfect bodies are worthwhile. While children may be taught during an hour-long health class that too much fat and sugar are bad for the body, this hardly constitutes a sufficient antidote to thousands of expertly designed advertisements that encourage consumption of the sugary, high-fat foods. The capacity of adults to wreak great havoc on others is at an all-time high. Ethical decisions have always been crucial, but the consequences of unethical behavior have taken on even greater significance.

Discussion Children normally develop morally as well as cognitively as they mature (Piaget 1965; Power, Higgins, and Kohlberg 1989). Ideally this comes about through acting in the social world, observing consequences, and interacting with peers. Turiel (1983) pointed out that children develop judgments in two separate but interrelated domains: the conventional and the ethical. The appropriateness of clothing is a question of convention that varies from society to society and from setting to setting. The appropriateness of killing is an ethical issue in every society. However, disregarding a recognized convention (e.g., appearing nude in inappropriate circumstances) can cause sufficient disruption and discomfort to raise genuine ethical issues.

Education is often thought of as a process that helps individuals gain knowledge (vocabulary, rules of syntax, geographic locations, events of historic significance) and skills (parsing sentences, doing research, organizing results, writing, typing). While this is true, education also necessarily promotes values. Values are involved in curriculum choices, the materials chosen within the curriculum, how the material is presented, and the range of "correct" answers. For example, primarily focusing history studies on the history of one's own country promotes the value of chauvinism. Moreover, placing emphasis within that history on presidents, generals, wars, and victories (with little to say about changes that arise from and affect people in general) promotes the values of authoritarianism and militarism. Material focused on white Christian males promotes racism and sexism. Presenting subject material using a lecture style with little chance for debate, discussion, or dialogue reinforces the value of authoritarianism. Evaluating student progress based primarily on the ability to recite specific known facts also promotes the value of authoritarianism.

An interesting case study of the degree to which values are inherent even in so-called objective matters comes from the Ph.D. dissertation of T. G. Evans (1968), a student of Marvin Minsky, the prominent artificial intelligence researcher at MIT. Evans built an artificial intelligence program to solve multiple-choice figure analogy problems: A:B::C:D1, D2, D3, D4, or D5. The program found relationships mapping between A and B and then tried to apply those same relationships mapping C to each of the possible D answers. His program worked. In fact, his program worked too well–all answers were correct. In order to make the program pick the same answers as the test developers, he had to inculcate his program with the same value priorities as the test developers. For instance, according to test makers, it was (implicitly) more "elegant" to rotate a figure within the two-dimensional plane than to rotate out in three-dimensional space.

The inculcation of values is pervasive and subtle. Much of the value indoctrination that occurs in schools is unconscious. Even when conscious attention is given to values, there seems to be little appreciation of the extent to which children are subjected to much more powerful indoctrination by paid advertisements in print, TV, radio, games, and movies.

Solution Educational institutions, individual teachers, parents, concerned citizens, and children themselves must work to uncover and understand the values that are being taught, as well as to design the entire educational experience to foster those values that will help make for a sustainable and healthy future. (For a whole school approach to values, see http://www.valueseducation.edu.au/values/). In addition, a constructivist approach to education, while arguably important for deep understanding in topics as various as science and mathematics to poetry interpretation, such an approach is particularly vital to values education, and especially when values of the past may have to be rethought for their appropriateness to the future. (For examples, see http://www.education.monash.edu.au/profiles/ghildebr and http://www.rcdg.isr.umich.edu/faculty/eccles.htm.)

Linked patterns   Linguistic Diversity (16), Teaching to Transgress (20), Media Literacy (35), Open Action and Research Network (45), Peace Education (56), Digital Emancipation (60), Ethics of Community Informatics (67), Positive Health Information (74), Civic Capabilities (85), Experimental School (89), Service-Learning (90), Citizenship Schools (96), Informal Learning Groups (98), Community Animators (102).

Problem   Our current economic system that provides for our material needs works only by producing and selling things. The more we produce and the more we purchase, the more we have so-called progress and prosperity. However, the production, processing, and consumption of commodities require the extraction and use of natural resources (wood, ore, fossil fuels, water). They also require the creation of factories and factory complexes whose operation creates toxic by-products, while the use of commodities themselves (e.g., automobiles) creates pollutants and waste (Robbins 2004). The number of consumers and their individual and collective behaviors drive materialization (Wernick et al. 1996).

Context   Human societies face unintended and ironic consequences of their own mechanical, chemical, medical, social, and financial ingenuity (Zira 2003). The production and consumption of products is destructive in the long run to the environment and is a contributing factor to poverty and hunger around the world. A long list of social and ecological problems cannot be solved without a less consumptive society and the dematerialization of the resources we use.

Discussion   *Dematerialization* is a technological term that defines the reduction of material used per unit quality of life. You may have noticed the plastic sack at the grocery store getting thinner, but it is still strong enough to carry groceries. Over the years, it may seem that you can squeeze the soda can you drink from more easily with your hand, though you may not have gotten any stronger. These types of changes in products are the result of dematerialization: using fewer natural resources in products, using more recycled resources, and extending the life of products.

Industrial ecology is the study of the totality of the relationships of different industrial activities, their products, and the environment. It is intended to identify ways to optimize the network of all industrial processes as they interact and live off each other, in the sense of a direct use of each other's material and energy wastes and products as well as economic synergism. The macroscopic picture of materialization can help raise key research questions and set priorities among the numerous studies of materials flows and networks that might be undertaken. It puts these in a dynamic context of technical and market change (Wernick et al. 1996).

Dematerialization of unit products affects, and is influenced by, a number of factors besides product quality. These include ease of manufacturing, production cost, size and complexity of the product, whether the product is to be repaired or replaced, and the amount of waste to be generated and processed. These factors influence one another. For example, the ease of manufacture of a particular product in smaller and lighter units may result in lower production costs and cheaper products of lower quality, which will be replaced rather than repaired on breaking down. Although a smaller amount of waste will be generated on a per unit basis, more units will be produced and disposed of, and there may be an overall increase in waste generation at both the production and the consumption ends (Allenby 1992). Through industrial ecology, we can determine best outcomes using a wider, more global outlook of the effects of our activities on the environment.

In a functional economy, consumers can purchase function, rather than a physical product, from a service provider. "For example, we do not want the washing machine, we want clean, dry washing; we do not want the drill, we want to have a picture hanged" (Jucker 2000). Through dematerialization, a physical product is replaced by a nonphysical product or service reducing a company's production, demand, and use of physical products and the end user's dependence on physical products. This strategy realizes cost savings in materials, energy, transportation, consumables, and the need to manage the eventual disposal or recycling of a physical product. Dematerialization may involve making a product smaller and lighter, replacing a material product with an immaterial substitute. One common example is the replacement of postal mail with e-mail. Reducing the use of material or infrastructure-intensive systems allows us to make changes like telecommuting versus the use of the automobile for work purposes.

The ease and speed of travel is a large contributing factor to the materialization of our world. As a society, we have spread out and continue to create a built environment all over the map because it is so quick and easy to get from here to there. As we create wider, better roads, more cars fill the roadways. The use of plastics in society is the by-product of using too much oil to fuel our automobiles. As a result, the disposal of plastic waste is an increasing problem, not to mention the effect on the environment due to the amount of industrialized metals, plastics, electronic materials, rubber, and glass it takes to manufacture each car. A recent television ad with a woman talking about the need to protect the environment ended with this endearment: "But, I love my car!" Attempts to dematerialize the automobile by using high-strength steel and plastics to decrease mass but increase structural integrity are negatively offset by this kind of sentiment that consumers hold.

The starting point for any sensible theory or practice of consumption has to be the insight that every time you buy and/or consume something—be it a tiny battery to keep your watch going or be it a TV, a car or a hamburger, you are making an impact on the social, economic, and ecological environment. In the words of Anwar Fazal, former president of the International Organization of Consumer Unions (IOCU): "The act of buying is a vote for an economic and social model, for a particular way of producing goods. We are concerned with the quality of goods and the satisfactions we derive from them. But we cannot ignore the environmental impact and working conditions under which products are made." Our relationship with these products or goods does not end with our enjoyment of possessing or consuming them. We are linked to them and perpetuate them and therefore share some direct responsibility for them (Jucker 2000).

Lifestyles also shape demand. Today only a small fraction of consumption in wealthy nations (or communities) is for basic survival; most is for pleasure and to express one's standing in society (Wernick et al. 1996). In a standup monologue, comedian George Carlin used humor to increase our awareness of society's obsessive behavior for material objects: "That's all I want, that's all you need in life, is a . . . place for your stuff, ya know? A house is just a pile of stuff with a cover on it. . . . I can see it on your table, everybody's got a . . . place for their stuff. . . . This is my stuff, that's your stuff, that'll be his stuff over there. . . . And when you leave your house, you gotta lock it up. Wouldn't want somebody to come by and take some of your stuff. . . . That's what your house is, a place to keep your stuff while you go out and get . . . more stuff! Sometimes you gotta move, gotta get a bigger house. Why? No room for your stuff anymore." Sometimes the beginning to an answer for a serious problem like too much materialism and consumerism is to create personal awareness.

Of the three factors environmentalists often point to as responsible for environmental problems—population, technology, and consumption—consumption seems to get the least attention. One reason is that it may be the most difficult to change; our consumption patterns are so much a part of our lives that to change them would require a massive cultural overhaul, not to mention severe economic dislocation. A drop in demand for products, as economists note, brings on economic recession or even depression, along with massive unemployment. This is so ingrained into the cultures of the wealthy nations, that the thought of massive adjustment of lifestyles and economic systems to a more sustainable consumption seems too much to consider (A. Shaw 2005). Taking a moderate approach with gradual or incremental changes in lifestyle could increase the probability of an actual decrease in consumption.

Substantial progress has been made over the past century in decoupling economic growth and well-being from increasing primary energy use through increased efficiency. With this success, some economists may come to think that *dematerialization* is a term for scientific processes and economic strategies alone and has nothing to do with materialism as a philosophy. But there is also increased realization that "decoupling materials and affluence will be difficult—much harder than decoupling carbon and prosperity" (Wernick et al. 1996). The term *dematerialization* applies to the individual act of buying less, consuming less, and finding more meaning in our lives than the acquisition of material goods. Downsizing homes, automobiles, technological toys and entertainment systems, clothes closets, and the consumptive habits taught to children can help people simplify their lives and find other interests that create more meaning, value, and happiness. Understanding the historical roots of materialism that have resulted in modern affluence could also be key to decreasing the personal use and obsession with material goods in the built world.

Solution Consumption needs to be intentionally curbed. The growing role of knowledge, information, and culture should also it possible to displace materials and energy with human intelligence and ingenuity, satisfying more basic human needs with far fewer resources. It would ostensibly also allow human economic activities to be fit within natural processes without disrupting them. Dematerialization is the future of an ecologically and economically balanced world. (Robbins 2004).

Linked patterns   Global Citizenship (6), Back to the Roots (13), Whole Cost (28), Strategic Capacity (34), Technocriticism (39), Design Stance (44), Wholesome Design for Wicked Problems (82), Design for Unintended Use (84), Appropriating Technology (108), Environmental Impact Remediation (124).

19 Transforming Institutions

Problem Traditional management models used to develop and sustain institutions and their services are often based on the corporate concept of centralized and tightly controlled operations. They are led by people who are often chosen for their position only because they fit easily within the institution. Institutions become focused on their own survival rather than their original and evolving missions and visions. Institutions and organizations replicate themselves through their hiring practices and competitive practices, preventing diversity and, hence, innovation. Institutions become resistant to change, maintaining the belief (at least implicitly) that what they are now is what they should remain.

Context A distributed management and operational model for institutions is required to support and sustain remote and rural communities. Establishing innovation as a way of doing business to engage remote and rural communities in all regions requires an appreciation where people are employed and producing valued products as well as delivering services that are an important part of the social and economic fabric of the region. In many cases, success in fulfilling the mission of an institution can actually mean the transformation of their organization. Institutions that have some specified life span to fulfill their mandate can either disappear or change to accommodate the next challenge that is identified from its work and services.

Discussion Most institutions are positioned to deliver services from their operation center out to the region and the masses. Often these institutions, their leaders, and their corporate management models protect and maintain their existence without any regard for those they were intended to serve. Their development and sustainability strategies are built and maintained on the basic values of greed and exploitation of the people and regions they claim to serve. The exploitation and destruction of the environment, people, and rural communities are long-term results of these types of efforts by institutions.

Regional hospitals, colleges, and universities are three examples of institutions that sustain their operation centers in larger urban environments. They sustain their operation by drawing people to their facilities under the myth that they will be better served if they move to these centers. The professionals who work with clients in these institutions create a level of dependency that people have grown to accept. These efforts protect their positions and create wealth for the institution while draining local and regional resources. The reality that these institutions and corporations depend on communities to supply the resources required for their existence challenges their traditional model.

The real costs of developing and sustaining centralized, concrete environments have never been incorporated into the balance sheets of the institutions. These are real costs to the environment: the costs of destroying forests and the earth to extract natural resources for creating man-made environments. The artificial comforts that some experience as a result of these environments should reflect these real costs of producing the food and water that sustain the lives of the people who work within these institutions, the energy they consume to have these comforts, and the poverty that others must experience so they can be comfortable within these artificial environments. The list of costs is long and requires significant research to reflect the real exchanges that occur among the sectors of society.

Once these real costs are included in any true management system, institutions and governments will need to look outside their glass bubbles to work with others to find truly sustainable and equitable solutions. Management and program developers will need to find creative strategies to accommodate, work with, and sustain communities, cultures, and environments that have always existed and have been struggling to survive.

Being able to look outside their comfortable worlds to support innovation and development with their neighbors requires a new set of values and priorities. These institutional values and priorities will be different from those that are now in place to protect and sustain artificial and temporary facilities and environments. Partnering with others, trusting other people, understanding others, and respecting other environments, cultures, and people are values that should become part of every modern institutional culture and environment.

This transformation will benefit the institution by creating new opportunities and relationships, but it will also probably require some short-term pain to establish long-term gains. Finding creative ways to purchase and support services and products from other groups outside the institution also requires finding creative ways to pay the real price for these products and services. Learning how to value and respect people and environments in remote and rural communities helps create these new opportunities and relationships.

Working with existing institutions and supporting their required change is a challenge. Starting over to create new institutions is an option only when there are opportunities and support for innovative groups and organizations that are able to overcome or counter the traditional institutional management model. But for most existing institutions, the entrenched infrastructure and investments created over the years require that they remain in place.

Institutions located in most small urban centers are an integral and historical part of their environment. Over the years they have contributed jobs and significant investment to the communities where they are located. By their very nature, they will continue to exist. The question becomes, however, whether they will be able to make the necessary adjustments for successfully accommodating these real operational costs within their own environments.

This type of change, with its associated challenges and opportunities, requires a transformation at all levels within existing institutions. This transformative work needs to be led by innovative thinkers and new leaders who understand and respect the impact of their institution at the local, regional, national, and international levels. The global village demands this type of relationship within institutions. As these new institutions evolve from within existing institutions or as new institutions are started, the required transformations are facilitated and supported by factors and forces both within and outside the organization:

Leaders of older organizations often selected in the past are constrained by institutional routines, and may have resources that allow them to operate in counterproductive insulation from the environment. As leaders persist, they form bonds among themselves, develop common understandings of "how things work," and select others like themselves to lead. Access to internal organizational resources can insulate them, in the short run, from environmental change. For a time, these resources may even give them the power to shape that environment—but only for a time. Changes in organizational structure that reduce leaders' accountability to or need to mobilize resources from constituents—or changes in deliberative processes that suppress dissent—can diminish strategic capacity, even as resources grow. The strategic capacity of an organization can thus grow over time if it adjusts its leadership team to reflect environmental change, multiplies deliberative venues, remains accountable to salient constituencies, and derives resources from them. (Ganz 2003)

As Ganz and others note, there is a need for permeable organizations that are flexible, contain reliable processes for evaluating work in terms of mission and objectives and are able to accommodate and reward innovative thinking (Thomas 2002, Tresser 2002, Wortley 2002, Michaelson 2002, Brown 2006, Dutfield 2006). Working with groups and constituents outside the institution provides leadership with unique opportunities to adjust their goals and priorities. Providing appropriate reward structures for those within and outside the institution offers the opportunity for building new relationships and collaborative development. Being able to respond to these changes and opportunities in a timely and appropriate manner requires a special team comprised of partners in development.

Solution   Institutions should begin to:

• Develop innovative and sustainable relationships with remote and rural communities that are built on the principles of trust, sharing, respect, and strength to ensure an equitable and fair existence for all to support a sustainable, transformative institutional model.
• Establish a transformative change within their environments to engage as well as effectively communicate and share with the region their products and resources. The resulting exchange becomes a model for cooperative and collaborative development across regions and elsewhere as innovative strategies and creativity benefiting all become entrenched and commonplace in all relationships.
• Create flexible institutional management models that can adjust to the changing and evolving needs of people so everyone has the opportunity to become engaged in these transformative efforts.

Linked patterns   Political Settings (7), Social Responsibility (8), Public Agenda (30), Economic Conversion (41), Peace Education (56), Patient Access to Medical Records (95), Sustainability Appraisal (100).

Problem   Obviously good teachers try their best to teach what they believe to be correct. Yet the world changes, so that what was once true is no longer true and what was once irrelevant becomes important, even vital. Furthermore, even with respect to things that do not objectively change, new knowledge is continually created. It is natural for students to identify with good teachers and value their knowledge highly. A possible side effect of this basically good process, however, is that the student may become reluctant to "go against" the teaching of his or her mentor, hero, or professor. This reluctance occurs not just with respect to individual teachers but also with respect to society as a whole.

Context   The world is changing rapidly and critically. For example, the human population has exploded in the past few hundred years. The consumption of fossil fuels continues basically unabated despite signs of global warming and the finite nature of these fuels. The destructive nature of modern weaponry means that fights for limited economic resources or over restrictive and doctrinaire religions can produce unprecedented levels of human misery. Nevertheless, many individuals, groups, and societies seem just as conservative and rigid as ever.

Discussion   Living organisms have existed on earth for at least 10^9 years, while modern human institutions like government have been around for only about 10^4 years. Living organisms have the capacity to change with each new generation through mutation and recombination. We would do well to emulate what has worked.

The U.S. Constitution, although a best-efforts work at the time it was created, also carries within it provision for change through amendment, and many of these have been critical to the broadening of American democracy to a wider range of citizens.

The Walking People (Underwood 1997) describes the journey of one branch of the Iroquois tribe over several millennia. In the process, they were forced to learn to accommodate to different physical and cultural situations. They developed numerous mechanisms for retaining learned wisdom and for challenging and changing when new situations arose.

The need for challenge and change has probably never been greater. Nonetheless, many mechanisms tend to prevent change. At the individual level, change can be uncomfortable. Typically a targeted change in one area or domain has unintended consequences not only in that same area or domain but in others as well. If an individual changes, this may require compensatory changes in those close to the individual. Thus, there is often resistance to change at the level of family and friends as well. Furthermore, there is often institutional resistance to change. Institutions, including corporations, work to keep any and all advantages that they already enjoy. And governments and religions often work to keep the status quo.

Given the numerous levels at which resistance to change occurs, it is necessary to have active mechanisms that work toward change at numerous levels as well. The impacts of change need to be carefully evaluated, however, because not all changes, even well-intentioned ones, work well.

Education means preparation for the future, not submission to the past. As prominent educator and author bel hooks (whose enlightening 1994 book provided the title for this pattern) has made clear, transgression is a movement that is "against and beyond boundaries." She also places this movement at the core of the educational enterprise: "It is that movement which makes education the practice of freedom."

Solution   In order to help prevent stagnation of knowledge, one useful strategy is for the teacher, as an integral part of teaching, to teach "transgression;" that is, to go against the received wisdom—to test and rebel against it. The scope of such transgression should encompass all of a society's rules, prejudices, and attitudes.

Linked patterns   Civic Intelligence (1), Education and Values (17), Design Stance (44), Citizen Access to Simulations (48), Peace Education (56), Experimental School (89), Service-Learning (90), Citizen Journalism (91), Informal Learning Groups (98), Sense of Struggle (104), Arts of Resistance (111), The Power of Story (114), Illegitimate Theater (123), Power Research (128), Media Intervention (132).

Problem   Economic globalization is repainting the face of international trade. World trading has mushroomed into an unfair economic trend separating the developed and underdeveloped worlds. Around the globe, production, trade, and retailing of most goods and services are increasingly concentrated under the control of a small number of corporations. To offset the steaming engine of this powerful global economic force, fair trade associations made up of fair trade wholesalers, retailers, producers, and consumers are needed to foster a more equitable and sustainable system of production and trade that benefits people and their communities.

Context   Fair trade means that trading partnerships are based on reciprocal benefits and mutual respect; that prices paid to producers reflect the work they do; that workers have the right to organize; that national health, safety, and wage laws are enforced; and that products are environmentally sustainable and conserve natural resources. "Trade can either contribute to the process of sustainable development or undermine it. Given the rapidly accelerating destruction of the earth's natural resource base, there is no question what the choice must be" (Fair Trade Federation 2006).

Discussion   Backed by conventional economists, large corporations have convinced most of the world's governments that they should maximize global competitiveness through freer trade. Corporate and government officials often theorize that free trade will be beneficial for workers, whose wages and benefits can rise as foreign markets expand for their goods and for consumers who can buy cheap foreign imports. Following this theory, regional trade agreements like the North American Free Trade Agreement and the General Agreement on Tariffs and Trade are reducing barriers to trade and investment for firms. These free trade agreements offer firms global protection for their intellectual and property rights, but there are currently no equivalent enforceable global standards to protect workers and the environment. Furthermore, as barriers to entering local markets are removed, large-scale manufacturers edge small businesses and local cooperative enterprises out of the market. Local economies suffer when these firms' profits are channeled out of the country rather than being reinvested locally (Wedge Co-op Newsletter 2006).

As a result of these trends, the gap between the rich and the poor has increased dramatically in recent decades. The benefits of trade are similarly concentrated among the wealthiest segments of the world's population and a handful of developing countries. Even in many countries that are experiencing high growth rates from expanded trade, the benefits of growth are not trickling down to the poor (Fair Trade Federation 2006).

Another problem is that the bulk of exports from developing countries tends to be in primary product commodities, such as sugar, cocoa, and coffee, whose prices generally rise much more slowly than the prices of manufactured goods imports. Free trade agreements do little to enhance the trading positions and commodity prices of these poor countries. In many cases, the world market price for commodities such as coffee and cocoa falls below the cost of production, forcing farmers to sustain huge losses. Fair trade organizations offer a crucial alternative by paying farmers a price that always covers at least production costs (Wedge Co-op Newsletter 2006).

Deregulation allows corporations to benefit at the expense of the people in a nation or region with the relaxation of environmental rules, health, and educational services, including control of natural resources and energy (Fair Trade 2006). Meanwhile, subsidies in developed countries allow producers to sell their products at discounted prices and make it difficult for producers in developing countries to compete in the global market place. Protectionism issues such as unreasonably high tariffs restrict developing countries from exporting their products to developed countries.

Market prices do not reflect the true costs of producing products because external economic factors like environmental and social costs are not figured into production costs. Fluctuations in commodity prices make it difficult for producers in developing countries to maintain a living wage, forcing them into debt. Marginalized workers and producers work from a position of economic vulnerability and insecurity. Unethical labor practices such as gender inequality, child labor, and sweatshop practices contribute to unfair profits.

Equitable trade relations need to be established between governments, nongovernmental organizations, multinational corporations, and international institutions that promote the principles and practices endorsed by alternative free trade organizations. Fair trade advocates and associations support trading relationships by creating opportunities for economically disadvantaged producers. Fair trade is a strategy for poverty alleviation and sustainable development. Its purpose is to create opportunities for producers who have been economically disadvantaged or marginalized by the conventional trading system. Fair trade involves transparent management and commercial relations to deal fairly and respectfully with trading partners. Fair trade promotes transparency and accountability throughout the business operation. It helps build capacity as producers develop their own independence. Fair trade relationships provide continuity, during which producers and their marketing organizations can improve their management skills and their access to new markets (Fair Trade 2006).

Payment of a fair price in the regional or local context should be agreed through dialogue and participation. It not only covers the costs of production but enables socially just and environmentally sound production. Fair trade actively encourages better environmental practices and the application of responsible methods of production. Fair traders ensure prompt payment to their partners and, whenever possible, help producers with access to preharvest or preproduction financing (Fair Trade Zone 2006).

Fair trade provides fair pay to the producers and takes into account the principle of equal pay for equal work by women and men. It means that women's work is properly valued and rewarded: women are always paid for their contribution to the production process and are empowered in their organizations. Fair trade means a safe and healthy working environment for producers. Worker safety and environmental protection are pursued diligently. The participation of children (if any) does not adversely affect their well-being, security, educational requirements, and need for play and conforms to the U.N. Convention on the Rights of the Child, as well as the law and norms in the local context (Fair Trade 2006).

The idea of labeling fairly traded products needs to be expanded into a more widely used standard in business. The easiest way to support fair trade is to purchase fairly traded products. The actions of consumers support or discourage actions by businesses, even large corporations. Even small acts like purchasing a cup of coffee from a business that is fair trade certified help move the world economy in a more positive direction.

Solution Adhering to social criteria and environmental principles can foster a more equitable and sustainable system of production and trade that benefits people at the local level. Small as it may be, the rapidly growing fair trade movement is setting standards that could redefine world trade to include more social and environmental considerations. Fair traders believe that their system of trade, based on respect for workers' rights and the environment, if adopted by the big players in the global economy, can play a big part in reversing the growing inequities and environmental degradation that have accompanied the growth in world trade (Fair Trade Federation 2006).

Linked patterns Social Dominance Attenuation (4), Global Citizenship (6), Matrifocal Orientation (9), Working-Class Consciousness (12), Whole Cost (28), Durable Assets (58), Powerful Remittances (73), Voices of the Unheard (83), Self-Designed Development (106), Engaged Tourism (107), Labor Visions (112).

Problem   Human welfare depends on using the earth's physical resources, material cycles, and biological processes, yet human techniques, understanding, decision making, and perceptions of need are profoundly blind to their destructive effects on these essential functions of the earth. The reverse is also a problem: attempts to protect the earth are often blind to their impact on human welfare.

Context   This pattern addresses people whose work involves direct or indirect interactions with the environment, that is, with earth's regenerative systems of all kinds.

Discussion   It is not news that the earth's environment is under assault at all scales, from the planetary (global warming, overfishing, ozone depletion, and the like) to the local (toxic waste sites, extinction of rare species, oil spills, and so on) and everywhere in between. Nor is it news that all of these assaults are intimately entwined with the welfare of human groups or even whole populations. Whether evil masterminds are making the basic decisions (probably negligence is much more often to blame than malevolence), industry and agriculture, together with modes of finance and organization, provide the framework for billions of people to engage in livelihood, child rearing, recreation, even spirituality. This framework cannot be abolished without great suffering.

Fortunately, the nearly four decades since the first Earth Day in 1970 have seen the linking of a mode of thinking—design—and a set of values—sustainability—to seek new ways of building, making products, and providing utilities and services with reduced or no destructive effects on the planet. Examples of this sustainable design include the "living machine" concept for sewage treatment, "green roofs" of soil and plants, and passive solar techniques for managing indoor temperatures.

In a green roof, hardy plants in a layer of soil form the first surface between the weather and the building. Underneath is an impervious layer that does the rest of the waterproofing and keeps roots from growing down into the building. Like a conventional inorganic roof, this assembly protects the building interior from the elements, but it is better in some important ways. The presence of a large planted surface softens the building's appearance and brings nature much closer to hand. Evaporation from plants and soil keeps the roof cooler in summer than normal surfaces, which benefits building occupants and reduces the heat island effect for the surrounding town. The planted layer also protects the impervious surface from solar ultraviolet light and swings of temperature, so it lasts longer.

Green roofs are a particularly clear case of sustainable design. The direct environmental effects on energy, urban air quality, longer life of materials, and the like are positive, and intangible effects such as contact with nature go in good directions as well. Simultaneously, human welfare, at least as understood by the occupants of buildings, is also supported. Sustainability as a set of values accepts human purposes and an inevitable degree of human impact on the rest of nature, even while it hopes to minimize destruction and pollution. Sustainability is a compromise between environmentalism and economic development.

Design enters the picture because sustainability has never been conceived in terms that are both concrete and applicable everywhere, and it probably cannot be. The range of environmental and human situations across the planet is too wide, and each situation has too many delicately related variables for any general formula to apply. The discussion of sustainability has identified topics of attention, such as energy, toxic emissions, local production, and resource equity, but it can voice only ideals, not definite rules. To express sustainability in a specific time and place requires a mode of thinking that can synthesize general values like sustainability with local constraints and opportunities. Design is just such a mode. (See the Design Stance pattern (44) for more on this point.)

Sustainable design is much like conventional design, but sustainable values replace novelty, fashion, and mastery of nature as priorities. There are also several important new emphases. Sustainable design is much more open to community involvement than the conventional expert-centered design approach, and it assumes that older traditional practices can contribute much to existing designs. Finding ways to synthesize expert knowledge and community wisdom and bring together traditional and innovative methods are active areas of experiment and investigation.

Sustainable design needs to be integrative in brand-new ways, because such a wide range of environmental and human values in each project needs attention. Whereas an architect could previously draw a form and instruct engineers to find a way to build it and heat it, with everyone relying on cheap energy and industrial materials to permit a solution, sustainable design usually needs to be a team effort from the start, allowing a mutual influence of energy, materials, form, and other considerations. As a simple example, solar energy in the United States calls for a southern orientation, while good access from roads at a given location may call strongly for a northern orientation. Sustainable design does not place one of these values automatically higher than the other: the right integration for the project and its users has to be worked out each time, with relevant voices represented from the beginning.

Taking nature seriously also guides the time perspective of sustainable design. Whereas architects or engineers have often conceived their work as timeless and independent of nature's processes, the sustainable designer understands the work as an intervention in the natural flows of the planet. It creates impacts but also receives them. Even heroic engineering, like the New Orleans system of levees, cannot defy nature indefinitely. And even the most profitable (or most humanitarian) project of the present can inflict enormous costs on the planet, including its people, in the future. Sustainable design does not regard the future as superior to the present, but it regards it as the involuntary heir to what happens now, for good or ill.

Solution   Consider each building or product as a double intervention—in the earth's cycles and processes and simultaneously in the human culture of needs and techniques. Make use of available understanding, both innovative and traditional, both natural and social, to gauge the proper balance of human and nonhuman effects for each intervention. Remember that culture today builds from the work of the past, and future culture will have to build from what the present provides. The ethic of sustainable design is not only that future existence should be possible, but that it should exhibit justice and beauty for humans and for the rest of nature.

Linked patterns   Civic Intelligence (1), Global Citizenship (6), Back to the Roots (13), Antiracism (23), Spiritually Grounded Activism (24), Earth's Vital Signs (26), Whole Cost (28), Indicators (29), Participatory Design (36), Design Stance (44), Sustainability Appraisal (100), Environmental Impact Remediation (124).

Problem Perceived physiological and cultural differences are easily exploited by political elites for the purpose of gaining and maintaining social control. Discrimination and violence are a common consequence of perceiving one group of people as less trustworthy, moral, intelligent, or civilized (and ultimately less human) than another group. Imbalances of power are seen as reflections of individual strength and cultural merit rather than systemic injustice. Efforts toward creating a desirable society continue to be hindered by unquestioned privilege, fear, and prejudice across race, caste, and ethnic divisions.

Context There are few cultures in the world that have not been affected in some way by European concepts of race. In some cases, European colonizers layered race on top of long-standing caste hierarchies or religious prejudices to further subjugate, divide, and control colonized people. In the United States, alliances between blacks and poor whites, for example, were intentionally subverted by elites who bestowed minimal advantages on lower-class whites to prevent class-based uprisings. The historical legacy of long-maintained racial divides and inequalities continues to affect any organization attempting to create a more just and sustainable society, even when racism is not the primary issue that an organization or movement wants to address. As with gender divisions, race, caste, and class hierarchies often intertwine to erode the effectiveness of organizations and their communication, especially when patterns of privilege and bias go unnoticed.

Discussion This pattern has two major dimensions: antiracist awareness and antiracist action.

Awareness begins with seeking a deeper understanding of the multiple ways that racism and race privilege operate in the lives of individuals and organizations. Antiracist books, movies, workshops, lectures, discussions, and observation can all be useful tools for raising awareness. Multicultural history books (e.g., Takaki 1993) or social and economic analysis (e.g., Oliver and Shapiro 1997) can help us see beyond the myth of the melting pot and understand how social structures maintain racial inequity generation after generation. Films like *Banking on Life and Debt* help us understand the international forces that maintain global inequalities built on European colonialism and how those inequities reinforce domestic racism. Reflective essays like *White Privilege and Male Privilege* (McIntosh 1988) can help us see how privileges are bestowed on whites on a daily basis, even when they do not seek racial advantage.

By analyzing social and historical dynamics of power and privilege, we understand why few people reach adulthood without internalizing social hierarchies that shape their unconscious perceptions of one another. At the same time, it is important to become more aware of the possibilities for change and resistance. We must learn about the successes of communities of color that have struggled against racism, and we must learn about interracial solidarity that has aided antiracist efforts at numerous times and places in history.

Armed with a better awareness of the dynamics of racism, members of an organization can become more reflective about their own practices. Developing and maintaining an antiracist consciousness is an ongoing process for most people, but it is especially challenging for members of dominant racial groups. Because information and communication represented in the dominant culture are likely to reinforce the racial status quo, whites in the United States, for example, must take extra care to seek the perspectives of people of color who are critical of mainstream policy, discourse, and ideology.

Action begins with recognition that we are not powerless in the face of institutionalized or interpersonal racism and that challenging racism is both an individual and collective responsibility. Examples of antiracist action are plentiful—from individuals interrupting racist jokes to transnational organizations uniting against contemporary colonialism.

An antiracist orientation can help guide many facets of an organization: outreach practices, service providing, hiring, resource allocation, and group communication, for example. With an antiracist perspective, individuals can work to create organizations that embrace ethnic diversity and model a commitment to racial justice. Organizations whose members are primarily from privileged communities can seek guidance from leaders who represent grassroots organizations in other communities. Groups can form alliances across racial or national boundaries, making shared use of differing access to information, experiential knowledge, economic resources, and political power.

Organizations can promote antiracist solidarity by investigating the racial dimensions of any issues they are working on. For example, antiracist environmentalists have exposed the disproportionate effects of toxic waste on communities of color (see, e.g., Bullard 1996). Information technology activists interested in racial justice have designed projects to accommodate differing needs in differing ethnic communities. Within the antiwar and antiglobalization movements, activists with an antiracist orientation have drawn attention to the role that racist discourse and ideology play in maintaining public support for international policy.

The greatest challenge to antiracism is the discomfort, defensiveness, and animosity that it often engenders among whites (or other racially privileged groups—depending on the context). Rejection often happens when individuals from privileged groups do not see themselves as responsible in any way for the conditions that other racial groups experience. Talking about race privilege and unconscious racial biases can seriously threaten people's positive sense of self. Many people are more comfortable believing that innate characteristics of racial groups cause the problems or successes that each group experiences, and some people even perceive themselves to be discriminated against when members of other racial groups demand social change to alleviate injustices. Whites who are economically disadvantaged (or experience discrimination related to age, gender, sexual orientation, physical ability, or other characteristic) sometimes see antiracism as a denial of their own hardships. In extreme cases, oppressed whites may react so negatively to antiracist critiques that they turn toward white supremacist or neonationalist ideologies to shore up their low self-esteem (see Gilroy 1987 for a critique of British antiracist education of working-class youth). People of color also sometimes oppose antiracist perspectives when they have been convinced by the dominant culture that racism is no longer a significant, institutionalized problem. For people of color, becoming more aware of racism can be particularly painful and disempowering.

In order to be successful, antiracists must recognize the strength of dominant racial attitudes and ideology. Antiracist education and discourse should be geared toward the forms of denial and dismissal that are most common in a particular context. Educational activities should include follow-up support to help people process new, sometimes disturbing, ways of seeing the world. Resources that put a human face on the experience of racial oppression can be particularly useful. Focusing on the shared costs of racism (and the shared benefits of ending it) may be the best way to encourage interracial solidarity. When both whites and people of color recognize that ending racism is in their interests, they begin to see themselves as part of the long history of resistance to racism. This sense of solidarity across time and racial boundaries adds meaning and a sense of hope to the difficult, and sometimes emotionally painful, process of recognizing and challenging race privilege and racism.

Solution   Only by recognizing racism (personal and institutional) and actively challenging it can we hope to overcome the racial divisions that inhibit effective problem solving and weaken progressive movements. An antiracist orientation to social change can help organizations successfully challenge policies and practices that mask power, exploitation, and resource grabbing behind the guise of liberal individualism and national interests.

Linked patterns   Social Dominance Attenuation (4), Sustainable Design (22), Cyberpower (25), Opportunity Spaces (33), Culturally Situated Design Tools (49), Voices of the Unheard (83), Sense of Struggle (104), Power Research (128).

Problem   Some social change agendas and strategies are derived from sacred texts, religious doctrines, and traditional spiritual practices. Grounding public engagement in this way can lead to productive and insightful action, but such efforts are often highly charged. Contemporary societies and communities vary widely in how well they receive such initiatives; a martyr to one group will seem like a dangerous radical to the opposition. Intermingling politics and religion can taint both, leading to false pieties in politics and making mundane the prayers and rituals that were originally spiritual in purpose.

Context   Groups and individuals seeking to structure social agendas have to create a sense of their purpose, and spiritual convictions often offer constructive guidance. Activists can find allies in the public debate by framing their position in religious terms. Personal resilience can be sustained by strong religious belief. Constitutional separations between church and state in North America and Europe are decidedly ambiguous about whether and how particular congregations should participate in public affairs. Other societies, notably those Muslim ones that base their law and the state itself on religious doctrines and sacred texts, can find secular ethical criteria offensive. Furthermore, activism motivated by religion is often denounced as extremist by those whose motivations are strongly secular.

Discussion   This pattern is illustrated by a series of historical examples intended to suggest its scope. The possibilities are many and varied. Read these stories while remembering that secular organizing can be just as powerful, legitimate, and insightful.

Gandhi practiced and advocated Ahimsa, the nonviolent struggle for truth, inspiring his part of the anticolonialist movement to center on that strategy. Derived from Hindu tradition, Ahimsa applied to all features of their lives, from confrontations with the British to the ways they lived and ate and worked together. Martin Luther King Jr., working within the Christian tradition, was able to find religious inspiration for a similar approach to nonviolence in the U.S. civil rights movement. Thich Nhat Hanh and his fellow Buddhist monks used self-suffering in the Gandhian tradition to oppose the war in Vietnam. All three movements followed a religious injunction against doing violence, although in each it was recognized that they themselves might die. The strategy continues in use at the state level in the struggle between Tibetans under the leadership of the Dalai Lama and the Chinese government.

For centuries Catholic nuns, monks, and brothers have been engaged in providing health care, hospitality, and basic succor to the poor and needy. In recent years, that work gained worldwide recognition as a result of Mother Teresa's order in India. Their practice, like the nonviolence movement, is both a strategic imperative and an injunction for activists to live a certain way, in this case sharing poverty and privation with those they help.

For the past fifty years, women's reproductive systems and rights have been at the center of a wide range of conflicts. Papal encyclicals and local health center policies are alike in their ability to stimulate confrontations about contraception and abortion. In parts of Africa, religious traditions have been the basis for both challenges to and support for female genital mutilation, referred to by Africans as circumcision. Religion, life, and birth have always been linked. The relationships between medicine and religion have become quite uneasy, as much at the end of life as at the beginning.

Debt and monetary interest payments mark another area where religions have guided and inspired action on the global scale. The Christian notion of Jubilee provided the doctrinal basis for groups around the globe to press the largest banks and richest nations to support debt relief for poorer nations in the Jubilee 2000 campaign. Meanwhile, working from the Buddhist perspective, writers and activists have begun to reconfigure the definition of wealth and materialism.

Sacred environmentalism is well rooted around the world. Connected in the United States to the transcendentalists of the nineteenth century, this movement has found a responsive reaction in many areas since place and sacred experience are so often linked.

At their best, religious practices serve not only to shape the mission but also to guide organizational behavior. Silent retreat or a prayer meeting can offer respite from the mundane. Singing together, marching together, or sitting quietly in Quaker meeting together can strengthen the sense of community. Charitable giving, cooking for the poor, and visiting prisoners can feel like religious practices when inspired by a spiritually grounded activism. Priests, imams, and other religious leaders offering blessings over an action can ease the qualms and concerns of their followers. In all of these ways, organizational resilience gains support from adherence to a religious or spiritual path. Marshall Ganz (2003) reminds us to see religion "not only as a source of "understanding" about what was right but also as a source of the solidarity, willingness to sacrifice, anger at injustice, and courage and leadership to take action—in other words, not only of moral understanding but the capacity to act on that understanding—or, as St. Augustine said, not only of "knowing the good" but also of "loving it" enough to act on it."

The stories in this pattern were chosen to illustrate constructive work undertaken by adherents in a variety of traditions. These same traditions have of course often been the basis for cruel, intolerant and self-righteous oppression, government and justice.

Solution   Remember the hymns and prayers of the American civil rights movement, which exemplify ways that a healing religious practice can build solidarity among activists while holding them to laudable ethical standards. Several injunctions are embedded in this pattern. By all means, ground your own work in the values, the mysteries, and the heritage of a religious community. At the same time, hesitate to judge others whose motives and practices are different. If secular values justify and guide your actions, assume the best of those driven to act by religious convictions, and if you are religious, give credence to the secular. In either case, remember that ritual, whether sacred or secular, can strengthen bonds among organizers and provide them with the respite necessary to keeping on with the work of change.

Linked patterns   The Good Life (3), Social Responsibility (8), Memory and Responsibility (11), Demystification and Reenchantment (14), Sustainable Design (22), Peace Education (56), Citizen Diplomacy (93), Sense of Struggle (104), Everyday Heroism (116), Retreat (136).

25 Cyberpower

Problem   The inability to send e-mail or browse the Web in the age of the Internet is comparable to using an "X" for a signature in the age of print. Many people and communities are still catching up to the information age and discovering what digital tools have to offer, which in a word is cyberpower, that is, power in cyberspace (Alkalimat and Williams 2001). The usefulness of this term can be understood in comparison to another expression: e-commerce. E-commerce began as a term summarizing the interactions of businesses, coders, and consumers. On the basis of that idea, many more people were encouraged to participate, which strengthened the advances in e-commerce. Millions of people now buy and sell online, with the goods delivered in the real world. Our experience with the word cyberpower is much the same: the word came into use based on practical experience, then mobilized more people to exercise their cyberpower. As with e-commerce, when people wield cyberpower, the "goods"—power—are delivered in the real world, in a cycle from actual to virtual to actual.

Context   Digital inequality often has an impact on the same people as older inequalities such as poverty, oppression, discrimination, and exclusion. The new tools, however, are so powerful that the inability to use them sets individuals, groups, and communities even further back. Hardware and software continue to evolve, and only those who are able to use them can guide their current application and shape their future development. And a global conversation is taking place online every day. Those who are being talked about but cannot answer need cyberpower.

Discussion   Digital inequalities persist even as technology evolves, becomes more broadly available, and costs less. The reality for certain populations is restricted or no access, lower levels of skill, a lack of support, or relatively irrelevant tools and resources. How are we to maintain democracy if core conversations and the wealth of information sources are all online, but not everyone is able to participate or even observe? Recent calls for a dialogue of civilizations, starting with the United Nations (1998), rather than a clash of civilizations (Huntington 1988) could be taking place online, but only if everyone can see, hear, and speak in cyberspace.

Although it is not yet well understood, communities in crisis—from poverty, disaster, war, or other adversities—are known to turn to technology for response and recovery. Cell phones, impromptu cybercafés, and the Internet all assisted in the recovery from the Gulf hurricane. Farmers on quarantined farms quickly mastered use of the Internet in their homes during England's foot-and-mouth disease outbreak. The U.S. armed forces now strategize in terms of land, sea, air, and cyberspace. Immigrants all over the world have created digital diasporas (Miller and Slater 2000). Whatever language people use to describe it, cyberpower is the driver in all these cases.

Hip-hop can be seen as a technology-based response to crisis and a cyberpower project. Participants in a community-based seminar created a CD of original rap about information technology. Students and community members were skeptical—one said, "We do not know anything about computers"—but all the music was digitally made, the tools were gathered in bedrooms and basements, and the result was a compilation of fifteen tracks (http:// www.toledohiphop.org/reboot). Here is an example of lyrics by S. Supreme, the lyricist for one of the REBOOT CD tracks, who at the time was a student and community member:

Information technology
Skipping the Black community with no apology
Flipping the power off
On an already alarming deficit,
So please, please, PLEASE, PASS THE MESSAGE KID!
Ohh Umm Diddy Dum Dum
If he do not turn his Ice off
And turn his head past the gas of Microsoft
He'll really be lost like the tribe, 'cause the time is now and that's a bet
How you throwing up a set and you ain't on the Net,
Yet you say you're a G?
I said I'm not Chuck D, but welcome to the terror
If you ain't ready to build in this information era
Survival of the fittest, our rights get diminished, cats be on their Crickets
But do not know about Linux

This track reflects the use of cyberpower to speak about cyberpower.

Another example of cyberpower is the experience with a proposed auction of Malcolm X's papers. When the sale, planned for March 2002, was discovered online, thousands protested online and the sale was stopped. The process began when an eBay auction house, Butterfields, was about to sell thousands of pages of Malcolm X's diaries and notes, recovered from a storage locker, for an expected price of $500,000. This news was distributed across multiple communities of scholars, librarians, activists, and others using the H-Afro-Am listserv. The American Library Association then released a story on its online news site, which is linked to more sites and individuals. The next day, the *New York Times* published a story. On the third day the *Guardian* newspaper ran a story about the impending sale and the online groundswell opposing it. The listservs and the news articles alerted the family and the Schomburg Center for Research in Black Culture at the New York Public Library, and they were able to negotiate the postponing of the sale and its ultimate cancellation. An agreement was negotiated with the seller to place the materials in the possession of the family and be housed at the Schomburg's archives. To summarize, important historical papers (actual) were being auctioned (virtual); thousands of people were mobilized (virtual); traditional media carried the story (virtual and actual); and ultimately the materials were withdrawn from sale and placed intact in a public library archive for scholars and the public (actual).

Another example of cyberpower is told by Mele (1999). Faced with the prospective demolition of their housing project, tenants in Wilmington, North Carolina, wrangled the key to a long-locked community room and Internet access through a single computer (actual), and using e-mail and listservs (virtual) recruited architects and planners to help them obtain regulations and other legal documents, understand the issues, and address the developer and housing officials. They won a seat at the negotiating table and, more important, key changes to the demolition plan that included interim and long-term housing for residents.

All sorts of new tools for exercising cyberpower are in wide use, including MySpace, blogs, wikis, and YouTube. Any of these tools locates users in a lively community. Putnam's (2000) fear that we are "bowling alone" and not connecting with other people in an atomized world is, as Lin (2001) asserted, may ultimately be trumped by the fact that we are not computing alone.

Solution   *Cyberpower* refers to two related activities related to empowerment: (1) individuals, groups, and organizations using digital tools for their own goals and (2) using digital tools as part of community organizing. The general idea is that people can use cyberpower in virtual space to get power in actual space. Cyberorganizers help people acquire cyberpower just as community organizers help empower communities.

Linked patterns   Social Dominance Attenuation (4), Antiracism (23), Whole Cost (28), Opportunity Spaces (33), Culturally Situated Design Tools (49), Accessibility of Online Information (75), Mobile Information and Computer Technology Learning Facilities (77), Citizen Journalism (91), Power Research (128).

Problem Society's great scientific capacity to measure and interpret the world and the role of humans in nature has failed to translate into improved environmental stewardship. Modern environmental challenges that threaten global consequences are often difficult to see and distant in time and space from their sources. The increasing complexity and chronic rather than acute nature of today's environmental problems requires a revolution of decision making: the systematic integration of earth's vital signs.

Context Signals detected by scientists about earth's natural patterns and processes and the impacts of humans on these processes are earth's signs—indicators of what can be seen as either ecological health or the capacity of the earth to accommodate human demands. The conditions of the earth's systems tend to be worsening on a global scale but vary dramatically from place to place. Human decisions about how to live on earth drive these trends and can potentially reverse their negative directions. Policymakers, public interest organizations, universities, and governments can use earth's signs to better manage human and environmental well-being. Policymakers' decisions about sustainable practices in land- and resource-dependent sectors can be backed by scientific understanding about the effects of policies on resources. Citizens can demand better environmental stewardship from their leaders at local and global scales with improved access to and translation of relevant earth information at the proper scale. Governments and enforcement bodies can strengthen their monitoring capabilities and base development decisions on the latest information about trends in human impacts on earth.

Discussion   Three distinct approaches to integrating earth's vital signs come from the scientific community, public interest organizations, and enforcement bodies.

Scientific institutions can collaborate to reach audiences in need of earth-related information to solve problems. The work of earth observation agencies to collect and disseminate data and images to important users like humanitarian aid agencies provides one example. Disaster prevention, response, and rebuilding are information intensive. This fact is illustrated time and time again in the wake of natural disasters. For example, in Asia in 2005, an immediate need emerged in tsunami-affected areas for earth observation and environmental data to help in assessing damage, reaching victims, and rebuilding resilient communities. In response to this need, an alliance of European and international organizations is working with the humanitarian community to improve access to maps, satellite imagery, and geographic information (the CGIAR Consortium for Spatial Information 2004). This kind of effort by the scientific community to ensure that this information is widely available opens a host of possibilities for more sustainable decision making if scientists in other fields can repeat it. Scientists from communities researching water, pollution, and future risks from global warming could create similar initiatives to ensure the information that they gather becomes integrated in decision making in water-scarce areas, in clean water and air policies, and for promoting climate change adaptation in development strategies, to name a few.

Another way earth's signs are integrated into decision making is by concerned public interest groups and universities in gathering, translating, and communicating trends that reflect environmental sustainability to motivate improved environmental governance. The outcomes of resource and land management policies such as energy, fisheries, forests, water, urban planning, and rural development can be extrapolated from existing environmental data. A key challenge, however, is translating scientific information to connect to the public and policymakers. In examples from around the world, organizations locate data reflecting the condition of affected resources, create indicators of stewardship or sustainability from these data, and translate their findings into insightful measurements, models, and maps that are publicly available and understandable to broader audiences. Clarifying the connections between political and business decisions and environmental outcomes can promote environmentally sustainable decisions and reverse negative trends if decision makers are held accountable to these indicators. Scorecards of environmental performance (Environmental Performance Index, Millennium Challenge Corporation 2006), policy-wise ecological assessments (Hudson River Foundation 2008), and regional indicators and indexes of sustainability (Cascadia Scorecard, Sightline Institute 2007) have the potential to become a systematic part of policymaking if leaders are held accountable for their performance on these measures of earth's vital signs. Currently information is not available at the right scales and frequently enough for such assessments to be carried in every context, but an increase in reporting has been proven to stimulate better information gathering.

Earth monitoring information has also been used by enforcement agencies, environmental organizations, and governments to improve accountability for the environmental impacts of business practices. Satellite imagery and other sources of management practices can be used to monitor natural resources on public lands, in protected areas, in human settlements, and other areas. One example comes from an initiative in Central Africa's Congo Basin, an important wood products exporting region to Europe (Global Forest Watch, World Resources Institute 2008). European procurement standards are the highest in the world, and buyers often demand legally and sustainably harvested wood from their suppliers. A system to monitor the legality and sustainability of forestry operations has emerged that uses satellite imagery, tracking whether harvested areas conform to legally agreed boundaries and harvest rates. By making the findings publicly accessible, consumers use the information in procurement decisions, and market pressure can promote better management by companies. Similar innovative applications of earth information can capitalize on market forces and encourage sustainable resource management if public concern is tangible.

Solution   Integrating earth's signs throughout decision making requires that environmental information is widely available, connections between management practices and environmental outcomes are understood, environmental implications of policies are translated to the public and policymakers, and the environmental performance of governments and companies is publicly disseminated. Replication of existing initiatives and further innovations can help to ensure that decision making balances human impacts with the health of the planet.

Linked patterns   Civic Intelligence (1), Back to the Roots (13), Sustainable Design (22), Indicators (29), Citizen Science (37), Meaningful Maps (47), Emergency Communication Systems (121).

Problem   Health information cannot focus solely on individual change. Many detriments to health cannot be eradicated without changes to the physical and social world that people inhabit. If environmental and social changes are necessary for people to get well, individual patients cannot do so solely by seeking health care and avoiding health risks. Expert medical information and advice is inadequate to create a healthy environment that creates healthy people.

Context   Poor people bear a disproportionate burden of global ill health, such as diabetes, malaria, HIV/AIDS, and tuberculosis. Health discrepancies between rich and poor will not be solved through better access to information alone. Good food, less stress, clean air and water, and a life with a purpose will increase health and healthy behaviors. Real change to improve health comes from a shift away from acknowledging only expert clinical opinion and toward a real-world awareness of the effect of environment on health: a shift from passive diagnosis and treatment to active engagement with the causes of and solutions to health problems.

Discussion   We are not, for the most part, born unhealthy. We become unhealthy. And even for those born unhealthy, a great deal of ill health may have been preventable. The campaign to find the cure for breast cancer is a good example of health information that neglects any causal connection between ill health and the environment (in this instance, an environment that includes the use of estrogen in prescription medication), and ignores political or social change that might address environmental causes of the disease. This pattern of information, in which action comes only after the individual becomes ill while nothing has been done to prevent illness in first place, focuses on individual responsibility with no questioning of the established social order. The unspoken message is that breast cancer just happens. It is up to the individual to get involved with a screening program for early detection and treatment. Information on research that investigates environmental effects to the development of breast cancer is not part of mainstream health information.

Public health information about diabetes further illustrates the lack of emphasis on the connection between environment and health. Among Native Americans, diabetes (like most other noninfectious chronic diseases) was virtually unknown before World War II. Now, in some tribes, over 60 percent of adults have diabetes, and the age of onset is decreasing with each generation. Much of the research on diabetes among Native Americans focuses on genetic causes or molecular-level differentiations of diabetic types. It gives short shrift to how the disruption in traditional diet and lifestyle and the devaluation of traditional medicine correspond with the dramatic increase in the disease. The connection of indigenous people to the environment that they come from, the types of foods they eat, and activities they perform to prepare those foods are not considered an active component in their health.

Diabetic health information focuses on what the individual can do to access mainstream diets and medicine. It does not validate traditional knowledge that prevented diabetes in the past and ignores how the community as a whole can work together to recreate that knowledge. This does not mean trying to reestablish life as it was sixty years ago, but it does mean putting the current problem in a holistic context that includes history, indigenous knowledge, the interaction between diet and environment, and reasons for lack of access to even nontraditional healthy food.

In 1854, John Snow removed the handle from a London neighborhood water pump that was located a few feet from a sewer (UCLA Department of Epidemiology 2006). He believed that this sewage was causing the epidemic of cholera deaths in the neighborhood. Epidemiology textbooks emphasize Snow's connection of cause and effect as the first public health intervention of the modern era. They ignore an analysis of cause: industrialization and dislocation, poverty, and overcrowding, for example. What options for water did people in the neighborhood have without the pump? Seldom mentioned is that due to the demand of a thirsty public, the handle was replaced six weeks after its removal.

Public health programs must include methods to share power with communities they hope to help. What are the contributors to ill health in their communities? What are the barriers to good health that the communities identify? Information needs to realistically address what is within the control of the individual and what will take groups of people working together to solve. Methods to improve health in disadvantaged communities must reflect the larger social change and shift in power needed.

Health information such as in *Fast Food Nation* (Schlosser 2002) needs to be the norm, not the exception. This book chronicles the entire environment that produces fast food, including social norms and values. Similarly, the documentary film *Life and Debt* shows the destruction of healthy, local food production in Jamaica by the combination of multinational food businesses and international government policy.

Health information needs to do more than simply inform. What does not question the existing state of affairs will not, for example, bring affordable nutritious food to poor neighborhoods and will not create safe neighborhoods in areas where children have no place to exercise. Better access to information may improve health care decisions to some extent; but unless it also generates momentum and optimism for social change, it simply perpetuates a focus on individual behavior and treatment of symptoms that have already occurred. Health information needs to look honestly at the conditions that cause ill health and engage not only those who suffer illness but the entire social and regulatory apparatus that can play a role in improving the conditions that people live in.

Solution   Demand and produce health information that identifies environmental and social causes of ill health. Analyze the interconnection between these causes and their solutions, and bring individuals, communities, and governments together in putting the solutions into effect. If the struggle with disease includes a struggle with established power, the possibility of ultimate success is increased considerably.

Linked patterns   The Commons (2), Health as a Universal Right (5), Indicators (29), Public Agenda (30), Big Tent for Social Change (32), Citizen Science (37), Mutual Help Medical Web Sites (54), Powerful Remittances (73), Positive Health Information (74), Civic Capabilities (85), Strategic Frame (86), Shared Vision (101), Power Research (128).

Problem   Through the clothes we buy, the food we eat, the cars we drive, the way we dispose of our trash or sewage, where and how we live, and how we make a living or spend time in recreation, people every day and everywhere make impacts—large and small, good and bad—on the world. Many of the problems in the world are compounded by people who are unaware of the damage they are inadvertently perpetuating through their daily lives. They are probably determining the costs in overly simplistic ways such as immediate monetary costs or the seeming convenience of using plastic eating utensils.

Not only are these problems debilitating to people in less developed countries who are often the people who first experience the costs (thus presenting moral and ethical challenges to their more fortunate brethren), they also have an uncanny way of ultimately affecting developed countries as well; for example, over 20 percent of the air pollution in the Pacific Northwest region of the United States has blown in from China. If people had a better idea of what the entire costs of their actions were—not just their own personal costs at that moment—there is a higher likelihood that they would change their behavior to encourage positive changes and discourage negative ones.

Context   People in developed countries are always buying things, often from developing countries, and are generally unaware of the particulars of the product's life-cycle before and after they owned it. People may be morally opposed, for example, to the child labor that went into, say, a pair of athletic shoes, yet they implicitly condone the practice with their purchase. Would consumers change their behavior if they know the "whole cost" or if they actually had to bear more of the "true cost?" And, if yes, how should society employ this concept? One economic point of view suggests that the whole cost should be reflected in the price tag, but this is rarely possible. Many of the costs are impossible to put a number on, and they may even differ depending on the point of view of different people. What is the true cost of taking away a wetland used by geese on their migration, for example? This pattern incorporates in some sense common economic tenets but transcends simplistic economic reasoning.

Discussion   In an increasingly globalized world, people are connected to each other in ways that are often unknown to each other. One of the main ways that people in developed countries and less developed countries are linked is through products. When a person in a developed country buys clothing, consumer electronics, or other items, all the buyer sees is a purchase price. Missing is the entire chain that was effectuated in order to place that product within purchasing range and its enduring effects on the environment. Often the price on the product obscures a sordid legacy that could include child labor, environmental abuse such as pesticides in groundwater, air pollution or soil depletion, or aspects that are harder to quantify, like migration of youth to urban areas or loss of cultural heritage.

One of the basic uses of this pattern is understanding the whole cost of an object or a service that one is purchasing. Ultimately the intent of this pattern is identifying the whole cost of something and using the information that a single price obscures to promote broader public consciousness and ultimately improved social good. There are a great number of ways that the information can be used—and a great number of ways left to be discovered. Ideally the information behind the price tag will take on greater significance while the price tag itself can also be made to reflect the previously hidden information more accurately, including, for example, labeling that tag to include information about contents or relevant environmental effects or labor practices.

Understanding the whole cost is primarily a process of education that can be done individually (by people of virtually any age) or in more public ways. This understanding can be through a narrative or story, or it can be more quantified, including, for example, information about who got paid how much for what work at every step in the chain. One approach is using the origin of the product as an indicator and not buying a product, for example, if it were made by nonunion, child, or slave labor or because it was produced by a repressive regime.

A more nuanced process with a distinctively quantitative feel is illustrated by the work done by the International Center for Technology Assessment in its report, "The Real Price of Oil" (Harrje, Bricker, and Kallio 1998). In that report based on gasoline prices from a U.S. perspective, the authors reveal how ultimately deceptive the idea of the price at the pump is to the actual monetary cost expressed in a specific currency, dollars, for example. And while their approach, like other economically based approaches, ignores (or at least reinterprets) the human story, it goes a long way toward developing and ultimately using a unitary price as a meaningful attachment to a commodity or service available for purchase. In the case of gasoline, the authors show how multiple government subsidies to oil companies (huge tax breaks, direct support for research development and other business costs, and "protection subsidies," often of a military nature) and a multitude of externalities (problems as diverse as air pollution, automobile crashes, suburban sprawl and climate change that are costs the oil industry is not going to address and are not reflected in any way by the price one pays at the pump) result in a public price tag for gasoline that distorts the real price by five to fifteen times. The "free" television programming that occupies so much of the time of the U.S. citizenry shows another perversion of the ideas of price and costs. The various offerings of course are not free at all—at least not to the viewers (and nonviewers), who pay for the ads every time they purchase something advertised on television. (Television's role in the decline in social capital [Putnam 2000] and the overall "dumbing down" of society [Morgan 2002] also raise the whole cost of electronic addiction.)

A simple use of the information (at least in the gasoline case) would be to eliminate or otherwise lower the government subsidies—especially the ones that hurt the environment and lead to wars and other problems and let the price creep (or leap) up to the actual price, or at least closer to it. This at the least would test the citizenry's commitment to the automobile in a fair comparison with competing approaches to transportation. A related approach is un-externalizing the externalities by bringing the costs back home to the companies that are making them possible. This can be done by imposing a green tax on the companies, which would be used to help try to reverse the damage caused by the company's business practices. Unfortunately, as Peter Dorman (personal communication, December 3, 2006) explains, "There is a general distrust of the effectiveness of government, a fear that green taxes will be more regressive than some of our current ones. The alternative is the creation of environmental trusts, which would collect the money on behalf of the beneficiaries, which could include current people, future people and natural entities. The trust would pay back some of the money directly (per capita rebates) and also finance ecological conversion. Vermont and Massachusetts are in the process of setting up a trust of this sort for carbon, and New York and California are possibly going this route too."

The city of San Francisco showed another innovative use of the whole cost concept. In the spring of 2005, San Francisco became the first city in the United States to enact legislation requiring the city to consider environmental and health implications when making purchases for the city. Since the city spends about $600 million every year on a multitude of purchases (including, for example, 87,000 fluorescent light tubes), this type of legislation could conceivably have some effect, especially since city officials are hoping that the Environmentally Preferable Purchasing for Commodities Ordinance will serve as model for other cities. The city is working with community groups, technical experts, and other city staff to establish criteria. Debbie Raphael, the city's toxics reduction program manager, stated, "Traditionally, we have a list of specifications we use to decide which computer to buy. Those specifications do not include things like how much lead is in them? Can you recycle them? What is their energy use? What it does not mean is that cost and performance is ignored. We're expanding the universe of criteria" (Gordon 2005).

A final use of the whole cost pattern is to consider the whole cost in more of a global way. Looking just in the area of health reveals the importance of this approach. In "The Price of Life," Glennerster, Kremer, and Williams (2005) point out that Africa "generates less than one half of 1 percent of sales by global pharmaceutical firms but accounts for nearly 25 percent of the world's disease burden." The lion's share of pharmaceutical research and development is for the health (and cosmetic) problems of rich countries. Sadly the economic equations of the world's corporations exclude the vast majority of world's population. Lacking money, the whole costs that they bear do not show up on any balance sheet or business plan.

Solution   The first thing to realize is that the price one sees on a price tag is rarely the whole cost. The second is that knowing the whole cost of a good or service is educational as well as inspirational. People have been innovative in this area, but there is room for much more. It is important to publicize the whole cost of a product, as well as the monetary price. This could include what percentage of the monetary price goes to workers and other costs to the environment, quality of life, and other important factors. All people need to live consciously in this world, and having better information about the effects they have on it can play a key role in this.

Linked patterns   Health as a Universal Right (5), Dematerialization (18), Fair Trade (21), Sustainable Design (22), Cyberpower (25), Public Agenda (30), Economic Conversion (41), Alternative Progress Indexes (46), Durable Assets (58), Community Currencies (63), Environmental Impact Remediation (124), Follow the Money (135).

Problem Citizens are often bystanders in their own lives. Research, even that which is putatively conducted in their behalf, is often irrelevant or even damaging to the livelihoods of ordinary people and marginalized groups alike. Since it is intended to promote academic aims, such as publication in an academic journal, rather than community goals, the idea of actual benefit based on the results of the research often takes a back seat. This lack of genuine community involvement or connection helps lead to the self-perpetuating cycle of citizen disempowerment.

Context This pattern could be used in any situation in which citizens need to come together to better understand complex dynamic situations and develop meaningful responses. This pattern can be used in a focused or more distributed way; it can be used as the basis for a long-term project or a project of short duration.

Discussion "We view the process and product as interwoven and equally valuable. Part of our task is to practice and develop the skills of civic democracy and volunteer participation," writes Richard Conlin, Sustainable Seattle cofounder (Sustainable Seattle 1995).

Doctors take a patient's temperature to help get an understanding of the person's general health. Although this is only one measure among numerous other possible measurements, it is judged to be important enough, and acquired easily enough, to warrant its use. An indicator is typically a single measure that can be acquired over time to help ascertain the general health or condition of a larger, more complex entity, like a lake, city, or society. It helps serve by being a stand-in or proxy for that whole.

Indicators are often devised and used by scientists, economists, and other professionals to help inform them about the status of what is important to them. And just as the medical community has selected temperature as one indicator among many possibilities, these professionals have selected theirs. Like other measurements, these can have far-reaching consequences, which basically depend on how they are interpreted, what meaning is ascribed to them, and what is done with them. Communities, especially those that are struggling to stay alive, generally play no direct role in the development of these indicators and rarely design their own.

In 1991, a group of social activists in Seattle launched an ambitious multiyear project around the idea of sustainability. Though many people today view sustainability as largely an environmental paradigm, it is one that can capture the long-term cultural, economic, civic, and educational health and vitality of a region as well. Because *sustainability* is a complex term and difficult to define and comprehend, the first goal was the development of a set of critical indicators of sustainability that would assist in defining the term and Seattle's general status.

Since that time the project has matured into a community-wide program divided evenly into research and community action. One commendable aspect of this effort has been the patient, evolving, consensus-driven manner in which the project has taken shape and unfolded over time without being driven by set agendas.

When the project was launched, the indicators of sustainability were designed to form its intellectual and motivational foundation. Indicators are measurable values that accurately reflect and incorporate several factors deemed to be important. The selection of indicators as core constructs of the endeavor demonstrates the founders' commitment to a long-term rather than a quick-fix effort, for it is only by examining how the values of the indicators change over time that an understanding of trends can arise. Examining changes over time may also help identify relationships between indicators. Two indicators, for example, may actually bear inverse relationships to each other.

When people in the community identify indicators that are important to them, the indicators are more likely to carry personal and operational meaning than when social scientists in an ivory tower identify theoretical constructs that are significant only to an academic community. The indicators are carefully chosen to reflect activities within a community that are desired or not desired by that community. Furthermore, because the community identified the indicators, there is a feeling of ownership and confidence in them.

While Sustainable Seattle's report on Seattle's critical indicators presents a useful snapshot of several important aspects on the community's agenda, it does not by itself create a sustainable society. According to its newsletter (Sustainable Seattle 1994), "Understanding trends in our community is only the first step in the journey toward sustainability. The next step is to change the community." To that end, Sustainable Seattle initiated a community outreach project "to create measurable improvements in the behaviors and practices that drive the indicators, both on large and small scales, as a result of homes and organizations changing their behavior in response to this project." Its ambitious goal "is to enable and inspire people in the many different communities in greater Seattle to transform the values of sustainability into actions that will move Seattle, the region, and the planet toward long-term cultural, economic, and environmental health and vitality."

The Worldwatch Institute identified and assessed fifty social, economic, and environmental trends that it labeled the earth's "vital signs" (see pattern 26) to help show the important role consumers can play in demanding environmentally friendly products. Indicators can also be used in international or other large-scale collaborative projects. A new international effort between the United States and Canada that monitors the health of Puget Sound Georgia Basin, where salmon and orcas are endangered in Washington State and in the province of British Columbia, shows another use of indicators (Stiffler 2006). Of the nine indicators that the project has established, five of them are declining (Urbanization and Forest Change; River, Stream and Lake Quality; Marine Species at Risk; Toxics in Harbor Seals; and Marine Water Quality); the remaining four have not shown progress (Population Health;

Solid Waste and Recycling, Shellfish; and Air Quality). Scott Redman from the U.S. team stated that the indicator project "puts pressure then for us to catch up, or the other way around." There is a Web site (http://www.epa.gov/region10/psgb/indicators) that includes data as well as a large number of suggestions for people and groups that want to help improve the situation.

The *Bulletin of Atomic Scientists* through its "Doomsday Clock" offers a variant on this concept. The clock measures the state of worldwide nuclear danger (not just from a U.S. perspective) and graphically reports its findings on a clock whose hands are approaching midnight—nuclear apocalypse. Moving the hands is not taken lightly. "Because the Doomsday Clock is the world's most visible symbol of nuclear danger, any decision to reset it is taken with great care and only after significant deliberation by the *Bulletin*'s board of directors, in consultation with the board of sponsors" ("It is 5 minutes to midnight" 2005). It is interesting to note the infrequency within which the clock has been reset: seventeen times in fifty-six years. The two boards reset the hands infrequently to demonstrate significant developments; the clock does not respond "to every change in the global security environment. If it did, it would be in almost constant motion and would lose much if not all of its symbolic resonance.

Many of the patterns in this pattern language, including this one, could be used as indicator generators. What indicators, for example, could be used to show whether humankind's civic intelligence (pattern 1) is increasing or decreasing? Virtually any area, conceptual or actual, could be a source of indicators. And in any area, it will be important to think of what possible actions could come after the indicators are developed before they are identified. What to do with information? Who could use the information? What resonance could the information have with various people and groups?

Solution   Citizens should construct indicators that measure what is important to them. The values of these indicators should be readily obtainable. Then, with the values of the indicators in hand, citizens can publish them, discuss them, analyze them, publicize them, and develop policy and projects that address them. Indicator projects seem to be best coordinated through organizations and groups.

Linked patterns   Collective Decision Making (10), Sustainable Design (22), Earth's Vital Signs (26), Big-Picture Health Information (27), Public Agenda (30), Citizen Science (37), Alternative Progress Indexes (46), Meaningful Maps (47), Citizen Access to Simulations (48), Community Currencies (63), Ethics of Community Informatics (67), Grassroots Public Policy Development (78), Users' Information Technology Quality Network (80), Citizenship Schools (96), Self-Designed Development (106), Emergency Communication Systems (121), Environmental Impact Remediation (124).

Problem   At any given time, there are a few issues that are receiving public attention. These issues change dramatically from day to day, offering the public very little time to think about one issue before another one takes its place. In addition to the manic novelty, the stories offer little real information, especially about alternatives or opportunities for public involvement. Even the "news" is entertainment. In the United States (and other places) the market is credited with or blamed for "giving the people what they want." Thus while television and other commercial media command the attention of people for a large percentage of their nonworking, nonsleeping hours, the owners merely shrug their shoulders and say that they are just giving people what they want. This turns out often to be grisly murders, cheesy voyeurism, celebrity romance (or, better, infidelity and divorce), and advertisements. In less free societies, the governing elites make all decisions about what is news and governmental misdeeds are not deemed newsworthy. Who decides what issues are important? What issues are on the public agenda?

Context   If the public agenda is simply the set of issues that people happen to have in their heads at any given time, then we can say that a public agenda exists. If the public agenda consists of issues that ought to be considered in a public way, particularly how society uses limited resources and what is truly important, then the public agenda today is a far cry from it could be.

Discussion   During a 1999 interview on the local Seattle public radio affiliate, a woman who was involved in the demonstrations against the World Trade Organization in Seattle was asked "why it was necessary to break glass" to get the issues on the public agenda. She first mentioned that she and her colleagues had been trying unsuccessfully to get these issues on the public agenda for a decade and that she was opposed to using violence against people or property. She went on to say, however, that one could not help but notice that after windows were smashed in Seattle, the media, pundits, and others seemed to acknowledge the issues more readily—at least for a week or so. Nevertheless, it should not be necessary to break glass for citizens and citizen groups to get a public airing for the issues that they feel are important.

   Where do the "pictures in our heads" (Lippmann 1921) and the issues that we are contemplating at the moment come from? Certainly we are all free to come up with something that is all our own, but this is not likely to be commonplace. When we see something, something else in our mind is triggered. We may interpret the information in our particular way, but the new information, not something else, is the driver. Yet it is not the idiosyncratic and disconnected thought that is important; it is the focused, diverse, engaged, and thoughtful collective mind that democracy requires. The sounds and the images that the big electronic billboard, always there and always on, holds aloft for the world to view will obviously garner more attention ("mind share") than something with less visibility, which, of course, is every-thing else. The press, as Bernard Cohen (1963) points out, "may not be successful much of the time in telling people what to think, but it is stunningly successful in telling it is readers what to think about."

Maxwell McCombs and Donald Shaw (1972) proffered the notion that the mass media are instrumental in agenda setting. They demonstrated that the public's answers to the peren-nial Gallup Poll question, "What is the most important problem facing this country today?" could be predicted quite clearly by looking at the news as presented by the newspapers, net-work television news, and news magazines published in the month prior to the poll. More recently, McCombs (2002) reported that since the original article, "more than 300 published studies worldwide have documented this influence of the news media."

Now, some thirty-five years after McCombs and Shaw wrote, the media landscape has changed considerably. People (at least in the United States) have more choices, and many apparently choose to be ill informed. The mass media with their collage of seemingly ran-dom information about celebrity divorces, dog food, genocide, game shows, laugh tracks, mass starvation, cell phones, climate change, "shock jocks," trailer fires, bus plunges, talking heads, celebrity chitchat, and invasions may be actually doing more to muddle than to inform.

The Internet is providing an interesting challenge to the hegemony of the mass media. Community networks and Indymedia show glimpses that other ways of producing and con-suming news are possible. The explosion of blogs of every type is the latest salvo along these lines. In fact, as of the end of the 2003, two-thirds of the blogs were political (Delwiche 2005). The blogging phenomenon suggests many things, including the blurring of the divi-sion between producers and consumers of journalism and the continuing fragmentation of journalism roles and venues. Some of the more interesting questions, explored by Aaron Delwiche (2005), are whether the blogs are or can be agenda setters in their own right and whether they can serve as a tonic and an alternative to mass-produced media.

It would be naive to think the mass media will provide citizens with the information that they need without pressure from the citizenry. They will say first that their first responsibility is their stockholders. And there is certainly a danger (as well as a temptation) to disregard all mass media. The realization that traditional mass media are ready and willing (and generally capable) of diverting attention from the important to the superfluous is a significant first step, but it is just a start. Monitoring the media systems and constructing a broad and com-pelling alternative agenda must be an ongoing enterprise.

Solution   We need to think about what belongs on the public agenda and what we can do to put it there and keep it there. This may mean working in opposition to—and in co-operation with—existing media systems. It must certainly involve developing diverse and specialized public agendas, including ones related to research, as Raffensperger, Peters, and Kirschenmann (1999) advise.

Linked patterns   Health as a Universal Right (5), Matrifocal Orientation (9), Transforming Institutions (19), Big-Picture Health Information (27), Whole Cost (28), Indicators (29), Big Tent for Social Change (32), Citizen Science (37), Strengthening International Law (42), Alternative Progress Indexes (46), Transparency (64), Powerful Remittances (73), Accessibility of Online Information (75), Grassroots Public Policy Development (78), Future Design (88), Citizenship Schools (96), Great Good Place (119), Media Intervention (132).

31 Democratic Political Settings

Problem Democratic political action is difficult where social inequality is great. People low on the social scale are often barred, formally or informally, from political meetings. And in meetings women, poor people, and members of low-status groups often fail to voice their views because they feel vulnerable to reprisals inside and outside the meeting. How can democratic political action be initiated under conditions of marked social inequality?

Context Many governments that give some respect to the rules of electoral democracy silence the voices of people of low economic and social standing. Many meetings where people raise and debate matters of public importance are structured to block their effective participation and reinforce existing hierarchies of class and social standing.

Discussion Even where most political settings are biased against certain people (the poor, women, youth, stigmatized groups, recent immigrants, disabled people), some institutions and cultural values support wider participation. It takes great energy, persistence, and strategic action to expand democratic practice. For example in fishing villages in southern India, the long-established Catholic church, newer fish-worker unions, and women's associations contain values and practices that innovators could use to increase participation by disfavored groups, often by starting new political settings such as neighborhood assemblies. Trying to change formal and informal rules of participation in existing political settings usually runs up against entrenched elite power. New and reformed settings can establish a base of democratic experience for pressing change in older, powerful settings.

Solution Strengthening already democratic settings and starting new democratic settings and organization are ways to sidestep the customs and practices that reinforce the existing social hierarchy. A new setting open to all offers people with little experience of expressing and advocating their ideas and interests an opportunity to gain experience and confidence.

Linked patterns The Commons (2), Political Settings (7), Big Tent for Social Change (32), Opportunity Spaces (33), Participatory Design (36), Conversational Support Across Boundaries (50), Digital Emancipation (60), Participatory Budgeting (71), Grassroots Public Policy Development (78), Voices of the Unheard (83), Civic Capabilities (85), Citizen Diplomacy (93), Citizenship Schools (96), Community Animators (102), Self-Designed Development (106), Great Good Place (119), Citizens' Tribunal (129), Peaceful Public Demonstrations (133), Activist Road Trip (134).

Problem   When separate groups work on social issues without learning of what similar groups are doing on related issues, opportunities for exchanging ideas are lost. Historically it has been difficult to bring diverse groups together to discuss and mobilize on social issues of shared concern. Worse, groups that should be working together have a tendency to argue fiercely over philosophical or other points of disagreement, thus making collaboration nearly impossible.

Context   There are many groups, in many localities, addressing many issues and themes related to global social issues. This pattern helps to promote coordination among these not-so-disparate groups. Often people at the grassroots level have a better understanding of issues, especially those that have an immediate effect on their local areas. At the same time, many issues that play out at the local level also have a global context.

Discussion   Principle 1 of the World Social Forum Charter of Principles (Sen et al. 2004) states that the forum "is an open meeting place for reflective thinking, democratic debate of ideas, formulation of proposals, free exchange of experiences, and interlinking for effective action by groups and movements of civil society that are opposed to neoliberalism and to domination of the world by capital and any form of imperialism, and are committed to building a planetary society directed toward fruitful relationships among Humankind and between it and the Earth."

By offering a "big tent" setting such as the World Social Forum (WSF) where these groups can come together, synergy can happen, and solutions to social programs can be developed. The basic idea is that social forums, like parties or conferences or other gatherings, provide an occasion for people of similar interests to get together. What people choose to do with the information they receive is ultimately a decision that they will make. But by the same token, the forums do what they can to make the events successful in the sense of spawning collaborative and collective actions and projects without heavy-handed social engineering. The big tent pattern encourages other "smaller tents" (with, for example, regional or thematic focus) to form within the event, and these smaller tents can ultimately provide issue and geographical space to support the work of additional groups with other forums.

The big tent scale of the WSF and the growth (starting with 20,000 in 2001 and up to 100,000 in 2005) has helped foster respect from mainstream media and other entities that may be seen as oppositional to the forum principles, as it demonstrates that there are large numbers of people and organizations committed to working on these issues. Another positive attribute of this pattern of a large gathering of many social issue groups for mobilization is that the scale is big enough that individuals can participate and be somewhat anonymous, which can reduce the pressure to represent a certain group ideology and offer more freedom to express alternatives, listen, and learn.

Conceived as an counterforce to the elite World Economic Forum held annually in Davos, Switzerland, the World Social Forum picks up where the 1999 demonstrations against the World Trade Organization (WTO) in Seattle left off by providing a setting for activists to create alternatives to corporate dominance. The economic agenda was not the only issue discussed at the WSF when it was held in Mumbai, India, in 2004. Government repression (in Burma, for example) was examined in workshops and demonstrations, as was discrimination based on gender, race, sexual orientation, or caste. The presence of Dalits, the "untouchables" at the bottom of India's elaborate (and technically illegal) caste system, was a reminder that basic human rights are far from universal. Regional issues like so-called honor killings and dowry practices were also discussed, as were the rights of children. Jabala, a group that works with children in red-light districts, led a rally with the chant: "*Aloo becho, machchi becho, par bachchon ko mat becho*" ("sell potatoes, sell fish, but do not sell children"). Thousands of children are inducted into the sex industry every year.

Throughout the four-day gathering in 2004, labor groups, human rights advocates, anti-war campaigners, and many others conducted boisterous processions accompanied by dancing, sign brandishing, and drumming. Along with rallies, films, and photography exhibits, delegates from over 130 countries had organized scores of workshops, seminars, information-sharing, sessions, and debates. They discussed strategies, areas of mutual concerns, and opportunities for collaborations based on newly discovered linkages between issues.

The WSF is the most prominent meeting of this type in the world. It has shown itself to be replicable (at least so far) in its totality as a world social forum, but also in a variety of constituent regional and thematic fora. Although not all big tents are required to adopt the tenets of the WSF, two of its principles may be useful to those considering the idea of convening big tent events.

The first principle is that the forum is an open meeting place, or agora, where issues are raised, not necessarily deliberated or used to directly plan actions. The second principle is that power is not intended to reside within the organizational structure of the WSF. The governing body of the WSF, for example, is prohibited from making statements in the name of the forum. Also, the original charter of principles states that the WSF "does not constitute a locus of power to be disputed by participants in its meetings." While both of these ideas are designed to forestall certain problems, they ironically raise other types of challenges or tensions within the WSF community. One of these is related to action versus talk orientation, with the action-oriented people saying that after seven years, it is time for an action agenda. Another objection is related to participation versus elitism. Although most events are organized by participants, some plenary events are generally convened, and these are likely to populated by star activists.

Those who attend a big tent event like the WSF certainly have a better understanding of the enormity of the world's problems but also can begin to entertain some cautious optimism. Airing the problems of the world with dedicated people who are working to create "another world" that is more equitable, sustainable, and peaceful than our current world is a necessary step in the solution of these problems.

Solution   Bringing groups together in a big tent where a multiplicity of perspectives is encouraged fosters numerous opportunities for discussion of solutions to social problems and sharing of ideas that help other groups working on the same or similar issues.

Linked patterns   Global Citizenship (6), Social Responsibility (8), Working-Class Consciousness (12), Big-Picture Health Information (27), Public Agenda (30), Democratic Political Settings (31), Opportunity Spaces (33), Strategic Capacity (34), World Citizen Parliament (40), Strengthening International Law (42), Community Networks (61), Transaction Tax (72).

33 Opportunity Spaces

Problem   Inequality can be understood to a large degree as unfair access to opportunities. In the United States, opportunities for education, employment, and health are invariably tied to economic status. Current social and technological systems are generally not developed to create or support equitable opportunity spaces even though these are the hallmark of a just society. Without adequate opportunity spaces, marginalized people will almost certainly be prevented from meaningful participation in the society at large.

Context   Although opportunity spaces can be physical places (e.g., a public library or a community garden), the term is intended to be used metaphorically. It simply represents a convenient way to talk about sets of opportunities that exist for people. This pattern can be used in any community. After all, every community depends on opportunities. Some communities have ample opportunities that are open for all people, while some have all but the most demeaning opportunities reserved for its privileged members. Although applying this pattern is intended to lead to concrete action, it can also be useful as a focus for thinking about equity and social progress.

Discussion   How can society develop more and better opportunities for its citizens? An opportunity space presents one or more possible steps that a person might take as he or she plans for and moves into the future. It describes a potential "contract" between an offering entity and a person looking for future possibilities. Opportunities take many forms: classes and seminars, volunteer positions, jobs, paid trips, contests, access to the media, timely announcements, mentoring, scholarships, grants, and many others.

Opportunities dictate the possible paths to the future that are available to people. Hence the opportunities that society offers are of critical importance. What opportunities exist? Do they exist for all citizens or just privileged ones? How are these opportunities developed and maintained? How do people learn about them? In many cases, spending a little more effort making the existing opportunities more widely known will help considerably.

There are often mismatches in a society between the opportunities that exist for individuals and opportunities that individuals believe exist for them. It is very important to understand the great distinction between realizable opportunities and ones that are perceived to exist but do not and ones that exist but are not known. Sometimes the actual opportunity space is larger than the perceived one, and sometimes the reverse is true. An obvious example is the generally unfulfilled hope of a successful career in professional sports.

Ironically opportunities for individuals can sometimes be detrimental for society as a whole. Consider opportunities that encourage people from less developed countries to move to more developed ones to pursue higher education. While the individual is likely to gain educationally (and economically), the society from which he or she originated is losing significant human resources and contributing to an ongoing "brain drain."

Opportunities and certainly opportunity spaces are rarely provided by a single entity. The provision of opportunity spaces in a community is accomplished by a web of people and organizations who don't always even know that they're working together. Opportunities should be linked to each other, even if informally. If somebody accepts an opportunity and fulfills the obligations, new opportunities should become available to them. In addition, opportunities should generally be well known and available on a predictable basis. If opportunities are only known to a few, and if they are only sporadically available, they won't serve the community as effectively as they could. Ideally opportunities would beget more opportunities. That is, people who have benefited from opportunities should appreciate this concept and help provide opportunities for others. The phenomenon of people helping with the expectation that they'll be helped sometime—but not necessarily by the same people they helped—is known as "generalized reciprocity."

Opportunities require resources of all types, and money is among the most prominent. At the same time, however, money is certainly not the only resource that can be used. Opportunities are not just formal ones that are announced in the newspaper or sponsored by large philanthropic foundations. Any skill, spare time, art supplies, books, a spare room, tools, or even an idea or suggestion could be the core of a new opportunity. Every need suggests opportunities. It might even make sense to think of these resources as underutilized if they are not part of a society's opportunity space. The idea of an English speaker and a Spanish speaker teaching each other their language seems to be an obvious though underused arrangement.

Communities and institutions need to think tactically and strategically about implementing new or improving existing opportunity spaces. The number, diversity, and distribution of opportunities provide significant social indicators (see Indicators, 29). Their absence or vastly unequal distribution in society would in all likelihood represent a community or society in crisis.

Solution   People and communities need help realizing their potential. They also need support as they work to repair social and environmental problems. It is important to devote attention and resources (including policy, services, media, and technological systems) to help create new (and improve existing) opportunity spaces for people and communities that need them.

Linked patterns   Social Dominance Attenuation (4), Global Citizenship (6), Political Settings (7), Demystification and Reenchantment (14), Antiracism (23), Cyberpower (25), Democratic Political Settings (31), Big Tent for Social Change (32), Participatory Design (36), World Citizen Parliament (40), Indigenous Media (55), Public Library (59), Digital Emancipation (60), Community Networks (61), Community Currencies (63), Positive Health Information (74), Accessibility of Online Information (75), Mobile Information and Computer Technology Learning Facilities (77), Patient Access to Medical Records (95), Citizenship Schools (96), Self-Help Groups (105), Self-Designed Development (106), Labor Visions (112).

Problem   Occasionally in the course of human history, a small group with meager resources fighting a powerful foe wins. One of the most famous of those struggles is that of the biblical shepherd David, who vanquished the seemingly invincible Goliath. A thousand other struggles, against poverty, against oppression, against environmental degradation, retell the David and Goliath story with equally improbable outcomes. What is the secret to these unlikely successes? Resources (financial, organizational, cultural, and many others) alone, though useful, do not tell the whole story: the group with the biggest war chest sometimes fails where the seemingly more impoverished group succeeds. The idea of political opportunity does not explain everything either; sometimes groups fashion their own opportunity seemingly our of the air. And individual characteristics such as dedication, drive, and emotional commitment, although also quite important, do not necessarily portend success or failure of activist struggles or social movements. There must be more to understanding why some efforts fail while others succeed beyond all expectations.

Context   Groups of people, formally organized or not, strive to make a positive impact on the world. Any group devoted to social change must sustain the organization, largely through marshaling and replenishing resources, over the course of its existence. To move beyond mere existence and to achieve its goals, the members of a group must work together effectively to make decisions. This pattern is intended to help groups increase the probability that they will make good decisions at each stage of the group's development and in its engagement with the rest of the world. According to Marshall Ganz (2004), the person who developed the concept of this pattern, it is most useful in "turbulent environments where rules, resources, and interests are emergent and links between ends and means are uncertain."

Discussion   Discerning the macro tides of history is a risky business. Fortunately for those who undertake this avocation, those attempting the readings of the tea leaves writ large have generally been quite dead years before the evidence emerges that demonstrates the unforeseen flaws in their reasoning (or, in rare cases, vindicates their astonishingly spot-on observations). Perhaps riskier is the business of responding purposefully, punctually, piercingly, and resoundingly to the micro tides of the here and now, the unexpected opportunities that arise from nowhere and vanish as rapidly. The best responses often demonstrate a shocking disregard for conventional wisdom. They often demonstrate a preternatural anticipation of the next event and the next event after that, and so on, while everyone else is seemingly caught unaware.

In the early 1960s, Marshall Ganz set aside his undergraduate studies at Harvard to work within the civil rights movement in the U.S. South. Twenty-eight years later, he returned to Harvard, finished his undergraduate and doctoral degrees, and developed the concept that this pattern is based on. Strategic Capacity specifically focuses on the question of why and how some people and organizations happen to adapt so wisely, and often guilefully, to new circumstances. Indeed, some appear to thrive on them. Strategic Capacity is too elusive to yield to mechanical analytical probes. For one thing, as Ganz (2004) points out, we can observe "choices about targeting, timing, and tactics," but "the strategy that frames these choices—and provides them with their coherence—must often be inferred, using data drawn from interviews with participants, oral histories, correspondence, memoirs, charters, constitutions, organizational journals, activity reports, minutes of meetings, and participant observation."

While it is true that a specific strategy can probably be understood after the fact, the general strategic capacity of an organization's or movement's resistance to analysis is undoubtedly part of its power. Thus Ganz focuses more on the conditions that engender successful strategizing within an individual or group (its strategic capacity) than on the strategies themselves. (Of course, how a strategy is put into action is not trivial.) Ideally a group will use its strategic capacity to simultaneously build its strength while accomplishing its objectives.

Ganz explains that decisions are expressions of strategy and that successful strategy is related to "the times, the people who act upon them, and the organizational settings in which they act." His theory of strategic capacity uses motivation, access to salient knowledge, and the heuristic processes that organizational leaders use as the key factors behind effective strategic capacity. Motivation is important because it describes how willing the group is to work toward its goals and what types of goals are established in the first place. Ganz further states that motivation based on "intrinsic rewards" and on the moral meaning of the enterprise is very important. Access to salient knowledge is important because, without this knowledge, particularly knowledge about resources and opportunities, the group would be using inadequate and misleading information that it assesses and interprets to make its decisions in the heuristic processes, the third constituent of strategic capacity.

Ganz then steps back to consider the two driving forces, leadership and organization, that will be employing the strategic capacity that the model describes. According to Ganz, "Leaders devise strategy in interaction with their environments." He stresses that leadership teams are more likely to have effective strategic capacity when they include "insiders" and "outsiders," have strong and weak ties (connections) to a variety of sociocultural networks, and have "knowledge of diverse collective action repertoires." On the organization side, Ganz points out that "leaders interact with their environment from within organizational structures." Leadership teams that are regularly involved in open deliberations with outcomes that determine organizational actions have more strategic capacity, and leadership teams that rely more on people than money are cultivating sustainable strategic capacity by encouraging leaders who can effectively strategize.

Solution   A group or organization that makes good decisions will be more effective than one that does not. Marshall Ganz's concept of strategic capacity identifies the underlying attributes behind a group's ability to make these decisions. By improving these attributes, a group can likely improve its ability to make good—and sometimes surprisingly good—decisions. Based on Ganz's reading (2004) of Bruner (1990), "Strategic thinking is reflexive and imaginative, based on ways leaders learn to reflect on the past, attend to the present, and anticipate the future."

Linked patterns   Civic Intelligence (1), Working-Class Consciousness (12), Dematerialization (18), Big Tent for Social Change (32), Mobile Intelligence (38), International Networks of Alternative Media (43), Open Action and Research Network (45), Meaningful Maps (47), Community Currencies (63), Powerful Remittances (73), Mirror Institutions (94), Citizenship Schools (96), Community-Building Journalism (97), Appreciative Collaboration (99), Sustainability Appraisal (100), Shared Vision (101), Self-Help Groups (105), Labor Visions (112), Power Research (128).

Problem Bias-free media may be impossible. For that reason, people need to be able to identify and assess media bias. Some have argued that the media have become so vivid, so real, that people can "live" in them. Media literacy is the process of decoding and making sense of all media. It allows us to critically view media and evaluate the role that media play in our lives. Someone who is media literate has the skills to identify the ideological implications and manipulative means of media systems and practices. Unfortunately, exposure to media does not necessarily suggest that people have the critical skills to understand how media systems work or how they are relating to media messages. Further, there is very little training in media education. In most places in the world, public education ignores or resists the changing media environments. Also, teachers are not given specific instruction in the workings of media and are not trained in the methods of media practices. In some places in the world, media have a foothold in the curriculum of public education, but rarely does this curriculum come with the pedagogical training educators need to reach their audiences. The study of media has developed into complex systems of understanding, analysis, and synthesis. Yet media study is not thought of within the context of traditional academic disciplines. As a result, we live in a world where ubiquitous media messages, without critical appraisal, bombard our world.

Context Masterman (1985), in particular, stresses the student's development of critical autonomy as a primary objective of media education. In *Teaching the Media*, he argues that the key task of media teachers is to "develop in pupils enough self-confidence and critical maturity to be able to apply critical judgments to media texts which they will encounter in the future." Thus, the primary objective of media education is not simply to foster critical awareness and understanding, but to develop a student's awareness of his or her role as an active agent when engaged by all media, no matter the context. The critical autonomy approach to media education differs from its predecessors in three ways. First, the pedagogical practices of this approach stress investigative strategies: teaching and learning are emphatically student centered and inquiry oriented. Second, the process of making meaning through critical investigation is emphasized: strategies of decoding are stressed within pedagogy. And third, visual literacy and media literacy, rather than an exclusively print-oriented literacy, function as the criteria for evaluation of student work.

Discussion Until recently if somebody complained about the media, the typical response was, "Turn off the TV." Nevertheless, it has become commonplace to think of media not as an autonomous system but as an important element in a cultural environment that, like the physical environment, needs to be monitored for degradation and corruption. We need to be able to recognize biases and other problems that we encounter with existing media systems.

All messages are made with some sense of the people receiving them. People filter these messages based on their beliefs, values, attitudes, behaviors, and experiences. Every media message is communicated for a reason: to entertain, inform, and usually persuade. Behind every message is a purpose and point of view. The advertiser's purpose is more direct than a program producer's, though both may seek to entertain. Understanding their purposes and knowing whose point of view is being expressed and why is crucial to being media literate. Yet the basic motive behind most media programs is profit through practices like the sale of advertising space and sponsorships. These reasons are also important to consider because all media messages are owned. They are designed to yield results, provide profits, and pay for themselves. Nonpublic news and entertainment programming, including film and television, tries to increase audiences to attract advertising dollars. Understanding the profit motive is key to analyzing media messages. Messages are communicated through the use of elements like sound, video, text, and photography. But most messages are enhanced by the use of visual and technical elements such as camera angles, special effects, editing, or music. Analyzing how these features are used in a message is critical to understanding how that message attempts to persuade, entertain, or inform. Because messages are limited in both time and purpose, rarely are all the details provided. Identifying the issues, topics, and perspectives that are not included can often reveal a great deal about the purposes of media messages. Because media messages tell only part of the story and different media have unique production features, evaluating multiple messages on the same issue can identify multiple points of view, some of which may be missing in any single message or medium.

These are but some of the issues to discuss when considering the problems and challenges associated with the term *media literacy*. The following questions provide a good start for an individual who wants to become more media literate as well as an educator or other individual or group that wants to understand and apply media literacy principles and skills.

1. Who is communicating and why?

Every media message is communicated for a reason: to entertain, to inform, and usually to persuade. A basic motive behind most media programs is profit through the sale of advertising space and sponsorships.

2. Who owns, profits from, and pays for media messages?

Media messages can be measured in terms of economic value. Most media messages are owned, designed to yield results, provide profits, and pay for themselves. For example, news and entertainment programming, including film and television, try to increase their audiences to attract advertising dollars. Understanding the economic factor, including who owns the companies and how they are linked into the political economy, is key to analyzing media messages.

3. How are media messages communicated?

Messages are communicated through the use of forms, conventions, and techniques such as sound, text, and image. But most messages are enhanced by the use of visual and technical elements, like camera angles, special effects, editing, or music. Analyzing how these features are used in any given message is critical to understanding how that message attempts to persuade, entertain, or inform.

4. What are the intended or underlying purposes behind the media message?

Behind every message is a purpose and point of view. The advertiser's purpose is more direct than a program producer's, though both may seek to entertain. Understanding their purposes and knowing whose point of view is being expressed and why is crucial to understanding the motivation behind any media message.

5. What are the effects, both intended and nonintended, of media?

This question, although not easy to answer, is crucial. Is media educating people or the reverse? Does it promote violence in society? What effects does it have on attention spans, self-identity, and attitudes toward the elderly, people in other countries, or the environment?

6. Who are the target audiences for media messages?

All messages are made for some group of people or audience. People filter these messages based on their beliefs, values, attitudes, behaviors, and past experiences. Identify the target audience for any given message to learn how its audience may engage in a range of interpretations.

7. What is *not* being said and why?

Because messages are limited in both time and purpose, rarely are all the details provided. Identifying the issues, topics, and perspectives that are *not* included can often reveal a great deal about the purposes of media messages. In fact, this may be the most significant question that can uncover answers to the other questions.

8. Is there consistency both within and across media?

Does the political slant, tone, local/national/international perspective, and depth of coverage change across media? Because media messages tell only part of the story and different media have unique production features, it helps to evaluate multiple media outlets and channels that cover the same issue. This allows you to identify multiple points of view, some of which may be missing in any single message or medium.

9. Are the needs of the citizen being met?

Although people have a legitimate need to be entertained, there are other needs—such as the ones discussed in this pattern language—that deserve at least as much as consideration as the need for leisure. The particular needs that people have in a democratic society and how to address them is crucial. In today's world, looking for answers to these questions means necessarily looking at media—and one of the ultimate aims of media literacy is to develop systems that more capably address the needs of the citizen.

A critical autonomy approach to media education addresses these concerns within an educational context. As part of the school reform movement of the past decade, media education scholarship assumes a student-centered pedagogical practice in which the student is viewed as an active, aware participant in learning, a lifelong learner, and a self-motivated and self-directed problem solver. This image of the learner is an essential consideration not only in the design of media education, but also within the larger pedagogical frame in which the curriculum is negotiated. According to Boomer, Lester, Onore, and Cook (1992), negotiating the curriculum means deliberately planning to invite students to contribute to and modify the educational program so that they will have a real investment in both the learning journey and the outcomes. Negotiation also means making explicit, and then confronting, the constraints of the learning context and the nonnegotiable requirements that apply. Masterman (1985) argues further that "if students are to understand media texts ... then it will obviously be helpful if they have first-hand experience of the construction process from the inside." To this end, media education includes media production, or what Masterman dubs "practical work," as a pedagogical practice that enables students to create media products. Thus, students are actively engaged with both the production of media and the workings of the classroom.

As a result of their interest in student-centered learning, scholars of media education aim to develop curricula that consider the forms and practices of education and pedagogy. Curricula that are inquiry oriented tend to offer activities that stress critical strategies, and pedagogy centers around the creation of a dialogue—not just discussion, but the kind of talk that leads to dialectical thinking. In this context, divergent readings of texts are positively valued for their potential to stimulate further analysis, and thus growth in understanding. The aim of media education is to encourage a heightened self-consciousness about the processes of interpretation and meaning making and provide people with an opportunity to recognize that everyone uses a selective and interpretive process to examine media texts. This process and the meanings obtained depend on psychological, social, cultural, and environmental factors. In this view, media education strives to enable people to understand how media texts come to have a range of meanings or readings ascribed to them and develop even richer, more critical readings.

Contemporary media educators are also beginning to challenge traditional notions of literacy. Literacy, by definition, refers to the ability to read and write. But scholars insist that there are "languages" other than print, such as those related to the mass media, that also need to be considered within the definition of *literacy*. Visual literacy, for example, has been described by Messaris (1994) as "greater experience in the workings of visual media coupled with a heightened conscious awareness of those workings." And Masterman (1985) has argued that since both print and visual literacy involve "the deconstruction of texts by breaking through their surface to reveal the rhetorical techniques through which meanings are produced," any education for "literacy" should focus on that process, rather than on the symbolic form of a particular set of texts.

Solution   Education and educational practices need to shift to address the changing media environments. We need to perform more public media criticism. We need to engage with media more closely to keep them in check and to be informed as to how we are responding and why. We need to be more serious about our media environments and foster greater awareness of the impact and influence media systems have on daily life. We must arm all people with the knowledge, skills, and values a media education program provides, granting people access to new technology and information about its workings and ideological impli-cation. Finally, we need more alternative communication systems to counter these problems.

Linked patterns Demystification and Reenchantment (14), Education and Values (17), International Networks of Alternative Media (43), Ethics of Community Informatics (67), Accessibility of Online Information (75), Service-Learning (90), Citizen Journalism (91), The Power of Story (114), Public Domain Characters (115), Tactical Media (131).

Problem   A large number of artifacts that people use every day are ill designed and they do not appropriately address the needs of the people for whom they are designed and produced. The problems range from the inconvenient (in setting an alarm on an unfamiliar alarm clock, for example) to the dangerous (an inadequately marked pedestrian crosswalk or scalding water from the tap when cold was expected). And in the design of groupware, software systems that facilitate group collaboration, developers can inadvertently create systems that embed users in a system like cogs in a machine where a more human-centered system that was more user friendly—and more effective—could be developed.

Context   This pattern is intended to be used in any situation in which a service, policy, or other artifact is being designed. Those who will use the artifact and those who will be affected by it should be included in the design process.

Discussion

The very fact of exclusion from participation is a subtle form of suppression. It gives individuals no opportunity to reflect and decide on what's good for them. Others who are supposed to be wiser and who in any case have more power decide the question for them and also decide the methods and means by which subjects may arrive at the enjoyment of what is good for them. This form of coercion and suppression is more subtle and more effective than are overt intimidation and restraint. When it is habitual and embodied in social institutions, it seems the normal and natural state of affairs. (Dewey 1937)

This "subtle form of suppression" that Dewey identified in the quotation above shows up in sociotechnological systems and in various arenas including the workplace. Without genuine participation in the design process, class, managerial, or other privileges become designed in. That is, sociotechnological systems often carry forward the perquisites and propensities of the designers, intentionally or unwittingly. Cases abound in both cases. Robert Moses, New York City's "construction coordinator," ensured that the bridges over the highways leading to the beaches from New York City were low enough to prevent buses from traveling under them (Caro 1975). This ensured that African Americans and other minorities who often had to rely on public transportation would, in large measure, be confined to the city while the more financially well-to-do could periodically escape to the seaside. There was no need to pass laws when a permanent physical structure could silently and invisibly enforce the color bar Moses preferred.

Frustrated by what they saw as unresponsiveness of software and the impending institutionalization of management prerogatives into software systems, Scandinavian researchers in the late 1970s conceived a new paradigm for software development called participatory design in which end-users worked as co-designers of the systems that they would ultimately use. They believed that adopting a participatory design approach would result in systems that better served users, initially workers in industrial settings. According to PD researchers Finn Kensing and Jeanette Blomberg (1998), "At the center of the critique was the neglect of workers' interests—those most affected by the introduction of new technology. PD researchers argued that computers were becoming yet another tool of management to exercise control over the workforce and that these new technologies were not being introduced to improve working conditions (see, e.g., Sandberg, 1979; Kyng and Mathiassen, 1982)." The Scandinavian researchers and workers also worked on the legislative front to establish "code-termination" laws in Scandinavia that ensured that workers had the right to be involved with technological decisions in the workplace (Sandberg et al. 1992). They promoted user empowerment through education and "researchers developed courses, gave lectures, and supervised project work where technology and organizational issues were explored (see, e.g., Kyng and Mathiassen, 1982)" (Kensing and Blomberg 1988).

Participatory design is an integration of three interdisciplinary concerns that span research and practice: "the politics of design; the nature of participation; and method, tools and techniques for participation" (Kensing and Blomberg 1998). In their paper "Participatory Design: Issues and Concerns," Finn Kensing and Jeanette Blomberg discuss two primary aspects of this work.

Increasingly, ethnographically inspired fieldwork techniques are being integrated with more traditional PD techniques (Blomberg et al., 1996; Bødker 1996; Beyer and Holtzblatt 1997, Kensing et al., forthcoming). The primary techniques of ethnography include open-ended (contextual) interviews and (participant) observations, often supported by audio or video recordings. These techniques are employed to gain insights into unarticulated aspects of the work and to develop shared views on the work. ... Complementing these tools and techniques for work analysis are those focusing on system design such as scenarios, mock-ups, simulations of the relation between work and technology, future workshops, design games, case-based prototyping, and cooperative prototyping (Kensing 1987; Ehn 1989; Greenbaum and Kyng 1991; Trigg et al., 1991; Mogensen 1992, 1994; Blomberg et al., 1996; Grønbæk et al., 1997). These tools and techniques avoid the overly abstract representations of traditional design approaches and allow workers and designers to more easily experiment with various design possibilities in cost effective ways.

The nature of participatory design has changed over time. In the software world, for example, the focus has shifted from the development of site-specific software systems to the design of Web applications and, perhaps more important, to the entirety of the information and communication infrastructure, including policy development. The idea shows up in many guises, and even open source communities could be considered a type of participatory design.

Participatory design has been advocated in a number of areas besides software. Architects Lucien Kroll (1987), John Habraken (1972), Christopher Alexander (1984), Michael Pyatok (2000), and others developed a number of techniques for allowing people to design their own working and living spaces. Artist Suzi Gablick, writing in *The Reenchantment of Art* (1992), describes a number of ways that the creation of art could be more participatory, while many others are advocating participatory approaches to media, policy development, and citizen participation journalism (Gillmor 2004).

Several books, including *The Design of Work Oriented Computer Artifacts* (Ehn 1988), *Participatory Design: Principles and Practices* (Schuler and Namioka 1993), and *Design at Work* (Greenbaum and Kyng 1991), helped provide some early guides for the use of participatory design of software, and the biennial Participatory Design Conference sponsored by Computer Professionals for Social Responsibility helps to foster its continued evolution.

Participatory design is not a panacea. People may not want to participate; in many cases they quite plausibly determine that the disadvantages outweigh the advantages. Participatory design can certainly be time consuming, and higher quality of the end product cannot be guaranteed. Participatory design projects can go awry in a number of ways (as do traditional and more orthodox software development efforts). Software users using mental models based on the software are accustomed to using may enter a design session believing that they have already fully designed the system (down to the last key-stroke short-cut). Because of this possibility (and other reasons), many PD approaches focus on general, high-level exercises that are far removed both conceptually and physically from computers.

In some cases, a participation trap may be said to exist. This could happen when people are being brought into an effort that will ultimately make matters worse for them. In cases like this a less cooperative, more confrontational approach may be more likely to bring satisfactory results. Participation gives rise to several issues that probably must be resolved on a case-by-case basis in practice. Potential participants understand this instinctively. If, for example, the participative arena is for show only, and no idea that originates with a participant has any chance of being adopted, people can't be faulted for being dubious of the process. Genuine participation should be voluntary and honest; the relevant information, rules, constraints, and roles of all stakeholders should be well understood by all. (A person may still decide to participate even if any and all benefits would accrue to the organizers.) Ideally, the participants would be part of any decision making, including when to meet, how to conduct the meetings, and other processes. Kensing (1983) and Clement and Van den Besselaar (1993) describe several requirements for effective PD.

PD principles, techniques, and methodologies will continue to improve and be better known over time. PD will likely continue to involve bricolage, the ability of the participants and the people organizing the process to improvise. Unfortunately, as Kensing and Blomberg (1998) point out, building on the work of Clement and Van den Besselaar (1993), "the experimental nature of most PD projects often leads to small-scale projects which are isolated from other parts of the organization." (See Eevi Beck's "P is for Political" for more insight on this important observation.) The best way for the process to continue to improve is to build on successes and create incrementally a culture of participation on the job and in society, that is both equitable and effective at designing systems, services, tools, and technologies whose design better meets the real demands and needs of the people.

Solution   There should be a strong effort to include the users of any designed system (software, information and communication systems, administrative services and processes, art, city plans, architecture, education, governance, and others) into its design process in an open, authentic, and uncoerced fashion. Participatory design, according to Finn and Blomberg, "has made no attempt to demarcate a category of work called cooperative, but instead has focused on developing cooperative strategies for system design.... PD is not defined by the type of work supported, nor by the technologies developed, but instead by a commitment to worker participation in design and an effort to rebalance the power relations between users and technical experts and between workers and managers. As such PD research has an explicit organizational and political change agenda."

Linked patterns   Working-Class Consciousness (12), Sustainable Design (22), Democratic Political Settings (31), Opportunity Spaces (33), Meaningful Maps (47), Intermediate Technologies (57), Digital Emancipation (60), Online Community Service Engine (62), Participatory Budgeting (71), Grassroots Public Policy Development (78), Users' Information Technology Quality Network (80), Voices of the Unheard (83), Design for Unintended Use (84), Civic Capabilities (85), Future Design (88), Document-Centered Discussion (92), Shared Vision (101), Self-Designed Development (106), Engaged Tourism (107), Appropriating Technology (108), Community Telecenters (117), Open Source Search Technology (125).

Problem   The role of science will become increasingly critical in the years ahead as health care, energy, resources, and the global environment become ever more problematic. Science can appear to serve powerful institutions, such as stock markets and the weapons industry, more than it serves the people most affected by these problems. Meanwhile, the resources of society's professional scientists are overtaxed by the extent of the data to be collected and the need to distribute expertise over a wide area. Science needs greater participation from people at large, and people need a greater voice in science.

Context   Science is a human activity. Study of the physical world and of society itself has tangible effects on society. Scientific knowledge is provisional, subject to revision. The scientific profession is inseparable from society as a whole; science requires funding and regulation, contributes expertise to official inquiries and investigations, and helps create technological and social changes that affect everyone. Citizen groups and individuals experience the benefits, hazards, and missed opportunities of scientific development in the real world, not in the laboratory.

Discussion   Citizen Science has been with us for a long time. Since 1900, the Audubon Society has organized volunteers throughout the United States to count birds at Christmastime and used their data to build a huge database of early winter bird populations ("History and Objectives," 2004). This is a clear-cut instance of citizen science as "a partnership between the public and professional scientists" ("Citizen Science" 2003, para. 3); people benefit from learning about birds, society benefits from information it would otherwise lack the resources to obtain, and birds benefit from researchers' knowledge of which species require special attention ("Citizen Science" 2005).

Our relationship with science is not always so simple. Mistrust exists in public perceptions of science as offering scientific solutions to complex social problems, furthering various forms of social and environmental depredation, and inappropriately claiming certainty in judgments about risks associated with scientific and technological developments (Irwin 1995). The drug industry's investment in treatments seeking diseases of the rich (Blech 2006), for example, undermines the view of scientific development as "open-minded, skeptical and independent of institutional constraints" (Irwin 1995, 109). Agents of public policy too can contribute to popular mistrust, though supposedly representing the public interest. For example, a 1977 U.K. government inquiry into leukemia among workers at the Windscale nuclear plant was less democratic decision making than keeping up appearances of public participation in a decision that had already been made (Irwin 1995).

At the same time, science has cause to be wary of the public; in the United States, for example, the proportion of people overtly accepting the idea of evolution has dropped from 45 percent to 40 percent since 1985 (Miller, Scott, and Okamoto 2006). Popular media have a stake in public mistrust of science because they stand to profit from science-related scare stories (Cassidy 2006a).

What scientists learn under controlled conditions differs in important ways from what people experience in real life. For example, British government regulations on the use of the herbicide 2,4,5–T assumed circumstances unrecognizable as those under which farmworkers actually used the substance (Irwin 1995, Corburn 2005). Local knowledge—public experience and intuition—is a different kind of knowledge, differently gained, from the professional knowledge of scientific research and regulation (Corburn 2005).

Overcoming the rift between professional and local knowledge can be achieved by "a constructive renegotiation between science and the needs of citizens" (Irwin 1995, 110). In what Corburn (2005) calls street science, professional science and the people most affected by it collaborate to coproduce knowledge that benefits both. In the field of environmental health, this coproduction reveals hazards and provides information that professionals may miss, reduces mistrust of science, empowers community members, and creates positive engagement with problems instead of entrenched and polarized positions.

Local knowledge can both amplify and stimulate professional knowledge. The Watchperson project in the Greenpoint/Williamsburg section of Brooklyn, New York, combined government data sets and conducted surveys to map sources of air pollution at greater detail than regulators' models (Corburn 2005). Recent developments in wireless mobile sensors create possibilities for mapping pollutant levels at much finer detail than previously possible; one example using human volunteers is Area's Immediate Reading (AIR) preemptive media project (2007).

The scientific profession can further the coproduction of knowledge by reaching out to individuals, communities and citizen groups. BirdSource uses an Internet-based tool to help more than 50,000 birdwatchers develop a deeper understanding of science and the environment while they accumulate data that help identify priorities for conservation. This extends the reach of science by providing knowledge that scientists would lack the resources to gather by themselves (Fitzpatrick and Gill 2002).

Science shops and cooperative extensions offer groundbreaking resources for the coproduction of knowledge. Science Shops (such as http://www.scienceshop.org) provide university scientific expertise to the public, at the instigation of either students or citizen groups. The illustration for this pattern shows a citizen scientist, trained by the University of Rhode Island Cooperative Extension Watershed Watch program ("URI Watershed Watch" 2007), demonstrating water collection for participants in the Rhode Island Rivers Council Watershed Stewards program ("About the Watershed Stewardship Program" 2007), which in turn educates citizen volunteers in areas such as monitoring and managing water quality so as to build the leadership of grassroots river and watershed groups. Cornell Cooperative Extension provides scientific expertise and conducts scientific research as part of a mission to extend the democratic process by helping people participate in their communities (Peters, O'Connell, Alter, and Jack 2006).

Citizen groups can further their own aims while extending the reach of science. For example, the Ocean Conservancy conducts an international cleanup of marine debris on the third Saturday in September each year. While helping to clean the coastline, volunteers collect data that enable the Ocean Conservancy to learn about the causes of marine debris and use this information in public education and advocacy.

Because mainstream scientific research does not predetermine its conclusions, its use in advocacy is a double-edged sword. Activists may better spend their time in political lobbying than in scientific research whose results may not support their agenda. Just as the public mistrusts research funded by tobacco companies, for example, research by activist groups may appear suspect to policymakers and professional scientists. Despite this, many avenues are open for activists to initiate research that furthers their aims. Two examples follow.

Aiming to show a connection between pollution from incinerators, toxic waste storage, and other industrial sources in the neighborhood and asthma in Greenpoint/Williamsburg, the El Puente group trained community members as community health workers and in conducting surveys. Their twofold process, of gathering information on asthma in surveys and then discussing the results in focus groups, uncovered knowledge about a link between women's occupations and asthma not directly related to environmental pollution, differing levels of asthma among Hispanic groups, and underreported asthma rates because people avoided treatment at the local hospital (Corburn 2005).

The Center for Science and Environment uses the results of its own scientific research to publicize problems and solutions. A recent achievement has been the research-based development of rainwater harvesting methods, combined with community outreach and advocacy to policymakers, offering a "politics of hope" to those whose water supplies are declining in quantity and quality (www.rainwaterharvesting.org).

Solution   Use and develop means of collaboration between science and communities. People benefit by bringing both scientific knowledge and local knowledge to bear on the problems that they experience. Citizen groups, policymakers, and professional scientists all gain from proven ways to do this.

Linked patterns   Civic Intelligence (1), Working Class-Consciousness (12), Earth's Vital Signs (26), Big-Picture Health Information (27), Indicators (29), Public Agenda (30), Technocriticism (39), Open Action and Research Network (45), Meaningful Maps (47), Citizen Access to Simulations (48), Positive Health Information (74), Open Access Scholarly Publishing (76), Mobile Information and Computer Technology Learning Facilities (77), Grassroots Public Policy Development (78), Academic Technology Investments (81), Wholesome Design for Wicked Problems (82), Emergency Communication Systems (121), Community Inquiry (122), Environmental Impact Remediation (124).

Problem   While we make plans, opportunity can vanish. The world changes while you are still trying to figure out what the question is. We cannot think or act intelligently in relation to the world if we think statically. The main problem is that we think that things change one at a time in ways that can be readily foreseen; in actuality, things are constantly in flux. This can lead people to misunderstand the possibilities or underestimate the complexity of a situation.

Context   Mobile intelligence is the capacity to think about the mobilities of our era. Beyond that, it is the capacity to think with a mobile orientation, as a person or organization that exists, and can act, within a dynamic and fluid environment. This pattern addresses the need for exploring (with the hope of improving) mobile intelligence. It is intended for researchers, activists, citizens, and anybody else who is trying to make sense of the world that is in constant motion.

Discussion   John Urry (2000) articulated the need to reconceptualize sociology in such a way to better understand and explore the "mobilities" of our era. *Mobilities* characterize movement from one state to another in the broadest sense. A reconceptualization of social mobilities extends the core notion of people moving from one place to another, whether to fight—or escape from—a war, pursue economic opportunities unavailable at home, visit family, attend college, make a religious pilgrimage, conduct business, or visit resorts or museums as a tourist. Urry reminds us that people are not the only entities in the social universe. These new mobilities include the movement of commodities, raw materials, microbes, pilgrims and soccer hooligans, AK-47s and fissionable material, ideologies, tactics, criminal networks, social issues, social movements, money (legitimate and otherwise), brands, virtual communities, financial information, smuggled people, radioactivity, movies, pirated DVDs, pollution, oil, electricity, water, surveillance, terrorist cells, drugs, and credit card information. In addition to those mobilities, the social status of individuals, and even identity itself, can change through movement to a higher or lower economic class, becoming a citizen—or refugee—in another country, or undergoing a sex change or religious conversion.

   Urry points out that sociology places social interaction at its core and is therefore the proper intellectual home for these considerations. Yet sociology as it is currently construed was created at a certain point in Western history, and it often presupposes notions like structure or function that belie the inherent complexity of social interactions and forces. Its area of focus is like the old "flat earth" perspective where the areas outside the known territory are terra incognita. Urry advocates a new type of sociology that extends traditional sociological tenets to a new sociology that more accurately reflects today's realities. Specifically Urry adds networks and fluids to the traditional idea of "region" (on which metaphor the "sociological concept of society is based") as important constituents to be added to the new mix of phenomena and artifacts that need to be considered when interpreting new social realities. Networks contain structure, or what Urry calls "scapes," the "networks of machines, technologies, organizations, texts and actors that constitute various interconnected nodes," and "flows," which pass through the "scapes." Fluids, unlike networks, do not move discretely from node to node along scapes but are "heterogeneous, uneven mobilities of people, information, objects, money, images, and risks, that move chaotically across regions in strikingly faster and unpredictable shapes."

Some of the patterns in this language are ambiguous and hazy, and their recommendations can be summarized with noncommittal "more research is needed" statements. One may get the impression that "more research" is always needed if you ask an academic. Given the fact that all knowledge is incomplete, it may seem impossible to avoid that last refuge of a scholar who is seemingly unable to make recommendation until, he or she claims, new research, once funded, will certainly bring the results that would lead to recommendations. The Mobile Intelligence pattern is one of those (hopefully few) patterns that generally follow the line above. It will surely morph in future versions of the language, possibly by splitting into several patterns that exploit new opportunities or confront new threats undreamed of today. For now we basically note its critical nature.

The coverage of this pattern extends from the most abstract and theoretical to the nitty-gritty street level. It relates to how we think and converse in broad strokes about social change, the environment, and other topics when we take the time outside other work, as well as our thoughts and action when we are "thrown in" a situation (Heidegger 1962). In an example of the latter, Mary Jordan (2006) reports on an emerging type of mobile intelligence:

Cell phones and text messaging are changing the way political mobilizations are conducted around the world. From Manila to Riyadh and Kathmandu protests once publicized on coffeehouse bulletin boards are now organized entirely through text-messaging networks that can reach vast numbers of people in a matter of minutes.

The technology is also changing the organization and dynamics of protests, allowing leaders to control, virtually minute-by-minute, the movements of demonstrators, like military generals in the field. Using texts that communicate orders instantly, organizers can call for advances or retreats of waves of protesters.

And in 2003, when U.S. President George Bush on a visit to London was keeping as far from the public eye as he could, protesters set up a "chasing Bush" system that encouraged people to announce their Bush sightings using the short messaging service on their cell phones, which would then be relayed to protesters who would hasten to the location. The flash mob concept, in which a "spontaneous" gathering of a large number of people at a rug store or hotel lobby has been orchestrated with the aid of fast and inexpensive access to mobile communications, provides a glimpse into the future as to the absurd and amusing possibilities that new technology can bring. It is easy to see that mobile communications has its dark sides, a point that Howard Rheingold brings up in his aptly titled book *Smart Mobs* (2003). A mob consists of people who are operating wholly at the limbic level. While rationality and cool-headed reason may be flawed, overrated, and mostly mythical as operating concepts, consider a world in which they were totally absent.

New technologies are changing and are likely to continue to change our urban settings in particular (which are already undergoing massive changes due to globalization and new patterns of human settlements). Alex Steffen on his World Changing Web site quotes the following from the 2006 Breaking the Game conference both permeate urban spaces (changing their uses) and change the way we look at buildings and place (changing development).

An emerging group of artists deploying sensors, hand-held electronics, and faster Internet connections are developing projects that actively intervene in the shaping and reshaping of public spaces in contemporary cities. They are integrating digital technology into buildings in order to make them adaptive and responsive to the flows of human activity and environmental forces.... They are scanning the unseen electromagnetic spectrum that surrounds specific places, and turning these data into compelling audio/visual experiences that both heighten and change our perception.... Using PDAs and portable laptops connected wirelessly to databases, some artists are creating alternative social maps, counter-histories and individually annotated narratives about local populations in specific neighborhoods.... Still others are using mobile social software to coordinate large numbers of bodies for political action; or devising playful and imaginary spaces within the city.... We do not have to leave or disconnect from physical space in order to connect to digital spaces. Artists, architects, technologists, urban planners, and others are recombining the two, connecting individuals and groups together at a variety of scales and intensities.

It is an understatement to say that mobile communications represents a major historic shift from historical patterns of communications. The Internet and other information and communication technologies have helped usher in tremendous changes already, but these changes may represent just the tip of the iceberg. Mobile communication is fast and increasingly commonplace. It opens up new arenas of thought and action. Like many new technologies, the opportunities for abuse are legion, and critics should not be cowed into submission by new digital pitchmen and their cheerleaders in the media. Some of the dimensions by which to consider barriers, boundaries and opportunities are accessibility (costs of producing and consuming, location, and language, for example); relative size and influence and the relationship configuration between information producer and consumer (one or few or many or mass to one or few or many or mass); privacy, regulation, and control; motivation for use; and user demographics.

Sociologists, historians, and others are now realizing that social phenomena, like environmental phenomena, are inherently complex. This means that we cannot really know with certainty what the effects of our actions will be. Although this has always been the case, the realization is only now getting some traction. Moreover, many people (if not most) still seem to deny its reality and think and act according to older paradigms. Accepting its reality does not mean that we do not know anything or that anything can happen. What is different now is the increased speed, reach, and influence of the mobility. Imagine a missile latching on to the frequency of a cell phone or myriad consequences of remote observation, sensing, and surveillance. On a larger scale, consider the vulnerability or volatility of a complex physical, social, or technological environment where critical limits or tipping points in many important areas are likely to be breached at the same time.

While much of our time in the future will certainly be spent trying to repulse the efforts of people who will use (and attempt to use) mobile intelligence to increase their dominance over others, one of the main points of this pattern is to encourage the exploration of positive possibilities that the new technology opens up. One such area is in the realm of emergency communications. What difference could it make in a situation like the Chernobyl disaster or Hurricane Katrina? Unfortunately it seems quite likely that we will face many new challenges in the future in which our mobile intelligence will be put to the test.

Solution   We can think of mobile intelligence in at least three ways: (1) intelligence about a variety of mobilities, (2) intelligence that can be used in different situations (where the intelligence itself is mobile or "portable"), and (3) mobile intelligence that moves us forward; in other words the intelligence mobilizes people. As researchers, activists, and citizens, we can consciously ask about the "mobility" of our intelligences and reconceptualize them as necessary.

Linked patterns   Strategic Capacity (34), Open Action and Research Network (45), Digital Emancipation (60), Community Currencies (63), Mobile Information and Computer Technology Learning Facilities (77), Future Design (88), Emergency Communication Systems (121), Peaceful Public Demonstrations (133), Activist Road Trip (134).

Problem All technology is social technology. Technology is created by people and is used by people. It exists within a social environment and it has implications for society. Because technology and technological systems can play out in so many ways, this is one of the longest problem statements in the pattern language.

Technological systems are often portrayed as nearly miraculous solutions to problems both real and imagined. For this reason, people put faith in technology that is not always warranted. Moreover, the technologists peddling techno-utopian visions in which technology causes problems to vanish—essentially by magic—are not subjected to the same scrutiny that other societal prognosticators receive. For one reason, technologists, by virtue of their special knowledge and unfathomable jargon, are often intimidating to nontechnologists.

An unquestioning reliance on technology can result in a technocratic culture where people come to expect technological solutions. This over-reliance puts major decisions in the hands of the technologists; degrades public discussion; and diverts attention, discussion, and funds. Sociotechnological systems generally have implicit trajectories. They are often implemented as "total programs" when almost by definition they are partial solutions that do not adequately address the social aspects of the situation either through analysis, co-design, education, or funding. This is what is generally lacking when introducing computers into the classroom or in discussions about bringing inexpensive laptops to the children of Africa.

The use of technology often introduces new problems, including ones that humankind is not prepared for. (And then, of course, the expectations are that technology will solve the new problems.) Introducing mandatory laptop computers in a middle school or high school, for example, soon leads to additional issues. Should students be able to use Instant Messenger during class? Download movies? Play fantasy baseball? As was pointed out in the play *Mitzi's Abortion* (Heffron 2005), based on a true story, technology can tell a pregnant woman that the baby she is carrying has no brain, but it cannot provide any guidance on what she can do about the situation or how to negotiate with her insurance company to help her with financial burdens that may arise. Technology can be used for dumbing down, but having technology should not be an excuse for ignorance. Knowing, for example, that the information you need is on the Internet is not the same as having it in your own mind where you can use it to answer questions or pose new ones.

Moreover, it almost goes without saying that technology is a nearly perfect candidate for systems of exploitation, control, and surveillance. Machines will never be plagued with doubts about ethics or morality as a human pressed into an inhuman situation may be. Nevertheless, we must continually remind ourselves that technology breaks down. It is not perfect and never will be. The large number of failed tests of the Strategic Defense Initiative ("Star Wars"), the mixed results of laptops in schools, the quiet withdrawal of facial recognition systems for security at sports stadiums, and the potential for economic collapse due to unanticipated results of automated buying and selling all show the imperfection of our technological creations. The irony is, however, that technology might be most dangerous when it works correctly. For example, wouldn't a total failure of nuclear or biological weapons be preferable to "success"? Although Isaac Asimov presumed that humans would never allow robots to make life-or-death decisions or take the life of a human, the launch-on-warning computerized systems in the United States (and presumably Russia) are virtually the same, minus the anthropomorphic features we have come to expect in robots.

Context   Virtually anybody who is alive today will be confronted with new technology that is likely to change the circumstances of his or her life. Technology is too important to be left in the hands of the technologists.

Discussion   The interesting and more useful use of the word *criticism* is as it is used in art or literary criticism: the analysis, evaluation, interpretation, and judging of something. Technology, or, rather, its practice, including discourse, development, use, education, funding, regulation, and disposal, in addition to its physical embodiment, deserves this type of attention like all other aspects and creations of humankind.

Although technology, and information and computer technology (ICT) particularly, has a variety of attributes, or "affordances," that will allow or encourage certain capabilities (while discouraging others), and individual people obviously will play important roles in technology use, the extreme weight of the social context will always exert considerable impact. The mistake that people most frequently make is forgetting the fundamental fact that technology in all of its guises is applied within specific social contexts. In other words, the old bumper sticker message *Guns do not kill people, people kill people* could be more accurate if it read, *Guns do not kill people; they just vastly improve the ease and efficiency of doing so*. Without the "need" to shoot people, only a fraction of the world's arsenal would exist. There is no such thing as "technology by itself," and therefore it makes no sense to view it in those terms.

The Strategic Defense Initiative (SDI), commonly called "Star Wars," illustrates many of the reasons that technocriticism is so necessary. Basically untestable and demonstrably unreliable, the SDI effort escalated militarism at the expense of nonmilitary solutions while removing large sums of money from other more worthwhile enterprises. Additional militarization of space and the development of the next generation of nuclear weapons also cry out for very deep technocriticism.

One of the most visible current manifestations of techno-utopianism is that revolving around the prospects of a new "$100 laptop" ostensibly for the children of Africa. Although many people believe that computers would empower people around the world, it is not at all clear why African children would be less attracted to *Grand Theft Auto* or other violent, time-squandering video games than, say, their American counterparts if a brand-new laptop computer was suddenly in their possession. This is not to say that African children should not receive computers, only to stop seeing computers as magic, independent from the social system that creates, uses, and regulates them.

A last example provides a glimpse of what can happen when fast computers and knowledge of human behavior are combined within specific systems of power. In a provocative article, "AI Seduces Stanford Students" (2005), Kevin Poulsen describes a phenomenon called the "chameleon effect," in which "people are perceived as more honest and likeable if they subtly mimic the body language of the person they are speaking with." Now scientists at Stanford University's Virtual Human Interaction Lab have demonstrated that computers can exploit the same phenomenon, but with greater success and on a larger scale. Sixty-nine student volunteers interacted with a realistic human face, a computer-generated "digital agent" that delivered a three-minute persuasive speech. Unbeknown to and undetected by seven out of eight students, the talking head was mimicking their every expression: eye movements, head tilts, and others.

The ominous result of this experiment was that the students reported that the echoing "agent" was "more friendly, interesting, honest, and persuasive" than the one that did not blindly ape the facial movements of its mark. One does not need excess paranoia to imagine what might be in store when ubiquitous mass media systems, perhaps two-way, are joined with the system described above. Poulsen describes one way in which this could be accomplished:

Bailenson [the Stanford researcher] says the research not only shows that computers can take advantage of our psychological quirks, but that they can do it more effectively than humans can because they can execute precise movements with scientifically optimized timing. The killer app is in virtual worlds, where each inhabitant can be presented with a different image, and the chameleon effect is no longer limited to one-on-one interaction. A single speaker—whether an AI or a human avatar—could mimic a thousand people at once, undetected, transforming a cheap salesman's trick into a tool of mass influence.

Ironically the people who are best equipped to apply this pattern are the people who know the most about how technology is designed, deployed, and marketed. Technophiles probably make the best technocritics. This is an argument for technical education that is integrated with the humanities and the social sciences, a marriage that many people in the nontechnical disciplines might find as distasteful as those in the technical disciplines do. A technologically literate society would not "throw technology at problems" any more than they would "throw money at problems." That, however, is not at all the same as saying that technology or money never can help solve problem, as both resources when applied wisely can help immensely.

Organizations like Computer Professionals for Social Responsibility that have worked with issues like SDI and electronic voting and groups like the Union of Concerned Scientists and Electronic Privacy Information Center are working in this area. The bimonthly *Bulletin of the*

Atomic Scientists provides thoughtful discussion on matters of weapons and national security. The world is ready for discussions in this area that are not dominated by the media and the digerati. Many policy options come to mind, but in general, they should be based on informed public discourse. One intriguing example of this is the "codevelopment laws" in Scandinavia in the 1980s in which new technology could not be introduced without the consent of the workers who would be affected by it. Another ripe field is that of genetic engineering of seeds and other biological entities.

Luddism is not an answer to the question of autonomous technology any more than it is to embrace it uncritically. The solution is not to totally eschew the use of technology in society. Technology is an integral part of the human condition. At the same time, it is important for the reasons discussed above to acknowledge and consider how technology is presented, designed, discussed, implemented, and used, just as other activities, particularly ones with similar potential for large-scale disruption, should be subjected to this scrutiny. Unfortunately a surprising number of people are likely to interpret this discussion as being anti-technology. At any rate, this reaction has a chilling effect on the idea of actual conversations about technology (as would befit a democratic society) and the adverse effect of reinforcing the stereotype that technologists are binary thinkers who are incapable of more nuanced thought.

Langdon Winner (1986), one of the intellectual founders of technocriticism (along with Lewis Mumford, Norbert Weiner, and even Dwight Eisenhower), made these statements in relation to the advent of ubiquitous digital computer networks:

As we ponder horizons of computing and society today, it seems likely that American society will reproduce some of the basic tendencies of modernism:

- Unequal power over key decisions about what is built and why
- Concerted attempts to enframe and direct people's lives in both work and consumption
- The presentation of the future society as something nonnegotiable
- The stress on individual gratification rather than collective problems and responsibilities
- Design strategies that conceal and obfuscate important realms of social complexity

Although technological systems can be extremely powerful, they are subject to a number of limitations that must be understood and probed thoroughly if these systems are to be deployed effectively in society. A more visible, inclusive, and engaging practice of technocriticism could go a long way toward educating society on the myriad implications—both creative and destructive—of technology in today's world.

Solution   Technology often alters power relations between people, generally amplifying the power for some and not for others. The development of new military technology throughout history dramatically illustrates this phenomenon. The distribution of computers in society is yet another example. Generally rich people have them, and poor people do not. If computers enable people to be more productive (as computer-related companies assert), then economic benefits would obviously accrue to those that have them. People need to understand or at least anticipate to some degree not only the effects of specific technological artifacts but the sociotechnological systems that they support or destabilize.

Linked patterns   The Good Life (3), Demystification and Reenchantment (14), Dematerialization (18), Citizen Science (37), Economic Conversion (41), Appropriating Technology (108), Socially Responsible Computer Games (126), Power Research (128), Retreat and Reflection (136).

Enabling Systems

Problem   Although the world's economy has grown considerably over the past few decades, half of the world's population subsists on less than $2 (U.S.) per day. Economic inequality is steadily rising, and nearly everywhere the rich are getting richer and the poor are getting poorer. At the same time, meaningful representation among the world's population is steadily degrading. This lack of representation results from, and engenders, increasing power and diminishing accountability of the world's corporate and governmental institutions.

Context   The social world has vast needs and intriguing possibilities for citizen engagement with global affairs. The United Nations is an assembly for the world's nations. Business too has an incredible assortment of institutions and events, such as the World Economics Forum and the Chamber of Commerce.

Discussion   Richard Falk and Andrew Strauss (2001) have explored the possibility of a global parliament. It is their work that inspires this pattern, and many of the ideas advanced here originated in their writings.

This pattern is one of the few in this collection that does not seem to have a concrete analogue in the real world. This is due generally to its extremely broad scope: linking all of the world's inhabitants. The very fact of globalization provides the most solid support (and for the need) for the attainment of the World Citizen Parliament pattern. Smaller versions that approximate some aspects of this pattern do exist, and we can learn a lot from these experiments as we attempt to cultivate democratic processes and institutions that are more wide ranging. The European Parliament may be the most prominent example of a large civic society institution whose representatives are democratically elected by people from various countries.

This pattern, like many of the others in this system, is incomplete. This discussion ultimately must address the following questions:

- What evidence exists that demonstrates the degradation of citizen representation?
- What problems result from degraded citizen representation?
- How would increased representation help?
- What relevant experiments are now underway?
- What could, or should, we do now?
- What design principles should we use in designing new systems?
- What approaches to developing new deliberate bodies can we devise?
- How do evaluate our efforts?

Solution   Develop concepts, design principles, and engage in experiments that lay the groundwork for a world citizen parliament. The new deliberative bodies that are developed in the near future will necessarily be advisory only at the onset. Ultimately the recommendations that they issue will play important roles in policy development, as well as in ways of thinking. Each of the experiments undertaken will undoubtedly have drawbacks; many of these will be revealed only as people use them to address real concerns. Information and communication technology will play an important role in many of these projects, and people in these fields will need to work with social scientists, representatives from civil society organizations, and many others if a world citizen parliament that sensitively, fairly, and wisely explores and addresses the concerns of the world's citizens is ever created.

Linked patterns   Social Dominance Attenuation (4), Global Citizenship (6), Political Settings (7), Big Tent for Social Change (32), Opportunity Spaces (33), Strengthening International Law (42), Meaningful Maps (47), Conversational Support across Boundaries (50), Transparency (64), Free and Fair Elections (68), Document-Centered Discussion (92), Mirror Institutions (94), Power Research (128).

Problem   Approaching two decades after the disappearance of the only superpower rival to the United States, the U.S. military budget is almost as large as all other countries' military budgets combined. The United States continues to spend at cold war levels despite the fact that, as we are slowly learning, none of the most pressing twenty-first-century threats to security—terrorism, proliferation, climate change—are effectively addressed by military force. Why is this the case? In part the reason is that the livelihoods of millions of people in politically powerful military-dependent institutions and communities are tied to the flow of military dollars.

Context   This troubled world is very different today than it was even a few decades ago. We have more to fear from handfuls of determined terrorists and blowback from the environmental damage we have done than from attack by standing armies. Changing times call for changing strategies, yet people with vested economic interests in the status quo always feel threatened by change. Those convinced that our continued well-being depends on redirecting national priorities will find it easier to bring about change if they can reassure people tied into the current system that their economic well-being is not at risk.

Discussion   Economic conversion is the process of efficiently transferring people and facilities from military-oriented to civilian-oriented activity. Changing the consequences of substantial military spending cuts from massive job loss to a change in what people produce on the job removes the politically powerful "jobs" argument. By forcing military programs to be judged on their real contribution to security, conversion is important to more intelligent decision making on national priorities.

Huge military budgets are ineffective in facing down twenty-first-century threats to security. Obviously military spending offers no advantage in confronting the threat of increasingly severe weather events (hurricanes, tornadoes, droughts, floods) that, with other environmental disasters, appear directly linked to global warming. Less obvious but equally true, military force is of little use in confronting terrorist threats. The world's most powerful military did nothing to prevent or stop the terrorist attacks of September 11, 2001. Virtually every terrorist caught and every terrorist plot foiled has been the result of first-rate intelligence and police work, not the threat or use of military force. Military force has also been useless in preventing the spread of weapons of mass destruction.

Not only is high military spending ineffective in addressing the most pressing security threats, it is also a serious drain on economic strength, one of the most important sources of national well-being and international influence. This idea is hardly new in economics; it goes back to Adam Smith, the eighteenth-century founder of capitalism. Smith argued that military spending was economically unproductive. Decades ago, economists commonly used *military burden* almost synonymously with *military budget*.

Today the problem is the same, but some mechanisms are different. Large numbers of highly skilled engineers and scientists are needed to develop technologically sophisticated military weapons and related systems, but engineers and scientists are also critical to the civilian industry. They develop new technologies that improve products and processes, driving the growth of productivity, which allows producers to pay higher wages and keep prices low. Rising wages and low prices are the recipe for increasing economic prosperity. Quality products at low prices are also key to keeping industries competitive with rivals abroad, and therefore to keeping unemployment low and profits strong.

By directing the nation's technological talent away from developing the technologies that civilian-oriented producers need, huge military budgets drain a nation's economic vitality. This is one reason for both the collapse of the Soviet Union and the deindustrialization of the United States. Thus, there are compelling economic and security arguments for reorienting national priorities. Economic conversion facilitates this process.

When World War II ended, the United States transferred 30 percent of its economic output from military-oriented to civilian-oriented activity in one year (1945–1946) without unemployment rising above 3 percent. That remarkable feat, which depended on advance planning by the private sector and government, successfully reconverted an economy that had moved into military production during the war back to producing the civilian products it made before the war. Although the scale is smaller today, the problem is more complicated. Unlike the 1940s reconversion, most of those working today in what President Eisenhower called the military-industrial complex have never done anything but military-oriented work. And the difference between military and civilian-oriented activity has become much greater. The process is no longer one of going back to what is familiar; it is now a move to new work in a very different environment. For example, military sector engineers today are under enormous pressure to squeeze every ounce of performance out of products they design. With enormous military budgets, cost is not nearly as important an issue. Civilian sector products must perform well, but keeping cost low is absolutely critical. Engineering for maximum performance with little attention to cost is very different from engineering for low cost with reasonable performance. To successfully transfer from military to civilian work, engineers must be retrained (given some different skills) and reoriented (taught to look at engineering from a different perspective). In general, more specialized and skilled people require more retraining and reorientation.

Converting facilities and equipment requires assessing their character and condition to find the best match to productive civilian use. From 1961 to 1981, more than ninety U.S. military bases were closed and converted to industrial parks, research centers, college campuses, and airports—with a net 20 percent increase in employment. In the 1990s, Bergstrom Air Force Base in Austin, Texas, was converted to a booming civilian airport. In October 2005, the nuclear weapons complex at Rocky Flats, Colorado, was closed, and the land on which it stood is being turned into a national wildlife refuge.

The conversion movement in the United States began in the 1970s and grew through the early 1990s. In 1977, bipartisan sponsors introduced the National Economic Conversion Act in the Senate and, soon after, the House of Representatives. Repeatedly reintroduced through the years, it never became law. If it had, the decentralized nationwide private and public sector process of conversion planning and support it would have set up would have prevented the economic shock wave that military-dependent workers and communities felt in the late 1980s and early 1990s and made it politically much easier to forestall the subsequent return to cold war military spending levels.

Given the urgent need to redirect the nation's attention and resources to address the economic and security realities of the twenty-first century, economic conversion has never been more important. Through letters, town hall meetings, and personal visits, representatives in the Congress must learn that reducing the military drain on the economy is critical to rebuilding the American middle class, repairing the decaying national infrastructure, and addressing the real problems of national security. Working with existing citizens' organizations, conversion can help build alliances among the growing number of businesspeople who oppose the unilateralist militarism that has poisoned the nation's image abroad, workers who see themselves going backward, and environmentalists who want the nation to free the resources necessary to stop the slow-motion disaster of global warming.

Solution   Conversion defines economic alternatives for those tied into institutions of militarism and war anywhere, helping to build support for redirecting national priorities toward more effective, nonmilitary solutions to real national security needs. It is also critical to removing the economic burden of high military budgets and thus reinvigorating national economies.

Linked patterns   Social Responsibility (8), Collective Decision Making (10), Working-Class Consciousness (12), Transforming Institutions (19), Whole Cost (28), Technocriticism (39), Peace Education (56), Grassroots Public Policy Development (78), Online Antipoverty Community (103), Power Research (128).

Problem   In an era when international cooperation is critical, no overall reliable system of global governance is in place that enjoys universal respect and satisfies concerns about accountability of leaders, participation of peoples and their representatives, and transparency of the regulatory process itself. Particularly disturbing is the persistent tendency of political leaders to consider resort to war as their fundamental instrument for the resolution of international conflict and to divert vast resources to the preparation for war without being constrained by the limits set by international law governing the use of force.

Context   It is important not to overstate the role and contributions of international law, which in the past has been used to lend an appearance of legality to colonialism and aggressive war, as well as to serve the interests of oppressive governments that engaged in abuses of their populations, being shielded by the law that upheld the territorial supremacy of sovereign states. International law is relevant in many different settings that reflect the extraordinary diversity of transnational activity in the contemporary world. Legal professionals represent governments, corporations, banks, and international institutions to facilitate their activities, both by acting within the limits set by regulations contained in international law and by altering legal standards to the extent helpful for more orderly conduct of affairs. Ordinary citizens, nongovernmental organizations, and international civil servants all invoke international law to influence policy debates on a variety of global issues. International law is an important means for communicating claims and grievances and provides insight into whether particular demands are reasonable. The viability of international law has been drawn into serious question by the American response to the attacks of September 11, 2001. It has been claimed that the nature of international terrorism, combined with potential access to weaponry of mass destruction, especially nuclear weapons, makes it unreasonable for states to wait to be attacked. The U.S. government relied on such reasoning to justify its invasion of Iraq in 2003, which was widely regarded by international law specialists and world public opinion as a flagrant violation of both the U.N. Charter and international law. International law is partly motivated by considerations of mutual convenience (e.g., the immunity of ambassadors, safety signals at sea) and partly reflective of the accumulated wisdom of seasoned statesmen.

Discussion   From the perspective of the United States, the country that is most responsible for establishing the legal framework governing war after World War II and also the main challenger in the light of recent global developments, the resolution of the debate about whether to limit foreign policy by reference to international law is of great importance. It should be noted that the two greatest failures in American foreign policy in the past fifty years have resulted from the Vietnam and Iraq wars. These failures would not have occurred if American policy had been self-limited by reference to international law. It is a general fallacy to suppose that in the twenty-first century, a powerful country is better off if it is not restricted in its policy options by law. The evidence suggests that the restrictions contained in international law reflect the encoded wisdom of several centuries of statecraft. The narrowing of the availability of war by international law over the course of the past century is an acknowledgment, in large part, of the growing dysfunctionality of war as an instrument for the resolution of conflict.

It is not only war and uses of force that need to be regulated effectively by international law; it is also necessary for advancing the human security of peoples throughout the world afflicted by disease, poverty, environmental degradation, and oppressive governance. Respect for law and international institutions encourages cooperative problem solving that is increasingly necessary given the realities of globalization. In this regard, it is necessary to adapt the lawmaking procedures of the world to the significant roles being played by a variety of nonstate actors, including market forces, regional organization, and civil society organizations. Whether incorporating this globalizing agenda and these nonstate actors is achieved by an enlarged conception of international law or by a transition in legal conceptualizing that adopts the terminology of global law is less important than the realization that the law dimension of world order is of critical importance in the struggle to achieve a less violent, more equitable, and more sustainable future for the whole of humanity.

The prospects for strengthening international law have two important current centers of gravity. The first is the unresolved debate in the United States as to whether to pursue security within a framework that respects international law and the authority of the United Nations. The learning experience associated with the failure of the Iraq policy needs to be converted into a renewed appreciation that reliance on military dominance and discretionary wars is dysfunctional at this stage of history and that a voluntary respect for international law would simultaneously serve the national and global interest. The resolution of this debate is of great importance to Americans and the rest of the world because of the leadership role that the United States plays on the global stage. The evidence supports the view that American global leadership will recover its claims of legitimacy only if it is able to revive its earlier enthusiasm for promoting the rule of law in world politics.

The second is that this specific debate, heightened in intensity after 9/11, hides an underlying set of issues associated with achieving a more effective and equitable approach to global governance in the light of a series of world order challenges that have been generated by such problems as global warming, an imminent energy squeeze, mass migrations, and an array of self-determination struggles. At present, contradictory trends are undermining efforts to fashion a humane approach to these challenges. On the one side, globalization in all its forms is rendering the boundaries of states increasingly irrelevant to the patterning of many substantive concerns, while at the same time border controls are growing harsher and walls are being created to fence some people in and others out.

This requires a new set of international legal initiatives, ambitiously conceived, to address these problems in a manner that does not produce chaos, oppressive violence, and ecological collapse. It is no longer acceptable to consider that world order can be entrusted to sovereign states pursuing their short-term interests. Protecting the future for the peoples of the world presupposes an ethos of responsibility, which rests on the willingness to replace traditions of unilateralism and coercion with improved procedures of cooperation and persuasion. It is here that the past and future of international law offer hope to humanity provided that the turn away from law can be reversed.

The growing fragility and complexity of international life provides a fundamental argument for strengthening international law and moving toward the establishment of global law that is able to regulate for the common good activities of market forces, regional organizations, international institutions, civil society actors, and the behavior of states. With a growing prospect of an energy squeeze requiring a momentous shift to a postpetroleum world society, the strains on regulatory regimes will be immense. Trust in and respect for international law will encourage approaches that are more likely to be fair and effective than the sort of chaos and resentments that will follow if relative power and wealth are relied on to shift the main burdens of adjustment to the weak and poor.

Solution   The lessons of failed wars over the course of recent decades need to be converted into a sophisticated appreciation that reliance on military superiority and discretionary recourse to wars has become increasingly dysfunctional at this stage of history and extremely wasteful with respect to vital resources needed to achieve other essential human goals, including the reduction of poverty, disease, and crime. Protecting the future for the peoples of the world presupposes an ethos of responsibility, which rests on the willingness by both the powerful and the disempowered to replace, whenever possible, coercion with persuasion and to rely much more on cooperative and nonviolent means to achieve order and change. Law is centrally important in providing guidelines and procedures for moving toward a less violent, more equitable, and more sustainable future for the whole of humanity. With the rise of nonstate actors (market and civil society actors, international institutions of regional and global scope), there is underway a necessary transition from an era of international law to an epoch of global law. It will be beneficial for the citizens and governments of the world to encourage this transition.

Linked patterns   Health as a Universal Right (5), Global Citizenship (6), Political Settings (7), Social Responsibility (8), Collective Decision Making (10), Translation (15), Public Agenda (30), Big Tent for Social Change (32), World Citizen Parliament (40), Conversational Support across Boundaries (50), Truth and Reconciliation Commissions (51), Transparency (64), Free and Fair Elections (68), Multiparty Negotiation for Conflict Resolution (79), Citizenship Schools (96).

Problem   A key challenge facing movements for social change is the global commercial media. A handful of Western-based transnational media corporations, working in tandem with regional companies, control most programming, emphasizing entertainment to recruit urban consumers, and circulating news primarily framed by the interests of corporate business and Western foreign policy. Public programming to encourage dialogue and debate of public issues has withered. Stark inequalities are increasing, in both poor and rich countries, between those with the full means to produce communications and those without, especially if we factor in the violence of poverty, illiteracy, and patriarchal, racial, and caste oppression.

Context   A global network of communications activists, advocates, and researchers is emerging to address these problems (Kidd, forthcoming). This network of networks operates simultaneously on at least three planes: the construction of alternative communications media, the reform of the mainstream corporate and state media, and the support of transnational communications networks for social change movements. Alternative media projects (zines, radio, video, television, and Internet sites and blogs) not only serve people seldom represented in the corporate media; they also demonstrate what democratic media might look like in their alternative content, modes of operation, and overall philosophy. Communication reformers campaign to make existing local, national, and global communications systems more accessible, representative, accountable, and participatory. Finally, media activists work in support of social change movements whose transnational communications networks also provide additional links for the movements to democratize media. Why now? This is due to at least three interrelated global trends. First, the global shift to neoliberalism presents people all over the world with a complicated but clear set of common problems. Second, the communications networks first emerged as links among social justice movements to address these common problems. Finally, the network of communications networks began to take its own shape as groups everywhere inventively adapted the glut of consumer hardware and software from the transnational corporate market.

Discussion   The transnational movement to transform communications predates the shift to global neoliberalism. During the 1970s, led by the Non-Aligned Movement (NAM), a coalition of national governments of the global South, mobilized to challenge the old imperial status quo in which news, information, and entertainment media were controlled by Western governments and corporate powers. They called within the U.N. system for a New World Information and Communications Order (NWICO), for an end to the dominance of the Western colonial powers, the equitable distribution of the world's information resources, the right to communicate, and the support of alternative and community-based media in democratizing communications. Rejecting this multilateral consensus, the U.S. and U.K. governments withdrew from the commission, arguing with the commercial media industry that any measures to limit Western media corporations or journalists represented state censorship of the free flow of information.

The United States instead shifted to neoliberalism, or the Washington agenda. It called for market rules (privatization of public resources and deregulation of government oversight of corporations) at home and abroad. The Reagan government successfully gutted antitrust and public interest rules, as well as public supported programs at home, and pushed for the implementation of similar policies in other countries through its powerful voice in the International Monetary Fund (IMF) and World Bank. However, the U.S. government was still unable to win in the multilateral arena, failing to get culture (audiovisual services) onto the trade block in the General Agreement on Trades and Tariffs (GATT), the precursor to the World Trade Organization (WTO). Instead, it decided to work on the less powerful countries one or two at a time and began unilateral free trade talks with Taiwan, Canada, and Mexico.

During the 1980s, the number and sophistication of alternative media projects and networks grew around the world. These networks emerged from both the confluence of links between social movements, primarily from the countries of the South, mobilizing against the Washington agenda; and alternative media groups inventively seizing the newly available consumer production media. Primarily based in local geographic communities, media activists began to link across their own countries and across national and regional boundaries to share resources and campaign for greater access to radio, cable, satellite, and the newly emerging computer-linked systems. They also began to support one another on common issues, including massive cuts in public spending and state-run services, growth in global media conglomeration, and U.S., Japanese, and European calls for global standards in digital systems and copyright rules.

The transnational networks begun in this era include the World Association of Community Radio (AMARC) and the Association of Progressive Communicators (APC). AMARC now operates through regional organizations, program sharing through special theme-connected collaborations (against, for example, racism and discrimination against women) and global media reform coalitions. Formed to support the global network of women, labor, ecologists, indigenous peoples, and activists organizing against free trade and corporate globalization, APC continues to build on the idea of communication rights, prioritizing the capacity building of women, rural and poor people, and the media reform efforts of member groups.

During the 1990s, a new set of activists demonstrated the more tactical use of the technologies and networks in political change. In 1989, the prodemocracy activists of Tiananmen Square in Beijing, China, used fax machines to get their message out to the world. In 1994, the Zapatista National Liberation Army built on what Harry Cleaver (1998) called the emerging transnational "electronic fabric of struggle," employing old and new media and global media networks, to challenge the North American Free Trade Agreement (NAFTA). In 1997, Korean labor and social movement activists used highly sophisticated broadband media to demonstrate against the IMF and also opened Jinbonet, the first Web-based interactive people's news service. This alternative vision of communications took another leap forward in 1999 when the first Independent Media Center (IMC) formed in Seattle to support the protests against the WTO. Drawing from the Zapatistas, the IMCistas created a global news network. Building on the existing networks opposed to corporate globalization and providing easy-to-use open-publishing software, the global IMC quickly grew to over 150 centers around the world.

Since 2001, the network of networks has begun to flex its collective muscles to reform the dominant global media system. Coalitions of activists, often in tandem with progressive government representatives, are calling for more democratic communications at the World Summit on the Information Society; against the U.S. push for the free trade of culture, with a Convention on Cultural Diversity, adopted by UNESCO in 2005 (http://www .cdc-ccd.org); and for the protection of the global knowledge commons with a development agenda and a treaty on access to knowledge and technology at the World Intellectual Property Organization.

Solution   This new network of networks demonstrates that another communications is possible and already happening. Its strength is based in cooperation through social movement organizing, media reform campaigns, and the adaptation of information and communications for the greater use of all. Almost all are severely challenged by their lack of sustainable funds and technical resources, and continuing inequities between members of racialized and gendered class differences and of cultural capital. However, faced with the stark realities of neoliberal immiseration, the network continues to build, creating a complex lattice of local-local, regional (especially South-South), and transnational links that circumvent the old colonial North-South linkages and power dynamics. If there is one glaring structural vacuum, it is the lack of involvement of U.S. activists, and particularly those based in U.S. communities and social justice movements. In the next five years, one of the key challenges will be for U.S. activists to bring together efforts for media justice in the United States, recognize the leadership of the rest of the world, and assist in mobilizing against the Washington agenda at home. What can people do to help build this network? In their own area, they can help support or produce programming for their local alternative communications media. They can also find and support the existing local, national, and global campaigns to reform the mainstream corporate and state media. This is especially crucial in the United States, whose media and media policy affect so much of the world. Finally they can educate themselves about what is going on in their own communities, national and especially international, and then help link the work of the local and global justice networks.

Linked patterns   Global Citizenship (6), Working-Class Consciousness (12), Strategic Capacity (34), Media Literacy (35), Alternative Media in Hostile Environments (53), Indigenous Media (55), Digital Emancipation (60), Community Networks (61), Online Community Service Engine (62), Media Diversity (66), Citizen Journalism (91), Community-Building Journalism (97), Homemade Media (110), Citizens' Tribunal (129), Tactical Media (131), Media Intervention (132), Activist Road Trip (134).

Problem Conscientious social and environmental activists try to understand the issues or problems they confront rather than act blindly. However, significant issues are typically intricate, ill defined, and conceptually complicated, to the point where whole careers are devoted to sorting out small portions of them and action is delayed indefinitely or activist energy dissipated. But the alternative of rushing to action, substituting passion or outrage for understanding, is counterproductive in its own well-documented ways.

Context This pattern is for people, on their own or within organizations, who are ready to initiate meaningful action. They have done enough analysis of whatever issue or problem they are concerned with and have developed enough conviction to be sure that action is needed. Their question is, What action? or perhaps, How can I focus the notions, wishes, and urges that surround this issue into specific, meaningful steps? This pattern does not give detailed answers; instead, it suggests a mode of thinking that can generate such answers.

Discussion The complexity of significant issues today is overwhelming. This is obvious for national issues such as health care, outsourcing of jobs, or energy policy. But small-scale problems, such as a derelict lot, are often equally complex (think of drug dealing, vandalism, invasive plants, liability, and city departmental turf battles) in relation to the energy and goodwill available to deal with them. Seemingly obvious moves ("Let's all clean it up!") get blocked in unexpected ways ("Who are you to order us around?") or generate further issues (the lot becomes a better place to play hooky). The activist has to escape the paralysis of analysis, but also must be accurate about the effects and costs of actions, which can radiate far beyond the immediate zone in which they occur.

Large- and small-scale social and environmental problems in the United States have come under concerted assault before, most notably in the Progressive era of the early twentieth century. The great successes of that time in clean water, safe housing, conservation of natural areas, and much more also established dispassionate expertise as the preferred approach to such issues (at least by liberals). Gather enough data, include enough considerations, weigh the evidence objectively, and sensible, legally defensible decisions will emerge—or so goes the argument. However, as the complexity of issues has increased and as affluence has permitted many more parties to mobilize their own experts, the ideal of dispassionate expertise is becoming unreachable. Technicalities breed subtechnicalities, and the latter sub-subtechnicalities, in a fractal process of escalating delay and cost. And it turns out that many of the actors have more uses for the delays than for smooth functioning.

There is a way forward, embodied in the long tradition of physical design. Buildings, ships, bridges and dams, water systems, and waste disposal are objects of transcendent complexity if one tries to assemble in advance all the knowledge and techniques that might be required to make them, but yet they do come into existence and serve their diverse tasks effectively.

The process that generates buildings and bridges, design, is quite different from expert-based decision making, even though expertise plays an enormous role in it. Instead of assuming that the answer can be deduced definitively from the evidence, the designer takes a different stance. The designer constructs, in imagination, an intervention in the world and then uses powerful representations of the world, such as drawings, mathematical models, or simulations, to assess the ways in which the contemplated intervention would change the world. Usually modifications are indicated, and the process goes around again, often numerous times, before the design settles into final form.

This design stance can be used for many different kinds of problems, from house building to social activism. Houses are a straightforward example to start with. The early stages of designing a house are typically to have some general ideas about its features and character, to choose a location, and to make some rough sketches or diagrams about how the features might be physically embodied. Already at this point, constraints and limitations begin to show themselves, such as high cost or the difficulty of all rooms having the same dramatic ocean view. Client and designer reimagine the house in ways that address these challenges somehow and may also reveal opportunities, for example, a convenient location for storage. New drawings emerge, often with labels as to sizes, materials, and the like. There may be several rounds of imagining and drawing. Eventually the drawings have become detailed and definite enough to guide construction. The dream has evolved into a reality.

Social activists often use much the same process to establish a program or campaign for a reform. The locus of action is societal, say, a budget decision, rather than physical; the constraints may have more to do with politics or social history than with drainage or carpeting; the number of people affected may be much larger than a household; there may be spreadsheets or maps or organizational charts rather than sketches or blueprints. But the same cycle of constructing an intervention in the world, using imagination aided by concrete representation, is there.

Solution   Approach issues with the stance of the designer: construct, in imagination assisted by concrete representation, ways to intervene in the world for the better. More specifically, choose a client, a locus of action, and a form of intervention; use static or dynamic simulations to indicate how the setting will react to the intervention; gather information and make analyses (but limit the scale to the smallest allowed by the setting) to shape the details of the contemplated intervention; modify, adjust, and refine repeatedly, evaluating effects at each round. Assume few limits at the start, and use the iterative process of modifying and evaluating to determine which real limits exist and how to cope with them. When the right balance of timeliness and effectiveness presents itself, follow the advice of Samuel Mockbee, the noted architect of housing and community buildings for rural and poor America: "Proceed and be bold."

Linked patterns   Dematerialization (18), Teaching to Transgress (20), Sustainable Design (22), Meaningful Maps (47), Citizen Access to Simulations (48), Wholesome Design for Wicked Problems (82), Design for Unintended Use (84), Civic Capabilities (85), Future Design (88), Thinking Communities (118).

Problem   As local and global problems become more numerous and more intractable, people and groups of people are working together to take appropriate action to address these urgent problems. Unfortunately, the increasing size and complexity of these problems and the corresponding actions that are required introduce a set of thorny issues that must be addressed for these actions to be effective.

Context   This pattern can be used in situations where a distributed, diverse, dynamic group of people is working toward complementary goals in complex, collaborative efforts.

Discussion   The ability of people to form effective open action and research networks is critical to the success of any attempt at significant social and environmental amelioration. It is also an approach that is only now being explored. For that reason, the concept—and this pattern—reflect the uncertainty and ambiguity inherent in the situation.

Most of the daunting problems that we face today are large and complex. Grappling with large and complex problems is invariably best served when addressed by many people working together. Indeed this is often the case, as each stakeholder in any situation can be said to be working on the problem. Yet each person and organization working on the problem has a unique orientation that can be at odds with others. *Orientation* is a broad term that includes reward structures; goals, tactics, and strategies; areas of interests; obligations and allegiances; values and norms, status, legitimacy, and power; and ultimately the very language that the community uses to discuss the issues. Consider, for example, the wide range of people who are working to minimize the negative effects of global climate change, or what Margaret Keck (2002) calls an "ecology of agents." These people include scientists, activists, inventors, "green" businesspeople, educators, politicians, and ordinary people among others, and these people are as often as not members of other organizations and networks with diverse goals and varying resources and abilities to influence others.

It is against and within this complex environment that the stakeholder players must act and interact. This diverse group of people of continually shifting size, shape, orientation, and modus operandi can scarcely be called a team since teams (particularly in sports) have a single objective. It is clear that many of the players working in these new open networks have similar objectives, working, for example, for social and environmental ameliorization, and these players will come from a multitude of communities: some are interested in research, some action, some the creation of policy, and some physical or material changes right now, while others are interested in abstract goals to be attained in the indeterminate future. In the worst case, the diversity of the players destroys the team. Ideally the diversity is the source of its strength. (Indeed diversity of thinking is essential to effective strategy. See the Strategic Capacity pattern.)

According to Ganz (2004), "The task of devising strategy in complex, changing environments may require interaction among team members like the performance of a jazz ensemble. As a kind of distributed cognition, it may require synthesizing skills and information beyond the ken of any one individual, making terms of that interaction particularly important." Nearly opposite to the ensemble idea is the impossible vision of herding cats "in which each "cat" is totally unconcerned about the doings of the other "cats."

The networks that this pattern must address vary tremendously. At one end of the scale are networks with few members and resources, short duration, and informal procedures. At the other end are networks like the LTER (Long Term Ecological Research) Network that was started in 1980 and involves twenty-six sites in the United States, and over 1,800 scientists and students (Karasti and Syrjänen 2004). Although the network is fairly well financed (by the National Science Foundation) and is more formal and less diverse than some other groups, the networks on both ends of the scale share many points in common befitting their structure as networks of semiautonomous peers.

Some of the questions that this network approach should ultimately address are as follows:

- How can differences of opinion be "managed," that is, encouraged to some degree, while not allowing them to become destructive?
- How are coordination and cooperation accomplished without coercion?
- How can we cooperatively develop useful modes of organization and engagement that are especially suited for these new environments and ensembles?
- How can people maintain respect for allies who have other perspectives and capitalize effectively on the diversity of the ensemble?
- How do efforts survive personnel change by ensuring that relevant information, including facts, lessons learned, and intriguing opportunities, is made available to new members?
- How can environmental scientists and other types of researchers (including social scientists) conduct research that meets the demands of their profession and the needs of the communities they are working with?
- How are conflicts and misunderstandings over the short-term and long-term goals reconciled?

Each organizational type (and each organization) has its own orientation that encompasses its thinking and acting, and it is this orientation that is likely to be challenged when working with others.

Shared concerns and principles help bring people together into groups, organizations, and networks. Beyond that, however, other things are also critical. The individuals within the network should be able to work with other people to solve problems collectively and help maintain cordiality and integrity within the group. Also because the membership of these networks is dynamic, there must be ways to bring in new members easily. Besides shared values and shared ideas about the roles, interests, and constraints of the other players, there should be shared goals. Goals and other forms of collective, documented statements or plans, however symbolic they might be, can provide coherence over time.

Margaret Keck's work in Brazil provides an excellent example of the power that these documents can have. In 1971, the Solução Integrada (Integrated Solution) was included as the sanitation component of the metropolitan development plan. However, it was abandoned by the following government and replaced by a more expensive, less popular, and more environmentally degrading plan called SANEGRAN. According to Keck, the very existence of the plan made it "possible for nontechnical social and political actors to challenge public authority on water policy." In fact, in more striking terms, "Like a shadow government existing in counter point to sitting ones, the plan has functioned as a shadow sanitation plan for São Paulo for more than a quarter century, making critical action more possible" (Keck 2002).

Girard and Stark (2007) point out the importance of agreeing on general philosophical aims among disparate groups without descending into micromanagement or debate. Sharing of ideas, documents, and information was the also general aim of the Telecommunications Policy Roundtable that met monthly in Washington, D.C., in the 1990s to help build a general public interest policy for the Internet and other information technologies. The LTER Network, as a body of researchers, places data in a central position for their work and has developed specific formats to encourage the development and sharing of data as well as policies for its use in a loosely coupled network configuration (Karasti and Syrjänen 2004).

Today's phenomenon of creating movies with a team that was assembled for the purpose of making a single movie is instructive. Clearly reputation and connections play some part in the selection of individuals. Once on the set, however, the person's skill set, role in the enterprise, and ability to work with others in a dynamic milieu where unexpected events may arise is put to the test. While the open networks we discuss here are not identical, the agility, intelligence, and effectiveness that these groups can potentially manifest is huge.

Solution   Acknowledge the importance of this pattern, and work consciously to identify the inherent dilemmas of the situation, as well as the emerging wisdom that is to be learned from the practice. We must take note of the avenues that are likely to yield important and useful insights about working together as we move forward.

Linked patterns   Civic Intelligence (1), Collective Decision Making (10), Working-Class Consciousness (12), Education and Values (17), Strategic Capacity (34), Citizen Science (37), Mobile Intelligence (38), Digital Emancipation (60), Open Access Scholarly Publishing (76), Grassroots Public Policy Development (78), Informal Learning Groups (98), Appreciative Collaboration (99), Self-Help Groups (105), Thinking Communities (118), Open Source Search Technology (125), Open Source Everything (127), Activist Road Trip (134).

Problem   Economic indexes of various kinds attempt to measure the well-being of nations, markets, corporations, individual people, and society. Most of these economic indexes express return only in monetary format, and risk is calculated on the standard deviation of this monetary expression. These economic indexes also need to include information that makes life worth living, natural and social capital (living capital), so nonmonetary rewards are also included in the standard deviation and risks to human well-being can be indicated more accurately.

Context   Trading on the benchmark of indexes has become increasingly popular. As indexes become more widely used than ever before, they become easy indicators, for those they benefit, in measuring how our world is doing, according to them, and skew the honest reality for humanity that we hope to protect. It is imperative to accurately measure the well-being of nations, corporations, individual people, and societies through indexes that adequately reflect the true costs and benefits contributing to the well-being of the world.

Discussion   Indexes take on a market theory notion that the efficient frontier has all the information needed to calculate an accurate return (reward) versus risk (cost) index. Following this notion is the idea that filtering the market for certain criteria of a specialized index lowers the amount of return received for risk taken, because filtered information is inefficient. This raises questions about the efficiency of markets because active managers filter economic information every day to create specialized portfolios to increase return. On this, it would theoretically stand that an index measuring the well-being of society could filter for criteria rewarding the common good with little to no ill effect from lack of the so-called efficiency imbibed by the market.

Around the globe, there is an increase in the number of sustainability and social responsibility indexes (SRI). These indexes came out of first-generation socially conscious investing that excluded corporate stock from investment portfolios on the basis of particular activities deemed to be unethical. From this, a second generation has emerged, and the focus of SRI has changed primarily to identifying social and environmental issues that are material to business performance. This is an increased attempt by companies to assess the materiality of sustainability issues on (stock) value creation. These indexes paint a picture that socially responsibility is important only when a financial gain is made by corporations or stockholders. This is not exactly what we are looking for when we hope to use indexes to help measure the well-being of the world. When individual investors purchase SRI traded securities and indexes, they still have to deal with the reality that the costs to living capital are making life less valuable even while their portfolios grow.

Gross domestic product (GDP) and gross national product (GNP) per capita have most lately been used as an index of standard of living in an economy. They measure only the population's ease in satisfying their material wants (an index of reward for risk taken); all else that contributes to the sustainability of people and the environment is lost. "Adding up the monetary transactions in an economy and calling this prosperity obscures an honest account of the well-being of nations" (Anielski 2000).

Quality of life and standard of living should not be separate measurements in an index. "A more complex index of standard of living than GDP must be employed to take into account not only the material standard of living but also other factors that contribute to human well-being such as leisure, safety, cultural resources, social life, mental health, and environmental quality issues, to name a few" (Anielski 2000).

Simon Kuznets's idea, "[in] favor of more inclusive measures, less dependent on markets" (Anielski 2000), rings true as a more realistic approach to well-being. "The eventual solution would obviously lie in devising a single yardstick of both economies [virtual wealth, that is, money, debt, and stock markets; and real wealth—human, natural and social capital] . . . that would perhaps lie outside the different economic and social institutions and be grounded in experimental science (of nutrition, warmth, health, shelter, etc.)" (Anielski 2000). The business for this millennium is to take up this empirical economic challenge for a single bottom line index for national well-being:

The U.S. Genuine Progress Indicator (GPI) and its predecessor, the Index for Sustainable Economic Welfare (ISEW) provide the basis for developing a new accountancy to address Kuznets' challenge. The U.S. GPI released in 1995 and since updated . . . is one of the most ambitious attempts at calculating the total benefits and costs related to [economics for community] for the U.S. First developed by Clifford W. Cobb, GPI/ISEW remains one of the most important attempts to measure sustainable current welfare. . . .

The GPI adds a cost side to the growth ledger, begins to account for the aspects of the economy that lie outside the realm of monetary exchange, acknowledges that the economy exists for future generations as well as for the present one and adjusts for income disparities. The GPI begins with personal consumption expenditures as a baseline, the way the GDP does. Personal spending by households makes up roughly 65 percent of the U.S. GDP. The GPI then make a series of 24 adjustments for unaccounted benefits, depreciation costs (for social and natural capital) and deducts regrettable social and environmental expenditures. Specific elements of the GPI include personal consumer expenditures, income, value and cost of consumer spending on durable goods and household capital, cost of household pollution abatement, cost of commuting, cost of crime, cost of automobile accidents, cost of family breakdown, value of housework and parenting, value of voluntary work, loss of leisure time, services of streets and highways, cost of underemployment, air pollution, ozone depletion, water pollution, noise pollution, cost of depletion of non renewable, loss of forests, long term environmental damage, loss of wetlands, net capital investment, net foreign lending/borrowing. (Anielski 2000)

The GPI has also set goals for itself "to improve its framework in the areas of human capital, technology, government spending, social infrastructure, natural capital and environmental accounts, ecological carrying capacity, genetic diversity, water projects, workplace environment, underground economy, and pollution and lifestyle induced disease" (Anielski 2000).

The results of the GPI reveal that "well-being has declined while virtual wealth (debt, stock markets) have grown exponentially. One could say that while we are making more money we are effectively eroding the living capital which makes our lives worthwhile. "The primary benefit of the GPI is to provide decision makers with a more holistic account of the economic well-being of their community" (Anielski 2000). Anielski continues, "Any accounting system of well-being must be aligned with the values, experiences, and physical realities of the citizens of a community. The challenge in future GPI/ISEW accounting will be the ability of constructing accounts that are consistent with the held values, principles, and ethical foundation of a community or society."

Solution   Alternative indexes like the Genuine Progress Indicator that include natural and human capital can illuminate the real picture of human well-being, which can be obfuscated by traditional economic indexes. "The ultimate utility of such measurement efforts is that the information provides evidence of trends in the welfare of society" (Anielski 2000).

Linked patterns   The Commons (2), The Good Life (3), Social Responsibility (8), Matrifocal Orientation (9), Whole Cost (28), Indicators (29), Public Agenda (30), Positive Health Information (74), Grassroots Public Policy Development (78), Sustainability Appraisal (100), Shared Vision (101).

Problem   People are often unaware of the state of the world around them. (especially "invisible," second-order or abstract relationships). Many of the important issues for the community, the environment, and humanity are difficult to see. Improving the world requires understanding the current situation, highlighting the important factors, and helping others understand the issues. How can we collect up-to-date information and present it in a way that people find easy to understand?

Context   This pattern is useful for community groups, advocacy groups, and campaigns that are working to improve the world around them. This might be about local environmental quality, promoting international respect for human rights, ensuring basic needs such as clean water or nutrition, or providing access to opportunities in a neighborhood, city, or country. Groups need to target their resources carefully to achieve maximum impact. They also want to communicate their concerns and encourage others to support their work. To be effective, they need to reveal and suggest potential relationships. A person in a neighborhood could find out where he or she could buy locally grown produce or learn about worm bins and composting.

Discussion   To act effectively to improve a situation requires understanding that situation. Using a map is a way of monitoring the current situation in an area and showing how this is changing. It is also a way of presenting issues to other people to raise their awareness and encourage them to support the work.

Examples of using maps in this way include green maps (www.greenmap.org) of cities that show information about local open space, green transport options, pollution problems, renewable resources, sustainable or fair trade businesses, or cultural facilities; *The State of the World Atlas* (Kidronl, Segal, and Smith 2003), which includes a large set of global maps covering topics such as political systems, transnationals, climate change, biodiversity, human rights, war and peace, malnutrition, and life expectancy; locally produced maps such as the Sheffield Food Map (Fletcher, Mills, and Gaskill 2005), which shows locations of community cafés; healthy and socially responsible eating places; opportunities to grow food, buy seeds, or get advice on growing; and places to get advice on healthy nutrition, cooking, and health.

It is important that the map is easy for readers to understand. Distinctive icons, graphs, and other visual features should be designed to represent the key topics. The Green Maps project provides a set of icons that can be used for maps concerned with environmental issues. Displaying such icons on a map can make inequalities between different areas easy to see.

It may be helpful to make the map available on the Internet, but giving the information away freely requires considering how the funding to keep the map up to date will be sustainable. There may also be online approaches available in the future that would encourage collaborative map development among community activists and other civil society organizations.

It is important that the map is seen as a reliable source of information. The project needs to define a clear set of criteria for what is and is not to be included on the map. These criteria should be publicly available.

The map also needs to be kept up to date, so the project will need to identify a person or group of people who will be responsible for assessing items against the criteria and revising the map on a regular basis. Online versions can be made database driven.

To ensure that the map is seen as unbiased, the mapping project must be careful to remain independent of political or commercial interests that a reader might interpret as influencing the content. This can make it difficult to use advertising as a source of funding for the project. Alternative sources of funds may be selling the printed version of the map, providing the map to schools or education centers in return for a fee, or funding from local government or planning authorities.

Solution   Create a map that displays the information you care about in the area where you are working. Design easily readable icons and visual features to make the map interesting to look at and the facts easy to see. Establish a group of people to maintain the map so that information is up-to-date and someone is monitoring how things change over time. Ensure that this group is able to give unbiased reports, independent of pressure from interested parties.

Linked patterns   Collective Decision Making (10), Earth's Vital Signs (26), Indicators (29), Strategic Capacity (34), Participatory Design (36), Citizen Science (37), World Citizen Parliament (40), Design Stance (44), Citizen Access to Simulations (48), Public Library (59), Accessibility of Online Information (75), Grassroots Public Policy Development (78), Community Inquiry (122), Activist Road Trip (134).

48 Citizen Access to Simulations

Problem   It can be difficult to understand and bring into public deliberation the long-term consequences of major public decisions, for example, the consequences of building a new rail system or a freeway in an urban area. Simulations can help illuminate these consequences (for example, a simulation of the long-term effects on land use, transportation, and environmental impacts of different choices). To be compelling and useful, the simulation results should presented in a way that they can be understood and used by a range of interested citizens. Further, ideally not just the results but access to running the simulation should be available to the public, to allow experimentation with alternatives. To aid in understanding and credibility, the simulation should be constructed in a transparent fashion, so that its operation is open to inspection and discussion.

Context   This pattern is potentially useful to advocacy groups, other community organizations, business associations, and local and regional governments. Using this pattern depends on a suitable simulation and available data . Another factor (less important but useful) would be the existence of a community indicators program that tracks current trends using indicators, so that the same indicators can be used to both track current trends and present the simulation results.

Discussion   Community indicators (see, e.g., Hart 2006) can provide an important tool for monitoring current trends in a community. However, we will usually be interested in the values of these indicators in the future, not just the present, and which actions will result in more desirable outcomes as measured by the community indicators. Simulation and modeling can provide a powerful tool for informing such discussions, particularly if the results from the simulation can be presented using the same indicators as selected in a participatory community and civic indicators project.

The results of the work should be made available using the Web or printed reports. Using the Web has the advantage that definitions of indicators, documentation, and related information can be conveniently linked together.

Supporting public access to running the simulation, as well as the results, might be provided in several ways, depending on the complexity and size of the simulation and input data. Particularly for complex simulations, with substantial data requirements, accessing a simulation hosted on a server using a Web interface is a good technique. Smaller simulations might be downloaded and run on an individual's computer.

This is in general not an easy pattern to use. In addition to developing the set of indicators (including careful definitions and documentation), a simulation of the phenomenon of interest must exist or be developed, including the necessary data and calibration to apply it in the given community. For the example used here (land use and transportation), this typically requires that the local or regional government agency in charge of land use and transportation planning either undertake the simulation work itself or be willing to work closely with another organization that does so.

The game SimCity demonstrates that many people, including grade school children, can be highly engaged by what might have been thought to be a dry topic: urban planning. While games such as SimCity can provide valuable inspiration and interaction ideas, there are key differences between such games and the simulations suggested in this pattern. First, this pattern is concerned with producing simulations of actual phenomena, for example, simulating a specific, real urban area, with the intent of producing useful forecasts of its long-term development to inform public deliberation and debate. Second, the interaction techniques available to its users should expose only the actions and policy levers available to real citizens and governments (for the urban simulation example, such as building light rail systems or changing zoning). Users of these simulations cannot simply declare that an area will be redeveloped (or bring in Godzilla); rather, all they can do is change relevant policies in a scenario in hopes of influencing people in the simulated environment to redevelop the area and residents to move there.

Potential challenges to the result include challenges to the accuracy and reliability of the simulation.

Solution   Develop a simulation of the system of interest (for example, of urban land use and transportation) and make the results of the simulation accessible to interested stakeholders using indicators. When possible, make running the simulation accessible to the public as well.

Linked patterns   Teaching to Transgress (20), Indicators (29), Citizen Science (37), Design Stance (44), Meaningful Maps (47), Online Community Service Engine (62), E-Consultation (70), Future Design (88), Emergency Communication Systems (121), Socially Responsible Computer Games (126).

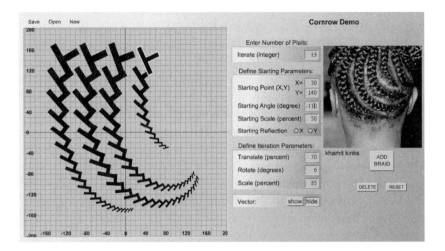

Problem   The characterization of inadequate information technology resources in disadvantaged communities as a "digital divide" was a useful way to bring attention to a critical issue. At the same time, this metaphor is often taken to imply a problematic solution: the one-way bridge. The one-way bridge sees a technology-rich side at one end and a technology-poor side at the other end. The one-way bridge attempts to bring gadgets to a place of absence, a sort of technology vacuum. This view can have the unfortunate side effect of making local knowledge and expertise invisible or devalued.

Context   An alternative approach that avoids the one-way assumption is that of culturally situated design tools: using computer simulations of cultural arts and other practices to "translate" from local knowledge to their high-tech counterparts in mathematics, computer graphics, architecture, agriculture, medicine, and science. Current design tools include a virtual bead loom for simulating Native American beadwork, a tool based on urban graffiti, an audio tool for simulating Latino percussion rhythms, and a Yupik navigation simulation. Each design tool makes use of the mathematics embedded in the practice—for example, the virtual bead loom uses Cartesian coordinates because of the fourfold symmetry of the traditional loom (and many other Native American designs such as the "four winds" healing traditions and the four-pole tipi). Applications are primarily in K-12 math education, but they also can be applied to design projects such as architecture or used as a research tool in investigations such as ethnomathematics, that is, a study of the relationship between mathematics and culture.

Discussion Although there has been some strong success with these tools, their deployment, particularly in the field of education, has not been easy. The educational context requires first working with community members to find a cultural practice that can be simulated. In the case of Native American practices, some of the best examples in terms of ethnomathematics turn out to be sacred practices that cannot be simulated, such as Navajo sand painting and Shoshone whirling disks. Second is to make sure youth recognize the cultural practice; for example, several African examples were questioned by teachers who said African American children would see them more as dusty museum artifacts than as something they had cultural ownership of. Third is to satisfy the requirements of standard curricula. Many interesting examples of ethnomathematics, such as Eulerian paths in Pacific Islander sand drawings and fractals in African architecture, are difficult to use because they are outside the standard curriculum. Fourth, the software support must be easy for teachers to use because many math teachers (particularly those serving large minority populations) do not have ready access to good-quality computers for their students and lack good technological training. The students must be provided with cultural background information and tutorials, and the teachers must be provided with lesson plans and examples of use.

Solution An early design tool was developed for the an African fractals project (Eglash 1999). Mathematics teachers with large African American student populations reported that they could not use fractals (there was too much pressure to conform to the standard curriculum), and they felt that many of the examples were too culturally distant from the students. They all felt that the examples of hairstyles would work well, however. Thus a tool focused on hairstyles and used the term "iterative transformational geometry" rather than "fractals." The graphic above shows the result, called "Cornrow Curves." Each braid is represented as multiple copies of a Y-shaped plait. In each iteration, the plait is copied, and a transformation is applied. The series of transformed copies creates the braid. The example shows the original style at top right and a series of braid simulations, each composed of plait copies that are successively scaled down, rotated, and translated (reflection is applied only to whole braids, as in the case where one side of the head is a mirror image of the other). One of the interesting research outcomes was that the students discovered which parameters need to remain the same and which would be changed in order to produce the entire series of braids (that is, how to iterate the iterations).

The cultural background section of the Web site (http://www.csdt.rpi.edu) is divided into "how to" (for those unfamiliar with the process of creating cornrow hairstyles) and an extensive cultural history of cornrow hairstyles (http://www.csdt.rpi.edu/african/CORNROW _CURVES/index.htm). Many students, even those of African American heritage, will say that cornrows were "invented in the 1960s." The history section of the Web site was developed to provide students with a more accurate understanding of that history, starting with their original context in Africa (where they were used to signify age, religion, ethnic group, social status, kinship, and many other meanings), the use of cornrows in resistance to the attempt at cultural erasure during slavery, their revival during the civil rights era, and their renaissance in hip-hop. Most important, the goal is for students to realize that the cornrows are part of a broader range of scaling designs from Africa (Eglash 1999) and that they represent a part of this African mathematical heritage that survived the middle passage.

A wide variety of design tools is now available, ranging from simulations of Mayan pyramids to virtual baskets. Evaluations have been based on pretest/posttest comparisons of mathematics performance, average grades in mathematics classes (comparing a year with the tools to the previous year without), and scores on a survey of interest or engagement with information technology (specifically computing careers). All three measures show a statistically significant increase ($p < .05$ or better) with use of these tools.

Any attempts to revalue local or traditional knowledge in the face of oppressive histories will be challenging, and all the more so if the revaluation has to compete with current mainstream global practices. The Culturally Situated Design Tools pattern offers an important new position in which to engage that struggle.

Linked patterns   Antiracism (23), Cyberpower (25), Intermediate Technologies (57), Design for Unintended Use (84), Control of Self Representation (109), Community Telecenters (117).

Problem   As Herbert Simon pointed out in "The Architecture of Complexity" (1962), a common heuristic for dealing with complexity is to break complex problems into smaller, more or less independent components. When a complex organization is broken down into smaller units (such as divisions, departments, or teams), each unit specializes. People are selected, trained, and motivated to optimize the performance of that unit. However, there remains a need to coordinate across units to deal with changes, exceptions, and errors in organizational design. In these cases, it is necessary for human beings to solve problems across organizational boundaries. However, since people in different organizations have been selected, trained, and motivated differently, such conversations can be difficult.

Context   Organizations strive to become more efficient partly through automation and partly through specialization of function. Organizations train one group of people to perform a function and then hand off the process to another group trained to perform another function. Integration often extends across formal organizational boundaries so that, for example, various participants in supply chains attempt to coordinate their efforts. Such larger-scale integration can result in greater efficiency. Systems are not designed, however, with complete knowledge of every possible contingency. When design assumptions break down, it is important for people on both sides of a functional boundary to have a cooperative conversation in order to solve the problem left by the gap between reality and the design assumptions.

Discussion   To understand more completely how and why a particular effort is necessary to support conversation across boundaries, it is useful to consider explicitly some of the forces and constraints that typically influence the behavior of people in organizations. For example, many processes are too complex to be understood in detail by one person. This is one reason why organizations assign different tasks to different individuals. People differ in terms of native talents and experience. Furthermore, performance on a task is generally a logarithmic function of time on task so initial differences tend to become even more pronounced over time. For these reasons, complex systems are typically designed and built by decomposing systems into subsystems and tasks into subtasks.

However designs can never anticipate all contingencies. Thus, unanticipated problems will arise that require new cooperative behaviors across the boundaries inherent in any design. Luckily, human beings can use conversation to negotiate and solve novel coordination problems. Indeed, people find conversation in the service of finding and solving problems rewarding. At the same time, however, people are also subject to forming in-groups and out-groups. The groups formed by any organizational design tend to be subject to this "us vs. them" mentality. Once formed, each group will try to "win" by forcing the solution that is optimal for its subfunction rather than negotiating a solution to a problem that is globally optimal. If conversation across boundaries only begins during a crisis or breakdown, these tendencies will be especially strong. In contrast, if regular conversation across boundaries is facilitated, normal human bonding and desires to learn will tend to form important social connections that will serve well in crisis situations.

Historically, many organizations have recognized the need for informal conversational ties and have provided both special places (officers' clubs, traditional pubs, company cafeterias) and events (company picnics, religious retreats, holiday parties, clubs) to facilitate these interchanges. As organizations attempt integration across ever wider scales, however, providing appropriate venues becomes increasingly challenging. In some cases, two related functions report to a single manager, and the manager may serve as a communication bridge. But in complex organizations, formal management methods alone will be insufficient for coordination across all the boundaries.

When links in a processing chain do not converse, inefficiency results. For example, customer service reps from a telecommunications company gave out credit card numbers to business customers, and they had to get these numbers from the accounting department. The customer service representatives were allowed to make outbound calls only between noon and 1:00 P.M, but the accounting department generally had lunch at that time. As a result, it was often many days before customers were able to begin using their business accounts. The accounting department and the customer service representatives also disliked each other, had no informal contact, and generally blamed each other when other coordination problems arose.

The same general difficulty arises in attempting to deal with any complex problem, for example, attempting to voluntarily and democratically facilitate social change. For instance, it is possible for various communities to develop plans that inadvertently interfere with each other. That is why it is useful, on a regular basis, to have conversations that cross community boundaries.

An IBM researcher used to play a lot of tennis with other IBMers, including those in an intercompany league. Here, he met someone in the corporate tax department named Frank. He also used a system that returned the abstracts of scientific and technical articles that contained keywords of interest. Such systems return many false positives, and one in particular had nothing whatever to do with his interests; it was about a new federal program that allowed highly profitable companies to trade tax credits with companies that were losing money. Because of the conversations he had had with Frank, he forwarded the abstract to Frank instead of throwing it in the trash. Frank looked into this program and saved a lot of money for IBM. This case illustrates that ideally, even people with no obvious process connection should have opportunities to converse informally.

Those who planned the first Universal Usability Conference, ACM SIGCHI (Special Interest Group on Computer-Human Interaction), in 2000 found it necessary to delegate functions to various parties. They attempted to plan ahead of time by standard tools such as budgets and project time lines. A weekly conference call proved crucial in allowing them to identify and solve unanticipated problems effectively and efficiently.

In WorldJam, an online, three-day, companywide electronic meeting for all IBMers, moderators and facilitators used Babble (an electronic blended synchronous/asynchronous chat) and Sametime (a synchronous chat system) as backchannels to collectively solve problems and coordinate information among jam topics.

In Hanna Pavillion, a children's psychiatric hospital, each change of shift is marked by a short joint staff meeting to discuss critical issues so that a continuity of knowledge extends across shift boundaries (common in most medical settings). In addition, at least some people work double or rotating shifts and get to know people from various shifts. There are ample opportunities for informal conversation during the day as well as special outings. Then staff members can coordinate treatment for a specific child across the boundaries of profession and shift.

Solution   At a minimum, time, space, and means, as well as motivation, must be provided for people who need to coordinate across boundaries to carry on continuing informal conversation. They must have time to carry on such conversations and a space in which such conversations can take place. If a physical space convenient to both parties is not feasible, some means of support for informal distant collaboration and conversation is necessary. Payoffs must accrue to the parties across a boundary for jointly for solving problems, not for proving that the other party is to blame.

Linked patterns   Collective Decision Making (10), Linguistic Diversity (16), Democratic Political Settings (31), World Citizen Parliament (40), Strengthening International Law (42), Online Deliberation (52), Media Diversity (66), E-Consultation (70), Multiparty Negotiation for Conflict Resolution (79), Shared Vision (101), Engaged Tourism (107), The Power of Story (114), Great Good Place (119), Activist Road Trip (134).

Problem   Trauma and destruction are common results of war, religious conflict, gender oppression, and natural disaster, and the way that societies deal with these issues can make a bad situation worse. Traditional systems of blame and punishment and even reparations all too often create additional harm.

Context   Formal judicial systems centered on a national government and the courts are losing ground to new models of adjudication and problem solving. Some communities are reverting to long-standing traditions for healing, cleansing, and restoring community balance. Others are creating a truth commission to take testimony from the victims and perpetrators in a conflict. These bodies range in scope and scale from the famous South African hearings covering thousands of cases spanning thirty years, to U.S. hearings in Greensboro, North Carolina, about a single local catastrophe (Mayer 2006). Commission hearing rooms offer a forum for contact across previously insurmountable barriers of hostility, which can inspire traditional enemies to build a newly shared investment in the future.

Discussion   Community organizations dealing with local traumatic events, families with a personal story of injustice, and even an entity as large as the United States with its dark history of slavery can consider creating a truth, reconciliation, and amnesty commission. A commission holding hearings will allow the actual history to be revealed by taking testimony from a wide variety of perspectives and will also become a forum in which adversaries can approach each other without insisting on punishment or revenge. Perhaps surprising, a narrative, anecdotal yet full recounting of painful truth contributes substantially to restoring the harmony and vitality of the community for the future.

South Africa is the site of the most famous Truth and Reconciliation Commission (TRC), but there have been dozens of others (Hayner 1994). Many have played an important role in repairing community rifts without furthering the suffering for most people. In South Africa, an indigenously inspired and funded project heard testimonies from thousands and disposed of over 3,000 requests for amnesty (Reid and Hoffman 1999). Guatemala's TRC was more centralized and sponsored by the United Nations. A key outcome of its work came in an apology from the United States for its abusive interventions in Guatemalan affairs.

TRCs offer a substitute for traditional disaster adjudication systems, which usually take one of the following three forms: insurance payments and liability lawsuits, government investigations and hearings, or criminal trials and punishments. Although each of these has its place, all three are concerned above all with blame for the past. Furthermore, legal and official procedures traditionally depend on arcane jargon and tend to be expensive, drawn out, and highly centralized. Since they are dominated by experts, traditional dispute forums tend to marginalize the ordinary people who experience traumatic events. U.N. war crimes tribunals for Rwanda and Bosnia, which refuse to consider amnesty, have been bedeviled by the failings of court-based systems.

TRC-style hearings are quite different. They are relatively informal, so they are commensurately cheaper and can take place anywhere in an affected area. If they follow the South African model, hearings are not adversarial, they do not assign guilt or innocence, and they are carried out in the local language. In 2004 in Greensboro, hearings about the 1979 slaughter of four civil rights activists offered an opportunity for people to continue with a process that had been cut off in the courts (Mayer 2006).

TRC commissioners need to attend openly to the voices of suffering and ask probing questions about responsibility and action so as to determine if the truth has indeed been told (Tutu 2000). Their success depends on the integrity of these commissioners. It also depends on careful recording and distribution of the testimonies. Participation, for both witnesses and those accused of doing harm, has traditionally been voluntary, in the sense that no one faces additional legal sanctions from their society for failing to appear, though community hostility can be hard on those who reject the commission's request to appear.

The strongest argument against TRC proceedings is precisely the strongest argument in favor of them: that such hearings are not the forum for punishing a perpetrator. Victim opponents of TRCs fear being deprived of justice. Perpetrators worry that the hearings are merely fishing expeditions to search out the guilty, who will then be punished. Theorists are concerned that perpetrators who are not prosecuted under such a system will find they can act with impunity. In South Africa some victims remained critical of the process to the end, but many discovered that the new knowledge they gleaned at the hearings about what happened and why proved much stronger in easing their hearts than they had expected. And nothing about these hearings need prevent judicial action. Indeed in recent years there have been examples of reopening judicial proceedings with a similar intent, for example, the 2004 re-creation and new "trial" of Nisqually Chief Leschi leading his exoneration in Washington State, a hundred years after his execution by hanging. The charge of murder was dropped as the charge was later determined to be an act of war.

Establishing a successful commission depends on preparing the groundwork on many issues. The Truth Commission Project (2002) has identified the following factors as important:

- By whom or under whose name the commission is established
- When the commission is established and how far back it reaches
- The prevailing focus on healing or justice
- Public support for a truth commission
- A geographical horizon for investigation
- Legal powers of investigation
- Rejecting anonymous and confidential testimonies
- Visibility of hearings

- Degree of formality of hearings
- Whether to offer amnesty
- Completion, publication, and distribution of report

Although most actual TRC hearings have been conducted in former war zones, it is easy to discern other issues that could benefit from this process:

- The U.S. government and the American people could reexamine the costs of the slave trade and the centuries of slave labor and yet minimize the likelihood that the acknowledgment of history becomes the basis for furious revenge.
- The people and the different levels of government could investigate the events of the New Orleans 2005 catastrophe without focusing narrowly on blame and thereby prompting an onslaught of liability lawsuits.
- The residents and former residents of Hanford, Washington; Chernobyl, Ukraine; Bikini Island; and other nuclear sites could craft public history out of the secrecy that surrounded the nuclear programs of the twentieth century. At the same time, they would create a forum for dialogue with the builders of the weapons and power plants that have left behind a radioactive legacy that will last for millennia.

Solution A community that faces a festering historical trauma can create a truth, reconciliation and amnesty commission using informal or official channels. A commission can hear victim testimonies about past suffering as well as explanations from those responsible, and it can provide a forum in which adversaries can meet without fear of further harm or punishment.

Linked patterns Memory and Responsibility (11), Strengthening International Law (42), Alternative Media in Hostile Environments (53), Peace Education (56), Transparency (64), Multiparty Negotiation for Conflict Resolution (79), Community Inquiry (122), Citizens' Tribunal (129).

Problem   People working together to conduct business as a group are often plagued by the clash of personalities and shifting rivalries of factions and subgroups within the group. Also, without structure, a discussion can become random and rambling, and it can be dominated by powerful individuals or other factors. The emergence of these negative group dynamics can have an adverse impact on the ability of the group to achieve its shared objectives. Other factors, such as distance to the meeting, inconvenient scheduling, or costs of getting to the meeting, can obstruct effective and inclusive participation. Online systems currently do not provide the structure that groups of people engaging in deliberative meetings or discussions need to help them efficiently move through a decision-making process that is accessible and ensures equal participation by all.

Context   This pattern could be profitably employed in board meetings, committee meetings, administrative panels, review boards, volunteer organizations, nonprofit community groups.

Discussion   Everyday conversation, though often purposeful, is informal; it does not rely on an agenda, defined roles, or precisely delineated rules of interaction. To overcome the unpredictability of this type of human interaction, systematic rules have been created to facilitate purposeful group meetings whose objective is to produce collective decisions. One of the earliest set of parliamentary procedures was formulated in 1876 by Henry Robert in *Robert's Rules of Order*. Robert's Rules, as they have come to be known, have been widely adopted as a means to fairly and equitably conduct the business of group meetings and provide a method to ensure that all parties within the group have the opportunity to participate in the decision-making process (Robert's Rules of Order, Revised 2008). At the same time, the rules ensure that no minority interest can exert undue influence on the process.

The advent of the Internet has provided an opportunity to combine democratic principles and procedures (such as Robert's Rules of Order) with interactive communication technologies to provide new Web-based meeting facilitation systems. Ideally, online deliberations systems would allow people to come together as peers in an online environment and conduct official business meetings without being present in the same physical location. The plethora of online discussion systems, especially when contrasted to the scarcity of deliberative systems, suggests the difficulty of this enterprise.

While working in and with a team of students at The Evergreen State College, the authors of this pattern were involved in the development of e-Liberate (http://www.publicsphereproject .org/e-liberate/), a working prototype developed using Linux, MySQL, Apache, and PHP. The application provides facilities to create groups and create and schedule meetings. Then, using written (typed) rather than spoken input, the system facilitates meeting by coordinating user interactions (such as making motions), conducting and tallying votes, and providing an archive facility for official minutes.

Online deliberation substitutes one set of advantages and disadvantages for the set that face-to-face deliberation offers. In general, the broad criteria of either approach include access to the process, efficacy of the process (including individual involvement, and process as a whole, and the context (including legal requirements). Of course, these criteria overlap to some degree and influence each other.

Although face-to-face deliberation is basically low-tech, physically getting to meetings may involve costly travel. And effective participation at face-to-face meetings depends on the skills (including, for example, knowing how to use Robert's Rules of Order), intentions, and knowledge of the individuals. It also depends on the skills, intentions, and knowledge of the other participants in the meeting, including the chair who acts as the meeting's manager.

By making access to a computer (connected to the Internet) a prerequisite to participation, online deliberation adds an access hurdle of cost, geography, and computer fluency. Depending on the characteristics of the potential attendees, this barrier may be more than offset by the advantages that online deliberations could provide. If, for example, the meeting attendees are drawn from western Europe and the United States, it is likely that costs associated with computer communication will be lower than transportation costs. In fact, online deliberation makes the prospect of more-or-less synchronous discussions and deliberations among people around the world possible, although here the tyranny of time zones and humankind's intrinsic circadian rhythms (which encourage us to sleep at night and stay awake in the daylight hours) becomes a mitigating factor: making decisions while many of the attendees are sleeping is one formula for dysfunctional meetings. The very fact that worldwide meetings become possible, however, provides an enormously fertile ground for civil society opportunities. (See, for example, the World Citizen Parliament pattern, 40.)

Knowledge of the topics under discussion, knowledge of the process (Robert's Rules of Order, for example), and command of the languages being used in the discussion can also be obstacles to effective and equitable face-to-face as well as online deliberation. Online environments, however, have the potential of alleviating, at least to some degree, some of the disadvantages that seem to be intrinsic to face-to-face settings. In the e-Liberate example, attendees can select a "language pack" so that the appropriate Robert's Rules process word or phrase (such as "I second the motion") will be presented in the attendee's own language. This is not machine (on-the-fly) translation. Moreover, it has no bearing whatsoever on the content of the meeting, that is, what the participants actually contributed; it determines only which of several equivalent language sets of the Robert's Rules meta-language is displayed to each user. The possibility of using automatic machine translation on all attendee input so that each attendee only saw input to the meeting in their own language is an intriguing one that is currently not feasible. Machine translation is imperfect at best and may always remain so. Try, for example, transforming some verbiage into another language and back again using a machine translation system on the Web. The result generally bears no resemblance to the original. Of course, translation by humans is not perfect either, relying as it does on the skills of the human translator. It may be well advised for reasons of transparency and integrity of the process to make both (or all) original and machine-translated language versions available for inspection with the other meeting contributions in the database. So while free and reliable electronic translation is desirable, high-quality human translation could be inserted into the process as appropriate. This could be only as simultaneous and as accurate as the skills and availability of the human translator interposed within the process would allow. The need for maintaining all language versions are appropriate in the case of human translation as well.

The online environment offers other potential advantages. One obvious benefit is that only the actions that are allowable within the deliberation process at that time are displayed to the individual participants. This, in theory, can help reduce problems that are commonplace with meeting attendees who are not thoroughly familiar with the Robert's Rules conventions. Online systems can also provide online help systems. Within e-Liberate, for example, users can view descriptions of how and when specific actions are used. Also, a meeting transcript can be automatically created and votes automatically tabulated as well.

Work has begun on e-Liberate 2.0. This new version will allow groups to edit the version of Robert's Rules that comes with the system to support the particular ways that groups prefer to conduct meetings. This also opens the door for integrating other collaborative software tools such as brainstorming or collaborative document development into a meeting.

Solution   A network-based application should provide nonprofit, community-based organizations with the technology they need to conduct effective deliberative meetings when members cannot easily get together in face-to-face meetings. Ideally the tools should increase their effectiveness in addressing their mission while requiring less time and money to conduct deliberative meetings. See Davies and Noveck (forthcoming) for a good overview of these issues.

Linked patterns   Political Settings (7), Conversational Support across Boundaries (50), Online Community Service Engine (62), E-Consultation (70), Citizen Journalism (91), Document-Centered Discussion (92).

Problem   Despots despise the visibility that a truly free press can provide. It is their unchallengeable iniquity that would receive the most intense airing. Under oppressive regimes, the circulation of information, literature, and other art forms can be dangerous. People can be harassed, beaten, imprisoned, or even executed for possession of forbidden information or the means to create, reproduce, or distribute it. Journalists face even greater challenges and require an extensive collection of techniques to get the news out to all who need it.

Context   This pattern focuses on journalism during hostile conditions in which citizens have a great need to engage with the forbidden knowledge and share it with members of their community. The future of reform often depends on the success of this collaboration between journalists and citizens. The ideas in this pattern (including new distribution practices, for example) also can be used in countries that have a nominally free press yet one that is dominated by a few strong voices with deep pockets.

Discussion   The world can be hostile to independent and alternative journalists and to people who read and think. Even countries where there are no legal restrictions to a free press have major problems. The journal *Index on Censorship* and the organization Reporters without Borders regularly report on the barbarities visited on journalists worldwide. Despots know that the truth can damage their reputations and ultimately their regime. Although the truth is difficult to hide forever, postponing its arrival, limiting its exposure, and casting aspersions on its accuracy may be adequate for their purposes.

A hostile environment is one in which coercion or force, either formally through laws and police or informally through thugs or contract killers, is employed to stifle the free flow of ideas. The most common form of choking off the flow of information that could be damaging to the government, corporations, or wealthy individuals is distraction. Serbian media during the Milosevic years, with their breezy lightweight confections of schmaltzy pop as well as nationalist songs and slapstick, served up in many cases by scantily clad women, provide a good example.

One appendage of the unfree press (at least as conceptualized in the United States) is a ruthlessly efficient secret police that stomps out every aspect of alternative point of view the instant that it surfaces. That modus operandi seems to be uncommon in practice (and would no doubt be the envy of all the despots). The defenders of the status quo, though loutish and dangerous, are often capricious and incompetent, and they are generally stymied by insufficient resources. The ambiguity of the laws and the ambiguity of the presumed offenses also can work in favor of journalists.

The former Soviet Union and its satellites provided fertile soil for an independent press that operated on the margins of the law for several decades. This is the classic samizdat distribution in which readers painstakingly and secretly copied by hand or typewriter and carbon paper multiple copies of entire books, which were then passed on to others, who would also duplicate and pass on the material.

In the developed world, journalists and other media workers are specialized: one person intones the news of the day, using video clips that another person edited, which was shot by another person during an interview conducted by another person as ordered by another person. When the political climate turns nasty and journalists are beaten, threatened, or killed by government soldiers, paramilitary troops, or thugs or when resources dry up or disaster or wartime situations erupt, journalists habituated to the strict division of labor may have difficulty adapting to the more flexible and improvisational mode of news production when that becomes necessary. Journalists with overspecialized and deep but narrow skills may find that they are unable to respond quickly and flexibly when their tried-and-true practices fail due to unexpected circumstances.

Alternative news distribution involves a canny cat-and-mouse game between those who believe in the free distribution of information and those who do not. Life within an actively hostile environment will need to keep changing the way that business is done to meet new challenges. Unlike journalists in the United States and other developed countries, journalists must be adept in many modes of reporting, many approaches to distribution, a variety of tactics and strategies, and the inventive use of what is available to get the job done, as befits what Veran Matic, a journalist at B92, an independent radio station in Belgrade, Serbia, opposed to the Milosevic regime, (2004) calls a "universal journalist, not an encyclopedic polymath who is informed in different fields, but a professional familiar with print journalism, radio and television, online journalism and information distribution mechanisms." This is what might be called a *bricoleur-journalist*, somebody, for example, who sends the sounds that accompany the scene at a voting station in Africa directly over the air using a cell phone with an open line to the radio station. Audiocassettes, printed broadsides, or, more commonly today, DVDs can be distributed when the plug is pulled on a radio station (as it was three times during B92's early years of confronting Milosevic). And bricoleur-journalists in different cultures and settings, such as Chinese prodemocracy or environmental activists, may adopt or invent any number of local variants.

An interesting unexpected issue seems to surface from time to time by the underground media (and society in general) after the fall of an oppressive regime. Ironically, many people who worked closely with clandestine media over the years now feel unsettled in the post-Soviet environment. After communism fell, the former trickle of information became a tsunami of mostly commercial offerings. When information was scarce and in danger of extinction, it possessed an almost sacred allure. Now the same type of information is lost in the flood, just more anonymous flotsam and jetsam in a torrent of images and sounds.

Samizdat or clandestine journalism does not always succeed. Translating the success of the samizdat or underground press to other regions under oppressive regimes is far from automatic. A potential audience that is interested in the material must exist (as with the media in any situation), and there must be a way to get the material to them. Some of these people earnestly want social change and believe there is some degree, however small, of hope that this outcome is achievable. Interestingly, and somewhat contrary to conventional wisdom, some people in the potential audience are motivated by their desire to know the truth, whether it helps to actually change the situation or not. The larger and more active and supportive the audience is, the more likely that the alternative press will succeed. On the other side of the equation are the journalists, and the absence of either audience or journalists can prevent the enterprise from being successful.

Although it is precarious, alternative media production actually builds civic capacity. According to Anna Husarka (Smillie 1999), who worked for Poland's Solidarity Information Bureau in 1989, the journalism practiced "was a political blueprint for the democratic struggles that dismantled communism." It is also important to note that traditional news is not the only product of an alternative media project. The B92 enterprise, which started as a college radio station in Belgrade, now includes Radio B92, Television B92, B92.net (Web site), B92 publishing (books and magazines), B92 music label, B92.Rex cultural center, B92.concert agency, and B92.communications (Internet provision and satellite links), amply illustrating the rich potential of media that choose to embrace the widest range of outlets. One of its biggest and most successful projects was Rock for Vote, the biggest rock tour in Serbia's history, "a traveling festival with 6 to 8 bands playing in 25 cities and towns throughout the country." The tour was organized while organizers and activists "were being molested, harassed and detained by the police on a daily basis." In spite of that, 150,000 citizens attended the concerts. Most important, the results of the 2000 elections demonstrated that the main objective was attained: "80 percent of first-time voters did go to the polls after all … casting their ballots to bring about fundamental changes in the country" (Matic 2004).

Some media operations that developed during a period of hostility have had a difficult time making the transition from a postwar or postoppressive regime. On the other hand, *Gazeta Wyborcza,* one of Poland's leading underground newspapers in the 1980s, which was started in a kindergarten classroom, became one of the most influential and commercially viable dailies in Poland (Smillie 1999). B92, at least in the immediate aftermath of the troubles in Serbia, continued innovative programming that reflected their terrifying past. For example, it launched a truth and reconciliation process (see pattern 51) that included radio shows and a series of books about the wars (including the Srebrenica crimes) and the disintegration of the former Yugoslavia. It also convened a conference, In Search for Truth and Reconciliation, in 2000 that was attended by journalists, intellectuals, and representatives of nongovernmental organizations from all former Yugoslav republics, and another conference, Truth, Responsibility and Reconciliation, the following year that featured experiences of other countries in similar processes. Radio B92 set up a special documentation archive on the wars, which included testimonies, documentaries, video footage, books, and other documents. It arranged "exhibitions, screenings of documentaries and public discussions on these topics are being organized throughout Serbia" (Matic 2004).

Solution   Producing (and consuming) cultural or journalistic media within hostile societies can be hazardous to emotional as well as physical health. It is often an unrewarding enterprise yet can be absolutely critical.

Linked patterns   International Networks of Alternative Media (43), Truth and Reconciliation Commissions (51), Indigenous Media (55), Citizen Journalism (91), Mirror Institutions (94), Sense of Struggle (104), Arts of Resistance (111), The Power of Story (114), Follow the Money (135).

Problem   People suffering from chronic medical conditions need both information about their condition and the support of others who share their problems. How can such groups of people use the Internet to address their needs, and how can they design and operate a Web site for the best possible outcome?

Context   The Internet allows users to become content providers as well as users. A medically based Web community can become a powerful source of collective intelligence about a particular medical condition, with thousands of people sharing research results, articles, and personal observations with each other, thus breaking down the monopoly that doctors once held on medical information. Such a community also can be a source of comfort, wisdom, new friendships, and material assistance. However, the nature of the medium also allows for casual, even abusive, use of the information space.

Discussion   Breast Cancer Action Nova Scotia's (BCANS) interactive site (http://www.bca.ns.ca) is the world's largest and oldest breast cancer discussion site, indeed one of the oldest medical mutual help sites in existence, dating from 1996, when it was started by a volunteer. The site began a period of fast growth in 1998 and in 2002 was reported to have about 400 closely involved regulars, a wider circle of people who drop in now and then, and an unknown number of lurkers, some of them long term. Not only women but a few men with breast cancer post to this group, as well as family and friends. Although the majority of users are American, with about one-fourth Canadian, the site also hosts visitors from other continents, notably a large and active contingent from Australia and New Zealand, numerous Europeans, and participants from Turkey, South Africa, India, Hong Kong, and elsewhere.

   Participants in the Web site can give and receive:

- Reassurance and caring
- Informal advice to cope with the myriad subacute problems that arise
- Encouragement to stick with medical treatment regimens
- Professional medical information, such as details of new clinical trials
- Support for questioning conventional medical wisdom
- Material goods such as cards, gifts, and funds

The site also includes tributes to those who have died, a collection of links to specific breast cancer topics, and a glossary of more than 400 breast cancer–related terms.

   Since its launch with a single discussion forum, an interactive calendar for local (Halifax, Nova Scotia) activities, and a mission statement, BCANS has grown into a community that has written books, given conference presentations, appeared on TV and radio, launched a fundraising arm, and fostered numerous in-person friendships.

To account for the success of BCANS, community informatics activist and researcher Patricia Radin (2006) turned to social capital theory, which analyzes the elements of beneficial social networks (Coleman 1990; Putnam 2000). According to the literature, trust is at the heart of a "virtuous circle" of activity wherein people voluntarily help each other, receive benefits in return, and again reach out to provide assistance. Although social capital theory was developed by looking at networks of people working face to face in bounded situations, it appears applicable to any context where mutual assistance is being rendered, such as an online medical mutual help group (Blanchard and Horan 1998; Street et al., 1997).

Some specific features of site design and operations help to move visitors progressively toward a state of greater trust and reciprocity:

• An alert webmistress fiercely protects the community from hurtful messages, spam, and exploitation, thus promoting a high level of trust and goodwill.
• As well as the main forum discussing breast cancer issues, there are now additional subforums—for example, one to accommodate groups planning get-togethers and one to allow for the swapping of recipes, jokes, and other material.
• A prayer chain section is available for users to post spiritual messages.
• Chatrooms are open twenty-four hours a day, but particular times are specified when a host will be available to welcome newcomers to the chatroom.
• There are two ways for participants to post permanent self-introductions (including photos): filing a profile, which is then automatically linked with each message, and posting an autobiography in a password-protected section accessible only to others who have filed a "biog." Many personal friendships have been formed, and some community members visit the discussions as often as three times a day.

These features allow new visitors to size up the costs and benefits of participation in a risk-free environment; allow longer-term users to stage their level of self-disclosure; choose from many ways to contribute and receive from the group; and take part in shared experiences, both virtual and face-to-face. The Web site also gives the more established community members chances to develop personal relationships and initiate projects of mutual benefit.

Solution   Seek to build trust in stages. First, attract and reassure new visitors by giving visual messages explaining why the Web site was built and who it is for. Avoid advertising, and show sponsorship from individuals clearly. Provide messages from others who share the condition. Second, allow users to choose when and how to give out personal information. Separate publicly available profiles from password-protected areas where more personal information might be shared. Chatrooms can allow a more ephemeral form of conversation. Sites should also permit people to send personal responses to posted comments instead of posting to the whole forum. Third, be alert to the potential problems of lurkers or abusive material. Active editors are needed to edit out abusive material, act as hosts in chatrooms, and maintain the site as a safe space. Finally, seek to build "thick trust" by supporting joint activities; doing things together gives people the opportunity to size up each other in a variety of situations.

Linked patterns   Big-Picture Health Information (27), Service-Learning (90), Shared Vision (101), Self-Help Groups (105).

Problem   Lack of representation in media production results in reduced diversity of ideas and perspectives in the media, in addition to manipulation and lack of political participation and knowledge about rights. It also results in fewer opportunities to engage in politics or assume responsibilities in government. Indigenous people who are denied their voice will find it difficult to fight oppression, work with allies, or maintain their culture. Without the means to make their voices heard, communities become atomized within themselves and invisible to the outside world.

Context   Indigenous people in rural and urban areas in developing and developed countries around the world need to create, as well as use, information and communication systems to promote education, health, governance, cultural life, and many other important values.

Discussion   This pattern can be applied in urban and rural areas where communities have suffered years of economic and social exclusion. Indigenous media are different from media produced by and for other underserved groups such as ethnic and sexual minorities, women, and youth. Indigenous people often do not know how to engage the media from their village far from electricity, telephones, press, or radio or television stations. Moreover, the knowledge that is intrinsic to their culture may be localized. It may be centuries old, embodied in stories or other nonwritten forms and endangered.

Information is essential for development, and it is now urgent to empower indigenous people with media technology and knowledge. There are many activities that indigenous farmers could undertake to help improve their lives with better access to media. If, for example, the farmers of Chiapas in southeast Mexico could sell their products directly to companies, they could improve their economic situation. Currently intermediaries buy coffee in poor villages at low prices, which they then sell to big companies at great profit. Access to the market depends on knowledge and the technological means to capitalize on it.

This is not only a problem for the poor. Many people around the world have problems related to lack of media access. The fact that large corporations control the media becomes a matter of life and death because the media are the de facto gatekeepers of important information related to health and safety. Indigenous people often lack the power, knowledge, and technology to produce their own information and their own media. The Internet could provide a new way to communicate. For example, in the south and southeast areas of Mexico, there are new Internet access centers, but these are for people who already know how to use computers and the Internet, knowledge that many indigenous people do not have.

Indigenous media simultaneously address many needs of marginalized indigenous groups. Thus, embracing this pattern entails education and training, policy, and resources (time, money, and people, for example) in addition to access to the technology itself. An e-mail campaign or a panel discussion on a radio show can help organize a campaign against a group of intermediaries or denounce poor or corrupt legislators. In Mexico's rural communities such as Chiapas, Guerrero, and Oaxaca, radio stations managed by indigenous farmers and satellite gateways to the Internet can make the difference between intimidation and free speech. Some notable examples from around the world include Radio Tambuli Radio Network in the Philippines, the Deadly Mob aboriginal organization of Alice Springs, Australia, and the Koahnic Broadcast Corporation in Alaska.

Nonindigenous people can play a role in support of this pattern. They can organize training programs in the 3,100 new access points installed in the municipalities around Mexico and in Internet cafés. Many institutions and international agencies with programs promoting technology in rural areas can donate equipment, access to the Internet (maybe using satellite gateways), and Internet streaming. Nongovernmental organizations with training and learning programs can work with indigenous farmers and others to teach them how to apply media access technology. Mino (Eusebio Castro) of the Ashaninka native people in Peru, who was instrumental in establishing Internet access for his people, stresses that indigenous people must not allow nonindigenous people to monopolize information. For that reason, he and others in his group carefully observed every technical installation carried out in his village (Mino, public presentation, Seattle, Washington, May 16, 2002).

Unfortunately the pattern language and other educational tools are not available in native languages and are useless to most indigenous people. Many of these stakeholders who have experience with information and computer technology can share their stories of success and failure, but they cannot express their thoughts in English. Indigenous media and collaborative partners who may be outside of the indigenous group can help address these issues.

Radio, print media, and television all have the potential to help shape public opinion. When rural farmers acquire Internet skills and can access media, they can apply this knowledge to create their own information and communication systems. Ultimately indigenous people can promote success by communicating with other indigenous people around the world about their experiences.

Solution Encourage the development of indigenous media controlled by indigenous people themselves. People outside the indigenous community can become involved, but only in consultation with the indigenous community.

Linked patterns Health as a Universal Right (5), Linguistic Diversity (16), Opportunity Spaces (33), International Networks of Alternative Media (43), Alternative Media in Hostile Environments (53), Media Diversity (66), Community-Building Journalism (97), Self-Designed Development (106), Control of Self-Representation (109), The Power of Story (114), Public Domain Characters (115), Everyday Heroism (116), Tactical Media (131).

Problem   People seem to have studied war more than peace. The energy devoted to peace studies, whether in school history classes or in the allocation of government research and university budgets, is commonly so small as to be virtually invisible. Furthermore, an interest in peacemaking is often taken as a sign of weakness. Hence, peace education is unattractive to people with power. On the largest historical scale, there is a strong correlation between the acquisition of the full rights of citizenship and warrior status. Furthermore, the right to command violence and wage war is a core prerogative of governments and political leaders, so peace education is easily defined as antigovernment, and in many places there is constant pressure to sustain the commitment to patriotic and sometimes bellicose sentiment.

Context   The United Nations Peace University in Costa Rica, UNESCO's educational, research and cultural agenda, and the Nobel Prize for Peace offer evidence that international agencies are making a serious contribution to understanding how to achieve and keep the peace. Nagasaki, Hiroshima, and The Hague have become centers for peace education as a result of the significant historical events that took place there. However, in most countries, peace studies remain peripheral, confined to a few universities and the professionals in conflict management and reconstruction who are asked to repair the damage of war once the fighting has ended. Rampant bullying in schools, abusive relationships in families, and litigious business relationships testify to the failure to do peace education in the United States. And the media in many cultural contexts are much more willing to tell and retell war stories than to teach peace.

Discussion   Young people are encountering peace education in a variety of modes. Volunteer lawyers in Washington and other states teach mediation in the public schools. Community groups working with teenagers in trouble teach "straight talk," a system for engaging directly with potential critics. Families too have a choice between authoritarian parental powers and developing their members' negotiation skills, although if children are to learn to negotiate, parents must be willing to respond to their child's arguments.

Since peace and justice are intertwined, peace education requires also that younger generations learn about achieving justice. Addressing topics relating to economic, ethnic, class, religious, and other injustices remains controversial in U.S. public education, but many schools and colleges have begun to open discussion of these issues.

Japan makes a significant investment in peace education for the young through a large network of museums and peace sites. Most school programs are focused on peace as it relates to World War II, and indeed some of the facilities Japan describes as peace museums, others might label war museums or memorials. Nonetheless, through the cities and citizens of Hiroshima and Nagasaki, Japan has been a world leader in reminding people of the perils of nuclear weaponry.

Peace education and peace research are linked, and in 1981, under the leadership of Senator Spark Matsunaga of Hawaii, the U.S. government set up the Institute of Peace. Since the end of the cold war, when it became legitimate once again to think more about peace, U.S. universities have founded significant programs, including undergraduate studies at Hampshire College and graduate programs at George Mason University and Antioch University. Europe too has seen considerable investment in university-level education in peace studies, and Europeans seem more willing than Americans to take an assertive stance in favor of peace. One outstanding program in Great Britain is at Bradford University, and another is at Lancaster. Among international institutions, Vienna is host to the UNESCO-supported European University Center for Peace Studies, and the United Nations Peace University is centered in Costa Rica, with affiliated institutions in Geneva and Toronto, among other places.

Large-scale, institutionalized settings for peace education are complemented by dozens of smaller venues in temples and shrines, churches and mosques, peace camps for youngsters from war zones, anger management courses and other therapist communities, contemplative practices and even martial arts training. The right environment for peace education can be found to match almost any age, mood, and orientation.

Peace-oriented schools teach negotiation skills and empathic respect for different perspectives, often using in-class simulations, theater, and other action-learning methods. The histories we teach can demonstrate that making social change does not have to be synonymous with aggressive action. Peace education is urgent because in many societies competitive and vengeful energies dominate in the media, in business, in commerce, law, and sport.

Solution   Parents on behalf of their children and adults on their own behalf must make an explicit and continuous effort to get enough access to peace education and also to hold back the strong militaristic energies in most contemporary societies. Controlling gun play is important, of course, but so is teaching peaceful negotiation and challenging the notion that the good citizen must be ready to go into combat.

Linked patterns   The Good Life (3), Social Dominance Attenuation (4), Education and Values (17), Transforming Institutions (19), Teaching to Transgress (20), Spiritually Grounded Activism (24), Economic Conversion (41), Truth and Reconciliation Commissions (51), Experimental School (89), Soap Operas with Civic Messages (120), Socially Responsible Computer Games (126).

Problem   Often technologies used in development or transferred to poor communities do not fit the needs of the community that these technologies are designed to help. Instead these tools go unused or are not properly used to maximize their benefits due to a lack of knowledge about their use or, more commonly, their relevance to people's needs.

Context   Often the simplest level of technology that can effectively achieve the intended purpose in a particular location will be the most relevant. These intermediate technologies are particularly useful to underdeveloped rural areas, which may lack the specialized expertise or infrastructure to operate and maintain high technology.

Discussion   Intermediate technology, as asserted in the book *Small Is Beautiful* (Schumacher 1973), tends to promote values such as health, beauty, and permanence.

The idea of intermediate technology, or appropriate technology, is meant to highlight an approach to the concrete tools pushed in development practice. For example, in a rural area where literacy is low and there is a lack of communication lines and even electricity, it would not make sense to implement a telecenter to promote information awareness. Rather, a small, local radio station by which people could obtain information through battery-operated radios would be much more relevant to information transfer.

In essence, the role of an intermediate technology is to allow peoples to take advantage of technology in ways that do not drastically disrupt the cultural integrity of the community. It is ultimately respectful and mindful to understand that a treadle pump for accessing water rather than walking two miles to the river five times a day is going to be more relevant to rural women with a household to care for than a computer. In fact, there is no shortage of reports of technology transfer programs that failed miserably due to inadequate assessment of community needs. Instead, tools that were perceived to be most relevant based on a variety of biases were given; when they were later evaluated, they were found to be dysfunctional or not in use. The reason was that they lacked relevance to the lived experiences of the people they were intended to help.

Unfortunately, it is difficult to produce a list of appropriate technologies since their deployment is context specific. In some cases, a rural wireless network may be very relevant, and in others underground water collection stations for use during the dry season will be most applicable.

Solution   Those seeking to promote the livelihoods of peoples through the process of technology transfer must be careful and creative in mapping out projects and types of technologies to be placed in a community to reach maximum use and benefit to those it is intended to support. Consultants and development advocates must ensure that proper measures are taken to ensure relevance and usefulness. It would seem appropriate for communities and technologists to come together in a participatory process for mapping out needs, infrastructure, and culturally relevant solutions.

Linked patterns   Participatory Design (36), Culturally Situated Design Tools (49), Durable Assets (58), Community Networks (61), Powerful Remittances (73), Wholesome Design for Wicked Problems (82), Appropriating Technology (108), Community Telecenters (117), Environmental Impact Remediation (124).

Problem   Poor people who depend on day labor and other forms of hourly employment can find it difficult to provide a livelihood for themselves and their families. They have little to support themselves in the event that employment becomes scarce or food prices skyrocket, undermining their capacity to feed their families. Similarly, these assetless peoples often find it impossible to acquire credit for opening small businesses because they are dependent on fluctuating levels of income.

Context   Development that pursues an emphasis on building the durable assets people have, such as land, machinery, or livestock, can empower people to be self-sufficient even in times of hardship because it provides the materials necessary for ensuring their livelihood regardless of the larger economic climate.

Discussion   Durable assets in sustainable development can be divided into four categories: natural capital (natural resource assets), reproducible capital (durable structures or equipment produced by human beings), human capital (the productive potential of human beings), and social capital (norms and institutions that influence the interactions among humans). The idea of durable assets is that they are capable of generating flows of goods and services (Rust 1985).

Here is a list of some concrete examples of durable assets that people can acquire to support their overall economic security:

- Automobiles
- Land for cultivation
- Computers
- Sewing machines
- Tools
- Livestock

This list, by no means exhaustive, shows the types of durable assets that can provide peoples and families greater means of supporting their livelihoods in times of relative prosperity and times that prove to be not so prosperous.

Overall this pattern emphasizes both a focus (and approach) and a concrete goal of engendering livelihood development for those left without the means to ensure their own survival. The foundation of a durable assets approach follows from the understanding that fully relying on one's own labor can be problematic in regions in which the economy is vulnerable to dramatic transitions. Giving people the power of ownership over their own lives in the good times as well as the bad adds another layer of protection to avoid worse poverty.

For example, one movement of development throughout South Asia is driven by the creation of women's self-help groups. In these groups, women collectively save in order to acquire loans or assets to acquire the tools to initiate income-generating activities. Many start up shops as seamstresses, or begin poultry farming; some go on to open small stores, and others, as in the case of the Grameen Bank's cell phone program, to provide cell service to local people. In each of these examples, a common thread is the tools used. The seamstress must possess a sewing machine to pursue her business, just as the poultry farmer needs livestock and land. The cell phone women in Bangladesh would not be there if it were not for their ownership of the cell phones they use to run their businesses. Just as the fisher would go hungry without tools, so too would a farmer without land and the taxi driver without a taxi.

This pattern highlights a useful view on how to facilitate the inherent creativity of people for pursuing livelihoods for themselves and their families. As long as there exists any durable asset, it is capable of possessing monetary attributes and therefore of giving rise to the characteristic problems of a monetary economy (Keynes 1936). Therefore, this pattern could be perceived as reinforcing oppressive or unfair economic systems. Nevertheless, the reality remains that over 1 billion people live in extreme poverty without the means to feed or protect their families in times of greater economic hardship. To ignore this fact based on arguments against the current economic system is perhaps to make a bad situation worse and perpetuate socioeconomic inequalities.

Solution   Development practitioners, community members, and individuals can participate in ways to consciously pursue the acquisition and sustainability of durable assets to promote income-generation activities and support a greater level of economic security to the most vulnerable populations. Such approaches could conceivably be achieved through the linkage of other patterns such as self-help groups, cooperatives and collectives, or a variety of other relevant patterns. Ultimately officials in government could, through pressure from social change advocates, develop policy initiatives to enable individuals and communities to both acquire durable goods and assist in protecting those assets that they do possess, such as land, from external threats.

Linked patterns   Fair Trade (21), Whole Cost (28), Intermediate Technologies (57), Community Currencies (63), Powerful Remittances (73), Civic Capabilities (85), Self-Help Groups (105), Open Source Everything (127).

Problem   Obstacles to diversity of ideas and freedom of thought are obstacles to human development, whether in wealthy countries rich in Internet connections or in rural regions short of roads and electricity. Not all people have access to information and ideas from which they might benefit, and the proliferation of ideas does not guarantee that people will encounter them. Information does not always want to be free.

Context   Public libraries have a history of successful struggle against obstacles to access to information and ideas. Among the findings of a recent research report in the United States, they remain trusted and valued by the public, even though funding is becoming increasingly difficult. Public libraries are increasingly becoming a community space; while demand for traditional library services remains strong, public libraries are widely perceived as offering solutions to community problems, and they have the potential to do more in future (Public Agenda 2006).

Discussion   More than 150 years ago, public libraries started to provide people with information and knowledge that would otherwise have been out of reach. Through a publicly funded lender, ordinary people such as Samuel Johnson's "common reader" could discover more and better books. At a library open to all, any ambitious working-class youth could seek self-improvement; Andrew Carnegie, future benefactor of public libraries around the world, educated himself as a young immigrant through the kindness of the owner of a private library.

Broad public support for the sober and egalitarian institution of the public library allows citizens to encounter difficult, provocative, and unpopular ideas. Public libraries embody both the characteristics of their communities and the principles of intellectual freedom. More of one may lead to less of the other. The challenge of liberating libraries is to benefit from the justified pride that communities take in their public libraries while encouraging greater efforts toward intellectual freedom.

Article 19 of the Universal Declaration of Human Rights declares the right of intellectual freedom: "to hold opinions without interference and to seek, receive and impart information and ideas through any media and regardless of frontiers." This freedom of opinion and expression for all citizens underlies a society's capacity to recognize and realize new possibilities. Civic participation requires access to information and life-long education. Prosperity in a free society depends on the creativity that comes from diverse and challenging ideas. Democracy's survival over time calls for adaptability and critical thought in the face of change.

Through professional associations such as the American Libraries Association and the International Federation of Library Associations, librarians advocate the principles of intellectual freedom. The pressures that they experience point to the obstacles to these principles:

money, location, coercion, private interests, lack of privacy, and pressure toward conformity, among others.

Public libraries provide services regardless of the ability to pay; they serve everyone equally, including those for whom money would otherwise present an obstacle. Although the public library may enjoy broad public approval, funding for this free and open source of information is seldom easily come by.

Public libraries provide services regardless of location. Whether in inner cities or remote rural outposts, they reach people who might otherwise not encounter the information and ideas that libraries offer. Public libraries provide services regardless of coercion and censorship. They exist to bring people and ideas together, not to separate them. Public libraries operate at arm's length from their sponsors, whether government, taxpayers, volunteer fundraisers (such as friends' groups), or private donors. Despite this, they often struggle with the restriction of information by governments, self-censorship among librarians, and those who seek to impose their standards or tastes on others.

Public libraries provide services independent of private interests. While respecting intellectual property, they give priority to their patrons over commercial concerns, advocates of particular views, and any other interests that may distort the free flow of information and ideas.

Public libraries protect the privacy of their patrons. They encourage people to access information and ideas by maintaining the confidentiality of what they look for, look at, and communicate.

Public libraries resist pressures toward conformity that arise even where the diversity of information and ideas is growing. They take pride in providing ideas and information that are "unorthodox, unpopular, or considered dangerous by the majority" (American Library Association and Association of American Publishers 2004).

As an "information commons" (Kranich 2004), the public library provides a forum for information and ideas, offers new ways to access information, and recognizes freedom of opinion and expression as the basis of democratic society. Although its strategies and services go beyond the printed word and beyond the walls of the library building, the public library also offers those who love "that magical hinged object, the book" (Holroyd 1999) a refuge from the possibly less subversive distractions of technology and contemporary media.

Public libraries develop access to information in many ways. Individual libraries provide computer access and guidance to patrons, including those who have no other means of using the Internet. Regional aggregation of library catalogues and databases offers patrons a collection much richer than any one library could maintain. Libraries are active in making government information more available, and they work to influence legislation to prevent intellectual property rights from adding new obstacles to access.

Public libraries have long worked to develop skills, most often needed by their underserved constituents, in language, literacy, and technology. As more information of increasingly variable quality becomes available, it is more and more necessary to evaluate its integrity and independence. With their staff and their patrons, public libraries are beginning to cultivate information literacy: the skills necessary to find, use, and critically evaluate information from many sources.

Side by side with public libraries' broad mission for an informed and active citizenry is a focus on the local community and civic dialogue. The typical public library offers a public gathering space, available to all regardless of opinion or creed. It may provide a network connection to the local school so that youngsters can use library computers to do their homework assignments. It may maintain an archive of local history and records and care for cultural artifacts (such as paintings) of local significance. This local focus can lead to collaborations with other local stakeholders; for example, in the case of a major local environmental issue such as industrial river pollution, the library may work with a government agency to host community meetings and include copies of the agency's reports in a collection of documents related to the issue.

Public libraries have a special mission to serve their underserved or "information poor" (Kranich 2004) constituents. Groups such as urban minorities and rural communities have special difficulty in surmounting the obstacles to accessing and using information and ideas. In some parts of the world, such as the rural north of Peru served by the Rural Library Network (Medcalf 1999), library services develop literacy through books and storytelling. In situations such as this, public libraries transport books on foot or by pack animal—camels in Kenya, donkeys in Zimbabwe.

The public library is an established institution that offers a model for building new institutions and services. It enjoys broad public respect and support and promotes principles central to democracy and development: intellectual freedom, access to information and to ideas both fashionable and unfashionable, and serving the needs of the underrepresented. If the Navajo call the library a "house of papers," it can be much more; through new technologies, new partnerships, and new services, it offers what Josh Cohen (1990), director of the Mid-Hudson Library System, calls "one of the cornerstones of democracy and one of the building blocks of a strong community."

Solution   To create access to information, civic participation, and life-long education, use what public libraries already offer and work with them to implement new services. Support public libraries by volunteering, forming friends' groups, and establishing networks with other community institutions. Where there is no library, use the power of books to build public support. Wherever there is a public library, work with it to further the principles of intellectual freedom for all.

Linked patterns   Opportunity Spaces (33), Meaningful Maps (47), Community Networks (61), Privacy (65), Design for Unintended Use (84), Informal Learning Groups (98), Universal Voice Mail (113), Community Telecenters (117), Great Good Place (119), Community Inquiry (122), Open Source Search Technology (125).

Problem   The opposition between local and global as well as the relative deemphasizing of space and region in the face of the ubiquity, mobility, portability, and interconnection provided by numerous digital networks has become a major aspect of globalization and the virtualization of life. Yet there is a well-known saying concerning universality: describe your backyard, and you will reach humanity. These same features of our increasingly digital and connected world also support decentralization, telecommuting, and the intangible revaluation of each local space, of actually "being there" or at least making a connection to a specific spot (a hot spot) for the sake of material and immaterial interaction. Thus a new space-time dimension, on a "glocal" level (global in reach but ultimately local in its value-producing competencies), creates new human development challenges. This new space-time requires new skills and generates its own styles of employment and ownership, control and freedom.

Context   According to Glocal: Glocalization (Robertson 1995), a portmanteau world of globalization and localization entails one or both of the following:

• The creation or distribution of products or services intended for a global or transregional market, but customized to suit local laws or culture.
• The use of electronic communications technologies, such as the Internet, to provide local services on a global or transregional basis. Craigslist and Meetup are examples of Web applications that have a globalized approach.

The global and the local may be regarded as two sides of the same coin. A place may be better understood by recognizing the dual nature of glocalization. Often localization is neglected in the shadow of the omnipresent veneer presented by globalization. Yet in many cases, local forces constantly strive to attenuate the impact of global processes. These forces can be seen in efforts to prevent or modify plans for the local construction of buildings for global corporate enterprises, such as for Wal-Mart. *Glocalization* as a term, though originating in the 1980s from within Japanese business practices, was first popularized in the English-speaking world by the British sociologist Roland Robertson (1992, 1995).

Discussion   The "glocal" dimension relates to specific areas of economic development models, such as local productive arrangements and industrial and sectoral clusters (from the electronics district in Tokyo to software and information technology–related hubs in Bangalore).

It is clear that the combination of local and global, concrete and universal, remote and present, material and immaterial, tangible and intangible is not clearly demarcated in the glocal development model. Other classic distinctions also become blurred, such as private, public, the third (or philanthropic) sector, and academic or technoscientific. Telecenters, public spaces in third world countries that offer free access to the Web as well as other social and educational services, are examples of new glocal development tools. These information and computer technology (ICT)–enabled hubs of social and economic engineering also tend to create and design new social artifacts, thus opening opportunities for self-knowing, life-long learning, and employability.

Digital emancipation, as opposed to digital inclusion, aims at income generation and identity creation rather than access to networked infrastructures, a common tenet among "digital divide" critics and researchers. While access to digital networks has been on the rise, especially within developing countries, there is less confidence and actual, verified results when it comes to job opportunities, entrepreneurship, solidarity, and organization of civil society. Emancipation refers to greater autonomy and skills to avoid, when necessary, automation and digitalization when necessary, rather than an overall commitment to a "digital life." The emancipated individual or community should be able not only to create income and opportunities as a result of digitalization but also through a rejection of excessive digitalization of processes and projects.

Mediatic capitalism is a new regime of capital accumulation. The term *mediatic* stresses not only the growing role of media (ICTs) but also the key function of intermediaries in the organization of production and distribution networks. It is regulated by the value aggregation of knowledge-creating activities and the development of intangible assets (brands, consumer habits, technological standards, and service-based value chains). This new form of capital accumulation has also led, for policy purposes, to the increasingly relevant clustering of creative industries. Telecenters can also play a role in the production of images (and self-representations) in peripheral regions of the world, given appropriate regulatory and technoeconomic incentives and subsidies.

Infomediaries, regulators, knowledge-based business consortia, and local informational clusters are examples of economic agents and institutions defined by their skills in the production and management of information, communication, knowledge, and cultural networks in value chains, power dynamics, and organizational structures. This perspective requires new approaches to governance in the context of rapid globalization and emerging organizational semiotics and new forms of finance that value social, cultural, and intellectual capital.

For the peripheral nation-states of the world system, a new threat emerges: there is a growing concern not only with gaps in technology and knowledge, but also with the emergence of a digital divide within developing societies. On the other hand, neoilluminists (or proponents of an "integrated" reaction to mass media and cultural industries as discussed in Eco (1977)) preach about the creation of development opportunities led by new technologies. This would include the celebrated $100 computer concept, later rephrased as One Laptop per Child (http://laptop.org/), a technology-focused project that responds to the needs of the industry rather than addressing the pressing issues of underserved communities in the developing world In Brazil, one of the latest countries to attempt an implementation of the low-cost, educational laptop, the OLPC itself came to the auction with machines valued at about $300, amidst a faltering alliance of suppliers.

Digital emancipation was proposed as a theoretical perspective for policymaking related to glocal development in December 2005 at the first international conference on digital emancipation, held in Brazil by the City of Knowledge at the University of São Paulo. Human development as emancipation places the burden of action in the local dimension, stressing traditional and informal knowledge whenever possible, so that human development under mediatic capitalism can lead to sustainability, identity, and civic intelligence. These characteristics have often been highlighted by development funding agencies, which are increasingly conscious of the rising importance of glocal economics for the appropriate design and implementation of development policies. In this context, micro and nanoeconomics may be more relevant than classic macro and microeconomics.

Solution New forms of exchange, gifts, collaboration, and collective action involve not only technical choices but a fundamental consideration for the emancipatory potential of every policy and technological option. Empowerment in the creation of representations may be as important as job creation for youth and may be a precondition for jobs to emerge. The critique of local, regional, and global, as well as other (gender, faith, language), representations of the world in the media becomes as crucial as access to software codes and network engineering. Emancipation is also defined as an antidote to the limiting and binary digital divide paradigm, so that a philosophical and political turn moves technological advances into human development tools at both local and global dimensions.

Linked patterns Global Citizenship (6), Education and Values (17), Democratic Political Settings (31), Opportunity Spaces (33), Participatory Design (36), Mobile Intelligence (38), International Networks of Alternative Media (43), Open Action and Research Network (45), Community Currencies (63), Mobile Information and Computer Technology Learning Facilities (77), Informal Learning Groups (98), Self-Designed Development (106), Open Source Everything (127).

61 Community Networks

Problem Communities often lack the information and communication infrastructure needed to support and sustain social networks of clubs, organizations, associations, groups, agencies, families, and individual citizens that constitute the structures, organization, and activities of community life and enable effective organization, planning, and enactment of local campaigns when threatened by external agency. Although network technologies present interesting opportunities to support community networking activities, they are not, in themselves, community networks. Furthermore, the dominant information and computer technology (ICT) agenda of both public and commercial sectors is often hostile to the mutuality, collaboration, and communicative processes required for using ICT in support of community networking (Day and Schuler 2004).

Context Building, organizing, and sustaining active relationships within the social, cultural, and economic networks of the community require appropriate and effective strategies. Building and sustaining community networks require strategies that facilitate community appropriation of communication technologies in support of community networking. This pattern is intended as a contribution to, and perhaps even as a catalyst for, a dialogue about community networks. Dialogue participants should include community members, local activists, practitioners (community developers and community technologists) community researchers, policymakers, and local businesses and community economic developers. Although this list is not exhaustive, it illustrates the diversity and levels of knowledge and expertise needed to plan and develop community networks that empower and strengthen community relationships and processes through democratic communications.

Discussion Community networks are frequently referred to as technological artifacts (Community Artifacts 2006) and appear to be understood in terms of the connectivity they give to ICT rather than the links they facilitate within communities. Yet in his seminal text on the emergence of ICT-based community networks, Schuler (1996) explains that the term *community networks* is a sociological concept that referred to community communication patterns and relationships, long before the emergence of the community bulletin boards of the late 1970s (Morino 1994), that is, the forerunners for the Web-based community networks of the 1990s onward (Kubicek and Wagner 1998).

Establishing what lies at the heart of community networking, that is, the purpose and nature of the relationships within communities and the processes of communication, is central to understanding community. Generating knowledge of what shapes and energizes community life by making connections and interacting with people of diverse values and belief systems is pivotal to developing effective community networks. In this respect, the effectiveness of community networks is understood in terms of how they support and sustain community communications, relationships, and activities.

An example of how knowledge of community networking in its broadest sense can be generated and how this knowledge might inform the development of community networks is illustrated by the Community Network Analysis (CNA) project in the Poets Corner community of Brighton and Hove, U.K. Early in the project, a community profile (Hawtin, Hughes, and Percy-Smith 1994) was conducted to develop a picture of community assets, community needs, and community relationships. Interestingly, the 104 groups, clubs, associations, centers, and organizations often interpreted their shared social environment in different ways. Acknowledging the existence of such diversity is a central part of beginning to understand and work with it as a source of community strength rather than community threat.

Analysis of the community infrastructure revealed eight main clusters of groups, clubs, and other organizations and four smaller clusters. These clusters, or affiliation networks, were organized by a parent organization, such as community associations and places of worship. Affiliation appeared to be based around organizational support mechanisms and the availability of physical space. A number of isolated nodes or didactic networks were also identified; for example, the two schools were exemplars of a didactic network, although both were eager to develop stronger ties within the community.

Informal network structures in the community are altogether more open and dynamic than their formal counterparts but are also transient in nature. Familial or friendship ties usually predominate, and networking often occurs in public spaces, such as the park, local pubs and coffee shops, or serendipitous street meetings. This "agora effect" provides opportunity for knowledge exchange, comfort, and mutually supportive transactions.

Informal social network exchanges tend to be self-organizing and mutually reinforcing, falling into one of two categories. The first is spontaneous, for example, someone's cat is missing, and the neighbors organize a search of the neighborhood; neighbors leave bags of good-quality but unwanted clothes or toys on the doorsteps of families new to the area as a welcoming gesture; groups of people pop in to each other's houses for coffee and a chat, all reinforcing and developing social bonds. The second category is organized but with no formal membership; examples are networks of babysitters and parents requiring sitters that evolve through the local grapevine; a curry club, where participants try new curry recipes, is organized at irregular intervals by e-mail; a book club run along much the same lines as the curry club is organized by cell phone; or there are networks among neighbors on the same street in which spare keys are cut and distributed among trusted neighbors.

Both network types play a significant role in developing relationships of trust and social cohesion in the community. The communication technologies that people feel comfortable with are increasingly being used to support both network links and exchanges. If community networks are to support the diversity of social realities in a community, then they must provide safe and welcoming spaces that encourage and facilitate participation and engagement. Enabling people to tell their stories and interact with one another in ways meaningful to them and in comfortable environments is central to effective community networking.

A prototype community communication space (CCS) being developed as part of the CNA project attempts to create such spaces. Those working with the community to build both the context and the content for the CCS have been asked to support video and audio podcasting, digital storytelling, digital art, poetry, and music. Local communication forums are being established to support the face-to-face forums of community development and building activities. Blogs, wikis, and other social software such as social networking applications are also being explored for potential community benefits.

Drawing on Rogers's diffusion of innovation theory (1995) the stages of CCS diffusion in Poet's Corner can be envisioned as a set of concentric rings. The innermost ring represents the Poets Corner Residents Society's (PCRS) invitation to CNA and the subsequent invitation from its executive committee to work in partnership to map and improve community communications. Much of this period was spent getting to know people in the community, building trust, raising awareness, and supporting the activities of PCRS and other community groups. A group of enthusiastic project advocates emerged as CCS innovators. With their assistance, the project became grounded in and supportive of community activities and needs.

Slowly trust and respect developed among the partners. A number of community groups displayed interest in the project and began collaborating. The second ring shows early adopters within the community infrastructure. By this time, the project was participating in and supporting the planning and organization of a second summer festival and family fun day. The third ring illustrates the resultant increased involvement from the community infrastructure and the beginning of some involvement from local residents. This is second-stage early-adoption activity.

During the project, the CNA partnership raised awareness of the potential of the CCS, and interest within the community increased. The partnership is now in what Rogers (1995) would describe as the trial and evaluation phases of community assessment. Whether the CCS will be adopted and can be sustained beyond the funding of the project will depend largely on the community itself. The CNA team will continue to collaborate with the community, but its long-term objective has always been to design and build a prototype CCS in participation with the community and explore how the community will take ownership of and sustain that space.

Solution   The potential scope for ICT to support, enhance, and sustain community communications is immense, but effective community networks can be built only through meaningful and mutual partnerships of knowledge exchange. Communities are contested spaces rich in diversity. They embrace or reject technologies at their own pace and in their own way. These processes cannot be rushed and must be respected. Accepting that they might have to step out of their community comfort zone in order to embrace new technologies can be threatening. Achieving a willingness to participate requires patience and dialogue. Community engagement will be sustained only if the community understands the benefits to community life. If community networks are to emerge as significant components of modern community life, external partners must understand this in context and content. Only then can they contribute in a meaningful way.

Linked patterns Big Tent for Social Change (32), Opportunity Spaces (33), International Networks of Alternative Media (43), Intermediate Technologies (57), Public Library (59), Online Community Service Engine (62), Community Currencies (63), Powerful Remittances (73), Civic Capabilities (85), Citizen Journalism (91), Community-Building Journalism (97), Informal Learning Groups (98), Universal Voice Mail (113), Community Telecenters (117), Great Good Place (119), Emergency Communication Systems (121), Community Inquiry (122).

Problem   Researchers and practitioners often trivialize the relevance of software in deter-mining the sustainability and success of online communities. Opinions differ widely be-tween two extremes: some implicitly assume that any software for managing online forums is sufficient (cf. Kim 2000); others, including Wenger (2001), suggest that a large set of fea-tures (up to seventy-three) must be included in software for managing online communities —encompassing several different applications, from access to expertise and synchronous interactions, from e-learning spaces to project spaces, and resulting in complex and expen-sive proprietary solutions. Between these two extremes, it is necessary to identify a set of basic macrofunctionalities that an online community service engine should provide, as well as a framework for extending these functionalities as required. In the course of this effort, support for communicating across community boundaries is as vital as focusing on individ-ual communities.

Context   Communities are increasingly seen as powerful means for addressing significant problems in many fields of human activities. Virtual and online communities extend these possibilities as they remove the time and space constraints of physical communities while preserving the advantages of sharing knowledge and experience, developing mutual trust and ultimately cooperation. Local communities in developed as well as developing countries, communities of practice within and across enterprises, and learning communities represent very different situations that can be extended and enriched by an online counterpart. More recently, communities have arisen directly online, as in the case of blogs and blogger com-munities. Regardless of these different contexts, online communities are complex sociotech-nical systems. However, while significant efforts have been made, and are still being made, to investigate the implications of online communities from a sociological perspective (see, e.g., Preece, Abras, and Maloney-Krichmar 2004), much less has been done on the technology side.

Discussion   While the sociotechnical nature of online communities is manifest and a mas-sive volume of literature on online communities deals with topics such as their sociological aspects and organizational impacts, as well as the role they can play in a variety of contexts (within organizations as well as in the society), much less attention has been paid to techno-logical issues. Actually otherwise satisfactory sociological analysis and identification of gen-eral requirements technologies already available, such as usability studies (Preece 2000) do not provide clear hints for software developers.

Etienne Wenger has probably advanced the most relevant attempt to identify an appropri-ate technological platform for the features online communities should provide. In his exten-sive survey (Wenger 2001), now revised and updated (Wenger et al. 2005), Wenger identifies a set of critical factors for the success of a community of practice (CoP) and the technological implications for supportive tools in terms of a list of features (seventy-three items) that an online community environment should have if it wants to satisfy its members' needs.

Inspired by Wenger's work and through an analysis of software used for managing virtual community (PhpBB, PhpNuke) and community networks (such as FreePort and CSuite), as well as through direct experience of managing several online communities (primarily related to community networks, as a basic competence; De Cindio et al. 2004) with different software, De Cindio, Sonnante, and others developed a higher-level classification of the macrofunctionalities an online community services engine should provide, that is:

• Homogeneous, since each macrofunctionality is at the same level of abstraction as the others
• Complete, since the seven macrofunctionalities capture the essential elements of a fully featured online community service engine
• General enough to be applied to any kind of online community, for example, communities of practice, community networks, communities of interests, and learning communities

The result is the following list of macrofunctionalities an online community service engine should provide:

• Users' management characterizes community members and provides differing and personalized views, and it allows discriminating levels of access to community resources. This group of functions includes member directories, access rights, and profiles.
• Communication and dialogue include all the typical synchronous and asynchronous communication tools such as e-mail, discussion boards, blogs, private messages, and chats
• Information and publishing allow community members to manage content for publishing, as with a standard content management system (CMS), but with an effective integration with the communication and dialogue dimension, which is essential in an online community services engine (Benini, De Cindio, and Sonnante 2005).
• Community awareness gives members the sense of belonging to a community that is characterized by rules, roles, history, customs, and other characteristics. Examples of these features are presence awareness (knowing who is online), reputation and ranking, personal history, subscriptions, and a distinctive appearance.
• Calendaring includes features for storing personal or community events or appointments by date, together with reminders features, and the possibility of sharing calendars among members based on access rights.
• Work group support features. These features are based on the ability to restrict member access to community resources like forums, upload file areas, and calendars.
• Monitoring and statistics gathering features that keep track of access, the number of posts, liveliness of forums, and moderators' reliability, and other indicators are needed to trace the vitality, diversity, and overall "health" of the online community.

In addition to these general-purpose macrofunctionalities, an online community services engine should be able to be integrated with modules that offer features relevant for any specific type of community, such as teaching modules for learning communities or deliberation facilities for civic and community networks.

To facilitate the integration of basic functionalities with dedicated features necessary to support specific types of communities, the online community services engine must have an overall modular architecture for integrating functionalities that were not built in. It also must include a user management component capable of supplying authentication and authorization services to external add-on components or tools (most of the user management components of the software used to implement online communities do not accept authentication requests from external modules). Both requirements have the effect of opening the online community services engine through standard protocols, thereby facilitating cross-community communication. For the same reason, the online community services engine should include features such as RSS (really simple syndication) feeds, which enhance information exchange.

All of these functionalities are possible if the online community services engine is implemented on standard base technologies, such as the lightweight directory access protocol to handle authentication and authorization and Web services for providing standard interoperability among modules.

Solution   This classification of the macrofunctionalities that an online community services engine should provide, together with the associated architectural requirements, challenges researchers and practitioners to implement and deploy an online community services engine that can be tailored by the community that uses it. Each deployment of the engine should be created as an instance of the engine, including the set of functionalities necessary for each specific online community. The opening requirement naturally calls for developing software using open source tools. Alternatively, the resulting classification can be viewed as a checklist for selecting from available software (proprietary or not) rather than for development purposes.

Linked patterns   Participatory Design (36), International Networks of Alternative Media (43), Citizen Access to Simulations (48), Online Deliberation (52), Community Networks (61), E-Consultation (70), Accessibility of Online Information (75), Civic Capabilities (85), Document-Centered Discussion (92), Homemade Media (110), Universal Voice Mail (113), Community Telecenters (117), Emergency Communication Systems (121), Open Source Search Technology (125), Open Source Everything (127).

Problem People have always traded or bartered with each other, using different tools and materials to represent and store value in various kinds of transactions: trade, investment, consumption, production, marriage, kinship, and sacrifice, for example. In complex urban and global capitalist societies, money expands the potential for growth and accumulation while also creating new forms of wealth and power concentration, regulated by central banks and other supervisory authorities at national and international levels. Community currencies, or "complementary currencies," offer a solution for local markets deprived of or unserved by global or national currencies.

Context Thomas Greco (1994) states three basic ways in which conventional money malfunctions: there is never enough of it, it is misallocated at its source so that it goes to those who already have lots of it, and it systematically pumps wealth from the poor to the rich. The symptoms of a "polluted" money supply are familiar: inflation, unemployment, bankruptcies, foreclosures, increasing indebtedness, homelessness, and a widening gap between the rich and the poor. Nevertheless, the ultimate resource of the community, the productivity, skills, and creativity of its members, is not limited by lack of money (Meeker-Lowry 1995)

Discussion According to Michael Linton, "Money is really just an immaterial measure, like an inch, or a gallon, a pound, or degree. While there is certainly a limit on real resources—only so many tons of wheat, only so many feet of material, only so many hours in the day—there need never be a shortage of measure. (No, you cannot use any inches today, there are not any around, they are all being used somewhere else.) Yet this is precisely the situation in which we persist regarding money. Money is, for the most part, merely a symbol, accepted to be valuable generally throughout the society that uses it. Why should we ever be short of symbols to keep account of how we serve one another?" (Meeker-Lowry 1995).

"The proper kind of money used in the right circumstances is a liberating tool that can allow the fuller expression of human creativity. Money has not lived up to its potential as a liberator because it has been perverted by the monopolization of its creation and by politically manipulating its distribution—available to the favored few and scarce for everyone else" (Greco 1994). Creating community currencies may foster exchanges among people that need it most.

Conventional money is strictly regulated by central authorities at a federal level. Its regulated scarcity is a major source of powerful economic policy (e.g., raising interest rates to curb inflation) that plays on the rules of capitalist competition. Community currencies are designed to counterweight scarcity by promoting exchanges founded on cooperation or collaboration. The emergence of new information and communication technologies has promoted numerous local projects that use "open source money" or "collaborative money." (Author Douglas Rushkoff (2006) provides a definition for these terms: "Open Source or, in more common parlance, "complementary" currencies are collaboratively established units representing hours of labor that can be traded for goods or services in lieu of centralized currency.") Both conventional money and community currencies, however, rest on the same foundation: confidence in the agreed-on rules of production and supply of monetary and financial instruments (credits, loans, and time sharing, for example). Both are conventions designed and operated by living human communities.

Community currencies may also be qualitative rather than quantitative, so that the purchasing power of the currency takes advantage of specific ranges of skills and resources (child and social health care, environmental campaigns, or edutainment projects), unlike the conventional economy, which values certain skills and devalues or ignores others as effects of blind market forces. The move toward community currency is motivated by the desire to bridge the gap between what we earn and what we need to survive financially.

Local currencies are seen as a community-building tool. Communities may range from solidarity economies in economically disadvantaged and vulnerable social areas, to game players, to collectors or charity donors and are spread throughout the world as digital networks promote new forms of community life. Community currencies not only prove a commitment to community building and to supporting what is local but also may function as a path toward a greater experiential understanding of the role of economics and money in daily lives. Any community can, in principle, design currencies backed by something, tangible or intangible, that the community agrees has collective value.

Hundreds of community currency models are at work. These are a few of the community currency reference sites:

http://en.wikipedia.org/wiki/Bernard_Lietaer
Resources for Community Currency Activists, http://www.communitycurrency.org/resources .html

Luca Fantacci, "Complementary Currencies: A Prospect on Money from a Retrospect on Premodern Practices," http://akira.arts.kuleuven.be/meijifin/node/52
Social Trade Organization, http://www.strohalm.net/en/site.php
Open Money, http://www.thetransitioner.org/wiki/tiki-index.phppage=Open+Money+home +page

Ithaca Hours, where everyone's honest hour of labor has the same dignity, and LETS, Local Exchange Trading Systems, are examples of such models. These two community currency models illustrate new forms of social and communicative practices that have an impact on living structures at a local level.

The Ithaca Hours system was created in 1991 by Paul Glover, a community economist and ecological designer. With Ithaca Hours, each hour is equivalent to $10.00, the approximate average hourly wage in Tompkins County, Ithaca, New York. Participants can use hours for rent, plumbing, carpentry, car repair, chiropractic, food (two large locally owned grocery stores as well as farmer's market vendors accept them), firewood, child care, and numerous other goods and services. Some movie theaters accept hours, as do bowling alleys and the local Ben and Jerry's ice cream shop (Meeker-Lowry 1995).

The LETS model was created on Vancouver Island, British Columbia, Canada, as a self-contained network in which members buy and sell services to other members and are paid in the LETS currency. Every member has an individual account that records his or her debit or credit. Members do not "owe" the person or business providing the service; instead their debt is to LETS, and their debt is thus socialized (DeFilippis 2004).

Currencies are powerful carriers of feedback information, and potent triggers of adjustments, but on their own terms. (Jacobs 1984). "A national currency registers, above all, consolidated information on a nation's international trade" (Jacobs 1984). National dollars tend to flow out of local communities where they are needed the most to those who already control large pools of wealth like banks and corporations. Community currency is also a tool that can help revitalize local economies by encouraging wealth to stay within a community rather than flowing out. It provides valuable information about the community's balance of trade and collective values. (Meeker-Lowry 1995)

People who are time rich and cash poor can be socially and economically productive without necessarily using only national or international, centrally regulated money. If community currencies can also be used in conjunction with national currency, their use does not have to become an all-or-nothing proposition, thus leading to the notion of complementary currencies.

Local currencies empower their members to improve their circumstances and environment while protecting the general community from the negative influences of other capital flows. This gives the community more control over investments and allows the poor to become emancipated in the economic choices and conditions that affect their daily lives. Local currency systems offer the opportunity of transforming labor power or working time into local purchasing power (Meeker-Lowry 1995).

Solution   There are unique challenges in implementing a community currency system, both technical and political. Shared values and a longterm commitment by many community members are needed to build a sustainable currency. Adequate management at the local level may involve monetary policy issues similar to those experienced at national or international spheres. The community may be local, but also involve participants from distant places acting toward a common goal that can be social, educational, and cultural. If successful, a community currency system can leverage local projects in economically depressed areas of the map and put them on the road to a hopeful and fruitful future.

Linked patterns   Whole Cost (28), Indicators (29), Opportunity Spaces (33), Strategic Capacity (34), Mobile Intelligence (38), Durable Assets (58), Digital Emancipation (60), Community Networks (61), Grassroots Public Policy Development (78), Strategic Frame (86), Shared Vision (101), Community Animators (102).

Policy

Problem   The lack of authentic and principled accountability of corporations, government, political processes, and the media provides irresistible opportunities for corruption. Unfortunately this most often deprives whole societies and the world's poorest people of their right to opportunity and a sense of well-being.

Context   Corruption is a common mechanism of social domination. In one basic form it exacts a price from people with little power in exchange for a favor from someone with more power. In another form, two or more people or organizations with power swap favors for mutual advantage. The favor can be large or small, and it can be granted or denied at the pleasure of the power holder, whose criteria, rationale, and legitimacy for the decision are hidden and therefore unavailable for review or criticism. Although the degree of corruption varies from place to place, everybody at one time or another can be a victim, however indirectly. Journalists, businesspeople, government officials, activists, educators, as well as ordinary people, that is, citizens, are affected by corruption and can play a role in its prevention.

Discussion   At its most basic level, transparency is the quality of being able to be seen through. When used in a social context, it means "easily detected, understood: obvious, evident." To exhibit transparency means that the reality of how things actually work is not occluded by false or misleading layers of artifice. Transparency thus helps shed light on corrupt practices that thrive on secrecy.

At a time when concern is mounting over the seemingly overwhelming range of problems facing the world, the principle and initiatives of transparency advocates are gaining momentum and significant interest within a broadening global discourse. While rights to privacy and protection are critical benchmarks in evaluating the relative health of a democracy, deterrents and penalties to corruption are essential if efforts designed to invigorate social justice are to become more successful.

It turns out that the relatively simple approach of making transactions, both monetarily and information based, of the powerful visible has the desired effect of discouraging corruption and encouraging good works. Learning about corruption is a first step toward rooting it out, often a long, frustrating, thankless, and sometimes dangerous enterprise. A corrupt court system, for example, is likely to free guilty people in certain instances, and noncorrupt judges may pay with their lives when they act to convict guilty people.

Niccolò Machiavelli introduced the familiar social equation, "Power corrupts, absolute power corrupts absolutely," which asserts that corruption is an inevitable consequence of power and that the greater the power, the greater the resultant corruption. Machiavelli's perspective reminds us why citizens are naturally suspicious of, for example, secret meetings between government officials and corporate executives, as when Bush administration officials met in 2001 behind closed doors with lobbyists from The American Petroleum Institute,

The American Gas Association, and other corporations and industry associations to discuss U.S. energy policy and propose legislative language, some of which was incorporated into law ("The Cheney Energy Task Force" 2004).

In truth, Machiavelli's wisdom provides governments with ample incentive for making such meetings more open or transparent. Corruption is not intrinsically the province of one political party or another. It does thrive, however, in situations where secrecy and fear are prevalent. The Enron and WorldCom scandals certainly provided lessons that were largely responsible for the whistle-blower protection provisions of the Sarbanes-Oxley Act in the United States.

On the international front, groups that adopt transparency as a prerequisite to their work while providing expert advice include the International Institute for Sustainable Development, whose model Multilateral Agreement on Investment for Sustainable Development brought the convention of sustainability to influence within the Organization for Economic Co-Operation and Development by helping design both legal and policy instruments on foreign investment.

While numerous projects and events have focused on transparency, two are especially relevant to this pattern's big picture at a most sensitive time in human history: the United Nations Convention against Corruption (UNCAC) which was adopted by the General Assembly in 2003 (Resolution 5814) and the ongoing Union of Concerned Scientists Transparency Project ("UCS-China Workshops on Transparency" 2005) that has been working for over a decade to foster the "intellectual and institutional capacity to increase transparency through participation in international arms control negotiations."

The transparency pattern is very general and can be applied in a variety of cultures and situations, including:

- Disaster aid and reconstruction, such as that related to the Southeast Asian tsunami
- Decisions about what articles to run in newspapers or on television news shows
- Sources of funding for media columnists and other pundits
- Decisions about corporate executive salaries and severance packages
- Inspectors of new construction, fish harvests, food quality, and tax returns
- Building permits and other land use decisions
- The revolving door between executives in weapons corporations and government officials who place orders with them
- Lobbying government officials (versus bribes for legislative support)
- Welfare systems
- Judicial systems
- Money laundering, or support or opposition to banking transparency legislation
- Attendance at government meetings by corporate executives to decide policies where they are the direct beneficiaries
- Arms control and other international trust development initiatives

One of the greatest strengths of transparency as a social pattern can be found in its inclusiveness. Highlighting this point are grassroots activists who are elevating public awareness and forming alliances with many people and groups. As a result, the practice of transparency is becoming a model of increasing influence.

For instance, in 1999, the Poder Ciudadano (Citizen Power), a nongovernmental organization based in Argentina, "negotiated an integrity pact with the city government of Buenos Aires," to monitor a $1.2 billion subway construction project to "root out corruption." Across political, economic, industrial, scientific, legal, and civic sectors, numerous reform initiatives are being coordinated, providing benchmarks for accountability and success that are being applauded. These evolving strategies have resulted in a holistic integrity approach toward waging a unified struggle against corruption. The resulting victories provide a great ray of hope for countries and peoples ravaged by decades, even centuries, of tyranny. Hence, transparency is now poised to have a greater and greater influence on enforcing civil society values over time.

Transparency International (TI) is a global civil society organization that was founded in 1993 and is providing leadership in the battle against corruption worldwide. Over the years TI has developed a wide range of useful tools and information resources, including these:

• TI Corruption Perceptions Index, the best known of TI's tools, has been credited with putting the issue of corruption on the international policy agenda. The index ranks more than 150 countries in terms of perceived levels of corruption, as determined by expert assessments and opinion surveys.
• Global Corruption Barometer, a survey that assesses general public attitudes toward and experience of corruption in dozens of countries around the world.
• *Global Corruption Report: 2006*, which focuses on the health sector, where lack of integrity can be a matter of life and death.
• TI Integrity Pact, a tool aimed at preventing corruption in public contracting. It consists of a process that includes an agreement between a government department (at the federal, national or local level) and all bidders for a public contract. It also introduces a monitoring system that provides independent oversight and accountability.
• TI Bribe Payers Surveys, an annual tool that evaluates the supply side of corruption: the propensity of firms from industrialized countries to bribe abroad.
• Business Principles: A comprehensive reference that aims to provide a practical tool to which companies can look for ways to counter bribery. It was designed as a starting point for businesses to develop their own antibribery systems or as a benchmark.

Transparency is fundamental to the evolution of a just and humane civil society. Focusing on transparency should help thwart corruption at the root and help create new solutions to age-old problems stemming from greed, fear, anger, and stupidity.

A concentrated effort to foster visibility is fundamental to the success of this project. Humanity has much to learn from the many tangible gains and policy shifts that are taking effect. Corruption in its various guises can deprive whole societies of opportunity and a sense of well-being. This reality beckons us to develop constructive innovations that can help open the doors of change. If we are successful, this work holds the promise of giving new life to the testimony and values of peace, justice, and solidarity for generations to come.

Solution   Using traditional as well as new forms of online media and ICT, we can continue to raise public awareness about specific struggles over transparency while exposing, protesting, and defying corruption at all levels. It is important to continue to broaden the support for transparency initiatives and enforcement. In this way, more accountability can be demanded, which can be translated into the development of equitable practices, and policies.

Linked patterns   Civic Intelligence (1), Social Responsibility (8), Demystification and Reenchantment (14), Public Agenda (30), World Citizen Parliament (40), Strengthening International Law (42), Truth and Reconciliation Commissions (51), Privacy (65), Free and Fair Elections (68), Participatory Budgeting (71), Powerful Remittances (73), Grassroots Public Policy Development (78), Academic Technology Investments (81), Civic Capabilities (85), Shared Vision (101), Sense of Struggle (104), Self-Designed Development (106), Whistle-Blowing (130), Follow the Money (135).

Problem   Everybody has information, activities, thoughts, and events from their lives that they would rather keep to themselves. Unfortunately for them, corporate marketeers, government security forces, and criminals, both amateur and professional, are working hard to uncover and exploit these secrets. While it is clear that some information of this sort needs to be uncovered for the common good (news of an impending terrorist attack, for example), this need is sometimes invoked as a pretext for trampling on privacy protections. Without adequate safeguards, dictators and other authoritarians (including many in putatively democratic societies) spy on critics of their regimes, an activity that can result in harassment or even torture or death of the critics in many places around the world.

Context   Legitimate governments, civil society, and concerned individuals must work together to prevent the all-too-common privacy abuses where the powerful prey on the less powerful. Thanks to what the British rock band, The Kinks call "the wonderful world of technology" in their song "Twentieth-Century Man," the basic ingredients—massive amounts of personal information in digital form, ubiquitous communication networks, and inexpensive and minuscule surveillance devices, coupled with the social equation of overzealous snoops and unsuspecting dupes—have helped fuel an explosion of privacy abuses and the potential for untold others. The fact that human identities themselves are now routinely stolen reveals the severity of the threat and how far privacy abuse has advanced.

Discussion   In 1763, the noted English Parliamentarian William Pitt, in his Speech on the Excise Tax, declared that "the poorest man may in his cottage bid defiance to all the force of the Crown. It may be frail; its roof may shake; the wind may blow through it; the storms may enter; the rain may enter—but the King of England cannot enter; all his forces dare not cross the threshold of the ruined tenement."

Now, nearly 250 years after Pitt's speech, rulers use technology to easily enter the tenements, both ruined and intact, of millions of people without a warrant or the problems associated with actual physical entrance. In the campaign to reelect Arnold Schwarzenegger to the governor's office in California, according to Michael Blood (2006), "The Schwarzenegger campaign has stockpiled millions of names, phone numbers and addresses with consumer preferences, voting histories and other demographic information." Then, based on assumptions about consumer preferences (a Democrat, for example, is more likely to drive a hybrid vehicle, while a Republican is more likely to drive a pickup truck or Cadillac), the campaign employed microtargeting to carefully craft messages to appeal to individual people based on their interpretation of the information they had gathered. According to Blood, "The idea is an outgrowth of techniques that businesses have long used to find new customers.... Few people might realize how much information is publicly available, for a price, about their lifestyles. Companies collect and sell consumer information they buy from credit card companies, airlines and retailers of every stripe."

Why is technology so crucial—and so threatening right now? The short answer is "plenty of product and buyers." The list of new technology is growing daily, and institutions are not afraid to (ab)use it. Some, if not most, of the technology is plagued by problems that are either built in (or otherwise inherent or inevitable) to the technology or subject to misuse. Face recognition software, at least currently, falls into the first category. John Graham, for example, of the Giraffe Project, a project discussed in the Everyday Heroism pattern (116), faced a problem in the second category when his name showed up on the U.S. "no fly list" for no discernible reason. After several letters to the government, he finally received word that his "identity has been verified," meaning, presumably that, yes, *he* is the "John Graham" he says he is. Currently his name has not been removed from the list; whether this is attributable to incompetence, work overload, or basic mean-spiritedness is not easily determined.

According to Privacy International (2006),

Privacy is a fundamental human right. It underpins human dignity and other values such as freedom of association and freedom of speech. It has become one of the most important human rights of the modern age.

Privacy is recognized around the world in diverse regions and cultures. It is protected in the Universal Declaration of Human Rights, the International Covenant on Civil and Political Rights, and in many other international and regional human rights treaties. Nearly every country in the world includes a right of privacy in its constitution. At a minimum, these provisions include rights of inviolability of the home and secrecy of communications. Most recently written constitutions include specific rights to access and control one's personal information. In many of the countries where privacy is not explicitly recognized in the constitution, the courts have found that right in other provisions. In many countries, international agreements that recognize privacy rights such as the International Covenant on Civil and Political Rights or the European Convention on Human Rights have been adopted into law.

Privacy International also points out that "the recognition of privacy is deeply rooted in history. There is recognition of privacy in the Qur'an and in the sayings of Muhammad. The Bible has numerous references to privacy. Jewish law has long recognized the concept of being free from being watched. There were also protections in classical Greece and ancient China."

Although privacy is seen as a fundamental and universal right, it is not easily defined. For one thing, it depends to some degree on culture and context. Privacy protection in the workplace, for example, is very important, yet employers would argue that they "own" the time of the employees on the job and hence have the right to surveil all their activities. New communication and surveillance technology has shown also that privacy, and the threats to it, change over time. Generally "privacy protection is frequently seen as a way of drawing the line at how far society can intrude into a person's affairs" (Privacy International 2006). U.S.

Supreme Court Justice Louis Brandeis explained privacy simply as the individual's "right to be left alone."

Privacy can be divided into the following separate but related concepts (Banisar and Davies 2008):

• Information privacy, which involves the establishment of rules governing the collection and handling of personal data such as credit information, and medical and government records. It is also known as "data protection."
• Bodily privacy, which concerns the protection of people's physical selves against invasive procedures such as genetic tests, drug testing, and cavity searches.
• Privacy of communications, which covers the security and privacy of mail, telephones, e-mail, and other forms of communication; and
• Territorial privacy, which concerns the setting of limits on intrusion into the domestic and other environments, such as the workplace or public space. This includes searches, video surveillance, and ID checks.

Each of these types of privacy concepts has a variety of ways in which the privacy can be abused or invaded. Can anything be done to stop or slow down these abuses? Or does the following variation on the statement attributed to former U.S. president Abraham Lincoln that begins, "You can fool some of the people all of the time" capture the reality of the privacy issue? *You can spy on some of the people all of the time and all of the people some of the time. You cannot spy on all of the people all of the time ... yet.*

The ultimate aim is self-restraint where government and other groups and institutions that have a propensity to invade privacy stop doing it. There was a sense, for example, that "gentlemen do not read other people's mail" actually was an operative notion within some governments. Although it is not always obvious, there are presumably always limits to what people or institutions do that are either self-imposed by habit or by fear of retribution or other penalties.

Unfortunately it is not the case that people should just trust governments, businesses, employers, or other people or institutions that might feel obliged to invade someone's privacy. What can individuals do to protect their rights? And what can they do to rectify problems where privacy has already been invaded? As individuals and as members of organizations like the American Civil Liberties Union, Electronic Privacy Information Center, and Privacy Rights International that stand up for privacy rights, we must anticipate abuses, monitor powerful (and otherwise snoopy) institutions, develop policy, negotiate and engage with authorities (law enforcement, legislators), and redress abuses. There are many ways in which people can—and should—take personal initiative. These include encrypting e-mail, shredding documents, taking precautions to prevent identity theft, and generally not falling for scams. Initiating lawsuits against the government and corporations for breaches in privacy can be an effective tool of the citizenry in behalf of privacy, although ideally it would be much preferred if these institutions could be counted on to police themselves adequately beforehand.

The idea that an innocent person has nothing to fear is an illusion. Worse, it shows a lack of knowledge that is almost breathtaking. If privacy is the right to be left alone, then different people will draw different boundary lines, but everybody will draw one. On the other side of that boundary are institutions and people who will cross that line if they are emboldened to do so. There are of course times when government or police are legitimately obligated to cross that line, but they will need to do so in a manner that is legitimate for the times. There is never a time when there is no line. Thus privacy is important to everybody in the world. It is also an important policy to consider for groups of people. When, for example, would it be necessary to forcefully bring a small group that existed communally for centuries into a cash economy? When is it ethically acceptable to bring the "word of God" (one version at least) to people of another religion? When does one country bomb another to bring the benefits of democracy to it?

We would like to think that people would not have to resort to extraordinary measures to protect themselves from privacy intrusion and invasion. After all, in the best of all possible worlds, people would not bother about privacy. But we do not live in the best of all possible worlds, and there is ample evidence that the assault on privacy has only just begun. There are a number of problems that are simply waiting to happen. Google, for example, owns an immense amount of information about virtually everybody who has ever searched for anything online. While it may be true that, as its mission statement asserts, that it will "do no evil," how can anyone be sure about the company in five or ten years? And just as spammers keep finding way to send electronic dreck, the future collection of personal information may be accomplished by new automated spying viruses and other software, which could be part of e-blackmail rackets, possibly in conjunction with faked digital evidence. Although some people have less reason to fear government, business, or criminal impinging on their privacy, no one is immune from problems of real and potential abuse. For that reason privacy rights are often strongly associated with human rights. Privacy is not, however, just an issue for dissidents or political activists.

Solution   We are living in an era when new technology and security concerns, both genuine and feigned, raise tremendous threats to privacy. The struggle against these must be as strong. Everyone should be cognizant of the critical importance of privacy and work conscientiously on all fronts to protect privacy rights. Public education is important in this area, as are public campaigns against privacy invaders.

Linked patterns   Public Library (59), Transparency (64), Patient Access to Medical Records (95), Control of Self-Representation (109), Power Research (128).

Problem Democratic societies rely on diversity of viewpoints and ideas for the intelligence, engagement, enthusiasm, and wisdom that sustains them. This is particularly important during this current era of globalization and critical public issues that require public engagement. At the same time, people all over the world are receiving more and more of their information from the mass media, which are becoming precipitously less diverse. The control of many of the world's media is becomingly increasingly concentrated in a handful of giant corporations.

Context Although the exact situation varies from place to place, virtually all communities are affected by the lack of media diversity, and all communities have opportunities to help promote this diversity. In the consolidating world of corporate mass media, large companies are touting mergers and monopolistic ownership practices as being conducive to diversity of programming and community representation in broadcasting. This claim of diversity is a facade that circumvents and ignores the idea of true community access and involvement.

Discussion A rich, dynamic universe of public thinking helps to ensure that all sides in public matters will be taken into consideration, thus promoting social, as well as economic, innovation. A paucity of diversity does not just jeopardize societal innovation, however. It becomes a threat to democracy itself. When media diversity is too low, public opinion is less likely to provide the oversight that democratic societies require, less likely to be engaged in public affairs, and less willing to entertain new ideas.

Ben Bagdikian is generally credited with the sounding of the alarm on media concentration in the United States. His book, *The Media Monopoly* (1983), revealed the disturbing fact that fifty corporations owned the majority of U.S. media companies. This trend toward consolidation has continued unabated since the book was published; Bagdikian reported that in 2000 (the 6th edition) 23 corporations own approximately 80 percent of media output in the United States. Today media corporations argue that when a company is able to monopolize a market, it can provide a more diverse array of cultures and voices than if that media landscape was broken into independently owned outlets. To use radio as a simple example, executives claim that when a corporation owns the majority of a market, the number of formats increases dramatically. While it may be true that the number of different formats increases slightly, it is doubtful that this reflects an increased diversity of opinion since the vast number of radio programs fall into a small number of predictable formats such as classic rock or easy listening. Many media corporations seize the opportunity that their conglomerate status affords them to record one radio show, which they then rebroadcast from all of their other stations with similar formats, sometimes localizing the show with a few references (perhaps pronounced correctly).

A lack of media diversity invariably means media concentration, and media concentration exacerbates problems of media homogeneity. The problem of media concentration extends beyond mere banality; it represents a major threat to the ability of citizens to act conscientiously and govern themselves as democracy requires. Media concentration brings power above and beyond what mere information provision would demand; illegitimate political and economic power invariably comes with the territory, and the nearly inevitable cozy connection with political elites leads to a self-perpetuating cycle that is extremely difficult to break. When media concentration reaches certain levels, it can keep an issue out of the public eye and, hence, off the public agenda. An important and relevant fact is the virtual blackout on stories involving media consolidation over the past two decades. Intense media concentration also allows companies to more easily work with government to pass legislation in its favor, notably overturning laws that combat media concentration, and not stepping on government toes because of possible retribution. It may already be too late. As Bagdikian notes, "Corporate news media and business-oriented governments have made common cause."

The United States is not the only victim of media monopolization: Conrad Black in the U.K. and Canada, Silvio Berlusconi in Italy, Rupert Murdoch in Australia (and, now, after renouncing his Australian citizenship in order to purchase U.S. television stations, in the United States as well), and many others around the world are huge players in national markets, and global media consolidation is proceeding in increasingly troubling ways.

In the 1990s, when use of the Internet was beginning to explode among the general population—or, more accurately, among people who were relatively well off economically, especially those who live in countries that are relatively well off economically—some of the digerati were quite eager to dismiss any protestations over media monopolization in the "smokestack" (that is, non-Internet-based) media industries. They reasoned that the inherent nature of the Internet made it more or less immune to human tinkering, in striking contrast to humankind's other inventions. Not only was the Internet inalterable, but it would soon prove the obsolescence of the old-fashioned media and, at the same time, provide diversity of viewpoints despite corporate or government efforts. The reality is that within several years of the Internet's inception, it became incredibly commercial; now, a mere handful of sites accounts for half the number of sites a user first sees on their Web browser. This is not to say that the Internet is not important. It is absolutely critical, as millions on millions of political actions initiated by civil society have demonstrated. And it is absolutely clear that citizen activism will be indispensable to prevent control from being seized gradually, or not so gradually, by corporate or government bodies. It is also clear that older forms of media should not be abandoned to corporate entities.

Media and information systems do not exist independent of the capitalist structure. Because having any semblance of control over the content of a news or entertainment company requires either owning or holding a stake in it, the rich control news and entertainment. While community-operated media exist in nearly every city, their saturation and distribution into the communities are extremely low because of financial constraints. The news and entertainment offered by these resources are vastly diverse from the corporate-owned outlets, often representing conflicting accounts and stories. Because the conflicting programming often represents the viewpoints of a different social class from that which owns the corporations, this programming rarely makes it into the mass media. The corporate owners claim they can provide an adequate diversity of community voice, when in truth the diversity they provide is severely limited by their moneyed interests.

People can get involved in the struggle in many ways. One of the most direct is to create and support independent media. This not only means developing videos, comics, zines, and blogs with alterative points of view; it means developing funding and distribution approaches and fighting for representation within the political system. For while it may be true that globalization and new communication technologies change the rules of the game, there are still likely to be rules, and for this reason civil society must be vigilant. Changes in protocols, domain name registry, domain servers, and other components of the infrastructure can have vast repercussions.

One of the most effective approaches remains the development of public interest policy that promotes media diversity. Although critics of this approach are likely to scoff at its quaint, "smokestack" modus operandi, governments in democratic societies have an obligation to support democratic systems, and the democratic experiment may be terminated earlier than anticipated by its original proponents if they fail in this duty.

The policies that governments can enact fall into two broad categories: those that limit the incursion by the big corporations into various regions or markets and those that promote media diversity by promoting alternatives to corporate monocultures such as government subsidies or tax breaks to independent media or specific set-asides for radio or television spectra. Media diversity represents a desired state for the media environment and an absence of concentrated ownership of media. For that reason, people need to fight for both media diversity and diversity of media ownership.

Solution   Democratic societies require diversity of opinions. Although government is often negligent in this area, media corporations cannot be allowed to assume too much concentration. As in other realms, power corrupts, and media corporations are not exceptions to this rule. Citizens must be vigilant to ensure that a diversity of opinions is available and that citizens have access to the media. Diversity of ownership of media is one approach that is likely to promote diversity of opinion in the media.

Linked patterns   Civic Intelligence (1), Matrifocal Orientation (9), International Networks of Alternative Media (43), Conversational Support across Boundaries (50), Indigenous Media (55), Citizen Journalism (91), Community-Building Journalism (97), Homemade Media (110), Public Domain Characters (115), Socially Responsible Computer Games (126).

Problem   Community informatics, which focuses on deploying information technology in support of community objectives, often imposes technology on communities without building the leadership and knowledge of community members to control the technology. Whether researchers or practitioners, community informaticians too often enter communities having already decided what the issues and solutions should be, reducing rather than contributing to community empowerment.

Context   Any time that a professional is working with place-based, virtual, or identity community attempting to improve its ability to gather, use, and communicate information, there is a risk that the professional's involvement can undermine rather than strengthen community empowerment.

Discussion   The developing field of community informatics occupies an intersection between information and communication technologies, community development, and community-based research. All three fields are attempting to improve community life, especially in communities excluded from normal access to power and wealth, and all can inform a code of ethics for community informatics.

In the information and communication technology field, corporate-driven design has been ethically bankrupt, but participants in the open source software movement and related organizations such as Computer Professionals for Social Responsibility and the Free Software Foundation have highly developed ethical principles. The focus of those ethics is that people have the right not to just information itself but also to the means of producing information. Thus, they have the right to use software and access the software source code to understand how the software works with information. This right carries the obligation to improve the software and to make these improvements public (Free Software Foundation 2007).

Community development focuses more on the relationship between the practitioner and the community. The Community Development Society (2006) emphasizes that the practitioner should promote participation of all community members, work to develop their understanding of the complex dynamics affecting their community and how those factors may relate to options for community development, and build their leadership capacity to take charge of their own community development process.

The field of community-based research lacks a singular code of ethics, but past problems with the practice, particularly in First Nations contexts, have led the Canadian government (2005) to develop an ethical code that can apply to all research with communities. This code emphasizes that any research should be a partnership between the community and the researcher, with a research design that fits the community culture, where control over the research is shared by the community, and benefits from the research flow to the community.

The following principles for community informaticians flow from these sources:

• Build the community's information power. This requires that the researcher-practitioner assist the community in knowing how to decide what information it needs, how to make informed choices about how to get that information, and how to access and adapt the tools needed to achieve their information objectives.
• Build the community's relational power. This requires that the researcher-practitioner assist the community in building its own democratic practices, developing leaders who can shepherd those practices, and organizing interventions in ways that build relationships among community members.
• Build the community's public power. This requires that the researcher-practitioner assist the community in knowing how to focus its information and relational power on the broader external conditions imposed by corporations and governments that oppress and exploit communities, thus democratizing the broader society.

Under these principles, traditional research that extracts information from communities, processes it elsewhere, and builds only the careers of academics or traditional practice that practices the same information extraction and then returns to sell the community on an externally designed intervention are no more acceptable than the multinational corporation that extracts raw materials and then tries to sell back finished products. Such purposeful underdevelopment is the antithesis of these ethical principles.

These principles can have uncomfortable implications, particularly for researchers. Building a community's information power and relational power means, minimally, that at the end of the project, the community knows enough so that it can do the next project on its own if it wishes. That achievement requires a researcher who can help community members develop their research and program design skills. Researchers must also give up culturally rigid standards of what constitutes good research and understand that the community may have its own research processes and its own standards of what constitutes good information, such as oral traditions and folk art, that require the same status as positivist science. Researchers or community members, then, must have special skills in community organizing in order to direct the research process (Stoecker 1999).

For practitioners, who may be used to applying a common tool kit to problems in communities flung far and wide, these principles can also require important changes. Following these ethics requires that the practitioner work with community members not just to apply a tool but to understand how it is created and can be adapted to their unique circumstances.

As an example of these ethics, consider a project to help a group of nongovernmental organizations, where one organization has incompatible databases and another wants to communicate more efficiently with its membership. The first step may be to convert the first organization's data to a common format and set up an e-mail list for the second. But because these interventions would violate the principles outlined, the correct first step is to bring all the organizations together to talk about their issues and trade ideas with each other, both to build relationships between the organizations and empower the knowledge that people already have. This can also help identify knowledge gaps that the group can collectively work to fill. Perhaps no one there really knows about databases, and so they start a process to educate themselves in their options, perhaps to the point of developing enough expertise among the organizations that they can design and manage their own databases. As the other organization talks about its need to communicate with its members, it may discover that the more efficient mechanism of e-mail will actually be less efficient because fewer members pay any attention to the mass e-mails. Telephone calls may be much more successful because more people get the information even though they take more time.

The processes illustrated require a much longer time frame to complete and require much more time of community members and organizations. Importantly, however, they produce much greater and more sustained capacity in the community.

Solution   Within the field of community informatics, achieving lasting community empowerment requires that community informaticians practice the principles of building the community's information power and their own relational power to build public power. This means making sure that community members can find, use, and control information tools and build relationships among themselves in the process. The result will be stronger, more information-self-sufficient communities that can build a stronger and better-informed democratic society.

Linked patterns   Memory and Responsibility (11), Education and Values (17), Media Literacy (35), Mobile Information and Computer Technology Learning Facilities (77), Voices of the Unheard (83), Value-Sensitive Design (87), Citizen Journalism (91), Patient Access to Medical Records (95), Citizenship Schools (96), Informal Learning Groups (98), Control of Self- Representation (109), Homemade Media (110), The Power of Story (114), Community Telecenters (117), Thinking Communities (118), Community Inquiry (122), Power Research (128), Activist Road Trip (134).

Problem   The process by which the votes of the people are gathered and counted is critical to the government's claims of legitimacy and the continued faith of people in their government. Although vote counting sounds straightforward, ensuring the accurate counting of votes in an entire country is quite difficult. Many obstacles can obstruct the democratic process, including inadequate access to the voting process, inaccurate counting, late results, and results that are not convincing to the electorate. Some of these obstacles are structural, others are due to human error, and others result from intentional manipulation and intimidation. Computers, which seem to offer the promise of increased speed and accuracy of collecting and counting votes accompanied by the possibility of decreased costs, introduce new challenges to the legitimacy of the voting process, including possible high-tech election fraud.

Context   Democratic states offer their inhabitants the important potential for self-governance. Their legitimacy and their effectiveness suffer when the actuality falls short of the ideal. The responsibility for free and fair elections falls on all citizens, although some are in better positions for promoting and maintaining authentic democracy.

Discussion   In national democracy, essentially the entire population of a nation above a certain age is entitled to vote on one or more questions put to the electorate, usually including what party or individuals will govern the nation. National democracy is the means of generating government for almost all industrialized nations. Furthermore, it is the stated objective of the world's great economic powers to eventually see national democracy in all the world's nations. For this and many other reasons, democracy is the most effective approach to producing legitimate government.

Democracies by definition face three major tasks. This pattern is concerned with the second task, determining the will of the people, while others concern themselves with informing the will of the people and implementing the will of the people. Any deviation in any phase of the process calls into question the entire process. A nomination process, for example, that unfairly denies the nomination of certain people poisons the process. How could voting be meaningful when the candidates on the ballot are the product of a corrupt system?

While the forms that democracies assume vary widely, voting is a key component of each. Thus, the process by which the votes of the people are gathered and counted is critical to the government's claims of legitimacy and the continued faith of the people in their government.

Voting is nearly always a critical milestone in the process of determining the people's will. It is the critical culmination of an ongoing deliberative process where decisions are made, for example, between candidates vying for a position or for a new proposal to support or limit something. Because voting often determines significant issues, it is subject to immense attention and pressure. While some of this pressure is normal politicking (which varies from place to place), other is unethical, illegal, and unfair. The voting process presents an irresistible opportunity for people who want things to go their way regardless of issues of fairness or legality. At the same time, the voting process seems to offer innumerable opportunities for unfair interventions at nearly every stage.

Elections vary from place to place, in jurisdiction, in primary or final (general) elections, in selecting officials from candidates or approving or disapproving legislative changes, and most kinds of elections have a whole range of complex activities associated with them. The best recommendation depends on the goals. Beyond that, one can talk about things to avoid. So an antipattern is easier than a pattern if a pattern is a type of recommendation. In every case the goal is still fair elections, however.

The expression "free and fair elections" originated in the first postapartheid elections in South Africa in 1994. The idea is that the outcome should be generated by a process that gives people free access to their franchise and then fairly calculates the result.

How can fair elections be guaranteed? What technology and administration are required to support national democracy? How can elections be trusted? What danger signs of unfair elections can be detected? What recommendations can be made? While vote counting sounds straightforward, ensuring the accurate counting of votes in an entire country is quite difficult. The requirements and constraints associated with fair elections introduce numerous challenges. Voters must have adequate access to the voting process, and this access must not be politically biased. The vote counting must be accurate and the results produced promptly.

Elections present a special problem in that it must be ensured that every voter voted at most once and each voter's vote was accurately counted. However, the vote of any particular voter must remain forever secret. This combination of accuracy and secrecy is unusual outside voting.

Elections produce results that are just vote totals (plus undervotes if they are permitted and overvotes if they are possible). Results imply outcomes: who (or what) won. Results have two metrics of quality: (1) accuracy (which obviously cannot be measured directly) measures how closely reported results match true results, and (2) confidence (which is closely related to transparency) measures the feeling in the electorate that the reported results are correct.

Total accuracy and no confidence is about as good (or as bad) as the reverse, but they lead to very different kinds of adverse outcomes. The goal of an elections process is to produce, for an affordable cost, outcomes that are very rarely wrong, even though everybody recognizes that results are seldom perfectly correct. Also, the results must be worthy of confidence. It is useless to produce a perfectly accurate result if people are not persuaded that it is accurate. So there must be good reason to believe the election results. The election process must be conducted in public view, and each step of the process, as well as the process as a whole, must be comprehensible to most ordinary voters. Nonpartisan officials should monitor the entire process, and voting equipment should be based on open specifications and untarnished by partisan and commercial interests. The chain of custody must be carefully maintained and documented for a wide variety of materials, including ballots, unvoted ballot stock, and the poll book. Furthermore, this must be accomplished on a limited budget. Elections administration is never a particularly high spending priority.

Solution In democratic societies, everybody has the responsibility to help ensure free and fair elections. Voters in democratic societies deserve a process that is easy, safe, and private. Voting—and running for office—in democratic societies should be universal and encouraged. All aspects, in other words, should be free and fair.

Linked patterns Global Citizenship (6), World Citizen Parliament (40), Strengthening International Law (42), Transparency (64), Civic Capabilities (85), Follow the Money (135).

Problem The fundamental principle of full and equal access to the justice system, particularly for those who suffer disparate barriers or are otherwise vulnerable, faces new opportunities and challenges from the advances in information and communication technologies, which can provide increased pathways for access but can also perpetuate or exacerbate existing barriers or even create new ones.

Context This pattern is based on a trailblazing effort by the Washington State Access to Justice Board, an agency of the state supreme court, to define principles and develop implementation strategies, means, and methods for ensuring that technological capabilities and advances are effectively incorporated throughout the state justice system in ways consistent with the fundamental principle that all persons should have equal access to justice. A recent legal needs survey had revealed that 87 percent of all low-income people in the state who had civil legal problems were unable to secure legal help and that residents of rural counties had substantially less access to technology-based resources than their urban counterparts (Task Force on Civil Legal Justice Funding, 2003). Therefore the overriding intent of the effort was to develop, implement, and institutionalize principles within all justice system agencies to increase access to justice system information, resources, and services for all, and especially those who most need it.

Discussion Technology is creating opportunities for people to find out about, initiate, or respond to court- or other law-related needs, obligations, or requirements from their home or a nearby library branch or community center. They can also communicate and exchange documents with their legal service provider or others in or associated with the legal system less expensively, using less time and effort, without having to travel to a central city, and with less time away from work or other necessary resources. This can be especially important for the elderly, persons with disabilities, persons with limited financial means, and those who cannot afford to miss time from work for reasons of financial need or jeopardizing their employment. Similarly, a person with limited mobility or hearing may be able to get information electronically about his or her rights as a tenant; a victim of domestic violence can learn on the Internet what she can do and in fact be able to start the legal process of protecting herself. The courts and other parts of the justice system can operate more productively and less expensively, making court and legal records and information more readily available, and receive all filings, fees, documents, and information electronically.

However, the means of using these very possibilities also create the risk of worsening old barriers or erecting new barriers to access, causing greater disparities. While the opportunities described seem positive, these innovations assume that users have access to a computer, reasonable proficiency at using it and the necessary software programs, reading capability, fluency in English, and sufficient phone or cable and electricity availability and capacity at affordable cost to support sufficient connections and streams of information and interactivity. Without all of that, those who have the tools and means, the proficiency, and the necessary infrastructure get further ahead, and those without fall further behind in having the justice system work for them. The lack of equality between the haves and the have-nots expands rather than shrinks.

On December 4, 2004, the Washington State Supreme Court became the first court in the United States, perhaps the world, to formally adopt by court order a set of authoritative principles to guide the use of technology in its justice system (Access to Justice Technology Principles Implementation Strategy Group 2006). The stated purpose was to ensure that the planning, design, development, implementation, and use of new technologies and the management of existing technologies by the justice system and associated organizations protect and advance the fundamental right of equal access to justice. Over a three-and-a-half year period, the Washington State Access to Justice Board drew on the input and involvement of a diverse group of approximately 200 people and organizations from a variety of disciplines and backgrounds to develop formal access to justice technology principles to serve as the practical operating norm for justice system organizations and entities throughout the state.

The access-to-justice technology principles broadly define access to justice as the meaningful opportunity to (1) assert a claim or defense and to create, enforce, modify, or discharge a legal obligation in any forum; (2) acquire the procedural or other information necessary to improve the likelihood of a just result; (3) participate in the conduct of proceedings as a witness or juror; and (4) acquire information about the activities of courts or other dispute resolution bodies. Access to justice, moreover, must include timeliness, affordability, and transparency.

Briefly paraphrased, the six access-to-justice technology principles are:

1. Requirement of access to justice. Introduction of technology or changes in the use of technology must not reduce access or participation and, whenever possible, shall advance such access and participation.

2. Technology and just results. The justice system shall use and advance technology to achieve the objective of a just process by impartial and well-informed decision makers and reject, minimize, or modify any use that reduces the likelihood of achieving that objective.

3. Openness and privacy. Technology should be designed to meet the dual responsibilities of the justice system of being open to the public and protecting personal privacy.

4. Assuring a neutral forum. All appropriate means shall be used to ensure the existence of neutral, accessible, and transparent forums compatible with new technologies.

5. Maximizing public awareness and use. The justice system should promote ongoing public knowledge and understanding of the tools afforded by technology to access justice.

6. Best practices. Those governed by these principles shall use best practices procedures or standards to guide the use of technology so as to protect and enhance access to justice and promote equality of access and fairness.

A broad-based interdisciplinary implementation strategy group then developed a set of practical strategies and initiatives to transform the principles from the words of a court-ordered statement of vision into a pervasive operational reality through the state justice system. Once the principles are truly institutionalized in justice organizations, the design for every new technology project will incorporate accessibility and usability and increase transparency of and information about the justice system for all users, especially those who are or may be excluded or underserved, as well as those experiencing any barrier to accessing justice system services. Essential actions include (1) development and maintenance of a Web-based resource bank, (2) initial and ongoing communication to and training for justice system and associated agencies about the ATJ Technology Principles and available resources for implementation, (3) demonstration projects, and (4) public awareness and usable information. Additional requirements address policy-level governance and guidance as well as ensuring the continuing relevance, effectiveness, and use of the principles over time.

Solution   A great deal has been said and written about what has come to be called the digital divide. Respect for and use of the rule of law is an essential way to move to a less divided, more equitable society and world. Accessible quality justice for all individuals and groups is a recognized worldwide value that crosses cultural as well as geographic lines. Meaningful access to justice can and does empower people to be part of creating their own just societies. This effort is the first such undertaking and can provide a useful example that can be adapted and used not only in other places but in other sectors of basic public need, such as access to health care, access to food, access to safety, and other essentials.

Linked patterns   Accessibility of Online Information (75), Grassroots Public Policy Development (78), Civic Capabilities (85), Value-Sensitive Design (87), Citizenship Schools (96).

Problem   Current public consultation is deficient in a number of ways. Few people have the time or language skills to respond in writing to 20-page consultation documents. It is mainly professionals with a financial interest who do so. Rarely are public meetings attended by more than a few local retired people. The language of the documents is often obscure and couched in public sector jargon. The questions asked are the ones the officials feel safe asking, not the ones local communities would ask. The style is not one that engages the interest of anyone who is not a committed activist, let alone young people. Current consultation techniques do not reach all groups in society and do not always produce fair democratic dialogue. Current techniques rarely help find consensus between different interests. It is easy to find out what people are campaigning for, but not what they will settle for if they have to compromise. In short, the problem is: *how can we facilitate the participation of groups who currently don't take part, and use their input to find policy consensus?*

Context   This pattern applies to any e-participation process that might fall under a wide definition of public consultation. This may be a formal public consultation initiated by government agencies, councils, or parliaments on a new policy. It could also be a regular rule review or regulatory impact assessment required by legislation. But it is not limited to the formal processes required by legislation in many countries. It also covers any process in which an organization seeks to solicit the views of people affected by its decisions and actions (the stakeholders) and engage them in helping improve the organization's policies, decisions, and work. Some of these processes include: informal communications between representatives (members of parliament, councilors, senators) and their constituents; community and voluntary organizations attempting to consult their members and clients to determine their response to a policy initiative or government consultation; media or community-sponsored discussions on a local issue; mediation between antagonistic communities who have conflicting interests (e.g., unionists and republicans in Northern Ireland; loggers and environmentalists in British Columbia, Canada; drivers and local residents along the route of a new road; employers and workers in Irish social partnership negotiations).

Note that this pattern is most relevant in situations where a government body is mediating between competing interests (e.g., in a planning inquiry). It is one of a number of patterns that can be followed in the other situations mentioned.

Discussion   How can we improve public consultation between citizens and their public servants? Here public consultation means any of the ways a policy maker engages the public in the decision-making process. This extends from simple surveys of citizen satisfaction with public services to full citizen participation in decision making, such as town budget setting or New England town meetings. But the most common situation is when an official or politician wants to find out citizens' views on a proposed new development or policy change, such as producing consensus plans for town and regional developing in Germany or the Netherlands, reorganizing the school system in Northern Ireland, or running an inquiry into citizens' views on active citizenship or what should be in broadcasting legislation in Ireland. This is not always called public consultation, but processes of engaging stakeholders in shaping the decisions that will affect them exist in every democratic country.

These problems are becoming very clear in places, such as devolved regions of the UK, where public consultation has suddenly grown very fast. In Northern Ireland, equality legislation forced 120 public authorities to consult on how they were planning to measure the equality impact (gender, race, religion, age, class) of each of their policies over the next five years. This led to 120 long documents being sent to the same 80–120 voluntary organizations, each given eight weeks to reply. Their choices include ignoring the documents (whereupon the officials could continue to do what they had done before) or spending every day drafting replies, with very little time to talk to the people who would be directly affected.

Contrast this with experimental use of ICTs in public consultations in the Netherlands, the use of Internet chat to hold discussions between young people in East Belfast (the only neutral venue at the time) on human rights, research into on-line mediation support systems in Germany (for planning disputes), and electronic public meetings that bring together 6,000 New Yorkers to discuss the future of the twin towers site.

Can we design software that supports electronic public consultation, that improves both its effectiveness in reaching different people and its efficiency in controlling information overload and consultation fatigue? Ideally this software would help guide people through a natural process that resulted in decisions that were acceptable (though not necessarily ideal) to all.

When mediators get opponents to meet and discuss issues, they take the group(s) through a number of stages. Here are some of the things that happen at each stage.

1. Open discussion
• People meet and become familiar with other participants
• They discuss the issue(s) of concern
• They explain their own needs and listen to other's needs
• They do *not* set out positions and solutions at this stage
• They agree on the key issues to be discussed further
2. Structured problem solving
• Participants start to explore the issues
• They identify many possible solutions
• They work out how well these alternatives help or hinder them in meeting their needs
• They try to modify and synthesize the options into ones that meet the important needs of each group
3. Evaluation and choice
• Independent mediators combine similar options to come up with a short list to choose from

• The participants evaluate the choices through a consensus voting system
• The mediators report on the results of the vote, picking out the options with the most consensus support
4. Implementation
• Develop the top choices into a workable plan
• Complete the work—done by one or more of: the participants themselves; independent mediators or planners; civil servants and legislators; decision makers who have accepted the report on 1-3

This process is designed to encourage the development of practical plans through orderly and uncoerced engagement, a process arguably at the heart of democracy. The stages of this process are shown in the table along with the type of activity that is necessary along the way. This depiction helps suggest ways in which groupware could be employed to help the process.

Level of group-ware needed to support stage	Stage of consultation process			
	1. Open discussion	2. Structured problem solving	3. Evaluation / choice	4. Implement
1. Communicate (exchange messages)	What are the issues and needs?	Explore problem; creatively generate potential solutions; create multiple maps of alternative options		
2. Understand others			Evaluate options and synthesize solutions	
3. Develop shared models				Develop into practical plans

The types of communication and depth of understanding required to make the stages work are listed along the left of the table, and the different stages in the process are listed across the top. We need to use different levels of groupware to support each stage of the consultation process. The levels of groupware (and characteristics of the level) are:

1. Communication
• Can send and receive messages, overcoming distance or time problems
• Recipient may not read, listen, or understand
2. Mutual understanding
• Understand others' ideas and positions
• Need not agree with them
3. Shared mental models
• Shared maps of ideas, beliefs, or possible solutions

• In functioning team, all share the same model(s)
• In conflicting group(s), there may be alternative models

When looking for techniques or technologies to improve consultation, we should start with simple tools that make it easy for participants to communicate their needs and the issues they are concerned about. They may want, for example, to be able to upload video clips of poor services, or participate in Issues Forums.

If the consultation intends to bring in stakeholders to explore the problem and suggest solutions, we need techniques and tools to help them build "maps" of what they come up with, which could be physical or abstract maps of the issues, positions and arguments for and against the positions.

Once options have been identified, consulters want to find out which options people prefer. There are now, thanks to the use of computers, more subtle ways of exploring their preferences than a majority vote, such as the de Borda preferendum (de Borda Institute 2006), which can find what they will settle for if they do not get their first choice.

When there are strong disagreements between different groups, a mediation or negotiation model is appropriate, based on what we understand about dispute resolution in communities that have been affected by conflict. This can be used to build a pattern of the process and identify technologies to support different stages in that process.

Solution   Consider consultation as an interorganizational learning process that is characterized as a series of mediation and negotiation processes. Knowledge is transferred between citizens and government as they learn from each other. In particular, the policymakers need to better understand the needs, life experiences, and preferences of different actors in civil society (sometimes called stakeholders). In doing that, they act as both apprentices, learning from citizens, and mediators, managing disputes between different groups of citizens. When these basic dynamics are understood, it should be possible to participatively design software that supports these human processes, in the stages identified in the preceding table.

Linked patterns   Citizen Access to Simulations (48), Conversational Support across Boundaries (50), Online Deliberation (52), Online Community Service Engine (62), Grassroots Public Policy Development (78), Multiparty Negotiation for Conflict Resolution (79), Wholesome Design for Wicked Problems (82), Voices of the Unheard (83), Document-Centered Discussion (92), Informal Learning Groups (98), The Power of Story (114), Thinking Communities (118).

71 Participatory Budgeting

Problem   Developing a budget is a task often left to financial experts even though the decisions that result from the budget-making process affect everyone, and the ideas that inform budget decisions often are improved by the experience and insights of a wide range of individuals. Budget development is in fact a political act, with winners and losers, most of whom never participate in the process.

Context   Budgets and the budget development process are tools through which social values are expressed and manifested in useful public activity. This pattern explains the importance of budgeting and encourages participation in all stages of budget development. Public budgeting connects to several other patterns. For example, participating in the creation of budgets is an ideal way to foster Civic Intelligence (pattern 1); joint budget development helps create Shared Vision (pattern 101); public budgeting using online tools is an example of Online Deliberation (pattern 52); and understanding budgets is one aspect of Power Research (pattern 128).

Discussion   A fundamental step in the life of any organization is the design of a budget. The decisions made early in the process (for example, What is to be budgeted for? What are the sources of income? Who is to be paid? What are the categories of effort that are highly compensated, and what effort is to be considered voluntary?) often set core parameters for the future and help determine not only the ways in which time and money are spent, but also the values and reputation of the organization, and even its soul.

But budgeting is often treated as a technical process that should be handled by experts rather than as a political activity in which many people should be invited and encouraged to participate. One way in which budgets can be more easily discussed publicly is to use online tools to disseminate budget information, host public discussions, and create sample budget variations; this should be coupled with face-to-face discussions whenever possible.

The best-known example of participatory budgeting is found in Porto Alegre, Brazil, where community residents (now numbering in the thousands) have cooperated since 1989 in annual deliberations about the allocation of a portion of the municipal budget. Poor citizens are vastly more engaged in this process than is typical in budgeting processes, and increasing proportions of the city's revenue have been directed toward improving the most impoverished parts of Porto Alegre. Although there is some disagreement over how much of this outcome to attribute to the participatory budgeting process, there is no doubt about the increased sensitivity of all citizens to the importance of budgeting decisions. In June 1996, the United Nations declared the "popular administration" of Porto Alegre as one of forty urban innovations at the Second Conference on Human Settlements.

Various related experiments in participatory budgeting have taken place on several continents since Porto Alegre, typically fine-tuned to local circumstances, with an evolving set of principles promoting conditions that enhance the effectiveness of the process.

Several important attempts at involving typically excluded citizens in the budget allocation process have occurred in the United States, often during progressive periods. Two of
the most significant were the Affirmative Neighborhood Information Program during Mayor
Harold Washington's tenure in Chicago (Kretzmann 1992), which failed to survive succes-
sor administrations, and the Seattle Public Schools multiyear experiment in decentralized
school-based budgeting, supported by an online budgeting tool (Halaska 2000).

In the Seattle experiment, a vastly increased proportion of district resources was redistrib-
uted from the central administrative offices to individual schools. School principals were
encouraged to engage in a public budgeting process where trade-offs (for example, reduced
class size versus after-school music programs) were actively debated in public meetings and
online. The process was messy because "democracy is messy" and was controversial at every
stage, in part because it surfaced hidden assumptions about core values in public education.
Some participants believed that this process had the potential to provoke a fundamental
rethinking of the purposes of the education process itself.

Key findings from the Chicago and Seattle experiments align with the principles of Porto
Alegre and elsewhere. For example, it is important that significantly different approaches to
budgeting such as these become so embedded that they cannot readily be set aside by later
regimes. Equally critical is that traditional budget staff be convinced about the importance of
participatory budgeting. While philosophical and political discussions about larger-scale
budget issues can be done without technical assistance, detailed information about current
costs and funding formulas typically reside with budget staff. Without their support, key
budget information can be difficult to obtain. Moreover, while the ideology of participatory
budgeting has wide appeal, critical studies should be undertaken to determine under what
circumstances participatory strategies have lasting effects and whether, in the case of participatory budgeting, for example, systemic changes such as in the labor market must occur for
poorer citizens to benefit from these new strategies in the long run.

Solution   Budgets for organizations in the public sphere should be developed openly and
inclusively, in public meetings and using publicly accessible online tools. Budget assumptions should be discussed, and rethinking of assumptions, priorities, and allocations should
be encouraged, no matter how far they depart from current practice. At every stage, the
results of the process should be made public for feedback and refinement. Attention should
be paid to what has been learned from experience (for example, about the wisdom of convincing traditional budget staff of the utility of public budgeting), and studies of the long-
range impact of participatory budgeting are essential.

Linked patterns   Civic Intelligence (1), Social Responsibility (8), Shared Vision (9), Democratic Political Settings (31), Participatory Design (36), Online Deliberation (52), Transparency (64), Transaction Tax (72), Academic Technology Investments (81), Shared Vision
(101), Power Research (128).

Problem   Transaction taxes have been proposed on both international and national levels as a development tool to help groups of people with low financial strength. An international cash transaction tax could help the global good by raising substantial funds to support the Millennium Development Goals set by the United Nations. This tax also has the potential of stemming damaging speculative attacks on the currencies of middle-income developing countries, aiding in their financial stability. National transaction taxes have also been suggested to create even-handedness and fairness by allowing the wealthy to carry the larger share of the tax burden.

Context   The implementation of transaction taxes is seen as a way to broaden the tax base by the collection of tax on the voluntary exchange of money that is not currently taxed. Primary examples are the purchase and sale of stocks, bonds, and foreign exchange transactions. Transaction taxes have been proposed on national and international levels for various reasons.

Discussion   Many support the idea of an international currency transaction tax (ICTT) on voluntary currency transactions as an innovative financing tool to raise money for international development. One of the most urgent local problems that needs to be addressed is starvation in the sub-Sahara region of Africa, though the United Nations has defined several other areas of need around the world with the Millennium Development Goals (MDGs): "The MDG's are as follows: Eradicate extreme poverty and hunger, achieve universal primary education; promote gender equality and empower women; reduce child mortality; improve maternal health; combat HIV/AIDS, malaria and other diseases; ensure environmental sustainability; and, develop a global partnership for development" (Spratt 2005). The Group of 8 has also pledged money for the achievement of the MDGs by the year 2015. Whether that money becomes a reality or not, there is still a huge need for funding to help implement these important goals.

The idea of a transaction tax was presented in London in 1936 by John Maynard Keynes. However, a transaction tax is commonly known as a Tobin tax, named after Nobel laureate James Tobin. In 1970 Tobin recommended the use of a transaction tax to discourage speculation in the foreign exchange market. Reducing speculation has the expected result of lowering market volatility, which can be damaging to developing countries when their currencies are unstable. In this way, the transaction tax has a second development function in bringing middle-income countries in line with underlying fundamentals that promote long-term investment in their country. India has already implemented its own national transaction tax on securities trades as a means to simplify the tax regime and reduce speculation in Indian financial markets.

Even in wealthier nations like the United States, the idea of instituting a transaction tax is floated as a means to broaden the tax base, eliminate the marginal tax, and overhaul a complex tax system. This type of national transaction tax allows the wealthy to carry a larger share of the tax burden based on their easy access to financial markets and the less fortunate to carry a smaller burden in relation to their lower income and assets.

There are many critics of the Tobin tax. Some economists say the reduction of speculation also means the reduction of liquidity, which can have its own damaging effects. Other economists have produced studies to show that curbing speculation does not reduce currency volatility. Often critics are those who would be most affected by paying the new tax, and their criticisms tend to echo their desire for maximum self-enrichment. However, there are many around the world, including wealthy people who would be affected by the tax, who like the charitable development that could be funded by this type of financing.

New technology and communications systems along with the Internet make it possible to collect a transaction tax with efficiency and make avoidance extremely difficult. Electronic technology of the bank clearing system already in place could be digitally fitted with a financial equivalent of the pass that is now used to speed traffic through toll booths on highways. International payment and collection systems like the CLS (continuously linked settlement) bank already link automated domestic large-value payment systems, making the collection of a transaction tax a realistic idea.

Solution   By allowing a transaction tax at a national or international level, disparities between the rich and poor can be mitigated to some degree. The poor will not bear an overproportionate amount of tax in relation to their incomes. Needs of people in developing countries can be served by taxes reaped from the wealthiest, who perform large national or international transactions. Financial markets can also be strengthened in developing countries, creating a win-win situation.

Linked patterns   Global Citizenship (6), Social Responsibility (8), Matrifocal Orientation (9), Big Tent for Social Change (32), Participatory Budgeting (71), Powerful Remittances (73).

Problem   The amount of remittances that people working in the developed world send home to their families is huge, estimated to approach $232 billion in 2006. This figure surpasses by far the total of direct foreign investment and overseas development aid. In fact, many countries around the world rely on remittances as a major source of foreign exchange. World Bank technical reports fret about how best to leverage remittance income. While remittance transfers has become a growth industry (e.g., "banking the unbanked"), public policy to date has been reluctant to regulate this phenomenal resource flow apart from the usual concerns about money laundering. Remittance transfers grow annually, but this growth curve is not indefinite. Low-paid guest workers (many working without documents) in richer countries send a portion of their paychecks to their families back home. Their cheap labor allows many industries to remain competitive. In the recipient countries, this foreign exchange often represents a large percentage of gross domestic product. Although the amount of money is large, the percentage of funds siphoned off as commissions at various points during the transfer process is also significant, although it is steadily dropping. In 2000 the average transfer cost was often close to 15 percent, whereas in 2008 it is around 5.5 percent. Nevertheless, there is considerable room for further transfer cost reductions through innovative information technologies and regulatory reform. Remittance transfers from the migrant refugees from recent structural adjustment policies and "market failures" represent the flip side of global capital flows.

Context   Poor countries generally have few job opportunities, and their best and brightest leave the country in what amounts to a new form of resource extraction (if not a new form of inverse colonialism). This process seems to be self-perpetuating, as the respective national diaspora circuits become consolidated and young men, and increasingly women as well, migrate northbound, to the United States or Europe, or westbound to the Gulf States, on reaching adulthood. Migration patterns may vary significantly within countries. Village cultures and family and ritual life have adapted to these new circumstances, often less than a generation old. Transnational communities are now the norm in many regions of Mesoamerica, Mexico to Nicaragua, the Caribbean microstates, regional pockets in northern South America and sub-Saharan Africa, among South Africa's neighbors, India and Pakistan, the Philippines, and Micronesian states dependent on Australian dollars.

Discussion   National elites quietly applaud these incoming resources; unfortunately, some would like to tax them as income as some U.S. state legislatures also propose. This money is an aggregate of private family funds that paradoxically provoke a positive multiplier effect for local merchants and economies, while somewhat reducing demands for social services from public funds and improving the balance of payments in national accounts. Remittance flows in hard currency reinforce central banks' stock of foreign exchange, in effect reducing interest rates for the minority with access to credit. Banks and money transfer operators (MTOs) now accept foreign government identification cards (e.g., Mexico's Matrícula Consular), thereby bypassing strict migration controls in some countries. Global remittance flows may be a contemporary form of social Darwinism, whereby "remittances seem to be taking care of local needs." In the job- and remittance-generating host countries, workers from poor countries are often exploited, denied basic rights and services while paying local taxes, and increasingly, demonized by racist "seal the borders" ultranationalists.

Mexico has taken the lead in leveraging migrants' remittances using a three-for-one program now operating in sixteen states of its federal system. Begun in Zacatecas in 1992, for each dollar a migrant organization earmarks for investment in public improvements in specific locations back home, the municipal, state, and federal governments contribute another dollar. Gradually many *municipios* are paving their plazas, building sidewalks, refurbishing the churches, adding bathrooms to primary schools, and installing other amenities. This program can be exported, and other countries are discussing its implementation.

The emergence of these remittance economies is a function of emigration patterns that attest to the failures and limitations of the capitalist development model. Near-monopoly MTOs (e.g., Western Union and Money Gram) dominated the early phase, but the profits to be made have attracted many new players, including regional companies and, most recently, commercial banks and credit unions. Workers deliver cash to an MTO receiving window, often in franchises located in small businesses and storefronts in migrant urban neighborhoods or small towns next to labor-intensive industries (furniture, poultry and meat packing, fruit and vegetable farms). The licensed MTO moves the funds using its electronic network, situating the remittance at the assigned location on the receiving end in the migrant's home country. Often the remitter is unaware of the foreign exchange rate used (U.S. dollars or euros to his or her local currency), and MTOs have been sued for offering exchange rates well below the market value on the day of the transaction. In addition to service commissions, exchange rate spreads are a major component of MTOs' bottom line.

In the United States, undocumented workers often use a fake social security identification card and number. Employers accept them at face value and send obligatory salary deductions to the Social Security Administration, which deposits these funds in a special earnings suspense fund (ESF). This account now receives over $7 billion a year, a significant sum that will never be reclaimed by workers in the future. The ESF is a de facto migrant subsidy to the U.S. social security capital budget. It remains an open question if this amount equals or is less than the value of the social services that nontax-paying migrants receive at the state and local levels.

This pattern of massive remittance transfers can be more transparent and cost efficient while leveraging resources for migrant families and organizations committed to growth back home. Information technology can substantially reduce remittance transfer costs and improve transparency if both financial and telecommunications regulatory reforms were in place. Experts in the field admit that commissions and exchange rate spreads totaling 2.5

percent of the amount sent home allow a healthy profit for MTOs. Commercial and financial elites, in both the North and the South, at present profiting from the poor, are probably not going to innovate in this fashion. Accelerating the citizenship process and then mobilizing former migrant voter turnout may lead to immigration policy reforms in the North. Simultaneously, migrant organizations need to continue to fight for their rights, services' access, job safety, and civic respect in the framework of each respective national guest worker policy. Also, there is immense potential in using the power that can be derived from the aggregated sums of small proportions of remittances to bring pressure to bear on political elites in the home countries. This is beginning to happen in Mesoamerica, where returning migrants manage collective remittances, run for public office, win, often reconfigure local priorities, and lobby for reforms at other levels. The power of leveraging this amount of money through political lobbying and policy reform will have impacts in both the North and South.

Solution   Nonprofit foundations working with migrant organizations could set up alternative networks of cost plus transfer mechanisms and otherwise protect remittance transactions while lowering costs still more. Stored value cards will play a strategic role in this process. Voice over Internet protocol free or low-cost phone calls will contribute to lower communications costs, a significant aspect of each migration circuit. International financial institutions could offer matching funds for specific investments back home. There is room for innovation and experimentation for migrant organizations and their supporting transnational communities. Emerging remittance economies may reconfigure local politics over time.

Linked patterns   Fair Trade (21), Big-Picture Health Information (27), Public Agenda (30), Strategic Capacity (34), Intermediate Technologies (57), Durable Assets (58), Community Networks (61), Transparency (64), Transaction Tax (72), Grassroots Public Policy Development (78), Voices of the Unheard (83), Sense of Struggle (104), Community Telecenters (117), Power Research (128), Follow the Money (135).

Problem   Health information in the developed world exists in vast quantities, not only for the general public but also for health professionals. Much of this information depicts good health in terms of vigilance against the failings of our own bodies. This serves to create dependency on a high-tech, commodity health system.

Context   The style of language and the content of information are very important in how information makes people perceive the world. Authors in many fields have noted patterns of communication that create distrust and enforce dependency by emphasizing danger from external, uncontrollable forces. If people have a sense of helplessness in the face of this threat, they do not act on their own feelings and perceptions.

Discussion   Negative language has the effect of emphasizing threats, magnifying fears, and creating dependency. Reminding people of their mortality tends to make them hold more closely to traditional culture (Pyszczynski, Solomon, and Greenberg 2003); this has implications for mental health and can also be used to influence mass opinion and behavior. A recent example is the Bush administration's use of language to create fear and mistrust among the public by creating the specter of a constant external threat (Brooks 2003).

Much health information, especially advertising from hospital corporations and pharmaceutical companies, uses this technique. A paternalistic and commodity-driven medical system produces an endless stream of information that encourages the perception that natural processes, such as growing older or pregnancy, are fraught with danger. This inhibits the spread of health information that is not based on the treatments that this system has to offer.

Language may not only be negative; it can also be empty (Brooks 2003). Complex issues are broken down into broad statements with little meaning. In health care information, this pattern of communication places the cause of ill health on the individual. The complexity of individuals' relationships to the world they live in and the effects on individual health of pollution, poverty, and unhealthy social norms and values are ignored. People come to construe healthy behavior in terms of dependency on a medical industry that constantly invents not only new cures but new diseases for the cures it already possesses (Blech 2006).

Empty language is like empty calories: it tastes good and you can eat a lot of it, but you do not obtain much benefit. A great deal of health information tempts us to feel that we are well informed. We are bombarded by advertising and public health campaigns that do little more than create mistrust of the inherent healthy processes we possess. To reduce complex health issues to taking a pill ignores people's emotional needs and the complex connection between body and mind; instead it emphasizes the negative aspects of their health.

The use of estrogen replacement in postmenopausal women illustrates this. Estrogen replacement was pushed on women as a way if combating the "problems" of growing old, such as osteoporosis, heart disease, memory loss, and drying skin. The unspoken message was that there was something wrong with growing old that taking medication could correct. Preventative approaches that emphasized a lifetime of healthy behaviors and the inherent correctness of aging were ignored.

In their Health Center pattern, in *A Pattern Language* (1977), the first major pattern language effort, Alexander et al. describe a medical system that emphasizes sickness over health. By contrast, they show the Pioneer Health Center in Peckham, England, an experiment from the 1930s, as an example of medical care that focuses on health instead of sickness. In the same manner, health information must distinguish between healing and medicine. We need to hear messages of what is right with us and what needs to be done to stay in touch with the inherent health of our bodies.

Many alternative health practices, such as yoga, polarity treatment, and acupuncture, focus on the inherent healthiness of the body. In these practices, the underlying concept is healing, the natural process by which the body repairs itself. The rise of alternatives to conventional medicine reflects in part the lack of substance people feel from the information they receive during a visit to a doctor. Health-related discussion forums that include both lay and professional perspectives offer a way to make sense of information from various health-related sources without falling victim to negative language and information; people put information into the context of everyday life and validate positive perceptions of themselves. This type of information has substance to it not only because it is active rather than passive; it has the positive effect of engaging people in independent, creative thinking.

Solution   Health information should emphasize the idea that people are inherently healthy. It must inspire trust in the body's ability to heal itself once the person has taken a healthy path. Where information of this kind is insufficient, either create it or supplant it with participant-controlled interactive forums.

Linked patterns   Health as a Universal Right (5), Education and Values (17), Big-Picture Health Information (27), Opportunity Spaces (33), Citizen Science (37), Alternative Progress Indexes (46), Grassroots Public Policy Development (78), Value-Sensitive Design (87), Future Design (88), Patient Access to Medical Records (95), Shared Vision (101), Control of Self-Representation (109), Soap Operas with Civic Messages (120).

75   Accessibility of Online Information

Problem   There are many digital divides—those based on economics, gender, race, class, and ability. We can understand these divides by dividing them into two main categories: accessibility to and accessibility of information and communication technologies (ICTs). Accessibility to ICTs means having access to the technologies that connect one to the network society. Accessibility of ICTs means that these technologies of access are accessible to those with disabilities.

Context   "For people without disabilities, technology makes things convenient, whereas for people with disabilities, it makes things possible.... [This] fact brings with it an enormous responsibility because the reverse is also true. Inaccessible technology can make things absolutely impossible for disabled people, a prospect we must avoid" (Heumann 1998).

Discussion   Just as buildings are built with accessibility factored into their architecture from the ground up, so too must the Web and Internet architecture factor in accessibility initiatives from the outset to ensure equitable access to online resources. Accessibility standards such as the World Wide Web Consortium's Web Accessibility Initiative (W3C WAI) offer developers guidelines for designing inclusive information infrastructures.

The WAI guidelines provide a blueprint for ensuring that information and computer technology (ICT) used to access them are accessible to all. They are meant to prevent digital divides from growing disproportionately to the continued use of new technologies. By taking into account accessibility considerations, people with physical or learning disabilities are encouraged to become producers of information, not just passive consumers. This is an important point and a distinction worth making. It is one thing to ensure that ICT and online media are rendered accessible for those using assistive devices (screen readers, special keyboards, mouse devices). It is another thing entirely to ensure that people with disabilities can actively participate in creating content for the online world. A key factor of accessibility is ensuring that those with disabilities can access both the information produced for and in the electronic world and, equally as important, can access and use the tools needed to produce this content.

Here we can return to our accessibility *to* and *of* distinction. Accessibility *of* means making electronic information accessible according to the W3C's WAI guidelines. Accessibility *to* ICT means making the tools required to produce electronic content accessible also. These two taken together mean ensuring that all people, regardless of ability, can participate equally in the production of the network society, that is, the information produced and broadcast through communication technologies. Creating knowledge from this information defines the network society. To our accessibility bifurcation we must add the ability to assess, decode, and use information, central components of digital literacy. Ensuring that this knowledge benefits from all voices ensures that this network society is inclusive, representational, and reflective of the society at large.

A review of accessibility issues by various disability groups highlights the barriers faced by a significant proportion of the population. It is useful to remember that the percentage of people with either a physical or learning disability that may impair access is around 20 percent (54 million people in the United States alone) (Waddell 1999) and grows significantly according to age group:

Age Group	Proportion of People with Disabilities
0–21	10 percent
22–44	14.9 percent
45–54	24.5 percent
55–64	36.3 percent
65–79	47.3 percent
80 and over	71.5 percent

Visual and hearing impairments are among the disabilities associated with ageing. U.S. Census Bureau (Quoted in "Accessibility in Web Design" 001).

Disabilities that may impair access include visual, hearing, mobility, and cognitive impairments:

• Vision disabilities include blind and low-vision people who use screen readers to access electronic information. A number of items may be inaccessible to or cause difficulty for vision-impaired people—for example, some Java elements, browse buttons, poorly labeled form elements, inconsistencies in layout, inconsistencies in language, surprise pop-up windows, and multiple frames and nested tables. Other problems are the illogical display of steps required for task completion and confusing and ambiguous use of terminology.
• Hearing-impaired people need closed captioning for audio so this information will not be lost to them.
• People with mobility impairments may use screen readers, laser and infrared head mouse devices, special keyboards, and other products to access online and electronic information. They face problems similar to those that the visually impaired encounter.
• People with cognitive and language and learning disabilities use a variety of access devices to help improve access and cognition. Difficulty with language use, the manner in which text and links are encoded, and the use of colors, fonts, sounds, and graphics may have an adverse impact on these users. Other issues include inconsistencies in layout and language, absence of alternative formats (no redundant display of information), difficulty with multistep activities, confusing terminology (e.g., "click here"), and complexities in page or site payout and lack of clear and consistent instructions or other navigational aids.

Other factors affect all disabled users (and, to a lesser degree, some people without disabilities):

- Lack of experience with Internet and Web technologies
- Lack of experience with assistive and adaptive technologies
- Operating system and software conflicts and difficulties
- Sites and technologies that do not support alternative access devices and strategies

Solution   Following the W3C WAI guidelines is one way to ensure that all online information is accessible to persons with disabilities and those who rely on adaptive and assistive technologies. Voluntary compliance on the part of all online providers will help the evolving standards of the Web keep pace with the population. However, it is imperative to seek ways to encourage the accessible design of Web materials from their first iteration. Inclusive design practices must take an active role in directing the development of accessible technology. Equally important is the need to educate all users and developers of ICTs on accessibility. This includes focusing on the ways in which the network society (the culture in which ICTs are embedded) can best respond to the needs of all people. It includes looking at the social contexts in which technology sits and examining the broader issues of access and living in a culture increasingly dominated by various mediating technologies. It means focusing less on individual accommodations and more on providing inclusive network infrastructures from the ground up. We need to develop a cultural or environmental approach to providing accessible ICTs and online environments. Similar to the curbcuts in sidewalk curbs that allow easier transit for people using wheelchairs, walkers, or other mobility aids (including baby strollers), it is possible to build in "electronic curbcuts" from the ground up, to allow easier access to online media and ICTs. This helps fulfill the opportunity for all people to participate in digital information exchange. Accessibility affects us all—some of us directly and all of us indirectly.

Linked patterns   Social Dominance Attenuation (4), Translation (15), Cyberpower (25), Public Agenda (30), Opportunity Spaces (33), Media Literacy (35), Meaningful Maps (47), Online Community Service Engine (62), Equal Access to Justice (69), Patient Access to Medical Records (95), Informal Learning Groups (98), Universal Voice Mail (113).

Problem   Although open distribution of ideas is fundamental to the scholarly enterprise, this flow has been increasingly constricted at a time when arguably humankind needs the information most. The price of journals and books has risen to the point where libraries, let alone individual scholars, can barely afford them. Nancy Kranich, former president of the American Library Association, reports that "Journals like *Nuclear Physics*, *Brain Research*, and *Tetrahedron Lettters…* now cost close to $20,000 a year." These prices have risen far faster than the cost of living. Some have argued that this is an outgrowth of a dramatic consolidation in the publishing industry. In addition, with the consolidation in retail bookstores as well as publishers, publishers often concentrate their efforts disproportionately on textbooks with large markets. Moreover, even if publishing profits were driven to zero, there would still be many people in the world who would not be able to gain access to important scientific and scholarly information in the form of paper books and journals because of the costs of distribution to remote places and translation into myriad native languages.

Context   There are many scholars, scientists, and teachers in a wide variety of fields. Only a very small percentage of authors gain a significant amount of income from the publication of their scholarly works. In some cases, authors have to pay to have their work published in scholarly journals. At the same time people who could gain greatly from the knowledge in books and journals often cannot afford them. This is particularly true for people in highly specialized fields, remote locations, and or who communicate in languages that are relatively uncommon. Not only do most scholars receive little or no income for publishing their work in scholarly journals and conference proceedings, the amount of work required of authors has increased over time. Not too many years ago, authors sent in a paper manuscript, and the publishing companies were responsible for typesetting and copyediting. Today, publishers of journals and conference proceedings often require computer-readable files completely formatted, and expect the author to carefully check for typos, grammatical errors, and word use. For example, if one examines the Proceedings of the first ACM conference on Human Computer Interaction (the 1982 Gaithersburg Conference) one sees many different formats and fonts. To be published in more recent CHI Conferences, the authors are all required to submit "camera-ready" manuscripts in a prescribed format and font.

Discussion   The Internet provides the foundation for a radical redesign of scholarly publishing that more effectively and equitably meets the needs of the communities that produce, consume, and otherwise use the knowledge, rather than the needs of commercial gatekeepers that often impede widespread distribution and open access.

Open access is the name given to the movement to increase the equity, effectiveness, and incidence of scholarly publishing. Probably the best introduction to the important concepts in open access (OA) scholarly publishing is the overview provided by Peter Suber (2006), a former philosophy professor now working at the Scholarly Publishing and Academic Resources Coalition (SPARC). Among other important points, he debunks some myths about OA. OA is not cost free, for instance, although clearly it can be less expensive than traditional for-profit, paper-based publishing. Even if it is not completely cost-free, it can still be free to the readers. There are a number of models of funding. In some cases, the authors pay a small fee; in others, institutions pay; in still others (e.g., the National Science Foundation), granting agencies make OA a condition of acceptance. It is also pointed out that there is no necessary relationship between quality and whether something is published in paper. Specifically, any and all approaches to review can be incorporated with open access. Stringent peer review by experts in the field is possible as is the exact opposite where anybody can publish anything. Educational institutions, nonprofit organizations, scholars, and software developers are working together to create online software systems (such as Open Journal Systems (2007) for journal management and publishing) and processes that support an extremely wide variety of models for journals, digital repositories, and other approaches. OA journals support peer review, high standards, and the editing process as easily as paper media do. OA archives typically permit researchers to post nonreviewed white papers and drafts. OA projects do well to use the OAI metadata standards so that others may search works seamlessly across organizational boundaries.

In addition to OA journals (whose number has been growing rapidly—see Directory of Open Access Journals, 2008), there are other ways that scholars are cooperating on the publication of scholarly materials. Perhaps one of the best-known current examples is the cooperative project known as the Wikipedia, but there are many others. MIT is making all of its course material available online; MERLOT is a cooperative project across many universities in the United States for sharing course materials. There are similar projects in Europe and Canada.

One example illustrating some of these concepts is the Global Text Project, whose goal is the provision of a library of 1,000 free electronic textbooks for the developing world, comprising all the texts needed for undergraduates in every major. Many of the participants have experience with creating a free textbook about XML. The next two planned projects are for texts on management and on information technology.

The Global Text Project and others like it seem feasible. Most scholars in the developed world are relatively wealthy compared with those in the developing world. Contributing to education in developing countries can potentially help lower disease rates and improve economic conditions and lessen the likelihood of civil war, corruption, and starvation. In turn, this increases the opportunities for more education. In addition, contributing to such projects offers scholars the opportunity for enhancing their reputation and getting valuable feedback from other colleagues.

There are some advantages to print media. Owning a printed book or journal that can be annotated and carried from place to place can be beneficial. In some ways, the covers and design of a book can serve as a helpful retrieval cue to the material inside in a way that Web sites typically do not. However, having books and journals online also has distinct advantages over and above the tremendous difference in costs. With online books, readers can search for keywords, put related passages on the screen side by side, apply automatic summarization techniques; and easily reformat, for example, to display in a larger font. Online books can also contain hyperlinks to other scholarly (or nonscholarly) work and to Web sites.

There are other significant advantages to OA publishing. Because the overall price is so much lower (due to lower cost and less concern with profit), publishing in a multitude of languages becomes more feasible. In addition, a much wider variety of materials may be published. By way of contrast, textbook publishers tend to focus their efforts on books for very popular and required courses.

A study by Antelman (2004) indicates that this form of publication may offer substantial benefits to authors as well. In her study of citations for articles in four fields (philosophy, political science, electrical engineering, and mathematics), she found in each case a highly significant difference in favor of OA articles.

Solution   Provide means for scholars to jointly create and improve scholarly materials, have them peer-reviewed and disseminated to those who can learn and critique the information without always engaging the additional costs and gate-keeping properties of traditional paper publishers.

Linked patterns   Civic Intelligence (1), The Commons (2), Translation (15), Citizen Science (37), Open Action and Research Network (45), Experimental School (89), Informal Learning Groups (98), Open Source Search Technology (125), Open Source Everything (127).

77 Mobile Information and Computer Technology Learning Facilities

Problem   In many countries, the lack of access to technology, and information and communication technology (ICT) in particular, is an acute problem of both resources and location. Solutions must focus on making scarce resources cover as much ground as possible.

Context   Placing fixed computer facilities in communities with government or donor funding limits the benefits to the communities in question.

Discussion   One solution that has long been available in the sphere of basic literacy is the mobile library, whereby suitable motor vehicles carry libraries on wheels to those unable to otherwise access them. This makes good use of financial resources and allows a scarce and important asset to be brought to where it is most needed and reused continually.

The provision of similar traveling computer laboratories, whose drivers are trained computer literacy educators, could play a similar role in bringing the ICT "mountain" to the disempowered. Self-contained units with their own power generation ability can grant ICT access to many people in remote locations or in other communities too poor to support such access in other ways. Encouraging community participation in the program will help to ensure that those in the community who could most benefit by the program will be helped first. The goals of such a program would be to:

• Bring scarce and economically empowering assets to communities desperately in need of them because of poverty or geographical remoteness.
• Help reduce the geographic and economic isolation of many communities.
• Begin to bring the wider world to communities that wish to gain knowledge of it and interact with it.
• Contribute to the knowledge and skills of those joining the exodus from rural to urban areas in an attempt to provide survival strategies that move away from begging, menial labor, and crime.

In South Africa a similar initiative that focuses on bringing science and technology to disadvantaged communities is already in place. A bus called the Discovery Mobile travels to communities and gives young people the opportunity to interact with a wide range of exhibits inside the bus.

Solution   By working together, government, donors, and communities can establish mobile computer laboratory facilities to begin to answer the needs of many communities for exposure to and training in the use of information and communication technologies.

Linked patterns   Cyberpower (25), Opportunity Spaces (33), Citizen Science (37), Mobile Intelligence (38), Digital Emancipation (60), Ethics of Community Informatics (67), Informal Learning Groups (98), Universal Voice Mail (113), Activist Road Trip (134).

Problem   Ironically, public policy development is very unpublic. It is often silent, invisible, and developed behind the scenes. This results in poor public policy that favors narrow interests and blocks progress. As power and wealth become more and more concentrated, the people and institutions that possess them will become more and more dominant in the policy arena. When that happens, local and marginalized voices are not heard; people feel disempowered and disengage further from the political process. Ordinary people generally stay far from the public policy arena. They feel isolated and are unaware that others are striving toward positive change. When there are public policy successes, they are not shared with other communities, and the people who do strive to enter the public policy arena often must needlessly reinvent the wheel.

Context   As our world becomes more and more complex, governance also grows more complicated. Meanwhile, the need for sound policy becomes essential. Whatever the policy issue at stake is, there are opportunities for grassroots political engagement. Increasingly this will involve the intelligent use of new media and the Internet. Moreover, with that in mind, the development of the Internet and policies regarding citizen use of information and computer technology (ICT) in general make this a critical area for citizen engagement.

Discussion   Public policy determines whether a new library is built and where, and how a new clinic for homeless people is funded or not. It even determines to a large degree who has access to communication services and who has the right to control them. Although it is often public policy that silently promotes or discourages certain public actions, the development, maintenance, use, and, often, the very existence of the public policy is about as far from "public" as can be imagined.

Policy is governance. It helps address questions like, How will we live together in a complex society? How will we deal with the problems of our time, and how do we collectively define what those problems are? Will governance be of the people, by the people, for the people, or will it succumb to the defects resulting from a concentration of power and wealth?

Public policy often has a technocratic air about it. It is often constructed by "wonks" just as computer code is produced by "geeks," and both geeks and wonks are stereotypically portrayed as social misfits who prefer complicated and artificial arcana to the real world of flesh, blood, and emotions. But while it is true that policy development (like computer development) does have its degree of inherent complexity (especially as it assumes a final form), an important part of its development involves the crucial task of determining what one would like to see in society and how it might be encouraged to happen.

Grassroots public policy development involves local engagement that is generally contrary to top-down approaches. It occurs when the problem and the solution are defined by the active local parties rather than imposed from outside. Jason Corburn (2005) discusses why people, especially nonprofessionals working in the local community, are unlikely to get involved in policy work:

One difficulty that local knowledge presents is that its insights are often very contextual, while policy-making tends to make general rules. Much of the work on local knowledge is ethnographic and deeply conceptual, and few general patterns or lessons are offered. Advocates of local knowledge have been understandably hesitant to "scale up" or generalize their findings and insights—largely out of fear of inaccurate decontextualizations, oversimplifications and unjustified generalizations.

Corburn goes on to point out that it is not just local communities that lose out when they are excluded from the process. Society at large suffers, as do, interestingly enough, the policy "wonks" whose job it is to develop these policies:

Professional decision makers have not found ways to incorporate the important understandings from studies of local knowledge into the more generalized practice of policymaking. Scaling up knowledge from local settings is a necessary task in environmental health because of the extreme heterogeneity in ecosystems and human-environment linkages. But local knowledge can be used to improve environmental-health decisions while maintaining a heightened sensitivity to the contextually specific qualities of this knowledge.

The W. K. Kellogg Foundation (2006) lists four types of public policy: statutory (including constitution, charter, or laws), fiscal (including annual budgets, acts, and resolutions), regulatory (administrative rules), and institutional (such as policy manuals and standards, and tenure and appointment). For each public policy type, the foundation describes broad characteristics, including scope, applicability, duration, process characteristics, and primary policymakers. Note that different jurisdictions have different public policies and a variety of types within them. Nevertheless, the public policy landscape of any given jurisdiction can be described and understood using this framework, albeit with some variation. Using a table based on the approach above—with the four policy types as column headings and the five broad characteristics as row headings—as a way to focus one's learning in the public policy arena, especially as it pertains to one's own area of interest, is a prerequisite for effective public policy engagement.

The Children's Partnership organization offers "Six Essential Elements Derived from The Children's Partnership's Experiences" that show the basic steps in a process of moving "from an idea to a successful public policy":

1. Research base that is grounded in what local communities want and need.
2. Policy proposal that responds to findings from research—one that is saleable and scaleable.
3. Ways to communicate the policy idea effectively.
4. Demonstration that the policy idea can work in the real world.
5. Organizing/advocacy for the idea—using strategic partnerships
6. Follow-through to implementation of the new policy

The inherent problem that people are approaching similar problems from diverse perspectives will continue to crop up. People working on similar problems may not find each other or be aware of the efforts and intentions of the other. There are also questions related to who gets to do what, whose ideas are taken into account, what attitudes (respectful, paternalistic, domineering) prevail, in whose name or on what basis decisions are made, and whether they are enforced or neglected that need to be addressed.

People often do not know how to get involved and have limited experience of being effectively involved. They will therefore probably require additional information about context or channels in which to get involved and an invitation to participate. There are numerous sociological and psychological dimensions at play here, and people need to advance their individual development within this social exercise.

Although face-to-face encounters remain important, tools of the Internet era can be used to facilitate new modes of organizing. For one thing, we can develop more open space for dialogue and engagement. It may also be possible to coordinate with other communities that are involved in similar activities. The Internet can be used to promote the idea of moving decision-making power toward smaller and local assemblages while maintaining flexibility and freedom to connect in local assemblages. In other words, new online media can allow people and communities to organize more effectively on their principles and values.

Once it has been established what type of policy should be developed and at least the rough form that the policy should take, the plan for getting the policy implemented should be developed. The process, including both the formal or legal aspects of the process and the informal, tacit, and behind-the-scenes aspects of the process, must be considered, especially in conjunction with a consideration of the primary policymakers and how they generally operate.

Note also that although some action or procedure or decision might be properly enshrined as part of public policy, it may have little bearing on how things are actually done. Public policy is valid only to the degree that it is enforced or respected and abided by. The use of this pattern is probably reasonable only to the extent that public policy is actually respected in the setting in which the policy is intended to be used. For that reason, the reality of the policy's actual deployment in society, in addition to any other relevant circumstances surrounding the development and use of the policy, ought to be considered as a separate characteristic called *context*. Finally, we also need to consider the form (or structure) that the public policy will ultimately take.

This pattern is closely related to the Power Research pattern because the information uncovered through power research is likely to be useful in determining how policy is often developed and what alternative practices may be effective in developing alternative policies from the grassroots.

Solution   *Public policy* is often a misnomer. It often functions as policy imposed on the public rather than policy achieved by the public. Public policy should reflect cultivated public wisdom. The discipline required of policy work must be distributed through the body politic: civil discourse, research, and inclusive creative deliberation. The exercise of grassroots public policy development is the ongoing work of (re)constituting the public (sphere).

Linked patterns   Civic Intelligence (1), Collective Decision Making (10), Linguistic Diversity (16), Indicators (29), Public Agenda (30), Democratic Political Settings (31), Participatory Design (36), Citizen Science (37), Economic Conversion (41), Open Action and Research Network (45), Alternative Progress Indexes (46), Meaningful Maps (47), Community Currencies (63), Transparency (64), Equal Access to Justice (69), E-Consultation (70), Powerful Remittances (73), Positive Health Information (74), Users' Information Technology Quality Network (80), Civic Capabilities (85), Future Design (88), Document-Centered Discussion (92), Patient Access to Medical Records (95), Citizenship Schools (96), Self-Designed Development (106), Labor Visions (112), Community Telecenters (117), Power Research (128).

Problem Any challenge to the status quo can lead to conflict, which raises a key problem: how to shift the conflict creatively to achieve real change. Even within like-minded social change communities, participants can find themselves in conflict with each other. To negotiate over disagreements on the basis that only one of the affected parties can gain at the expense of all the others is to perpetuate the status quo, and often leads to everyone involved feeling that they have lost more than they have gained.

Context Organizations and communities dedicated to social change will encounter intense disagreements since they are working among people with strongly held beliefs and differing agendas. Many strategic action choices set up conflicts that do more to perpetuate the status quo than to change it: protests, negative media campaigns, lawsuits, and regulation battles are time-honored tactics, but their win-lose dynamic tends to polarize opinions around long-standing hostilities. Problems can also arise when attempting to resolve conflicts by relying on a third party to mediate the issues, particularly if the dispute affects multiple divergent and distinct parties. Increasingly social change actions are developed in settings at which participant decision makers represent people from around the world. The U.N. Decade of the Women's meetings in Kenya, Mexico, and China and the World Social Forum called for participants to finalize strategies and decisions then and there. Under such conditions, genuine consensus calls for skilled, culturally aware multiparty negotiation.

Discussion Starting in 1981 with the publication of Fisher and Ury's *Getting to Yes: Negotiating Agreement without Giving In,* Americans, in particular, learned to imagine solutions to conflicts in which constructive win-win solutions replaced the win-lose model. Fisher and Ury centered on negotiation, and negotiation remains a critical conflict strategy. Their Program on Negotiation at Harvard University Law School operates as a training and research center with a particular focus on large-scale and international conflicts, using a fourfold process: (1) separate the people from the problem; (2) focus on interests, not positions; (3) invent options for mutual gain; and (4) insist on using objective criteria. Central to this process is the ability to recognize whether a proposed agreement is in one's interest; the best alternative to no agreement (BATNA) is a clear understanding of what one will do if no agreement is reached.

Good communication skills and versatile approaches to problem definition are critical to negotiation and to conflict resolution in general. There is no single posture or style that connects across all cultures and power differences, but many people have found Marshall Rosenberg's (2003) training useful for learning to listen effectively and learning to ask clearly. Michelle Le Baron (2003) offers detailed descriptions of good practice for respecting specific cultural factors that will impact any negotiation. Meyer-Knapp's (2003) analysis of attempts to end wars highlights some additional factors: secrecy can facilitate progress in difficult talks, key leaders must be involved, and success often depends on all parties publicly agreeing to end retributive and punitive actions.

Some conflicts become so embedded in communities that it comes to seem impossible even to discuss them. Two programs illustrate options for opening up the dialogue. The Public Conversations Project has set up forums for private and extended dialogue on abortion in the United States. In the cities where they have worked, there is an increasing willingness to reach across the divisions. The Health Bridge Project in the former Yugoslavia achieved a similar effect by setting up clinics and health care recovery projects staffed by professionals from among the hostile Serb, Croat, and Bosnian Muslim communities. One particular peacetime derivative of military gaming uses an intensive negotiation and planning protocol in which the stakeholders are explicitly required to negotiate from the perspective of someone other than themselves.

Intraorganizational disputes can be softened if workers and board members routinely engage in mediation and facilitation training. Then, should a disagreement arise, they can use the skills on their own behalf. However, managers must remember that in U.S. law and culture, once an organizational dispute has arisen, decisions that withstand legalistic challenges are based in well-grounded due process. The essentials of due process are timely handling of complaints, neutrality of decision makers in relation to the dispute, the right of appeal, and an opportunity for all sides to have their point of view heard.

Solution   Conflict can supply a positive impetus to improve the situation, often through negotiations among a variety of opposing parties. So, approach change prepared to acknowledge and actively deal with conflict. To generate lasting change, use an imaginative array of conflict strategies and skills, including negotiation, multiparty process, and cross-cultural dialogue. To enable constructive outcomes, negotiate with flexible and compassionate attitudes to opposing parties. Organizations should develop and regularly review their capacity for negotiation and dialogue, both internally and externally. Schools at all levels should be teaching skills in negotiation, conflict resolution, and communication. In complex situations, each participant must be willing to assume the responsibility of negotiating for himself or herself.

Linked patterns   Global Citizenship (6), Collective Decision Making (10), Strengthening International Law (42), Conversational Support across Boundaries (50), Truth and Reconciliation Commissions (51), E-Consultation (70), Voices of the Unheard (83), Citizen Diplomacy (93), Appreciative Collaboration (99), Peaceful Public Demonstrations (133).

Problem Competitive software suppliers need demanding customers who can articulate sophisticated user requirements for the software they use in their daily work. However, it takes people from different professions to articulate requirements that serve the employees, the (co)owners, and the customers of tomorrow. If the contact between the end users and the people who purchase their software is too loose, then the purchasing personnel get their information only from the dominant software suppliers.

Context The competition between suppliers of communication services is different from that between suppliers of physical goods, since what the former deliver is not just a platform for communication, but the access to service providers and other users who have already invested in that platform. Other economic forces tend to further decrease competition in the software market. This makes it even more important to support the articulation of end user quality demands.

Discussion An example of an emerging users' information technology (IT) quality network is the Users' Award network (www.usersaward.com) initiated in 1997 by a group of trade union activists and researchers who wanted to address the problem of expensive and centrally controlled workplace IT systems. Many such planning and control systems had become a bureaucratic hindrance for both employees and employers in Swedish firms. In 2002, the project, which by then engaged a consortium of researchers from four universities, had developed a quality certification method and demonstrated its viability by certifying two software packages in Sweden.

The Users' Award network is open for employees who want to take part in efforts to raise the quality of software for use in the workplace. The network arranges user conferences where exemplary software is showcased and discussed. It initiates periodic user surveys to gain hard facts about user preferences and user satisfaction with the major software services in the marketplace. A yearly users' IT prize contest has been held since the year 2000. Since 2002 the user-certified certificate has been issued to software suppliers that have passed the certification process developed by the research consortium which is an important part of the network.

The former software design manager at Apple, HP, and Next, Donald Norman, sums up his design philosophy in the epigraph of his book, *Things That Make Us Smart* (1993): "People Propose, Science Studies, Technology Conforms." This viewpoint contrasts sharply with what Norman claims to be the dominant division of roles today: that industry proposes, science studies, and consumers conform. The critique is elaborated in the book *The Invisible Computer* (1998), where Norman argues that (1) the typical computer user over the past ten years has been a person with substantial technical expertise; (2) due to the fast dissemination of IT services, the typical user in the coming years will be a person without technical expertise;

and (3) this will force a fundamental reorientation on the hardware and software industries, bringing policies of user orientation to the fore.

Norman's analysis has been one of the inspirations for the Users' Award initiative. Norman identified three social institutions as key actors in the overall process of innovation. But there is a fourth crucial actor, the media, which can be further divided into three categories. Thus, the following social forces interact in complex ways to support the articulation of problems and solutions, an ongoing process that could be further institutionalized in user-driven software labeling, (as it already has been for computer hardware):

- User groups complain about recurrent software problems and point out alternatives.
- Popular media inform the general public about complaints and alternative solutions.
- Research groups study the complaints and invent solutions.
- The trade press scrutinizes the research results.
- National media comment on the research results.
- User-oriented software suppliers implement proposed solutions.
- Regulators and standards organizations confirm the principles behind the solutions.

Solution Support initiatives in workshops, offices, schools, and universities to articulate user requirements for software. Take part by formulating concrete demands that enhance the quality of the software you use in your group. Make it fit the decentralized teamwork organizations of tomorrow. If a users' IT quality center already exists in your region, support it by participating in its many activities. If it does not exist, take part in forming one.

Linked patterns Indicators (29), Participatory Design (36), Grassroots Public Policy Development (78), Academic Technology Investments (81), Appropriating Technology (108).

81 Academic Technology Investments

Problem New technologies have been making rapid inroads in higher education, and, in many ways, they are changing methods of teaching, learning, and research. Yet strict segregation of academic disciplines, industrial age concepts of technological ownership and control, and entrenched silos across institutions place limits on the kinds of innovation and extension of learning and research that computer-mediated communication networks can help facilitate.

Context Institutions of higher education provide significant benefits to students and researchers within their walls as well as the broader public. At the same time, economic downturns have resulted in diminishing revenue streams for legislative support of higher education, and for-profit as well as international educational institutions offer increasing competition. Academic institutions need to explore the greater opportunities enabled by information technologies for interdisciplinary and interinstitutional pedagogical and administrative partnerships in order to revitalize their economic circumstances and reestablish their social relevance.

Discussion Institutions of higher education play a critical role in the maintenance and advancement of a nation and a culture. They are also often mired in organizational fiefdoms and disciplinary rivalries arising from competition over scarce resources. In turn, opportunities for collaboration are neglected that can advance the education of students and the production of knowledge.

Information and communication technologies (ICTs) enable faculty and students to interact with others in academies across the nation and around the world. Courses engaging other institutions are being taught through videoconferencing and computer-based classrooms; group activities for students using databases and computer-generated learning objects are revolutionizing large lecture courses in physics and other sciences; researchers are using high-performance computing to conduct experiments with international colleagues; and the extra computing power is leveraged to make available to students at their desktops expensive software through virtual computing labs.

Yet the rapid and continual development of ICTs leave administrative budgets and personnel at universities struggling to adapt to constant change. In an age of vastly distributed information networks that can speed data and news around the globe, transparency and accountability are still lacking at academic institutions. Despite the proliferation of communication devices and channels, faculty, staff, and students too often feel that their needs and views go unheard. Although the complexity of technological advances makes it impossible for any one person or group to know all that is needed to make the best implementation plans, for example, ICT investment decisions continue to be made without soliciting other viewpoints.

At the same time, academic communication systems such as e-mail and electronic calendaring that have become inextricably interwoven with the day-to-day operations of universities are still being run by multiple units and departments, which have developed a sense of distrust and distance from central operations. Educational institutions within the same region and state continue to run routine technology networks individually instead of investigating the significant cost sharing that is possible through interinstitutional cooperation, and beliefs in the necessity of institutional branding outweigh the advantages to be found in intercollegiate curricula and teaching.

Part of what hinders the realization of more of the collaborative advantages communication networks can offer is an administrative hierarchy that tends to favor corporate-style decision making in the hopes of producing corporate-style efficiencies, especially in the light of the huge costs and rapid change of educational technologies. Yet institutions of higher education are built on principles of peer review of evidence and communal sharing of knowledge. When the diverse constituencies of the academy—students, faculty, administrators, technical staff—are not consulted in top-down decisions and have no forums in which to engage with each other, those foundational principles are discarded, and progressive initiatives can be resisted and even sabotaged.

A *Chronicle of Higher Education* article, "The Role of Colleges in an Era of Mistrust" (Yankelovich and Furth 2005), lays out ten communication principles by which colleges can provide leadership and maintain good faith in the public eye. Reporting on a University of California controversy over the cancellation of an invited speaker by the university's president without consulting faculty or students, the authors press for a process of communication that includes diverse perspectives: "When it is possible to make deliberations open and transparent, colleges must do so. When open-door meetings are not prudent or practical, colleges must be careful to ensure that all the affected parties have a place at the table. Just as important, they must emerge with a clear account not only of what was decided but of how that decision was reached."

Multiplying communication channels do not necessarily yield greater communication. An inclusive environment that fosters transparency and accountability within all academic sectors can go a long way to eliciting the sense of mission and dedication that characterizes the motives of people in choosing to be part of an educational community. Collaborative learning opportunities, interinstitutional partnerships, and interdisciplinary scholarship are all developments supported by ICTs; creating a climate of openness and engagement across the university enterprise will further their realization.

Solution   ICTs can facilitate the development of new models of teaching, learning, and research that take advantage of interdisciplinary and interinstitutional collaborations in higher education and contribute to the quality of an information society. Such developments can be hindered by the persistence of traditional top-down decision making that excludes the voices of the wider academic community and perpetuates a climate of disciplinary rivalry and entrenched silos. The constructive realization of the network capacities of new communication technologies in higher education needs to be guided by insights and perspectives from a diverse collective.

Linked patterns Citizen Science (37), Transparency (64), Participatory Budgeting (71), Users' Information Technology Quality Network (80), Strategic Frame (86), Sustainability Appraisal (100), Shared Vision (101).

Collaboration

Problem   One often regards difficulties or issues as problems to be solved, but one must not blithely accept the implication that the first step is to define the problem and the next is to find one or more solutions to it. The significant issues and difficulties in the world do not sit still for this orderly strategy: every attempt to define these problems changes them, and so does each step in any attempted solution. Moreover, there are no sound rules to tell when a solution to such a problem is complete or any way to test it offline.

Context   This pattern addresses the mind-set one brings to a problem. It may be especially useful for people weighed down by the complexities of the problem they confront and by the accumulation of previous failed solutions that complex problems tend to accumulate about themselves.

Discussion   The system theorist Horst Rittel coined the term "wicked problem" in the early 1970s as a corrective to the rationalist approach to planning and design of large-scale systems. The late 1960s and early 1970s were a heyday for rationalist planning, which can be summarized as the process of fully and explicitly laying out goals, assumptions, and constraints of a problem situation; generating and evaluating alternative solutions; and expecting that the preferred solution will emerge clearly, backed by good reasons. This approach grew, among other things, from the rise of digital computation, the activist federal mood of the 1960s, and the prospect of bypassing bitter political struggles over such matters as urban extensions of the interstate highway system. Among its applications were low-cost public housing projects, flood control initiatives, moon missions, and the Vietnam War strategy. The hope was that objective, data-driven analytical approaches would provide a broadly applicable tool kit for solving large-scale social and environmental problems.

Rittel saw that this hope was doomed because the problem situations in view could not be defined in agreed, unchanging ways (Rittel and Webber 1973). These problems are intrinsically ill defined, and attempts to define them are already actions that reshape the problem and commit the analyst to a course of problem solving that omits legitimate alternatives—and there is no way of escaping this. An extreme example is the Israel-Palestine question: a storm of protest and counterprotest greets every attempt to say what "the question" is, much less propose answers. But much milder situations exhibit wickedness. Consider low-cost housing, middle school math curriculum, or the length of the salmon fishing season. Indeed, every building project and most social action, down to the smallest scale, has elements of wickedness. In each case, the interests in play, the intangibility of key values, and the elusiveness of key information mean that a commonly agreed base for problem solving is not objectively available.

There are, however, ways forward. The first is to shift the goal of action on significant problems from solution to intervention. Instead of seeking just the right moves to eliminate a problem once and for all, one should recognize that any actions occur in an ongoing process, in which further actions will be needed later. This is not to accept injustice or suffering quietly. If there are ways to eliminate smallpox as a public health problem, and the vaccination campaigns of the 1970s proved there were, one should pursue them by all means. But one should realize that smallpox will remain part of the global health situation in some way. (And so it has, most recently as a potential bioterror weapon.) The intervention mentality recognizes that situations tend to continue, even if their form changes radically.

There is a natural fit between the wicked-problem mentality and the Design Stance (pattern 44). While design has often aimed at closed, once-and-for-all solutions, the multifactor, iterative, imagination-based process of generating designs is very congenial to what is needed for intervening in wicked problems. Design naturally generates multiple possibilities before settling on one proposal; it naturally engages in a sort of dialogue with the problem situation, in which drawings or other representations of the design idea reveal consequences or relationships that call for changes in the design idea, and vice versa. The precise definition of the problem evolves alongside the ideas for interventions until they converge on action.

A second way to work with the wickedness of significant problems is to admit the significant actors to the design process. A typical wicked problem is shaped and reshaped by multiple actors whose influence cannot be closed out. The long maneuvering over the reconstruction of Ground Zero in New York City is a classic example. Both the rationalist tradition in architecture, engineering, public policy, and most other fields and what could be called the now-we-need-a-genius tradition in those same fields have relied on an expert (or sometimes a team of experts) generating a solution in isolation. But the multiple actors in wicked problems cannot only obstruct such a solution, they can change the problem's definition while the solution is being generated.

A third step is to design loose-fit actions. Instead of tailoring an intervention tightly to the understood conditions of a problem, for example, choosing sealed windows and central air-conditioning for an office building, one should allow for uses, costs, and regulations to change in unforeseen ways, for example, drastic escalation in energy costs. Architecture is one area where the rationalist, optimizing mood of the 1970s (and after) has saddled businesses and communities with rapidly obsolescing buildings of many kinds, but the need for loose-fit designs or plans occurs in any area with wicked problems.

A powerful example of successful handling of a wicked problem is passive solar design of buildings. The problem area emerged from the oil crises of the 1970s, as activists' strong desires to make use of solar energy as a renewable, free alternative to oil encountered technical difficulties such as low efficiency and daily and seasonal variability, economic challenges such as high first cost and low availability of experienced suppliers, and political and cultural resistance, including vested interests, suspicion of unfamiliar technologies, and opposition to ideas perceived as countercultural. This mix of difficulties and disparate actors is typically wicked.

Slowly, over two decades, the problem and goals shifted (e.g., from replacing oil heat to reducing the need for it), experimentation revealed unforeseen directions of development (e.g., building orientation and control of overheating became more critical than total window area), knowledge from traditional practices as well as from engineering measurement began to accumulate, and designers found more and more ways to blend solar performance with standard building functions. A growing consensus on good practice included building code officials and contractors, as well as solar enthusiasts and academics. Discovery, development, and a degree of controversy continue, but the United States is now at a point where passive solar guidelines are widely available and used at times in such routine guise as to be invisible.

Solution   Address significant problems with a design mentality that expects them to be "wicked," recognizes the kinds of wickedness at work, and understand the design process, from initiation to proposals, as an intervention in a flow of events, not a fixed change in a static scene. Admit the significant actors to the design process. Pursue "loose-fit" interventions that have good potential to adapt to unforeseen changes in needs or impacts.

Linked patterns   Dematerialization (18), Citizen Science (37), Design Stance (44), Intermediate Technologies (57), E-Consultation (70), Voices of the Unheard (83), Value-Sensitive Design (87), Future Design (88), Appreciative Collaboration (99), Self-Designed Development (106), Appropriating Technology (108), Community Inquiry (122).

Problem   Despite the significant effort and thought that go into decision making and design, bad decisions and designs are frequently conceived and implemented primarily because a critical and relevant perspective was not brought to bear. This is especially true if the missing perspective represents that of someone who holds a stake in the outcome.

Context   Complex problems such as the construction of new social institutions or the design of multifaceted interactive systems require that a multitude of viewpoints be brought to bear. Unfortunately, this is all too often not the case. One group builds a "solution" for another group without fully understanding the culture, user needs, extreme cases, and so on. The result is often a technical or social system that creates as many problems as it solves. This process is often exacerbated when those building the solution interact more intensely with each other than with those affected by the solution.

Discussion   Several forces are at work in the situations requiring this pattern:

• Gaps in requirements are most cheaply repaired early in development. For this reason, as well as the need to gain acceptance by all parties, all stakeholders must be allowed to participate in any development or change process. This is an ethical issue as well.
• It is logistically difficult to ensure that all stakeholder groups are represented at every meeting.
• A new social institution or design will be both better in quality and more easily accepted if all relevant parties have input.

The idea for this pattern comes from a Native American story transcribed by Paula Underwood (1993) entitled, "Who Speaks for Wolf?" In brief, the story goes as follows. The tribe had as one of its members a man who took it on himself to learn all that he could about wolves. He became such an expert that his fellow tribe members called him "Wolf." While Wolf and several other braves were out on a long hunting expedition, it became clear to the tribe that they would have to move to a new location. After various reconnaissance missions, a new site was selected, and the tribe moved.

Shortly after, it became clear that a mistake had been made: the new location was in the middle of a breeding ground for wolves. The wolves were threatening the children and stealing the drying meat. Now the tribe was faced with a hard decision. Should they move again? Should they post guards around the clock? Or should they destroy the wolves? Did they even want to be the sort of people who would kill off another species for their own convenience?

At last it was decided they would move to a new location. But as was their custom, they also asked themselves, "What did we learn from this? How can we prevent making such mistakes in the future?" Someone said, "Well, Wolf would have prevented this mistake had he been at our first council meeting."

"True enough," they all agreed. "Therefore, from now on, whenever we meet to make a decision, we shall ask ourselves, 'Who speaks for Wolf?' to remind us that someone must be capable and delegated to bring to bear the knowledge of any missing stakeholders."

Much of the failure of process reengineering can be attributed to the fact that models of the "as is" process were developed based on some executive's notion of how things were done rather than a study of how they were actually performed or asking the people who did the work how the work was done. A "should be" process was designed to be a more efficient version of the "as is" process, and then implementation was pushed down on workers. However, since the original "as is" model was not based on reality, the "more efficient" solution often left out vital elements.

Technological and sociological imperialism provide many additional examples in which the input of all stakeholders was not taken into account. Of course, much of the history of the U.S. government's treatment of Native Americans reflects a refusal to truly include all the stakeholders.

A challenge in applying the "Who Speaks for Wolf" pattern is to judge honestly and correctly whether someone has the knowledge and delegation to "speak for Wolf." If such a person is not present, those making the decision may do well to put off the design or decision until such a person or, better, "Wolf" himself can be present.

As a variant of this, a prototype creativity tool has been created. The idea is to have a "board of directors" consisting of famous people. When you have a problem to solve, you are supposed to be reminded of, and think about, how various people would approach this problem. Ask yourself, "What would Einstein have said?" "How would Gandhi have approached this problem?"

Solution   Provide ways to remind people of stakeholders who are not present. These methods could be procedural (certain Native Americans always ask, "Who speaks for Wolf"), visual (e.g., diagrams, lists) or auditory (e.g., songs).

Linked patterns   Social Dominance Attenuation (4), Social Responsibility (8), Collective Decision Making (10), Memory and Responsibility (11), Demystification and Reenchantment (14), Fair Trade (21), Antiracism (23), Democratic Political Settings (31), Participatory Design (36), Ethics of Community Informatics (67), E-Consultation (70), Powerful Remittances (73), Multiparty Negotiation for Conflict Resolution (79), Wholesome Design for Wicked Problems (82), Value-Sensitive Design (87), The Power of Story (114), Whistle-Blowing (130).

Problem   A designable and open technology like the Internet is never finished or final. This type of open technology invites ongoing creative use, which drives the evolution and development of the technology. While creative use is associated with active and engaged users, it can present severe challenges in the design of public systems. From the perspective of the designer, the creative user is unpredictable and random and uses the system in unintended ways that can be detrimental to the overall functionality and robustness of the system. Unfortunately this often leads designers to create closed systems with little or no room for user action outside the intended scope. This approach can result in systems that are unattractive to a creative and imaginative community that desires ownership and opportunity to developing a system that is effective from their perspective.

Context   Unintended use exists wherever open and designable technology is used. People tend to use systems in creative ways insofar as the design of the technology allows it. The Internet and related technologies have historically benefited from a concept and infrastructure supporting unintended use. We continue to be surprised on a daily basis by new and inventive applications of the Internet. Although the Internet has changed over time, this essential foundation remains. This technology is well suited for large, open communities that grant people (as users) ample freedom in the ways they can relate to and apply it. This technological foundation can be exploited for a creative user-driven design.

Discussion

A successful tool is one that was used to do something undreamed of by its author.
—S. C. Johnson (attributed)

Many observations, both scientific and anecdotal, describe how people use technology in unintended ways. Studies show this happens within organizational settings as well as on the open Web. However, the predominant concept is that the design of a technology should make its use obvious, that it should be user friendly. Studies have shown that in many cases, such systems leave users feeling that they are just users (or even customers) of a community system, not participants (Ciborra 1992, Carroll and Rosson 1987).

Instead of viewing unintended use as a problem, it is possible to define it as an opportunity; instead of designing to protect the system for creative use, design the system to support and withstand creative use. A system that can handle unintended use will be well equipped to evolve over time and to be updated, and thereby continue to be relevant to users in the community.

To be able to design for unintended use, we must study how people as users deal with and approach technology in everyday life rather than focusing on what they should do when using it in the intended way. Creative unintended use is and will always be context and situation specific, and it will probably not be possible to produce abstractions that could subsequently be used to produce generalized knowledge or concise design principles.

The important thing, however, is to find out how people understand, imagine, and approach technology. Since Internet technology is designable, community support systems can never be moved from one community to another without adaptation. This means a tool or a specific use that is simply copied will not work the same way under two different circumstances. The tool must be redesigned. The most important knowledge question is therefore what kinds of knowledge and understanding of the technology are needed to create a solid foundation for these kinds of context-specific redesigns.

A community is always changing. People develop new needs and wants. The technology for supporting such a community must build on the idea of unintended use. Unintended use is not a threat to the supporting system; instead it should be understood as a creative driving force. Creative unintended use is a way for users to take control of the technology and make it relevant to them. Unintended use is a fact of life in a community support system, not a problem.

Solution   The solution is to design intentionally for creative unintended use. Design principles for creative unintended use can be formulated and used to inform new designs (Stolterman 2001). Some examples of such principles are that (1) the system must be sufficiently robust to withstand creative use "attacks" from users; (2) the system must be forgiving, which means it has some ability to accept creative use changes without demanding complete safety; (3) a system whose purpose is to elicit creative and radical use must present a sufficiently rich, inspiring, and complex environment and (4) provide the user with tools for exploring and changing the system itself; and (5) the system must be designed as an open system, through, for example, open protocols, software hooks, and toolkits, so that it is possible for users to expand the scope and breadth of the system without demanding too much structure and administration. These high-level design principles must be developed and expanded. There is a need for experimental approaches to design for unintended use that are relevant to the situation at hand.

Linked patterns   Dematerialization (18), Participatory Design (36), Design Stance (44), Culturally Situated Design Tools (49), Public Library (59), Self-Designed Development (106), Appropriating Technology (108).

Problem   Peoples can often find the path to social and economic empowerment blocked to them due to any number of circumstances: lack of literacy and information, limited access to health care, a low level of durable assets, political marginalization and so forth.

Context   From the grassroots level up toward the international sphere, peoples are seeking ways to encourage and develop the capability of individuals and communities to actively engage in creating the life they desire to live through promoting access to health, higher literacy, and ability to collectively engage in public political action.

Discussion   Nobel laureate Amartya Sen asserted that the "expansion of basic human capabilities, including such freedoms as the ability to live long, read and write, to escape preventable illnesses, to work outside the family irrespective of gender, and to participate in collaborative as well as adversarial politics, not only influence the quality of life that the people can enjoy, but also effect the real opportunities they have to participate in economic expansion" (Drèze and Sen 1999).

In essence such a statement highlights both the ends we seek to achieve in the process of development and the path by which we achieve that end. If people do not have access to health, how will they be able to participate in society or the civic life of their geographical community? And if they cannot participate, how can they ensure that they will encourage and generate a level of action necessary for developing the access to health they need?

In taking a closer look at Sen and Drèze's statement above, Jan Garrett (2003) believes that there are important freedoms that have an instrumental role in making positive, substantial, freedom possible.

• Political freedoms. These are "the opportunities that people have to determine who should govern and on what principles, and also include the possibility to scrutinize and criticize authorities, to have freedom of political expression and an uncensored press, to enjoy the freedom to choose between different political parties, and so on. They include ... opportunities of political dialogue, dissent and critique as well as voting rights and participatory selection of legislators and executives."
• Economic facilities. These are "the opportunities that individuals ... enjoy to use economic resources for the purpose of consumption, or production, or exchange." The quantity of income as well as how it is distributed is important. Availability and access to finance are also crucial. (Not being able to get credit, for example, can be economically devastating.)
• Social opportunities. These are the arrangements society makes for education, health care, and other services.
• Transparency guarantees. These relate to the need for openness that people can anticipate and the freedom to deal with one another with a justified expectation of disclosure and

clarity. These guarantees play a clear role in preventing corruption, financial irresponsibility, and violation of society's rules of conduct for government and business.

- Protective security. A social safety net prevents sections of the population from being reduced to abject misery. Sen (2000) refers to "fixed institutional arrangements such as unemployment benefits and statutory income supplements to the indigent as well as ad hoc (temporary) arrangements such as famine relief or emergency public employment to generate income for destitutes."

As a pattern of development, engaging civic capabilities can exist as both an approach and a map for distinct and concrete implementation of development projects and empowerment campaigns, whether they be economic, political, health, and gender-centric or an integrated collection of all of these. The term *engaging* refers to the normative stance that these are fundamental aspects of enabling individuals to lead lives worth living.

It is a call to those who are blocked from realizing these capabilities in their day-to-day lives to engage and work to actualize these in their lived experience; similarly it is a call to social activists, community animators, governments, and international organizations working to pursue not only the economic betterment of peoples, but to address the more holistic reality that makes up people's lived experience.

Sen's work has placed much emphasis on the individual, but capabilities also point to the civic or community sphere in which groups of participants engage in the process of not only achieving such substantial freedoms but also collectively enjoying and exercising such freedoms.

While much development may indirectly encourage the creation or realization of such freedoms, the purpose of engaging these capabilities as a pattern is meant to emphasize awareness of such fundamental freedoms and promote their centrality to a consciously constructed pattern language that seeks to empower individuals and communities at all levels of society.

This means identifying and pursuing direct interaction with local as well as national-level officials to engage in cooperative and adversarial politics. Ideally this would help in bringing about accountability, or at least making some progress toward a more responsive form of government. Affiliation with regional and transnational advocacy groups can access leverage for marginalized groups. Through engagement and a direction toward freedoms and capabilities, people can prioritize their political battles that pressure government to pursue policies that produce results in education, health, and economic opportunity for those who lack these building blocks.

Solution   Ultimately the idea of civic capabilities is a critical component to almost any pattern language we might wish to construct. Therefore, when constructing a pattern language that is meant to address development in any way, it is necessary to consider the ways in which these projects will use the individual as well as collective civic capabilities of a community (and associated development partners) and how they will be used to support and encourage the further realization of these freedoms in peoples lives.

Linked patterns   Collective Decision Making (10), Education and Values (17), Big-Picture Health Information (27), Democratic Political Settings (31), Participatory Design (36), Design Stance (44), Durable Assets (58), Community Networks (61), Online Community Service Engine (62), Transparency (64), Free and Fair Elections (68), Equal Access to Justice (69), Grassroots Public Policy Development (78), Citizenship Schools (96), Self-Designed Development (106), Thinking Communities (118), Emergency Communication Systems (121), Community Inquiry (122), Power Research (128), Peaceful Public Demonstrations (133), Follow the Money (135).

Problem   The complexity of the world and multiplicity of perspectives with which to view it can often stymie people's attempts to interpret it in ways that make sense and suggest meaningful action. People cannot see the connection between their own thinking and the situation they wish to address. Groups seeking to work together in some broad arena may not identify a common basis for doing so effectively. Sometimes groups can't even agree on what they would like to accomplish, much less how to go about accomplishing it. At other times, their efforts may not resonate with the people and organizations they are trying to influence. A similar problem arises when people reactively base their interpretation on some prior, and frequently unconscious, bias or stereotype, a fact that is consciously exploited through deceptive use of language. In all of these cases, a poor understanding of strategic frames hinders the ability of people to make progress in their pursuits.

Context   This pattern can be used whenever people and groups need to interpret complex information or develop approaches to communicating with other groups or the public.

Discussion   People all over the world are confronted with events and information that they find overwhelming. Without frames, they quite literally would not know how to make sense out of what their senses provide. Frames provide the connection between information and data and the way that the information and data are interpreted. In other words, frames of one sort or another are necessary for every aspect of daily life. Human brains lack the processing power to interpret each new situation from scratch.

Social psychologists, linguists, political scientists, and others routinely use the concept of frames and framing to help understand how people interpret information. Social scientists and neuroscientists are now recognizing that the context or framing of a event has a major effect on how it is interpreted and, hence, what course of action or inaction is pursued (De Martino et al., 2006). Frames are apparently an economical way for the brain to process large amounts of information quickly, a skill undoubtedly linked to human survival. A frame is deeply connected to cognition in individuals and is helpful in understanding other social phenomenon (such as learning) as well.

The concept of frames was developed by anthropologist Gregory Bateson (1972) and was popularized by sociologist Erving Goffman (1974). More recently, based on the work of George Lakoff (2004), a linguist at the University of California at Berkeley, framing has taken a prominent position in progressive political discourse. On a general level, a frame in a social or political sense is a story distilled to its basic elements. It could be related to the family, father as protector, fairness, fatalism, laziness, freedom, a favored football team, nostalgia for the past, or fear of the unknown. The possibilities are limitless.

Recognizing the ubiquity of frames and the fact that different frames can be employed by different people for different reasons to describe the same story or event has led to a strong interest in frames and *framing*, the conscious act of characterizing a situation, event, or idea by specific frames that help encourage the interpretations that the framer desires.

How do frames work? When a person selects a frame (usually subconsciously), other aspects of that frame are automatically called into play. Labeling a person an "illegal immigrant," for example, causes connotations to arise that the term "refugee" would not. Framing the person in that way places the focus on that person and his or her "illegality," not, for example, on the societal forces that caused him or her to leave home.

Although political and economic elites and mass media are the major users of frames, the framing lens can and ought to be turned around and focused upward as well. Mass media systems are the primary purveyors of frames, and their choice of frames can have important consequences. The use of frames by journalists can be conscious or unconscious; conscious use can suggest manipulation, while unconscious use may reveal fatigue, laziness, or a lack of understanding of the subject. A "strategic communication terms" Web site (Tamatsu 2007) refers to an example from Charlotte Ryan's *Prime Time Activism* (1991) that illustrates multiple ways in which an incident of a child in a low-income neighborhood who was repeatedly bitten by rats could be covered by the local television news stations. Because frames shape interpretation, they also contain implications for what types of action are acceptable responses. Who, for example, should be held responsible for this unfortunate occurrence? Is the child's mother the culprit, or should the apartment manger, the government heath department, or even society at large be reprimanded?

A strategic frame is a specific type of frame that has been developed as an important element within an overall strategy to encourage people to see things in a certain way. In this sense, the concept is neutral. In fact Susan Niall Bales (Mooney 2003) stated that her approach to "strategic frame analysis" could be used to promote tobacco use, but added that she probably wouldn't consent to help with that effort.

When frames are shared with people or organizations, they promote group action and similar interpretations while acting to discourage disputes and incompatible interpretations. When developed collaboratively, a strategic frame can be a useful tool for groups. Keck and Sikkink (1998) illustrate the potential of frames to bring together disparate groups under one coalescing concept. The unifying theme of opposing violence against women became an important frame in the 1995 United Nations Conference on Women in Beijing.

When people respond without reflection to an externally imposed strategic frame, they are being exploited. Different frames can be constructed for any given story, message, or event. How well those frames resonate with people and what they choose to do with the ideas contained within the frame is of interest to people who are trying to influence others. Opposing forces employ different frames with different people to win the particular battle they are engaged in. This is reflected in a *New York Times* article entitled, "Framing Wars" (Bai 2005). Unfortunately many strategic frames that are available to the public serve to reinforce existing stereotypes, thus preventing people from developing effective agendas for the future. Frames allow people to quickly assess a situation, but they can also allow people to quickly assess a situation incorrectly. Unfortunately, too, the new evaluation, although easily and painlessly obtained, is not as readily abandoned. Strategic frames work in two directions: they can channel progressive action but can also constrict and distort thought.

When frames are acknowledged as independent entities, people who are interested in persuasion can begin asking such questions as: What frames do people use? How are they initially constructed or modified? What is the outcome when two or more frames compete? When does it make sense to create new frames? How does one know when people are trying to manipulate you using frames or if the frames you use are impeding creative thought?

Solution Although frames are powerful, they are not destiny. The first step toward changing frames is understanding the frames that influence our actions and behavior. Activists are interested in identifying and in some cases creating frames that have specific functions of interest. These strategic frames help build coalitions, provide useful interpretations, and promote useful transformations from one set of interpretations to another (Tarrow 2005). New frames are typically bridged from the old ones. In other words, the new frames must not reach too far beyond the capability of people to grasp and shape them.

Linked patterns Civic Intelligence (1), Social Responsibility (8), Matrifocal Orientation (9), Memory and Responsibility (11), Working-Class Consciousness (12), Back to the Roots (13), Big-Picture Health Information (27), Community Currencies (63), Academic Technology Investments (81), The Power of Story (114).

Problem   Human values and ethical considerations no longer stand apart from the design and development of information and communication systems. This shift reflects, at least in part, the increasing impact and visibility that information and communication technologies have had on human lives. Computer viruses have destroyed data on millions of machines. Large linked medical databases can, and often do, infringe on individuals' privacy. The fair outcome of the national elections may hinge in part on the design and management of computerized election ballots. On and on, the media portray such problems. In turn, software engineers, designers, and developers must engage not only the technical aspects of their designs but the value and ethical dimensions as well. Yet how should they do so? What theories, methods, tools, and techniques might they bring to this challenge?

Context   Values are at play in all phases of envisioning, designing, developing, implementing, deploying, appropriating, and ongoing reappropriation and reinvention of computer and information technology. In all these activities, there exists the need for explicit consideration of values, value tensions, and value trade-offs. The Value-Sensitive Design pattern can be used throughout all of these phases. Moreover, it is expected that value-sensitive design will be used in conjunction with other successful methodologies (such as participatory design, systematic debugging and testing practices, and rapid prototyping) and with a variety of practitioners, including software engineers, usability engineers, interaction designers, information solution professionals, and concerned direct and indirect stakeholders.

Discussion

That technology itself determines what is to be done by a process of extrapolation and that individuals are powerless to intervene in that determination is precisely the kind of self-fulfilling dream from which we must awaken.... I do not say that systems such as I have mentioned [gigantic computer systems, computer networks, and speech recognition systems] are necessarily evil—only that they may be and, what is most important, that their inevitability cannot be accepted by individuals claiming autonomy, freedom, and dignity. The individual computer scientist can and must decide. The determination of what the impact of computers on society is to be is, at least in part, in his hands.... It is possible, given courage and insight, for man to deny technology the prerogative to formulate man's questions. It is possible to ask human questions and to find humane answers. (Weizenbaum 1972, 614)

Heeding the call of computer scientists like Joseph Weizenbaum and cyberneticist Norbert Wiener before him, the emerging field of value-sensitive design seeks to design technology that accounts for human values in a principled and comprehensive manner throughout the design process (Friedman 1997; Friedman and Kahn 2003; Friedman, Kahn, and Borning 2006). Value-sensitive design is primarily concerned with values that center on human well-being, human dignity, justice, welfare, and human rights. This approach is principled in that it maintains that such values have moral standing independent of whether a particular person or group upholds such values (e.g., the belief in and practice of slavery by a certain group does not a priori mean that slavery is a morally acceptable practice). At the same time, value-sensitive design maintains that how such values play out in a particular culture at a particular point in time can vary, sometimes considerably.

Value-sensitive design articulates an interactional position for how values become implicated in technological designs. An interactional position holds that while the features or properties that people design into technologies more readily support certain values and hinder others, the technology's actual use depends on the goals of the people interacting with it. A screwdriver, after all, is well suited for turning screws, and yet amenable as a poker, pry bar, nail set, cutting device, and tool to dig up weeds. Moreover, through human interaction, technology itself changes over time. On occasion, such changes can mean the societal rejection of a technology or that its acceptance is delayed. But more often, it entails an iterative process whereby technologies are invented and then redesigned based on user interactions, which then are reintroduced to users, further interactions occur, and further redesigns implemented.

To date, value-sensitive design has been used in a wide range of research and design contexts, including an investigation of bias in computer systems (Friedman and Nissenbaum, in Friedman 1997), universal access within a communications company (Thomas, in Friedman 1997), Internet privacy (Ackerman and Cranor 1999), informed consent for online interactions (Friedman, Howe, and Felten 2002), ubiquitous sensing of the environment and individual rights (Abowd and Jacobs 2001), computer simulation in support of democratization of the urban planning process (Borning, Friedman, Davis, and Lin 2005), social and moral aspects of human-robotic interaction (Kahn, Freier, Friedman, Severson, and Feldman 2004), privacy in public (Friedman, Kahn, Hagman, Severson, and Gill 2006), value analyses in reflective design (Senger, Boehner, David, and Kaye 2005), and the place of designer values in the design process (Flanagan, Howe, and Nissenbaum 2005).

Methodologically, at the core of value-sensitive design lies an iterative process that integrates conceptual, empirical, and technical investigations. Conceptual investigations involve philosophically informed analyses of the central constructs and issues under investigation. Questions include: How are values supported or diminished by particular technological designs? Who is affected? How should we engage in trade-offs among competing values in the design, implementation, and use of information systems? Empirical investigations involve both social-scientific research on the understandings, contexts, and experiences of the people affected by the technological designs, as well as the development of relevant laws, policies, and regulations. Technical investigations involve analyzing current technical mechanisms and designs to assess how well they support particular values, and, conversely, identifying values, and then identifying or developing technical mechanisms and designs that can support those values.

How then to practice value-sensitive design? Some suggestions follow (see also Friedman, Kahn, and Borning 2006):

• Start with a value, technology, or context of use. Any of these three core aspects easily motivates value-sensitive design. Begin with the aspect that is most central to your work and interests.

• Identify direct and indirect stakeholders. Direct stakeholders are those who interact directly with the technology or with the technology's output; indirect stakeholders are those who are also affected by the system, though they never interact directly with it.

• Identify harms and benefits for each stakeholder group. Systematically identify how each category of direct and indirect stakeholder would be positively or negatively affected by the technology under consideration.

• Map harms and benefits onto corresponding values. At times the mapping between harms and benefits and corresponding values will be one of identity; at other times the mapping will be multifaceted (that is, a single harm might implicate multiple values, such as both security and autonomy).

• Conduct a conceptual investigation of key values. Develop careful working definitions for each of the key values. Drawing on the philosophical literature can be helpful here.

• Identify potential value conflicts. For the purposes of design, value conflicts should usually not be conceived of as either-or situations but as constraints on the design space. Typical value conflicts include accountability versus privacy, trust versus security, environmental sustainability versus economic development, privacy versus security, and hierarchical control versus democratization.

• Technical investigation heuristic: value conflicts. Technical mechanisms will often adjudicate multiple, if not conflicting, values, often in the form of design trade-offs. It may be helpful to make explicit how a design trade-off maps onto a value conflict and differentially affects different groups of stakeholders.

• Technical investigation heuristic: unanticipated consequences and value conflicts. In order to be positioned to respond with agility to unanticipated consequences and value conflicts, when possible, design flexibility into the underlying technical architecture to support post-deployment modifications.

Solution   Human values and ethical considerations are fundamentally part of design practice. Value-sensitive design offers one viable principled approach to systematically considering human values throughout the design and deployment of information and other technologies. Through its theory and methods, value-sensitive design asks that we extend the traditional criteria (e.g., reliability, correctness) by which we judge the quality of systems to include those of human values.

Linked patterns   Ethics of Community Informatics (67), Equal Access to Justice (69), Positive Health Information (74), Wholesome Design for Wicked Problems (82), Voices of the Unheard (83), Future Design (88).

Problem   By acting as though the future will never arrive and things never change, we are subconsciously creating the future with the seeds that we are unwittingly sowing today. Whether by actively embracing the conventional wisdom that has created these socially and environmentally precarious times or by succumbing to the dictates of habit, instinct, or necessity, humankind seems to sleepwalking into the future. Indeed it is quite plausible that we are creating the ideal conditions today for unspeakable disasters tomorrow.

Context   This pattern can be used in unlimited situations, especially when people feel strongly that the directions they are following are not the ones that they think they should. Employing this pattern often takes the form of a collaborative envisioning exercise with a variety of stakeholders.

Discussion   Looking at the future with open, imaginative, and critical eyes can open up the possibility of, if not the demand for, fundamental social change. After all, why would anybody bother to contemplate the future if there were no possibility of change, if every step taken was an echo of some past step?

The purpose of this pattern is to get people actively engaged envisioning better futures and making plans on how to get there. Through rehearsing for the future, we can create a wealth of possible scenarios that could become the positive self-fulfilling prophecies of tomorrow rather than the violent and exploitive scenarios that seem to rule today.

Educational settings are not the only setting for introducing and advancing a rich future-oriented agenda, but they may be the best. Unfortunately, current educational practices seem to be oblivious to the future. Schools present topics such as mathematics or science with no historical context. History, though based on human events, becomes an authoritative recounting of past facts, while the future is a mere abstraction (Slaughter and Beare 1993). And since everything seemingly and inexorably unfolded in an inevitable way, the sequence of human events appears largely unalterable.

One failing of an educational approach that is not oriented to the future is the lack of inquiry into the causes of the world's problems (Slaughter and Beare 1993). Nor is there any effort to develop or consider theories or strategies that could help alleviate these problems. Beyond a cursory look at history, where the impact of people who are not elites is never evident, many people worldwide live in an eternal now, a temporal cocoon that cultivates amnesia of the past and ill preparedness for the future. Both elites and ordinary people seem unwilling to acknowledge that they have roles in shaping the future. Forgetting that fact in the face of immense twenty-first-century challenges strips humankind of its fundamental capacity to consciously make plans (Slaughter and Beare 1993).

Future design helps surface the internal models of the future that have been ignored, repressed, or deliberately kept from view and attempts to understand how they play out and how they came to be. At the same time, and somewhat independently, future design builds new models that help liberate us from dangerous inertia and help us be more effective in our thinking about and acting on the future.

There is an endless variety of exercises, games, workshops, and other activities that we are calling "future design." Many of these could be organized and convened in just about any setting. Lori Blewett and Douglas Schuler recently used a "Design a Society" workshop to organize a large team project in the Global Citizenship program at the Evergreen State College. Schools, of course, should not be the only place where future design can be pursued. Future design activities are needed that could be done individually (and, shared), on the job (government, nongovernmental organizations, businesses, and others), with activists, and as broad-based, possibly phased, longer-termed projects, with or without government involvement and support.

Open Space Seattle 2100, a project that seeks to develop a "comprehensive open space network vision for Seattle's next 100 years," contains elements (including the need for participants and resources, even if it is just time) that could be considered typical of future design activities. Since the Seattle plan is ambitious, it requires broad support and ample resources. The University of Washington and the City of Seattle are key players, as are a variety of environmental, civic, neighborhood, professional, and other groups. Many of the future design projects that have civic goals are participatory and inclusive. At the same time that the community is developing a collective vision, the organizers also aim "to catalyze a long-term advocacy coalition and planning process for Seattle's integrated open space."

The Seattle project consciously invokes the work of the Olmsted brothers, the visionary park and landscape designers whose work include New York's Central Park as well as Volunteer Park in Seattle, in the early 1990s that greatly contributed to Seattle's livability. The time line for this project, which is longer than standard planning horizons, frees participants from a variety of constraints on their thinking. By encouraging people to think beyond what can be done in a fairly short time horizon, they are more likely to be creative. Still, if the time frame is too far in the future, participants are likely to feel detached from the enterprise. The Seattle project gets around this by including tasks for the short term as well as visions for the long term.

In order to strike a balance between the real and the imagined, those working on future design projects must provide a structure for less-structured activities to take place within. The projects must provide prompts (for example, scenarios, instructions, and props) that encourage people to imagine a future without forcing them down certain paths. Since people cannot simply be instructed to be creative, these prompts are used to promote futures thinking among the participants. This pattern can be used in many settings, but research has shown that future design needs a supportive atmosphere, and, as open space technology literature suggests (Owen 1997), participants need to have passion, commitment, and an open mind. A broad spectrum of community groups needs to be represented, or at least recognized, or the outcome can reaffirm prejudices and help perpetuate old conflicts.

Future design processes often provide a variety of participatory opportunities. The seven- to ten-person teams that addressed open space issues in one of the neighborhoods outlined on the Seattle Charrette Map are key to the effort but organizers have organized a lecture series and a blog (http://open2100.blogspot.com) to encourage alternative ways to participate.

Massive challenges await this undertaking at every turn. How effective is future design? How do games and other future design approaches translate into action? How do future designers from one group build on the results of others? Interestingly a project whose recommendations are not implemented can still be a success. Margaret Keck (2002) describes the Solução Integrada (Integrated Solution), a plan for sewage treatment and environmental restoration in Brazil; although the government shelved it, it lived on in the public's eye as an example of sensible large-scale solution in the face of ill-conceived projects. Success must be judged in a variety of ways, and this includes the inclusivity and richness of the future design process, its immediate impacts, and its indirect contributions to the overall imagination and civic culture of a community.

Finally, as the e-mail tagline of cyberspace pioneer John Perry Barlow reminds us: "Man plans, God laughs." Human history is full of twists, enlightened and macabre, tragic and heroic. The future is unlikely to come out the way we think it will or want it to, but that should not prevent us from trying to work toward the goal of a more just and healthy future.

Solution   Develop participatory activities that address four major objectives: (1) develop visions of the future and ideas about how to achieve them; (2) bring into the light and critically analyze the current models of the future that people, society, and institutions are employing, both explicitly and implicitly; (3) help instill feelings of empowerment, compassion, hope, and courage in futures thinking and action; and (4) cultivate humility in regard to the unknowability of the future and the limits to human reason and understanding.

Linked patterns   Public Agenda (30), Participatory Design (36), Mobile Intelligence (38), Design Stance (44), Citizen Access to Simulations (48), Positive Health Information (74), Grassroots Public Policy Development (78), Wholesome Design for Wicked Problems (82), Value-Sensitive Design (87), Experimental School (89), Mirror Institutions (94), Labor Visions (112), Environmental Impact Remediation (124), Retreat and Reflection (136).

Problem Schools can become institutionalized and unresponsive to the real needs of their students, the community, or even society at large. Schools with static and immutable assumptions and values are unlikely to meet society's changing needs. This is particularly unfortunate at a time when the need for public problem solving is the most acute. If schools are not innovative and people do not seriously think about how education can play new roles in new ways, it is unlikely that the society will be innovative in cultural, technical, scientific, or civic thought or action. Schools also tend to assist privileged subsets of society. Typically older people cannot attend school, nor can poor people, working people, or rural people. Many colleges and universities (at least in the United States) are more becoming commercially oriented, thus promoting economic aggrandizement of individuals and corporations while ignoring the common good.

Context This pattern applies to any situation where education or some type of schooling is necessary. It has almost universal coverage because learning is a universal phenomenon. Humans are built for learning.

Discussion For this pattern, we can define an experimental school as one that broadly attempts to accomplish certain aims (such as social and environmental amelioration) while adopting experimentation as an abiding and guiding orientation. This implies that the school is not perfect, and it affirms that the school will at least try to adapt to changing societal circumstances and needs, all while maintaining its values. Moreover, it will work toward its goals through a thoughtful experimentation that involves careful and ongoing evaluation of the approaches that the school is trying.

School, according to John Dewey, should be an experiment in collective action, and it should break down walls between academia and practical work. Although this pattern is quite broad and actually contains several patterns in their own right, several themes or trajectories stand out that support Dewey's contentions, whether the student is ten years old or eighty and whether the student is classically educated or illiterate. Adopting an experimental orientation reflects a belief in meliorism—that things can improve through directed effort —and an acknowledgment that nothing is perfect; the need for adjustment is an unavoidable and normal fact of life. Beyond that, the general orientation is compassionate engagement and integration with the world. In a general and nondogmatic way, an experimental school would be concerned with the common good and would stress solidarity and activism. It would be much more permeable. The boundaries between the institution, between teacher and student, between theory and practice, and between the academic disciplines themselves and the disciplines and the other systems of knowing that people have devised would all be less distinct and more forgiving. In addition, there would be more variety as to when and where the educational setting would be and who was eligible to take part. Costs would be as

Table 8.1

Experimental and Traditional Educational Models

	University model	Experimental school
Site	Centralized, stationary, and formal	Various locations, movable, informal
Student body	Elite, all same age	Open to anybody, life-long learning; mixed classes
Assessment	Defined by faculty; consists of tests, grades	Self-assessed by student as well as by faculty member through oral and written narrative evaluation
Curriculum	University directed, discipline based; disciplines kept separate	Student directed; inquiry based; discipline boundaries blurred and broached
Role of teacher and role of student	Authoritative (teacher) and receptive (student)	Teachers and students are both colearners
Costs	Expensive for middle- and lower-income people	Free
Instruction mode	Lecture	Peripatetic, seminar, group work
Credential granting	Often the most important reason for attending	Does not necessarily grant credentials; learning is primary
Focus	Individual focused	Group or community focused
Goals	Learning facts, getting degree	Learning how to learn, thinking across the curriculum
Faculty	Credentialed with Ph.D.	Knowledge, skill, values, commitment, and values as important as credentials
When	Two semesters or three quarters per year (no summer classes); established beginning and end dates for unit of time, weekdays, 9:00 to 5:00	Weekdays, evenings, or any other time
Theory and practice	Kept separate ("practice is for trade schools")	Integrated

low as possible to encourage everybody to attend. Education is not just for some small segment of the population who are destined for power, prestige, and money.

Table 8.1, admittedly overgeneralized, highlights some of the ways in which a typical university can be contrasted with an experimental school.

Walter Parker (2004) believes that "idiocy is the scourge of our time and place." Idiocy was defined by the ancient Greeks to mean the state of being "concerned myopically with private things and unmindful of common things." Idiots are like rudderless ships that are not grounded in the local or the global community. Unable to see beyond their parochial interests, they are likely to do damage to themselves and the communities in which they live. In his consideration of how idiots come about their idiocy, Parker asks whether our public "schools marshal their human and material resources to produce idiots or citizens? Does the school curriculum, both by commission and omission, cultivate private vices or public virtues?"

Parker proposes several important remedies: "First, increase the variety and frequency of interaction among students who are culturally, linguistically, and racially different from one another. Second, orchestrate these contacts so that competent public talk—deliberation about common problems—is fostered. In schools, this is talk about two kinds of problems: social and academic. Social problems arise inevitably from the friction of interaction itself (Dewey's 'problems of living together'), and academic problems are at the core of each subject area. Third, clarify the distinction between deliberation and blather and between open (inclusive) and closed (exclusive) deliberation. In other words, expect, teach, and model competent, inclusive deliberation."

It is also important for students to take some responsibility and interest in their own education early. People with these attitudes and capabilities can undertake their own ongoing education (even in the absence of schools and teachers) and work with others to get them involved. One of the best ways to do this and help install the sense that the student is part of the process is self-assessment of learning at all levels.

If the point of evaluating students' work were only to rank them, give faculty a lever for encouraging their efforts, or even describe the strengths and weaknesses of what they had produced, then it would seem clear that teachers should do it by themselves. The deepest reasons for asking students to formally assess their own work pertain to the students' development over the long run. For one thing, the student may have learned some things that are relevant to learning that the teachers do not know about. If students have learned how to write a paper without agonizing over the first paragraph for hours, or pay a new kind of attention to the clouds when they go for a walk, or think about the late Roman Republic when they read the newspaper, these changes may say more about their education in literature or physics or history than their essays or exams do yet be invisible to the teachers.

The practice of self-assessment is a central way for students to acquire the reflective habits of mind essential to their ongoing capacities to do good work and improve their work over time. Growth in intelligence, or thinking, is precisely growth in the capacity for ongoing reflective self-assessment. This point is the center of Dewey's analysis of the difference between mere activity and educational experience in *Democracy and Education* (1916): "Thinking ... is the intentional endeavor to discover specific connections between something which we do and the consequences which result, so that the two become continuous."

But formal education is considered complete at a certain age. Does this mean that people who have missed this one chance or are otherwise interested in additional education are simply out of luck? Popular education, developed in the 1960s and 1970s by the Brazilian educator Paulo Freire, helps to answer that question positively. Popular education is a nontraditional method of education that strives for the empowerment of adults through democratically structured cooperative study and action. It is carried out within a political vision that sees women and men at the community and grassroots level as the primary agents for social change. It aims to enable ordinary people to define their own struggles and critically examine and learn from the lessons of past struggles and from concrete everyday situations in the present. It is a deeply democratic process, equipping communities to name and create their vision of the future for which they struggle.

The popular education process begins by critically reflecting on, sharing, and articulating with a group or community what is known from lived experience. It continues with analysis and critical reflection on reality aimed at enabling people to discover solutions to their own problems and set in motion concrete actions for the transformation of that reality. In Freire's model, the teacher becomes a facilitator, the traditional class becomes a cultural circle, the emphasis shifts from lecture to problem-posing strategies, and the content, previously removed from the learners' experience, becomes relevant to the group.

Popular education has always had an intimate connection to organizing for social change. In the early 1960s, Freire began his work in this area by using the principles of dialogue and critical consciousness raising, fundamental to popular education: teach literacy to peasants struggling for land reform in Brazil. He argued that action was the source of knowledge, not the reverse, and that education, to be transformative, involved a process of dialogue based on action and reflection on action.

Although starting a new, or supporting an existing, experimental school might be the best use of this pattern, the concepts of an experimental school can be useful to anybody who is establishing new programs in a traditional school or involved in virtually any way in the education of themselves or anybody they know. The key concepts are respect for learning, reflection, and a faith in the importance of reasoning, and especially, reasoning together.

Solution   Integrate the ideas from this pattern into educational settings that exist or can exist. We can think about how we think and we can learn about how we learn.

Linked patterns   Education and Values (17), Teaching to Transgress (20), Peace Education (56), Open Access Scholarly Publishing (76), Future Design (88), Mirror Institutions (94), Informal Learning Groups (98), Engaged Tourism (107), Control of Self-Representation (109), Thinking Communities (118).

Problem   The people who are the most affected by the digital divide typically need to have access to information from nonprofit organizations. However, many nonprofit organizations do not have the time, personnel, or skills to create and maintain Web sites. Thus, the service-oriented information that lower-income community members need the most is often not online. In addition, many lower-income community members lack the skills necessary to use Web sites effectively. Finally, data supporting the local impact of the digital divide are often insufficient or even nonexistent.

Context   This problem has a unique solution in regions surrounding college campuses with service-learning programs.

Discussion   The groups most likely to be on the wrong side of the digital divide are, paradoxically, the groups that need access to basic service-related information the most. Quite often members of these groups also lack the skills needed to use the Internet effectively. In addition, nonprofit organizations often have the information that these groups need but, paradoxically, are unable to make this information available online. The needs of both groups are in conflict and create a context in which it is extremely difficult for either group's needs to be met.

The groups without access to computers need:

- Easily accessible and up-to-date information
- Information and communication with service providers
- Online resources with intuitive navigation systems and appealing design
- Training

For their part, nonprofit organizations need or lack:

- Personnel to put information online while still meeting clients' needs
- Additional time to create and maintain Web pages
- Knowledge and skill to create effective Web sites
- Funds to pay for server space or a Webmaster

One possible solution is for the nonprofits to rely on volunteers from the community to create and maintain Web sites. However, relying on volunteer labor for Web sites is risky due to the turnover rate and varying skill levels of volunteers. What is needed is a pool of skilled but cost-free assistance.

One place to find this pool is on college campuses with service-learning programs. Service-learning is a pedagogical method designed to link course content with external experiences. Students learn the course-related materials through traditional learning in the classroom and through practical projects in and with the community, as well as about the reality and significance of the social issues that the community faces, while simultaneously providing a service to the community by meeting specific needs of the agencies or the populations with which they work.

A service-learning class intentionally links the content of the course to a relevant nonprofit's goals. Students benefit from the chance to apply their skills to a real problem and learn about the needs of the community; the nonprofits benefit from the chance to have some of their goals and needs met and to influence the next generation of leaders (Campus Compact 2003). In the long run, research has shown that students who take part in service-learning courses feel a greater sense of connection to their local communities, as well as an understanding of their interdependence with their neighbors (Jacoby 1996). Connection and interdependence are building blocks of responsibility, and responsible citizens are in turn the building blocks of strong communities.

The initiative for a service-learning course can come from a number of different places. Individual professors can choose to use this pedagogical method in their courses, universities may require service-learning in certain classes, or community agencies may propose projects that fit with the learning objectives of a class. Regardless of the source, effective service-learning requires collaboration between the members of the community and the academic institution; it should be done with the community, not on the community. The goals and needs of the community must be combined with the goals and needs of the course. This process of collaboration is often facilitated by offices on the campus specifically designated to assist with service-learning (Appalachian and the Community Together).

The service can take one of three forms:

Direct service   Students work with the community members served by local agencies. In the case of the digital divide, students in a wide range of courses could train local community members to access and evaluate online information. This training could be done at the local library, senior centers, retirement homes, elementary schools, and any other locations with the necessary facilities (connected computers).

Indirect service   Students work with local community agencies to provide them with some needed assistance, which indirectly benefits their clients. In the case of the digital divide, students in Web design courses can be required to create or update Web sites for local nonprofits or run workshops training agencies representatives to maintain their own sites.

Community-based research   Students (with faculty support) conduct research for and with a local community agency. In the case of the digital divide, people trying to change the existing systems sometimes lack the hard evidence needed to prove that a problem exists. Students in a wide range of research-methods courses could conduct survey research into the impact of the digital divide at the local level.

Most important, the impact of a service-learning course goes beyond the immediate project: it results in changed lives. This is because a critical component of any service-learning course is reflection. Research shows that we do not really learning anything from experience (we often make the same mistakes repeatedly); we learn from thinking about our experiences (Speck and Hoppe 2004). Students in service-learning courses are required to reflect on their experience in rigorous, thoughtful, and evaluated ways. This process drives the learning home, increasing the integration of knowledge they have gained in the course with the way they live their lives in the future. For example, to create Web sites, students must understand the agency, which means they must research the role that the nonprofit plays in the community, the populations that it serves, and the social issues that underlie its mission. This research helps students understand how critical access to the right information is for everyone and how information is always related to power. Putting students in contact with members of the local community can also help dispel stereotypes. Students' easy access to computers often leads them to mistakenly believe that the digital divide is just a "Mercedes divide." Requiring students to work with underfunded and understaffed nonprofit agencies, which are themselves working with disadvantaged groups, can open their eyes to the informational needs in the communities in which they live.

Solution   Service-learning provides a way to use the resources of a college or university to meet community needs, such as designing Web sites for nonprofits or training community members to effectively access and evaluate information online. Students can create valuable resources for the community while simultaneously becoming more aware of the social issues in that community. This ensures that once people are able to cross the digital divide, they will find the information that they need, and not just more places to shop. This also creates the possibility for the next generation of leaders to have a better understanding of the information needs of their local community.

Linked patterns   Global Citizenship (6), Social Responsibility (8), Education and Values (17), Teaching to Transgress (20), Media Literacy (35), Mutual Help Medical Web Sites (54), Informal Learning Groups (98), Engaged Tourism (107), Community Inquiry (122).

Problem   For democracy in a complex society to work well, journalism is necessary. Citizens need information about the political, economic, and cultural systems that structure their lives in order to act on them effectively. However, traditional news institutions have had major failures in their ability to adequately cover news.

Context   Distributed information on the Web opens new possibilities for citizen information. Some say that we are at the "beginning of a golden age of journalism" in which the online audience, "armed with easy-to-use Web publishing tools, always-on connections and increasingly powerful mobile devices, has the means to become an active participant in the creation and dissemination of news and information" (Bowman and Willis 2003). Other observers claim we are in the midst of navigation from older forms of fact-oriented reporting to opinion journalism. This pattern would be interesting to any citizen who reads journalism or is interested in writing journalism, and organizations that want to participate more actively in the news stream. The Web is the most active site for citizen journalism and can cover local communities or communities of interest worldwide.

Discussion   The magnitude of and interest in citizen journalism is quite new, although forms of it have existed through much of modern history. The pamphleteers of the American Revolution were, in their way, citizen journalists. Many of the newspapers that cropped up in the nineteenth century were started by nonprofessionals who saw a need in local communities and began publishing a mix of news, advertising, and gossip. Newspapers were professionalized in the twentieth century, leading to a relatively independent corps of journalists oriented to fact-based objective reporting. But professionalization also discounted the underlying truth claims on one side or another and led to a decline of independent judgment and, sometimes, support for the status quo.

Beginning in the 1990s, public or civic journalism constituted a major reaction to this state of affairs. The movement grew from the principle that while news organizations could and should remain independent in judging particular disputes and advancing solutions to problems, they ought not to remain neutral on democracy and civic life itself. About a fifth of all American newspapers and some television stations experimented with civic journalism from the early 1990s to the early 2000s, but other pressures subverted it.

By the mid-1990s, the Web began to offer a different alternative. Blogging offered new networks of opinion writing, as well as criticism of traditional media outlets. Some considered it journalism, others editorializing or soapboxing. But what was clear was that the new writing could carve out its own space of attention on the Web (although it remained largely dependent on the reporting of the mainstream media).

Citizen journalism as a distinct movement emerged in early 2000s. Journalists like Dan Gilmor left the *San Jose Mercury News* to start Bayosphere, an independent journalism blog.

At the same time, political blogs grew rapidly in number and influence on both the left and right sides of the political spectrum.

The emerging practices of citizen journalism run the gamut from new forms of audience participation in traditional media to citizen expression in the blogosphere. In terms of content, they alternate fact-oriented reporting of locally based participants in the context of a global network to self-expression of opinion. What defines citizen journalism, then, is not specific content, a given business model, or a form of reporting. Rather, it is a networked structure of storytelling based on openness of information, horizontal linkage structures rather than vertical flows of information, blurring lines between content production and consumption, and diffused accountability based on reputation and meaning rather than on structural system hierarchies.

One of the best examples of a mainstream media institution practicing citizen journalism is the *Spokane Spokesman Review*, which systematically incorporates the views of Spokane's citizens in every aspect of its reporting, from hard news to sports. The *Review* has even put its morning news meeting on the Web.

Another strand of citizen journalism is a hybrid in which professional and citizens interact in the production process. The exemplar in this realm is *Ohmy News* from South Korea whose motto is, "Every Citizen Is a Reporter." *Ohmy News* has a paid editing and reporting staff that works on more than 200 daily submissions from citizens. More than 40,000 citizens overall have contributed to the site. U.S. sites like the *Twin Cities Daily Planet* and the *Voice of San Diego* are seeking to replicate its success, and *Ohmy News* is investing in its international site. In 2006 Jay Rosen (2006b) in *PressThink* proposed *New Assignment,* a hybrid model in which citizens will submit issues and topics they want to see reported on, and professional editors will pursue the story along with citizen journalists.

The Madison Commons project in Wisconsin has developed another type of hybrid model. It trains citizens to do neighborhood reporting and gathers reporting from mainstream media aggregates it on a local Web site. Another good example of academic-citizen partnerships is represented by Mymissourian, in which journalism students serve as editors for citizen journalists.

Finally, the blogosphere emerges as a massive example of citizen journalism as part of a large conversation that either makes or comments on the news. Of course blogs—their content, their significance, and recognition—vary widely, from general blogs of professional journalists like Gillmor's to pundits on the left and right, to community-level aggregators to more personal expressions (e.g., http://www.baristanet.com/).

Citizen journalism allows anyone who wants to contribute to public debate as an active participant. There are a number of relevant motives: the intrinsic enjoyment of interviewing, reporting, and writing; the civic rewards of contributing informed knowledge to a larger public discussion and debate; and the reward of building an alternative institution, whether local news alternative or worldwide public.

First, citizen journalism offers the ability to collaborate to make many small contributions to what is essentially an ongoing conversation among many people, most of whom know each other only through the common project. Second, the so-called wisdom of crowds holds that many people know more than a few, that even experts have only limited knowledge, and that a broad, open domain with many contributors will produce useful and valid knowledge.

Third, and closely related to these, is the idea of "the people formerly known as the audience" (Gillmor 2004, Rosen 2006a). This is to say that the audience for news media (media in general) is no longer passive. Rather it is an active group that will respond in a continuum to the news, ranging from simple active reading, linking and sending stories to friends by e-mail and lists, and commenting on stories, to contributing factual knowledge that can flesh out or correct a story, to actual writing as citizen journalists. Across all these levels of activity, citizens become more engaged with their communities.

An active and engaged citizenry can expand the range of topics discussed and improve the quality and extent of information about any given issue by opening it up to anyone. Citizen journalism creates the possibility for civic action to be deliberative instead of hierarchical. By participating directly in the production and dissemination of journalism, citizens help, even in small ways, to set the news agenda.

Alternatives to citizen journalism such as face-to-face community-level deliberation exercises and electronic dialogues are important and complementary to citizen journalism, but they lack the fact-based component that is critical to democracy and should not be solely in the hands of traditional media.

For citizens to use this pattern, there are a number of things they can do. They can go to Web sites like www.j-lab.org to find out how to begin doing citizen journalism themselves and have access to many tools and examples. The best overall resource for thinking about citizen journalism is Press Think, which links many layers of citizen journalists, mostly in the United States. Those interested in the international movement can go to Ohmy News International or Wikinews. There are also Web resources such as the News University, which was originally conceived to enhance the training of journalists but can also improve the journalistic skills of citizens.

There are three main challenges to citizen journalism: sustainability, inclusion, and traditional journalism. Probably the biggest challenge to doing citizen journalism is sustaining a distributed enterprise that requires time, attention, and skill from producers, contributors, and readers. A second challenge is to avoid ending up in many small communities of group monologue rather than in a broader community dialogue. And finally, citizen journalism may accelerate the erosion of traditional journalism without replacing it with a new model powerful enough to center attention on core social problems in a society that is already highly distracted.

Nevertheless, it appears that a pattern that brings together the networked discussion of citizens in the blogosphere with fact-oriented reporting will be a more fitting model to build a vibrant public sphere than the centralized and hierarchical model of the printed media and mass television that we have now (Maher 2005). Benkler (2006) has made a powerful argument that the baseline for our evaluation should be the mass media model that has, in many ways, failed to report on the most critical issues of our day, not an idealized model of citizen journalism. Further, for the foreseeable future, they will continue to complement each other, willingly or not.

Solution   Build new models of citizen journalism nationally, internationally, and locally to create new forms of reporting and public accountability. In local communities, build information commons to support the active learning and participation of citizens in changing the traditional media ecologies to ones that blend the best of citizen and traditional media. For individuals, learn new skills of reporting through the Web, and become an active reader, commenter, and contributor. The citizen journalism pattern is already being realized worldwide. It takes only a sufficient number of citizens with access to technology and an interest in some story. Citizen journalism is growing daily as the increasing number of projects worldwide and the expanding blogosphere attest. Whether it will continue to grow depends on the solutions posed by these projects to the challenges of sustainability and inclusion. Although it is early to assess the impact of citizen journalism, it would appear that in Korea, it has served to open the political spectrum and in the United States to redefine the news agenda. It remains to be seen whether and how citizen journalism can develop in nondemocratic countries. At least in theory, it could represent an important pathway in the development of a networked civil society that brings about democratization change.

Linked patterns   Civic Intelligence (1), The Commons (2), Teaching to Transgress (20), Cyberpower (25), Media Literacy (35), International Networks of Alternative Media (43), On-line Deliberation (52), Alternative Media in Hostile Environment (53), Community Networks (61), Media Diversity (66), Ethics of Community Informatics (67), Community-Building Journalism (97), Thinking Communities (118), Community Inquiry (122), Open Source Everything (127).

Problem   Supporting group interaction around a shared document is challenging for designers of two-dimensional interfaces and asynchronous, text-based groupware. The need to deliberate (collaborate, make decisions, or make comments) around documents appears to be one of the main reasons that groups that could otherwise interact virtually and asynchronously using the Internet choose to meet synchronously, either in person or online, often in a richer environment than text only (e.g., including audio, video, or a three-dimensional environment). When some or all stakeholders are unable to participate in synchronous meetings, distributed asynchronous interaction offers many advantages to groups deliberating about documents: more time for reflection, revision, and information seeking (cf. Holland and Stornetta 1992); the ability to accommodate people's conflicting schedules; flexible interaction modes through conversion of text to and from speech (e.g., for disabled or less literate users); the easier access, storage, and search afforded by digital archives; and the empowerment of those who are at a disadvantage when participation involves speaking in a live group (Price and Cappela 2002). But mapping in-person meetings onto an asynchronous interaction through distributed two-dimensional text displays entails several types of lost richness, including nonverbal grounding cues (Clark and Brennan 1991), spatial depth, the natural use of separate perceptual modalities for document (visual) and discussion (auditory), and the use of a shared temporal progression to guide attention.

Context   In our usage, a *document* can be in any format, including images, audio, and video, but our primary focus here is on digital documents in which most of the information is in text. Discussion that takes place around a document consists of comments that pertain to either the document as a whole or some part of it. The document may be fixed or evolving as the discussion around it proceeds, but the document assumes an elevated status over the comments made about it because, for example, it has been chosen for careful discussion, its final version will have governing consequences, or it will represent the outcome of a collaboration. In the latter cases, the group must somehow reach a decision relating to the document (e.g., whether to adopt it). This pattern focuses on interfaces for visually abled users. Adapting the analysis presented here for visually impaired users might be possible, but our feeling is that that will require quite a different approach, one we hope to investigate in the future.

Discussion   The projection of a three-dimensional, multimodality, co-located, synchronous deliberation experience (i.e., communicating face to face in a nonvirtual place) onto a two-dimensional, primarily visual, distributed asynchronous interaction requires essential aspects of face-to-face deliberation to be remapped onto a screen interface. The needed mappings can be judged according to two broad goals:

Visible relationships   Relationships between comments and the texts they reference, between different comments, and between group members and the document and discussion should be as visible as possible.

Distinguishable boundaries   Separations between contextually related and unrelated text and comments and between individual authors of documents and comments should be as distinguishable as possible.

We first consider visible relationships. Exhibiting relationships between the components of document-centered deliberation (document, comments, and participants) implies a number of refinements of this goal. First, the document text that is the target of deliberation should be covisible (displayed simultaneously) with comments around it, and the identities of comment authors and document text, when relevant, should also be covisible with their output. Second, the referencing relationship between a comment and its target text should be visible, that is, the interface should incorporate ostensive pointing (meaning that a pointing relationship is displayed on the screen rather than being enacted through a peripheral device) and in-text placement of comments. Third, response relationships between comments should be visible through threading. And fourth, the reactions of deliberation participants should be visible through polling and decision features.

The other goal is distinguishable boundaries. Visible relationships can be inadequate, as anyone would know who has used a map with ambiguous place labelings. The interface should also mark boundaries between text that is and is not the reference target of a comment, for example, though text highlighting. Text authored by different people at different times should be distinguishable through textual boundaries. The topic of a text should be able to be viewed separately from its main body through headers. And obsolete comments (those made on a previous version) should be recognizable through pertinence markers that indicate which versions a comment pertains to, as well as those to which it does not apply, for example, because it has been addressed in the revision process.

The Deme environment for online deliberation is a tool for document-centered discussion, polling, and decision making that incorporates all of the elements derived above in a dynamically updating (no-page-reload) interface. The introductory image shows the most recent design of the meeting area viewer in Deme. The shaded-in header of a comment in the discussion view pane on the right points to a shaded-in comment reference in the text of a document shown in the item view pane on the left. Deme provides covisibility between document and comments through an optional split-screen view. In-text comment references are transiently pointed to (the dotted-line arrow goes away as soon as the user scrolls) when clicked on, and comments are displayed in the context of hierarchical threads. Members can vote on documents under a variety of decision rules. Boundaries are provided through highlighting, text boundaries, headers, and a versioning system that remembers when comments become obsolete and marks them as such. The design takes advantage of no-page-reload Web server calls to provide dynamic relationship visibility and boundary distinguishability.

Solution   Applying the principles of relationship visibility and boundary distinguishability in an integrated way puts online deliberators at less of a disadvantage relative to their face-to-face counterparts.

Linked patterns   Collective Decision Making (10), Participatory Design (36), World Citizen Parliament (40), Online Deliberation (52), Online Community Service Engine (62), E-Consultation (70), Grassroots Public Policy Development (78), Thinking Communities (118), Community Inquiry (122).

Problem   When countries are antagonistic to each other and have ceased diplomatic relations or are cultivating other distrustful or threatening attitudes, the countries may drift into war by accident or by design. When this antagonism becomes institutionalized through policy, public attitude, or propaganda, warfare or other violence becomes a natural consequence. The unique powers of individual people to help overcome these rifts by calming tempers, building ties, promoting reason and dialogue, or healing wounds is rarely acknowledged or promoted. And sometimes the efforts of the rare person who strives to develop personal connections with "the enemy" is demonized by people on both sides.

Context   This pattern can be applied whenever a country's stance toward another country is antithetical to the needs and values of civil society. This can happen before, during, or after a war or other period of hostility and mistrust.

Discussion   The use of the concept of citizen diplomacy was apparently first applied when U.S. citizens journeyed to the former Soviet Union in the 1980s and met with activists, educators, scientists, health professionals, and ordinary citizens. These citizens, and their Soviet counterparts, did not want to accept the "inevitability" of war, either hot or cold, and sought to find common ground on which to build a more peaceful future for everybody. Citizen diplomacy offers the promise of peace by building on actual, hopeful, and optimistic face-to-face encounters by citizens of the designated enemy states.

The idea for this pattern, like others in the language, arose in the 1980s in a specific historical context: the protracted cold war between the Warsaw Pact nations (most notably the Soviet Union) and the member nations of the North Atlantic Treaty Organization (NATO) countries (most notably the United States). Although the information reported here is based on experiences from that time, this pattern will be applicable in a great variety of situations in which two or more states or other large groups are enemies. Several antagonistic dyads come to mind—India and Pakistan, Israel and the Arab states, the United States and Cuba or Venezuela—and each situation contains its own unique opportunities and risks. People who engage in projects along these lines certainly fit Richard Falk's (2004) description of a "citizen pilgrim" who is willing to go on a quixotic journey for a seemingly improbable goal.

Interestingly, especially in a pre-Internet era, many of the collaborative efforts (described in Jeffrey 1989) were related to the use of information and communication. Some of the projects include Children's Art Exhibit and Book, US-USSR State Bridge Citizen Diplomacy, Moscow-DC Live Broadcast: *Soviet Citizen's Summit*, Peace Lines: Computer Supported Networking, US Kids to Siberian Computer Camp, Electronic Peace Mail Project, Video Conference: *Doing Business with USSR*, and World Civilization and Education Centers.

The collaborative projects themselves are subject to enormous challenges. Simply meeting with people from "the other side" presents great obstacles (including financial costs, legal restrictions on travel to and within the other country, privacy of communications, and access to people). Furthermore, any collaborative project, unless it is done clandestinely, will exist at the pleasure of the governments involved. In fact, one of the ultimate risks inherent in a project like this is that of individuals being used or manipulated by traditional powers (such as the media, state power, think tanks, political parties, or religious institutions) in ways that overwhelm the hopes and energy of the citizen-diplomat.

Since the unraveling of the Soviet Union in the early 1990s, the global situation has changed considerably. The rough parity of power (exemplified to some degree by the size of their nuclear weapon stockpiles) between the Warsaw Pact countries and the NATO countries and the promise of mutually assured destruction helped prevent direct confrontation and led to numerous proxy conflicts supported in part by the combatants' respective superpower allies. The military parity has now largely dissolved, and the arms race between the United States and the Soviet Union has given way to a one-sided arms race where the United States appears now to be competing with the rest of the world; its military expenditures (including several new nuclear weapon programs) amount to nearly half of the world's military expenditures.

Finally it is not obvious that collaborative projects like these will yield any long-lasting benefits. An interesting observation is that when the U.S. media entered the Soviet Union after Glasnost, they followed the routes that citizen-diplomats established. While it is true that relations were finally normalized between the two countries, the citizen-diplomat may be well advised that setbacks may outnumber gains.

Solution   Establish contacts and develop collaborative projects between individual citizens and groups in countries or regions where relations are severely strained or nonexistent.

Linked patterns   Global Citizenship (6), Spiritually Grounded Activism (24), Democratic Political Settings (31), Multiparty Negotiation for Conflict Resolution (79), Mirror Institutions (94), Citizenship Schools (96), Appreciative Collaboration (99), Thinking Communities (118), Activist Road Trip (134).

Problem   There are millions of organizations and other institutions that are responsible for important decisions and policy development on behalf of the public trust. There are also organizations and other institutions that violate the public trust or otherwise wield illegitimate power. Both types (and they often overlap) must be monitored closely—persistently and nonsuperficially—to encourage them to exert their powers appropriately. Moreover, all of these groups (and, indeed, all of us) are faced with uncountable problems (and problems in the making) within the environment that are not well understood, often for lack of a useful framework. The institutions that civil society establishes are often too diffuse or too narrow to face these problems effectively, some seem to be reinventing the wheel, and many are unable to change as times change. Institutions of government and business can be too powerful or politically beholden to perform their duties responsibly; they can also be conceptually or administratively misaligned with their mission for many reasons.

Context   Many sets of problems, situations, and contexts can be addressed with the same pattern. Institutions (in the sense of people who are organized around certain goals in a persistent way) are ubiquitous as is the need to monitor or confront them. Sometimes these actions are best accomplished with mirror institutions.

Discussion   The world of mirrors—and, hence, any discussion of them, metaphorically or not—leads to reflections and reflections of reflections and reflections of reflections of reflections, and so on.

Mirrors reflect, but not perfectly. At the very least they reverse the image that they are reflecting. Here, *mirror* is being used as a metaphor for reflection and replication. Mirror institutions are institutions that can be thought of in terms of reflection and replication, and both of these actions are necessarily selective in what aspects are reflected and replicated.

Due to the size and complexity of most of these mirroring challenges, formal or informal organizations are established to tackle the job. For many reasons, organizations that mirror to some degree the area within the overall environment that they are focused on are likely to have more success than those that do not. An institution is society's attempt to make a machine whose output is of a desired type. It reflects (however imperfectly) the desires of its creators and maintainers, and its "products" are mirror images of each other (or at least have the same family resemblance). Mirror institutions reflect or reflect on other institutions or other realities. As such, this pattern covers a wide range.

Four important facets cover this wide range: the reflective mirror institution, the critical mirror institution, the alternative and generative mirror institution, and the flattering mirror institution. The boundaries between these different institutional mirror types are not clear. It is hard, in other words, to know exactly where one ends and another begins. And the mirror itself (at least the metaphorical mirror) is a constructed object whose selective approach to reflection and replication is implicitly or explicitly what it is set up to be and what it has come to be.

The *reflective mirror institution* is used to help us understand without bias some aspects of the real world. This institution needs to reflect the most salient aspects of its object back to the people who need to understand the object. Scientists ideally employ this type of mirror institution when they endeavor to understand the complex and intricate relationships within the physical environment.

James A. Wilson (2006) states that the "mismatch of ecological and management scale makes it difficult to address the fine-scale aspects of ocean ecosystems, and leads to fishing rights and strategies that tend to erode the underlying structure of populations and the system itself." He continues: "This is likely to be achieved by multiscale institutions whose organization *mirrors* the spatial organization of the ecosystem and whose communications occur through a polycentric network."

Problems can result if people believe that they are using a reflection that has perfect fidelity or if their ideology prevents them from perceiving the degree of infidelity that does exist.

The *critical mirror institution* is used to uncover, analyze, and expose the failings of another institution. Using the explicit philosophy, goals, and practices of the institution itself to show the stark contrast between their often noble rhetoric and what they are actually doing is a common approach. In the United States, for example, the OMB Watch organization performs a watchdog function on the Office of Management and Budget (OMB) within the U.S. government. The Bretton Woods Project uses the decisions made by global economic powers at the 1944 Bretton Woods meeting as the basis for its critique of international capital and its institutional handmaidens.

The *alternative or generative mirror institution* is used to develop and propagate alternatives to existing institutions. Governments in exile are one example of this pattern, as are community banks, whether they are in Venezuela or other countries. Sometimes the alternative is then mirrored into multiple versions of itself. Federated institutions that are loosely connected to each other and more or less the same type of species represent a good way to develop strength globally while maintaining local control. This was used in independent, noncommercial communication, including community access television, community networks, and the independent media centers movements.

The World Social Forum is a blend of two mirror institution facets: the critical, and the alternative and generative; it was established as a counterforum to the World Economic Forum, which promotes alternative ideas and visions. The World Social Forum itself is also being mirrored in the form of regional and thematic forums.

The *flattering mirror institution* is an existing mirror, sometimes called an infinite mirror, that is self-referential, often self-indulgent, self-deceiving, self-reinforcing, and sycophantic. That is, to a large degree, the state of the media today, endlessly fascinated with its own flawless version of itself, perpetually reflecting on itself in an echo chamber of its own device.

There are several ways by which to look at any mirror institutions, especially when establishing one.

- The object or environment: What is standing in front of the mirror?
- The reflection: What is being reflected?
- Reflecting on the reflection: What are you seeing in the reflection? Should you be looking for other things?
- The audience: Who is (or should be) peering into the mirror institution? How will the institution present its reflections?

Does relying exclusively on reflections mean that wholly new institutions cannot be devised? Although this pattern can be used to modify existing institutions or develop new ones, developing a new one is a probably a better choice if novelty is important. In general, the pattern is less likely to impose constraints on innovation than the habits of people who would like to employ the pattern and the context, institutional or otherwise, in which they are working. Consider, for example, the possibilities that are unleashed when contemplating an alternative mirror institution called the Decentralized Intelligence Agency, a sort of people's variation on the U.S. Central Intelligence Agency, whose mission statement could be created through some simple editing commands using the CIA's mission statement as the original. If "President" is replaced with "people," "America" and "United States" with "the planet," "covert" with "overt," "action" with "nonviolent action" and "adversaries" with the more specific but less U.S.-centric "nations and other institutions who promote environmental, economic, and other violence" an alternative mission statement emerges, one that is unlikely to describe a replica of the existing CIA.

We are the earth's first line of defense. We accomplish what others cannot accomplish and go where others cannot go. We carry out our mission by:

- Collecting information that reveals the plans, intentions and capabilities of nations and other institutions that promote environmental, economic, and other violence, and provides the basis for decisions and nonviolent action.
- Producing timely analysis that provides insight, warning, and opportunity to the people of the world charged with protecting and advancing the interests of the people and the planet.
- Conducting overt action at the direction of the people to preempt threats or achieve world policy objectives.

The challenges include knowing when adopting and realigning is necessary and maintaining a network with like-minded organizations, mirror or not. The mirror approach is ecological, since it explicitly promotes and recognizes the variety of institutional life-forms that exist within a diverse social environment. But what organizations are doing the higher-level coordination between the institutions? Governments exist to (or should exist to) sort out (or at least assist with the process) issues related to rights and responsibilities: who (and what) *can* do something and who (and what) *should* do something. Associated with this is the task of developing (and exercising) incentives to encourage people to do the right thing and penalties for those who do not. Values and human intelligence come into play: we cannot leave it up to government, and we must not leave it up to "survival of the fittest."

This is a pattern for conscious adaptation, and it is a pattern that encourages transformation, since culture is propagated by its institutions. This pattern is evolutionary as it focuses on replication with variation. Mirroring implies copying, but generally copying with changes made to one or more aspects of the original in the process. *Liberating Voices* is a mirror of *A Pattern Language* (Alexander 1977).

Solution   Although this pattern may be a bit heavy on abstractions, the institution-as-mirror metaphor can be useful primarily due to the questions it raises. The German playwright Bertolt Brecht (2001) held that "art is not a mirror held up to reality, but a hammer with which to shape it." Mirror institutions to a large degree must also be applied to similar ends.

Linked patterns   Civic Intelligence (1), Matrifocal Orientation (9), Strategic Capacity (34), World Citizen Parliament (40), Alternative Media in Hostile Environments (53), Future Design (88), Experimental School (89), Citizen Diplomacy (93), Open Source Search Technology (125), Citizens' Tribunal (129).

Problem   Patients and the public traditionally have very poor, if any, access to information in their medical records. Unless they are with a personal doctor who knows them well, many patients have great difficulty describing their condition accurately. At the same time, the clinician whom they are seeing is expected to provide excellent care without having up-to-date information about a patient's health. To compound the problems, medical records often contain inaccuracies of which neither patient nor medical providers are aware.

Context   Over many centuries, medicine has identified and studied diseases and developed treatments that benefit individuals and societies. However, the more treatments there are, the more they need careful monitoring for serious side effects or interactions with other treatments or conditions a patient may have. Patients therefore need increased contact with the medical profession, and this contact is increasingly fragmented among many practitioners and disciplines. This complexity creates unnecessary tests and clinician appointments, as well as an increasing risk of litigation. Patients and the public face rising costs, more demands on their time, and decreasing understanding of their health.

Discussion   As health care in developed countries becomes more complex, more sophisticated and expensive systems are being put in place, but with no proof that delivery of care is improving. Inasmuch as these systems succeed in reducing costs, they tend to benefit the large public and private health care providers that sponsor them. They constitute ever more effective electronic filing systems for information about patients, but patients neither see nor use these systems.

We live in a world of choice, and if there is little access to information about patients, there is plenty of other information for them. More and more, the public seeks information so as to choose among options for treatment. At the same time, more and more is available on the Internet (at, for example, www.nhsdirect.nhs.uk) for those who want high-quality information about health and well-being.

Simply providing information is a job half-done. Until patients can work with their own health indexes, such as blood pressure, blood sugar, cholesterol, and diabetes status, for example, they will find it difficult to relate information they find on Web sites to their own health. Secure systems already exist for patients to add blood pressure and blood sugar data to their records (Pincock 2003). Clinicians welcome such information when determining a patient's treatment management plan, especially if it can be easily found in one place. Clinicians who have experienced patient-maintained personal health records become enthusiastic about the practice (Protti 2005).

Traditionally the medical practitioner has provided a bridge between medical knowledge and the patients themselves. If a treatment plan did not perfectly match the patient's needs or if the patient was challenged by changes or crises, the practitioner would take responsibility. Today there is seldom a single clinician involved in any patient's care, that is, no single person in a position to mediate between the complexities of medical technology and the actual experience that the patient has. Patients themselves are willing to contribute to this role; they are clamoring for access to their full electronic health records so as to see for themselves what clinicians have written about their individual consultations, the results of tests they have undergone, letters that have come back from specialists, and medications they have been prescribed.

Fulfilling the goal of active patient involvement in health care through access to medical records offers many opportunities and challenges. Patients could verify the accuracy of their medical records (Cross 2005) and access their medical records wherever in the world they happened to be. Given proper controls for privacy and confidentiality, patients could share their information with others if they so wish. Given professional protocols between medical practices (the lack of which has led to bad outcomes for patients in the past), availability of information on patients should be protected at all points of health care service delivery. Some patients may find some information in their records upsetting, while equivalent information may help in the treatment of other patients or other conditions. Patients may need protection from seeing some information about themselves before a clinician has discussed it with them, and this may limit a patient's choice to access full information. Information about a patient gleaned from a third party requires careful treatment before it is entered into the record.

The clinician's role as mediator between medical expertise and the patient's experience will endure, but it will change. Some of the opportunities of patient access to medical records may save clinician time, and others may not. Some patients will thrive on the ability to combine health information on the Internet and elsewhere with information about themselves from their medical records; others will not. With the right of online access to medical records comes the responsibility to deal with the information presented. The informed and responsible patient, comfortable with interpretive tools for making sense of medical data, has greater trust and confidence in the medical profession. Such changes in health behavior cannot be left to technology and information; they may require emotional support that depends on some degree of human intervention.

Online recording of medical information by patients is already being done (www.ihealthrecord.org; www.healthspace.nhs.uk), and online patient access to medical records is beginning (www.paers.net; Bos, Fitton, and Fisher 2006), and it presents a cutting-edge challenge for practical trust between patient and clinician and among medical providers. Medical records are being put online anyway, and over time they will become increasingly interoperable; the challenge is to make record access not merely a cost reduction measure for administrators and providers, but a tool for patients and their families to participate in their own health care.

Solution Use patient access to online medical records as a bridge between professional medical discipline and its practice as the patient experiences it. Let the public, patients, and clinicians and other health care providers have up-to-date access to accurate medical information, regardless of where the patient is located. Develop robust systems to protect privacy and confidentiality. Above all, educate and encourage practitioners and the public in patients' use of online medical records to manage their health.

Linked patterns Transforming Institutions (19), Opportunity Spaces (33), Privacy (65), Ethics of Community Informatics (67), Positive Health Information (74), Accessibility of Online Information (75), Grassroots Public Policy Development (78), Control of Self Representation (109).

Problem   Some of the skills of citizenship, like basic communication and cooperation, grow from skills learned in daily life. Others, like deliberating with others, defining problems, collaborating on common projects, and organizing are not so basic: they often need to be learned. Not long ago, associations and intermediary institutions–social and professional clubs, religious congregations, neighborhood schools–rooted in local communities were the main places where these skills were learned. Today there are fewer contexts in everyday life to learn them. People are less connected in and to local communities and often learn about what is important from the media. Increasingly, general discussion about political and civic issues is occurring on and through the Internet. But it is easier to find information on the Net than to learn reflexively with others. The Net only partly lends itself to learning collaborative citizenship skills. Further, many lower-income people around the world lack access to the Net. Therefore citizenship schools are needed to build civic skills in both local communities and on the Net.

Context   In order to act effectively, people need to learn and apply the skills of citizenship. Everyone who wants to find a democratic and lasting solution to deep and complex problems needs these skills, and they are open to anyone to learn and teach. But there are also experts—civic practitioners, government officials and civil servants, teachers and scholars, civic and community organizers—who have applied civic skills and learned how to teach them. Needed are contexts in which citizens in their everyday lives can come together with expert practitioners and learn from each other. This pattern is useful in a media-saturated society, where time and attention are scarce and citizens are pulled in hundreds of directions.

Discussion   Citizenship schools originated in South Carolina in 1959 and quickly spread throughout the South through the Highlander Folk School in Tennessee. In the late 1950s many southern states had literacy tests that required people to be able to read and write and sometimes answer "citizenship" questions that were generally designed to exclude blacks from voting. Teaching large numbers of African Americans in the South to read, write, and learn about citizenship was critical in the larger struggle for civil rights, including the right to vote. According to Andrew Young and Ella Baker (Levine 2004), movement leaders, the citizenship education program was the "foundation on which the entire movement was built." But communities with citizenship schools had few ways to make connections with other communities that lasted over time. Eventually, as the early fights for civil rights were won, the schools faded (Evans and Boyle 1992).

The spirit of the schools lived on through the decades that followed in hundreds of civic training programs conducted by organizations and local communities. Faith-based community organizations like the Industrial Areas Foundation train local clergy and lay organizers, who learn to conduct campaigns and forums to build consensus on issue agendas like housing, school reform, or job training. Environmental watershed, forestry, ecosystem restoration, and justice movements, among others, teach citizens and youth to collect data and monitor environmental quality while building skills of civic trust and cooperation. And civic movements to build a new model of the public and civic university are growing, like the Council on Public Engagement at the University of Minnesota (Sirianni and Friedland 2005).

Citizenship schools have also been tried online. In 1994, the American Civic Forum met to try to address a widely perceived crisis in political life and civic culture in the United States. The Citizenship Schools were an important model, and the Civic Practices Network (CPN) was built, to use the newly emerging technology of the Internet to build skills of citizenship. CPN, launched that year, sought to facilitate broad and multimedia sharing of best cases, civic stories, mutual evaluations, and mentoring opportunities. Other independent civic networks also emerged around this time, including LibertyNet in Philadelphia and Civic Net in Washington, DC. Despite the growth of the Internet, however, no broad network connected and nurtured these activities.

As the Web matured beginning around 2000, finding information on many topics of civic interest (public deliberation, the environment, youth, education, health care, communication) became relatively easier for individuals. The new problem was how to link these groups together not only to provide information in their own specialized subfields but to create an active environment for teaching, learning, and collaboration while also building a larger sense of solidarity in citizenship. National civic portals to aggregate the growing number of civic sites and discussions on the Net were one proposed answer. But by 2003 or so, with the emergence of the blogosphere, the topology of the Web itself suggested that distributed links among widely dispersed civic sites might lead to new kinds of collaboration in which a great deal of the work of gathering and connecting is done by sites in the midrange. This is the level most appropriate for new citizenship schools on the Web.

Therefore, to establish citizenship schools in local communities and institutions requires building a framework that can support many local organizing efforts with curricula and training routines that are distributed, shared, inexpensive, flexible, and sustainable. These can be done in local communities, through institutions like schools and universities, and on the Web.

Local citizenship schools would necessarily be the result of pooled efforts among many active local civic organizations across different areas. Many could benefit from local government support. In Seattle, for example, the Department of Neighborhoods provides leadership and skills training to many neighborhood, environmental, and other civic groups.

Citizenship schools through university extension and outreach could train new expert practitioners rooted in local communities. For example, at the University of Minnesota, the Council on Public Engagement reaches out to both scholars and academic staff to redefine the teaching and research mission of the public university. Potentially, certificates and university credit through university extension services and community colleges could provide individuals valuable learning resources that also support and reinforce the extended investment of time, attention, and civic commitment.

New citizenship schools on the Web could allow collective learning in a distributed, asynchronous environment, help frame a broad civic agenda collaboratively through distributed discussion, and form a midrange network of portals to focus attention without the initial high costs of building national space. Schools on the Web could support and integrate both local and statewide efforts. The CPN is one online model indicating that there is significant demand online for serious learning material about civic practice. Deliberative-Democracy.net demonstrates how key blogger-editors can be recruited for a civic site and distribute the labor of a serious, ongoing conversation. The Liberating Voices pattern language project is also a key example of a distributed learning collaborative.

For the pattern to be realized online, moderate-sized hubs with committed editors will need to be seeded and a few models created. Possibly citizenship schools on the Web could ally with university partners, particularly in civically oriented extension programs, to provide credentials and a modest flow of support. Their life cycle is potentially renewable. If a network of citizenship schools succeeds, it could become self-sustaining using commons models with relatively little ongoing external support.

The biggest challenge in building citizenship schools on a commons model is sustaining energy and collaboration and maintaining a high quality of information. A commons model requires moderate levels of commitment from a wide core. Many of the contributors will be citizens, academics, policymakers, and administrators with other jobs and commitments. Rewards will be intrinsic. A second challenge is to get citizens to commit time to learning, not merely seeking information.

Solution   There are five basic steps to promoting this pattern: (1) build citizenship schools in local communities, institutions, and online that can aid collaborative learning; (2) develop sites (local and virtual) that include active learning and civic curricula that can be widely shared; (3) find citizens (lay leaders and experts both) who can serve as teachers and editors who can make minimal but real commitments; (4) build templates to aid the spread of learning; and (5) create new forms of civic credentials that provide value to both individuals and communities.

Linked patterns   Civic Intelligence (1), Global Citizenship (6), Education and Values (17), Indicators (29), Public Agenda (30), Democratic Political Settings (31), Opportunity Spaces (33), Strategic Capacity (34), Strengthening International Law (42), Ethics of Community Informatics (67), Equal Access to Justice (69), Grassroots Public Policy Development (78), Civic Capabilities (85), Citizen Diplomacy (93), Community-Building Journalism (97), Community Inquiry (122).

Problem How do activists, would-be activists, and those interested in learning about and participating in any movement or community of practice get a sense of what the best practices are, what the underlying philosophies are, who the leaders are and what they are thinking, what the key institutions and organizations are and how they are developing, what the most useful resources and tools are, and what is going on in other communities? How do people learn how to participate with a critical and reflective perspective?

Context The journalistic pattern and communication tools noted here can be used in any field, narrow or wide, where public education and outreach, as well as discussion and information sharing among key contributors and other participants, are important to the vitality and development of the field.

Discussion There are many ways of speaking to this family of problems, issues, and concerns: face-to-face get-togethers, from conversations to conferences; e-mail and discussion lists, blogs, Web sites, and bulletin boards; books and articles; faxes and radio. Tying into all of these, regular publications have come to serve a key role in movement development and community building. Tom Paine's *Common Sense* at the beginning of the American Revolution, arousing the colonists in a radically new "common sense" way, and *The Federalist Papers,* the country's first major newspaper op-ed series, designed to convince people to support the newly drawn up Constitution, were crucial works of popular journalism that helped set our country's founding. They are indicative of what can be found in any social and political movement, large or small, specialized or general. Regular publications that cover the events and developments of a movement are indicative of the depth of thought and commitment that people have to their work and their interest in sharing it and learning from one another.

Movement and community-building journalism and their publications are most often written and produced by the actors and participants in the movement and provide reflections on the roots and meanings of specific contributions to the field. They tie particular events and achievements, programs, institutions, and actors to a wider field of interconnected activities that together point toward renewed possibilities for people to create a healthier and more democratic common world. Consider professional academic disciplines: all have their many journals (international, national, regional) and their growing online availability and distribution, and they are important to developing cohesion and direction in their respective communities of practice. Consider the situation among artists, social workers, leftists, conservatives, and citizens of a viable community of any size. In American political life, consider the longevity of key political journals and how they have not only reflected trends and movements but helped define the movements themselves and provided an arena for its participants to learn about and from one another. That strand of radical liberalism that has characterized the *Nation* from its inception as a vocal antislavery voice, the descent from progressive liberalism to neoconservatism represented by the *New Republic,* and the development and fracturing of the radical political culture and politics of eastern European Jewish immigrants as found in the *Partisan Review, Dissent,* and *Commentary.*

In the field of community media and technology, the *Community Technology Review* (CRT) reflects several useful pattern features of current community-building journalism. CTR has served as the formal and informal publication of both the Community Technology Centers' Network, the country's oldest and largest association of nonprofit and community organizations dedicated to providing emerging technology resources for those who do not ordinarily have effective access, and the Association for Community Networking, the affiliation of institutions and individuals interested in developing community-wide information resources and tools. CTR has covered key directions and issues of its two prime organizational partners by placing them within the developments of the wider field of community media and technology. For example, the fall 1999 issue was a joint production of CTCNet, AFCN, and the Alliance for Community Media (ACM), the national association of community cable public, education, and governmental (PEG) access centers; ACM and community cable access center development receive ongoing coverage. CTR has maintained close relations with the *Community Media Review,* ACM's official publication; with the fairly recently established *Journal of Community Informatics*, the international journal of the emerging academic discipline of the field, especially outside the United States; with the Digital Divide Network, the online communication environment that has done so much to address issues involving the problem identified in its name; and with the Nonprofit Technology Enterprise Network, the association of nonprofit technology assistance providers. It also has offered ongoing coverage of NTEN, Circuit Riders, CompuMentor/TechSoup, and other organizations and developments in this part of the field. To the degree it is a model, CTR suggests that coverage of key organizations in a field provides a useful map that can be of assistance to both experienced actors and he new participants looking for information and guidance.

CTR is published simultaneously online and in hard copy, using state-of-the-art tools most appropriate to each environment. The developing online environment has been designed with open source publishing tools (Movable Type/Drupal) that provide a large number of embedded hyperlinks for readers to easily explore special areas and references in depth, extensive searching capacity throughout the archives, interactive options for reader comments and additions, and communication with authors and editors. Desktop publishing is tied to appropriate printer and print-on-demand options for hard copy production and distribution, providing a tangible publication for those readers and occasions where hard copy availability is especially appropriate and useful. With the growing number of links to community-produced audios and videos, CTR provides an integrated multimedia platform that models a variety of approaches that can be used.

Articles are written by a combination of recognized leaders in the field and first-time authors who have worked on innovative projects and new resources. With first-time authors, editorial staff have expended substantial time in providing writing and editorial assistance. Overall the tone and approach toward readers is one that assumes an interest and some familiarity with the field but one that seeks to provide explanations and meanings when technical or field jargon or acronyms are used. In general, the CTR seeks to welcome readers into an ongoing conversation among some of the major practitioners and leaders in the field (hence the inclusion and important role of photos of authors and individuals who are participants in the events covered). In contrast to so-called objective or neutral journalism and reportage, movement-building journalism engages both the producers and readers in a way that builds and strengthens their communities.

Solution   Develop journalism and communication venues that present news, events, and developments in a field in depth, covering key organizations and institutions to offer a map and guide and using the most appropriate communication tools for participant leaders and actors. For those interested in using hard copy or online tools for community building in a field that does not currently make use of them, discuss the situation with colleagues and compatriots and find an associated field where such tools are used. Those who have developed them will almost always provide useful advice and even volunteer assistance.

Linked patterns   Working-Class Consciousness (12), Demystification and Reenchantment (14), Strategic Capacity (34), International Networks of Alternative Media (43), Indigenous Media (55), Community Networks (61), Media Diversity (66), Citizen Journalism (91), Citizenship Schools (96), Labor Visions (112).

Community and Organizational Building

Problem   Overemphasis on formal education can lead to an oversight of alternative learning methods that could be more appropriate within certain contexts. Particularly for adult populations looking to increase their understanding on relevant subjects, the option of pursuing formal training is not conducive due to the investment in time and extra resources it takes. As a result, people find it difficult to acquire the skills necessary for them to address a radically changing global economy, and thus many capable people continue to remain behind.

Context   In cities, in villages, in the workplace, or an Internet café, even in a coffee shop among friends, learning can and does take place. Individuals and groups of people can come together to share their knowledge in structured or unstructured ways to actively engage one another and mutually build each other's understandings. When other methods of learning are not available, and yet the skills necessary to gain better employment or the building of awareness on specific issues facing a community are needed for achieving greater livelihoods, informal learning processes can serve as an effective alternate route to meet the needs of communities and individuals.

Discussion   In a variety of settings, from the workplace to village development initiatives, informal learning through group interactions and individual self-teaching can be an effective tool for developing new skill sets, alternative ideas, and even new approaches to advancing livelihoods.

There is a hot debate among many educators as to what informal learning is, especially since its practice has become more commonplace within developed countries as businesses and employees attempt to stay abreast with the latest developments in technologies and management practices so that they can collectively and individually remain competitive in a market-driven environment.

Informal work-related adult education activities take place without an instructor. Examples of such activities include on-the-job demonstrations by a supervisor or coworker; on-the-job mentoring or supervised training; self-paced study using books, videos, or computer-based software; attendance at informal presentations; and attendance at conferences, trade shows, or conventions related to one's work or career (nces.ed.gov/programs/coe/glossary/i.asp). It occurs in everyday life and may not even be recognized as learning by the individual. For example, using a television guide may not be equated by an individual as having learned how to use a table.

It has been claimed that "many times we can find the answer in the world around us, through either people, or formal courses, or bits of information. When it is not found (whether it does not exist or a search is incomplete), we go into a problem-solving mode. Then we need data, and analytical frameworks. If we do it in conjunction with others, we need collaboration and/or communication tools. Finally, if we solve it, we (should) close the loop by either adapting the materials to account for this problem in the future, or to create new material" (Quinn, 2002).

In a developing country, informal learning has gained a reputation as a tool for meeting a number of goals that include not only skills training but also civic and health-related education that can be acquired through individual inquiry, as well as through group interactions. Similarly, adult literacy projects that use an informal education approach (predominantly among women) have gained increasing prevalence. In fact, women participants of local self-help groups often support one another through imparting knowledge to one another; they can help to tutor each other in their homes for building up literacy and educating each other on personal finance.

When done in a group context, an informal learning project can consist of a number of group-led demonstrations that relate to managing one's personal finances, starting a business, using a computer for e-mail, and accessing political representatives. The learning spaces are as dynamic and varied as the topics and the people involved in them. Sometimes these groups start through simple conversations among neighbors, or the group is seeded with support by an outside agency that brings some structure to the initial group development but after time allows the groups to be autonomous and define its own interests and pursuits.

Similarly, online learning groups can assist members in learning new software or computer programming. Consider the number of user forums dedicated to asking and answering technology-related questions. This exchange among participants constitutes an informal learning group in which information is shared that ultimately builds on the skills of the participants. In this online dialogue, individuals bring to the group their own experiences and expertise to share with other members of the group to help support a mutual sharing of knowledge. Even those not openly communicating with the group can benefit from finding answers to their own questions. As new doors are opened through this process, new levels of curiosity emerge that can aid the group.

Whereas these types of learning communities are contingent on access to information technology, in other contexts, these groups can meet within their geographical proximity. A community animator (pattern 102) can act as a facilitator by asking participants questions that help them ask new questions or find answers to questions that they may have not known how to answer before.

Regardless of how it is organized, the informal learning group serves two basic functions: providing access to information and knowledge creation and evoking a deeper level of individual curiosity among participants to prompt them toward greater levels of self-enrichment, whether for financial gains or inner personal gains.

Although informal learning has gained greater attention over the years within development-related education and beyond, technologies and access to information resources can make this pattern difficult to use effectively. While usage of these groups in development initiatives is high, it is difficult to ascertain whether they have had the level of benefit being represented through the increased effectiveness among employees with the corporations of more highly developed countries. This does not mean that informal learning groups are inadequate, but it perhaps highlights the acceleration of learning possessed by those who have greater access to information on a larger scale. For this reason, this pattern could be made more effective within a development-related context through the linking with other patterns that emphasize technology infrastructure and alternative access to information for groups.

Solution   As an approach to improving the capacities of peoples involved in any number of development schemes designed to address local livelihoods, informal learning groups can provide an alternative avenue for supporting life-long learning spurring individual curiosities, and acquiring new skills.

Community leaders, self-help groups, development agencies, and local employers can all act as initiators of informal learning groups and encourage an overall culture of participatory learning geared to meet the interests and needs of the community. These opportunities can be pursued and developed at the local Internet café, or time can be set aside by employers who realize the benefits of supporting a more educated and curious workforce.

Overall the pattern tends to be mutually reinforcing: as knowledge is created, curiosity tends to be ignited, furthering greater levels of self- and group-directed investigations. It is up to individuals, groups, communities, and businesses to promote these endeavors and increase the intellectual capabilities of local residents.

Linked patterns   Education and Values (17), Teaching to Transgress (20), Open Action and Research Network (45), Public Library (59), Digital Emancipation (60), Community Networks (61), Ethics of Community Informatics (67), E-Consultation (70), Accessibility of Online Information (75), Open Access Scholarly Publishing (76), Mobile Information and Computer Technology Learning Facilities (77), Experimental School (89), Service-Learning (90), Community Animators (102), Self-Help Groups (105), Community Telecenters (117), Thinking Communities (118), Community Inquiry (122).

Problem   Collaboration toward a shared goal is not always an uplifting experience; sometimes the problem is that there always seem to be problems. People can become discouraged in their work toward some common good. They suffer a dissonance between their enthusiasm for an uplifting cause and the gritty reality of bringing it about. What seems at the outset to be a life-enhancing enterprise can produce frustration, burnout, and turnover of group members.

Context   To pursue a shared goal is to seek a positive impact on the world: what David Cooperrider (1990) describes as a "heliotropic movement," toward the light of a positive image of the future. As long as the group visualizes the positive contribution that its work will make, it will approach its work with optimism and hope. If pursuing the goal appears as the remediation of a deficit rather than movement toward a positive image, a focus on the negative will emerge over time.

Discussion   Conflict can affect a group of people positively or negatively; it can be functional or dysfunctional. Some level of conflict can lead to creativity, responsiveness to change, and learning from experience. Conflict becomes dysfunctional when it produces feelings of hostility, interferes with honest communication, and distracts from the shared goal. People become frustrated when conflict prevents them from achieving what they want to achieve. They may react through aggression, compromise, or avoidance; each of these makes the situation worse than it was. The result is a diversion of the group's attention to perceived problems with the collective enterprise: a language of deficit in which not merely the shared goal but the group itself becomes a problem to be solved.

Geoffrey Bellman writes of the commitment, passion, and "aspiration for a larger life" (2000) that energize people who seek to change the world for the better. If we can see the beauty in our collaborations, we can release the creativity that comes from a compelling vision of a future worth working for.

Human beings, the groups and organizations we work in, and the world we inhabit all contain the potential for this larger life. Through consistent attention to what is alive and what can be alive in the future, we can become more alive. The belief that people are good and that they respond positively to being treated accordingly is well grounded in research on the Pygmalion effect (Cooperrider 1990). We respond to positive images of ourselves by regarding others more positively: by noticing their successes, remembering their strengths, and seeing challenges from a positive aspect.

An appreciative approach adopts a fourfold cycle of discovery, dreaming, design, and destiny (Cooperrider and Whitney 1999). It starts not by identifying a need or deficit but by discovering the best of the current situation. It dreams or envisions what a better future might be rather than analyzing what caused the deficit. In place of planning how to redress a deficit, it collectively constructs a design for a better future. Instead of acting to resolve a problem, this approach enacts a better future as its destiny.

To enact a better future suggests that a life-affirming end is a natural outcome of life-affirming means; we aspire to larger life in the world through larger life in ourselves and in our collaborations. If we learn to be drawn together by a positive image of each other, our collective effort "enhances the potential for creative, fresh human action toward a life-enhancing purpose" (Srivastva and Barrett, in Srivastva and Cooperrider 1990).

This can succeed if we continually revise our expectations of what we can achieve: to open new possibilities for ourselves, for those we collaborate with, and for the world we hope to improve. This requires that we continually learn by developing and revising "the norms, strategies and assumptions which specify what work gets done and what work is important to do" (Dixon 1999). We need to maintain a dialogue, with ourselves and others, about our individual and shared assumptions.

To better understand the value of others, we must suspend our own assumptions. People are seldom malicious or idiotic, but they often work from different assumptions; once we can understand these assumptions, we can appreciate their value. For this reason, appreciating differences is critical to collaboration. Once we appreciate others' concerns (Spinosa, Flores, and Dreyfus 1997), we can embark on a dialogue about how to work together.

Appreciative collaboration assumes that differences are valuable and focuses attention on what is positive in any situation; in place of a vocabulary of deficit, it offers a forward-looking language of hope. Combined with a clear shared vision, appreciative collaboration allows us to achieve life-affirming goals through life-affirming means.

Solution   Positive images of the future lead to positive actions. Consistently build positive expectations for the future on the basis of positive attributions to what has been achieved in the past. Constantly learn the value of others, and be prepared to change cherished assumptions if they undermine the larger life of the group.

Linked patterns   The Good Life (3), Strategic Capacity (34), Open Action and Research Network (45), Multiparty Negotiation for Conflict Resolution (79), Wholesome Design for Wicked Problems (82), Citizen Diplomacy (93), Shared Vision (101), Community Inquiry (122).

Problem   There are many limitations to the take-up and use of information and communications technologies (ICTs) in nonprofit organizations. Technical, social, and management
issues are frequently involved, but the complex, interconnected mix of factors at work is
often confusing. There is not a common language for understanding and modeling a particular organization's situation. Furthermore, until understanding is achieved, action planning
and change are even more problematic. However, ideas of sustainability drawn from the
worlds of sustainable development, sustainable communities, and environmentalism are
familiar to many civil society activists and nonprofits. Can these ideas be imported to form
a holistic sense-making framework for understanding nonprofit ICT use? More important,
can the use of sustainability indicators also help inform action planning and change on the
basis that diagnosis is halfway toward a cure?

Context   This pattern has emerged from extensive research, development, and consulting
on ICT in nonprofit organizations (Plant 2003). Nonprofit organizations are key to organized
social action and increasingly reliant on ICT in pursuing their missions, especially as they
move from internal, efficiency-oriented applications to those that support service delivery
externally. But small nonprofits are frequently vulnerable to, yet dependent on, external
expertise due to limited internal knowledge. Outside support is, furthermore, often technically biased and solutions focused. There is a need to facilitate internal capacity development
and learning, especially on the organizational and political, not just technical, factors associated with ICT. The notion of sustainability as imported into this field embraces a holistic
range of organizational, social, and technical factors. These affect success and autonomy in
the use of ICT, as well as technological longevity. The application of sustainability indicators
to appraise ICT use in nonprofits should interest both nonprofit staff and outside helpers
committed to a facilitative approach. Those needing a holistic understanding of a particular
organizational situation and those looking to move toward action planning for change and
improvement in ICT use should benefit.

Discussion   A sustainability model was originally constructed as an analytical abstraction for
research purposes to model the suggestion that three main factors, each with subfactors,
might explain sustainability or its absence in nonprofit ICT. The top-level factors were
inspired by the triple bottom line in sustainable development (Henriques and Richardson
2004) combined with information systems theory. They are: longevity (technical factors
that affect information technology quality and life expectancy); success (management factors that affect the overall impact of ICT use on the organization); and autonomy (empowerment factors that affect the extent of appropriate relationships with outside expertise).

A method of appraising sustainability operationally in any given nonprofit was derived
from the theoretical model. A questionnaire asks respondents to agree or disagree with asser-

tions associated with sustainability in each of the three main areas using a five-point Likert scale. Drawing on Bell and Morse's (2003) approach to sustainability indicators, these qualitative responses are plotted on a diagram representing the theoretical modeling in graphical terms. This results in a visual impression of sustainability as subjectively interpreted by the organizational stakeholders taking part.

A full "information systems health check" service was then designed (Plant 2001). The consultant first gathers and preliminarily analyzes sustainability appraisal data from completed questionnaires. A face-to-face meeting then takes place, at which feedback is offered, and the situational diagnosis is discussed with client representatives. The consultation then moves toward initial action planning and change. Possible areas for improvement are drawn directly from the graphical sustainability appraisal plot and respondents' annotations.

Specific action plans that might bring about change and improvement are identified, focusing on segments where sustainability appears to be weakest. The follow-up to this part of the process involves canvassing a wider cross-section of the client organization's staff, if possible, in order to confirm, enrich, or challenge the situational diagnosis and the action-planning steps emerging.

Evaluation of the health check service suggests that it leads to new insight for client organizations. Key phrases appearing on evaluation questionnaires emphasize the strengths of a "completely outside perspective" that "forces the issue" to give participants an "understanding of context" and "make recommendations" from an "unbiased viewpoint" following "critical review." Insight appeared to be based largely on bringing to the surface ideas that were already latent within the organization, newly articulated, and legitimized as a result of the engagement. It was therefore argued that internal capacity can be unlocked by employing the external facilitator in the role of a sounding board. Drawing out multiple perspectives through this participative approach appeared particularly important.

The crucial requirement for the client to take ownership of the process cannot yet be taken for granted. For this reason and others, further action research is needed to confirm or challenge the findings. Follow-up work is time-consuming and demanding for clients, particularly if, as suggested during the health check, the consultant's definitions of *health* and *sustainability* are to be challenged, reviewed, and appropriated to suit local conditions and culture.

The qualitative basis of this work also leads to its own challenges. The most effective sustainability appraisals have been those involving questionnaire responses from multiple stakeholders that express divergent views. Productive outcomes have resulted from the debate and discussion over the multiple subjective interpretations of sustainability that have emerged. Focusing on disagreement as well as agreement can of course generate conflict instead of consensus, so sensitive facilitation and careful management are required.

Furthermore, given that as follow-up, clients are encouraged to engage organizational stakeholders at all levels (a move that could generally be considered healthy), such conflict can be problematic for those in less powerful positions. More generally, the process may influence the existing power balance; this could be either positive or negative in any given organization. As a minimum, this possibility must be taken into account.

Solution   Sustainability ideas were originally imported into the nonprofit ICT field in order to construct an explanatory model for research purposes, but their utility goes beyond this. The use of sustainability indicators has led to a practical grounded tool for understanding real-world nonprofit ICT situations. A common language for making sense of and modeling the organizational, social, and technical factors involved in ICT sustainability in individual nonprofits is now available. It has been used successfully to achieve situation diagnosis and understanding and has also led nonprofits toward practical action for change and improvement in ICT use. Although there is more work to be done, the core method, an "information systems health check," involves a visual representation of sustainability that promotes accessibility and a facilitative approach that can lead to empowerment and organizational learning. Furthermore, researchers concerned with industrial or other sectors have observed similarities with ideas such as capability maturity modeling, and this work may well have application beyond the nonprofit sector.

Linked patterns   Transforming Institutions (19), Sustainable Design (22), Strategic Capacity (34), Alternative Progress Indexes (46), Academic Technology Investments (81), Shared Vision (101).

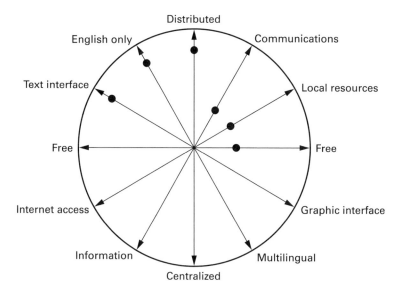

Problem   In any collective enterprise, the participants have diverse goals and points of view. Not everyone will agree that a given course of action is the best available, and the results of collective action may not meet all expectations. Not knowing that they are pursuing dissimilar goals, people may work at cross purposes. Over time, especially where involvement is voluntary, commitment to the enterprise may erode or the group may become less diverse.

Context   Organizations dedicated to a social or environmental issue attract people from diverse backgrounds, with strong feelings and differing levels of experience and interest. Such a group is bound together by the common concerns of a diverse membership, and those who feel underserved within the group may dissipate the efforts of the group or take their energies elsewhere. Building on and integrating shared concerns into a shared vision helps members focus their involvement in the group so as to better orient their energies toward the collective enterprise.

Discussion   A McKinsey report on nonprofits states that nonprofit organizations have a special need for a vision as a means to guide their actions and evaluate outcomes. A "compelling, easy-to-understand description of how the nonprofit would like the world to change in the next three-to-five years, what role the organization will play in that change, and how the nonprofit will measure the success of its role" (Kilpatrick and Silverman 2004), the vision should pervade the organization's activities: an ultimate guide for making decisions and setting goals in alignment with collective values and aspirations.

A vision should express values, purpose, and progress toward a better future. It should be neither too specific nor too general. Detailed goals, though necessary, do not belong in the vision itself; they easily become outdated once they are attained or when unforeseen opportunities and unexpected consequences occur. And noble sentiments and statements of principle do not always easily translate into action under complex circumstances.

A shared vision should be clear and compelling, aspirational for a better world in the future, and describable in simple terms. It should be capable of being understood as a common purpose and of acting as a guideline for evaluating decisions and outcomes on a continuing basis. Nanus (1992) recommends that a vision be challenging but realistic, and developed by people throughout the organization.

The content of a shared vision is less important than the life it brings to the organization. Peter Senge quotes Robert Fritz that "it is not what the vision is, it is what the vision does" (Scharmer 1996). A shared vision comes from the individual visions of group members; it becomes a force for action through the process of becoming shared. The difference between the shared vision and current reality should generate energy for change. Through its use, a shared vision should ensure that strategic decisions and specific goals are aligned with the organization's values.

To provide both accountability and allegiance to collective values and goals, a vision must be put into practice. According to Etienne Wenger, "One can design visions, but one cannot design the allegiance necessary to align energies behind those visions" (1998); members' allegiance can, however, be encouraged in the way a group or organization enacts a shared vision—how its members live out their accountability to collective values and goals. One way to promote allegiance to a vision is to use and communicate it constantly; another is to promote behavior, both inside and outside the organization, that is consistent with the vision.

A shared vision lives constantly in tension with fast-changing and unpredictable circumstances. To pursue vision while ignoring what is practical and relevant cannot sustain an organization, yet the vision is an essential guide to action through a succession of new circumstances and possibilities. Brinckerhoff (2003) believes that nonprofit organizations should respond flexibly to external demands, while remaining in alignment with the collective purpose. By maintaining the shared vision, an organization learns not only how to do better, but also what better to do. "The world changes, and so must the vision" (Nanus 1992).

A shared vision helps to guide an individual project with specific tasks and a finite life span (Christenson and Walker 2004). Developed in conjunction with stakeholders both within and outside the project members (e.g., developers, funders, and the community at large), it helps people make sense of the project plan and their contributions to it. An easily understood, inspiring, credible, and challenging vision can create and sustain the alignment of members' energies, their enthusiasm and allegiance to the group, and their accountability to shared values and specific goals.

When a community or civic project begins, participants may be highly enthusiastic, each with a strong conception of what the project should be. It is tempting to jump right in and assume that everybody shares the same vision. Proceeding from this ambiguous and contradictory beginning may lead to division and hard feelings within the group and to unsound early decisions that become built in to the system.

Developing a shared vision may be the most important task for the group to accomplish at the outset. Developing shared perspectives on both the vision and the process for enacting it are indispensable for success. Good communication is essential; face-to-face group meetings, brainstorming, and other methods of envisioning a collective future provide a forum for dialogue that e-mail, for example, cannot address adequately.

Steve Cisler (1994) suggests the use of a spoked circle as a graphical decision aid to fine-tuning the vision. The circle represents the space of decisions and goals, and the end points of the spokes represent the two possible extremes of each decision. Cisler shows an example of the spoked circle used by the Silicon Valley Public Access Link Project (reproduced in the graphic above). The upright spoke, for example, might be labeled "architecture," and the location of the small circle on the spoke near the "distributed" end point depicts the decision to use a distributed architecture instead of a centralized one. A point on the middle of a spoke would indicate an intermediate position between the views represented by the end points.

There are no stringent requirements as to how to use the tool. Simply identifying the spokes can be an important first step, as the spokes clearly show which decisions are to be made. It may not be critical to determine the exact location of the spot indicating a decision. In some cases, a group may decide to postpone a decision, but it is a group decision and ultimately must be made with others in the group. If it had not been resolved, for example, whether the network should be free to use or whether there should be fees, the organizers could say, "We're still trying to resolve this. Which approach do you think is best?" The tool can be used as a way to explain compromises or transitional circumstances by showing the current point in relation to the direction along which the developers plan to proceed. For example, when the system is launched, it might be deemed necessary to charge users a small fee, but ultimately the system would be expected to be free to use.

Solution Create, communicate, enact, and maintain a shared vision. Create the vision early in the life of any collective enterprise; it will guide the actions of the group or organization as a whole and for individual projects that the group undertakes. Clearly communicate the vision, and use it to guide strategy, decision making, and goal setting. As circumstances change, be prepared to modify the vision to keep it alive and capable of energizing group members.

Linked patterns Social Responsibility (8), Big-Picture Health Information (27), Strategic Capacity (34), Participatory Design (36), Alternative Progress Indexes (46), Conversational

Support across Boundaries (50), Mutual Help Medical Web Sites (54), Community Currencies (63), Transparency (64), Participatory Budgeting (71), Positive Health Information (74), Academic Technology Investments (81), Appreciative Collaboration (99), Sustainability Appraisal (100), Sense of Struggle (104), Self-Designed Development (106), The Power of Story (114), Public Domain Characters (115), Thinking Communities (118), Follow the Money (135).

Problem   Development professionals often find it difficult to adequately assess the broad spectrum of problems a community faces, as well as understand and use the assets the community has to work with. The lack of grassroots knowledge has proven problematic in that development schemes are often mismatched in scale and relevance to the community's needs, abilities, and liabilities. Thus, the conceived solutions for encouraging community capacities and livelihoods fall short of their objectives.

Context   Through their lived experience, community members trained in assessment techniques and information gathering can provide contextual understandings of the assets and liabilities a community possesses that would otherwise go unnoticed by outside professionals. Similarly they can act as agents for the process of consciousness raising and subsequent mobilization for people to pursue change and empowerment.

Discussion   In response to the failures of top-down approaches to development, a shift toward emphasizing participation and empowerment has begun to make its way into the mainstream of development practice. This move toward bottom-up, farmer-to-farmer, and grassroots communication has been a fundamental reorientation. Following the 1970s and 1980s, years often associated with the dark ages of development, a new light has come about through alternative practices that seek to employ the communities themselves in defining their needs, mapping out their assets, and coming to terms with their own liabilities (Richardson and Rajasunderam 1999).

   Through a variety of participatory processes, both community members and development professionals have had the opportunity to jointly design community improvement schemes that are appropriate to the community's needs and wants as well as sustainable and empowering. As a result of relative success, the role of the community animator has become increasingly important for enabling this process of cooperation and participation between the development practitioner and the community members themselves. In some ways, the animator acts as both initiator and ongoing advocate for the community's development through regular open communication with community members and the representative staff working in the area (Bessette and Rajasunderam 1996).

   In the past, highly educated teams of researchers and development fieldworkers would enter a community and employ any number of assessment tools to identify community needs, some of them participatory in nature. When they returned to their offices, these assessments would be used to design projects ranging from indoor lavatories, to treadle pumps, to community telecenters. In many cases, these projects failed to support the kind of long-term growth in people's livelihoods they were expected to bring. Rather than looking at what the community wanted or needed from their cultural and social point of reference, these professionals designed projects relative to their own point of reference.

Instead of persisting with this paradigm, nongovernmental organizations such as the Institute for Integrated Rural Development (IIRD) have pursued vigorous development campaigns in Bangladesh. In this example, the community animator has become a central agent for helping to identify and express the needs and desires of a community, as well as initiating and supporting change to include informal education, microenterprise ideas, and even the creation of women's self-help groups, which have enabled a number of women in rural areas to gain access to credit and thus empower them to pursue income-generating activities.

Organizations such as IIRD could send exploratory panels out to the communities as a get-to-know-you campaign. Over a period of time, they could identify predominantly young men and women whom they would sponsor for further education. The pool of students could serve as the primary group that would go on to perhaps become powerful community animators. Not only could they be given a valuable education, they would still retain familial bonds to their community, which often gives them an immediate advantage in having the lived experience of their particular area, as well the rapport of being a community member.

However, problems of jealousy and apprehension can be potentially problematic, and it is important that groups and agencies that seek to draw advocates from the field they want to assist find ways to mitigate potential social conflict. Unfortunately, it may not be possible to completely eliminate it, but the community-oriented approach presented here is perhaps a far better approach than previous alternatives.

Solution   The community animator can act as a critical link between the community and any nongovernmental organization collaborator. Those in the field for social change have noted that local citizens and activists can often better activate a community's sentiments and bring about awareness of the possibility to realize change than an outsider, who may be perceived to have little understanding of the real issues at stake.

Beyond the processes of consciousness raising that a community animator can bring to the process, nongovernmental organizations can also assist community members in training for information gathering and needs assessments to help refine the basic kinds of projects and programs that might be of benefit to a community.

Linked patterns   Civic Intelligence (1), Back to the Roots (13), Education and Values (17), Democratic Political Settings (31), Community Currencies (63), Informal Learning Groups (98), Self-Help Groups (105), Self-Designed Development (106), The Power of Story (114), Everyday Heroism (116), Community Inquiry (122).

Problem   Antipoverty advocates and activists are isolated in their own communities. They often do not have the communication capabilities, education, and training resources they need to do their work. Poor people do not have the information they need to exercise control over their lives and get the resources to which they are entitled or to advocate effectively for themselves. Lack of access to communication severely limits opportunities for building communities where poor people can help themselves access the resources they need and for advocates and activists in the antipoverty community to be involved in organizing for social change locally, nationally and internationally.

Context   The players in this online movement in Canada include poor people and advocates involved with community advocacy groups, settlement workers, multicultural groups, organizations of seniors, disability groups, legal aid, test case interveners, labor organizations, public libraries, women's centers, injured workers' and workers' rights groups, Native friendship centers and other First Nations and Aboriginal organizations, Inuit groups, research and policy groups, and tenants' organizations.

Discussion   Poverty is a debilitating worldwide problem that affects people directly as well as society at large. Although access to information and resources is critical to overcoming poverty and alleviating the problems of people living in poverty, poor people and antipoverty advocates traditionally have limited access to the Internet and other communications technologies. Although poverty and computers do not make for an obvious alliance, it is clear the two worlds must connect, or we will have a society where access to information and resources is only for those who can afford it.

Public access sites are rarely adequate to satisfy public need; users need people to help them do online research and free printers to print out forms and information. Hosts of public access sites need funding to keep equipment up-to-date and tech support to keep computers and Internet connections running smoothly. Lack of access to communication makes it difficult to connect communities in the antipoverty world outside their local regions.

PovNet, a nonprofit society created in British Columbia, Canada, in 1997, is an online resource created to assist poor people and antipoverty advocates through an integration of offline and online technology and resources. It works with advocates and activists across Canada involved in direct casework and social action and justice. Some of these groups include:

• The National Antipoverty Organization, a national voice for poor people that is working to eliminate poverty in Canada
• The Canadian Center for Policy Alternatives, a left-wing think tank doing research for change in social policy
• Canadian Social Research Links, an all-inclusive resource for social policy information about poverty in Canada
• DisAbled Women's Network of Ontario, an online inclusive community fostering virtual activism and individual empowerment locally and globally
• The Canadian Feminist Alliance for International Action, a coalition of over fifty Canadian women's equality-seeking and related organizations organized to further women's equality in Canada through domestic implementation of its international human rights commitments
• The Toronto Disaster Relief Committee, a group of social policy, health care, and housing experts, academics, businesspeople, community health workers, social workers, AIDS activists, antipoverty activists, people with homelessness experience, and members of the faith community who provide advocacy on housing and homelessness issues and lobby the Canadian government to end homelessness by implementing a fully funded national housing program.

PovNet has become an online home for advocates across Canada. Its Web site provides regularly updated information about issues and policy changes.

Using PovNet resources is an interactive process. Advocates learn the tools because they find them useful in order to do the social justice and casework that they care about. Poor and otherwise marginalized people find the Web site when they need information that is relevant to their lives. For example, PovNet e-mail lists have grown over the years into invaluable resources for specific campaigns (e.g., the Raise the Rates campaigns in both Ontario and British Columbia to raise welfare rates). They also provide an online support network for advocates working in sometimes quite isolated areas in British Columbia or in other parts of Canada. As one advocate put it: "I love the PovNet list—on the lighter side there's the kibitzing going on among the subscribers which often brings me to laughter—always a good thing in this job. On the serious side—the exchange of ideas and generous sharing of experience is a huge boon to those of us who often do not have time to pick up the phone to seek advice from our colleagues." Another subscriber says: "The lists that I am a subscriber provide me with first-hand current information on what issues are affecting BC residents and/or newcomers. I am able to provide useful information and referrals to some of the requests coming through PovNet lists. They are an invaluable and efficient resource for community advocates, settlement and family workers, especially those issues that are time-sensitive and need an immediate response."

Other PovNet tools include a Web site that is updated once a month with new information, online education and training courses (PovNet U) for poor people (e.g., "Be Your Own Advocate") and for advocates ("Introduction to Advocacy," "Disability Appeals," and "Tenants' Rights"), as well as an online space for antipoverty community groups to have their own Web spaces, calendars, and discussion boards. PovNet can adapt to needs as specific campaigns emerge. For example, it set up an e-mail list for a new campaign to raise welfare rates and created an online hub for papers and press releases when a group of antipoverty activists traveled to Geneva in 2005 to meet with the United Nations Human Rights Committee and the United Nations Committee on the Elimination of Discrimination Against Women to speak on behalf of the social and economic rights of poor people in Canada. The following year Committee on Economic, Social, and Cultural Rights groups met with the United Nations Committee on Economic, Social, and Cultural Rights.

Building a successful online movement in antipoverty communities includes, first and foremost, the people. It starts by finding local community workers who want to broaden their connections. Then it gathers together key people (without computers) to talk about what is needed and identify the technological limitations, and it communicates with advocates and activists in diverse antipoverty communities as listed above.

Next, the barriers are identified. These could include access to the technology (education, money, literacy, language); how to share information, resources, and skills between have and have-not advocacy communities (e.g., community advocates and advocates in funded agencies); and research on how to provide online resources in languages other than English and how to provide an online space for poor people to communicate and access information using public access sites and interactive Web-based resources.

Barriers for advocates and activists using PovNet tools have changed over the years. Initially, fear of technology was a big factor. But as advocates observed its use as a communications tool, they taught and continue to teach each other. Money for computers and printers is an ongoing problem as the technology demands higher-end equipment. For example, advocates in rural communities with dial-up access get frustrated with attachments that take up all their dialup time. The antipoverty work becomes harder as governments slash social services because the advocates have fewer resources to do their work. Technology cannot address such needs.

Despite the difficulties, the network continues to grow, establish links with other organizations in Canada and internationally, and exchange ideas and strategies for advancing social change.

Solution   The most effective online antipoverty communities are constructed from the bottom up rather than the top down. Their resources are defined and created by advocates and poor people to address the need for online antipoverty activism as it arises. Electronic resources can provide additional tools, but they are activated and made useful by the underlying human and locally based networks where the work of advocacy is actually being done.

Linked patterns   Social Dominance Attenuation (4), Health as a Universal Right (5), Economic Conversion (41), Sense of Struggle (104), Self-Help Groups (105), Control of Self-Representation (109), Everyday Heroism (116).

Problem There are myriad forces in the world. Some are working to create an alternative future, while some are working to preserve the status quo and perpetuate injustice and privilege. Many of the forces that are the strongest are the ones that must be challenged. A casual response is inadequate; a sense of struggle is necessary to meet those challenges.

Context This pattern is applicable to any person or group working toward the solution of a seemingly intractable social or environmental problem.

Discussion Social change is not easy. Effecting change is long term and not trivial. The change that is needed may not occur until long after the deaths of the people who first seek it. A sense of struggle can bind together a group dedicated to justice and positive social change. The striking miners in the photo above faced innumerable challenges that would be unsurmountable without their sense of struggle and the solidarity they shared.

A sense of struggle emerges from the realization that the problem is very deep and the appreciation that there will be setbacks over the long term. A sense of struggle lies midway between unwarranted optimism and helpless despair and cynicism.

A sense of struggle, which is often necessary in social activism, can change over time into something less desirable. Sometimes a too grim sense of struggle can result in not acknowledging a genuine opportunity when it comes along. A sense of struggle unrelieved by humor and camaraderie can even give way to dogmatism, paranoia, or messianic thinking. Being flexible and open to new approaches and to new people who share concerns is the best way to avoid these problems.

Frederick Douglass wrote, "If there is no struggle, there is no progress. Those who profess to favor freedom and yet deprecate agitation, are men who want crops without plowing up the ground; they want rain without thunder and lightning; they want the ocean without the awful roar of its mighty waters. Power concedes nothing without a demand!"

Solution   We need to cultivate a sense of struggle and at the same time make it easier for those who do struggle.

Linked patterns   Health as a Universal Right (5), Working-Class Consciousness (12), Teaching to Transgress (20), Antiracism (23), Spiritually Grounded Activism (24), Alternative Media in Hostile Environments (53), Transparency (64), Powerful Remittances (73), Shared Vision (101), Online Antipoverty Community (103), Arts of Resistance (111), Labor Visions (112), Everyday Heroism (116), Power Research (128), Media Intervention (132), Peaceful Public Demonstrations (133).

Self-Representation

Problem   Individual capacity among poor peoples in the developing world, particularly women, to establish credit and develop self-sufficient businesses is problematic. Lack of assets and stable employment lend a view that these peoples are not credit-worthy, and so they are barred from a variety of economic opportunities.

Context   Organizing groups to support collective and individual credit acquisition, as well as formal and informal skills training, can assist people in accessing the capital necessary to develop small businesses and ultimately help build livelihoods for families and communities.

Discussion   A basic description of the self-help group (SHG) has been offered by the Rural Finance Learning Center:

Self-help groups are usually informal clubs or associations of people who choose to come together to find ways to improve their life situations. One of the most useful roles for a self-help group is to provide its members with opportunities to save and borrow and it can act as a conduit for formal banking services to reach their members. Such groups can provide a guarantee system for members who borrow or they may develop into small village banks in their own right. In rural areas self-help groups may be the only way for people to access financial services. (2006)

The structure of the SHG is meant to provide mutual support to the participants by assisting one another in saving money, opening up cooperative banking accounts that help women and others to build credit with a lending institution. The SHG also functions to support members through maintaining consistent contact among them to aid individuals' savings goals and help support the creation of microenterprises. Often the SHG helps in the conception of these businesses and even the implementation of these enterprises on receipt of the microloan.

The SHG also supports accountability for ensuring that the loans are paid back and the SHG can continue to include other members and support greater access to credit and capital to those within their community. SHGs also provide a space that facilitates the discussion of many issues pertaining to the community's socioeconomic, educational, and health status. Thus, the formation of this group provides a forum to initiate many participatory activities, including training and awareness camps.

This process has been shown to increase confidence among participants and help support greater levels of decision-making status in their society, particularly within South Asia. This should encourage members to participate and contribute to decisions about general social and political matters in their respective villages.

As people are supported in building their credit, they are able to apply for microloans geared toward a number of self-sufficiency-based business ventures. Among the businesses commonly financed are seamstress shops and beautician parlors. In rural areas, these businesses can be as diverse as natural healing clinics, chicken farms, aquaculture projects, silk weaving, or any number of other handcraft-based ventures.

While a great number of SHGs have been initiated by communities themselves, many of the SHGs are implemented through the help of a nongovernmental organization that can provide the initial information and support to establish these groups. Such information and support often consists of training people how to manage bank accounts–for example, how to make deposits and withdrawals and balance cooperative and individual accounts. Informal education regarding a number of possible trades can take place in order to build up the capabilities of the participants to function as business owners.

The SHG has also shown in some instances problems that must be addressed when considering its use as a pattern of community empowerment. For instance, many of the people it seeks to help live in absolute poverty, and the little that they do save can put the family that is in an already precarious financial situation in a worse situation. It can force them to make tough choices as whether to purchase necessary goods such as food, clothing, and fuel and risk defaulting on their microloans, or, in the case of SHGs, hurt the entire group's ability to take out small loans as these are dependent upon the entire group's ability to save and collectively support each other through the generation of credit.

Other issues revolve around the nature of work and the family in developing countries where women are often the primary householder and men work outside the house. The creation of these businesses often burdens women with greater levels of work because they are committed to the SHG and the creation of their business yet their husbands expect them to do all the household duties. In these situations the pressures related to juggling the business, household chores, and child care can be immense.

In response to some of these problems, many nongovernmental organizations have sought to play a critical role in helping with that burden by offering to provide school to children, thereby giving women time to pursue their career goals by providing a place for their children to go while simultaneously providing education to children who would otherwise be working at home. Despite some of the drawbacks, the role of the SHG is a vital and growing component of bottom-up development.

Solution Despite the problems some of the participants have faced due to the changing nature of their socioeconomic status, SHGs offer one approach to creating associations of support for some of the most economically marginalized groups within society. Through the desire of women and other members of the community, these SHGs can establish an organized structure for providing employability and ownership for peoples otherwise left out.

Overall, communities themselves can act to develop similar groups (or with the aid of nongovernmental organizations working in the area), as these programs can be realized with relatively little resources from the outside.

The SHG is not a panacea to social and economic development and should be only one part of a larger solution to addressing poverty in communities. Other patterns must be called on to address some of the social consequences that can arise from creating SHGs.

Careful attention must be paid particularly to women; they are often the primary benefactors of the SHG, and yet the amount of work involved can be stressful and difficult for them. Other steps might also be taken to addresses these issues to pursue and integrated approach to supporting development.

For an in-depth guide to SHGs, see Jain and Polman (2003).

Linked patterns Political Settings (7), Matrifocal Orientation (9), Opportunity Spaces (33), Strategic Capacity (34), Open Action and Research Network (45), Mutual Help Medical Web Sites (54), Durable Assets (58), Informal Learning Groups (98), Community Animators (102), Online Antipoverty Community (103), Self-Designed Development (106), Everyday Heroism (116), Emergency Communication Systems (121).

Problem   All too often, development initiatives are designed and implemented by outside professionals, politicians, and wealthy elites. Neither community empowerment nor fundamental sustainability plays a central role in many of these interventionist projects. And just as bad, they fail to honor the basic desires and knowledge possessed by these people. Thus displacement, increased unemployment, and the overall degeneration of livelihoods become the actual result of this misplanned, misinterpreted, and misimplemented development. Similarly, even among well-meaning development nongovernmental organizations (NGOs), a culture of dependence tends to emerge, with communities being perpetually tied to the expertise and monetary assets that these organizations bring with them.

Context   Before governments, international development agencies, and corporate stakeholders attempt to define the nature of development for a particular community or region (or for the world, for that matter), peoples must assert their own paradigm as a challenge to the problematic realities that have come from vertically planned development schemes and break out of dependency.

Discussion   Stepping away from the interventionist model of development, self-designed or autonomous development emphasizes at its core development designed and implemented by the people it is intended to affect. While this pattern presents an orientation toward the practice and approach of development at one level, at another it is meant to be translated into the direct actions of people pursuing the right to define the trajectories of their lives, the lives of their families, and their overall communities. It tries to avoid the assumption that all people want to be developed; rather, it assumes that people wish to enjoy a certain type of life defined on their own terms, and the hope is that they will have the opportunity to realize that desire in their lifetime.

The words *self-designed* and *autonomous* are meant to address the fundamental notions of power: who has it, who uses it, and how it is used and to what end. As a pattern that values autonomy but also a notion of development toward greater well-being, traditional as well as modern knowledge must be acknowledged, with the understanding that they do not always have to be competing forces. When approached carefully, they can be used to promote a viable path toward community transformation that honors the social, cultural, and political realities a community exists within. Thus, self-designed development places both the responsibility and power of change in the hands of those who have been historically disempowered through the processes of traditional developmentalism.

At the level of philosophically orienting this process, it is necessary to reframe development and redefine the roles between peoples in communities seeking transformation and the various outside agents working for authentic social and economic change. Here we emphasize facilitation over the management and design on the part of development practitioners and community independence and autonomy over dependence.

As an example, participatory rural appraisal (PRA), so often thought of as the mainstay of the development practitioner seeking to design projects, becomes instead an awareness tool for community members to guide their own decision-making process on what steps are to be taken to better their livelihoods and offer clear paths to achieving that. In fact, communities can use this tool without the need for complex levels of understanding into social research and can be used in a relatively low-tech way in a variety of settings. Therefore, the role of the outside agent can be to act as an observer and help identify ways in which to help a community realize its mutually defined goals.

At the level of implementation, the pattern can guide specific actions to be taken by communities to include any number of projects: for example, a system of check dams used to provide electricity to power a rural village, the construction of a primary school or health center for women, or the creation of farming cooperatives to ensure the community not only achieves the ability to provide sustenance but can also generate income by selling products to others.

Undoubtedly the use of this pattern at this level will be context specific and must be shaped by the various needs and desires, plus the capacities and capabilities, of people seeking to pursue this pattern of development. This recognizes that not all communities possess the same needs or desires or the same levels of capacity or capabilities. In a community with a high level of civic capacity, as well as a great deal of cohesion and participation among community members, a more autonomous approach to development is going to be more easily realized. A community with lower capacity and cohesion may need to seek the assistance of an outside agent to facilitate the process. This could include consciousness raising, financial support, transfer of knowledge, and so forth. Any such assistance must be a result of the wishes of the community and brought forth based on the terms and desires of the people these plans are meant to assist.

In some situations, this pattern may not be at all viable or only minimally so. This is particularly true in situations of displacement, through war, famine, or other outside forces that fragment the capacity of the community to coordinate and act collectively. In these situations, the pattern may still be used, but it will be much more of a goal to be actualized by development agents who are seeking to ameliorate the problems associated with fragmented communities. The pattern thus becomes a guiding force for the interventionist, and care must be taken not to cross the boundary of creating development dependence among peoples.

It can be difficult for agencies to relinquish control over development initiatives as communities reconstitute themselves and gain a level of independence and cohesion that will allow them to participate in a process of autonomous development. And since it is difficult to say when the work of a nongovernmental organization is done in an area, there is a tendency to maintain an interventionist role long after the community has acquired the capacity to define its own goals. It therefore begins to become the kind of development the outsiders, not the community, envisions.

Thus, this pattern becomes not only an orientation to community-driven development but an orientation and guide by which nongovernmental organizations themselves can pursue a process to empower communities by emphasizing any number of projects designed to empower peoples to regain control over their lives in a rapidly modernizing world.

Solution Those in the professional development community should not always assume that a community wishes to be or needs to be developed. Rather, support to communities should be pursued based on invitation. For the communities themselves, this is an opportunity to empower themselves and project the ways in which they wish to interact and be defined in the process of modernization. It is an opportunity to exert their own sense of identity and influence their livelihoods as best and most effectively as possible in the face of so many outside forces that are consciously and unconsciously seeking to define their collective futures.

Those who are pursuing a development project must come together, discuss, plan, and decide what they want. If the community chooses to maintain a traditional way of life, it is up to them to determine how they will protect that. And in the event that a community does seek outside assistance, it is up to the residents to define the nature and terms of that relationship of those working with them from the outside. For those with a low capacity for truly implementing such an approach, any initiative must incorporate the necessity of capacity building for communities to achieve a level at which they can envision their own development. Ultimately the realization of a community's independence rather than dependence should be at the fore.

Linked patterns Collective Decision Making (10), Fair Trade (21), Indicators (29), Democratic Political Settings (31), Opportunity Spaces (33), Participatory Design (36), Indigenous Media (55), Digital Emancipation (60), Transparency (64), Grassroots Public Policy Development (78), Wholesome Design for Wicked Problems (82), Design for Unintended Use (84), Civic Capabilities (85), Shared Vision (101), Community Animators (102), Self-Help Groups (105).

Problem Tourism has largely developed unhindered by environmental and community concerns. Its sole basis is economic growth, with the majority of profits funneled to already rich industrialized nations. At its worst, tourism devastates rich landscapes, displaces long-established and thriving communities, causes pollution, creates a culture of drug and sex trafficking, diminishes access to clean water, and eradicates culturally unique lifestyles and livelihoods.

Context Individuals or organizations seeking to take part in travel and tourism that benefit local communities should investigate the many resources for engaged or responsible tourism. The hallmark of engaged tourism is that it is community determined and sustainable and draws on the existing people and environmentally centered resources of the community.

Discussion The challenges to participating in responsible tourism are many. A Westerner's perception of travel and vacationing is already formed to expect a certain kind of product. Swimming pools, air-conditioning, lavish meals, subservient staff, staged traditional activities, and the like leave little room for discovering the many wonders of foreign cultures or experiencing the complexities of a different lifestyle. Foreign governments share in the global race to classify tourism as a national export, paving the way for multinational corporations to build a tourist infrastructure at the expense of whatever may be in its way.

Tourism Concern, a nongovernmental organization (NGO) based in the United Kingdom, is a primary source of information about the social, environmental, and economic impacts of tourism at the same time that it advocates and provides information about alternatives. According to Tourism Concern's Web site, some of the main negative effects of tourism are displacement of people (particularly native peoples living on their traditional lands), environmental damage from uncontrolled development, and water abuse. In examining water abuse, it is easy to find that "the presence of tourists naturally means a much higher demand for water. Local communities normally do not benefit, and in most cases, are not allowed access to infrastructure built to ensure safe drinking water. The development of golf courses and hotel swimming pools are responsible for depleting and contaminating water sources for surrounding communities; this is especially true in Southeast Asia and the Middle East. An average 18-hole golf course soaks up at least 525,000 gallons of water a day—enough to supply the irrigation needs of 100 Malaysian farmers" ("Water Abuse" undated).

Equations, an East Indian NGO promoting responsible tourism, documents several tourism projects that are moving ahead without local support. The Bekal tourism project plans to convert Bekal, a northern rural coastal fishing district, into Asia's largest beach tourism resort of 6,500 units by 2011. As a consequence, four entire fishing communities would be destroyed, communities that are among the most sustainable in all of India. In addition, unique cultural practices are at risk:

The indigenous fishing community of Kasaragod is the last remaining community along the Keralam coast with traditional fishing techniques. They abhor over-fishing and adhere to sustainable harvesting practices. The community still practices the traditional "sea courts" where the community heads assemble at the place of worship every day to hear and decide on issues within the community. ("Bekal Tourism Project: An SOS Call" 1996)

The Bekal project illustrates more. The government of Keralam has already begun acquiring land as cheaply as possible under "public purpose" and intends to sell the land to private and multinational tourist organizations for this same price. To date, there is no environmental impact assessment despite the fact that as planned, the project would violate national coastal regulation zone rules. Local community members are being denied due process through hearings that are a sham.

Fortunately, there are organizations that are becoming involved in the process of revitalizing community efforts to direct tourism. An extensive list of responsible travel organizations can be found on Tourism Concern's Web site. Reference books include *Good Alternative Travel Guide: Exciting Holidays for Responsible Travelers* (2002) by Mark Mann, and the *Ethical Travel Guide* (2006) by Polly Pattullo lists ethical and sustainable tourism in over sixty countries.

Global Exchanges is a model organization in creating opportunities for engaged tourism. Its Reality Tours give people "the chance to learn about unfamiliar cultures, meet with people from various walks of life, and establish meaningful relationships with people from other countries" ("Frequently Asked Questions" 2008).

Solution   Engaged tourism represents a shift in attitudes and activity. Tourists traveling to developing nations shift their attitudes from experiencing inexpensive fun abroad to participating in meaningful experiences in international communities. Interestingly, it is exactly the presence of Western engaged tourists that assists in reestablishing the values, culture, status of local people, and communities adversely affected by commercial tourism.

Linked patterns   Global Citizenship (6), Fair Trade (21), Participatory Design (36), Conversational Support across Boundaries (50), Experimental School (89), Service-Learning (90), Activist Road Trip (134).

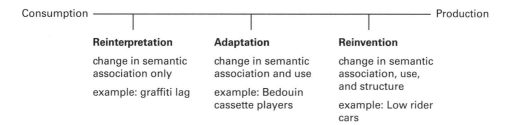

Consumption ———————————————————————— Production

Reinterpretation

change in semantic
association only

example: graffiti lag

Adaptation

change in semantic
association and use

example: Bedouin
cassette players

Reinvention

change in semantic
association, use,
and structure

example: Low rider
cars

Problem   We usually think of technology as that which is designed by elite groups, mostly male, mostly white, and mostly upper class. But the lay public can also be thought of as producers of technology and science. The "smiley face" emoticons used in e-mail, for example, were not designed by experts; rather, they came about as ordinary people took advantage of a flexibility in the system. Technology appropriation can be profound: Latino "street mechanics," who repair and customize cars generally outside of the mainstream and formal economy, for example, created the low-rider car or truck—modified to bounce, ride with exceptionally low clearance, and/or exhibit other "tricked out" aesthetics—that revolutionized their culture. Black teenagers created the "scratch" sound of rap by appropriating the turntable. Appropriated technology can help the disenfranchised gain social power. But there are three barriers. First, marginalized people often see science and technology as the enemy, a force to be resisted. Second, they often lack the education and physical resources for technology interventions. And third, designers (or at least the corporations they work for) do not necessarily see flexibility as something they should incorporate in their products. Of course, not all cases of appropriated technology are happy stories: neo-Nazi groups are also outside the centers of scientific production, and they too adapt and reinvent to gain power.

Context   The first barrier to helping the disenfranchised gain social power is a view of science and technology as the enemy. Social critics often cite technocracy as an evil that perpetuates disparity in social power. Thus oppositional groups that subscribe to this theory tend to desire less technology, not more. We see this in the 1960s counterculture, in the conflation of technology with patriarchy, and in race-based movements that see an original "natural" or "pure" identity that was later defiled by colonialism. The second barrier is a view of science and technology as unattainable. Our society tends to mythologize expertise, particularly that of science and technology, making lay interventions less attainable than they actually are. Many researchers suspect this serves to maintain elite privilege and passive consumption. The third barrier is designing for rigidity. Corporations can increase profits by forcing consumers to use their products or engage in limited behaviors; for example, Microsoft's operating system created barriers to competing Internet browsers.

Discussion   In collecting the various case studies for their anthology, *Appropriating Technology* (2004), Eglash, Croissant, and Di Chiro noticed that some examples made a stronger case for appropriation than others. Using that distinction, they developed three categories positioned along a spectrum from consumption to production (see graphic above).

The weakest case, reinterpretation, is defined by a change in semantic association with little or no change in use or structure. That is, the layperson has changed only the meaning of the artifact, not its physical makeup. Graffiti tags are a good illustration: the physical and functional aspects of a building are essentially unchanged, but the semantic claim to ownership, as a form of either cultural resistance or criminal turf war, is not trivial.

The next stronger case, adaptation, is defined by a change in both semantic association and use. For example, the bedouin society of Egypt, a relatively disempowered ethnic minority, found that cassette tape players, which were marketed for listening to music from the Egyptian majority, had an unused recording capability as well. They began to record their own songs, and this eventually led to the rise of a bedouin pop star and the creation of new economic and cultural opportunities (Abu-Lughod 1989). Adaptation requires two techno-social features. First is an attribute of the technology-user relationship that Hess (1995) refers to as "flexibility." For example, a calculator is less flexible than a word processor, which is less flexible than a personal computer. Second, it requires a violation of intended purpose. It is a mistake to reduce this to the intentions of designers; we also need to consider marketing intentions and commonsense or popular assumptions. In the case of bedouin cassette players, there is a preexisting flexibility for recording that was intended by the designers, but this was obscured by the marketing focus on playback only. Adaptation can be described as the discovery of a latent function, but that definition needs to be problematized in the same ways that philosophers have debated whether mathematics is invention or discovery. The creativity required to look beyond the assumed functions of the technology and see new possibilities is a powerful force for social change, yet one that receives insufficient theoretical attention.

The strongest case for appropriated technology is reinvention, in which semantics, use, and structure are all changed. That is, if adaptation can be said to require the discovery of a latent function, reinvention can be defined as the creation of new functions through structural change. Low-rider cars provide a clear demonstration of this combination. Although automobile shock absorbers were originally produced for decreasing disturbance, Latino mechanics developed methods for attaching them to electrically controlled air pumps, turning shock absorbers into shock producers (the cars can move vertically as well as horizontally). Low-rider cars violate both marketing and design intentions, but the new functionality was introduced by altering the original structure rather than discovering functions lying dormant in the original artifact.

After studying appropriated technologies, what should we do with them? First, it is important to understand that in distinguishing strong versus weak cases for appropriated technology, we make no evaluation of ideology or effectiveness. One might, for instance, find more political success with reinterpretation than reinvention in a given case. It is, rather, more a question of how much involvement the lay public can have in production versus consumption.

Second, appropriated technologies do not have an inherent ethical advantage. Not all forms of resistance are necessarily beneficial in the long run. Aihwa Ong (1987), for example, notes that Malaysian women using spirit possession as resistance to exploitation may be releasing frustrations that could have gone into collective labor organizing. And white supremacist groups might well be described as marginalized people who appropriate the Internet and other technologies. While free speech must be preserved at all costs, appropriation is not making a better society in the case of neo-Nazi Web sites.

Third, insofar as science and technology appropriations have potential contributions to stronger democracy (Schuler 1996), we need to understand how these positive attributes can succeed. First, there are obstacles to appropriation on the design side; most obvious are those created by totalitarian governments, but corporations can also dampen or discourage appropriation. The flexibility required to allow user adaptation, for example, is increasingly threatened in contemporary information technology marketing strategies. Encouraging designers to incorporate appropriation as a positive virtue means reversing this trend toward inflexibility. Second, there are obstacles to appropriation on the lay public side. We need to overcome not only the ideology barrier but also the barriers of education and access to physical resources.

Solution   In terms of the designer barrier, engineers and designers can be trained to think about appropriation as a positive goal. In terms of the ideology barrier, marginalized groups can be encouraged to strive toward positive conceptions of hybridization rather than relying on notions of purity. And in terms of the resource barrier, the creation of community technology centers, among other efforts, can be encouraged Finally, we should examine each case of the lay-professional relationship in terms of the dependence or independence fostered by various appropriated technology strategies. A consumer ombudsman offers more independence than a marketing survey, participatory design offers more than the ombudsman, and appropriating technology offers a maximum of independence. But this is not an ethical spectrum. There are cases in which groups are better off with an ombudsman than an act of appropriation. Increasing independence can free up new possibilities, but decreasing it can facilitate institutionalization. Rather than romanticize independence, both users and designers should strive toward lay-professional relationships that will move toward strong democracy in their particular context. In conclusion, we can encourage, inspire, and incite the use of appropriated technologies for opening new possibilities in culture and technoscience.

Linked patterns   Dematerialization (18), Participatory Design (36), Technocriticism (39), Intermediate Technologies (57), Users' Information Technology Quality Network (80), Wholesome Design for Wicked Problems (82), Design for Unintended Use (84), Labor Visions (112), Community Inquiry (122), Tactical Media (131).

Problem   How people are represented in speech, story, or image influences how they are perceived by themselves and others and, hence, how they are treated. Africa, for example, is typically presented to the rest of the world, and to Africans as well, by CNN and other Western media, not by Africans or African media. This problem, of course, is not confined to Africa. Poor people everywhere are portrayed (if they are portrayed at all) as nameless and voiceless, rarely as people with ideas, aspirations, creativity, culture, or values.

Context   This pattern is applicable in any setting where information about one group of people is being developed and distributed primarily by another group of people.

Discussion

More recently, in later modernity the theme of the everyday has been considerably more prominent. But this does not mean that questions about who is representing for whom and why and how have been resolved. Issues about legitimacy of representation remain crucial, and indeed I shall argue that how to articulate and represent the everyday is the main issue in the politics of culture. (Chaney 2002)

Nonwhites, convicts, the poor, sick, starving people, flood victims, the uneducated, the aged, and those who live in rural areas, as well as intellectuals, dissidents, gender, ethnic and other marginalized groups, are often victims of misrepresentation. Their representations are often paper thin and stereotypical at best. The net result is a compelling, free-floating image of normalcy that serves tacitly as a model to be emulated.

This pattern represents a concept that gets little notice. After all, there is really no way to fully control a representation or what people do with it. Ultimately it is an expression of power: Who is creating the representations, under what conditions, and how can they be maintained, changed, or challenged? When somebody else is determining how you will be represented, you have been robbed of your right to defend yourself, to make your own case for who you are. On some level, it is a type of identity theft. Who you are has been determined elsewhere and stamped on you.

Why bother with representations? Is there really anything to worry about? Are there any negative implications? Yes. For one thing, there seems to be substantial evidence that people start believing their own representations and act according to them. Representations can have unfortunately long life spans since culture tends to replicate itself. Also people individually see little reason to change the way they view the world unless there is a compelling reason to rethink themselves.

This pattern depicts the need for people everywhere to grab hold of their own representation and challenge the mechanisms (generally of media production) that perpetuate stereotypes. At this level of analysis the pattern recommends a more accurate and bidirectional approach to representation, often of entire countries and ethnic and other marginalized populations. At a deeper level this pattern seeks to remedy a problem much more insidious: that of a steady colonization from within.

The importance of this pattern is obvious. It is why people may be suspicious when others are talking about them. It is why big corporations and political parties spend enormous sums on public relations and spinning news and other information to their advantage. Corporations and government agencies have elaborate and professional strategies for ensuring that their public portrait is painted according to their specifications. Movies stars, writers, and others have their own publicists whose job it is to bring (or push) certain information to certain people. Of course, powerful people and institutions also go to great lengths to keep some information submerged and hidden.

There are several tools for addressing these problems. People in the group who may be perpetrating the stereotypes have the responsibility to acknowledge these transgressions and strive to overcome them. Media literacy and media critique are two skills worth developing, and media monitoring is a worthwhile way to develop a fact base that can be used to confront the misrepresenters. Much of this work should be done at a community level: the analyses should be shared, for example, with the community because it is often the community that is being misrepresented. Also, it may even be possible that members of the misrepresented community are unconsciously living down to the stereotypes of their community.

The media are major violators of this pattern's intent. In developed countries especially, their presence is ubiquitous. The "message" of the media is rarely acknowledged. Like a voice in your head, the message is compelling and persistent. It will not go away! It sows stereotyping and simplistic thinking while removing individual autonomy and opportunities for authentic social learning. Although the challenge is great, it's clear that the mass media systems must be challenged if this pattern is to be realized.

Solution   The first step to addressing this problem is to acknowledge that it exists. Since the media (and cultural representations generally) are ubiquitous, it may be hard to believe that there is a bias, however implicit. The second obstacle is thinking that nothing can be done about this. As you explore this problem, you may be amazed at the extent of the problem and your desire to help overcome it.

Linked patterns   Social Dominance Attenuation (4), Linguistic Diversity (16), Culturally Situated Design Tools (49), Indigenous Media (55), Privacy (65), Ethics of Community Informatics (67), Positive Health Information (74), Experimental School (89), Online Antipoverty Community (103), Homemade Media (110), Labor Visions (112), Soap Operas with Civic Messages (120).

Problem   People outside the major spheres of power are often denied access to the tools and technologies of self-expression. This is often the unfortunate by-product of poverty; education is out of reach of the majority of the world's population and access to media tools (including cameras, editing software, recording studios, and the Internet) and other systems is often prohibitively expensive. Although this situation can be debilitating to people who are caught in those circumstances, the rest of society suffers as well: they are deprived of stories and perspectives that could enrich their understanding of the world while preparing them to become better citizens of the world and their local community.

Context   Anybody with a story to tell (and this includes everybody) can benefit from this pattern. This pattern, however, specifically addresses people with little to no access to media production of any kind. Although this pattern focuses on the people who lack the access, implementation of this pattern often requires the assistance of people and organizations with both the resources and interest in working with people in a participatory way.

Discussion   The story told in the 2004 documentary *Born into Brothels* is an excellent example of this pattern. In 1997, New York–based photographer Zana Briski traveled to India to document the lives of women, children, and men who lived in Calcutta's impoverished red-light district. During the next three years, some of which she spent living in the brothels, Briski noticed that many of the children of the prostitutes were fascinated by her photographic equipment. Soon she started giving them cameras and helped the children use them as a new lens to look at their world. Later she organized shows at galleries for the photographs and made the photographs available on the Internet (and one as the introductory image for this pattern). The money from the sales is now being used to help support the children's education. While raising money for the worthy cause of education and raising the consciousness of millions of people who watched the documentary is exemplary, the most important outcome of the project may be the increased awareness and perception that seemed to be unlocked in the children by the acts of observing and recording their surroundings with the camera.

While the Homemade Media pattern is not a panacea, it does have many possible benefits. The first benefit is that learning to create media helps build skills and may lead to employment. In addition, it helps build confidence and self-esteem. These positive attitudes about oneself and the desire to keep persisting in the craft of creating media, whether photography, interviews, audio recordings, or newspapers, is a good defense against self-destructive behaviors such as alcohol or other drug abuse or gang activity or other criminal outlets. The act of capturing an image in a camera's viewfinder or writing down fragments of overheard conversations or otherwise recording promotes the idea of reflection on various aspects of life or the imagination.

Media are inherently shareable in some way. Photographs can be displayed for viewing in galleries, printed in magazines, or hung on public walls. Videos can be shown on televisions or in theaters. These can be artistic or informational, and they can lead to social change in some way. Most basically, they can be used to communicate with others. Homemade media can open up channels of communication with people as audience or as potential partners for additional collaboration.

A few other examples can show a more of the breadth of the pattern: Drawings of children in Darfur present the horror of genocide that is hard to shake off. Gumball Poetry allows people to buy a short poem from a gumball machine for twenty-five cents. One of the most remarkable projects took place in Bogotá, Colombia. Filmmaker Felipe Aljure developed the Rebeldes con Cauce project in which he worked with 140 young people with no filmmaking experience to help them learn how to make films (Dowmunt 1988). Most of the students were from economically disadvantaged backgrounds. They studied film, developed outlines, and created ten- to fifteen-minute films, which were ultimately aired on Bogotá's channel Canal Capital, where they received outstanding ratings.

The Plugged In Project in East Palo Alto, California, helped teach underprivileged youths how to create Web pages that told their stories (while teaching them a skill and self-confidence), from celebrating Thanksgiving holiday with their family to witnessing the seizure of a family member by immigration officials for not having the appropriate papers to remain in the United States.

The homeless newspaper movement is active in many cities around the world. Although it takes different forms in different cities, the basic model is the same: the newspaper concentrates on issues of homelessness and poverty, two subjects that are unlikely to be covered sensitively or in much depth by mainstream media. Beyond that, the newspaper is often actively engaged in the struggle for the rights of poor people and engages poor people and their communities in every aspect of the newspaper production and distribution. The *Real Change* weekly newspaper in Seattle is sold by people who are homeless or otherwise in underprivileged positions. The paper is sold for a dollar, and they receive seventy cents for each paper sold.

Solution   Homemade media can be applied in uncounted ways. Support and enjoy homemade media in your community and around the rest of the world.

Linked patterns   Memory and Responsibility (11), International Networks of Alternative Media (43), Online Community Service Engine (62), Media Diversity (66), Ethics of Community Informatics (67), Patient Access to Medical Records (95), Control of Self-Representation (109), Universal Voice Mail (113), Soap Operas with Civic Messages (120), Tactical Media (131), Media Intervention (132), Activist Road Trip (134).

Problem Repression and other forms of injustice and other social ills are often overlooked, dismissed in a cursory way, or deemed to be inevitable and immutable. Even when these problems are acknowledged, resistance to them can be shallow, erratic, uncoordinated, and ineffectual. Although art can be used to deliver a message of inspiration and information for the disempowered, it is often irrelevant; it can be a tool of the powerful and a diversion of the wealthy. In many cases, distracting and ubiquitous corporate media have replaced the tradition of people and communities telling their own stories.

Context People and societies around the world have developed their own versions of hell on earth that some subset of its inhabitants is obliged to endure. These regions exist within all societies, but vary in size and in magnitude of abuse ranging from neglect to active repression.

Discussion Artists occupy a unique role in society. Through a diversity of approaches, they explore new terrains that words alone are incapable of describing. Art can address issues, help solve problems, and even serve as a "public psychiatrist" that surfaces social anxieties. Art speaks to places that other languages cannot and affects consciousness on a level that we do not understand and cannot map. Some artists work for social and environmental justice. Notably artists can explore ideas of personal or societal importance, or they can operate within a world circumscribed by religious authorities, corporations, or the art-buying public, a decidedly privileged class economically.

The world that resistance strives to understand and confront provides an exhaustible fount of inspiration for artists, professionals and nonprofessionals alike. The media through which messages and stories can be conveyed include T-shirts (indeed, wearing the wrong T-shirt is an invitation to harassment, fines, and imprisonment in many regions and countries around the world), comics and zines, opera, ballet, graffiti, murals, sculpture, and film. Art can be immersive and engaging; it can help build community and involve the audience in rituals or processions. Art can be an individual or collective effort, big or small, public or anonymous, clandestine or furtive. It can be created by children or emotionally disturbed people, among many others. The art of homeless people, refugees, or incarcerated people is likely to present a view of the world that the rest of us may not see.

Resistance art brings hidden knowledge out of the shadows. The historic roots of contemporary experience, a common theme of Chicano murals, such as those created by Los Cybrids collective in Los Angeles and other southwestern cities in the United States, explore themes of identity and hybridity. (A mural created by the Rebel Chicano Art Front Collective is used as the introductory image for this pattern.) Another approach is to present the reality of a situation in a documentary style, such as Walker Evans's sparse, unadorned depression-era photographs of the rural poor. Another approach is exemplified by George Grosz's grotesque and piercing caricatures of militarists and war profiteers, or Hitler garbed in a bearskin.

In the 1980s, Artists of the World Against Apartheid, based in France, issued a broad appeal to artists around the world to contribute antiapartheid works of art. Ernest Pignon of France and Antonio Saura of Spain worked unselfishly for two years to make it happen. A major exhibition was mounted in late 1983 at the Fondation Nationale des Arts Graphiques et Plastiques in Paris. Since the organizers had stipulated in advance that the art would be held in trust and given to the people of South Africa on the occasion of "the first free and democratic government by universal suffrage" as the basis of an antiapartheid museum, the collection was moved to South Africa at the request of President Nelson Mandela.

A similar event took place in the United States two decades later. With the invasion of Iraq looming, first lady Laura Bush picked an inopportune time to invite poet Sam Hamill to a special White House event, Poetry and the American Voice, which was to celebrate the works of Emily Dickinson, Walt Whitman, and Langston Hughes. Instead of being seduced by the allure of power and prestige, Hamill refused Bush's invitation. Instead he e-mailed several friends, asking them for poems on the theme of war that would be bound and presented to Bush. This ignited a poetic firestorm that claimed no national border. Inspired by Hamill's defiance, a Web site (http://www.poetsagainstthewar.org) was established that provided a platform for poets around the world to express their feelings related to the impending war. The site proved immediately and enormously popular; at its peak it was averaging several new poems a minute. Now the site has over 20,000 poems online, including works by Adrienne Rich, W. S. Merwin, and Lawrence Ferlinghetti, and it spotlights several poems each week. The project ultimately published two volumes of poetry, and a documentary film, *Poets in Wartime,* was inspired by the effort. Moreover, the work engendered a nonprofit organization, Poets against War, formed with this mission statement: "Poets Against War continues the tradition of socially engaged poetry by creating venues for poetry as a voice against war, tyranny and oppression."

The Poets against War episode raises the general question of the role of occupational groups and whether there is an implicit or explicit obligation to help deter aggression and war. A short list of such candidates would include teachers, religious leaders, engineers, journalists, farmers, and doctors and nurses and other caregivers. A longer list would include almost everybody, for very few people in the world want to be within war's lethal compass as either participant or as innocent bystander.

Another example is the Beehive Design Collective, an anarchic and itinerant design collective based in Vermont that travels around the world to create region-specific murals. Members often work with indigenous or other people to develop murals that capture the circumstances in which they live. The murals they develop grow organically and contain a variety of elements, sinuously weaving indigenous plants and animals, historic referents, and symbols of corporate and colonial domination, with images of fanciful and realistic resistance.

Resistance art has many audiences. In the antiapartheid movement, for example, the audience obviously included the victims of apartheid and supporters of their struggle. It also included the people who believed themselves neutral or had not thought about apartheid from a moral standpoint and people who were actively promulgating it: politicians, policemen, the media, and business spokespeople who benefited from the cheap labor provided by the marginalized victims. Beyond that, the audience extended to the rest of the world. Many people outside South Africa worked on antiapartheid campaigns. Gill Scott-Heron's antiapartheid anthem, "Johannesburg," was played on the radio in U.S. cities, where its references to segregated cities in the United States like New York and Philadelphia showed that South Africa was not the only country in the world where prejudice and racism flourished.

From Goya and Picasso to Johannesburg's T-shirt artists and anonymous graffiti artists around the world, resistance artists, generally acting on their own, have portrayed the horrors of war and other abominations. Activists in Seattle, hoping to help cultivate a supportive community network for resistance artists, convened two Arts of Resistance conferences. Through workshops, presentations, videos, and, most important, face-to-face dialogue and debate, the idea that art can be socially transformative became more widely recognized and more thoughtfully practiced.

People ultimately also need to be reminded that they are not impotent, disconnected spectators but active and engaged participants in the ongoing vibrant fabric of life. Art can tell the story of the ongoing struggle while suggesting ways for people to work against it. It can also sketch out, in possibly indistinct and uncertain terms, a future that may exist, after successful struggles, where children, do not experience the daily injury of living in an unjust and unhealthy world.

Anglican Bishop Desmond Tutu, a long-time foe of apartheid, notes that when resistance art is successful, "People come to the forceful realization that they are not entirely the impotent playthings of powerful forces." According to Tutu, resistance art, whether it is a play, song, or T-shirt, represents, "a proud defiance of the hostile forces that would demean and dehumanize" (Williamson 1989).

Solution   Art can convey beauty, love, and joy. It can also convey justice, fairness, dignity, and resistance. Engaging in art can hone creativity by encouraging exploration within a plastic medium. The future itself is a plastic medium, and we will never know how malleable it is if we do not explore how to shape it. Resistance art can be a seed that helps people understand their situation and how they might work to improve it.

Linked patterns   Teaching to Transgress (20), Alternative Media in Hostile Environments (53), Sense of Struggle (104), Socially Responsible Computer Games (126), Power Research (128), Tactical Media (131), Media Intervention (132), Peaceful Public Demonstrations (133), Activist Road Trip (134).

Problem   Fifty years ago, there was little doubt that unions had dramatically raised living standards for workers. But while more than one in three American workers belonged to a union in the early 1950s, today scarcely one in ten workers do. As companies move jobs away from unionized workplaces, it is no coincidence that fewer workers have health insurance and that pay has stagnated. Nonunion workers are only one-fifth as likely to have reliable defined-benefit pensions as union workers. In their heyday, American unions became somewhat complacent, confident that they were an accepted part of American life and secure in their ability to bargain for middle-class living standards for millions of workers. Many neglected the need to vigorously organize new members or reach out to the public.

Context   New technology has helped businesses consolidate into huge multinationals that swiftly move jobs around the world to where labor costs are the lowest. This has vastly strengthened the power of employers to keep workers from unionizing and getting a fair shake. American workers watch their jobs transferred to Mexico, where workers can be controlled by management-run unions. When Mexican workers organize unions, they encounter government hostility and threats to move work to China. In this global race to the bottom, governments try to attract (and keep) investment by offering minimal resistance to company demands, privatizing operations, and weakening worker protection rules. Workers and their allies are using new communications tools to discover what is happening and build broader support networks.

Discussion   Recent surveys show that U.S. workers want to join unions (Teixeira 2007). But employers often prevent this from happening by illegally threatening or firing union activists (Lafer 2007). More than 23,000 U.S. workers are dismissed or punished each year for exercising their legal rights to form or join a union.

Trade agreements like the North American Free Trade Agreement (NAFTA) and the General Agreement on Tariffs and Trade further weaken worker power. Although they strongly protect corporate intellectual property and investment, they open up nations to unfettered competition in terms of jobs and living standards. Even workers in high-tech fields like programming see their wages and job security battered by international outsourcing.

Unions have historically helped workers overcome this competition by uniting them to win across-the-board justice for the majority. In the 1900s they won equal pay and benefits across entire industries like automobiles and steel. The challenge today is to overcome international competition and join hands to win good wages and conditions worldwide.

The challenge is daunting. The AFL-CIO split in 2005 when several big unions formed a new federation that pledged to organize more vigorously. This division, however, may also dilute the clout of labor to act in concert. Nonetheless, steps being taken today suggest ways to move toward the vision of global worker justice and unionism, aided by fast, global Internet communications. Here we look at several of these steps

• Build broad support for workers and communities, regardless of location or whether there is a union contract, and apply pressure to encourage government support for workers.

People can join AFL-CIO campaigns for better laws and worker rights at workingamerica .org. The Jobs for Justice coalition also rallies public support for worker-justice battles. The campaign against Wal-Mart, one of the most powerful economic forces on earth, is proof that the movement can reach beyond members. Wal-Mart paved the way for retailers to aggressively demand lower costs from producers around the world. The union movement is using the Internet to tap into a broad lode of resentment to such tactics, including small businesses and towns devastated by Wal-Mart super-stores, states that are stretched by paying the health costs of Wal-Mart's shortchanging of its own workers, and people upset with how Wal-Mart and its imitators are cheapening culture and diminishing opportunities globally, as the drive for ever-lower costs crushes more humane social standards. People have demanded laws in Chicago and elsewhere to make big retailers pay good wages and benefits.

• Connect with immigrants and workers across national borders to build permanent support networks and apply global pressure on companies and governments to respect workers.

Given the vast distances and differences in living standards, culture, and language, as well as interference from repressive governments, reaching across borders is not easy. To succeed, unions must connect with other social movements and take maximum advantage of technology to communicate quickly and cheaply around the world.

• Organize globally against corporate threats to play workers against each other.

The New York–based National Labor Committee exposes appalling conditions in foreign sweatshops through creative media events that attract support from churches and the public. The Campaign for Labor Rights in the United States, Britain's LabourStart, and the U.S.-based UE, the union for electrical workers (which publishes a virtual newsletter on Mexican labor and is allied with a democratic Mexican union), also organize powerful e-mail campaigns to support union struggles around the world, while groups like the Comitè Fronterizo de Obreros organize on the ground across borders.

• Challenge the commercialization of culture and inspire an ethical framework in which people are called on to make sacrifices, such as not buying products made in sweatshops, to press for gains that benefit all.

Students are organizing to support labor rights locally and globally. The first group of Mexican workers to organize at a *maquila* clothing factory (a factory producing products for export under conditions favoring multinationals) was at the Korean-owned Mexmode factory in Puebla. A strike by young women workers won a new union in 2001 through key support from the U.S.-based United Students against Sweatshops, which is allied with labor and global antisweatshop groups. They quickly mobilized using the Internet.

• Share technical ideas, information and organizing experiences with activists and labor supporters worldwide.

Academics have been sharing information globally on labor organizing, as evidenced at the Global Unions conference sponsored by Cornell University in 2006. And union supporters from several nations meet biannually at LaborTech conferences to showcase creative uses of modern communications.

• Push for trade agreements that protect not just corporate investment but workers' rights, with trade penalties for mistreating workers. Insist on union participation in all international trade negotiations.

Several Latin American governments have rejected the neoliberal basis of modern trade agreements and the antiworker conditions imposed by lending institutions. In 2006, a popular French revolt against watering down job protections for young workers won a surprise victory. Recent rounds of trade talks have failed, and Mexican voters in the 2006 presidential election turned out en masse for Lopez Obrador, who wants to renegotiate NAFTA.

The labor movement cannot and will not die. Workers are struggling for union rights around the globe against the greatest of odds, and the public is increasingly supportive.

Solution   After decades of losing ground, unions and advocates of worker justice are striving to overcome the competition for jobs that pits worker against worker in a global race to the bottom. A vision of global progress, based on humane values, solidarity, and local community, can motivate a union movement that transcends borders and involves all workers and allies. The Wal-Mart campaign, the antisweatshop movement, and international networking are evidence that unions, the public, foreign workers, and academics are reaching out in new ways to form support networks to raise standards for all workers. They are pressuring governments to reject the neoliberal trade policies that disadvantage workers and insist on trade rules that require justice for workers.

Linked patterns   Social Dominance Attenuation (4), Health as a Universal Right (5), Working-Class Consciousness (12), Fair Trade (21), Opportunity Spaces (33), Strategic Capacity (34), Grassroots Public Policy Development (78), Future Design (88), Community-Building Journalism (97), Sense of Struggle (104), Appropriating Technology (108), Control of Self-Representation (109), Thinking Communities (118), Power Research (128).

Problem   How do people find a job without a telephone? How do they avail themselves of services, receive timely information, or stay connected to loved ones if they do not have a reliable message number? Even in this very wired age, the need for a phone number remains; the lack of a constant telephone number becomes a very real obstacle for the homeless or phoneless.

Context   Communities around the world have different levels of technological sophistication for supporting the everyday conversations of their members. The health of a community is sustained by these conversations, and people who are blocked from this universe of conversations are, in a fundamental way, blocked from membership in the community. For that reason the integration of people into the broad community conversation network is important to all communities.

Voice mail is a low-cost solution that substitutes for dial tone for those unable to afford it. Providing voice mail to a community of people cut off from the communications infrastructure is technologically plausible and works well in urban environments where there is existing infrastructure (telephone service, community providers, and pay telephones); however, the need for the service exists anywhere there are disconnected people. The audience of users runs the gamut from the homeless to the working poor to people fleeing domestic violence or dealing with health problems in need of a confidential communication link that is easy to access.

Discussion   In 1991, two program directors at the Seattle Worker Center conceived of a small project that had an unpredictably potent impact. Called Community Voice Mail (CVM), the idea responded practically to a specific problem: How can a homeless person find work or housing, receive medical or social services, or navigate daily life without a reliable and direct point of contact? Furthermore, how can the job developer, the doctor, the advocate, in short, the social services system charged with the mission to respond to the needs of the poor and homeless, do so efficiently and effectively if they must devote hours to tracking down the individuals they serve?

Community Voice Mail responds to this need by acting like a home answering machine for thousands of people across a community. The CVM service is a shared resource operated by the CVM national office and a local community-based organization that takes on the role of host. This host builds a network of participating agencies to maximize the distribution of the resource cost-effectively. People in crisis and transition may enroll in CVM through any number of social, human, or health services agencies in the community. By providing multiple points of access, the service allows practical and flexible eligibility criteria while maintaining basic measurement standards.

As of 2008, the program operates in forty-one U.S. cities and in Melbourne, Australia, connecting more than 41,000 people annually. The CVM national office provides guidance on how to start a CVM service and supports the resulting federation of peer sites. Cisco Systems is the majority funder of the nonprofit program and donated equipment and software for a centralized network that uses Voice Over Internet Protocol (VoIP) to manage accounts for tens of thousands of users. The network's advanced capabilities include a broadcast messaging feature that is used to distribute information about job openings, training opportunities, community resources, and emergency weather warnings to the voicemail subscribers.

Connecting individuals via communication services integrates people into existing communication networks and also helps establish new networks. These networks could help support the community of people who use the system by allowing the users and the managers of the system to share relevant information and mobilize users in relation to specific issues and events.

Universal voice mail presents a meaningful pattern and objective that can assist communities by encouraging the integration of all people into the community. At the same time the employment of this pattern will necessarily take a wide variety of forms depending on many factors. These forms will be determined by the people who will use the services, organizations in the community that are providing the services, and the general nature and climate of social services in the community. Other things, including the technological infrastructure, social capital, and the ability to raise funds in the community, perhaps through an innovative commercial sector, are relevant as well. The dedication of the organizers is also key, as is their ability to collaborate and incrementally improve the level of support over time. Since technological systems are still changing rapidly (although they are unevenly distributed, with the more technically sophisticated systems concentrated in economically privileged regions) the nature of the service needs—and the technological support that is needed to support the service—will undoubtedly change as well.

Solution   Universal voice mail should be available as a low-cost alternative to telephone service so that all people, regardless of income, have a reliable point of contact that maintains dignity and restores connection to opportunity and support.

Linked patterns   Public Library (59), Community Networks (61), Online Community Service Engine (62), Accessibility of Online Information (75), Mobile Information and Computer Technology Learning Facilities (77), Homemade Media (110), Community Telecenters (117), Great Good Place (119), Emergency Communication Systems (121).

Problem   "The truth about stories is that's all we are," wrote Thomas King (2003). Stories are fundamental to being human. How do they change as languages and cultures evolve through different communication technologies? In the age of cyberspace, we often feel alienated from genuine stories—those we live with every day that tell us how to become decent human beings and live meaningful lives. Corporate media exploit story patterns that had originally evolved to pass on ethical codes, and we are now trapped into thinking about products instead of reflecting on our lives. Traditional myths explored dynamic relationships between humans and nature. How can stories help us adapt to our quickly changing world?

Context   This pattern addresses the concerns of organizations and individuals involved in education, culture, arts, society, mythology, technology, law, philosophy, humanities, psychology, science, environmental studies, religion, social and political science, and activism.

Discussion

One way or another we are living the stories planted in us early or along the way, or we are also living the stories we planted—knowingly or unknowingly—in ourselves. We live stories that either give our lives meaning or negate it with meaninglessness. If we change the stories we live by, quite possibly we change our lives. (Okri 1997)

Patterns in stories tend to reflect the environments we live in and the communication media we use. Indigenous peoples evolved patterns in oral traditions that resonated with the voices of the land and reinforced memory and meaning. The invention of writing and the phonetic alphabet played with the way language and images could be displayed as text. The advent of the printing press offered freedom to experiment with new narrative and poetic forms, as well as restraints, as texts and language became standardized. The structure of stories changed as they moved from the places they were told and captured on the printed page (Ong 1992).

In the image (above) from ancient Greece, a poet pours wine to the muse, Erato who appears in the form of a bird. Today can words again become "winged" as they fly through both time and space in new forms offered by electronic media? Speech is communal; it exists only as it is shared. As stories shift and change in response to new environments and technologies, who has access and jurisdiction to manipulate them? Can these new media offer opportunities to engage our senses and help us reconnect to the natural world? Can this enriched experience help us reflect on the deeper messages that stories contain?

Stories are conduits or vehicles that mediate our inner and outer worlds. When we tell stories, we are connected to live events and internal dramas. Modern cultures use technology to record ideas or performances and tend to value the analysis of texts, recordings, and other artifacts of expression. We cultivate methods of reflection that reinforce our capacity to respond, think, and explore symbolic messages, but our objectivity makes us feel removed or alienated from authentic experience. We often yearn for the mystery of stories to deepen our lives.

Oral cultures are immersed in ritual and experience; the time, place, and context in which a story is told are crucial to its meaning. Myths, which convey symbolic messages, are also repositories or living encyclopedias of practical knowledge and wisdom gained from sustainable relationships to the natural world. Oral traditions resonate with mnemonic patterns, poetic rhythms, tones, and inflections of local landscapes (Kane 1994, Abram 1996).

Richard Louv (2006) points out that studies of the songs of birds and whales reveal many of the same laws of composition as those used by humans. New scientific methods have enabled humans to learn about the intricate patterns of human and animal communication but have not given most children a deep or genuine experience of animals and the stories or songs grounded in the natural world. This results in what Louv describes as the modern child's "hyperintellectualized" perception of nature and other animals.

Technology gives us tools to analyze and preserve traditional stories, but also disrupts and alienates people from meaningful stories that connect them with sustainable patterns in the natural world. Modern myths are often caught up in the social, political, and economic systems created by new technologies. Those who control the stories, knowledge, and mediums of communication wield the power (Czitrom 1982).

Marshall McLuhan (1962) explored the shadow side of technological and economic success by arguing that popular culture is a source for diagnosing the "collective trance" of industrial society. Ads are a new kind of storytelling, "a social ritual or magic that enhances us in our own eyes." Rolf Jensen (1996) says, "The highest-paid person in the first half of the next century will be the 'storyteller.' Many global companies are mainly storytellers, and the value of products depends on the story they tell." Advertisers proclaim freedom of choice as the foundation of the American way of life; however, they gloss over questions of power and control. McLuhan (1962) suggested that individuals break the hypnotic trance of the media through tough-minded evaluation that probes the collective myths of our industrial folklore.

Mythologist Joseph Campbell (1972) says, "Not only have the old mythic notions of the nature of the cosmos gone to pieces, but also those of the origins of the history of mankind." He suggests that to give meaning to life, the modern person cannot simply reproduce inherited patterns of thought or action, but must create his or her own stories. Since many people start with seeds provided by the media, how do they proceed?

Words and stories are active agents. Ernest Cassirer (1946) wrote that the "word," in early cosmologies, is the primary force from which being and doing originate. Likewise, the cause and effect of media and print "word magic" in modern cultures determine our political and economic systems and can result in nationalism and colonialism. Traditional stories and myths that have evolved from oral, consensually shared standards and beliefs that value feeling and community interaction have come into conflict with technologies that value independence, analytical thought, and scientific or secular authority. Modern civilization is faced with a split between the head and the heart.

In the Greek myth of the phonetic alphabet, King Cadmus planted dragons' teeth (alphabetic symbols) that rose up as armed men. If the alphabet could have such effects, what is the effect of modern technologies? We face the challenge of dealing ethically with the power humans have manufactured through technology. Can we recover a sense of reverence for the word without fueling tribal or national myths that sow dragons' teeth?

Thoreau anticipated these arguments in "Walking" when he says: "There are other letters for the child to learn than those which Cadmus invented" (Atkinson 2000). Rather than learning letters in dusty schools, Thoreau wanted students to learn from wilderness. For him, mythology came close to expressing the language of nature. He advocates a kind of "tawny grammar" that celebrates what is wild and free. Through this, he says, "The highest that we can attain is not Knowledge, but Sympathy with Intelligence."

Perhaps McLuhan (1962) suggested a solution to our dilemma: "Two cultures or technologies can, like astronomical galaxies, pass through one another without collision; but not without change of configuration." Are we ready for a transformation of this magnitude?

Can we connect traditional stories and myths with new technologies in ways that do not hypnotize us into a trance but instead help us engage us more completely with community and the natural world?

Solution Storytelling, an ancient art, needs to be rediscovered and updated. Stories help humankind understand, reinterpret, and reframe the meanings that undergird its existence. Can we use new communications technologies to weave together words and images, scientific information and poetic inspiration, and incorporate multiple voices (including the larger community of plants, animals, birds, and elemental forces) to tell multifaceted stories of our communities? Can stories help us to weave together the communications and global challenges that face us as we learn to live creatively with each other and the natural world?

Linked patterns Memory and Responsibility (11), Back to the Roots (13), Demystification and Reenchantment (14), Translation (15), Linguistic Diversity (16), Teaching to Transgress (20), Media Literacy (35), Conversational Support across Boundaries (50), Alternative Media in Hostile Environments (53), Indigenous Media (55), Ethics of Community Informatics (67), E-Consultation (70), Voices of the Unheard (83), Strategic Frame (86), Shared Vision (101), Community Animators (102), Public Domain Characters (115), Everyday Heroism (116), Soap Operas with Civic Messages (120), Illegitimate Theater (123), Socially Responsible Computer Games (126).

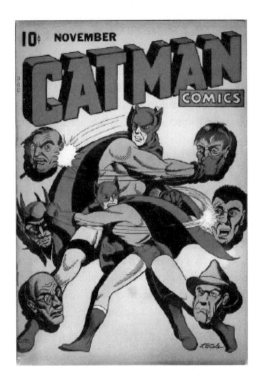

Problem   Stories are an ancient and still powerful technique for people to create and share knowledge across temporal and geographical boundaries. Stories may be conceptualized as having three major dimensions: character, plot, and environment. Traditionally societies have used and shared all of these dimensions. Today, in an effort to make the rich and powerful yet richer and more powerful, the natural processes of creating, sharing, and building on stories have been subverted into a process of claiming the world of stories as private property. This limits artistic creativity and stunts the growth of collective wisdom.

Context   Large, powerful corporations (many recently merged) control many of the media and have a huge influence on international copyright laws. In most cases, the characters used in movies and television shows (even if originally taken from the public domain) are restricted in terms of the ability of anyone else to use them. In fact, in some cases, people have been sued even for setting up fan Web sites for these characters, as well as for using them in satire. Arguably, there has never been a greater need for collective human wisdom. Yet the profit motive on steroids has put a host of economic, legal, and logistical barriers across possible paths of collaborative thought.

Discussion   Humankind has generated a magnificent pantheon of fictional and not-so-fictional characters over the millennia of its existence. But this rich legacy may be stopped cold through a transfer of the ownership of humankind's stories and images to corporate rather than shared commons ownership.

Civil society should establish a repository of characters who are available to all without charge. This could contain characters from our precorporate past as well as those of more recent vintage, such as Cat-Man (shown in the introductory graphic), who was raised in Burma by a tigress but abandoned by the corporation that spawned him. Ultimately it could even include those now embargoed behind commercial contracts. Novelists could legally allow the inhabitants of the universes they created to be enlisted in others. Cartoonists such as Matt Groening could donate Homer Simpson or a new type of American everyman complete with voices and descriptions of where he lived and what he liked to do. Frustrated novelists could supply names and descriptions that their colleagues could borrow for their own work. However, it is not only artists and writers who benefit from having access to stories and the characters who inhabit them. Characters can serve as sources of inspiration for all; they can give us hope in dire times and serve as models for ethical, effective, or clever behavior. One use of characters is to serve as a kind of "board of directors" that we can use imaginatively to help look at our problems and proposed solutions from various perspectives. (See "IBM Research: Knowledge Socialization" undated.)

The Disney corporation may be the most prolific borrower of stories (including Aladdin, Atlantis, Beauty and the Beast, Cinderella, Davy Crockett, "The Legend of Sleepy Hollow," Hercules, *The Hunchback of Notre Dame, The Jungle Book, Oliver Twist, Pinocchio,* Pocahontas, Robin Hood, Snow White, Sleeping Beauty, *Three Musketeers, Treasure Island,* and *The Wind in the Willows*) from the public domain. The number of stories Disney has added to the humankind's commonwealth is still at zero (thanks in part to U.S. legislation that granted Mickey Mouse another seventy-five years of service to the corporation).

Solution   Encouraging the open source creation and use of characters will enable artists to build on each other's work. Characters are not only an aspect of stories for entertainment; they also serve as sources of inspiration, community coherence devices, and tools of thought for creative problem solving. Open source characters help in all these domains.

Linked patterns   The Commons (2), Media Literacy (35), Indigenous Media (55), Media Diversity (66), Shared Vision (101), The Power of Story (114), Everyday Heroism (116), Soap Operas with Civic Messages (120), Illegitimate Theater (123), Socially Responsible Computer Games (126), Open Source Everything (127), Media Intervention (132).

Problem   In popular media, protagonists are usually richer, stronger, and more beautiful (or handsome) than ordinary people, who, even if they have names, are turned into stock characters. Many of the situations, moreover, in which the protagonists find themselves are extraordinary (situations of horror, action, thriller, or fantasy, to name just a few genres). This approach has the effect of making people feel that their own lives are boring and unimportant. Indeed, many people feel that escaping into a mediated reality, whether it is television, video games, or movies, is the only way to "live." This approach also distracts people from addressing real problems by directing their imaginations to situations that are irrelevant to their own lives.

Context   This pattern blends fact and fiction. It addresses the stories of people and settings in fiction and nonfiction and in real life as well.

Discussion   There are no reasons that stories involving ordinary people in everyday life cannot be genuinely beautiful, moving, and inspirational. The Everyday Heroism pattern was inspired by this passage: "Lispector (1925–1977) is best known for short stories and novels that are structured around small, epiphanic moments in the lives of Brazilian middle-class women" (Sadlier 1999; also see Lispector 1960, 1988).

Jean François Millet's evocative painting *The Gleaners* (1857) shows the simple heroism of staying alive. Toiling under the social stigma of gleaning for their food, three women scour the fields after the harvest for the leftovers to which they were entitled under French law. The film *To Be and to Have* provides another inspiring example. Through a simple and unhurried portrait of a teacher in a small French village, the viewer understands his concerns for the children in the one-room schoolhouse, his hobbies, and his connections with the entire village. No matter what the movies tell us, most real heroes do not fight intergalactic evil or psychopathic killers. The real struggles are at the human level.

Beverly Cleary, a well-known and prolific children's author, captures a great deal of the ordinary dangers that everybody must face with her wonderful books about a child. In *Ramona the Brave* (1975), when Ramona was just six, "She was tempted to try going to school a new way, by another street, but decided she wasn't that brave yet." In that same year, Ramona enters a new classroom with a teacher who does not seem to understand her or her imaginative ways of seeing things.

Although there is no evidence that Ramona became an activist, she probably would have respected the tough position it can put people in who take an unpopular stand and insist that changes for the good can be made. Clearly there would be no social change without heroism, especially the unsung, everyday kind. A small but significant piece of wisdom offers encouragement to those of us who hesitate when faced with this challenge: speak the truth even if your voice shakes.

The Giraffe Heroes Project promotes ordinary heroism (or, rather, heroism by people who might otherwise appear to be ordinary), realizing that no movement is due to a single leader. The project celebrates people who "stick their necks out for the common good" and has named over 1,000 "giraffes" in 27 countries thus far who have a vision of a better world. One of these heroes, shown being arrested during a demonstration in the introductory photograph, is Reverend Maurice McCrackin, who in 1945 built the first interracial Presbyterian congregation in the United States. He was still active in his nineties, protesting the mistreatment of mental patients who had been refused treatment because they lacked the funds. Each of the awardees has taken personal risks to initiate an ameliorative project on a grand scale, such as replanting a country's trees, or on a small scale, such as building bridges between two hostile groups in a community.

Solution   Produce—and consider—more popular media about ordinary people and everyday lives. Celebrate the heroes among us, and strive to be one yourself—even an ordinary one.

Linked patterns   Social Dominance Attenuation (4), Spiritually Grounded Activism (24), Community Animators (102), Online Antipoverty Community (103), Sense of Struggle (104), Self-Help Groups (105), The Power of Story (114), Public Domain Characters (115), Whistle-Blowing (130), Peaceful Public Demonstrations (133), Activist Road Trip (134).

Projects

Problem   Across the globe, new information and communication technologies (ICT) are increasingly perceived as elements essential to citizenship in contemporary society. However, numerous preconditions must be met before a person can make use of the applications and systems that represent the network society. Sometimes understood as contributing to the phenomenon known as the digital divide, these preconditions include, at the very least, an income level that facilitates payment for the equipment and its maintenance and operation; skills to use ICT; the availability of electricity; an awareness that ICT might matter; and confidence in oneself and in the possibility of an improvement in one's condition. Unfortunately, for the vast majority of people, these preconditions are not being met and are not likely to be in the near future.

Context   Projects to develop and maintain community telecenters, public access points for ICT, can exist at various levels, from small communities, for example, a neighborhood or grassroots organization in a village, to an entire large country, or even at the international level. Because circumstances vary from one community to another, recipes, best practice models, or the like cannot be mechanically replicated. Nevertheless, as telecenters emerge as significant network society phenomena some basic concepts and principles for the purposeful and appropriate use of ICT might strengthen efforts toward social progress.

Discussion   The idea that public facilities for ICT might be established within communities is now fairly commonplace around the world (Menou 2003). Modern public access points to ICT are often referred to as telecenters, though their diverse origins, ownership, purposes, and modes of operation might justify a typology of public access points, so that the commonalities and differences might be understood (Menou and Stoll 2003b).

Telecenters first emerged in Scandinavia and the U.K. during the 1980s and early 1990s and were known variously as telecottages, telehus, teleservice, centers, or electronic village halls (Day 1996a, 1996b). The first community computer center in the United States was established in 1981 in the basement of a housing project in Harlem in New York City (Schuler 1996). Intended to provide public access to computing technology, these initiatives were run as either community development projects, commercial ventures, or a bit of both (Day 2001, Day and Harris 1997). In developing countries, the development of telecenters took three forms. The most widespread are pilot projects initiated by international development agencies such as UNESCO and the World Bank, which commonly resulted in isolated facilities with limited community involvement; examples are in Timbuktu in Mali and Kothmale in Sri Lanka. Government programs claiming to overcome the digital divide by the implantation of a large number of telecenters in "underprivileged" communities (for example, in Argentina) experience similar drawbacks to those found in development agency telecenters; top-down approach, poor networking, and bureaucratic constraints. A third line combines individual initiatives by grassroots nongovernmental organizations (NGOs) in particular locales and a franchising model developed by the Red Científica Peruana in Peru, known as Cabinas Publicas Internet, which blurred the boundaries between community service and small business development.

Today the variety of public ICT access points (PIAPs) and the nature of their roles have expanded and can be distinguished in several ways:

- Their origin, ranging from the ad hoc initiative of an individual to national and international programs
- Their purpose, ranging from profit of business owners (often called cybercafés or Internet cafés) to free support to community development endeavors (true community telecenters)
- Their ownership, ranging from individual small entrepreneurs to community groups and local and central governments
- The community participation in their governance, ranging from none to full control
- The mix of ICT available, ranging from only one, say, public phone booths, to all (phone, fax, Internet, radio, Web TV, and others)
- The variety of services offered, ranging from independent use of ICT to a wide mix of economic, social, educational, and cultural activities
- Whether they stand alone or are part of a more or less extensive network

True community telecenters are part of the efforts undertaken by community members to build community and improve community conditions (Menou and Stoll 2003a). The centers are designed and managed with the full participation of the community (Roessner 2005). This pattern does not address noncommunity telecenters, concerned only with providing access to ICT at an affordable cost to people who are temporarily or permanently deprived of it.

Community telecenters typically get started in one of two ways. They are the brainchild of interested individuals or grassroots community groups that champion their development and implementation through various community strategies and actions, or they form part of a top-down (usually government or international agency) program with claims of bridging the digital divide.

Each community telecenter faces social, political, economic, and technical challenges. In the social realm the key issues are:

- The relevance of the telecenter and ICT use as a means to support development efforts undertaken by the community
- The appropriateness of its role, the social interaction it permits, and the information it makes available, especially with regard to cultural and gender biases
- The availability of people with required skills to operate and manage the telecenter and provide training and support to users
- The level of information and computer literacy in the community and the availability of intermediaries to offset their deficiency
- The availability and accessibility of local information.

In the political realm, key issues are:

- The degree of ownership that the community might have from the inception or progressively reach
- The level and continuity of community involvement in the management of the telecenter
- The support of or, conversely, conflict with local and national authorities and pressure groups
- The relationship with national programs in the area of universalization of telecommunications services and digital inclusion and a telecenter's ability to preserve its identity and autonomy while participating in such programs
- The attitude of telecommunication companies toward competition, universalization, and digital inclusion efforts

In the economic realm, key issues are:

- Funding for initial investments
- Regular income streams that can support the operation of the telecenter
- Resources for the maintenance and renewal of the equipment
- Employment conditions that are attractive enough for retaining the permanent staff

In the technological realm, key issues are:

- Reliability and cost of power supply
- Reliability and cost of telecommunications
- Reliability and cost of access to international Internet backbones
- Ability to implement a distributed network
- Capability of operating Free and Open Source Software (FOSS) applications
- Capability of deploying media integration, in particular radio

Community telecenter associations have been set up and are powerful instruments for sharing knowledge and experiences, mutual help, and establishing influence locally, regionally, and internationally (Menou, Delgadillo, Poepsel, and Stoll 2004). They are grassroots organizations,, not to be confused with top-down portals and support schemes that may claim to represent telecenters and disseminate second-hand knowledge for the sake of specific political and commercial interests.

Across the globe, governments and international agencies recognize telecenters as key instruments for achieving digital inclusion. Despite a proliferation of funding programs to support their establishment, top-down development does not address a telecenter's challenges of social, financial, and technological sustainability. In the 1980s and 1990s, for example, telecottages and electronic village halls (EVHs) were very much favored among government and funding agencies (Day 2001, Day and Harris 1997). However, they were short-term projects, expected to achieve sustainability with no support or training. Some transformed themselves into small commercial ventures, but most eventually closed, leaving behind a legacy of frustration and disillusionment in the community.

Few lessons from that period appear to have been learned. Many of the U.K. Online Centers have closed or are closing after massive amounts of public funds were pumped into them. The pressure toward securing financial sustainability in the short term (usually three to four years) may push telecenters to close or reinvent themselves as business enterprises, despite the fact that they serve a population with insufficient income to pay for nonessential goods and services.

Andrew Carnegie built libraries only for communities that committed to fund their continuing maintenance. Similarly, community telecenters require sustained operating revenue for purposes such as equipment and network maintenance and renewal, ongoing training, and advocacy work that keeps the telecenter at the hub of community activities and needs. Just as public library services facilitated increased participation in society for the socially excluded through universal access to knowledge, community telecenters can further citizenship in the network society not only through access to information but also through participation in content creation, communication exchange, and knowledge sharing.

Solution   Community telecenters should be as much a part of the social infrastructure as public libraries, education, and police services. Telecenters must be socially as well as financially sustainable and grounded in community engagement in their design, implementation, and development. Community members need skills in management, operation, fundraising, and in social networking so as to learn from the experience of others. Finally, local communities can assist themselves in these matters by electing public administrators and lawmakers who genuinely support community technology initiatives and understand the significance of their role in the community.

Linked patterns   Participatory Design (36), Culturally Situated Design Tools (49), Intermediate Technologies (57), Public Library (59), Community Networks (61), Online Community Service Engine (62), Ethics of Community Informatics (67), Powerful Remittances (73), Grassroots Public Policy Development (78), Informal Learning Groups (98), Universal Voice Mail (113), Community Inquiry (122), Open Source Everything (127).

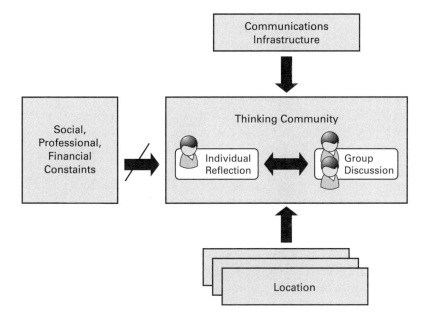

Problem   Creative thinking is a human activity essential for self-realization and for providing sustainable solutions to the myriad problems of our ever more complex global society. Three main factors prevent thinking communities (groups of people who work together on projects requiring substantial collaborative thought) from developing: lack of suitable locations for semisolitary deep thought, lack of affordable communications infrastructure for such communities to develop, and too many social, professional, and financial constraints that prevent people from breaking out regularly for a sufficient period of time.

Context   This pattern supports creative individuals and small groups with a pressing need for finding the time and concentration to work on a major project, but who lack access to locations and are inhibited by many personal constraints. The pattern helps them to connect with individuals and organizations interested in providing affordable thinking facilities, and then to design and build their thinking communities. These communities allow their members to concentrate deeply and meet peers who are working on their own projects. This semi-solitary mix of deep thought and social interaction should significantly increase individual and societal creative thinking capacity.

Discussion   Thinking, resulting in new knowledge, is an essential human activity. Most related community research has focused on knowledge management and knowledge construction communities, often in an organizational or educational setting. For example, a typical corporate knowledge management community acts as a custodian for a knowledge domain, nurturing the sharing and creation of practices and knowledge that is key to the achievement of both company and personal objectives (Von Krogh, Nonaka, and Aben 2001). Similarly, an educational knowledge-building community is a group of learners committed to advancing the group's knowledge of some shared problem through collaboration knowledge (Chai and Khine 2006). However, when shifting from such an institutional to a more individual-oriented type of knowledge community, not much is known. In such a community, not organizational goals but individual thinking requirements, preferences, strengths, and weaknesses predominate. The character of resulting communities is much more likely to be of an emergent nature that cannot be determined in advance and can be realized in a wide variety of forms. Thinking communities, even more so than other communities, cannot be fully designed in every detail. Instead, developers should provide the right conditions and just enough guidance for such communities to get started and then let them evolve (Preece 2000). A Thinking Community pattern can help outline such conditions and guidelines while leaving each community enough freedom to develop its own unique values, norms, structures, and processes.

Thinking communities require the right physical locations for individuals to reflect deeply by themselves while also being able to interact on their thoughts with peers. They need an electronic communications infrastructure to organize and coordinate their community and communicate between locations. Social, professional, and financial constraints need to be minimized.

With location, communication, and personal constraints satisfied, thinking communities should start to be established and grow. A great variety of communities, ranging from loosely connected, semisolitary individuals to large groups intensely focusing on solving a joint problem, will develop. Thinking communities could thus become catalysts of creative thinking processes urgently needed to deal with some of the many pressing problems facing our globalizing world.

Thinking communities can manifest themselves in numerous forms. Each of the dimensions identified in the pattern can have many possible values. The pattern acts as an analytical lens to help identify successful combinations of values, and possibly new types of thinking communities. Some examples show the breadth and depth of thinking communities:

• A researcher is overworked and overwhelmed by the continuous stress of teaching, the publication rat race, and projects. She decides to recharge by taking a two-month sabbatical after a conference she attended on the other side of the world. Since the semester is over, she can plan it between the two academic years. She looks up the country she is visiting in the ReCharge researchers' community Web site and discovers a scenic location close to the conference site, in the middle of a national park. It offers long-term accommodation for low monthly rent rates. It also has Internet connections, provides meals, and has a common room where she can meet fellow researchers. After two months of deep thinking and discussions with colleagues who provide fresh angles on her research since they are not in her field, she goes back home, full of new ideas that will sustain her in the years to come.

• Many people are inspired by the ways of living and thinking of indigenous peoples. However, it is often hard to establish relationships with such communities. A First Nation, however, hosts a simple hostel with a limited number of rooms on its domain, allowing thinkers to work on their projects, while inviting them for a selected set of meetings and activities with the local community. This offers visitors a low-intensity, unintrusive opportunity to get a realistic sense of the values, problems, and strengths of these communities, much beyond the understanding provided by the usual tourist visit to a reservation arts center. Simultaneously it offers these local communities an alternative source of income and access to a world of ideas and contacts provided by visitors sincerely interested in building bridges between cultures.

• Two countries go to war. Enlightened individuals from both sides want to discuss their differences in order to stop the madness, but discussions on an open electronic forum dedicated to the conflict inevitably derail into emotional rants and diatribes. Meetings in either country do not work for political and security reasons. Forum members from another country, which has managed to negotiate a peace agreement between its feuding factions in the recent past, invite a number of the most reasonable discussants to come to a resort in their country. A private foundation, sponsoring the discussion forum, pays most of the travel expenses. In the resort, the discussants gather in group sessions but also get ample opportunity to break out, go for walks, and have one-on-one discussions. Their meetings are structured by electronic meeting room software. Although in the short time frame available they cannot reach agreement on a road map to peace, they do agree on the most important issues to be worked out. In a closed electronic forum, supported by the same software, they continue their discussions on return to their respective countries. The personal relationships and face-to-face meetings in a peaceful environment have created the conditions to start building a thinking community across political borders.

Solution   A finely meshed worldwide network needs to be created of affordable locations where people can concentrate and work on their individual creative projects, while simultaneously being able to meet peers working on their own acts of creation. The Web will provide the communications infrastructure to develop the concepts of thinking communities and match supply and demand of thinking locations. Social, professional, and financial constraints need to be addressed by developing concrete guidelines and solution patterns.

Linked patterns   Working-Class Consciousness (12), Design Stance (44), Open Action and Research Network (45), Ethics of Community Informatics (67), E-Consultation (70), Civic Capabilities (85), Experimental School (89), Citizen Journalism (91), Document-Centered Discussion (92), Citizen Diplomacy (93), Informal Learning Groups (98), Shared Vision (101), Labor Visions (112), Great Good Place (119), Community Inquiry (122), Open Source Everything (127), Activist Road Trip (134), Retreat and Reflection (136).

Problem   People often do not have access to places in their neighborhoods that are outside their home or workplace where they feel at home. Yet they need places like coffee shops, community centers, or benches on the plaza or park where they can feel at home and hang out for extended periods without the need to spend lots of money. Unfortunately there is a scarcity of what Ray Oldenburg (1999) calls "great good places" that are convenient and welcoming. In many regions of the world people have forgotten how to "hang out" with friends, a lost art that refreshes the spirit and sometimes leads to social action as well.

Context   This pattern is applicable to any place where people live. Whether a community is rich or poor, it needs "third places" where people can comfortably congregate.

Discussion   This pattern makes the case that probably should not even need to be made: that people need the physical presence of others and that virtual spaces, however important and vibrant they can be, have not made physical meeting places obsolete. As Alexis de Tocqueville wrote, "The right of free assembly is the most natural privilege of man."

Although situations are different in different locations, the fact remains that communities need what sociologist Ray Oldenburg calls a "great good place" or "third" place, which is a physical location, a more or less public place, where people can hang out and talk. These locations are threatened in many places. Many factors can contribute to the decline in great good places. Some neighborhoods may be dangerous or have a mistrusting atmosphere. Some may be too economically disadvantaged to be able to afford a safe place with a roof overhead. Moreover, in the era of television and the car, the art of spending time around people who might be strangers may be dying. Sometimes a coffee shop, for example, may have such high rents that it becomes necessary to cycle customers quickly to increase the economic "efficiency" of the available seating capacity.

Oldenburg discusses many instances of the role of the great good place in history: German beer gardens in the United States in the early 1990s, Viennese coffee shops, and French café society, for example. It also discusses the role of taverns in the development of journalism, the media, business practices, and social change, including the American Revolution. Oldenburg quotes historian Sam Warner, who wrote that informal tavern groups "provided the underlying fabric of the town, and when the Revolution began made it possible to gather militia companies quickly, to form effective committees of correspondence and of inspection, and to organize and to manage mass town meetings."

Bradie Derrenger, a student where I teach, makes the important point that the great good place might not always be a traditional coffee or doughnut shop (personal correspondence, November 15, 2004). From the seat that he takes every day while waiting for the ferry to work, he can engage with people he sees regularly and with those who may be crossing Puget

Sound for the first time. And if and when other people started congregating there, it might happen that others would also do so.

Interestingly it may be the case that communities with more third places are more politically and economically active. Whether this is always the case, a third place often contributes to a community's "social capital," which, as Robert Putnam (2000) has shown generally, provides a wide range of benefits, including economic ones.

Solution   Communities need to ensure that third places, which are neither the home nor the workplace, exist where anybody in the community is free to go and stay for any amount of time. These places can be cafés, plazas, community centers, or simply places with chairs or benches. These locations can be privately owned, but their de facto policies must support the needs of the community if they are to serve as genuine third places.

Linked patterns   The Commons (2), The Good Life (3), Political Settings (7), Public Agenda (30), Democratic Political Settings (31), Conversational Support across Boundaries (50), Public Library (59), Community Networks (61), Universal Voice Mail (113), Thinking Communities (118), Retreat and Reflection (136).

Problem   Poor people in the developing world and elsewhere have high infant mortality rates and deaths from diseases that are preventable or readily treatable (as well as a host of social ills, such as domestic abuse). Moreover, lack of information, coupled with inflexible or outmoded social traditions and superstition, can perpetuate cycles of needless suffering for people of all economic sectors. Unfortunately the need for accurate health information is often addressed by ineffective public service announcements that seem preachy or uninteresting or otherwise fail to reach the entire audience or particular nexus of people who must be involved in important decisions.

Context   People all over the world face important life decisions with inadequate information that is often accompanied by overwhelming social pressure to behave in certain ways. Policymakers, media producers, and community activists are faced with the challenge of presenting that information to the people who need it, and in a form that is accessible and acceptable.

Discussion   This pattern was inspired by the work of Mexican television producer Miguel Sabido, who deftly weaves health and other socially responsible information into traditional soap operas to raise consciousness without compromising the compelling everyday drama that the genre exemplifies. Although this type of soap opera (called *Telenovelas* in Latin America) is not in the majority, there are examples of its use throughout Latin America, Asia, and Africa.

In 1967, the Peruvian telenovela *Simplemente Maria,* which chronicles twenty years in the life of a maid working through the travails of the day as a single mother preparing for a career as a fashion designer, was launched. It was apparently this show that opened up the possibility of social messages intertwined with popular culture. According to Hanna Rosin, whose *New Yorker* article, "Life Lessons," helped inform this pattern, "Peru's working-class women identified deeply with Maria; they saw her story less as a Cinderella fantasy then as a future that was possible for them, too. Thousands of maids wrote to the station to say that they were going back to school."

The hero or heroine of a Sabido soap is a transitional character in the drama, a "fallible character who struggles to behave decently" (Rosin 2006). In fact, the most important aspect of the telenovela is the barrage of *giros* (twists of fate), trials and tribulations, that continually tests the protagonist's perseverance. In China, the program *Bai Xing* ("Ordinary People") features Luye, an unmarried rural Chinese girl who has a baby and moves to the city. This perfectly ordinary story is filled with the real-life drama that people routinely face but is rarely portrayed on television or other mass media. In recent episodes, Luye discovers that two of her acquaintances have AIDS, a subject that is generally not treated on Chinese television.

The nongovernmental organizations Population Communications International and Population Media Center (PMC) have been involved in socially responsible soap operas for many years. The focus is usually related to population issues, which frequently involves health, sustainable development, and environmental issues as well. Both are involved in the development of television and radio shows and work in other media, media leadership issues, and communication strategy and theory as well. The PMC Web site explains that "the advantage of using long-running, entertainment serial dramas include their huge audience appeal and the emotional bonds that are formed between the audience members and characters, which can lead to strongly positive influences of the characters on attitudes and behaviors by audience members." Sabido has developed a methodology that was informed by the integration of several key communication theories.

Ideally the social messages in the soap operas and telenovelas are presented in the form of choices that can be consciously made, not injunctions or instructions that must be obeyed. The best of these soap operas are probably more like this, although the protagonist ultimately will make a choice, and that choice is likely to be the one favored by the producers of the program. For many reasons, everybody who is involved in formulating a response to a given situation would be party to the dilemma played out on the television screen and weigh all the relevant factors individually and collectively. In Nepal, for example, the mother-in-law and husband are key players in decisions involving childbirth and must therefore be part of any approach to offer new choices for life decisions. Because soap operas in developing countries are shown in prime time (rather than during the day, as in the United States) and are therefore seen by people across the spectrum of the population and because a high percentage of the viewers are illiterate or are otherwise unable to gain access to relevant information, socially responsible soap operas make ideal vehicles for the propagation of useful information on such topics as family planning, domestic violence, nutrition, home management, and emergency preparedness.

Socially responsible soap operas are clearly subject to challenges from many sources. In Burma, for example, the radio show *Thaby e gone Ywa* ("Eugenia Tree Village") was broadcast illegally over shortwave radio because Burma's military dictatorship declared the program illegal. In the examples discussed, the creators of the programs are aware of the dangers of using the media for propaganda. William Ryerson (2006), president of PMC, explains, "Unlike brainwashing, PMC's approach is to show a range of options—to broaden rather than to narrow the perspective of the viewing audience with regard to the choices available to them. For each of the options, the programs show realistic consequences."

It may be that the desire to fiddle with the content of popular shows could prove irresistible to overzealous governments intent in spreading their messages. Put in this context, the practice of inserting message into soaps seems Orwellian. Yet commercial message are increasingly commonplace, as are product placements in Hollywood films, television shows, and even books. Recently in the United States, a spot in a book for teenager girls was sold to the highest bidder, a makeup manufacturer. Also, subtle and not-so-subtle messages permeate much of the mass media, some explicitly designed for mass appeal, government appeasement, or as an expression of personal ideology, while others are unconsciously added to the mix.

Although many of the people who are likely to get involved in this pattern are policymakers or media producers, other people can help promote this idea by entering into a dialogue with those who are positioned to make changes. Although strong challenges exist, this pattern has rich potential as a tool for positive social change.

Solution   Information about family planning and other important life decisions can be integrated into soap operas in ways that strengthen the dramatic impact of the show while leading to beneficial social effects.

Linked patterns   Health as a Universal Right (5), Translation (15), Peace Education (56), Positive Health Information (74), Control of Self-Representation (109), Homemade Media (110), The Power of Story (114), Public Domain Characters (115), Socially Responsible Computer Games (126), Media Intervention (132).

Problem   Natural or man-made disasters reveal the fragile nature of social infrastructures, including the most advanced technologies, and require people to draw on their own resourcefulness. Given the destruction or significant compromising of basic civic infrastructures—electrical power, water and sewage, natural gas, roadways, and communications systems—individual and local capacities as well as external supports at every level must be prepared and effectively implemented to ensure personal and collective survival and well-being.

Context   Disasters require the attention of every level of society, from individuals, families, and neighborhoods to city, state, and national agencies, as well as international organizations. The content and flow of information are critical at every stage, from policy development to preparation, search and rescue, recovery, and the reconstruction of vital infrastructures. To some extent, everyone may be called on to participate in various aspects of this pattern, not only in the area of immediate impact but in the formal development of policies, procedures, and systems, as well as informal, voluntary emergency responses that help to extend the safety net for those directly affected.

Discussion   In one year, 2005, the world witnessed three major natural disasters—the Southeast Asian Tsunami, Hurricane Katrina in the Southeast United States, and the Pakistani earthquake—and the world was awakened to how even the most basic and essential structures can be swept away in moments. A spotlight was also cast on preexisting environmental conditions, policy decisions, inadequate preparation, and dysfunctional or nonexisting communication systems that either led to or intensified the extent of damage and loss of life.

This pattern encompasses three periods that focus on emergency situations: (1) the preexisting conditions and preparations prior to the occurrence of any disaster, (2) the actual disaster and immediate response, and (3) the longer-term recovery and reconstruction of physical and social infrastructures. Although all levels of society are involved, the focus of this pattern is on the initiative and actions of civil society.

In the period prior to any disaster, the focus is on advocacy for effective policies. This includes the remediation of social and environmental conditions that might prevent, or at least moderate, the damage of a disaster and the establishment of evacuation, response preparations, and the storage of food and medical supplies, as well as setting up emergency communications networks and facilities. For example, Seattle Disaster Aid and Response Teams (SDART) calls for neighborhoods to be prepared to be self-sufficient for at least three days by organizing teams that draw on local resources and skills. The program trains neighborhood teams and sponsors functional drills to rehearse roles and responsibilities. In terms of advocating for improved communications systems and facilities, the World Dialogue on

Regulation for Network Economies has compiled a special dossier on the role of regulators and policymakers in ensuring that adequate emergency communications are available.

In the immediate aftermath of a disaster, the delivery of food, shelter, and medical care can be hours, days, or even weeks away. Tasks that must be handled by the stricken residents, as outlined and assigned to teams under the SDART model, include damage assessment, first aid, safety and security, light search and rescue, and providing shelter and special needs. Communications responsibilities include monitoring emergency radio broadcasts, keeping neighbors informed of relevant information, relaying information about damage using amateur radio operators, satellite radio, cell phones, signs, or whatever other means are available. In the longer period of reconstruction following a disaster, when additional external resources can be brought into play, it is vitally important to ensure close coordination.

The very young and very old, as well as the poor, face the greatest risk in the short- and long-term aftermath of catastrophe, often related to the worsening of already existing conditions of poor health and nutrition and inadequate housing. UNICEF studies of groups hit by warfare and famine show it is critical to provide the correct mix and balance of relief services and not only food but public health assistance to prevent massive outbreaks of infectious diseases.

Civil society is capable of organizing large-scale efforts in the wake of disasters, as demonstrated by the Katrina PeopleFinder Project and the Southeast Asia Earthquake and Tsunami Blog SEA-EAT blog associated with the East Asian tsunami. Other projects to assist in the reestablishment of communications systems include the Center for Neighborhood Technology's Wireless Community Network project and supportive efforts by the Champaign-Urbana Community Wireless Networks for developed and developing nations.

One of the most common approaches for alleviating at least part of the challenge of communications around emergency situations is the idea of open, nonproprietary protocols, the ingredient behind the Internet's phenomenal success. The Common Alerting Protocol is one such data interchange protocol, and the Partnership for Public Warning (2006) is working on a wide variety of efforts to resolve national standards, protocols and priorities.

Even areas far distant from the disaster must be prepared to shelter massive numbers of displaced persons, possibly for extended periods of time.

Solution   Individuals, public agencies, environmental advocates, and international relief organizations need to continually reassess their level of preparedness and coordination in response to humanitarian emergencies. This means thinking and planning for the short, medium, and long terms, as well as continuing to address persistent issues of poverty and debilitating economic conditions. Information and communication technologies can play important roles in this area, but in order for the technologies to be useful, the people in areas where emergencies do or might occur and people outside those areas must assume leadership for genuine progress to be made.

Linked patterns   Civic Intelligence (1), Earth's Vital Signs (26), Indicators (29), Citizen Science (37), Mobile Intelligence (38), Citizen Access to Simulations (48), Community Networks (61), Online Community Service Engine (62), Civic Capabilities (85), Self-Help Groups (105), Universal Voice Mail (113), Media Intervention (132).

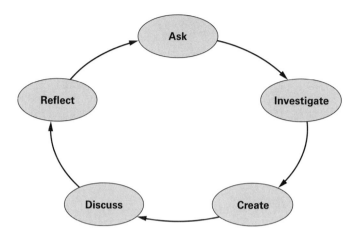

Problem   Communities face a wide variety of challenges in areas of health, education, economic development, sustainable environments, and social order. But regardless of the difficulty of these challenges, a necessary condition for addressing them is for communities to find ways for members to work together. Too often community members work at cross purposes and fail to develop what Jane Addams (1912) called "the capacity for affectionate interpretation," resulting in what John Dewey (1927) referred to as "the eclipse of the public." "Community inquiry" is what Addams and Dewey called their theory and practice for reshaping communities, and thus society at large.

Context   The challenges for constructive communities are as old as humanity, and there will never be an absolute or universal solution to them. One reason is that every member of a community has unique experiences in life and thus unique perspectives, beliefs, and values. This diversity can be a source of strength within communities, but it can also lead to frustration, disappointment, conflict, and even violence. Diverse institutions have been created to address community challenges, including public libraries, public schooling, procedures for democratic governance, and venues for free expression. Often, however, these institutions are reduced from their idealized conception. With community inquiry, diversity becomes a resource, and institutions are knit together productively.

Discussion   As Jane Addams pointed out in founding Chicago's Hull-House, the first settlement house in the United States (Addams, 1910), and Dewey examined through the creation of the University of Chicago Laboratory Schools, democracy has been more realized in its political than its social expression. That is, even when formal procedures are established and maintained, meaningful participation is by no means guaranteed. For example, a public library might offer a large collection of books available at no charge to members of the community, but meaningful use of those materials depends on available public transportation, broad-scale development of literacy skills, and a social organization that makes people feel welcome. In this and many other examples, it is clear that the problem goes beyond institutions, structures, and procedures, requiring instead the means by which every member of the community comes into the process of authority.

Community inquiry provides a theoretical and action framework for people to come together to develop shared capacity and work on common problems in an experimental and critical manner. The word *community* signals support for collaborative activity and for creating knowledge that is connected to people's values, history, and lived experiences. Inquiry points to support for open-ended, democratic, participatory engagement.

Consider the case of East St. Louis. Its widely noted dissolution and destruction (Kozol 1991) resulted from many factors, internal and external. The integration of housing in neighboring cities had the perverse effect of East St. Louis losing most of its middle-class and professional workers. Racism, both within and toward the city, was a key factor that led to its failure to get the resources it needed to maintain a vibrant community. Problems compounded as elements within the city began to pull in different directions, often serving their own ends at the expense of the larger community. For example, companies dumped hazardous waste, and landlords allowed buildings to become dilapidated and dangerous. From a community inquiry perspective, East St. Louis exhibited a failure of democratic, participatory engagement and demonstrated little evidence of people within the city or larger entities, state and national, coming together with shared values and goals.

Nevertheless, East St. Louis has survived and in some aspects has developed the capacity to thrive. Community members have come together to address the severe problems they faced. Substantial assets, such as the talent and dedication of Katherine Dunham, have taken enduring form in her museums and international dance workshops for children (http://www.eslarp.uiuc.edu/kdunham/). The community collaborates with other organizations, such the University of Illinois, and the joint East St. Louis Action Research Project has helped improve conditions in the city by setting up community technology centers, new housing, a light-rail station, and a youth-driven community theater. At the same time, the project has provided new opportunities for university students, staff, and faculty who have worked in the community.

A key element of the work in East St. Louis is that it reflects continuing inquiry by people who are invested in the community in a variety of ways. That is, successes to date have not come from outsiders who dictated and delivered solutions, but by bringing participants from diverse perspectives to work together. Moreover, this work, while it addresses such practical problems as jobs, the environment, health, education, cultural preservation, and enrichment, does not stop there. Local action becomes a means through which the residents and those outside learn more about the community and its possibilities. In that sense, inquiry is both action and understanding. The lesson from East St. Louis and similar communities is that the process of community inquiry is ultimately of greater importance than solving a specific problem.

Additional examples around the world show the power of community inquiry. In the domain of community development and learning, for example, a National Science Foundation study carried out in rural villages around Bangladesh related the finding that material from well-worn saris supplied a filtering material that worked better in reducing cholera than the nylon mesh that microbiologists had developed (Recer 2003). In Reggio Emilia, Italy, with few of the resources found in affluent and advanced communities, families and teachers developed an innovative approach to education, now heralded throughout the world, that recognizes the potential of all children to learn and grow "in relation with others, through the hundred languages of doing, being, reflecting, and knowing" (http://www.reggioalliance.org). Community inquiry can also be manifested in the development of information and communication technology. See, for example, the culturally situated design tools developed collaboratively between Rensselaer Polytechnic Institute and its community partners (http://www.rpi.edu/~eglash/csdt.html) and the Community Inquiry Laboratory software created collectively by the University of Illinois and its partners around the world, who come from all walks of life (http://ilabs.inquiry.uiuc.edu).

Solution A community that faces a problem should think of it not simply as something to be fixed but rather as an opportunity for the community to come together, build capacity, and learn about itself and its situation in a manner that can be joyful and intellectually stimulating. Every member of the community has knowledge that may be critical to solving that problem but can be discovered only if that individual has a voice in what the community does. Most problems are not solvable in one step, and even when they are, they may recur. Thus, it is critical for the community not only to fix its problems but to become capable of further inquiry. The community's knowledge about how to deal with challenges is not in fixed procedures but in the capacity to learn through ongoing action, or what Dewey called experimental knowing. We have created a diagram to represent this cycle of ongoing community inquiry (see above): a spiral of asking questions, investigating solutions, creating new knowledge as we gather information, discussing our discoveries and experiences, and reflecting on our new-found understanding.

Linked patterns Civic Intelligence (1), Political Settings (7), Memory and Responsibility (11), Citizen Science (37), Meaningful Maps (47), Truth and Reconciliation Commissions (51), Public Library (59), Community Networks (61), Ethics of Community Informatics (67), Wholesome Design for Wicked Problems (82), Civic Capabilities (85), Service-Learning (90), Citizen Journalism (91), Document-Centered Discussion (92), Citizenship Schools (96), Informal Learning Groups (98), Appreciative Collaboration (99), Community Animators (102), Appropriating Technology (108), Community Telecenters (117), Thinking Communities (118).

Problem   Theater is an ancient yet vital cultural force. Although legitimate or mainstream theater has traditionally been a gathering place for the exchange of ideas, it is largely irrelevant in today's world as a tool for social change. Forces that have contributed to this situation include economic factors, dwindling audiences, the talent drain to other media, the transformation of audience tastes and expectations as a result of film and television, and the decline of the avant-garde as an alternative to legitimate theater.

Context   Illegitimate theater can be a legitimate response in almost any setting of ordinary —and extraordinary—life. It can be practiced in any place where an audience might be found.

Discussion   Legitimate theater engages a paying audience sitting inside a theater with the expectation that they will watch the performance of a play or musical. These productions employ conventions normally associated with traditional theater: lights up and down, applause at the end of acts, a proscenium stage, professional actors working with prepared scripts, and no significant interaction between performers and spectators.

While legitimate theater has lost much of its relevance to our everyday lives (less than 2 percent of the population in the United States attends legitimate theater performances), theater (or performance) in the broad sense is a fundamental human experience. It represents a reservoir of immense potential that a mediated experience can rarely provide: the potential for human interaction. Film and video provide a stream of images to watch but no experiences in which the viewer can participate. Everyday life is often a sequence of ordinary, that is, expected, events. One's life experiences easily become insulated from important world events, along with the possibility of learning from new experiences as well. Ordinariness becomes a form of oppression, and a steady dumbing down of society is deleterious to culture and democracy as well. Performance provides an immediate human experience. Theater, particularly its "illegitimate" varieties, can also punctuate the ordinary and thrust new and unexpected experiences into everyday life. It has the power to bring a person into new, temporary realities in which the self is momentarily forgotten and submerged. Theater can empower spectators with insight and possibilities.

Baz Kershaw (1992), in his insightful study of the British alternative theater movement over four decades, explicitly addresses the role of theater as an instrument of "cultural intervention." His book "is about the ways in which theater practitioners have tried to change not just the future action of their audiences, but also the structure of the audience's community and the nature of the audience's culture." This pattern affirms Kershaw's observation that new theater should accompany a new society.

Other phrases—*theater without theater, antitheater, meta-theater, the world's a stage, social performance, guerrilla theater,* and *oppositional* (or *radical* or *provocative*) *theater*—are variations on the title of this pattern. Each of these alternative formulations focuses on some attributes and not on others. We use the term *illegitimate theater* primarily to highlight the differences between it and legitimate theater. Illegitimate theater can describe any performances in which one or more conventions of the legitimate theater are circumvented. For example, the convention of a single, discrete performance can be ignored in illegitimate theater. Thus, half of the cast can "perform"—at a coffee shop, at the zoo, or even a traditional the-atrical venue—while the other half of the cast can "accidentally" encounter the audience afterward and engage with them a second time, perhaps in dialogue, perhaps again as spec-tators, perhaps as actor-participants in a new performance that builds on ideas of the original one. The French group Le Grand Magic Circus devised a performance that gradually added spectators (while withdrawing their members) at the "end" of their performance until finally the spectators were the only ones left "performing" (Bennett 1990).

Performance is a broad term that characterizes an infinite number of situations, including sports, rituals, education, carnivals, politics, and protest. It can encompass everyday social events such as shopping, eating in restaurants, going to parties, or hanging out. Performance can be spontaneous or planned, obviously staged or masquerading as real life, or artistic, political, or cultural. The advent of performance studies as an academic discipline that tran-scends the traditional notion of the theater has contributed to our understanding of these myriad forms.

Bertolt Brecht, the most influential artist-advocate of theater for social change, rejected Aristotelian drama (the basis of legitimate theater) in favor of the epic or dialectical theater. His theories and plays, such as *Three Penny Opera* and *Mother Courage*, blur the line between real life and performance, reveal the mechanics of production, present actor and character simultaneously, and employ a wide range of techniques designed to rouse the audience to social action. The venerable San Francisco Mime Troupe, with performances such as *Fact Wino vs. Armagoddonman, Damaged Care,* and *Mr. Smith Goes to Obscuristan*, is a more recent incarnation of Brechtian rebellion. Augusto Boal from Brazil, a Workers' Party activist, pio-neered "theater of the oppressed" and other forms of participatory role-playing theater that have helped audiences explore and recognize their own predicaments while fostering coop-eration and critical engagement.

Many public protests, especially those that include role playing, dramatic encounters, or masks, puppets, and other props can be viewed as a type of performance. When Greenpeace's sailing ship *Rainbow Warrior* confronts a nuclear submarine or whaling ship, two symbolic worlds collide. Crosses symbolizing those killed in Iraq spring up in Crawford, Texas, near the ranch of U.S. president George Bush; Argentine mothers and grandmothers clothed in mourning black stand before the president's Casa Rosa in Buenos Aires. Social activists employing techniques of illegitimate theater have also confronted corporate globalization. These include the marching bands and giant puppets in the 1999 protests against the World Trade Organization in Seattle, Reverend Billy from the Church of Stop Shopping who orches-trates chain store "interventions" to "unlock the hypnotic power of transnational capital," and the "Yes Men," who have "played the roles" (as they satirically interpreted them) of various corporate and organizational officials to unsuspecting audiences around the world.

As Erving Goffman (1959) would say, and Shakespeare before him, the world is truly a stage, and everything we do in public is a type of performance. This means that in a trivial sense, everyday life provides a venue for exhibition and self-promotion. The media exploit people's desire for fame (or publicity—the desire to be made publicly recognizable) and exhibit those they consider offbeat enough for public display in the modern equivalent of a freak show.

Media are more easily commodified when they assume rigid forms. When a package exists, it is relatively easy and cost-effective to replicate it again and again with little effort or creativity. And when commercial broadcast media define what is legitimate, the imagination of the people decays, their capacity to create is harder to draw on, and their tolerance for experimentation and "amateurism" diminishes.

Illegitimate theater, like other patterns in this language, has unsavory manifestations as well: burning a cross in the yard of an African American or other ethnic minority, militaristic parades and rallies, public intimidation. Since performance likely predates language, its effects on people can be deep; it can unlock hate as well as love, anger as well as reason and compassion. Theater, legitimate or not, can be driven by emotion and therefore is less analytical than many other patterns in this language.

Illegitimate theater blurs or even negates the line between spectators and performers. In its extreme version, everybody, all of the time, is an actor. And actors in public performances can also be actors in social life, actors who help make things happen, for good or for ill. Although our life in public is a series of performances, our roles are often construed as "bit parts." Nevertheless, every moment is a teachable moment and every public appearance an opportunity to do and experience something new. Thus, anybody, at least in theory, can practice the craft of illegitimate theater. The performances that come from this practice can be simple or elaborate, impromptu or painstakingly rehearsed. The point is to cause ripples in the everyday stream of life.

Illegitimate theater, like its predecessors, legitimate or otherwise, can be used to provoke emotional reactions, discussion, or reflection. Practiced successfully and in a great number of venues, illegitimate theater could help foster positive social change and increased democratization of culture.

Solution   Illegitimate theater represents an intriguing set of possibilities for interactions between people that can lead to social change. Performance as a deeply human phenomenon can be explored by audience and performers alike in our quest for a better world.

Linked patterns   Social Dominance Attenuation (4), Teaching to Transgress (20), The Power of Story (114), Public Domain Characters (115), Citizens' Tribunal (129), Tactical Media (131), Media Intervention (132).

Problem   Although information and communication are often conceived as abstract, intangible, and immaterial, the systems that maintain them are, of necessity, constructed with solid things, such as paper, lead, concrete, rubber, glass, mercury, cadmium, and silicon, which are fabricated into delivery trucks, wires, library buildings, computers, chips, and CDs. The manufacture (and ultimate retirement) of all of these things is often accompanied with environmental damage, as the twenty-three Superfund sites in Silicon Valley will attest. In 2005, 63 million computers in the United States were replaced with newer models. Up to 80 percent of the waste is then sent to developing countries, where it often contributes to environmental and health hazards. Additionally, energy is consumed, often in immense quantities, throughout every stage in the life cycle of a product. As devices are made with shorter and shorter life spans and the uses of information and communication systems (ICS) increase worldwide, this problem will become more critical unless something is done.

Context   Vast numbers of people are affected by the increasing attention paid to ICS around the world. This includes people who are fortunate enough to capitalize on the new technology and those who are unfortunate enough to live with the refuse. This pattern can be used by people who have some control over the situation, including those who are in a position to develop laws and policies, producers who can lessen the effects of their products entering the waste stream, and local communities, which can develop policies and programs for responsible treatment of discarded technology. Community activists, health professionals, local governments, and neighborhood organizations will need to organize and work together in this effort. Other possible participants include computer geeks, social activists, environmental activists, and those wanting to learn more about computers and new technology.

Discussion   The use of ICS is expanding enormously around the world, which is causing immense demands on infrastructure and the environment. Computer technology has grown increasingly more sophisticated in a very short period of time. At the same time, the costs have dropped in relative and absolute terms, resulting in a massive number of obsolete computers and other technology, much of which has been dumped, with the result that their toxins (including lead, cadmium, and mercury) leach into the soil and water.

In addition to the new intellectual and social spaces that technology helps to provide, we need to think about the impact that ICS are having on the environment. Although we associate physical spaces like libraries and auditoriums with energy and resource use, the creation, storage, and distribution of information require energy and resource use as well. Some of this use does not square with conventional wisdom. Computer use, for example was supposed to lower the consumption of paper because everybody would simply read the computer screen. The amount of travel was also going to decline because business could be conducted electronically, thus substituting communication for transportation. The electronics industry was celebrated as an environmentally friendly industry, yet there are nineteen Superfund sites associated with high-tech industries slated for environmental remediation in Santa Clara County, California, home to more of these sites that any other county in the United States. IBM and Fairchild Electronics were disposing their waste products in underground tanks, which subsequently leaked trichloroethane, trichloroethylene, Freon, and other solvents into the drinking water of 65,000 people. There also seems to be an unhealthy link between the waste producers and the people who must deal with them, specifically prison inmates who work in for-profit prisons with inadequate protection and no health insurance.

Why pick on information and communication systems? After all, other sectors use energy and cause pollution. One reason is that "electronic waste is the fastest growing part of the waste stream," according to the Silicon Valley Toxics Coalition. Another is that it is important for people to realize that information and communication technology is not a utopian magical answer to all problems. Obviously we need to consider the entire life cycle of all products, including those related to information and communication. (Although this task is not trivial, thinking about the second-order effects, while extremely important, is even more difficult to do meaningfully. The effects of the automobile on all aspects of life, including attitudes on sex, as well as the effects of the size of the weapons industry in the United States on foreign policy, are intriguing examples of unforeseen side effects.) Understanding the entire cradle-to-grave (and beyond, as in the case of toxins that can reach out from the grave to poison air and water) is critical, but what should be done with the information? It may be easiest to require that every manufactured or imported product be covered under an ecologically sound "Take-it-Back" ("Electronics Take it Back!" 2001) policy that requires the manufacturer or importer to pay for recovery or safe sequestering of hazardous materials.

Free Geek was started in Portland, Oregon, in 2000 by members of the open source software community to bring resources to bear on the problems of e-waste and the digital divide by helping "the needy get nerdy." The Free Geek approach combines participatory education and environmentalism. It addresses the problem of discarded computers and other electronic waste, which can be diminished by reusing and recycling. Free Geek uses volunteer labor to give new life to discarded technology. Volunteers are eligible to receive a computer after finishing a tour of service that educates the volunteer about computers and the environmental impacts of ICS. The city government in Portland, as part of its effort to reduce e-waste, helps support the project. A broad range of people are working together to cross the economic and social divides by working toward a common goal. The Free Geek concept has quickly spread to other areas, including Washington, Indiana, Ohio, Pennsylvania, and Illinois.

The Free Geek approach is not the only way to address the problem of lacking a community recycling program. There are many similar projects throughout the country that may or may not use open source software. But Free Geek is worth mentioning here for many reasons. First, it was developed by civil society; second, it is a partnership of several sectors and thus helps bring all sectors of the local community into a common struggle; and third, it is an innovative approach that deftly addresses a multitude of issues within a common set of principles, assumptions, and actions.

Starting and running a Free Geek or similar program requires a variety of skills and activities. The pattern can be implemented only by a group of people. Putting together that group starts with posting meeting announcements and inviting members from local Linux user groups, college students, and others. Since the overall environment for this approach will vary from community to community, understanding the issues in the community and who is involved is important. The success of the project is likely to depend on how well the person who initiates this group understands the community and can work with people in it. Beyond that, there are many nuts-and-bolts issues, including finding space and funding and developing programs. Associating with Free Geek is probably a good idea because of its network of dedicated people, useful documents, and software for running a community recycling project.

The environmental problems associated with information and communication technology are severe, and no mutually agreed-on long-term, sustainable solution has been identified. People are developing a variety of creative and thoughtful responses to the problems of this pollution, but more are needed. Information and communication technology can probably be part of the solution, but part of this requires stopping being part of the problem.

Solution   As a necessary part of stewardship and responsibility, it is essential to come to terms with the environmental impact of information and communication systems and devise suitable strategies for minimizing their negative effects. Some combination of policy, consumer education, habits of consumption, and social and technological innovation and recycling will probably be necessary for this take place effectively.

Linked patterns   Dematerialization (18), Sustainable Design (22), Whole Cost (28), Indicators (29), Citizen Science (37), Intermediate Technologies (57), Future Design (88).

Problem   People rely on search engines to find the information they need on the Web. The motivation of the groups providing search engines, however, is securing profits for their owners; other motives necessarily and inevitably take a back seat. The negative implications of relying solely on commercial search engines, though vast, are generally not recognized. If the enormous gatekeeping potential of commercial search engines is not balanced with open and accountable public approaches, the ability to find noncommercial information, including that which does not appeal to broad audiences or is critical of governments and other powerful institutions, could diminish. The privatization of the means to access information could also lead to a situation where advertisements and other sponsored information could crowd out noncommercial information.

Context   People in their daily lives need, search for, and find a tremendous amount of information. Increasingly they are looking for this information in cyberspace. While Internet technology has opened up a vast amount of information and opportunities for communication for millions of people worldwide, the very fact that we are relying on technology that is out of our control is cause for concern, if not alarm. Although the application of this pattern is relevant to any system that people use to find information, our immediate attention is drawn to the Internet, which is poised to become increasingly dominant.

Discussion   Access to information can be made easier. Barriers to obtaining the information that people need can, at least in theory, be anticipated and circumvented. But like the chain whose ultimate strength is determined by its weakest link, access to information can be thwarted at many levels. Although nonpublic (commercial and otherwise) providers of information and communication services can be good citizens that prioritize the needs of their users, the temptation to become less civil may prove irresistible if and when the market suggests that uncivic behavior would result in higher revenue. In circumstances such as those, they may decide to relax their current high standards accordingly. Big Web portals are, for example, becoming increasingly cooperative with the Chinese government, presumably because of the growing and potentially huge Chinese market.

One approach to addressing this problem, an open source or public domain classification system similar to that used in the public libraries in the United States and other places coupled with open source, community-owned and -operated search engines, is simultaneously defensive and forward looking: defensive because it could serve as a hedge against information deprivation and commodification and forward looking because this approach could help usher in an exciting new wave of experimentation in the era of access to information. As the development of the Internet itself has demonstrated, the open source nature can help motivate and spur use through a focus on the complementary tasks of classifying information and its retrieval.

Existing classification approaches like the Dewey decimal system also have limitations (Anglo-centrism, for example), and approaches like Dewey are not strictly speaking in the public domain (although Dewey is readily licensable). Nevertheless the Dewey system might serve as at least a partial model. Schemes that are well known, such as the Dewey system, allow everybody to communicate quickly and at low cost. It is the open protocol nature of the Internet that has allowed and promoted easy and inexpensive ways to get connected and develop new applications that rely on the underlying protocols, which have no license fee.

Computing and the potentially ubiquitous availability of online environments provide intriguing possibilities that older approaches did not need or anticipate. The Dewey system, for example, tacitly assumes a physical arrangement of books: the code assigned by the librarian or technicians using the system declares both the book's classification and the location it will occupy in the library. Although having a single value is not without advantages, an online environment opens the door for multiple tags for a single Web page or for finer-grained elements (a paragraph, for example, on a Web page or the results of a database query) or broader-grained collections of elements. A federated collection of link servers (Malcolm, Poltrock, and Schuler 1991) could assist in this.

As far as search engines are concerned, civil society can hardly be expected to compete with Google's deep pockets and its server farms. Yet it may be possible to distribute expertise, knowledge, and computational capacity in such a way that a competitive people's search engine becomes conceivable. The idea of a single organization within civil society that can even remotely approach Google's phenomenal computing resources is absurd. But so in general is the idea of civil society taming the most powerful and entrenched forces and institutions. The problem here, though chiefly technological, is similar to the one that civil society faces every day: How can a large number of people sharing similar (though not identical) visions work together voluntarily without central authority (or centralized support), undertake a large, complex project and succeed? The answer, though diffuse, incomplete, and suboptimal, is for the workload (identifying, discussing, and analyzing problems to devising responses to the problems) to be divided up as intelligently as possible so people doing only pieces of the whole job can be successful in their collective enterprise.

This strategy is much easier to define and implement in the technological realm. One successful example is the SETI@home project, which employs the idle cycles of users' computers all over the world to analyze radio telescope data in a search for extraterrestrial intelligence. If, for example, 1 million computers working together on the people's search project could devote some amount of processing power and storage to the project, the concept might become feasible.

Although it would be possible for every participating computer to run the same software, breaking up the tasks and distributing them across a large number of computers is likely to provide the most suitable architecture for a people's search engine. For one thing this allows a dynamic reapportioning of tasks, changing the type of specialization that a computer is doing to make the overall approach more effective. At the beginning of the life of the people's search engine, for example, half of the computers might be devoted to finding (or "spidering") and indexing Web sites while the other half might work on identifying which Web sites meet the users' search criteria and presenting a list of pertinent results to the user. After a week or so, it may become clear that the first task (identifying and indexing sites) may require less attention overall, while the second task (handling user search requests) needs more processing power. In this situation, some of the computers working on the first task could be reassigned to the second task. This situation might then become reversed the following week, and another adjustment would be necessary. In a similar way, the contents of indexes could be shifted from computer to computer to make more effective use of available disk space more efficiently while providing enough redundancy to ensure that the entire system works efficiently even though individual computers are being shut down or coming online all the time and without advance notice.

The people's search engine would make all of its ordering and searching algorithms public. Google's page-ranking algorithm is fairly widely known, yet Google has adjusted it over the years to prevent it from being gamed in various ways by people who hope to increase the visibility of their Web pages by "tricking" the algorithm to gain a higher page rank than Google would presumably bestow. Ideally the people's search engine would offer a variety of search approaches of arbitrary complexity to users. Thus people could use an existing, institutionalized classification scheme like the Dewey decimal system or a personalized, socially tagged "folksonomy" approach, a popularity approach like that of Google, a social link approach like Amazon ("People who searched for X also searched for Y"), or searches based on (or constrained by) meta-information about the pages, such as author, domain, publisher, or date last edited.

Solution The development of open source, public domain approaches to information access is essential for equity and progress among the people of the world. The possibility of credible competition will serve as a reminder to for-profit concerns that access to information is a sacred human right. It would also help to maintain and extend the patterns of innovation that open protocols have made possible. Among other things, researchers and members of civil society need to work on classification systems for Internet resources. It is imperative that civil society focuses attention on open source approaches to searching, archiving, and other information access needs. For many reasons, this will help in the evolving process of opening up the world of information to people everywhere.

Linked patterns The Commons (2), Participatory Design (36), Open Action and Research Network (45), Public Library (59), Online Community Service Engine (62), Open Access Scholarly Publishing (76), Mirror Institutions (94), Open Source Everything (127).

Problem   Video games are frequently violent, sexually explicit and exploitive, and commercial. Whether their use leads inexorably to social exclusion or antisocial behavior and attitudes, the fact that their use occupies millions of people for billions of hours in a given year might make anybody question the wisdom of this preoccupation.

Context   Video games draw people in, but people (and society in general) do not necessarily get much in return. Is it possible that this medium can be reengineered to good purpose? Gamers and game designers should explore these possibilities, as should policymakers, nongovernmental organizations, and other people interested in new educational possibilities.

Discussion   The idea of using computer games for socially responsible purposes has some intriguing arguments in its favor. One is that people are already spending enormous amounts of time navigating through virtual space and shooting virtual villains. If people are going to spend that much of their time gaming, why not have them do something of value (or so that argument goes)? But perhaps these sorts of games would not attract them. Perhaps shooting is more fun than learning for some. And it is not obvious that even if people like playing an educational or socially responsible game that it would have any positive lasting effects.

Models and simulations provide ways for people to explore situations that cannot be experienced directly, like the future. At the same time, we must acknowledge that these tools are not as compelling as they could be. Well-designed interactive games have the potential to be educational, in that people learn about the world, as well as compelling; they thrust the gamer into the scenario.

Certain types of video games are not unlike simulations in which the computer extrapolates certain plausible outputs, both expected and unexpected, based on user selections or decisions. Simulations, however, are serious, while games by their very nature are frivolous, or so it would seem.

What, in theory, could socially responsible video games achieve? One possibility is that they could improve cognitive skills, including memorization of spelling and multiplication tables, as well as deeper skills such as analysis, interpretation, and evaluation. Another possibility is that users could learn a general understanding from the games, just as people get some type of general knowledge from visiting foreign countries. One could, for example, get an impression of what it would be like to, say, deliver relief food to refugees in a remote war zone.

A video game, like a movie, book, or even a story told aloud, is not real. It is a creation of a parallel artificial world or a world once removed from reality. In the early 1960s Yale psychology professor Stanley Milgram (1974) conducted a bold experiment that demonstrated (or was widely perceived as having demonstrated) how people were naturally inclined to follow orders from perceived authority figures, however illegitimate and immoral the orders might be. In those experiments, a "doctor" with official-looking garb tells the subject (misleadingly) that he or she will be involved in a memory experiment. In the course of this experiment, the subject will push buttons that purportedly deliver increasingly powerful electric jolts to an unseen person in the next room, a confederate who does not seem to be able to master the memorization of a few words at a level that sufficiently pleases the experimenter. After the hapless person with the poor memory cries out in feigned pain, the real subject understandably balks at delivering more pain to the person in the next room. After the authority figure explains that the person must continue with the experiment, the vast majority of the subjects elected to continue delivering the regimen of electrical shocks to the unseen victim. A notable sidenote to this excursion into a morally dubious zone involved a young man who participated in the "shock experiment" while a student at Princeton. He related to Milgram (1974) that his realization of his own susceptibility to authority had prompted him to seek conscientious objector status from the U.S. military. In other words he had learned about pitfalls of blind obedience, while those who had not been in such a situation had not. This suggests that video games could provide a type of rehearsal for situations that might arise in the future, serving much the same role as it is believed that play does for children.

The possibility that video games could provide meaningful instruction inspired Paul Rogat Loeb to propose a video game based on former U.S. Vice President Al Gore's *Inconvenient Truth* movie, which explores the looming prospect of global warming and massive climate change: "The game could build on Gore's existing movie, slide show, and Web site, adapting whatever elements were useful, but also making the process more interactive, more engaging for an audience for whom games are a prime language. Why not put people in the role of climate scientists assessing the evidence, governmental and corporate decision makers, citizens trying to keep our society from driving off a cliff? Why not let them try out different ways of acting?" (Loeb 2006).

Video games could (at least theoretically) help society learn how to deal with various problems that citizens might encounter: emergencies, stolen elections, or loss of civil liberties, for example. The fact is that our globalized, mediated, interconnected world thrusts a multitude of issues into our face that reveal our impotence. Although they demand a response, individually we have nothing in our experience that helps us truly grapple with it, let alone determine what should be done about it.

Several video games have been released, and several more are in planning, that are intended to teach people about real-world issues in ways that television new reports and formal education are unlikely to emulate. One game, Food Force developed by the United Nations World Food Program, puts players in the middle of a dangerous food relief mission on Sheylan, a fictional island in the Indian Ocean suffering from drought and civil war. Players air-drop food, drive down mine-infested roads, buy and distribute food, and help rebuild. Surprisingly, the game has been downloaded by over 3 million people and is second in the number of free downloads only to America's Army, a recruiting tool for the U.S. Army (Rosenberg 2006).

Several new games have socially responsible orientations. One, A Force More Powerful, is designed to teach nonviolent strategy. Others are based on the Israeli-Palestinian conflict (PeaceMaker), genocide in Darfur, and Adventure Ecology in which two children, Dash and Bay, fight eco-threats and villains like Agent Waste and Professor Ignorance and the environment is represented as a "a highly complex and interdependent system in which every life-form, air molecule and pebble plays a part" (Snoonian 2006).

While video games are often damned because of their total disconnect from the real world, this separation may also have its virtues. According to game designer and author Raph Koster (Wasik 2006), there is a "magic circle" surrounding games, and "it has to be a circle of no consequence." Formal education generally does not have a "magic circle of no consequence." In other words, failures, both small and large, at school have consequences that vary from minor annoyances and embarrassment to not being able to attend college or find meaningful employment after high school.

Solution   Will Wright, the designer of SimCity and other simulation games, commented on the goals he has for Spore, a video game now in development: "I want people to be able to step back five steps, five really big steps. To think about life itself and its potential-scale impact. I want the gamers to have this awesome perspective handed to them in a game. And then let them decide how to interpret it" (Johnson 2006b). While we cannot know how valid this perspective is and how his new game will promote those ways of thinking, it is clear that it represents a step up in relation to the majority of the other games that people play.

Linked patterns   Technocriticism (39), Peace Education (56), Media Diversity (66), Arts of Resistance (111), The Power of Story (114), Public Domain Characters (115), Soap Operas with Civic Messages (120), Media Intervention (132).

Problem   Commercial interests in the form of large multinational corporations strive to fulfill only the most profitable needs or wants. In many cases, the highest or easiest profit aims at wants that may not ultimately be in the interests of the targeted consumers (let alone the workers or the environment). For instance, many food companies focus on high-fat, high-sugar, high-salt products that humans find tasty based on an evolutionary history in which these substances were difficult to find. For people in the developed world, however, having access to such foods is unhealthy. Furthermore, the way these foods are produced, transported, and marketed involves unaccounted-for costs to humanity. This is just one example. In general, corporations are not only motivated but legally required to maximize profits, not meet actual human needs. Furthermore, the economies of scale lead large companies to focus efforts on those wants that are best met by mass-produced goods and services. There is a huge range of specific needs that much smaller groups or individuals have that do not provide sufficient inducement for large companies to provide. Thus, the corporate world fails to meet many human needs, and even when it does produce value, it tends to focus on wants rather than needs, and in a way that has many undesirable side effects.

Context   In a variety of arenas, including publishing scholarly work, the development of educational materials, and the development of useful, robust software, an open source process has shown itself to be very effective. Such a process is now timely for a variety of reasons. First, a large number of people globally have access to the Internet. This allows global communities with common interests to work together without the necessity of physical travel (which can be expensive in time and money). Second, there are examples of people from many fields volunteering their efforts to create value for the common good of their community. These examples serve as models for other communities. Third, a critical mass of people have time and knowledge to add value to such collective efforts. Fourth, although it has been common in the past for those in power to use their power to keep that power, social and legal processes have been put in place to consolidate power into structures that are no longer effectively regulated by countervailing forces such as local governments or community pressure. The first three factors make the use of open source feasible, and the last makes it mandatory. In addition, open source has the capacity to personalize and customize value to much smaller groups than is feasible for large companies. Thus, when open source materials are offered, people may collectively fulfill a greater proportion of human needs and wants. This is currently referred to as "the long tail." A very large number of people want a few common things and a very small number of people each want something different. Open source is much better positioned to fulfill those different things wanted by only a relatively few.

Discussion   Perhaps the most articulate introduction to the general concept of open source is the introduction to Eric von Hippel's *Democratizing Innovation* (2005):

When I say that innovation is being democratized, I mean that users of products and services—both firms and individual consumers—are increasingly able to innovate for themselves. User-centered innovation processes offer great advantages over the manufacturer-centric innovation development systems that have been the mainstay of commerce for hundreds of years. Users that innovate can develop exactly what they want, rather than relying on manufacturers to act as their (often very imperfect) agents. Moreover, individual users do not have to develop everything they need on their own: they can benefit from innovations developed and freely shared by others. The trend toward democratization of innovation applies to information products such as software and also to physical products. As a quick illustration of the latter, consider the development of high-performance windsurfing techniques and equipment in Hawaii by an informal user group.

Probably the most notable and widespread success story of open source is the development of open source software. The source code of any computer program is the complete set of instructions that the computer follows to provide its functions. There are two competing philosophies that determine the rules regarding the distribution of software source code. The basic business orientation dictates that, above all, the source code should be kept private and that only people who are allowed to make changes to it to add functionality or fix bugs are those authorized by the company that owns it. Although there are several variants, the free software or open source model is more or less the opposite of the corporation model in nearly all respects. Anybody can obtain the source code without cost, make changes to it, and distribute it without restriction.

Besides the fact that it is free, the open source model offers many advantages over the closed, corporate model. One is that many eyes can identify and fix many bugs. Software flaws such as bugs or security holes are more readily found and exposed. (This is the reason that fair voting advocates are generally in favor of open source voting software.) Another reason is that the open source model promotes innovation by allowing anybody to implement new functionality. Although many of the modifications may be unwanted, some may provide a foundation for desirable features. Although the open source approach has its own disadvantages (as do all other approaches), it offers surprisingly stiff competition against deep-pocketed corporations. Linux, for example, is more robust, less buggy, and on a faster release cycle than well-funded corporately engineered operating systems.

Although computer programmers have been at the forefront of this intellectual revolution, computer programs are certainly not the only complex artifacts that could be designed, built, maintained, and improved through an open source collective effort. With oil prices skyrocketing, open source automobile developers could work together on developing automobiles with super mileage and other environmentally friendly features. One obvious product to think about moving into open source development is the development of vaccines and other medicines. And in this arena, medicines that could reduce suffering caused by the worldwide HIV/AIDS epidemic come to mind readily. Of course, in so-called primitive societies, knowledge of how to find, prepare, and use medicinal plants was a precious gift handed down from generation to generation.

Because corporations are driven primarily to maximize profits, they tend to focus efforts on the very popular and tend to ignore small niche interests. For example, the open source music movement now allows individuals to create music collaboratively and globally. Probably the most popular of these, adding 200 users per week is MacJams. Albums can be built and distributed on a one-off basis without the high up-front costs of using a recording studio. Similar avenues exist for poetry, stories, photographs, video and artwork.

Solution Use the mechanism of open source to meet needs that are not well met by large institutions and corporations as well as areas where the social and environmental costs of market-driven competition outweigh the value provided.

Linked patterns Open Action and Research Network (45), Durable Assets (58), Digital Emancipation (60), Online Community Service Engine (62), Open Access Scholarly Publishing (76), Citizen Journalism (91), Public Domain Characters (115), Community Telecenters (117), Thinking Communities (118), Open Source Search Technology (125).

Problem   Powerful people and organizations tend to abuse their power. Without understanding who has power, how the power is wielded, and how that power can be kept within legitimate boundaries, people with less power can be ignored, swindled, lied to, led into war, or otherwise mistreated.

Context   This pattern should be considered in any situation in which institutionalized power is a strong influence.

Discussion   In 1956 sociologist C. Wright Mills provided an in-depth examination of power in the United States. He wrote in *The Power Elite*, "The powers of ordinary men are circumscribed by the everyday worlds in which they live, yet even in these rounds of job, family, and neighborhood they often seem driven by forces they can neither understand nor govern." A bit more than a decade later, in 1967, G. William Domhoff wrote *Who Rules America?* which he followed in 1983 with *Who Rules America Now?* These books contained a detailed analysis of who has power, how the power is exercised, and through what routes the powerful came to their positions. To some degree, the "who" of who has power is not as relevant as what they do with it and how they came to possess it. Their routes to power were so uniform as to suggest that specific, repeatable social mechanisms were at work to ensure that the same type of person, with the same ideologies, would be elevated to these positions and that other people from other circumstances would be denied entrance.

That social mechanisms at play are not news to sociologists, who make it their business to understand these mechanisms. The rest of us have vague suspicions but little concrete knowledge. Although the powerful may be visible to some degree, the representations that we witness in the media are likely to be sanitized, scrubbed clean of improprieties, stereotyped, and otherwise rendered useless for thoughtful consideration. This knowledge is vital to all participants in a democratic society. Knowing who and how people who occupy the seats of power wield the levers of social control is key to positive social change.

While the work of Mills and Domhoff uncovered the processes of the maintenance of power in the United States, it is undoubtedly the case that similar processes are being played out every day around the world. For that reason, it is imperative that these studies be undertaken throughout the world. The point of gaining an understanding of these processes is not to insert different people into the process (although in many cases this is desirable). Nor do we gain this understanding in order to derail the entire system or to throw the powerful out. (After all, not everyone holding power is a scoundrel.) An understanding of the process will help us adjust the system as necessary, know where the points of intervention exist, and in general increase the level of awareness, thus making it more difficult for the people with less power to be bamboozled by those with more.

There are many exciting examples of this pattern. One particularly compelling one is based on the Reflect theory developed in the mid-1990s by ActionAid, the international organization that is working to end poverty. The theory combines adult literacy and learning and social change using the theories of Paulo Freire integrated with participatory methodologies. Reflect builds literacy as well as critical analysis skills and community capacity by working with local knowledge and skills. Their report on *Communication and Power* (Archer and Newman 2003) describes how written and spoken word, images and numbers can be used by villagers in India in analyses of caste power.

According to Robert Dahl (1970), a longtime scholar of democracy, "the analysis of 'power' is not a merely theoretical enterprise but a matter of greatest practicality. How one acts in political life depends very heavily on one's beliefs about the nature, distribution, and practices of 'power'; to be misled about 'power' is to be misled about the prospects and means of stability, change and revolution."

Solution Although it is important to undertake research on this topic and make the findings freely available, it is at least as important to disseminate the ideas and techniques that help people initiate their own power research projects. This pattern particularly applies to government and corporations, but other people, institutions, and groups (such as hate groups, militias, or organized crime families) need to be thoroughly investigated as well.

Linked patterns Social Dominance Attenuation (4), Health as a Universal Right (5), Political Settings (7), Working-Class Consciousness (12), Teaching to Transgress (20), Antiracism (23), Cyberpower (25), Strategic Capacity (34), Technocriticism (39), World Citizen Parliament (40), Economic Conversion (41), Privacy (65), Ethics of Community Informatics (67), Powerful Remittances (73), Grassroots Public Policy Development (78), Civic Capabilities (85), Sense of Struggle (104), Arts of Resistance (111), Labor Visions (112), Tactical Media (131), Peaceful Public Demonstrations (133).

Problem   Powerful countries such as the United States and United Kingdom are seemingly free to ignore international law and other recognized norms of acceptable behavior when it suits their government. If other countries and international organizations are impotent against such transgressions, nongovernmental organizations and other civil society groups (which have even fewer resources) face almost insurmountable hurdles for legally challenging these actions.

Context   Nongovernmental organizations and other citizen groups with few to no means by which to challenge what they perceive to be moral wrongs are the main users of this pattern. Unfortunately the use of this pattern is limited generally to democratic societies or other places where its confrontational approach is tolerated. There are countries, for example, where a tribunal directed at the United States could be convened, while a tribunal directed against the government of the host country would be strictly prohibited. Unfortunately there are few, if any, public or legal means where citizens of countries like North Korea, Uzbekistan, and others that are isolated from the network of international relations can challenge their government's policy without fearing for their life and liberty.

Discussion   Civil society faced with what it perceives as serious crimes being perpetrated by governments has devised the concept of a citizens' tribunal. Part legal proceedings, part theater, part publicly speaking truth to power, the concept has been expressed most strongly with the World Tribunal on Iraq (WTI) condemning the invasion of Iraq by the United States.

According to Richard Falk (2005b), professor emeritus of Princeton University, "The WTI was loosely inspired by the Bertrand Russell tribunal held in Copenhagen and Stockholm in 1967 to protest the Vietnam War, which documented with extensive testimony the allegations of criminality associated with the American role in Vietnam. The Russell tribunal featured the participation of Jean-Paul Sartre, Simone de Beauvoir and other notable European left intellectuals. It relied on international law and morality to condemn the war but made no pretension of being a legal body, and its jury contained no international law experts." The WTI had its roots in a session of the Permanent Tribunal of the People before the war in Rome. The sessions of the WTI began in Brussels in March 2004 and finished in June 2005 in Istanbul. Sessions were also held in Berlin, Stockholm, Hiroshima, Rome, New York, and Barcelona.

The work of the WTI was divided into a Panel of Advocates and a Jury of Conscience. The role of the Panel of Advocates was to document the charges against U.S. president George Bush, U.K. prime minister Tony Blair, and others through analysis and testimony. This body would then present the case to a Jury of Conscience, "composed of distinguished moral authority personalities from around the world, to pass judgment on the actors and their actions from the perspective of international law."

One question is how the "other side" participates, if at all. Can they submit evidence or provide testimony? In other words, how does a tribunal differ from a trial? For one thing, the United States, for example, would undoubtedly skip a citizens' tribunal since it has declined to appear before the World Court as a defendant. A citizens' tribunal is not a court (it obviously has no powers of enforcement, for example) and is not obligated to emulate one. At least in the case of the WTI, a citizens' tribunal "is self-consciously an organ of civil society, with its own potential enforcement by way of economic boycotts, civil disobedience and political campaigns" (Falk 2005b). It is not designed to find the truth but to bring the truth to the light. As Falk (2005b) points, out, the WTI is an instrument of civil society: "[It] proceeds from a presumption that the allegations of illegality and criminality are valid and that its job is to reinforce that conclusion as persuasively and vividly as possible. Legitimacy, however, as in the legal system, is an important issue. If the tribunal does not seem legitimate, it can more easily be portrayed as a charade. Legitimacy can be maximized by including unimpeachable authorities and providing strong corroborating evidence, including documentation and expert testimony.

As a direct and public challenge to power and authority, the citizens' tribunal faces numerous challenges in addition to the difficult task of establishing legitimacy. One of the most important of these challenges is irrelevance. The unequivocal repudiation of those in power is unlikely to be covered in any serious way by the media. Additionally, the possibly marginal nature of the group sponsoring a citizens' tribunal places it even further from the centers of power.

Since the power of a citizens' tribunal relies on its symbolic nature, publicity is important. One approach is to bring in a broad coalition to organize the tribunal. It is important to get people to the event and to send out publicity afterward (through, for example, the Web and DVDs). The WTI submitted its report to the United Nations. Of course, exposure and publicity can be risky; counterdemonstrations, arrests, intimidation, and thuggery, in addition to media condemnation, might be in store for the conveners.

Many challenges present themselves in organizing and conducting the event: Who will participate? How is the agenda organized? Where will the funding come from? How will security issues be handled? And of course, the idea of multiple venues, however attractive the idea is, increases the magnitude of the logistical challenges considerably.

Although Falk's (2005a) statement below (from a WTI press release) is associated with the World Tribunal on Iraq, the basic approach and philosophy of that effort can serve as a basic model for people without extensive resources who are struggling with state violence and other urgent issues:

The WTI is opposing aggressive war, war crimes, and crimes against humanity. It is not opposing the governments or the United Nations. Indeed it hopes to create pressure from below that will encourage law-abiding governments and the UN to do their proper job of protecting weaker countries and their populations against such illegalities. And beyond this protection we are promoting a world movement of peoples and governments to realize a humane form of globalization that is equitable with respect to the world economy, legitimate in upholding the human rights of all, and dedicated above all else to creating the conditions for sustainable peace based on justice for every nation on earth.

Solution   In certain situations, civil society organizations are moved to protest perceived crimes of sovereign nations. The Citizens' Tribunal has the potential to become a powerful tool to raise issues to more visible levels than governments or the media are likely to do on their own.

Linked patterns   Global Citizenship (6), Memory and Responsibility (11), Democratic Political Settings (31), International Networks of Alternative Media (43), Truth and Reconciliation Commissions (51), Mirror Institutions (94), Illegitimate Theater (123), Whistle-Blowing (130), Peaceful Public Demonstrations (133).

Tactics

Problem   Corporations may flaunt legal or ethical guidelines by, for example, ignoring safety considerations on the job, harassing employees, or dumping toxic chemicals. Governments also engage in a multitude of transgressions, from the minor to the truly horrific. Many of these misdeeds are kept secret, cloistered within a strict organizational code of silence. *Whistle-blowing* is an expression that refers to exposing problems in an organization generally from within that organization. The act of whistle-blowing is essential to correcting problems in society, yet the whistle-blowers are often punished severely for their actions. Society benefits from but does not adequately protect whistle-blowers.

Context   This pattern can be used by anybody in possession of knowledge that is being kept secret when it should be made public. People who are not in this position—journalists and ordinary citizens, for example—can also use this pattern to support the people in this position.

Discussion   Whistle-blowers are often heroes of the modern world who undergo a mighty, and sometimes ultimate, sacrifice for the good of the rest of society. Tom Devine of the Government Accountability Project (GAP) wrote a thoughtful and informative book, *The Whistleblower's Survival Guide* (1997) with advice on how to blow the whistle on wrongdoing without becoming a martyr in the process.

Powerful (and not-so-powerful) institutions and organizations may engage in a variety of unethical or illegal activities to further their own goals, generally perceived to be important by the perpetrators. These activities are kept hidden from those on the outside until they are uncovered by somebody on the outside or exposed by somebody on the inside. The pressures on an insider to keep quiet about transgressions are immense. Although society as a whole benefits from the revelations, the whistle-blower is likely to be seen as a traitor to his or her community and punished for his or her efforts: shunned at work, fired, denied employment in general in the future, or even physically harmed. And even after it is revealed to the world, the damaging evidence can be ignored by the media or spun into irrelevance by the institution and its allies.

Devine discusses basic survival strategies for whistle-blowers:

1. Before taking any irreversible steps, talk to your family or close friends about your decision to blow the whistle.
2. Develop a plan so that your employer is reacting to you, instead of vice versa.
3. Be alert and discretely attempt to learn of any other people who are upset about the wrongdoing.
4. Before formally breaking ranks, consider whether there is any reasonable way to work within the system by going to the first level of authority.
5. Maintain good relations with administrative and support staff.

6. *Before and after* you blow the whistle, it is very important to protect yourself by *keeping a careful record of events as they unfold.*

7. Identify and copy all necessary supporting records before drawing any attention to your concerns.

8. Research and identify potential allies such as elected officials, journalists, or activists who have proven their sincerity and can help expose the wrongdoing.

9. Either invest the funds for a legal opinion from a competent lawyer or talk to a nonprofit watchdog organization about the risks and obstacles facing you.

10. Always be on guard not to embellish your charges.

11. Engage in whistle-blowing initiatives on your own time and with your own resources, not your employer's.

12. Do not wear your cynicism on your sleeve when working with authorities.

Whistle-blowing arises within government institutions as well as commercial concerns and has some legal protection in some countries. Some of the most important examples of government abuse are corruption, violation of human rights (by allowing torture, for example) or hiding decisions, such as a decision to start a war while publicly asserting that peace is being sought. Some connect the concept of protecting whistle-blowers with free speech rights secured by the First Amendment to the Constitution. Beyond a rights context, government transparency is necessary for a healthy democracy, in that accurate and timely information is vital for informed policymaking.

The whistle-blowing concept needs to be legitimized in different contexts, some of which are extremely hostile to the idea. In some cases, it will be important to come up with new expressions in other languages to talk about the concept. In addition, the very term *whistle-blower* does not translate well into other languages, such as Russian. It has been suggested that *truth-teller* may work better in that language than *whistle-blower.*

Solution   Support whistle-blowing and whistle-blowers. This is often done through support networks and by laws and media.

Linked patterns   Social Responsibility (8), Transparency (64), Voices of the Unheard (83), Everyday Heroism (116), Citizens' Tribunal (129).

Problem   Activist information campaigns and protests aimed at sensitizing the public to issues of social justice and politics often fail to reach an audience. In some cases, this is due to a reticence on the part of the mainstream media to tackle controversial issues. However, this can also happen because inadequate communication tactics prevent the public from identifying with or understanding the language used to convey the intended message. In other words, many actions organized by activist organizations go unnoticed, either because they do not succeed in showcasing their cause through means that cannot be ignored by the media or because their lines of argument cannot be easily connected with the ways non-activist audiences experience the world.

Context   Tactical media (TM) are a loosely defined set of practices that activists and community groups can use to engage with in producing counterinformation, as well as with its modes and possibilities of dissemination. In fact, the tactical circulation of information is a fundamental aspect of political intervention in the informational environment.

Discussion   According to "The ABC of Tactical Media" (Garcia and Lovink 1997), "Tactical media are media of crisis, criticism, and opposition. This is both the source of their power and also their limitation. Their typical heroes are the activist, Nomadic media warriors, the pranxter, the hacker, the street rapper, the camcorder kamikaze."

Because of their ad hoc character and their adaptability to different contexts, TM are hard to define. Hence, instead of asking, "What are TM?" a more useful question is, "How do TM work?" The following three examples illustrate some possible uses and outcomes.

This first example comes from the 2004 U.S. presidential campaign. President George Bush's official Web site was cloned, with the alternative site featuring a critique of his agenda to become president. This site was set up by the Yes Men, a group of actors who impersonate representatives of important organizations at official meetings in order to subvert their messages in the mainstream media. Their stunt prompted Bush to announce on television that "there ought to be limits to democracy."

In the second example, several labor activist groups in Europe fighting against unstable working conditions used TM for their campaigns. The Italian group Chainworkers (Chainworkers 3.0 N.d.) invented Saint Precario, the patron saint of workers in precarious circumstances. His statue appears at demonstrations, public events, and in public spaces, constructing precariousness through familiar symbols and leading the public to make its own connections between the procession, common people's problems, and today's world market. Through San Precario and other similar games and actions, the issue of precarious labor has gained visibility within the European Union and is now being discussed even outside its borders, while more sustainable forms of social struggle against social precariousness are the background on which such actions rest.

Telestreet, the third example, is a network of pirate television stations run by activists and community groups who use free UHF frequencies and low-cost technological devices to broadcast their video productions into Italian households. Telestreet programming was not solely aimed at counterbalancing Prime Minister Berlusconi's monopoly on the mainstream media with alternative content, but also at experimenting with the medium of television as a space for cultural production and community building.

Generally TM rely on artistic practices and "do-it-yourself" (DIY) media, created from readily available, relatively cheap technology and means of communication. A tactical medium is devised according to the context where it is supposed to function. This means that it is sensitive to the different sets of communicative genres and resources valued in a specific place, which may vary from street theater and banner dropping to the Internet or radio. For this reason, TM actions are very effective and can take a wide variety of forms. For instance, they can mimic traditional means of information while circulating alternative content, subvert the meaning of well-known cultural symbols, and create new outlets for counterinformation with the help of new media.

In many cases, TM practitioners borrow from avant-garde art practices (e.g., linguistic sabotage and *détournement*, a term first coined by Guy Debord and the Situationists who reused well-known images and symbols to create work with a different message), politics, and consumer culture to confront commonly held beliefs about everyday life. Such techniques, also called culture jamming, appropriate the language and discourses of their political target, which is familiar to the nonactivist audience. Therefore, the subversion of the meaning of the message pushes the audience to notice where some strategies of domination are at work in a given discourse, raising questions about the objectivity of what is believed to be "normal." TM actions creatively reframe known discourses, causing the public to recognize their limits. According to TM theorist David Garcia (2006), "Classical TM, unlike agit-prop, are designed to invite discourse." They plant the seeds for discussion by creating a fissure in what is considered to be objective reality, requiring a form of engagement to decode their message.

Despite many successes, TM practices like the Yes Men impersonations have often been criticized because their short-term interventions expose but do not attempt to address the weak points in the system. Nevertheless, TM should not be seen or employed as an isolated form of protest but as one tool for groups to reach wider audiences in a broader network of political struggle. In fact, even when they hijack the attention of the mass media, the Yes Men stunts and Saint Precario do not constitute emancipatory practices. Nevertheless, they are an example of how to bring topics to debate. As part of an organized campaign centered on a specific issue, such stunts can give resonance to voices otherwise unheard and possibly lead to a dialogue between minority and majority groups or between minorities.

Moreover, TM practices can help make transversal connections between context-related social, cultural, and political problems and various organized sites of resistance. For example, the Telestreet network enables different activist groups and coalitions to use their space to support or showcase their own cause. Similarly, TM practices can be useful to create new memes that raise awareness of unjust social conditions, as in the case of Saint Precario.

Ultimately it is important to maintain TM's emphasis on experimentation, collaboration, and the exchange of knowledge as part of a broader cartography of organized social struggle. For these reasons, there is a need to create more conditions where TM exploration of new possibilities for resistance can take place. Such projects can range from media literacy teaching to culture jamming (in which dominant cultural signs and images are intercepted and modified to encourage alternative interpretations) workshops in schools, to festivals and temporary media labs where people can come together and develop creative ways to engage in protest and critique of the systems which govern their lives from an ever-increasing distance.

Solution   TM practices are marked by an ongoing effort to experiment with the dynamics of media dissemination of information, searching for the most effective way to bypass the obstacles created during the diffusion of such information in order to reach an audience. Thus, TM actions can help activists attract the attention of the mainstream media, as well as enable them to convey their message in a way that the audience understands.

Linked patterns   Media Literacy (35), International Networks of Alternative Media (43), Indigenous Media (55), Appropriating Technology (108), Homemade Media (110), Arts of Resistance (111), Illegitimate Theater (123), Power Research (128), Media Intervention (132).

Problem   Corporate media exist to make as large a profit as possible; responsiveness to the public interest is secondary at best. The products of corporate media are scripted by people disconnected from ordinary people who consume it. Alternatives to corporate media exist, but the audiences are substantially smaller; the alternatives generally have lower production values (due to fewer resources) and are much harder to find. Consequently they are enjoyed only by the more determined among us. People and organizations that struggle to interject alternative messages into the public consciousness using the media, even with paid ads, will be soundly rebuffed. For example, the AdBusters Foundation has repeatedly attempted to get its "Buy Nothing" piece aired on television in the United States, only to be turned down by the major networks. MoveOn's "Bush in 30 Seconds" ads (which were created by MoveOn members and had been selected as winners in MoveOn's contest for best video arguing against George Bush's reelection) were also rejected by the networks. Environmental organizations have trouble getting their messages aired, but corporate ads on the same themes are aired without question.

Context   This pattern can be useful when access to media is blocked.

Discussion   Until fairly recently, it was a commonly held notion in the United States that "the people owned the airwaves." Although that notion has apparently vanished from the minds of many politicians and government regulators, people periodically reassert this right when other routes have failed. With few exceptions, access to media is generally blocked to citizen and, especially, alternative viewpoints. The choices of media often boil down to state-run media (often propaganda) or purely commercial (or a combination of the two) or none at all.

In the United States particularly, but in other countries as well, people are bombarded with images and ideas that are generally cut from the same cloth. Whether news, reality shows, police dramas, talk shows, or commercials, television is a seamless and impenetrable wall that is assiduously protected. Media intervention is one tactic to fight this particular and ubiquitous form of censorship. In this case, the media truly are the message: while the content itself is commercialistic, addicting, and intellectually and psychologically stultifying, the sheer immensity and second-order effects of the media as a societal phenomenon make it impossible to ignore. It is a problem for everyone when the vast wasteland grows vaster.

Media intervention comes in many guises, and new approaches are devised fairly frequently. There are vast differences in the ways that this pattern is employed, from the most polite and prescribed to the most overt and officially prohibited. This pattern is general enough to encompass culture jamming (Lasn 2000), in which cultural messages and symbols are interrupted and questioned; textual poaching (Jenkins 1992), in which characters and ideas from popular media are appropriated for other usages; subvertisements, where advertisements are parodied or false ones created; "disciplining the media," in which media outlets are brought to task for lying or other dubious practices; and "billboard adjustment," in which public billboards are modified in ways that expose a deeper and often more accurate reality to what's being advertised.

Randolph Sill, a Seattle artist and educator, carried out a brilliant media intervention with aplomb in Seattle in the summer of 2003. He attended a televised Mariners baseball game with a sign with the number of Mariner star player Ichiro Suzuki and some writing in Kanji. Unbeknown to the non-Japanese speakers at the game and, in particular, the people who were televising the game live to viewers in Japan who captured Sill and the sign that he enthusiastically brandished whenever Ichiro was at bat, the Kanji read on one side, "President Bush is a monkey's butt," and the other side claimed that "Americans are ashamed of their corrupt president" (Jenniges 2003).

In the late 1990s, the Barbie Liberation Organization (BLO) engineered a similarly clever caper that ultimately was covered with bemusement on the television evening news in a number of U.S. cities. The intervention began with the purchase of several ultrafeminine Barbie dolls and the ultramasculine G.I. Joe action figures. Back in their laboratory, the BLO surgically altered the dolls, performing a gender swap of the voice boxes of the two stereotypical avatars. Then the dolls were repackaged and placed ("reverse shoplifting") on various toy store shelves around the country, where they were purchased by unsuspecting shoppers. Back at home, the young recipients of the dolls were surprised when the Joe professed a love for shopping while Barbie, newly masculinized, wanted to "take the next hill," presumably with a hail of bullets. One intriguing postscript was that at least some of the recipients of the transformed doll/action figure preferred the new version to the old (Baldwin 1995).

Finally, the techniques of trying to get one's issue injected into the media and disciplining the media for content that people find objectionable (and, less frequently, praising the media for appropriate coverage) form the traditional core of this pattern and are not expected to go away or lose their importance in the face of the other approaches.

Solution   Sometimes it becomes necessary to nudge the media into new avenues that they might not have taken without the intervention. This can be done cleverly and effectively, but it is not easy. The tactic and campaign should be carefully tied to the aims and the particulars of the situation, and it still might not be successful.

Linked patterns   Teaching to Transgress (20), Public Agenda (30), International Networks of Alternative Media (43), Sense of Struggle (104), Homemade Media (110), Arts of Resistance (111), Public Domain Characters (115), Soap Operas with Civic Messages (120), Emergency Communication Systems (121), Illegitimate Theater (123), Socially Responsible Computer Games (126), Tactical Media (131).

Problem   Governments and large companies often ignore the will or well-being of the people. An election can be stolen, a war can be illegitimately launched, or an environmental disaster can be caused without significant challenge from legislatures, the courts, or other designated guardians of the people.

Context   When normal dissent is being ignored or imminent and possibly catastrophic initiatives are being undertaken, such as an unprovoked invasion of a sovereign country, traditional ways of registering dissatisfaction are not appropriate or effective.

Discussion   Although crowds of people can be, and are, denigrated by politicians, the media, and other powerful institutions, their existence is sometimes the most profound expression of a population whose rights or sensibilities are being ignored. People must sometimes take to the streets to express their dissatisfaction.

   Large public demonstrations are probably the most overt form of protest. It is hard to deny the reality of thousands or hundreds of thousands of people in the streets peacefully marching, with banners and signs, music, costumes, noisemakers, and other devices that have been spontaneously and individually designed. Although mass demonstrations (such as those in the Ukraine in December 2004) are often portrayed in the media as marginal or even dangerous, they are generally peaceful and indeed suitable for the whole family. In fact, the presence of families and older people helps ensure that the demonstrations are peaceful. Through their visibility, they help to legitimize the protest by showing that the concerns are not limited to one demographic, youths, for example.

In February 2003, the world witnessed the largest expression of this pattern in history. People gathered in over 600 cities in over forty countries worldwide to protest the U.S. invasion of Iraq. Although the Bush administration was undeterred by this unprecedented display of disapproval, the idea of peace as an ideal was brought forward by civil society worldwide and held aloft as a universal idea—one that citizens must not allow governments to pursue or ignore.

Mass peaceful demonstrations do not take place in a vacuum. They need to be tied to broader strategy. This often means engaging with the media and with established governing or intermediating entities. It is often helpful to have a clear set of demands. Finally, although this does not always happen, measures like gathering names and contact information can be used to help build a large activist network that persists beyond the duration of the protest itself. Patty Smith's rock and roll anthem on this theme (some of which is printed below) captures the elusiveness, importance, and potential of people power.

I was dreaming in my dreaming
Of an aspect bright and fair
And my sleeping it was broken
But my dream it lingered near
In the form of shining valleys
Where the pure air recognized
And my senses newly opened
I awakened to the cry
That the people/have the power
To redeem/the work of fools
On the meek/the graces shower
It is decreed/the people rule
—Patti Smith, "The People Have the Power" (1975)

Solution Peaceful mass public demonstrations, both large and small, in combination with other forms of dissent are sometimes necessary.

Linked patterns Democratic Political Settings (31), Mobile Intelligence (38), Multiparty Negotiation for Conflict Resolution (79), Civic Capabilities (85), Sense of Struggle (104), Arts of Resistance (111), Everyday Heroism (116), Power Research (128), Citizens' Tribunal (129).

Problem   It is surprising how little people experience and learn when they travel. They often seem to be in a hurry to get to a certain place where their friends or relatives live or where the media or other "expert" has told them they should go. Many people would like to see and learn about how other people live and the challenges they face, but it is often difficult to do. Since there is apparently scant profit in trips that would help bridge cultures and encourage understanding, there is little support for it. Also, for most people in the world, travel is costly, is sometimes perceived as dangerous, and there are lots of barriers in addition to physical borders that can impede forward motion intellectually as well as geographically.

Context   In an era of globalization, problems are no longer confined to local areas. Also, in an era of heightened fear mongering, paranoia, and suspicions about others, the importance of building bridges individually and in groups cannot be stressed enough. One of the best antidotes to propaganda is firsthand knowledge and personal ties to people in different regions.

Discussion Travel offers immeasurable insights if people are receptive to them and have meaningful experiences along the way. The trouble is, of course, that it is possible to travel all around the world and not get anywhere at all. The Activist Road Trip pattern is designed to prevent that from happening.

In 2006, Global Exchange led a tour to Caracas, Venezuela, one of the three locations of the polycentric World Social Forum, with side trips to Barquisemeto and the small hillside village of Sanare. This nonprofit organization in California leads "reality tours" to nearly thirty countries, including Afghanistan, China, Ireland, Mexico, India, Iran, the Mexican-U.S. border, and Cuba. This tour visited a number of community centers, health clinics, educational missions, agricultural cooperatives, and housing developments set up by the Chavez government. Also, during the bus drive from Barquisemeto to Caracas, the guide briefed participants about recent Venezuelan history from the point of view of Chavez supporters as well as detractors. Global Exchange set up numerous presentations including one from an economics professor (with opposition leanings) who explained some of the particularities of the Venezuelan economy. The participants also had ample opportunities to converse with people at the forum.

Activist road trips can provide more meaning than standard, nonactivist road trips. At a basic level, people can simply go on an activist road trip. This means pursuing activist activities, especially learning, while on the road. The preferred mode of transportation is by foot, bicycle, or car, possibly by bus or train, and probably not by airplane, because unscheduled stops and flexible timetables are not possible. This is not to suggest that the trip should be haphazard or random, just that serendipity is likely to come into play and chance favors the prepared mind. Thinking about the trip ahead of time, planning for it, and arranging to meet with various people and organizations in advance is very useful; just do not overschedule or otherwise become slave to your plan. A simple way to ground the trip is to attend events at the destination and at points along the way. Events could include anything from a mass rally to a simple breakfast with friends of friends. And do not forget to record your impressions during the trip and debrief and discuss on your return.

People can always elect to go on an activist road trip, but the concept itself must be institutionalized to make it easier for people in general to go on these trips and, ideally, build active networks of those who are interested in similar issues. This pattern, like the others, can be promoted incrementally, with little pieces that organically build toward larger networks or assemblies rather than through a grand, top-down plan. This means building on the basic components: physical locations, activists (hosts, guest, and guides), information, and means of getting from one place to the next. Many pieces of this pattern now exist. When, for example, punk rock aficionados travel, they often share information with each other: whose couch is available to sleep on, for example.

The goal of this pattern is to help promote processes and ideas to build a thriving alternative to existing approaches to travel that are disconnected and disengaged. Ideally each visit helps to build the network while advancing positive social change. How can the network promote people from different communities getting together? Some of the pieces include integrated calendars of events and atlases designed for this type of trip. These atlases would necessarily be dynamic to highlight events as well as the nonprofits, infoshops, and other host organizations, which are often short-lived.

One approach to an activist road trip is to visit activist sites along the way. Another approach is going on a road trip as activists. The Bee Hive Collective, which travels throughout Latin American and develops intricate and beautiful murals illustrating indigenous issues and struggles, and the Miss Rockaway Armada (featured in the introductory graphic above), which traveled down the Mississippi River in the summer of 2006 to share art, music, environmentalism, and an anarchist perspective with everyone they met, are examples. In both cases, the groups essentially brought their activism with them. The ultimate activist road trips in the United States were the Freedom Rides in the spring of 1961, when activists traveling on buses from Washington, D.C., to the Deep South to publicize their fight for civil rights were met with racist violence that was quelled only after federal intervention.

Those implementing this pattern should expect a number of challenges. For example, people working in one activist destination could be overwhelmed by large numbers of people passing through. It is incumbent on the traveler to make sure that the host is not taken advantage of. Visitors must be sensitive to their host's situation and aware of their responsibilities as guests. Encounters between visitor and host, important as they are, have several potential complications. Who knows, for example, whether a field trip to a purported workers' collective has been carefully staged in order to convey certain impressions to the guests, perhaps in a bid for funding? And how can a guide ensure that the visitors to a favela in Rio De Janeiro, a township in Cape Town, or the South Bronx are not simply treating what they are witnessing as a spectacle?

The possibility also exists that when any destination is made public, in an atlas, for example, hostile townspeople might choose to harass the travelers or the host. There could also be other types of vexing side effects. If, for example, people in the hosting situation were serving food to visitors, the local health department could decide to pay a call on what it deemed an "illegal dining establishment." Also, the network is built on social relationships, and the ones encountered on an activist road trip are more likely to be dynamic than more established venues.

There are dozens of possible places to visit on an activist road trip: activist organizations, collectives, shelters, migrant camps, small businesses, reservations, encampments, sanctuaries, labor halls, organic farms, conferences, concerts, environmental disasters, prisons, community media centers, barrios, and refugee camps, among many others. Ultimately the activist road trip orientation could help promote the development of new travel bureaus and embassies to further institutionalize this approach.

People also can add an activist road trip to another trip. Rather than fly in to their destination, they could explore the region en route to, or returning from, an event to observe firsthand the realities that the forum examines. This can even be done within the city itself.

Moreover, there is no need to travel very far physically to find unexplored regions. An activist road trip can be done in any local region or city.

Solution   Travel is generally viewed as being a necessary chore or an opportunity for pure escapism. But travel also represents an excellent opportunity to learn more about the world and ultimately make a positive difference. With a little additional thought and planning, it should be possible to interject some activism into your next trip.

Linked patterns   Global Citizenship (6), Back to the Roots (13), Translation (15), Democratic Political Settings (31), Mobile Intelligence (38), International Networks of Alternative Media (43), Open Action and Research Network (45), Meaningful Maps (47), Conversational Support across Boundaries (50), Ethics of Community Informatics (67), Mobile Information and Computer Technology Learning Facilities (77), Citizen Diplomacy (93), Engaged Tourism (107), Homemade Media (110), Arts of Resistance (111), Everyday Heroism (116), Thinking Communities (118), Retreat and Reflection (136).

Problem   Deep Throat was the mysterious character who said, "Follow the money!" in *All the President's Men* (Bernstein and Woodward 1974), a book about the Watergate scandal. More than thirty years since Watergate and now that Deep Throat has revealed his true identity, this scandalous political event should provide sufficient motivation to carry the torch for life, liberty, and the pursuit of happiness and against the corrupting power of money to democracy.

Context   The U.S. Congress passed the Uniting and Strengthening America by Providing Appropriate Tools Required to Intercept and Obstruct Terrorism (U.S.A Patriot Act) Act in 2001. This legislation expanded government powers to follow the money in an effort to intercept and obstruct terrorism around the world. Following the money has revealed money laundering and corruption by terrorist groups as allowed by the Patriot Act. The downside of this law is that government now has expanded authority for public surveillance, which creates right-to-privacy concerns.

Discussion   Following the money is a valuable technique to trace corruption and is used by political parties, religion, the military, social activists, farmers, the health care industry, education, the federal government, local governments, science, corporations, and just about everyone else who wants to track what opponents are doing. Money is liquid and powerful. The trail of a corrupt operation can often be determined by tracking the source and use of money.

In the Watergate scandal, an investigation of the links between James W. McCord, Jr., and the CIA determined that McCord received payments from the Committee to Re-elect the President (CREEP). McCord was one of the burglars discovered and arrested for breaking into the headquarters of the Democratic National Committee at the Watergate Hotel in 1972. The money trail quickly suggested a link between the burglars and someone close to the president. Richard Nixon was later impeached as the president of the United States because of the scandal.

Corruption is a general concept describing any organized, interdependent system in which part of the system is either not performing duties it was originally intended to or performing them in an improper way, to the detriment of the system's original purpose. Corruption happens in government when money is going to the wrong people or for the wrong reasons. This happens with both political contributions and federal subsidies. Watchdog groups in Washington D.C., and around the rest of the country follow the money of political campaigns and lobbyist groups to determine if corruption exists. One such group, Follow Your Money, has political giving information reporting that Wal-Mart is the ninth largest contributor to the Republican party, giving $3.5 million dollars during the 2004 election cycle (Basker 2007). On the flip side, government subsidies are also watched by activist organizations to determine if the system is being abused. Good Jobs First, a Washington-based subsidy watchdog group, found that $1 billion of government subsidies have gone to Wal-Mart over the years, helping it become the world's largest retailer.

The State of Maine passed a clean elections referendum in 2003 that encourages politicians not to follow the money. "Clean Elections is a practical, proven reform that puts voters in control of elections. Rather than being forced to rely on special interest donors to pay for their campaigns, candidates have the opportunity to qualify for full public funding which ends their reliance on special interest campaign cash. Being freed from the money chase means they have more time to spend with constituents, talking about issues that matter to them. When they enter office, they can consider legislation on the merits, without worrying about whether they are pleasing well heeled donors and lobbyists" (Clean Elections Campaign Reform, 1, 2, 3 2008).

"When the Maine legislature passed the Dirigo health care law, which would provide near-universal health care coverage for Mainers, a majority of legislators had won their offices under the Clean Elections system. "No private money meant no campaign contributions from hospitals, or insurers, or from any other big-money interest that might want to scuttle the Dirigo plan. "Publicly funded legislators were free to support this legislation without any concern for the big-money special interests that might oppose such a law," wrote Rep. Jim Annis, a Republican, and Rep. John Brautigam, a Democrat (2005).

Solution   Following the money is an effective tool to detect corruption and terrorism. However, making it harder for politicians and others to "follow the money" by enacting and enforcing more effective laws seems like an even better tool to accomplish positive goals like clean elections and universal health care without giving up important constitutional rights like the right to privacy.

Linked patterns   Social Responsibility (8), Working-Class Consciousness (12), Whole Cost (28), Alternative Media in Hostile Environments (53), Transparency (64), Free and Fair Elections (68), Powerful Remittances (73), Civic Capabilities (85), Shared Vision (101).

Problem   In developed countries the nonstop barrage of mass media promoting corporate-branded messages is never far away. How can people even hear themselves think under such conditions? How will smaller groups develop deep research or action plans, and how will society as a whole practice the due deliberation necessary for democratic work and progress? Without relief from the assault, how will people learn to appreciate what has value in life? How can they develop a self-identify that is truly theirs?

Context   This pattern applies to anybody or any group caught in a seemingly never-ending cycle of activity. Every person and every group and organization has a need to retreat from their everyday, often routinized, lives.

Discussion   This pattern is about escape, liberation, disengagement, and, necessarily, reengagement. Neither the name nor its discussion adequately reflects its enormity.

Both an instant of freedom and a year of freedom of disconnection from forces that are essentially inhuman and unnatural are covered by this pattern. What is not sanctioned by this pattern is permanent retreat. This pattern, the last in this pattern language sequence, is intended to help people get in touch with their own feelings, with a different pace, with a reality that is not mediated by mass media or by other distractions. It is intended to help people disengage, recharge, and reengage in ways that are lively, creative, caring, and wise.

Our species is millions of years old, and the universe we inhabit is incomprehensibly vast in size and in age. The rhythms of our universe and the seasons of the earth and our body seem timeless; they exist still, within what John Trudell (1999) calls our "genetic memory." The rhythms of timeless life are not the same as those of television, the Internet, and the workaday world.

The practice of cramming tasks into specific, discrete slots of time makes the declaration that the task will take that much time even when a slot with more or less time may be the right amount for the job. Educating people, for example, is not done best in an assembly-line fashion. Some students need more time, some less, and the type of lessons should vary as well.

When life is routinized, when all of one's actions are circumscribed by external events, canned responses, and internalized clichés, the ability to change direction and to pursue a different path is minimized. A retreat, a break in the process, is necessary, for it is during those times, however brief, that change can occur.

The digital realm, for social (as well as structural) reasons, has helped promote a culture where "answers" or "solutions" are sought. The Internet is good for finding facts, but cannot teach analysis, interpretation, critique, or common sense. Reality, even when addressed artificially through computer simulations (a proper use of the computer when its limitations are sufficiently appreciated) must cope with numerous levels of complexity and interaction.

The postmodern world of the Internet, mass media, virtual reality, globalization, spectacle, empty abstractions, and real-time data, on the one hand, and SUVs, AIDS, homeless children picking through garbage for food, landless peasants, mega-mansions, and vast slums, on the other hand, are both real. They exist in our individual and collective minds as perceptible information which has tangible implications. Our thoughts, ideas, and memories, no matter how incoherent, paranoid, or illogical, play themselves out in the real world.

The wilderness or other setting relatively unperturbed by humankind is probably the best setting for the practice of this pattern: "Alone in the forest, time is less 'dense,' less filled with information; space is very 'close'; smell and hearing and touch reassert themselves. It is keenly sensual. In a true wilderness we are like that much of the time, even in broad daylight. Alert, careful, literally 'full of care.' Not because of principles or practice, but because of something very old" (Turner 1989).

The following thoughts of German researchers Sachs, Loske, and Linz (1998) suggest a new slowness might be coming.

Beneath the official compulsions of acceleration a cautious interest in greater slowness is beginning to stir. Not as a program, not as a strategy, but rather as a subversive demand viewing all the glorification of speed as old-fashioned and out of touch with the times. If such experiences accumulate, then the familiar trend might conceivably be reversed and affluence become associated with deceleration. (Sachs, Loske, and Linz 1998)

The function of this pattern language is to acknowledge and celebrate seeds of life that can be used to generate more life in the face of violence and corruption. Remaining pure or removed, aloof from the sordidness of the world that has developed over the centuries, is not an option. Nor is it necessarily more admirable than retreating into the vast media wastelands, work, mysticism, sports, or drugs. Engagement and retreat together form an eternal cycle that we ignore at our own peril.

Solution　People need to set up times to think, step back, and recharge their batteries. After this respite, we are more likely to be happy, committed, and ready to reengage again. Retreat and reflection are necessary counterparts to engagement, and both are necessary if we are going to muster the strength we absolutely need for a "fierce struggle that will re-create the world" (Freire 1995).

Linked patterns　Civic Intelligence (1), The Good Life (3), Memory and Responsibility (11), Back to the Roots (13), Technocriticism (39), Future Design (88), Thinking Communities (118), Great Good Place (119), Activist Road Trip (134).

9 Evaluating the Language

In this chapter we look with an eye toward evaluating the first version of the Liberating Voices pattern language set out in chapter 8. Examining both the product (the individual patterns and the pattern language as a whole) and the development process used should improve understanding of the quality of this work and prepare for the next steps. One of these steps is enhancing the pattern language development online environment, which we hope will promote refinement, evaluations, and use of the pattern language.

Validity of the Language

Structurally, a pattern language is simply a linked set of patterns that contain the same elements: typically, the pattern name, problem, context, discussion, solution, and links to other patterns, although these exact terms might not be used, and two or more elements may be combined into one. Clearly Liberating Voices meets the structural requirements of a pattern language.

Patterns contain diagnoses and prescriptions: they are not neutral observations. They suggest that something is amiss and offer a course of action to correct the situation. From a content point of view, the patterns as a set (i.e., the pattern language) all must exist within a certain domain and should represent a holism of coverage within that domain. That holism is demonstrated by its coherence. This can be demonstrated when the patterns address problems at different levels of scale. Each pattern should represent a single idea, and each pattern should be a nontrivial and plausible response to a genuine problem within that domain. Furthermore, each pattern should be linked to a variety of other patterns that are not all the same type of pattern. Pattern languages are general but not specious. From a community point of view, a cross-sectoral pattern language like Liberating Voices should contain information for everybody interested in that domain. We are relatively confident that Liberating Voices meets these criteria but are resolved to the possibility that gaps exist and will be brought to light.

The main product of our work so far is the pattern language itself. Evaluating it entails looking at the individual patterns and a set of what we hope are coherent patterns.

Ultimately the pattern language must be evaluated in terms of what it is trying to accomplish. Hence, we are unable to perform this evaluation until we have acquired substantial feedback on the pattern language as it is used in practice. (There is a question of whether it can ever be demonstrated that any specific piece of information played a measurably meaningful role in meeting any long-term social change objectives, an issue examined in the next chapter.) More useful to the needs of this chapter are three questions specific to Liberating Voices. First, does it meet the criteria of a good pattern language? For example, is it complete? Does it adequately reflect its domain? Is it timeless (a claim that Alexander made for his architectural patterns)? Second, does it meet the objectives we have set for it? Does it provide a solid framework for effective progressive activities in the realm of information and communication? Third, is this framework (intellectually and materially) capable of adapting over time to maintain its usefulness? These three questions are deeply interrelated: if information or even structured collections of information are inadequate in general, then this enterprise is doomed. If the pattern language does not meet the criteria of a genuine pattern language, we cannot learn anything about whether pattern languages are useful for describing coherent, actionable knowledge in complex domains; if the pattern language is incapable of promoting progressive activity, then the whole enterprise is invalidated; and, finally, if it cannot evolve, it becomes out-of-date and obsolete earlier than need be.

Pattern languages do not exist in a vacuum; their validity cannot be ascertained merely by inspecting the pattern language itself. For a pattern language to be valid, there must be a valid correspondence with three entities: it should reflect the domain it is intended to address, fulfill the claims that the language developers put forward, and reach the community or communities that the language was intended to reach. The patterns and the pattern language should work for both the people who use it and for society at large. Based on this, we find three important factors that form the environment that the pattern language must exist within to be valid. The pattern language must balance the needs and demands of all three entities (figure 9.1). The discussion of the correspondence between the pattern language and these three factors follows a brief discussion of the factors themselves as they apply to both patterns and pattern languages. And, of course, all of this must connect to the real world—the world we wish to know and the world as we are able to know it. Significant changes in either should ultimately be reflected in future versions of Liberating Voices.

The word *domain* is used here to apply to the intellectual boundary that describes the field that the pattern language will address. The domain of a pattern language can be described in terms of a definition, boundary tests, and a model. The definition is concerned with how information and communication, chiefly its creation, distribution, modification, storage, destruction (or suppression), regulation (policy), interpretation, and use, can be employed by individuals and organizations within civil society to ameliorate social and environmental problems.

Patterns and pattern languages also have their particular way of being validated. According to the original conceptualization, they must reflect the "timeless way," in the sense that

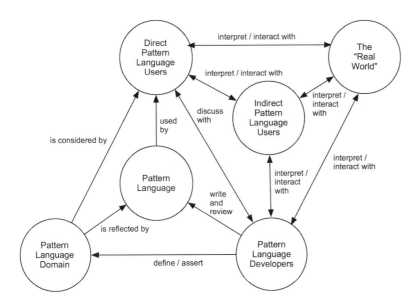

Figure 9.1
Validation components

Alexander articulated (1979), and have a moral center. The individual patterns should be nontrivial and reflect the values described. The patterns must also work together (be linked) and together describe a totality of a field, like towns and buildings for Alexander or information and communication for Liberating Voices. The boundary conditions can be used to help determine whether a pattern fits within the domain to which it is purported to belong. The model contains elements and interactions that reflect an interpretation of reality, including a critique of that reality (figure 9.1).

Developing Liberating Voices

During the seven years of developing Liberating Voices, a small group of people kept the fire burning for the project. There were long stretches when progress was barely perceptible and discussion about the patterns was more prevalent than work on the patterns themselves. But as time went on, the language as a whole took shape and became more coherent: the patterns became clearer and more fleshed out as patterns. Patterns from the "pool" environment were selected for patterns in the final Liberating Voices pattern language, the patterns were placed in order, and ultimately links were forged between patterns. In short, a pattern language gradually emerged from the chaos of cyberspace.

The core group, hailing from the United States, the U.K., and Australia (see the Pattern Authors section at the end of the book), was small—almost always smaller than half a dozen.

Also, there was little practical incentive for forward motion: everybody was a volunteer, and deadlines were rare. This was not to say that people were not interested, just that jobs that earned us our living and jobs with deadlines took precedent over this one, which offered neither (until, of course, this book project). This core group who became members of the advisory group did represent a community, albeit a small one, that sustained a conversation over time. This group also played a role in the sporadic conversations within the larger Liberating Voices electronic distribution list forum. As the workload increased and book deadlines loomed, this group became increasingly active. The amount of work that we accomplished increased dramatically, while the time that it took for tasks to be completed dropped correspondingly. The follow-on question then becomes what happens next to this community after the book is complete and people take notice of our effort. This question is taken up in the following section.

Another important and somewhat open question is how effective this project was as a participatory project. Earlier I noted that ultimate success would depend on the effective participation of the community. This venture is experimental, and there are few examples (at least that we know of) that share our broad objectives and global participatory approach. Thus we have not been able to simply adopt an existing process for our purposes. The success of Alexander's theory and books provided our best reference point for considering our possible success at producing a product that was compelling and worthwhile to a large number of people. But the previous work yielded few clues about how to develop a complex product like a pattern language in a distributed, participatory way.

This project raises many interesting challenges and contradictions. The first one is inherent in all participatory projects and programs (like being a citizen in a democracy): What does it mean to participate? Who can participate, and under what conditions? What are the rules, and can they be altered? Participation can be evaluated in three ways: (1) How much participation was there? (How many people participated in general, and how much participation was there among the people that did participate?) (2) How genuine was the participation? (3) How effective was the participation? In general we would like to answer all three questions positively.

As of November 2006, at least 350 people had directly participated in this project, not counting over 300 Directions and Implications of Advanced Computing conference attendees. Of these people, one put in over 2,000 hours, perhaps ten people had put in over 100 hours, perhaps eighty had put in between 10 and 99 hours, with the remainder putting in fewer than 10 hours. The project has been participatory, yet not radically so. Regardless of whether near total equality of participation is the goal or a standard by which to judge the project is a reasonable issue to address. Is it possible to develop a pattern language (a collective universe of knowledge) that is more balanced in terms of participation than the project so far? This would require less emphasis on leaders and would be developed more organically by people using their local knowledge and expertise, focusing on patterns that they are interested in, and using their own skills.

Wikipedia provides a powerful example of a collective universe of knowledge that was developed in seeming violation of my comments above on the importance of funding and deadlines as basic motivators for contributing to online projects. Although several people suggested that we should have used a Wiki for this effort, I thought, perhaps mistakenly, that our circumstances were different enough to warrant our own custom software. Briefly, the reasons that we did not use a Wiki included the fact that our patterns are not necessarily well-known encyclopedia-grade objects. In other words, while many people know what types of information belong in an encyclopedia, fewer have that knowledge about patterns. Wikipedia also has rules about objectivity, as befitting an encyclopedia. Many of its entries, including one on abortion, for example, have whipsawed back and forth as advocates on either side of the issue extended their battle into Wiki space. And although not all of the Liberating Voices entries are partisan in a narrow political sense, they do intentionally espouse a position or bias. Opponents of every pattern could be invited to edit the original authors' text in order to achieve a balanced position. Yet we also felt that authors would want autonomy of authorship because they are mostly academics (who generally eschew anonymous authoring) and because they were too busy to invest time providing verbiage for this book that could be removed summarily at any moment.

All participation is within some preexisting scope of involvement or engagement. Authentic participation allows the possibility of expanding the scope, of challenging the rules. Whether the rules can be changed or not, it is clear that initial parameters tend to exert influence over the lifetime of any project, organization, or even effects of any technological artifact. As Langdon Winner (1986) states, "Because choices tend to become strongly fixed in material equipment, economic investment, and social habit, the original flexibility vanishes for all practical purposes once the initial commitments are made." While people are free to set up a project any way they seem fit, if it is billed as participatory and the participants feel that their participation was not sufficiently encouraged or respected, the integrity of the project can be called into question.

Of course, if the vast majority of participants believe the project is valid, that provides one type of suggestive evidence. The fact remains that some submitted patterns do not belong in the finished pattern language; for example, where a pattern is known to belong to the system, its antithesis does not belong. If a pattern is judged to be unacceptable by whomever is allowed to make that judgment and the author is unwilling to make any necessary changes, then the pattern submission should be deleted. Some of the reasons that a submission would be unacceptable include irrelevance, incoherence, redundancy, insignificance, or being contrary to the objectives and philosophy of the project. Any such decisions need to be authorized in some way.

Arguably, having a single coordinator helps build personality or human voice compared with something created by the much-disparaged committee (which, as it grows in size, also grows in anonymity and vagueness). Regardless of whether that is true, the issue of asymmetrical participation arises in the development of a pattern language or any other collaboratively constructed artifact. In the course of this project, the issue did come up at least implicitly among the community. Although there was no formal agreement on how decisions large and small were to be made (or perhaps because of it), as the primary instigator, I made them. I believe that this did ultimately work out, mostly because I was willing to make and implement the decisions. The decisions that I did make were enough free of controversy to prevent people from voicing their displeasure too vigorously. This is not to say that there was no dissent and that big decisions were made without consultation, particularly with the advisory board.

Also because I conceived the plan and had some type of vision in mind, it seemed reasonable to continue—and too taxing to invent another way when forward progress was slow and difficult already. In other words, the other members of the pattern-making community and I were subscribers to the norm of pragmatism. We had a job to do and preferred doing that job to developing a standardized process for that job. The search for viable shared decision-making processes for pattern making—one that shares rights and responsibilities—continues. It remains a critical issue now and is likely to become increasingly critical in the future.

Interestingly, one example of participation asymmetry arose in the development of the chapters in this book. Since the chapters are intended to supply the context for the patterns, their role can be quite critical. As the author of these chapters, I recognize that I should not take advantage of this bully pulpit to either unduly frame the patterns within a parochial perspective of my own or make conclusions purportedly based on the patterns but not actually warranted by the patterns themselves. Therefore, after a brief mutiny on the part of the advisory board, I withdrew eleven pages that the board thought went beyond the presumptions of the pattern authors. I was admonished not to overstep the democracy of the interchange that takes place across patterns and took place among their authors and the discussants of their patterns, and to save those thoughts for the "next book," God willing. Moreover I have resisted summarizing the patterns in the chapters, allowing them to speak for themselves, so that they truly are the liberated voices specified in the book's title.

The evaluation of the process should focus on the quality of the participation as demonstrated by the openness or fairness of the process and its efficacy in producing the desired outcome. This desired outcome includes both a product, the patterns and their pattern language, and a strengthened community. Obviously a process that failed to create a good product could not be considered a success. Perhaps less obvious is that the development of a strong pattern language in this domain and with the values we espouse without an open and equitable process would be unsuccessful. If the process is not sufficiently open and equitable, it is unlikely that the end result can be legitimate.

Intellectual Ownership of Patterns

Another challenge that this work exposes is that of preserving intellectual ownership of the ideas during the evolution from pattern set to pattern language. At the onset, the issue was minor; patterns have authors and also refer to other authors, ideas, and sources in the

Table 9.1
Participation by phase

Phase	Community	Output
Conceiving project	Doug Schuler, Erik Stolterman	Original project description
Developing call for patterns	Program committee	Discussion suggestions
Entering pattern suggestions	Anybody with Web access	Pattern suggestions
Reviewing patterns for symposium	Program committee	Discussion, rating
Reviewing patterns (face-to-face)	DIAC-2002 Open Space session	Discussion, advice, clustering
Reviewing patterns (online)	Anybody with Web access	Discussion, advice
Language development	"Official" community	Review, advice
Language development	Advisory committee	Recommendations
Final edits	Editorial board	Pattern language

patterns. Sometimes the pattern author is not the idea author. In my own case, for example, I submitted a pattern on Whistle-Blowing (130) that was based on ideas put forward by the Government Accountability Project (Devine 1997). This pattern makes explicit the importance and risk of publicizing information that powerful people and institutions would rather keep quiet. It also points out the importance of protecting the publicizer of the information and not turning the publicizer into a martyr. In this case, I needed to make it clear that the basic idea was not mine; I was merely explaining the idea using the pattern structure.

One possible approach to ownership of the process is shown in table 9.1. The phases are listed in the left column and proceed downward as the project progresses. Further evolution of the language is not listed explicitly in table 9.1, but the process could begin again at practically any phase. All patterns submitted (and made public) along with their authors' names will be kept inviolate electronically and in print form. Although the form of the evolving language will continue to change, it is important to preserve all original thoughts as well as the legacy of who did what as the project evolved. This dictum suggests that potentially complex authorship exists for each pattern that ultimately becomes part of the language. These contributions could be acknowledged on a pattern-by-pattern basis in an appendix or acknowledged generally.

An interesting (and possibly inevitable) dilemma could arise in the next phase of this project's life. Although some of this is carried forward in next section on the next generation of Liberating Voices, it is also discussed briefly here. It is not difficult to imagine in the future that somebody could offer a challenge of some type to a pattern; an example within the discussion could, for example, be obsolete, or some text might be misleading or inaccurate. Pointing out a problem in a pattern is certainly a type of participation, as is creating a pattern on a topic that has already been represented. The online system and policies that guide its use should support this capability. Clearly we are not interested in making this a competitive event, although that would be one to way to address issues like this (and may even increase participation). One way to provide the underlying support would be to continue to use the existing online "pool environment" for submitting new pattern suggestions and freeze the patterns in the online "book" environment so the patterns in the book and in this environment would match. Then a new online environment could be established that would be engineered to behave more naturally as a pattern ecosystem.

Did Participation Improve the Project?

The answer to this question is yes. For one thing, the pattern language could not have been created by one person. It would not have been physically possible or broad enough. (As to whether a small team could do it, the answer is probably yes. Alexander did it this way. But that does not mean that we could have done it this way; it was not really a practical option.) However, the goal remained to achieve a type of collective wisdom because the whole is smarter than the individual.

Using Liberating Voices: Pattern Users and Nonusers

We identify pattern users in figure 9.1 earlier in this chapter. This group directly and consciously puts the patterns to work, while other people who do not directly or consciously use the patterns are outside the pattern system user community depicted in the figure. Both groups taken together constitute everybody on the planet. It is the spread of the patterns from users to "nonusers" that can extend the effectiveness of the patterns. To some degree, that success of the pattern language as a whole is dependent on the usefulness of the individual patterns. Certainly the pattern language cannot be successful if all its patterns are deficient. Yet it can still be very successful if there are a few bad apples in a basket containing mostly pretty good ones. But individual patterns can be excellent even if the pattern language itself is not. Ideally the patterns that people use successfully would naturally lead (through our links, for example) to others that are also useful.

Use Cycle

We envision a standard use cycle that is unlikely to change over time. First, a person hears about the project and, second, decides to follow up on it if he or she has sufficient interest. If the patterns are accessible, potential users can readily find the pattern system and especially the patterns that make sense to them. The potential user is then likely to try to use the pattern. Once this person determines to use the pattern, he or she will get satisfactory or unsatisfactory results. We may hear from this person if the pattern did not yield satisfactory results, but ideally we would like to hear about every success, every failure, and every opinion from a user.

The use cycle is basically a chain where failure in one step often means that the next step will not be taken. Something as simple as pattern names can present a barrier. For example, the Civic Intelligence (1) pattern is intended for general use. Unfortunately the word *civic* implies "city" or "urban" in some cultures, rather than broadly in a way that includes both small towns and rural people, as well as a citizenship orientation, and this alone may convince a person that the pattern is irrelevant to them.

Feedback: Questions in Need of Answers

Obtaining feedback is essential to the evolution of the system and we can identify the feedback information that we need in relation to pattern accessibility, efficiency, and portability. We need to know: Are the patterns useful? Which patterns are used the most? Which patterns are most useful? And how could they be improved? We also would like to find out if people are using patterns individually or several at a time. This question is related to one of the goals of our project, which is to convey the project (and its domain) as a whole. This means that the project scope is larger than a typical user believes it to be. Of course where this fails, it could be because the domain on which the pattern language was built was not viable or the individual patterns were not accessible. The first is a pattern developer issue; the second is (in a broad way) a pattern interface issue.

Other questions need answering too: How are pattern languages used? What goals do they have, and how successful are they in attaining them? What pitfalls (from the philosophical to the pragmatic) exist in such projects? How are they circumvented?

Building Community

One of the aims of this enterprise is the development of a community or communities of liberated voices. *Community* conveys the sense of being primarily social and providing the core social support around everyday as well as significant life-changing events. Ours is not likely to be all of those, however. Ideally ours would be inclusive, diverse, convivial, connected (to knowledge and ideas, other communities and networks, and activists), committed, and effective. Ideally this community would exhibit a form of collective or civic intelligence, as we discuss in the next chapter.

Saving the World? Or, at Least, Steps in the Right Direction?

Can Liberating Voices provide a solid framework for widespread and effective progressive activism? And perhaps more to the point, how would we know if it does? On some level, each pattern contains at least the germ of a way to test the phenomenon that it is trying to correct. One approach can be launched upon the completion of this version of the pattern language. One of our advisers, John Thomas, has estimated that there are 500 forces represented within the patterns. Forces are an important aspect of Alexander's approach to patterns as he and his colleagues frequently stated that patterns represented a way to resolve forces (Alexander 1979). Looking at these in the aggregate, especially with an eye toward how they might be measured, can provide a relatively large collective vision. Going further, the pattern authors and the pattern language community could try to identify indicators that demonstrated whether the context was changing and whether the pattern was having an impact. John provided a brief discussion of how the forces that are manifest in the patterns could be used to inform and improve analysis and planning.

As an example, let us consider one dynamic of *forces* that underlies a number of the problems addressed by several of the patterns in the book. On the one hand, in order to be more effective and efficient, humans have found that it is useful to divide labor. Division of labor allows people with special innate skills to focus on tasks that resonate with those skills. More importantly, through training, people become quite expert in very different domains. Then, people develop communities to exchange information and further improve special skills. As a natural consequence, these communities evolve special languages, attitudes, and even values. However, coordination and cooperation across communities is still necessary. The very "forces" that enable communities and individuals within these communities to become more efficient over time, also tend to lead to "in-groups" and "out-groups" and increased difficulty of communication across groups leading in many cases to non-productive arguments, struggles for resources, and in extreme cases, to war. In addition, one community often achieves a temporary power disparity over other communities which is then used to acquire resources at the expense of less powerful communities.

Many of the individual patterns are attempts to mitigate the various negative consequences of the interplay of these forces such as power imbalances or communication impediments. These include, for example, World Citizen Parliament (40), Strengthening International Law (42), Conversational Support Across Boundaries (50), Alternative Media in Hostile Environments (53), Peace Education (56), Free and Fair Elections (68), Equal Access to Justice (69), Voices of the Unheard (83), Appreciative Collaboration (99), Shared Vision (101), Online Anti-poverty Community (103), and Whistle Blowing (130). In a similar way, the interplay of other common sets of forces can be seen as underlying the problematic situations which other sets of patterns attempt, in a variety of ways, to address.

Liberating Voices Online

The online pattern management system was designed to support contribution, review, and presentation of patterns. Because we did not know in advance exactly where we wanted to go with the project and because our time and other resources were limited, the development of the online system has of necessity been incremental, in true bricolage fashion.

Although we are confident that the pattern language presented in the book is coherent and useful, it is not necessarily timeless. Limited time, page length, and other constraints on the book, our own lack of wisdom, not to mention the enormity (or even the impossibility) of the task, have prevented us from creating the last word on the subject. Moreover, the idea of explicitly stating socially ameliorative objectives acts more as gravitational pull than as a never-fail filter. Our assumption was (and still is) that you can keep your eyes on the prize without sacrificing integrity, rigor, or critique in a social action and research enterprise. This assumption informs our technological development in addition to the other decisions that we make as we proceed. Our basic philosophy advocates a do-it-yourself, experimental, probing approach to our entire enterprise, including, of course, our own technological support.

With these values informing all phases of the project, we will explore possible technological trajectories for this project, some of which may be implemented by the time you read these words. We have identified several broad objectives for the next phase of the project: (1) strengthening the community around this effort and complementary efforts, (2) improving the comprehensiveness and overall effectiveness of the Liberating Voices pattern language, (3) and adapting and enhancing our online environment to support the first two objectives. We discuss below some of the ideas that we intend to explore over the next few years in the technological realm. In general, we need to address questions like these: What can we do now to anticipate and build toward the continuing evolution of the pattern language as a useful tool? How does this system of knowledge coexist and coevolve with the world it is trying to change and to support? What follows in the remainder of this section should be considered more in the realm of speculation than specification.

General Approach

The intent is to maintain current focus on information and communication processes, systems, resources, and theories. Technologically we plan to keep using the incremental design approach and build on the existing pattern language system framework—the submitted patterns, ideas, and other data—and the system itself, including Web pages, tools, and programmatic and database support. The evolution into another incarnation may ultimately result in patterns and a support infrastructure that bear little or no resemblance to the system set out here. We also want to encourage the participation of people from all walks of life, all countries, and speakers of languages other than English. This process would ideally be fluid enough to allow people to participate in the areas and ways in which they feel most comfortable—in types of participation and areas of interest and expertise.

For our purposes, it makes sense to organize this discussion in terms of several fundamentals that are deeply interrelated but can be addressed separately: (1) the community of users, (2) the online environment that provides various services and capabilities to users, and (3) the technology infrastructure, including the objects that the system knows about.

Communities, Users, and Roles

The entire user community consists of all people doing anything with the system. The pattern language system, like many other interactive online systems, supports users who assume a variety of roles: author, reviewer, editor, researcher, board member (for governance and policy), system administrator, participation community member, and user. Each role has associated rights and responsibilities. The rights are enforced by the system (authors, for example, can edit their patterns and nobody else's) and by other people in the group (although this has always been informal). People in the group also had their own individual skills, interests, availability, and resources. Each of these roles is accompanied by different incentives for use and what tasks people in those roles are expected to do and what functions are available to them. Each of these roles also has implications for how the system is developed, as well as the formal and informal social policies for each role. A new role, apprentice, for example, could be needed in the future, and technological support (assigning permission within the system that allows apprentices to work on certain types of projects) would likely be needed, as well as new policies and expectations. And although the roles seem to be fairly distinct, individual people often shift from one role to another, and the software should seamlessly support the common need of allowing people to move from one role to another without obstacles. And although people are interested in the system for a variety of reasons and will have widely varying levels of involvement, the entire group does constitute a wider community. For that reason, it should be fairly easy to communicate with each other. Of particular importance is how information flows from one subcommunity to another.

Besides roles, the major factor in thinking about future users is whether they are interested in obtaining information—probably from patterns, for research, activism, or other reasons—or if they are interested in being an active member of a community. If the former, the system should be optimized for use; it should be easy for people to find patterns or other resources that are interesting or useful to them. Ideally pattern users would be able to ask questions and make suggestions that would be addressed quickly and appropriately. If community building is the focus, then there should be support for communication between interested people that is easy to use. Providing opportunities for face-to-face meetings and online approaches that promote collaboration and engagement is critical.

Environment

The Liberating Voices online environment (http://www.publicsphereproject.org/patterns/) is a collection of patterns and other objects surrounded by services that people can use to manipulate the patterns in various ways for the construction and use of pattern languages.

The system currently provides basic support for patterns and pattern languages. It is generally a repository model, where people can publish their pattern ideas for public perusal. It also provides rudimentary support for general discussion and focused pattern discussion. On top of the basic pattern repository, we have developed support for the creation of pattern languages from patterns. This is done primarily through importing, ordering, and linking patterns and by adding explanatory headers and captions to pattern lists. Currently the system provides no support for recommending (suggesting, for example, that a pattern be imported from the pool to the released environment) or other types of support that new Web-based social software systems provide.

For the next phase of the project, there are several services that we can envision to add to the system. All of these build on the basic infrastructure, and each is designed to promote certain types of activities or certain types of users. Although these are presented as independent services, ideally all would coexist, with the proviso that the presence of one would not have negative implications for the operation or usability of the others.

There are many ways that the online Liberating Voices system could be reconceptualized. These include focusing on, for example, repository services, practitioners, the exploratory environment, and collaborative learning space. With most of these models, we would like an ongoing inflow of new ideas and information that users could locate easily on the site.

If the system is seen as a repository, it could contain information on a number of things besides patterns. Some possibilities are events, news items, citations, relevant organizations, and projects. In essence, a digital library could grow up around the pattern language. If the system is seen as being optimized for novice users, it should be easy to use and should offer a welcoming environment. If the system is seen as an exploratory environment, we need to ask what objects we have, which ones we need, how we establish new ones, how we observe and manipulate them, and how they relate to—or interact with—other objects on the Internet. If the system is seen as a collaborative learning space, there should be active user forums. There could also be tools for collaboratively marking up patterns and developing patterns. And if the system is seen as a tool for feedback and data collection, we need to maximize the ability of gathering data about using the patterns and sets of patterns. We could then answer questions like, Which patterns work together? and others that were impossible to answer before the set was constructed.

New or Enhanced Services: Search , Retrieval, and Sublanguage Creation

If the facilities existed for people to specify what they were looking for, it would be relatively easy for the system to generate a graphic showing patterns and their links. Each pattern image would be a type of "front door" to the pattern, so a user could read the pattern easily. Justin Smith, a member of our advisory board, is currently working on an icon-based approach to the accessing the patterns. The pattern image could be colored in some way so users would not have to retrieve the pattern if the coloring signified that it would not be appropriate.

Annotations

The idea of allowing users to annotate patterns in some way comes up fairly often. The case could be made that since patterns are the "first-class citizens" in the system, why not use them as the primary locus for discussion? The reviewing system we developed can be used to send messages, which do not necessarily have to be about the patterns, to pattern authors. The annotation idea is similar to using the pattern as its own blackboard. If somebody used the pattern and learned something about how to use it more effectively, the user might want to let the author know so he or she could amend the pattern. Another potential user who was interested in using the pattern would also probably want to check what others had said about it.

Links

We have established the rudimentary database support for typed links (e.g., superset/subset links), multiway links (to, e.g., all patterns related to media), one-way links (e.g., "refers to" links), and others. We have also done some work toward supporting external links, meaning that the online patterns in, say *A Pattern Language* (Alexander et al. 1977) or *A Conservation*

Economy (What does a sustainable economy look like? N.d.), could be linked into our patterns in some way.

Infrastructure: Versions

One of the ideas that emerged from the project was the idea of pattern versions or "worlds" or "environments." When we first established the system, there was not anything called an environment, and so all patterns were in the same environment. We now call that initial environment the "pool" environment, and anybody can contribute their pattern concepts to that environment. When we realized that not all patterns were going to be included in this book, we created version 2, the released environment or the book environment. I envision a third version that is more of a Wiki-style system in which authors and readers can collaboratively construct a more vibrant ecology in which patterns are linked and interact with others. A fourth version could be the unabridged version of the patterns initially developed for the book that were then edited to conform to fairly rigid restrictions.

Each pattern in the database now has a version number associated with it. Although we have developed only two versions so far, this approach seems like a reasonable way to allow the system to become more of a collaborative test-bed and learning environment for people and patterns. This approach will allow us to set up a variety of worlds, each with different characteristics that the "owner" and others would determine—essentially the policy for the world. Each existing and future environment has policy rules that describe when certain actions are allowed (e.g., when a pattern can be imported from one environment to another) and who could initiate those actions and software functions that, for example, display patterns in novel ways. When this is coupled with customizable ownership, the system starts becoming remarkably flexible.

Customizable Ownership

One possible approach to explore different ways to support collaboration on pattern development would be to allow authors to be able to assign access privileges for each pattern. If, for example, the owner of a pattern allows all users (whether they were registered or not) to modify the pattern, that would be the equivalent of a Wiki. An author could also let everybody associated with, say, "world 9" (see "Infrastructure: Versions" section above), work on the patterns that he or she owns.

A favorite theme of speculative fiction is that of earthlings uniting against a common enemy, generally a murderous race of gruesome aliens from beyond our solar system. This faint hope of a real human brotherhood is held out by some people as a comforting sign that at least under some extremely unlikely circumstances, we might refrain from killing each other either individually or institutionally. The sad truth is that we are too frequently our own worst enemies.

More relevant to our concerns here than the prospect of an alien invasion is that the "united humankind" hypothesis is now undergoing several genuine tests. One such test is our own collective response to the threat of global warming. The belief that the earth is experiencing major climate changes, ushered in by humankind's seemingly casual disregard of environmental limits, is shared by nearly everybody whose business it is to know about such things. Yet the number of people who actively resist the idea forcibly and the number of those who are oblivious, do not care, or feel helpless is staggeringly immense. Other tests are also being conducted—humankind's response (or lack thereof) to AIDS and other public health emergencies and the proliferation of nuclear weapons, for example.

The human race seems to be engaged as subjects in the ultimate experiment. Teetering between competition and cooperation, toleration and genocide, we are eternally trying to reconcile the unsubtle fight-or-flight messages of our ancient brains with ideas that emanate from the more recent neocortex veneer of human logic, philosophy, art, religion, and science. Another source of tension is shown in the way we treat the earth, our nurturing host. Given over a million years of human life, we have had ample time to develop philosophies and policies that would simultaneously foster a good life for all humans without despoiling our host and depleting the resources that we inherited from the universe. From a population numbering perhaps 1 million in our distant origins, our fellow travelers on the planet have grown in number to 6.6 billion. For every person roaming the earth then, there are 6,500 people now, a small town. Given the incredible creativity and resourcefulness of the human race in facing unique challenges and opportunities over the centuries, it should come as no surprise that we as a species have developed vast numbers of cultures and belief systems. We could develop ideas that tolerate, even appreciate, the genius and wonder of other cultures, or we can listen to our inner reptile and choose ignorance, bigotry, suspicion, and death.

The Theory of Liberating Voices

The fundamental premise of this chapter is reflected in the title. We are asserting with this book that information and communication play a crucial role in positive social change. On the surface, this assertion may seem trivial. After all, any human action that involves more than one person requires some coordination—and, hence, communication—between them. On the other hand, the assertion that positive social change could be attained through intelligent use of information and communication places a burden on the people who propose agendas built on this premise. What information? What communication? We have taken the approach of not defining a single end state but a collection of transformative ideas. We are proposing, in other words, that the means will justify the ends. This project assumes that positive social change can be attained incrementally. This, of course, can never be achieved with the certainty that a theory of the physical world, where it is assumed that metal will behave in the same way in a million years as it does today, can attain. There are really no ends in history. Take, for example, a case where an organization working for social change is helping to build bridges between ethnic groups engaged in deadly conflict over territory. If at some point in the future, people from either inside or outside the territory initiate attacks that kill people or destroy property, they will rapidly undo whatever progress had occurred. This is what happened when World War I erupted, bringing with it the collapse of many international and cross-cultural linkages. Thus, one of the hoped-for outcomes of this project is to prevent violent and other events that forestall progress and, conversely, act to limit the damage that does occur after any such breach to the peace.

The approach we have taken promotes incremental improvements to the relationships within the social and environmental spheres. This approach runs the inherent risk of not being adequate to meet challenges set in motion by organizations predisposed to resorting to violence as a solution to a problem. The incremental approach may also be ill equipped to deal with challenges that require rapid mobilization and reorganization against, say, environmental disasters. Nevertheless, the recommended distributed, polycentric network organizational approach has many potential benefits as well.

Another assertion we make is that values that are made explicit can be legitimately used as motivation and criteria for change. Implicitly at least, the patterns reveal an emerging composite picture or natural history of how the world works in the information and communication sphere. Power plays itself out through social domination, media, social frames, and mental models, among others. The patterns reject the idea that today's dominant forces are likely to lead to positive change if left unchallenged and unchanged. Exploiting a person or people, intentionally or not, can be seen as a public health risk, not unlike breeding disease, developing the pathogens that encourage hatred toward others. An injury to one is thus an injury to all.

Our project also asserts that the ways we have partitioned knowledge are often inadequate (if not actual impediments) for the work that our times require. While the specialists in various areas of knowledge are important, generalists as well as other specialists will be needed in the future. In general, a hybrid mode of action and research will be necessary.

Finally, we advance the assertions that the pattern language approach is appropriate for the goals that we set out. It is sound in the sense that it approximated the goals we had established for it. Our methodology is also sound for the same reason. We also make the determination that Liberating Voices does in fact constitute a legitimate theory, although not the standard kind.

Since the pattern language is intended to accomplish so much, it will likely provide a fairly easy target for critics. For one thing, it appears to claim to address the whole of information and communication as applied to social change. Here a claim that the pattern language represents some basic essence is probably more convincing than a claim of comprehensiveness. Another claim is that the pattern language as a whole can be considered as a portrait of the situation as it is, albeit painted in critical hues. It could also be viewed as a catalogue of responses constituting a different portrait: the countertrends that rarely see the light of day. The language could be regarded as a collection of opportunities for individuals, groups, policymakers, journalists, and others, whether they accept the overall approach of the pattern language authors and editors or not.

Orientation

Regardless of whether the pattern language is a theory, an important issue to address is how well the orientation that we employed matches or suits our objectives. We have endeavored to make our goal of social and environmental amelioration overt and always present in our thinking. There are several reasons for this. The first is the belief that the orientation actually shapes the work. We have been trying to identify ways in which we as citizens of the world can work toward positive ends instead of academicism, hand-wringing, complaining, or escapism. We wanted to bring attention to the fact that whether the purpose or orientation is ever stated, all human activities are enacted within certain contexts. The scientific institution (or, perhaps, more properly, its submerged orienting principles) provides an interesting example of a context that is especially germane to this project. The three main contextual issues are funding (who gets it, who does not, and where is the money coming from), philosophical underpinnings of the nature of knowledge, and boundaries between scientific work and other types.

The first issue is that of funding. Clearly what types of research get funding has some effect on what gets done. The idea of science as the pursuit of truth unsullied by politics and money is to some degree a myth—not a myth in the sense that it is entirely false, but in the sense that it has broad effects on our thinking and action, operating largely on a sub-conscious level. Putting money into one area for research instead of another has a political dimension because it changes the dynamic of what gets done in the research field: funding one area creates researchers in that area.

More insidious perhaps are the assumptions of what science is and, significantly, how it plays out in society. Joel Garreau, writing in *Edge City: Life on the New Frontier* (1991), comments on Christopher Alexander's salient remarks on the insidiousness of reductionism: "Somewhere, Alexander says, we got to the point where any concern that did not fit into the machine model was tossed aside as not relevant. If it was not quantifiable in that fashion, it was not real. Even those who studied human behavior, such as psychologists and sociologists, felt compelled to ape the methods of physics, attempting to reduce the realities they observed to equations." In other words, the hard sciences became the exemplar for what science is. Their emphasis on repeatability and laboratory experiments implies a closed-system world (where all the variables are known and controlled for) that is absolutely knowable and context free. This reflects and helps perpetuate the idea of a controllable world, one where the future can be clearly seen and manipulated at a distance with knobs, dials, spreadsheets, and simulations.

The third point has to do with the boundaries of the disciplines. Knowledge and knowledge systems are not separable from each other or from the rest of society. For if scientists speak only to other scientists, stay out of realms not their own, and insist on pure science, they are effectively isolating themselves from major portions of society. Politicians and media pundits are thus relatively free to manipulate and misrepresent the findings of the scientific community. Whether the result of this isolation is interpreted as a gated, exclusive community or a banished group, the upshot is the same: scientists, either voluntarily or by decree, often stay out of policy debates. But how then do concerned citizens deal with scientific findings? Who is best positioned to help with this translation (see the pattern with that name)?

With these words, my objective is not to bury science but to praise it. I am appealing to the scientific community to become more engaged in social change struggles. This appeal does not request that scientists forgo their devotion to rigorous inquiry or pursuit of the truth, only that they reconsider some of the hidden assumptions of their culture and help ensure that their work is used for good ends.

Methodology

The product of the bricoleur's labor is a bricolage, a complex, dense, reflexive, collagelike creation that represents the researcher's images, understandings, and interpretations of the world or phenomenon under analysis. (Denzin and Lincoln 1998)

This project is largely qualitative research. It is nonrepeatable in the sense that we could never repeat the exact circumstances nor the broader historical context under which this project was carried out. The project itself may have altered the context. We will not have the opportunity to do it all again with a slightly different set of variables. Therefore, throughout the project, we have had to strike a balance of planning, participation, flexibility, efficiency, and the need for results. The subjects of the research are also contributors to the content and directions of the process. The project makes use of participant-observers, with every participant also an observer. It is also designed to give voice to a large number of people who are, in turn, attempting to give voice to a still larger group. It is an open-ended participatory program with the capacity to continue to collectively develop a shared vision that combines theory and practice. It is remarkable how much our work resembled the work of a bricoleur and, even more remarkable, how similar our work is to the description of the "bricoleur's labor" according to Denzin and Lincoln (1998).

We have tried to gather up and represent the voices of the people while appreciating and acknowledging the hazards that are inherent in such an approach, including the impossibility of the task. Nevertheless, I believe that this work is at least one step closer to a work where ordinary people with few resources (including few credentials) can be said to have participated in a research project in which they are subjects. And why shouldn't people be involved in some conscious way in the definition and construction of their own society? The bricolage approach that we embraced must continue to be an influence as the project includes an increasing number of people. The discussion of the scientific culture above could serve as a reasonable parable for nonscientists as well. The seeming independence of our roles in society, our general lack of responsibility to the greater good, and the limits to our influence as individuals all presuppose a boxed-up, circumscribed world. This represents a mechanistic and static perspective that may satisfy some psychological—as well as material—needs. It is, however, inaccurate, intellectually and morally strait-jacketing, and ultimately self-defeating on many levels.

The fact that our online system was fundamental to this enterprise also raises obvious questions about its appropriateness for our goals. The primary objection is that people without access to the Web were prevented from participating, but it was impossible to provide in any other way given our modest means. But the system helped primarily by providing an accessible public input and presentation system. We believe that the Web-based system ultimately offers a wide variety of pattern presentation and exploration approaches. Although we have not pursued this as vigorously as we had planned, our approach also suggests a number of avenues for deliberation and feedback. We suspect, however, that it was probably prudent not to have developed substantial resources for this effort that in the end might have been underused.

A Theory of *What*?

The Liberating Voices pattern language is a collection of knowledge, beliefs, and recommendations about the use of information and communication in the dawn of the twenty-first century. We of course hope it is relevant, compelling, and coherent. But what is it? It is clear that if Liberating Voices is a theory, it is a social theory; it describes or purports to describe something societal. The mechanism (the how) of the theory exists within the patterns and their interactions and, at the pattern language level, through the totality of the intentionality, values, observations and ideas. Each Liberating Voices pattern is a mini-theory. Each describes some general type of practice (with examples), frames it in a general way, and makes a claim that employing the ideas in the pattern can promote positive social change in some way. The broader assertion of the pattern language is that all of these mini-theories constitute a larger theory of social change, especially if the theory works systemically as intended and one pattern can pick up where another one left off. Note that neither a pattern nor the articulation from the use of one pattern to the use of another is intended to be mechanistic, an approach to social change that would be antithetical to the values and assertions of this book. We are arguing, however, that within an open systemic way that the patterns presuppose, the results proposed by the patterns have some higher possibility of occurring than through the use of other approaches. The pattern language can be viewed as a grand (though complex and imperfect) theory, a collection of minitheories (some better than others), a complex, collaborative, modularized ethnographic study of today's information society or any combination of the above. This particular theory of the information society is different from the others, as it is organized and built on a set of smaller theories that are also connected, however imperfectly, to each other. This keeps the theory from being too abstract by forcing actual experiences into the same conceptual package—the pattern.

Another intriguing question is whether Liberating Voices could be considered a theory of communicative space. This becomes particularly germane when looking at our effort in relation to Alexander's theory of living physical space. In another departure from traditional theories, this approach is both (selectively) descriptive and prescriptive. In other words, while the theory describes situations that currently exist, it also advocates changing them through explicit practices. In practical terms, the authors were not allowed to hide or disguise their advocacy. The purpose of the book was not only to create a scholarly recounting about what activists are doing in the realm of information and communication.

The tentative nature of the patterns and the pattern language suggests that it is a type of proto-theory or even an embryonic stew of ideas from which more formal or more developed theories may emerge. But since it is a theory composed of theories, it may be a metatheory. Since the patterns were generally contributed by their authors without considering the other patterns in the system, it is fair to say that new ideas are likely to emerge from considering the patterns in groups of two or more. As editor-in-chief, I was deeply involved with the potential of these connections, as were other advisers on the project.

It is clear that Liberating Voices goes beyond the "information society" and "network society" designations. Both of those characterizations are descriptive and ostensibly neutral. Both suggest that qualitative changes are occurring (as side effects), but no prescriptions or metalearning are involved: They are more or less a business-as-usual paradigm that focuses primarily on existing players in figuring out how to use new technology in order to do what they do better. Intelligence, and perhaps societal self-actualization, are good metaphors for what we are trying to do, but these designations are a loose, general orientation or trajectory, not mechanistic or overly constrained. Liberating Voices is a theory of how information and communication can be used for positive social change. It is an alternative theory to the information society.

Research and Action Agenda

Through this work, we have continually blurred the lines between thinking and doing, between research and action. For that reason, this chapter proposes an agenda that necessarily straddles and blurs the boundaries between the two. While we believe that the pattern language represents a significant and rich proposal or agenda in its own right, it also suggests an enormous amount of work beyond the use of the patterns.

One of the main side effects that we hope will emerge from this work is a concerted new focus on information and communication as a foundation for social progress, social problem solving, and social amelioration. Unfortunately simply asking, What information do people need for their survival and for their participation in democratic (and other) societies? and What types of communication systems are most likely to support the intelligent use of this information? is to invite widespread suspicion or, more likely, absolute silence from the large media companies and their clients in government and other powerful institutions. An intriguing historical example, the case of the U.S. Constitution, shows how loathe rulers are to encourage people to participate in government: "Designed at a time in which 'social problem solving' was not even in currency as a concept, the designers of the Constitution entertained no ideas of institutional capacity for general problem solving. They created a government capable of protecting the 'general welfare,' but with curbs on the state's capacity to pursue it" (Lindblom 1990).

The focus on information and communication as it relates to social change triggers a plethora of interdisciplinary issues, including the following:

• Social dominance. What are its origins, manifestations, and implications? How is it maintained? What policies help perpetuate it? Which ones can help level social divisions?
• Civic mobilization. How do ordinary people mobilize, for example, to confront inequality or war? What new opportunities and challenges exist?
• Monitoring and awareness. What types of information do people need, and in what form? How can ordinary people be part of this discussion and design?
• Collective discourse. How do we bring more people into productive discourse and collective learning, especially people from diverse backgrounds and across traditional or rigid boundaries? How do we increase participation and develop new participatory venues?
• Mental models and social framing. How can we reconstruct our mental models to reflect better models of reality and what we think we know?

- Collective metacognition. How does society learn? And how does society learn about learning? How can we correct self-defeating metacognitive habits? Can society change its paradigms consciously, proactively, and peacefully?
- Collaboration and new forms of collective organization. How are people working together in multidisciplinary ensembles?

Although these ideas can be explored in the absence of Liberating Voices or any other general theory, we believe that these questions might make more sense and be more useful when investigated in conjunction with the patterns. Each pattern can be thought of as an opportunity for social learning. In Lindblom's (1990) lexicon, each is a "probe." Probes propel "social learning without specifying an end—only criteria for action and evaluation and, thus, promote perpetual learning."

One of the next steps in this project should be dialogues around the patterns, using online systems and other forms of communication, including face-to-face venues. These dialogues with authors, users, and others could be used to foster collaborative research between the parties. The dialogues could also help bring the sprawling and unruly collection of patterns into line by transforming the set more fully into a theory and as a vehicle for surfacing new research and action initiatives. Any dialogue that arises through actual or imagined discussion between two or more patterns and their authors can help surface important shared research and action tasks and projects that help put the theory on firmer ground. And as the output of one pattern can be viably viewed as the input of another, the usefulness of the theory increases.

People from community groups with interests in specific themes could be involved in workshops to work with and critique the pattern language. Participants would access and analyze selected patterns, assessing their usefulness and usability for their own work and circumstances. A thematic and organizational mix of data from these experiences will help us perform some comparative analysis. Are there overlaps in the patterns that come up? Do the people from some groups prefer certain patterns that are different from those that are selected by people in other groups? What patterns come up in relation to themes such as health care, the environment, economic justice, and human rights? Ideally workshops like this would help build the capacity of community-based organizations in order to be more effective in their work and participate in larger collaborative and coalition efforts. Here are some possible questions to raise at a workshop (many were suggested by Hollander 2002):

- What patterns are the most immediately appealing—and why?
- Were the patterns that were linked to the patterns that people found useful also useful?
- What patterns seem to be the most useful for different types of activities such as theorizing, social critique, program or policy development, or other uses?
- What patterns are missing and need to be added?
- What problems do people and groups face that have information and communication aspects to them that are addressed in the pattern language? Which ones are not addressed?

• What can be done to make the pattern content more accessible?
• What type of outreach would be useful in getting the word out with the patterns?
• What type of training would help people use the patterns?
• What patterns that appeared to be outside an organization's direct focus or work practices seem useful?
• What can be done to make the Web site more accessible?
• How can the online system support community development and collaborative problem solving?

The use of a shared hypertext as collaborative space is a research area in its own right. We would like to discover, for example, how computer support and mediation can help—or hinder—the creation of a community largely through the collective construction of a rich resource bank (of patterns) that describes their particular body of shared knowledge. Communities, like the one created around this project are unlike traditional geographical communities. These communities of interest are formed in various ways. A scholarly community forms basically as a side effect of its efforts to develop a shared knowledge base of data, texts, precepts, paradigms, goals, and methodologies. In this project we hoped to leverage the increasing accessibility of the Web worldwide to help develop this community more rapidly (while not rushing to judgment or preempting deliberation or equitable participation).

Many questions will be confronted in this endeavor:

• What percentage of ideas put forth in the space of, say, one year, coalesce into something significantly useful?
• How is the problem of who is in charge to be handled, not just in this particular project but as a general practice if online pattern languages become prevalent?
• What kind of end products evolve?
• What kinds of concepts seem to be most amenable to this modality for building concepts?
• What is the motivation of participants to be involved? What incentives exist or could be developed? How effective are they, and are there unanticipated side effects?
• How are issues of intellectual property and ownership of coalesced concepts resolved?
• Are their legal ramifications of use? If so, what are they? How are they resolved?
• What kinds of ideas find this a useful medium for their development?
• What are the global or international implications of this kind of building of ideas?
• How do asynchronous (electronic) collaborative approaches reinforce or detract from synchronous (face-to-face) collaborative approaches and vice versa?

Pattern languages stress systems thinking, group problem solving, constructivist learning, discovery, creativity, and metacognition, and a pattern language orientation promotes collaborative and critical thinking. Pattern languages seem to be appropriate in the development of bodies of knowledge that differ from traditional paradigmatic bodies of knowledge. The idea of using a pattern language as the ongoing focus for a thematic orientation for interdisciplinary work in high school or college or beyond is appealing, as is the use of a pattern language to help networks of researchers focus on strategic research and action plans. Also, of course, there are numerous ways to involve students in research issues around Liberating Voices, such as using or evaluating individual patterns or researching the claims within patterns.

Students and researchers (and others) can be involved in their own collaborative development of ideas and knowledge particularly as they pertain to new fields of study (such as Global Citizenship (6) or Civic Intelligence(1)) that integrate theory and action and bridge traditional boundaries. I've used the pattern language approach in classes I've taught as a way to capture and embody holistic collections of information and ideas that represent collective learning. There is also a rich vein of work related to supporting collaboration, or distributed, collective cognition, which I believe is one of the most vital areas to understand and promote.

With this project we are consciously trying to spur interest, research, and action. The project is intended to inspire activism in several key ways. The first is by raising the consciousness of the diffuse communities that already exist and the communities that are forming and growing. This raising of consciousness is intended to provide many hints and ideas to the community, much like a how-to book in a given area. The pattern language is educational in the simple sense of providing useful information that will help people more easily achieve their objectives. Beyond that, however, this project—through the process and the end result—is intended to bolster civil society generally.

Social Evolution and Civic Intelligence

What we think and say and what we do are strongly linked. Each of us has power, both realized and unrealized, that varies considerably according to the context of our lives, thoughts, abilities, and motivation. The information and communication systems that we use can stifle that power or help free it in ways that are rewarding to individuals and the rest of the world as well. This book does not accept the notion that nothing ever changes or that people collectively are incapable of great achievements. The premise of the book is that through spotlighting the imagination and dedication of activists around the world, additional people will join the struggle to create systems of humanistic communication. Through use of the holistic language of ideas, these myriad efforts will be linked into a stronger and more effective tapestry of communication. It is through this new tapestry that humankind may get the upper hand on many of the problems that have generally been considered unsolvable.

The tapestry I referred to above can be described less metaphorically as collective intelligence. *Collective intelligence* basically refers to the way that society shares information, coordinates economic activity, develops culture, teaches its children, and in general demonstrates itself to be a vast collection of individuals that is much more than a collection of individuals. Collective intelligence, like intelligence in individuals, is not perfect. It can ignore important information, misdiagnose problems, be sluggish and lazy, and substitute habitual response for reason. The list can grow quite long. However, it is only through this tapestry that anything of any magnitude is accomplished. And although people are ultimately responsible for making changes, it will only be through this collective intelligence that a better society, along the lines discussed in this book, will ever come about.

The Internet and other new digital technology, as enabling technology for many intriguing information and communication innovations, deserves serious consideration as a potential facilitator of collective intelligence. This statement is not startling. Indeed, these words will seem positively stale to many Internet watchers, as the idea of collective intelligence on the Internet is the latest mantra. At the same time I will acknowledge the skepticism that I harbor in relation to the types of intelligence that are getting all of the attention. What type of intelligence is it? And intelligence applied to what purpose?

The fact that much of the talk of "collective intelligence" and even "collective wisdom" is positioned toward the business community and proposes a version of intelligence that I find wanting does not invalidate the entire idea or make it irrelevant. My hope is that Web 2.0 advocates and other potential sociotechnological innovators do not accept the prevailing wisdom or slogans as the last word on innovation. Computers can probably help support collective intelligence, but algorithmically constructing it from the online masses who did not even know they had it in them is not the philosopher's stone I am searching for. I am interested in versions of intelligence in which people are engaged in thinking and learning that can develop concepts that transcend rather than help consolidate the dominant paradigms. These new versions are not only more interesting but more useful. They can help us address questions like the following: Can the people in a democracy govern themselves if they do not know things and use their brain? Can we as one species among many figure out how to live together more amicably and tend the planet that sustains us?

One of the fiercest problems we face is whether this system of knowledge coexists and coevolves with the world it is trying to change and support. In general, what can we do now to anticipate and build toward the continuing improvement of the pattern language as a useful tool? How can we maximize the ability to gather data about using the patterns and sets of patterns? Which patterns work together? It was this evidence in particular that was impossible to gather before the set was constructed.

Challenges Ahead

One of the reasons that this book (and the Liberating Voices pattern language generally) contains a spectrum of patterns from broad theoretical and abstract ideas to practical nuts-and-bolts advice is that there should be—and actually is—a strong connection between theory and practice. In many cases, however, theory is submerged and therefore not subject to negotiation and contestation. For that reason, we have tried to provide explicit theoretical ideas that we believe will help provide a meaningful foundation for this effort. A second reason for placing attention on theory is that it may be necessary to embrace or introduce changes to humankind's multifarious lifestyles that result sooner or later in a social paradigm shift, a profound reorientation of our lives that results in the new world system that Immanuel Wallerstein described.

This presupposes that our collective efforts, coupled with the actions of corporations and governments, could play substantial roles in shaping this new world system. Unfortunately a good deal of evidence suggests that this new paradigm will not be consciously enacted and adopted (crafted by "reasonable people reasoning together") but will be more a result of accident, corruption, coercion, and possibly bloodshed. Langdon Winner's quotation (1986) in chapter 9 about the durability of design decisions explains the dramatic and long-lasting influence of certain choices in the development of sociotechnological systems. I believe that Winner's statement is correct. Every day and in nearly every way, we are carrying forward the genetic material in our bodies and also in our culture and our consciousness that will shape our future through our psychology, language and culture, technology, media, and institutions. All of the good—and bad—things that humans do is engendered by—and becomes part of—this genetic material as well. In fact, one of the maddening things about humans is our ability to engage with equal energetic and creative facility in selfless acts and evil deeds. For that reason, one of the lessons from this project is that all we have to do is do more of the good things and fewer of the bad.

A few words on the potential misuse of this knowledge is in order. All knowledge exists in a social context, and systems that dominate are generally ready to use new information if it helps them in this process. There is an interesting example in the nascent field of neuroeconomics in which scientists are exploring where and how the brain is involved in economic decisions. A *New Yorker* article (Cassidy 2006b) discussed the idea of "asymmetric paternalism," which is "a new political philosophy based on the idea of saving people from the vagaries of their limbic regions." One of the uses of this new idea might be, for example, to establish cooling-off periods that are required on purchases of expensive items. But without knowing much about the precise mechanisms in the brain that help urge people to make impulse purchases of new cars, clothing, or vacations, professional salespeople know a great deal already about how to capitalize on such behavior. It also seems plausible that a great number of business-oriented people and organizations (in the United States, for example) may be opposed to any legislated cooling-off period, just as they are opposed to the idea that Chinese workers should be able to join unions if they want (Barboza 2006). All this is not to say that all information could be misused; it is instead a reminder that much information can be misused. Perhaps scientists who bring forth this new information should be prepared to help form ethical guidelines as to its use and help develop policy to see that the guidelines are followed.

Although today is pretty much like yesterday, we would rather not identify habit as the most powerful characteristic of our species—individually and collectively—and thus condemn ourselves in the most profound of terms. Of course, if there were no habits, no built-in grooves or conventions, life would be indescribably chaotic. One would never know what to expect. But although habit and inertia are essential to all life and existence, we ignore this most powerful of forces at our own risk. If, for example, we were collectively about to fall over a precipice, plunging, for example, into nuclear war, environmental devastation, or climate change, it might be wise to alter the course. But can people and organizations voluntarily change? People living in the United States may supply the best refutation, although elites—and nonelites—throughout the world are also strong contenders.

Many, if not most, people in the United States consider themselves to be environmentalists—or at least would prefer a clean, healthy planet to a septic, abused one. Yet it is interesting, if somewhat dispiriting, to consider how unwilling many people are to alter their lifestyle at all, let alone profoundly. Hence there are books, articles, and ideas floating around that seem to capture the public's imagination simply by virtue of the fact that they are not asking readers to change any aspect of their life. My current favorite is Stephen Johnson's new book, *Everything Bad Is Good for You* (2006a), in which he argues that contrary to conventional wisdom, watching television and playing video games are wise uses of time. Shooting nasty virtual creatures for hours on end is proposed as a great way to develop your mind. The old notions that people ought to have some knowledge and skills—even values!—to participate meaningfully in the affairs of their family, region, country, and planet have become a little tiresome and stodgy. I can hear parents now: "I'm so proud of my little Jimmy. If the amount of time he spends shooting virtual aliens is any indication of his vast talents, he'll do very well in graduate school!" The scary part of the book's progress is that the media reports from the *New Yorker* praise the book, as well as others, such as *Blink: The Power of Thinking without Thinking* (2005) by Malcolm Gladwell. Thinking without thinking may be better than *not* thinking, though I still prefer thinking with thinking.

When President Jimmy Carter made the modest proposal for Americans to lower the thermostats on their home heating systems from 72 to 68 degrees, the howls from the right wing were so shrill (and apparently genuine) one might wonder if they had just been instructed to roast their family dog for dinner. In recent years, several sports teams have been asked to change their team names to names that are not offensive to Native American groups in the United States. Reminding them that the subject was sports and, even then, that a *name change* was proposed, not summary execution for everybody who entertained a fondness for sports, could not stanch their outrage.

Identifying "antipatterns" is an interesting way to be creatively idle. Of the dozens of these that have been casually conceived while writing this book, here are a few of my favorites: Social Darwinism, "God Likes Us Best," Technophilia, Proprietary Protocols, Media Monopoly, Conventional Wisdom, Idolatry of Power, Ignore the Unpleasant, "Just Turn It Off," Blame the Victim, and Servile Journalism. Unfortunately there are many more where those came from, and I am not the original source; I just packaged some common ideas as antipatterns. Here are some patterns of thinking that appear to be less provocative but ones that many of us have succumbed to at one point or another:

- Thinking that people can do nothing
- Thinking of people and institutions as being autonomous and strictly competitive
- Thinking of technology as being autonomous and immutable, as being something that technopundits alone are capable of creating
- Thinking of our own habits of thinking and acting as being as being correct and immutable
- Thinking about value in restricted ways
- Thinking that experts and professionals will solve all our problems
- Thinking that there is no need to develop a collective social agenda
- Thinking and speaking using a constricted set of allowable actions and vocabulary
- Thinking that propaganda, simplistic explanations, and toxic media are acceptable
- Thinking that the free market or vague ideas such as "progress" will rescue us effortlessly through side effects
- Thinking that we have no responsibility for other people and the planet now and in future generations

The people in the United States and around the rest of the world have to choose. Do we want a democracy where such a thing as a citizen exists, or do we want to surrender our awareness, integrity, humanity, and intelligence and pretend the life is a video game? Part of the answer is realizing that building civic intelligence is truly a collective enterprise, as is imagining how that might be accomplished.

Liberating Voices, Minds, and Actions

The work does not end with the book. The Liberating Voices pattern language will continue to evolve, and we intend to use the Web and other venues to ensure that the work remains vital. This book is intended to promote communication that is alive and life affirming. The pattern language that we have created and presented in this book must also be alive if the communication revolution it helps spawn will assist humankind in its struggles.

If this effort helps in some way, the authors of this work will be pleased. And regardless of the success of this particular venture, humankind's need to cultivate its collective wisdom remains crucial. All work is partial, and all thinking is only one step of a voyage, a voyage that one hopes is enlightening, productive, and engendering—and at the very least not destructive,

Liberating Voices, like life on earth, is intended to be part of the One Big Project. Have you enrolled?

Pattern Authors, Graphics, and Acknowledgments

1 Civic Intelligence
Douglas Schuler

Introductory graphic: Asthma Mural, NYC. Stewart Dutfield

Concluding graphic: Douglas Schuler. The figure was developed using the SeeMe socio-technical modeling approach developed by Thomas Herrmann and his colleagues. Thomas and Kai-Uwe Loser assisted with the development of the figure.

2 The Commons
David Bollier

3 The Good Life
Gary Chapman

4 Social Dominance Attenuation
Douglas Schuler

5 Health as a Universal Right
Douglas Schuler

6 Global Citizenship
Douglas Schuler and Lori Blewett

7 Political Settings
Jonathan Barker

8 Social Responsibility
Stewart Dutfield, Burl Humana, and Kenneth Gillgren

9 Matrifocal Orientation
Lori Blewett

10 Collective Decision Making
Valerie Brown

11 Memory and Responsibility
Douglas Schuler

Introductory graphic: Memorial of the Disappeared, Gilson Schwartz

12 Working-Class Consciousness
Steve Zeltzer

Introductory graphic: Mother Jones, mural by Mike Alewitz

13 Back to the Roots
Douglas Schuler

14 Demystification and Reenchantment
Kenneth Gillgren

15 Translation
Douglas Schuler

16 Linguistic Diversity
Douglas Schuler

17 Education and Values
John Thomas

18 Dematerialization
Burl Humana

19 Transforming Institutions
Brian Beaton

20 Teaching to Transgress
John Thomas

21 Fair Trade
Burl Humana and Anna Nakano

22 Sustainable Design
Rob Knapp

23 Antiracism
Lori Blewett

24 Spiritually Grounded Activism
Helena Meyer-Knapp

25 Cyberpower
Kate Williams and Abdul Alkalimat

26 Earth's Vital Signs
Jennifer Frankel-Reed

Introductory graphic: Earth Photo, Earth Image, 2007 Jupiterimages Corporation

27 Big-Picture Health Information
Jenny Epstein

28 Whole Cost
Douglas Schuler

29 Indicators
Douglas Schuler

30 Public Agenda
Douglas Schuler

31 Democratic Political Settings
Jonathan Barker

32 Big Tent for Social Change
Mary Reister and Shari McCarthy

Introductory graphic: World Social Forum, Mumbai, India, Reed Schuler

33 Opportunity Spaces
Douglas Schuler

34 Strategic Capacity
Douglas Schuler

35 Media Literacy
Mark Lipton

36 Participatory Design
Douglas Schuler

37 Citizen Science
Stewart Dutfield

Introductory graphic: Rhode Island water sampling, Margaret Kerr

38 Mobile Intelligence
Douglas Schuler

39 Technocriticism
Douglas Schuler

40 World Citizen Parliament
Douglas Schuler

41 Economic Conversion
Lloyd J. Dumas

42 Strengthening International Law
Richard Falk

43 International Networks of Alternative Media
Dorothy Kidd

44 Design Stance
Rob Knapp
Introductory graphic: City Repair Box, Rob Knapp

45 Open Action and Research Network
Douglas Schuler

46 Alternative Progress Indexes
Burl Humana and Richard Reiss

47 Meaningful Maps
Andy Dearden and Scot Fletcher

48 Citizen Access to Simulations
Alan Borning

49 Culturally Situated Design Tools
Ron Eglash
Introductory graphic: "Cornrow Curves" software, Ron Eglash

This material is based on work supported by the National Science Foundation under grant no. 0119880, the Fund for the Improvement of Postsecondary Education program of the U.S. Department of Education, and the Community Outreach Partnerships Centers program of the U.S. Department of Housing and Urban Development.

50 Conversational Support across Boundaries
John Thomas

51 Truth and Reconciliation Commissions
Helena Meyer-Knapp

52 Online Deliberation
Matt Powell and Douglas Schuler

53 Alternative Media in Hostile Environments
Douglas Schuler

54 Mutual Help Medical Web Sites
Andy Dearden and Patricia Radin

This pattern is dedicated to Patricia Radin, the original author of this pattern. Pat was an enthusiastic and compassionate activist and researcher.

55 Indigenous Media
Douglas Schuler and Miguel Angel Pérez Alvarez

56 Peace Education
Helena Meyer-Knapp

57 Intermediate Technologies
Justin Smith

For their support in my research, I thank Edward Violett, Marianus Kujur, Joe Xavier, Ranjit Kumar, and the staff at the Indian Social Institute, New Delhi.

58 Durable Assets
Justin Smith

For their support in my research, I thank Edward Violett, Marianus Kujur, Joe Xavier, Ranjit Kumar, and the staff at the Indian Social Institute, New Delhi.

59 Public Library
Stewart Dutfield and Douglas Schuler

60 Digital Emancipation
Gilson Schwartz

61 Community Networks
Peter Day

62 Online Community Service Engine
Fiorella De Cindio and Leonardo Sonnante

63 Community Currencies
Burl Humana and Gilson Schwartz
Introductory graphic: In Ithaca We Trust, Ithaca Hours

64 Transparency
John B. Adams and Douglas Schuler

65 Privacy
Douglas Schuler

John B. Adams did much of the original research for this pattern.

66 Media Diversity
Douglas Schuler

67 Ethics of Community Informatics
Randy Stoecker

68 Free and Fair Elections
Douglas Schuler and Erik Nilsson

69 Equal Access to Justice
Donald J. Horowitz

My deep appreciation to both Ken Gillgren and Doug Schuler for their considerable help in my getting this done at a very busy time, and to Doug for his encouragement and patience.

70 E-Consultation
David Newman

71 Participatory Budgeting
Andrew Gordon and Chris Halaska

72 Transaction Tax
Burl Humana

73 Powerful Remittances
Scott Robinson

74 Positive Health Information
Jenny Epstein

75 Accessibility of Online Information
Robert Luke

76 Open Access Scholarly Publishing
John Thomas

77 Mobile Information and Computer Technology Learning Facilities
Grant Hearn

78 Grassroots Public Policy Development
Douglas Schuler and Michael Maranda

79 Multiparty Negotiation for Conflict Resolution
Helena Meyer-Knapp and Stewart Dutfield

80 Users' Information Technology Quality Network
Åke Walldius and Yngve Sundblad

81 Academic Technology Investments
Sarah Stein

82 Wholesome Design for Wicked Problems
Rob Knapp

83 Voices of the Unheard
John Thomas

84 Design for Unintended Use
Erik Stolterman

85 Civic Capabilities
Justin Smith

For their support in my research, I thank Edward Violett, Marianus Kujur, Joe Xavier, Ranjit Kumar, and the staff at the Indian Social Institute, New Delhi.

86 Strategic Frame
Douglas Schuler

87 Value-Sensitive Design
Batya Friedman

Much of the material in this pattern was adapted from Friedman and Kahn (2003) and Friedman, Kahn, and Borning (2006).

88 Future Design
Douglas Schuler
Introductory graphic: Steven Hartson

89 Experimental School
Douglas Schuler, Steve Schapp, and Thad Curtz
Peter Dorman provided useful advice for this pattern and others.

90 Service-Learning
Norman Clark

91 Citizen Journalism
Lewis A. Friedland and Hernando Rojas

92 Document-Centered Discussion
Todd Davies, Benjamin Newman, Brendan O'Connor, Aaron Tam, and Leo Perry
Introductory graphic: Deme User Interface, Todd Davies et al.

93 Citizen Diplomacy
Douglas Schuler

94 Mirror Institutions
Douglas Schuler

95 Patient Access to Medical Records
Amir Hannan

96 Citizenship Schools
Lewis A. Friedland and Carmen J. Sirianni

97 Community-Building Journalism
Peter Miller

98 Informal Learning Groups
Justin Smith
For their support in my research, I thank Edward Violett, Marianus Kujur, Joe Xavier, Ranjit Kumar, and the staff at the Indian Social Institute, New Delhi.

99 Appreciative Collaboration
Stewart Dutfield

100 Sustainability Appraisal
Nick Plant
Introductory graphic: Nick Plant

101 Shared Vision
Stewart Dutfield and Douglas Schuler
Introductory graphic: Decision Wheel, Steve Cisler

102 Community Animators
Justin Smith

For their support in my research, I thank Edward Violett, Marianus Kujur, Joe Xavier, Ranjit Kumar, and the staff at the Indian Social Institute, New Delhi.

103 Online Antipoverty Community
Penny Goldsmith

Introductory graphic: PovNet: Building Online Community, Janice Acton.

104 Sense of Struggle
Douglas Schuler

This pattern was suggested by Erik Stolterman.

Introductory graphic: Brookside Coalminers Picket for UMWA Contract, Earl Dotter

105 Self-Help Groups
Justin Smith

For their support in my research, I thank Edward Violett, Marianus Kujur, Joe Xavier, Ranjit Kumar, and the staff at the Indian Social Institute, New Delhi.

Introductory graphic: Justin Smith

106 Self-Designed Development
Justin Smith

For their support in my research, I thank Edward Violett, Marianus Kujur, Joe Xavier, Ranjit Kumar, and the staff at the Indian Social Institute, New Delhi.

107 Engaged Tourism
Christine Ciancetta

108 Appropriating Technology
Ron Eglash

Introductory graphic: Three Types of Appropriation, Ron Eglash

109 Control of Self-Representation
Douglas Schuler

110 Homemade Media
Douglas Schuler

Introductory graphic: "Puja by Manik," Susan Song/Kids with Cameras, Inc.

111 Arts of Resistance
Douglas Schuler

Introductory graphic: Rebel Chicano Art Front, AKA the Royal Chicano Air Force. The mural was done by barrio children from the Barrio Art Program. At the time the Barrio Art Program, started by José Montoya at California State University at Sacramento, was being taught by Armando Cid, professor of art at CSUS.

112 Labor Visions
Nancy Brigham

113 Universal Voice Mail
Jenn Brandon

114 The Power of Story
Rebecca Chamberlain
Introductory graphic: Public Domain

115 Public Domain Characters
John Thomas and Douglas Schuler
Introductory graphic: Public Domain

116 Everyday Heroism
Douglas Schuler
Introductory graphic: Reverend Maurice McCrackin, Ann Medlock, The Giraffe Project

117 Community Telecenters
Michel J. Menou, Peter Day, and Douglas Schuler
Stewart Dutfield helped with some last minute assistance.

118 Thinking Communities
Aldo de Moor
Introductory graphic: Aldo de Moor

119 Great Good Place
Douglas Schuler

120 Soap Operas with Civic Messages
Douglas Schuler

121 Emergency Communication Systems
Douglas Schuler

122 Community Inquiry
Ann Bishop and Bertram (Chip) Bruce
Introductory graphic: Ann Bishop and Bertram (Chip) Bruce

123 Illegitimate Theater
Mark Harrison and Douglas Schuler

124 Environmental Impact Remediation
Douglas Schuler and Jim Gerner

125 Open Source Search Technology
Douglas Schuler

126 Socially Responsible Computer Games
Douglas Schuler

References

About the International Coastal Cleanup. 2007. Retrieved January 2, 2008, from http://www.oceanconservancy.org/site/News2?page=NewsArticle&id=8761

About the Watershed Stewardship Program 2007. Rhode Island Rivers Council. Retrieved January 2, 2008, from http://www.ririvers.org/wsp/index.htm

Abowd, G. D., and Jacobs, A. 2001, September–October. The Impact of Awareness Technologies on Privacy Litigation. *SIGCHI Bulletin. 2001: 9.*

Abram, David. 1996. *Spell of the Sensuous.* New York: Vintage.

Abu-Lughod, Lila. 1989, July–August. Bedouins, Cassettes, and Technologies of Public Culture. *Middle East Report* 47 (159): 105–112.

Access to Justice Technology Principles Implementation Strategy Group. 2006, June 30. Access to Justice Technology Principles. Retrieved March 19, 2007, from http://www.atjtechbillofrights.org/.

Accessibility in Web Design. 2001, March 1. Retrieved July 10, 2003, from http://www.wd4a.co.uk/HowMany.htm.

Ackerman, M. S., and Cranor, L. 1999. Privacy Critics: UI Components to Safeguard Users' Privacy. In *Extended Abstracts of CHI 1999.* New York: ACM Press.

Addams, Jane. 1910. *Twenty Years at Hull-House.* New York: MacMillan Company. Retrieved February 18, 2008 from http://digital.library.upenn.edu/women/addams/hullhouse/hullho use.html.

Addams, Jane. 1912, November 2. A Modern Lear. *Survey* 29: 131–137. Retrieved March 19, 2007, from http://womenshistory.about.com/cs/addamsjane/a/mod_lear_10001b.htm.

AIR preemptive media project (2007). Retrieved January 2, 2008, from http://www.pm-air.net

Alexander, Christopher. 1964. *Notes on the Synthesis of Form.* Cambridge, MA: Harvard University Press.

Alexander, Christopher. 1979. *The Timeless Way of Building.* New York: Oxford University Press.

Alexander, Christopher, Ishikawa, Sara, and Silverstein, Murray. 1968. *A Pattern Language That Generates Multi-Service Centers.* Berkeley, CA: Center for Environmental Structure.

Alexander, Christopher, Ishikawa, Sara, Silverstein, Murray, Jacobson, Max, Fiksdahl-King, Ingrid, and Angel, Shlomo. 1977. *A Pattern Language*. New York: Oxford University Press.

Alexander, Christopher, Davis, Howard, Martinez, Julio, and Corner, Don. 1985. *The Production of Houses*. New York: Oxford University Press.

Alexander, Christopher, Silverstein, Murray, Angel, Shlomo, Ishikawa, Sara, and Abrams, Denny. 1975. *The Oregon Experiment*. New York: Oxford University Press.

Alkalimat, Abdul. 2004. Social Cyberpower in the Everyday Life of an African American Community: A Report on Action-Research in Toledo, Ohio. In Peter Day and Douglas Schuler (Eds.), *Community Practice in the Network Society: Local Action/Global Interaction*. London: Routledge.

Alkalimat, Abdul, and Williams, Kate. 2001. Social Capital and Cyberpower in the African American Community: A Case Study of a Community Technology Center in the Dual City. In L. Keeble and B. Loader (Eds.), *Community Informatics: Shaping Computer-Mediated Social Relations*. London: Routledge.

Allenby, Braden. 1992. Dematerialization. *Green Business Letter*. Retrieved March 15, 2007, from http://www.att.com/ehs/ind_ecology/articles/dematerialization.html.

American Library Association and Association of American Publishers. 2004, June 30. The Freedom to Read Statement. Retrieved November 28, 2006, from http://www.ala.org/ala/oif/statementspols/ftrstatement/freedomreadstatement.htm.

A-Lo. 2004. *Telestreet* (online video). Retrieved March 19, 2007, from http://www.archive.org/details/Telestreets.

Anderson, B. 1993, April. Workshop Report—Towards an Architecture Handbook. *OOPSLA Messenger*. 4 (2): 109–114.

Anderson, B., Coad, P., and Mayfield, M. 1994. Addendum to the Proceedings of OOPSLA '93. Workshop Report: Patterns: Building Blocks for Object Oriented Architectures. *OOPS Messenger* 5 (2): 107–109.

Anielski, Mark. 2000. *Fertile Obfuscation: Making Money Whilst Eroding Living Capital*. Drayton Valley, Alberta, Canada: Pembrina Institute. Retrieved March 12, 2007, from http://www.pembina.org/pubs/pub.php?id=20.

Annis, Jim, and Brautigam, John. 2005, October 24. Clean Elections Work in Maine. *Hartford Courant. p 2.*

Antelman, K. 2004. Do Open Access Articles Have Greater Research Impact? *College and Research Libraries* 65 (2): 372–382.

Appalachian and the Community Together. 2007. Appalachian and the Community Together. Retrieved March 1, 2007, from http://act.appstate.edu/.

Archer, David, and Kate Newman (compilers). 2003. *Communication and Power: Reflect Practical Resource Materials*. London: ActionAid. Retrieved February 4, 2008, from http://www.reflect-action.org/compower/cphome.htm.

Atkinson, Brooks (Ed.). 2000. *Henry David Thoreau: Walden and Other Writings*. New York: Modern Library.

Bagdikian, Ben. 1983. *The Media Monopoly*. Boston: Beacon Press.

Baldwin, Craig. 1995. Sonic Outlaws. Video.

Banisar, David, and Davies, Simon. N.d. Privacy and Human Rights: An International Survey of Privacy Laws and Practice. Global Internet Liberty Campaign. Retrieved January 20, 2008, from http://www.gilc .org/privacy/survey/intro.html

Barabási, Albert-László. 2002. *The New Science of Networks*. Cambridge, MA: Perseus Books Group.

Barboza, D. 2006. China Drafts Law to Boost Unions and End Abuse. *New York Times*, October 13.

Barlett, Peggy F. 2002. The Emory University Walking Tour. *International Journal of Sustainability in Higher Education* 3 (2): 105–112.

Barlett, Peggy (Ed.). 2005. *Urban Place: Reconnecting with the Natural World*. Cambridge, MA: MIT Press.

Barrett, Tom. 2005, April 8. To censor pro-union web site, Telus blocked 766 others. LaborNet UK (http:// www.labournet.net). Retrieved February 20, 2008, from http://www.labournet.net/world/0508/canada2 .html.

Basker, Emek. 2007. The Causes and Consequences of Wal-Mart's Growth. *Journal of Economic Perspectives*, American Economic Association. 21 (3): 177–198, Summer.

Beare, Hedley, and Slaughter, Richard. 1993. *Education for the Twenty-First Century*. London: Routledge.

Beck, Eevi. 2002. P for Political. *Scandinavian Journal of Information Systems* 14 (1): 77–92.

Beck, K., and Cunningham, W. 1987. Using Pattern Languages for Object-Oriented Programs. Technical Report No. CR-87-43. Beaverton, OR: Tektronix. Retrieved February 17, 2008, from http://c2.com/doc/ oopsla87.html.

Bekal Samrakshana Samiti. 1996, November. Bekal Tourism Project: An SOS Call. Bangalore, India: Equations. Retrieved March 19, 2007, from http://www.equitabletourism.org/bekal.htm.

Bell, S., and Morse, S. 2003. *Sustainability Indicators: Measuring the Immeasurable*. London: Earthscan.

Bellman, G. 2000, May. The Beauty of the Organizational Beast. *Training and Development*. 54 (5): 66–73.

Benini, Marco, De Cindio, Fiorella, and Sonnante, Leonardo. 2005. VIRTUOSE: A VIRTual CommUnity Open Source Engine for Integrating Civic Networks. In Peter Van den Besselaar and Sotoshi Koizumi (Eds.), *Digital Cities III: Information Technologies for Social Capital: Cross Cultural Perspectives*. Lecture Notes in Computer Science 3081. Heidelberg, Germany: Springer.

Benkler, Y. 2006. *The Wealth of Networks*. New Haven, CT: Yale University Press.

Bennett, Susan. 1990. *Theatre Audiences: A Theory of Production and Reception*. London: Routledge.

Bernstein, Carl, and Woodward, Bob. 1974. *All the President's Men*, New York: Simon & Schuster.

Bessette, G., and Rajasunderam, C. V. 1996. *Participatory Development Communication*. ebook online. Retrieved December 12, 2007, from http://www.idrc.ca/en/ev-9302-201-1-DO_TOPIC.html.

Blanchard, A., and Horan, T. 1998. Can We Surf Together If We're Bowling Alone? *Social Science Computer Review* 16 (3): 293–307.

Blech, J. 2006. *Inventing Disease and Pushing Pills: Pharmaceutical Companies and the Medicalisation of Normal Life*. London: Routledge.

Blood, Michael. 2006. Schwarzenegger camp uses consumer data. *Seattle Post-Intelligencer*. Retrieved October 28, 2006 from http://seattlepi.nwsource.com/national/1110AP_Schwarzenegger_Targeting.html. October 26.

Bohm, D. 1996. *On Dialogue*. New York: Routledge.

Bollier, David. 2002. *Silent Theft: The Private Plunder of Our Common Wealth*. New York: Routledge.

Boomer, G., Lester, N., and Onore, C. 1992. *Negotiating the Curriculum: Educating for the 21st Century*. London: Falmer Press.

Borchers, J. 2001. *A Pattern Approach to Interaction Design*. Hoboken, NJ: Wiley.

Borning, A., Friedman, B., Davis, J., and Lin, P. 2005. Informing Public Deliberation: Value Sensitive Design of Indicators for a Large-Scale Urban Simulation. In Hans Gellersen, Kjeld Schmidt, and Michel Beaudouin-Lafon (Eds.), *Proceedings of the 2005 European Conference on Computer-Supported Cooperative Work*. Berlin: Springer. Retrieved February 17, 2008, from http://www.urbansim.org/papers/.

Bos, L., Fitton, R., and Fisher, B. 2006. Patient Record Access. Retrieved February 17, 2008, from http://recordaccess.icmcc.org.

Bowman, S., and Willis, C. 2003. The Media Center at the American Press Institute. Retrieved February 17, 2008, from http://www.hypergene.net/wemedia/weblog.php.

Brazil, Eric. 1997, September 30. Longshoremen Boycott Freighter. *San Francisco Chronicle*. Retrieved March 11, 2007, from http://www.labournet.net/sept97/sfpress1.html.

Brecht, Bertolt. 2001. *Brecht on Theatre: The Development of an Aesthetic*. New York: Hill and Wang.

Brinckerhoff, Peter. 2003. *Mission-Based Marketing: Positioning Your Not-for-profit in an Increasingly Competitive World*. Hoboken, NJ: Wiley.

Brooks, Renana. 2003, July 13. Power of presidency resides in language as well as law. *Seattle Post-Intelligencer*. E1. Retrieved February 25, 2008, from http://seattlepi.nwsource.com/opinion/130534_focusecond13.html.

Brown, V. A. 2006. *Leonardo's Vision: A Guide to Collective Thinking and Action*. Rotterdam: SENSE Publishers.

Bruner, J. S. 1990. *Acts of Meaning*. Cambridge, MA: Harvard University Press.

Bullard, Robert (Ed.). 1994. *Unequal Protection: Environmental Justice and Communities of Color*. San Francisco, CA: Sierra Club Books.

Campbell, Joseph. 1972. *Myths to Live By*. New York: Viking.

Campus Compact. 2003. *Introduction to Service-Learning Toolkit: Readings and Resources for Faculty.* Providence, RI: Brown University Press.

Caro, Robert. 1975. *The Power Broker: Robert Moses and the Fall of New York.* New York: Vintage.

Carroll, J. M. and Rossom, M. B. 1987. *Paradox of the Active User.* Cambridge, MA: MIT Press.

Cassidy, Jacqueline. (Ed.). 2006. *Science, Risk and the Media: Do the Front Pages Reflect Reality?* London: Social Market Foundation.

Cassidy, John. 2006. September 18. Mind Games: What Neuroeconomics Tells Us About Money and the Brain. *New Yorker.*

Cassirer, Ernst. 1946. *Language and Myth.* New York: Dover.

Center for Neighborhood Technology. 2006. Wireless Community Networks. Retrieved January 4, 2008, from http://wcn.cnt.org

CGIAR Consortium for Spatial Information. 2004. Asian Tsunami 2004. Retrieved March 12, 2007, from http://csi.cgiar.org/tsunami_intro.asp.

Chai, C. S., and Khine, M. S. 2006. An Analysis of Interaction and Participation Patterns in Online Community. *Education Technology and Society* 9 (1): 250–261.

Chainworkers 3.0 N.d. www.chainworkers.org. Retrieved July 11, 2008, from http://www.chainworkers .org/

Chaney, David. 2002. *Cultural Change and Everyday Life.* New York: Palgrave.

Christenson, D., and Walker, D. H. T. 2004. Understanding the Role of "Vision" in Project Success. *Project Management Journal* 35 (3): 39–52.

Ciborra, C. 1992. From Thinking to Tinkering: The Grassroots of Strategic Information Systems. *Information Society* 8 (4): 297–309.

Cisler, S. 1994. Community Networks: Past and Present Thoughts. In S. Cisler (Ed.), *Ties that Bind: Building Community Networks.* Cupertino, CA: Apple Computer Corporation Library.

Citizen Science. 2003. Cornell University Lab of Onithology. Retrieved January 2, 2008, from http://www.birds.cornell.edu/LabPrograms/CitSci/index.html

Citizen Science. 2004. Aububon Society. Retrieved January 2, 2008, from http://www.audubon.org/bird/citizen/index.html

Clark, H. H., and Brennan, S. E. 1991. Grounding in Communication. In L. B. Resnick, J. M. Levine, and S. D. Teasley (Eds.), *Perspectives on Socially Shared Cognition.* Washington, D.C.: American Psychological Association.

Clean Elections Campaign Reform, 1, 2, 3. 2008. Public Campaign. Retrieved February 1, 2008, from http://www.publicampaign.org/clean123

Cleary, Beverly 1975. *Ramona the Brave.* New York: William Morrow.

Cleaver, Harry. 1998. Computer-Linked Social Movements and the Global Threat to Capitalism. Retrieved March 12, 2007, from http://www.eco.utexas.edu/homepages/faculty/Cleaver/polnet.html.

Coad, P. 1992. Object-Oriented Patterns. *Communications of the ACM* 35 (9): 152–159.

Coad, P., and Mayfield, M. 1993. Addendum to the Proceedings of OOPSLA '92. Workshop Report: Patterns. *OOPS Messenger* 4 (2): 93–95.

Cohen, Bernard. 1963. *The Press and Foreign Policy*. Princeton, NJ: Princeton University Press.

Coleman, J. 1990. *Foundations of Social Theory*. Cambridge, MA: Harvard University Press.

Community Development Society. 2006. Community Development Society. Retrieved March 19, 2007, from http://comm-dev.org/.

Community Networks. 2006. *Wikipedia*. 2006. Retrieved March 19, 2007, from http://en.wikipedia.org/wiki/Category:Community_networks.

Cooperrider, D. 1990. Positive Image, Positive Action: The Affirmative Basis of Organizing. In S. Srivasta and D. Cooperrider (Eds.), *Appreciative Management and Leadership: the Power of Positive Thought and Action in Organizations*. San Francisco: Jossey-Bass.

Cooperrider, D., and Whitney, D. 1999. When Stories Have Wings: How Relational Responsibility Opens New Options for Action. In S. McNamee and K. Gergen (Eds.) *Relational Responsibility: Resources for Sustainable Dialogue*. Newbury Park, CA: Sage.

Corburn, James. 2005. *Street Science: Community Knowledge and Environmental Health Justice*. Cambridge, MA: MIT Press.

Cross, M. 2005, December 22. Health Records at Great Risk of Dodgy Diagnoses. *Guardian. Retrieved February 22, 2008, from* http://technology.guardian.co.uk/online/insideit/story/0,13270,1672038,00.html.

Crystal, David. 2000. *Language Death*. Cambridge: Cambridge University Press.

Czitrom, Daniel. 1982. *Media and the American Mind*. Chapel Hill: University of North Carolina Press.

Dahl, Robert A. 1970. *Modern Political Analysis*, 2nd. ed., Englewood Cliffs, NJ: Prentice-Hall.

Davies, T., and Noveck, B. S. (Eds.). Forthcoming. *Online Deliberation: Design, Research, and Practice*. Stanford: CSLI Publications/University of Chicago Press.

Day, Peter. 1996a. Information Communication Technology and Society: A community-based approach, In Gill, K. S. (Ed.) *Information Society: New Media, Ethics and Postmodernism*, London: Springer-Verlag.

Day, Peter. 1996b. The Human-Centred Information Society: A Community-Based Approach. *AI and Society* 10 (2): 181–198.

Day, P. 2001. The Networked Community: Policies for a Participative Information Society. Unpublished PhD thesis: University of Brighton.

Day, Peter, and Harris, Kevin. 1997. *Down-to-Earth Vision: Community Based IT Initiatives and Social Inclusion*. London: IBM/CDF.

De Cindio, Fiorella. 2004. The Role of Community Networks in Shaping the Network Society: Enabling People to Develop Their Own Projects. In Douglas Schuler and Peter Day (Eds.), *Shaping the Network Society: The New Role of Civil Society in Cyberspace*. Cambridge, MA: MIT Press.

DeFilippis, James. 2004. Collective Ownership of Money. In James DeFillipis. *Unmaking Goliath: Community Control in the Face of Global Capital*. London: Routledge.

Delwiche, Aaron. 2005, December. Agenda-Setting, Opinion Leadership, and the World of Web Logs. First Monday. Retrieved March 11, 2007, from http://www.firstmonday.org/issues/issue10_12/delwiche/index.html.

DeMartino, B., et al. 2006, August 4. Frames, Biases, and Rational Decision-Making in the Human Brain. *Science*. 313 (5787): 684–687.

Denzin, Norman, and Lincoln, Yvonna. 1998. *The Landscape of Qualitative Research: Theories and Issues*. London: Sage.

Devine, Tom. 1997. *The Whistleblower's Survival Guide: Courage without Martyrdom*. Washington, D.C.: Government Accountability Project.

Dewey, John. 1927. *The Public and Its Problems*. New York: Holt.

Dewey, John. 1937, April 3. The Democratic Form. *School and Society*.

Dewey, John. 1938. *Logic: The Theory of Inquiry*. New York, NY: Henry Holt and Company.

Diamond, Jared. 2003, March 28. *Why Do Some Societies Make Disastrous Decisions?* Retrieved January 25, 2008 from http://www.edge.org/3rd_culture/diamond03/diamond_print.html.

Diamond, Jared. 2005. *Collapse: How Societies Choose to Fail or Succeed*. New York: Viking.

Diamond, Jared. 2008, January 6. Solving Consumption Problems. *Seattle Times*. C1.

Directory of Open Access Journals. 2008. Retrieved February 11, 2008, from www.doaj.org.

Dixon, N. M. 1999. *The Organizational Learning Cycle: How We Can Learn Collectively* (2nd ed.). New York: McGraw-Hill.

Domhoff, William G. 1967. *Who Rules America?* New York: Simon and Schuster.

Domhoff, William G. 1983. *Who Rules America Now?* New York: Simon and Schuster.

Dowmunt, T. 1998. An Alternative Globalization: Youthful Resistance to Electronic Empires. In Daya Kishan Thussu (Ed.), 1998. *Electronic Empires: Global Media and Local Resistance*. London: Arnold.

Dovey, K. 1990. The Pattern Language and Its Enemies. *Design Studies* 11 (1): 3–9.

Drèze, J., and Sen, A. 1999. *India: Economic Development and Social Opportunity*. Oxford: Clarendon Press.

Dugan, Máire (Ed.). 2004, February. *Beyond Intractability: Power Inequities*. Boulder: Conflict Research Consortium, University of Colorado. Retrieved February 22, 2008, from http://www.beyondintractability.org/essay/power_inequities/.

Eco, Umberto. 1977. Mass Culture: Apocalypse Postponed. In Robert Lumley (Ed.), *Apocalypse Postponed*, 1994. Bloomington, IN: Indiana University Press.

Eco, Umberto. 2001. *Translating and Being Translated*. Toronto, Canada: University of Toronto Press.

Eglash, R. 1999. *African Fractals: Modern Computing and Indigenous Design*. New Brunswick, NJ: Rutgers University Press.

Eglash, Ron. 2003. Culturally Situated Design Tools. Retrieved March 12, 2007, from http://www.rpi.edu/~eglash/csdt.html.

Eglash, Ron. N.d. Appropriating Technology: Vernacular Science and Social Power. Retrieved February 23, 2008, from http://www.rpi.edu/~eglash/eglash.dir/apptech.htm.

Eglash, R., Croissant, J., Di Chiro, G., and Fouché, R. 2004. *Appropriating Technology: Vernacular Science and Social Power*. Minneapolis: University of Minnesota Press.

Ehn, Pelle. 1988. *Work-Oriented Design of Computer Artifacts*. Stockholm, Sweden: Arbetslivscentrum.

Electronics Take it Back! 2001. Retrieved February 4, 2008, from http://svtc.igc.org/resource/news_let/e_platform.htm.

Epstein, M. J., and Burchard, B. 1999. *Counting What Counts: Turning Corporate Accountability to Competitive Advantage*. Reading, MA: Perseus.

Epstein, Paul. 2006. Human Health and Global Environmental Change. Retrieved January 23, 2008, from http://chge.med.harvard.edu/education/programs/course_2006/topics/02_02/summary.html.

Evans, T. G. 1968. A Heuristic Program to Solve Geometric Analogy Problems. In M. Minsky (Ed.), *Semantic Information Processing*. Cambridge, MA: MIT Press.

Evans, S. M., and Boyte, H. C. 1992. *Free Spaces: The Sources of Democratic Change in America*. Chicago: University of Chicago Press.

Fair Trade. 2006. In *Wikipedia*. Retrieved March 11, 2007, from http://en.wikipedia.org/wiki/Fair_trade.

Fair Trade Federation. 2007. Welcome to the Fair Trade Federation. Retrieved March 11, 2007, from http://www.fairtradefederation.org/.

Fair Trade Zone. 2006. What is Fair Trade? Fair Trade Zone. Retrieved February 26, 2008, from http://www.fairtradezone.jhc-cdca.org/fair_trade.htm.

Falk, Richard. 2004. *The Declining World Order: America's Imperial Geopolitics*. London: Routledge.

Falk, Richard. 2005a, June 24. Opening Speech at the World Tribunal on Iraq. Retrieved February 5, 2008, from http://www.wagingpeace.org/articles/2005/06/24_falk_opening-speech-wti.htm.

Falk, Richard. 2005b, July 14. The World Speaks on Iraq. Retrieved February 5, 2008, from http://www.wagingpeace.org/articles/2005/07/14_falk_world-speaks-on-iraq.htm.

Falk, Richard, and Strauss, Andrew. 2001, January/February. Toward Global Parliament. *Foreign Affairs*. 80 (1): 212–220.

Farmer, Paul. 2003. *Pathologies of Power: Health, Human Rights, and the New War on the Poor*. Berkeley: University of California Press.

Ferry, Luc. 2005. *What Is the Good Life?* Chicago: University of Chicago Press.

Fisher, Roger, and Ury, William. 1991. *Getting to Yes: Negotiating Agreement without Giving In* (2nd ed.). New York: Penguin.

Fitzpatrick, J. W., and Gill, F. B. 2002. BirdSource: Using Birds, Citizen Science, and the Internet as Tools for Global Monitoring. In J. N. Levitt (Ed.), *Conservation in the Internet age: Threats and opportunities*. Covelo, CA: Island Press.

Flanagan, M., Howe, D. C., and Nissenbaum, H. 2005. Values at Play: Design Tradeoffs in Socially-Oriented Game Design. In *Proceedings CHI 2005*. New York: ACM Press.

Fletcher, S., Mills, J., and Gaskill, K. K. 2005. *The Sheffield Green Food Map*. Sheffield, UK: Sheffield Green Food Map Project. Retrieved March 12, 2007, from http://www.greenfoodmap.org/.

Florini, Ann. 2005. *The Coming Democracy: New Rules for Running a New World*. Washington, D.C.: Brookings Institution Press.

Food and Agricultural Organization. 1995. A Model Initiative: The Mexicali Experience. Retrieved March 19, 2007, from http://www.fao.org/docrep/W6840E/w6840e04.htm.

Fox, Michael. 2006, May 2. Opposition and Chavez Supporters March Separately for Mayday in Venezuela. Venezuelanalysis.com. Retrieved February 23, 2008, from http://www.venezuelanalysis.com/news/1721.

Frazer J. H. 1995, November. The Architectural Relevance of Cyberspace. *Architectural Design*. 65 (11–12): 76–77.

Free Software Foundation. 2007. The GNU Operating System—Free as in Freedom. Retrieved March 15, 2007, from http://www.gnu.org/home.html.

Freire, P. 1974. *Pedagogy of the oppressed*. New York: Continuum.

Frequently Asked Questions. 2008, January 20. Global Exchange. Retrieved February 4, 2008, from http://www.globalexchange.org/tours/faq.html.

Friedman, Batya. 1997. *Human Values and the Design of Computer Technology*. Cambridge: Cambridge University Press.

Friedman, B., Howe, D. C., and Felten, E. 2002. Informed Consent in the Mozilla Browser: Implementing Value Sensitive Design. In *Proceedings of the 35th Hawai'i International Conference on Systems Science*. New York: IEEE Press.

Friedman, B., and Kahn, P. H., Jr. 2003. Human Values, Ethics and Design. In J. Jacko and A. Sears (Eds.), *Handbook on Human-Computer Interaction*. Mahwah, NJ: Erlbaum.

Friedman, B., Kahn, P. H., Jr., and Borning, A. 2006. Value Sensitive Design and Information Systems. In P. Zhang and Galletta (Eds.), *Human-Computer Interaction in Management Information Systems: Foundations*. Armonk, New York: M. Sharpe.

Friedman, B., Kahn, P. H. Jr., Hagman, J., Severson, R. L., and Gill, B. 2006. The Watcher and the Watched: Social Judgments about Privacy in a Public Place. *Human-Computer Interaction Journal* 21: 235–272.

Friedman, Milton. 1970, September 13. The Social Responsibility of Business Is to Increase its Profits. *New York Times Magazine.*

Gablik, Suzi. 1991. *The Reenchantment of Art.* New York: Thames and Hudson.

Gabriel, R. 1996. *Patterns of Software: Tales from the Software Community.* New York: Oxford University Press.

Gamma, E., Helm, R., Johnson, R. and Vlissides, J. 1995. *Design Patterns: Elements of Reusable Object Oriented Software.* Reading, MA: Addison-Wesley.

Ganz, Marshall. 2003. *Some Reflections on Faith and Politics.* Cambridge, MA: Kennedy School of Government.

Ganz, Marshall. 2004. Why David Sometimes Wins: Strategic Capacity in Social Movements. In Jeff Goodman and James Jasper (Eds.), *Rethinking Social Movements: Structure, Meaning, and Emotion.* Lanham, MD: Rowman and Littlefield.

Garcia, David P. 2006, January 26. Learning the Right Lessons. Retrieved February 23, 2008, from http://www.metamute.org/en/Learning-the-Right-Lessons.

Gardner, Howard. 1983. *Frames of Mind: The Theory of Multiple Intelligences.* New York: Basic Books.

Garreau, J. 1991. *Edge City: Life on the New Frontier.* New York: Random House.

Garrett, J. 2003. Amartya Sen's Ethics of Substantial Freedom. http://www.wku.edu/~jan.garrett/ethics/senethic.htm.

Garrett, Laurie, and Rosenstein, Scot. 2005, Spring. Missed Opportunities: Governance of Global Infectious Diseases. *International Health* 27 (1): 64–69. Retrieved February 12, 2008, from http://hir.harvard.edu/articles/1327/.

Gerbner, G. 1998. Telling Stories, or How Do We Know What We Know? The Story of Cultural Indicators and the Cultural Environment Movement. *Wide Angle* 20 (2): 116–131.

Gibbs, Wayt W. 2002. Saving Dying Languages. *Scientific American* 287 (2): 78–85.

Gillmor, Dan. 2004. *We the Media.* Sebastopol, CA: O'Reilly Media.

Gilroy, P. 1987. *There Ain't No Black in the Union Jack: The Cultural Politics of Race and Nation.* Chicago: University of Chicago Press.

Girard, Monique, and Stark, David. 2007. Socio-Technologies of Assembly: Sense-Making and Demonstration in Rebuilding Lower Manhattan. In Viktor Mayer-Schönberger and David Lazer (Eds.), *Governance and Information Technology: From Electronic Government to Information Government.* Cambridge, MA: MIT Press. Retrieved March 17, 2007, from http://www.sociology.columbia.edu/pdf-files/newstark2.pdf.

Gladwell, Malcolm. 2005. *Blink: The Power of Thinking Without Thinking.* New York: Little Brown and Company.

Glennerster, Rachel, Kremer, Michael, and Williams, Heidi. 2005, May–June. The Price of Life. *Foreign Policy* 148: 26–27.

Global Forest Watch. 2008. Welcome to Global Forest Watch. World Resources Institute. Retrieved March 6, 2007, from http://www.globalforestwatch.org/.

Glocal: Glocalisation. N.d. *Wikipedia.* http://en.wikipedia.org/wiki/.

Goffman, Erving. 1959. *The Presentation of Self in Everyday Life.* New York: Anchor.

Goleman, Daniel. 1995. *Emotional Intelligence: Why It Can Matter More Than IQ.* New York: Bantam Books.

Good Life Center. N.d. Welcome to the Good Life Center. Retrieved March 9, 2007, from http://www.goodlife.org

Goodwin, J. and Jasper, J. (Eds.). 2004. *Rethinking Social Movements: Structure, Meaning, and Emotion.* Lanham, MD: Rowman & Littlefield.

Gordon, R. 2005, June 18. San Francisco: City Must Consider Environmental Impact of Purchases. *San Francisco Chronicle.*

Government of Canada. 2005. TCPS: Section 6. Research Involving Aboriginal Peoples. Retrieved February 13, 2008, from http://www.pre.ethics.gc.ca/english/policystatement/section6.cfm

Grabow, S. 1983. *Christopher Alexander: The Search for a New Paradigm in Architecture.* Stocksfield, Northumberland, UK: Oriel Press.

Grameen Foundation USA. N.d. Grameen Foundation: Fighting Poverty with Microfinance. Retrieved March 3, 2007, from http://www.gfusa.org/about_us/values.

Greco, Jr., Thomas. 1994, November 16. How to Create Your Own Money. *Green Left.*

Green Apple Map. 2006. Welcome to the Green Apple Map. New York: GreenMap. Retrieved March 12, 2007, from http://www.greenapplemap.org.

Green Map System. 2006, May. The Green Map System. Retrieved March 12, 2007, from http://www.greenmap.org/.

Greenbaum, Joan, and Kyng, Morton. 1991. *Design at Work.* Hillsdale, NJ: Lawrence Erlbaum Associates.

Grossman, Dave. 1995. *Killing: The Psychological Cost of Learning to Kill in War and Society.* New York: Little Brown & Co.

Grundner, T. 1993. Seizing the Infosphere: An Alternative Vision for National Computer Networking. In Ann Bishop (Ed.), *Emerging Communities: Integrating Networked Information into Library Services.* Urbana-Champaign, IL: Graduate School of Library and Information Science, University of Illinois at Urbana-Champaign.

Gurr, Ted Robert. 1971. Model Building and a Test of Theory. In James Chowning Davies (Ed.), *When Men Revolt and Why: A Reader in Political Violence and Revolution.* New York: Free Press.

Gurstein, Michael (Ed.) 2000. *Community Informatics: Enabling Communities with Information and Communication Technologies.* Hershey, PA: Idea Group Publishing.

Habraken, N. J. *Supports: An Alternative to Mass Housing*. New York: Praeger Publishers, 1972.

Halaska, C. (Ed.). 2000. *Community Participation in the Design of the Seattle Public Schools' Budget Builder Web Site*. Hershey, PA: Idea Group Publishing.

Hardin, G. 1968. The Tragedy of the Commons. *Science* 162: 1243–1248.

Harrje, Evan, Bricker, Amy, and Kallio, Karmen. 1998. *The Real Price of Gasoline*. Washington, DC: International Center for Technology Assessment. Retrieved March 11, 2007, from http://www.icta.org/doc/Real%20Price%20of%20Gasoline.pdf.

Hart, Maureen. 2006. Sustainable Measures. Retrieved February 24, 2008, from http://www.sustainable-measures.com/

Hawtin, M., Hughes, G., and Percy-Smith, J. 1994. *Community Profiling: Auditing Social Needs*. Milton Keynes. Buckingham, UK: Open University Press.

Hayner, Priscilla. 1994. Fifteen Truth Commissions: 1974 to 1994: A Comparative Study. *Human Rights Quarterly* 16 (4): 597–655.

Heidegger, Martin. 1962. *Being and Time*. New York: Harper and Row.

Heffron, Elizabeth. 2005. Mitzi's Abortion. Unpublished play. Performed at ACT Theatre, Seattle, July 27, 2006–August 20, 2006.

Henriques, A., and Richardson, J. 2004. *The Triple Bottom Line: Does It All Add Up?* London: Earthscan.

Herman, E., and Chomsky, N. 1988. *Manufacturing Consent*. New York: Pantheon.

Hess, D. 1994. *Science and Technology in a Multicultural World*. New York: Columbia University Press.

Heumann, J. 1988, February 1, 1998. Keynote Address to Microsoft Employees and Experts on Disabilities and Technology. Redmond, WA: Microsoft.

Hinton, Leanne. 2001. *The Green Book of Language Revitalization in Practice*. San Diego, CA: Academic Press.

History & Objectives. 2005. Retrieved January 2, 2008, from http://www.audubon.org/bird/cbc/history.html

Hoffmann, Jessica, and Petit, Christine. 2006, Spring. Fourteen Acres: Conversations Across Chasms in South Central Los Angeles. *Clamor*. 36: 12–17.

Hollan, J. and Stornetta, S. 1992. Beyond Being There. *CHI '92*, ACM 119–125.

Holland, Alex. 2006, February 11. Venezuela's Urban Land Committees and Participatory Democracy. *Venezuelanalysis.com*. Retrieved June 3, 2007, from http://www.venezuelanalysis.com/analysis/1611.

Holroyd, M. 1999. Places of Opportunity. *Index on Censorship* 28 (2): 139–143.

hooks, b. 1994. *Teaching to Transgress*. New York: Routledge.

Hudson River Foundation. 2008. Hudson River Foundation. Retrieved February 20, 2008, from http://www.hudsonriver.org/.

Huntington, S. P. 1988. *The Clash of Civilizations and the Remaking of World Order.* New York: Simon and Schuster.

IBM Research: Knowledge Socialization, Retrieved January 19, 2008, from http://www.research.ibm.com/knowsoc/.

IFAD. 2003, December 11. Fighting Rural Poverty: The Role of ICTs. Retrieved March 20, 2007, from http://www.ifad.org/events/wsis/media.htm.

Interagency Advisory Panel on Research Ethics. 2003, April 16. TCPS: Section 6. Research Involving Aboriginal Peoples. In Interagency Advisory Panel on Research Ethics (Ed.). Government of Canada. http://www.pre.ethics.gc.ca/english/policystatement/section6.cfm.

Irwin, Alan. 1995. *Citizen Science: A Study of People, Expertise and Sustainable Development.* London: Routledge.

It is 5 minutes to midnight. N.d. Bulletin of the Atomic Scientists. Retrieved June 19, 2005, from http://www.thebulletin.org/minutes-to-midnight/.

Jacobs, Jane. 1984. *Cities and the Wealth of Nations.* New York: Random House.

Jacoby, B. 1996. *Service-Learning in Higher Education: Concepts and Practices.* San Francisco: Jossey-Bass.

Jain, S. P., and Polman, W. 2003. *A Handbook for Trainers on Participatory Local Development: The Panchayati Raj Model in India.* New York: Food and Agriculture Organization. http://www.fao.org/docrep/007/ae536e/ae536e00.HTM.

Jeffrey, Sandy McCune. 1989. *Citizen Diplomacy: Progress Report: The USSR.* Boulder, CO: Clearinghouse for Citizen Diplomacy.

Jenkins, Henry. 1992. *Textual Poachers: Television Fans & Participatory Culture.* New York: Routledge.

Jenniges, Amy. 2003, September 11. Swinging at Bush. *The Stranger.* 6. Retrieved February 26, 2008, from http://www.thestranger.com/seattle/Content?oid=15568.

Jensen, Rolf. 1996, May/June. The Dream Society. *The Futurist.* 30 (3): 9–13.

Johnson, Stevem. 2006a. *Everything Bad Is Good for You.* New York: Riverhead.

Johnson, Steven. 2006b, October 8. The Long Zoom. *New York Times Magazine.*

Jordan, Mary. 2008, August 25. Going Mobile: Text Messages Guide Filipino Protesters. *Washington Post.* Retrieved March 12, 2007, from http://www.washingtonpost.com/wp-dyn/content/article/2006/08/24/AR2006082401379.html.

Jucker, Rolf. 2000. Toward Dematerialization: The Path of Ethical and Ecological Consumption. *OnWeb.* Retrieved October 13, 2007, from http://www.onweb.org/features/new/dematerial/dematerial.html.

Kahn, P. H., Jr. Freier, N. G., Friedman, B., Severson, R. L., and Feldman, E. 2004. *Social and Moral Relationships with Robotic Others?* Piscataway, NJ: IEEE Press.

Kane, Sean. 1994. *Wisdom of the Mythtellers.* Peterborough, Ontario, Canada: Broadview Press.

Kaplan, R. S., and Norton, D. P. 1992, January-February. The Balanced Scorecard: Measures That Drive Performance. *Harvard Business Review.* 71–79.

Kane, Sean (1994) *Wisdom of the Mythtellers.* Ontario: Broadview Press.

Karasti, Helena, and Syrjänen, Anna-Liisa. 2004. Artful Infrastructuring in Two Cases of Community PD. In Andew De Clement, Fiorella Cindio, Anne-Marie Oostveen, Douglas Schuler, and Peter van den Besselaar (Eds.). *Artful Integration: Interweaving Media, Materials and Practices (PDC 2004 Proceedings).* New York: Association for Computing Machinery.

Keck, M. 2002. Water, Water, Everywhere, Nor Any Drop to Drink: Land Use and Water Policy in São Paulo, Brazil. In Peter Evans (Ed.) *Livable Cities.* Berkeley, CA: University of California Press.

Keck, Margaret, and Sikkink, Kathryn. 1998. *Activists beyond Borders: Advocacy Networks in International Politics.* Ithaca, NY: Cornell University Press.

Keen, M., Brown, V. A., and Dyball, R. 2005. *Social Learning and Environmental Management.* London: Earthscan.

Kershaw, Baz. 1992. *The Politics of Performance: Radical Theatre for Social Intervention.* London: Routledge.

Keynes, John Maynard. 1936. *The Theory of Prices.* New York: Macmillan.

Kidd, Dorothy. Forthcoming. The Global Movement to Transform Communications. In Tony Dowmunt, Alan Fountain, and Kate Coyer (Eds.), *The Alternative Media Handbook.* London: Routledge.

Kidron, Michael, Segal, Ronald, and Smith, Dan (Eds.). 2003. *The State of the World Atlas.* London: Earthscan.

Kilpatrick, A., and Silverman, L. 2004. The power of vision. McKinsey & Company. Retrieved July 7, 2006, from http://www.mckinsey.com/clientservice/nonprofit/ourwork/pdf/Power_of_Vision.pdf

Kim, A. J. 2000. *Community Building on the Web.* Reading, MA: Addison-Wesley.

King, I. 1993, August. Christopher Alexander, and Contemporary Architecture, *Architecture and Urbanism.*

King, Thomas. 2003. *The Truth about Stories.* Minneapolis: University of Minnesota Press.

Kozol, J. 1991. *Savage Inequalities.* New York: Crown.

Kranich, Nancy. 2004. Libraries: The Information Commons of Civil Society. In Douglas Schuler and Peter Day (Eds.), *Shaping the Network Society: The New Role of Civil Society in Cyberspace.* Cambridge, MA: MIT Press.

Kranich, Nancy. 2004. *The Information Commons.* New York: Brennan Center for Justice at NYU School of Law.

Krauss, Michael. 1992. *The World's Languages in Crisis. Language* 68 (1): 4–10.

Kretzmann, J. 1992. *Affirmative Information and the Washington Administration.* New Brunswick, NJ: Rutgers University Press.

Kroll, Lucien. 1987. *An Architecture of Complexity*. Cambridge, MA: MIT Press.

Kubicek, H., and Wagner, R. M. M. 1998. Community Networks in a Generational Perspective. Designing Across Borders: The Community Design of Community Networks. Seattle, WA: http://www.scn.org/tech/the_network/Projects/CSCW-PDC-ws-98/kubicek-wagner-pp.ht.

Labournet Association and LabourNet Germany Net Daily. 2005, July 28. LabourNet Germany Raided. *LabourNet UK* (http://www.labournet.net/default.asp). Retrieved February 20, 2008, from http://www.labournet.net/world/0507/labnetde1.html.

LabourStart. N.d. LabourStart: Where Trade Unionists Start Their Day on the Net. Retrieved March 19, 2007, from http://labourstart.org/.

Lafer, Gordon. 2007, July. *Neither Free Nor Fair: The Subversion of Democracy Under NLRB Elections*. American Rights at Work, p. 4. Retrieved January 31, 2008 from http://www.americanrightsatwork.org/dmdocuments/ARAWReports/NeitherFreeNorFair.pdf

Lakoff, George. 2004. *Don't Think of an Elephant: Progressive Values and the Framing Wars a Progressive*. White River Junction VT: Chelsea Green Publishing.

Lancet Global Mental Health Group. 2007. Global Mental Health Scale Up Services for Mental Disorders: a Call for Action. *The Lancet* 370: 241–1252.

Lasn, K. 1999. *Culture Jam: The Uncooling of America*. New York: Eagle Brook/William Morrow.

Lea, D. 2000, November. Patterns-Discussion FAQ. Retrieved October 1, 2006, from http://g.oswego.edu/dl/pd-FAQ/pd-FAQ.html.

Le Baron, Michelle. 2003. *Bridging Cultural Conflicts: New Approaches for a Changing World*. San Francisco: Jossey-Bass

Levine, David. 2004, Fall. The Birth of the Citizenship Schools: Entwining the Struggles for Literacy and Freedom. *History of Education Quarterly*. 44 (3): 338–414.

Lewicki, Roy J., Gray, Barbara, and Elliott, Michael. 2003. *Making Sense of Intractable Environmental Conflicts: Frames and Cases*. Washington, D.C.: Island Press.

Light, Andrew, and Higgs, Eric. 1997. The Politics of Corporate Ecological Restorations: Comparing Global and Local North American Contexts. In Ann Cvetkovich and Douglas Kellner (Eds.), *Articulating the Global and the Local*. Boulder, CO: Westview.

Lin, Nan. 2001. *Social Capital: A Theory of Social Structure and Action*. Cambridge: Cambridge University Press.

Lindblom, Charles. 1990. *Inquiry and Change*. New Haven: Yale University Press.

Lispector, Clarice. 1960. *Family Ties*. Minneapolis, MN: University of Minnesota Press.

Lispector, Clarice. 1988. *The Passion according to G.H.* Minneapolis: University of Minnesota Press.

Loeb, Paul. N.d. An Inconvenient Video Game. *Huffington Post*. Retrieved November 1, 2006, from http://www.huffingtonpost.com/paul-loeb/an-inconvenient-video-gam_b_24681.html.

Louv, Richard. 2006. *Last Child in the Woods*. Chapel Hill, NC: Algonquin Books.

Macjams.com 2006. Macjams.com: Mac Music Community. Retrieved March 19, 2007, from http://www.macjams.com/.

Maher, V. 2005. Vincent Maher. Retrieved February 26, 2008, from http://www.vincentmaher.com/.

Maino, Eric. 2002. Self-Help Groups Empower Women. http://www.newsfromafrica.org/newsfromafrica/articles/art_864.html.

Malcolm, K., Poltrock, S., and Schuler, D. 1991. Industrial Strength Hypermedia: Requirements for a Large Engineering Enterprise. In Conference on Hypertext and Hypermedia. Proceedings of the third annual *ACM Conference on Hypertext*. New York: ACM.

Mann, Mark, and Zainem, Ibrahim. 2002. *Good Alternative Travel Guide: Exciting Holidays for Responsible Travelers*. London: Earthscan.

Marshall, J., and Aldhous, P. 2006, October 28. Swallowing the Best Advice? *New Scientist*. Retrieved October 30, 2006, from http://www.newscientist.com/channel/health/mg19225755.100-patient-groups-special-swallowing.

Masterman, L. 1985. *Teaching the Media*. London: Routledge.

Matic, Veran. 2004. Civil Networking in a Hostile Environment: Experiences in the Former Yugoslavia. In Douglas Schuler and Peter Day (Eds.), *Shaping the Network Society: The New Role of Civil Society in Cyberspace*. Cambridge, MA: MIT Press.

Mayer, Deanna Wylie. 2006, February 1. From Fear to Truth: America's First Truth and Reconciliation Commission Tries to Bring Healing to a Divided Community. *Sojourners* 35 (2): 32–37.

McChesney, R. 2000. *Rich Media, Poor Democracy: Communications Politics in Dubious Times*. New York: New Press.

McCombs, Maxwell, and Shaw, Donald. 1972, Summer. The Agenda-Setting Function of Mass Media. *Public Opinion Quarterly*.

McCombs, Maxwell. 2002. Agenda-Setting Role of the Mass Media. Retrieved on February 4, 2008, from http://www.infoamerica.org/documentos_pdf/mccombs01.pdf

McIntosh, P. 1988. *White Privilege and Male Privilege: A Personal Account of Coming to See Correspondences through Work in Women's Studies*. Wellesley, MA: Wellesley College Center for Research on Women.

McLuhan, Marshall. 1962. *The Gutenberg Galaxy*. Toronto: University of Toronto Press.

Meadows, D. 1997, winter. Places to Intervene in a System. *Whole Earth* 91: 78–84.

Medcalf, J. 1999. Barefoot Messengers. *Index on Censorship* 28 (2): 91–93.

Meeker-Lowry, Susan. 1995. The Potential of Local Currency. *Z Magazine* 8 (7/8): 16–23.

Mele, Christopher. 1999. Access to Cyberspace and the Empowerment of Disadvantaged Communities. In Marc Smith and Peter Kollock (Eds.), *Communities in Cyberspace*. London: Routledge.

Menou, M. J. 2003. Telecentres. In J. Feather and P. Sturges (Eds.), *International Encyclopedia of Information and Library Science*, 2nd ed. London: Routledge.

Menou, M. J., Delgadillo Poepsel, K., and Stoll, K. 2004. Latin American Community Telecenters: It's a Long Way to TICperary. *Journal of Community Informatics* 1 (1).

Menou, M. J., and Stoll, K. (Eds.). 2003a. *Basic Principles of Community Public Internet Access Point's Sustainability*. Hershey, PA: Idea Group.

Menou, M. J., and Stoll, K. 2003b. Community Development Telecenters. In M. Gurstein and S. Stafeev (Eds.), *Community Networking and Community Informatics: Prospects, Approaches, Instruments*. St. Petersburg, Russia.

Messaris, P. 1994. *Visual Literacy: Image, Mind, and Reality*. Boulder, CO: Westview Press.

Meyer-Knapp, Helena. 2003. *Dangerous Peace-Making*. Olympia, WA: Peace-Maker Press.

Meyerson, D. E., and Scully M. A. 1995. Tempered Radicalism and the Politics of Ambivalence and Change. *Organization Science* 6 (5): 585–600.

Millennium Challenge Corporation. 2006, January 26. Environmental Performance Index. Retrieved March 6, 2007, from http://www.yale.edu/epi.

Miller, D., and Slater, D. 2000. *The Internet: An Ethnographic Approach*. London: Berg.

Mills, C. Wright. 1956. *The Power Elite*. New York: Oxford University Press.

Mooney, Chris. 2003, March 24. Breaking the Frame: Susan Nall Bales Has a Lesson for Progressive Groups: Message Matters. *American Prospect*. Retrieved February 5, 2008, from http://www.prospect.org/cs/articles?article=breaking_the_frame.

Moore, J. 2003, March 31. The Second Superpower Rears Its Beautiful Head. Retrieved September 1, 2005, from http://cyber.law.harvard.edu/people/jmoore/secondsuperpower.html.

Morgan, Michael (Ed.) 2002. *Against the Mainstream: The Selected Words of George Gerbner*. New York: Peter Lang.

Morino, Mario. 1994. *Assessment and Evolution of Community Networking*. Cupertino, CA: Apple Computer Library of the Future. Retrieved February 25, 2008, from http://www.morino.org/under_sp_asse.asp.

Nanus, B. 1992, September-October. Visionary leadership: How to Re-vision the Future. *The Futurist* 26 (5): 20–25.

Nearing, Helen, and Nearing, Scott. 1970. *Living the Good Life*. New York: Schocken.

Norman, Donald. 1993. *Things That Make Us Smart: Defending Human Attributes in the Age of the Machine*. Reading MA: Perseus Books.

Norman, Donald. 1998. *The Invisible Computer: Why Good Products Can Fail, the Personal Computer Is So Complex, and Information Appliances Are the Solution*. Cambridge, MA: MIT Press.

Nucci, L., and Weber, E. (Eds.). 1991. *Handbook of Moral Behavior and Development*. Vol. 3: *Applications*. Mahwah, NJ: Erlbaum.

Nussbaum, Martha. 1994, Fall. Patriotism and Cosmopolitanism. *Boston Review*.

O'Reilly, Tim. 2006, December 10. Web 2.0 Compact Definition: Trying Again. Retrieved February 1, 2008, from http://radar.oreilly.com/archives/2006/12/web_20_compact.html.

Okri, Ben. 1997. *A Way of Being Free*. London: Phoenix House.

Oldenburg, Ray. 1999. *The Great Good Place*. New York: Paragon Publishing.

Oliver, M., and Shapiro, T. 1997. *Black Wealth, White Wealth: A New Perspective on Racial Inequality*. London: Routledge.

Ong, Aihwa. 1987. *Spirits of Resistance and Capitalist Discipline: Factory Women in Malaysia*. Albany, NY: State University of New York Press.

Ong, Walter (1982). *Orality and Literacy: Technologizing of the Word*. London: Routledge.

Oppenheim, James. 1973. Bread and Roses. In E. Fowke and J. Glazer (Eds.), *Songs of Work and Protest*. Mineola, NY: Dover Publications.

Ostrom, Elinor. 1990. *Governing the Commons: The Evolution of Institutions for Collective Action*. Cambridge: Cambridge University Press.

Owen, Harrison. 1997. *Open Space Technology: A User's Guide*, Second Edition. San Francisco, CA: Berrett-Koehler Publishers Inc.

Parker, Walter. 2003. *Teaching Democracy: Unity and Diversity in Public Life*. New York: Teachers College Press.

Partnership for Public Warning. 2007, August 3. Retrieved January 31, 2008, from http://www.partnershipforpublicwarning.org/ppw/index.html.

Pattullo, Polly. 2006. *Ethical Travel Guide*. London: Earthscan.

Peters, S. J., O'Connell, D. J., Alter, T. R., and Jack, A. L. H. 2006. *Catalyzing Change: Profiles of Cornell Cooperative Extension Educators*. Ithaca, NY: Cornell. Retrieved October 23, 2006, from http://www.cardi.cornell.edu/CatalyzingChangeFINAL.pdf.

Pew Research Center for the People and the Press. 2006, July 12. *Little Consensus on Global Warming*. Washington, DC: Pew Research Center for the People and the Press. Retrieved February 25, 2008, from http://people-press.org/reports/display.php3?ReportID=280.

Piaget, J. 1965. *The Moral Judgment of the Child*. New York: Free Press.

Pincock, Stephen. 2003, September 20. UK Doctors Still "Out of Office" to Patients Online. E-Health-Media. E-Health-Media Limited. Retrieved March 19, 2007, from http://www.e-health-insider.com/news/item.cfm?ID=531.

PlaceMatters. 2006. PlaceMatters. http://placematters.org/. Retrieved March 13, 2007.

Plant, N. 2001. An "IS Healthcheck" for Community Organisations. In M. Roberts, M. Moulton, S. Hand, and C. Adams (Eds.) *Information Systems in the Digital World; proceedings of the 6th UKAIS Conference*. Manchester: Zeuss Press.

Plant, N. 2003. Sustainability as a Tool for Understanding and Change in Community Information Systems. Ph.D. dissertation, University of the West of England.

Popper, K. 1972. *Objective Knowledge: An Evolutionary Approach*. Clarendon Press, Oxford.

Poulsen, Kevin. 2005, May 31. AI Seduces Stanford Students. *Wired News*. http://www.wired.com/news/culture/0,67659-0.html

Power, F. Clark, Higgins, Ann, and Kohlberg, Lawrence. 1989. *Lawrence Kohlberg's Approach to Moral Education*. New York: Columbia University Press.

Preece, Jenny. 2000. *Online Communities: Designing Usability, Supporting Sociability*. Hoboken, NJ: Wiley.

Preece, J., Abras, C., and Maloney-Krichmar, D. 2004. Designing and Evaluating Online Communities: Research Speaks to Emerging Practice. *International Journal of Web-Based Communities* 1 (1): 2–18.

Price, V., and Cappela, J. N. 2002. Online Deliberation and Its Influence: The Electronic Dialogue Project in Campaign 2000. Retrieved October 3, 2007, from http://www.stanford.edu/group/siqss/itandsociety/v01i01/v01i01a20.pdf.

Protti, D. J. 2005. NHS Connecting for Health. Retrieved February 25, 2008, from http://www.connectingforhealth.nhs.uk/worldview/protti7.

Public Agenda. 2006, October 1. *Long Overdue: A Fresh look at Public and Leadership Attitudes about Libraries in the 21st Century*. New York: Public Agenda. http://www.publicagenda.org/research/pdfs/long_overdue.pdf.

Public Campaign. N.d. Clean Elections Campaign Reform, 1, 2, 3. Retrieved March 19, 2007, from http://www.publicampaign.org/clean123/.

Putnam, R. D. 2000. *Bowling Alone: The Collapse and Revival of American Community*. New York: Simon and Schuster.

Pyatok, Michael. 2000, December. *Design of Affordable Housing: The Return of the Homestead Multifamily Trends* by the Urban Land Institute.

Pyszczynski, T., Solomon, S., and Greenberg, J. 2003. *In the Wake of 9/11: The Psychology of Terror*. Washington, DC: American Psychological Association.

Quinn, C. 2002. Informal Learning Model. Retrieved September 3, 2006, from http://ottersurf.com/InformalLearning/Informal.html

Raffensperger, Carolyn, Peters, Scott, and Kirschenmann, Fred. 1999, July 9. Defining Public-Interest Research. *Loka Alert*. Retrieved March 11, 2007, from http://www.loka.org/alerts/loka.6.3.htm.

Raymond, Eric S. 1999. *The Cathedral and the Bazaar*. Sebastopol. CA: O'Reilly.

Recer, P. 2003. Filtering Water Through Old Saris Can Halve Cholera Cases: Study. *C-Health News*. http://mediresource.canoe.ca/health_news_detail.asp?news_id=5734.

Reflect N.d. What is Reflect? Retrieved March 19, 2007, from http://www.reflect-action.org./enghome.html.

Reid, Frances, and Hoffman, Deborah. 1999. *Long Night's Journey into Day*. Iris Films. http://www.irisfilms.org/longnight/.

Reitman, Jason. 2006. *Thank You for Smoking*. Hollywood, CA: Twentieth Century Fox.

Rheingold, Howard. 2003. *Smart Mobs: The Next Social Revolution*. New York: Perseus.

Richardson, D., and Rajasunderam, C. V. 1999. Training Community Animators as Participatory Communication for Development Practitioners. *SD Dimensions*, FAO. http://www.fao.org/sd/CDdirect/CDre0044.htm

Richter, R. 1995. *Banking on Life and Debt*. Maryknoll, NY: Maryknoll World Productions.

Rittel, H., and Webber, M. 1973. Dilemmas in a General Theory of Planning. *Policy Sciences* 4: 155–169.

Robbins, Richard. 2004. *Global Problems and the Culture of Capitalism*, 3rd ed. Needham Heights, MA: Allyn and Bacon.

Roberts Rules of Order, Revised. Retrieved January 28, 2008, from http://www.constitution.org/rror/rror--00.htm.

Robertson, Roland. 1992. *Globalization: Social Theory and Global Culture*. Sage: London.

Robertson. Roland. 1995. Glocalization: Time–Space and Homogeneity–Heterogeneity. In Mike Featherstone, Scott Lash, and Roland Robertson (Eds), *Global Modernities*. Sage: London.

Roessner, C. 2005. *ICT and Development*. Hamburg, Germany: University of Hamburg, IT Infrastructure Telecenter. Retrieved March 20, 2007, from http://www.tele-centros.org/paginas/buscadorlist.php?start=1andbuscar=Roessner.

Rogers, E. M. 1995. *Diffusion of Innovations*, 4th ed. New York: Free Press.

Rosen, J. 2006. The People Formerly Known as the Audience. http://journalism.nyu.edu/pubzone/weblogs/pressthink/2006/06/27/ppl_frmr.html.

Rosen, Jay. 2006, July 25. Introducing NewAssignment.Net. Retrieved February 3, 2008, from http://journalism.nyu.edu/pubzone/weblogs/pressthink/2006/07/25/nadn_qa.html.

Rosenberg, Marshall B. 2003. *Nonviolent Communication: A Language of Life*. Encinitas, CA: PuddleDancer Press.

Rosenberg, T. 2005, December 30. What Lara Croft Would Look Like if She Carried Rice Bags. *New York Times*. Retrieved April 28, 2007, from http://www.nytimes.com/2005/12/30/opinion/30fri4.html?_r=1&scp=4&sq=tina-rosenberg.

Rosin, Hanna. 2006, June 5. Life Lessons. *New Yorker Magazine*. 82 (16): 40–45.

Rural Finance Learning Center. 2006. Rural Finance Learning Center—Training. Retrieved March 19, 2007, from http://www.ruralfinance.org/id/1036.

Rushkoff, Douglas. 2006. Open Source Currency. Retrieved February 1, 2008, from http://www.edge.org/q2006/q06_6.html#rushkoff.

Rust, John. 1985, July. Stationary Equilibrium in a Market for Durable Assets. *Econometrica* 53 (4): 783–805.

Ryerson, W. 2006. Are Family Planning Soap Operas Manipulative? http://www.populationmedia.org/docs/FamilyPlanningSoapOperaManip.pdf.

Sachs, Wolfgang, Loske, Reinhard, and Linz, Manfred. 1998. *Greening the North: A Post-Industrial Blueprint for Ecology and Equity.* London: Zed Books.

Sadlier, Darlene J. 1999. Theory and Pedagogy in the Brazilian Northeast. *Radical Teacher* 56: 35.

Sandberg, Åke, Broms, Gunnar, Grip, Arne, Sundstrom, Lars, Steen, Jesper. and Ullmark, Peter. 1992. *Technological Change and Co-Determination in Sweden.* Philadelphia: Temple University Press.

Saunders, William S. 2002, Winter–Spring. A Pattern Language (book review). *Harvard Design Magazine.* 16: 1–7. Retrieved February 26, 2008, from http://www.gsd.harvard.edu/research/publications/hdm/back/16books_saunders.pdf.

Scharmer, C. A. 1996. Closing the Feedback Loop Between Matter and Mind. [Interview with Peter Senge]. Retrieved July 7, 2006, from http://www.dialogonleadership.org/Senge-1996.html

Schlosser, E. 2002. *Fast Food Nation: The Dark Side of the All-American Meal.* New York: Penguin.

Schuler, Douglas. 1996. *New Community Networks.* Reading, MA: Addison-Wesley.

Schuler, Douglas. 2001, Summer. Cultivating Society's Civic Intelligence: Patterns for a New "World Brain." *Journal of Society, Information and Communication.* 4 (2): 157–181. Retrieved March 6, 2007, from http://www.publicsphereproject.org/civint/civic-intelligence.pdf.

Schuler, Douglas. Forthcoming. Community Networks and the Evolution of Civic Intelligence. *AI & Society.*

Schuler, Douglas, and Namioka, Aki (Eds.). 1993. *Participatory Design: Principles and Practices.* Hillsdale, NJ: Lawrence Erlbaum Associates.

Schumacher, E. F. 1973. *Small Is Beautiful: Economics as If People Mattered.* New York: Harper.

Sen, A. 2000. *Development as Freedom.* New York: First Anchor Books.

Sen, Jai, Enand, Anita, Escobar, Arturo, and Waterman, Peter. (Eds.). 2004. *World Social Forum: Challenging Empires.* New Delhi, India: Viveka Foundation.

Sengers, P., Boehner, K., David, S., and Kaye, J. 2005. *Reflective Design.* New York: ACM Press.

Shannon, C., and Weaver, W. 1949. *A Mathematical Theory of communication.* Champaign-Urbana: University of Illinois Press.

Shaw, Anup. 2005, August 10. Effects of Consumerism. Retrieved March 9, 2007, from http://www.globalissues.org/TradeRelated/Consumption/Effects.asp.

Shaw, Anup. 2007, March 5. Free Trade and Globalization. Retrieved March 9, 2007, from http://www.globalissues.org/TradeRelated/FreeTrade.asp.

Sidanius, Jim, and Pratto, Felicia. 1999. *Social Dominance: An Intergroup Theory of Social Hierarchy and Oppression.* Cambridge: Cambridge University Press.

Sightline Institute. 2007. The Cascadia Scorecard Project. Sightline Institute. Retrieved March 11, 2007, from http://www.sightline.org/research/cascadia_scorecard.

Simon, Herbert. 1962, December. The Architecture of Complexity. In *Proceedings of the American Philosophical Society*. 106: 467–482.

Sirianni, C., and Friedland, L. A. 2005. *The Civic Renewal Movement: Community Building and Democracy in the United States*. Dayton, OH: Kettering Foundation Press.

Six Essential Elements Derived from The Children's Partnership's Experiences [Handout]. N.d. The Children's Partnership. Santa Monica, CA: The Children's Partnership.

Skolnik, A. 2006, May 12. From Left and Right, Bloggers Let It Rip. *Seattle Post-Intelligencer*, p. A7.

Smillie, Dirk. 1999, October 20, *Husarska: Underground journalism was underpinning of communism's fall*. Retrieved January 31, 2004, from http://www.freedomforum.org/templates/document.asp?documentID =54

Smith, Patti. 1975. The People Have the Power. *Horses*. Arista Records.

Snoonian, D. 2006. Just Push Play. http://plentymag.com/features/2006/09/just_push_play.php.

SPARC. 2007. SPARC. Scholarly Publishing and Academic Resources Coalition. Retrieved March 20, 2007, from http://www.arl.org/sparc

Speck, B. W., and Hoppe, S. L. 2004. *Service-Learning: History, Theory, and Issues*. Westport, CT: Praeger.

Spinosa, C., Flores, F., and Dreyfus, H. L. 1997. *Disclosing New Worlds: Entrepreneurship, Democratic Action, and the Cultivation of Solidarity*. Cambridge, MA: MIT Press.

Spratt, Stephen. 2005. *The Tobin Tax in the 21st Century: Financing Development and Promoting Financial Stability*. London: New Economics Foundation.

Srivastava, Alka. 2004. *Self Help Groups and Civil Society: A Preliminary Study*. New Delhi: ISI Press.

Srivastva, S., and Cooperrider, D. 1990. *Appreciative Management and Leadership: The Power of Positive Thought and Action in Organizations*. San Francisco: Jossey-Bass.

Starhawk. 2002. How We Really Shut Down the WTO. In Mike Prokosch and Laura Raymond (Eds.), *The Global Activist's Manual: Local Ways to Change the World*, New York: Nation Books.

Stiffler, Lisa. 2006, October 27. New Web site tracks ecosystem's health. *Seattle Post-Intelligencer*. Retrieved March 11, 2007, from http://seattlepi.nwsource.com/local/290212_epa27.html.

Stoecker, Randy. 1999. Are Academics Irrelevant? Roles for Scholars in Participatory Research. *American Behavioral Scientist* 42: 840–854.

Stokois, Daniel, and Altman, Irwin. 1987. Handbook of Environmental Psychology. In Allen Wicker (Ed.), *Behavior Settings Reconsidered: Temporal Stages, Resources, Internal Dynamics, C*. New York: Wiley.

Stolterman, Erik. 2001. *Creating Community in Conspiracy with the Enemy*. In Leigh Keeble and Brian Loader (Eds.), *Community Informatics: Shaping Computer-Mediated Social Relations*. London: Routledge.

Sustainable Seattle. 2004. Sustainable Seattle—A Resource and a Catalyst for Urban Sustainability. Retrieved March 11, 2007, from http://www.sustainableseattle.org/.

Tainter, Joseph. 1988. *The Collapse of Complex Societies*. Cambridge: Cambridge University Press.

Takaki, R. 1993. *A Different Mirror: A History of Multicultural America*. Boston: Little, Brown.

Tarrow, S. 2005. *The New Transnational Activism*. Cambridge: Cambridge University Press.

Task Force on Civil Legal Equal Justice Funding. 2003, September. *Washington State Civil Legal Needs Study*. Olympia, WA: Washington State Supreme Court.

Taylor, Charmaine. N.d. Accessibility in Web Design. Retrieved July 19, 2003, from http://www.wd4a .co.uk/HowMany.htm.

Teaching, Learning and Technology Roundtable. N.d. Teaching, Learning and Technology Roundtable. Retrieved February 26, 2008, from http://ncsu.edu/tltr/.

Teixeira, Ruy. 2007, August 30. *What the public really wants is unions*. The Century Foundation/Center for American Progress. Retrieved January 31, 2008, from http://www.americanprogress.org/issues/2007/08/pdf/WTPRWunions.pdf.

Thinking Communities. 2006, July 31. ThinkingCommunities. Retrieved March 19, 2007, from http://thinkingcommunities.wikispaces.com.

Thomas, John. 2002. Reality Check. Retrieved March 12, 2007, from http://www.publicsphereproject .org/patterns/pattern.pl/public?pattern_id=48.

TLT Group. 2006, March 3. The LT Group. http://www.tltgroup.org/. Retrieved March 19, 2007.

ToledoHipHop. 2004. REBOOT: Pass the Message. Compilation CD of original tracks by Toledo, Ohio, artists. Retrieved March 6, 2007, from http://www.toledohiphop.org/reboot/

Tomatsu, Megumi. 2007, October 8. Strategic Communication Terms. Retrieved February 5, 2008, from http://www.uclaccc.ucla.edu/toolbox/terms-concepts/strategic-frame-analysis/strategic-communication-terms.

Tourism Concern. N.d. Info for Tourists. Retrieved March 19, 2007, from http://www.tourismconcern .org.uk/info-for-tourists/global-story.html.

Transparency International. 2006, May 1. Frequently Asked Questions about Corruption. Retrieved March 19, 2007, from http://www.transparency.org/news_room/faq/corruption_faq.

Transparency International. N.d. TI Corruption Fighters' Tool Kit: A Compendium of Practical Civil Society Anti-Corruption Tools. Retrieved March 19, 2007, from http://www.transparency.org/tools/e_toolkit/corruption_fighters_tool_kit_2002.

Tresser, Tom. 2002. Using Collaborative Technologies for Civic Accountability. http://www .publicsphereproject.org/patterns/pattern.pl/public?pattern_id=26.

Trocchi, Agnese. 2004, July 12. Mission Transmission. *Mute Magazine*. Retrieved March 19, 2007, from http://www.metamute.org/en/Mission-Transmission.

Trudell, J. 1999, March 13. We All Come From Tribes. Transcript of speech. Retrieved February 1, 2008, from http://www.warmcove.com/texts/all%20from%20tribes.htm.

Truth Commission Project. 2002. The Truth Commission Project. http://www.truthcommission.org/about.php?lang=en.

Turiel, E. 1983. *The Development of Social Knowledge: Morality and Convention.* Cambridge: Cambridge University Press.

Tutu, Desmond. 2000. *No Future without Forgiveness.* New York: Image Press.

Twist, Lynne. 2003, March 14. Waging Peace: A Story about Robert Muller. *West by Northwest.org.* Retrieved January 25, 2008, from http://www.westbynorthwest.org/artman/publish/article_340.shtml.

UCLA Department of Epidemiology. 2006, March 25. John Snow Pub. Retrieved October 29, 2006, from http://www.ph.ucla.edu/epi/Snow/snowpub.html.

Underwood, P. 1993. *The Walking People: A Native American Oral History.* San Anselmo, CA: Tribe of Two Press.

United Nations. General Assembly. 1998, November 4. Assembly Proclaims 2001 United Nations Year of Dialogue among Civilizations, Expressing Determination to Facilitate International Discussion. Retrieved September 25, 2006, from http://www.un.org/documents/ga9497.html.

University of Oregon. 2005, November. Frequently Asked Questions about the University's use of the Pattern Language. Retrieved August 29, 2006, from http://www.uoregon.edu/~uplan/faq/FAQPatternLanquage.html.

Urry, John (Ed.). 1999. Summer Special Issue on Globalization. Globalization and Citizenship. *Journal of World-Systems Research* 5 (2): 311–312. Retrieved February 26, 2008, from http://jwsr.ucr.edu/archive/vol5/index.php.

Urry, John. 2000. January. Mobile Sociology. *British Journal of Sociology.* 51 (1): 185–203.

von Hippel, Eric. 2005. *Democratizing Innovation.* Cambridge, MA: MIT Press.

von Krogh, G., Nonaka, I., and Aben, M. 2001. Making the Most of Your Company's Knowledge: A Strategic Framework. *Long Range Planning* 34 (2): 421–440.

Waddell, C. 1999. The Growing Digital Divide In Access For People With Disabilities: Overcoming Barriers To Participation In The Digital Economy. Retrieved 20 October 2000, from http://www.icdri.org/CynthiaW/the_digital_divide.htm.

Wallerstein, Immanuel. 1974. *The Modern World System: Capitalist Agriculture and the Origins of the European World Economy in the Sixteenth Century.* New York: Academic Press.

Wallerstein, Immanuel. 1999. *The End of the World as We Know It: Social Science for the Twenty-First Century.* Minneapolis, MN. University of Minnesota Press.

W. K. Kellogg Foundation. 2006. Types of Public Policy. http://www.wkkf.org/Pubs/Tools/Policy/Pub3795.pdf.

Walzer, Michael. 2002. Spheres of Affection. In Martha Nussbaum (Ed.), *For Love of Country?* Boston: Beacon Press.

wartribunal.org. 2007, January. Citizens' Hearing on the Legality of U.S. Actions in Iraq. *wartribunal.org.* Retrieved March 19, 2007, from http://www.wartribunal.org/.

Wasik, B. 2006, September. Grand Theft Education: Literacy in the Age of Video Games (moderated discussion). *Harper's*, 31–39.

Water Abuse. Undated. Retrieved February 4, 2008, from http://www.tourismconcern.org.uk/index .php?page=water-abuse.

Watts, Duncan. 2003. *Six Degrees: The Science of a Connected Age.* New York: W. W. Norton.

Watzman, Nancy. 2006, Fall. Getting Clean in Maine: The Power of Public Funding. *Yes Magazine.* Retrieved February 26, 2008, from http://www.yesmagazine.org/article.asp?ID=1514.

Webster, F. 1995. *Theories of the Information Society.* London: Routledge.

Wedge Community Co-Op. 2001, December/January. The Fair Trade Movement–Coffee and Beyond. *The Wedge Co-Op Newsletter.* Minneapolis, MN: Wedge Community Co-Op. Retrieved February 26, 2008, from http://www.wedge.coop/newsletter/article/201.html.

Weizenbaum, J. 1972. On the Impact of the Computer on Society. *Science* 176 (4035): 609–614.

Wenger, Etienne. 2001. Supporting Communities of Practice: A Survey of Community-Oriented Technologies. http://www.ewenger.com/tech/index.htm.

Wenger, Eienne, White, Nancy, Smith, John D., and Rowe, Kim. 2005, January 18. Technology for Communities. Retrieved February 20, 2008, from http://technologyforcommunities.com/CEFRIO_Book _Chapter_v_5.2.pdf

Wernick, Iddo, Herman, Robert, and Govind, Shekhar. 1996, Summer Materialization and Dematerialization: Measures and Trends. *Daedalus.* 125 (3): 171–198. Retrieved March 15, 2007, from http://phe .rockefeller.edu/Daedalus/Demat/.

Wertsch, J. 1988. *Mind as Action.* New York: Oxford University Press.

What does a sustainable economy look like? N.d. ConservationEconomy.net. Retrieved February 25, 2008, from http://www.conservationeconomy.net/

Whitford, N. E. 1905. *History of the Canal System of the State of New York*, Vol. 1. http://www.history .rochester.edu/canal/bib/whitford/1906/Chap20.html.

Wikipedia. N.d. Common Alerting Protocol. Retrieved March 17, 2007, from http://en.wikipedia.org/ wiki/Common_Alerting_Protocol.

Williamson, Sue. 1989. *Resistance Art in South Africa.* New York: St. Martin's Press.

Wilson, J. 2002. Scientific Uncertainty, Complex Systems, and the Design of Common-Pool Institutions. In Elinor Ostrom, Thomas Dietz, Nives Dolsak, Paul C. Stern, Susan Stonich, and Elke U. Weber (Eds.), *The Drama of the Commons.* Washington, D.C.: National Academies Press.

Wilson, J. A. 2006. Matching social and ecological systems in complex ocean fisheries. *Ecology and Society* 11 (1): 9. Retrieved January 21, 2008, from http://www.ecologyandsociety.org/vol11/iss1/art9/.

Winner, Langdon. 1986. *The Whale and the Reactor: A Search for Limits in an Age of High Technology.* Chicago: University of Chicago Press.

Wolner, C. 2003, April–June. Robert Muller's Joy. *Peace Magazine,* p. 25. Retrieved September 28, 2006, from http://www.peacemagazine.org/archive/v19n2p25.htm.

Women's World Banking. 2008. Women's World Banking. Retrieved March 3, 2007, from http://www.swwb.org/English/2000/performance_standards_in_microfinance.htm.

Woodruff, Paul. 2002. *Reverence: Renewing a Forgotten Virtue.* New York: Oxford University Press.

World Bank Group. N.d. Inequality, Poverty, and Socio-Economic Performance. http://www.worldbank.org/poverty/inequal/intro.htm.

Wortley, David. 2002. The Paradoxical Organization. http://www.publicsphereproject.org/patterns/pattern.pl/public?pattern_id=6.

WTI. 2006, October 22. World Tribunal on Iraq. http://www.worldtribunal.org/.

Yankelovich, D., and Furth, I. 2005, September 16. The Role of Colleges in an Era of Mistrust. *Chronicle of Higher Education.*

Zirra, Ioana. 2004, March. *Understanding Victorianism in Broader Cultural Terms.* Bucharest, Romania: University of Bucharest. Retrieved March 15, 2007, from http://www.unibuc.ro/eBooks/lls/IoanaZirra-VictorianAge/3.htm.

Index of Patterns

Index

Note on pattern indexing: Individual patterns are generally not indexed here since they are listed in a separate index (page 585). The page numbers of the Civic Intelligence pattern, for example, would not be listed here. Patterns that are listed in the "Linked patterns" section at the end of each pattern are also not indexed. Patterns, however, that are referred to within the context chapters (1–7, 9–10) or are referred to within a pattern and are *not* listed in the linked patterns section of the pattern are indexed here. Finally, when patterns from either *A Pattern Language* (Alexander et al. 1977) or *Liberating Voices* (this volume) are indexed here, they are annotated with either *APL* or *LV* and their number within their respective pattern language.

Index